BANKRUPTCY AND DEBTOR/CREDITOR

Examples and Explanations

BANKRUPTCY AND DEBTOR/CREDITOR

Examples and Explanations

Third Edition

Brian A. Blum

Professor of Law
Lewis & Clark Law School

1185 Avenue of the Americas, New York, NY 10036
www.aspenpublishers.com

> Permissions
> Aspen Publishers
> 1185 Avenue of the Americas
> New York, NY 10036

Printed in the United States of America

ISBN 0-7355-2809-8

1 2 3 4 5 6 7 8 9 0

Library of Congress Cataloging-in-Publication Data

Blum, Brian A.
  Bankruptcy and debtor/creditor: examples and explanations/
  Brian A. Blum. — 3rd ed.
    p. cm. — (Examples & explanations series)
  Includes index.
  ISBN 0-7355-2809-8
  1. Bankruptcy — United States, 2. Debtor and creditor —
United States. I. Title. II. Series.

KF1524.3.B58 2003
346.7307'8 — dc22

                                        2003063691

About Aspen Publishers

Aspen Publishers, headquartered in New York City, is a leading information provider for attorneys, business professionals, and law students. Written by preeminent authorities, our products consist of analytical and practical information covering both U.S. and international topics. We publish in the full range of formats, including updated manuals, books, periodicals, CDs, and online products.

Our proprietary content is complemented by 2,500 legal databases, containing over 11 million documents, available through our Loislaw division. Aspen Publishers also offers a wide range of topical legal and business databases linked to Loislaw's primary material. Our mission is to provide accurate, timely, and authoritative content in easily accessible formats, supported by unmatched customer care.

To order any Aspen Publishers title, go to *www.aspenpublishers.com* or call 1-800-638-8437.

To reinstate your manual update service, call 1-800-638-8437.

For more information on Loislaw products, go to *www.loislaw.com* or call 1-800-364-2512.

For Customer Care issues, e-mail CustomerCare@aspenpublishers.com; call 1-800-234-1660; or fax 1-800-901-9075.

Aspen Publishers
A Wolters Kluwer Company

To Helen, Trevor, and Shelley

Summary of Contents

Contents

Contents

Contents

Contents

Contents

Contents

Contents

Preface

Bankruptcy and Debtor/Creditor, Third Edition

This book deals with bankruptcy law and debt collection. I have aimed to keep the level of discussion and analysis appropriate to a basic bankruptcy or debtor/creditor course. I have been guided by my many years of teaching bankruptcy law and by the content of published casebooks. This book covers all the topics a student might encounter in a bankruptcy or debtor/creditor course.

Since the first edition of this book was published in 1993, there have been a number of changes in bankruptcy law. Quite apart from the development of case law, there was a fairly extensive amendment to the Code in 1994, as well as smaller, more discrete amendments at various other times. This edition incorporates these changes. Another significant development addressed in this edition is the 1997 report and recommendations of the National Bankruptcy Review Commission and the ongoing attempts in Congress since 1998 to pass bankruptcy reform legislation. The Commission's report and the successive bills introduced in Congress in response to it have generated considerable controversy, particularly as they relate to consumer bankruptcy. The reform legislation, which changes from one congressional session to another, and differs in separate bills introduced in the House and Senate, is a moving target. Nevertheless, students should be made aware of the issues that have caused controversy and the proposals for reform. Therefore, discussion of the Commission's report and the pending legislation are integrated throughout this edition. At the time of writing, it is unclear if the pending legislation will pass either in this or in future sessions of Congress, and if it does, what its final form will be.

Most of the alterations in this revision are intended to bring the book up to date without drastically changing the extent and nature of the material covered in the earlier editions. Material that had become stale has been eliminated to make room for issues that have come more sharply into view. Many new cases have been added or substituted for older ones. There has also been some expansion of coverage. In particular, this edition includes a new section on sovereign immunity.

Both State and Federal Bankruptcy Law

Debtor/creditor law encompasses both state debt collection and federal bankruptcy law. Although some law school courses omit the state law component in favor of more extensive bankruptcy coverage, most, it seems, devote some attention to debt collection under state law as well. This gives students the advantage, not only of acquiring a general knowledge of state debtor/creditor law — very useful for its own sake — but also of becoming familiar with concepts that are vital to an understanding of bankruptcy law.

This book, therefore, begins with coverage of the general principles of state law. It treats this subject in a broad and condensed way, and emphasizes general themes and key concepts. It focuses on aspects of state law that are key to the understanding of bankruptcy law. This level of detail should be sufficient for most courses that include a component on state debtor/creditor law. It should also make the concepts and procedures of state law accessible to students whose course omits state law, but who would like to do some background reading on the subject.

The Organization and Approach of This Book

Most law school courses call on students to do more than simply digest black letter law. Although legal rules are important, a full appreciation of the subject requires an understanding of the policy behind the rules, their efficacy, and their transactional impact. *Bankruptcy and Debtor/Creditor: Examples & Explanations* is not simply an outline of legal rules. It discusses the reasons behind the rules and the impact of their operation.

This book combines expository text with examples and explanations. The textual portion provides a clear and readable exposition of the topic, beginning with the basics, and moving in the direction of more intricate and advanced issues. It focuses on material that is likely to be covered in a Bankruptcy or Debtor/Creditor course. I have tried to ensure that basic assumptions are clearly articulated, that the transactional context is clear, and that technical language is explained. (There is also a glossary at the end of the book.)

Examples and explanations follow the textual discussion. The purpose of the examples and explanations is to provide concrete illustrations of how the principles discussed in the text would apply. They are also intended to be useful to students who wish to test their knowledge and understanding of the topic. A student who tries to resolve the questions asked in the examples before reading the explanations is likely to derive the greatest benefit from this feature of the book.

Acknowledgments

I owe thanks to many people who have helped me over the years with successive editions of this book. My work on the original edition and the revisions has been supported by summer research grants from Lewis & Clark Law School. I have had able research assistance from a number of Lewis & Clark students who have helped me to find and update material. In every edition of this book, I have benefited from the guidance and thorough editorial work of many members of the staff of Aspen Publishers. Finally, I am grateful to the many students and professors who have used this book and who have offered suggestions for changes or corrections.

Special Notice

To keep the text readable and uncluttered, I have been very selective in the citation of cases and have entirely omitted the citation of secondary sources, such as law review articles, treatises, and casebooks.

Sections of the Bankruptcy Code, Title 11 of the U.S.C., are simply cited by a section symbol (§) followed by the section number. Code chapters are cited by the abbreviation "Ch." followed by the chapter number.

BANKRUPTCY AND DEBTOR/CREDITOR

Examples and Explanations

1

The Formation and Framework of the Debtor/Creditor Relationship and an Introduction to Unsecured Debt

You owe me ten shillings,
Say the bells of St. Helen's.
When will you pay me?
Say the bells of Old Bailey.
When I grow rich,
Say the bells of Shoreditch.
Pray when will that be?
Say the bells of Stepney.
I am sure I don't know,
Says the great bell at Bow . . .
Here comes a candle to light you to bed,
Here comes a chopper to cut off your head.[1]

---

1. This is a nursery rhyme, not a poem by Karl Llewellyn.

§1.1   Debtors and Creditors

This book is about the relationship between debtors (people who owe money) and creditors (people to whom it is owed). More specifically, our concern here is with that relationship gone rotten. Frankly, this is a rather miserable tome. It all but ignores that large majority of transactions in which debtors faithfully perform their obligations and creditors garner the rewards of having proffered credit. Instead, it is concerned with the debtor/creditor relationship in shambles and with the law's attempt to resolve the conflicting rights and interests that must be accommodated when the debtor's resources do not measure up to the creditors' demands.

Who are these debtors and creditors who will trudge their way over the next few hundred pages? Abandon any stereotype that comes to mind and recognize that, in our complex and confusing society, almost everyone serves in one or the other role in numerous different transactions. For example, a wage-earning consumer, engaged in the simplest of business affairs, is likely at the same time to be a creditor (say, for wages payable in arrears by an employer, or for money on deposit at a bank) and a debtor (say, of the store that was paid by check or of the utility company that bills at the end of the month for services supplied). At the other end of the scale might be the mammoth corporation whose complex activities involve myriad relationships in which the corporation owes or is owed money.

A person who is conscientious about paying debts and who is current in the payment of all obligations is not likely to be flattered by being called a "debtor." Even though the term has a rather sterile legal meaning (it simply denotes the obligor on a monetary obligation), it can have a pejorative flavor because it is often used to describe not simply one who owes money but one who has failed to pay money when due. (This negative connotation has been reinforced by the Bankruptcy Code, which uses the word "debtor," rather than the traditional noun "bankrupt," to describe a person whose estate is being administered in bankruptcy.) In the area of the law with which this book is concerned, debtors are typically in default, and the unhappy associations of the word "debtor" are usually intended. It is worth remembering, however, that we will look only at the dark side of the debtor/creditor relationship: Most debtors are solid, solvent folk who will discharge their obligations.

§1.2   State Law and Federal Law:
An Introductory Note

The principal federal law in the area of debtor/creditor relations is the Bankruptcy Code.[2] However, the Bankruptcy Code is not applicable unless the

---

2. *See* section 5.2.1 for an explanation of why bankruptcy law is federal and a discussion of the role of state law in a bankruptcy case.

debtor has become bankrupt. In the absence of bankruptcy, the rights of debtors and creditors are governed by the law prevailing in the state that has jurisdiction over the transaction. This law consists of state law and any federal statutes (other than the Bankruptcy Code) that are applicable to the enforcement of debt. For example, federal statutes restrict the garnishment of wages, regulate debt collection practices, protect entitlements under federal benefits programs, and confer special rights on the federal government to collect taxes or other revenues.

Discussion of bankruptcy law is deferred until Chapter 5. In these first three chapters, the focus is on state debtor-creditor law. (The federal statutes just referred to are not covered in this book.) The treatment of state law here is condensed and presented in generalized form, using commonly accepted principles. Obviously, this overview cannot take into account all the variations in the laws of different states. Its purpose is to introduce and explain central principles and concepts of state law and to build a foundation for the later discussion of bankruptcy law.

§1.3 Formation and Planning Concerns

> Default, dear Brutus, is not in our
> stars, but in ourselves.
> — CASSIUS

Debtor-creditor law is essentially remedial in nature; it is concerned with the enforcement of debts rather than with their creation. However, the creditor's ability to enforce the debt and the debtor's power to resist payment are influenced by the circumstances and the terms under which the debt was created.

Where a debt is created contractually, the parties have some opportunity to plan the transaction. When the debt arises out of an unexpected relationship, such as that between a person who negligently inflicts injury and the victim of the negligence, opportunities for planning may not be present. One can hardly negotiate payment terms and check the credit of the occupant of a fifth floor apartment as the flower pot dislodged from the balcony comes hurtling down toward one's head. (Even here, some planning may have taken place in a more general way. For example, the potential debtor may have purchased liability insurance.)

In the contractual setting, the party who anticipates being a creditor under the contract will try to take precautions to minimize the risk of loss if the debtor fails to perform as promised. The debtor party will be concerned about protection against harsh enforcement action or intrusive creditor behavior.

The creditor's dominant concern is probably that the loan will be repaid with interest on the due date. Although the creditor realizes that it may have to resort to collection procedures, its principal goal is to get the benefit of its bargain with the least amount of cost and aggravation. To best achieve this goal, the creditor must ask itself at least two questions at the time the transaction is entered: First, is this prospective borrower likely to perform its obligations reliably? That is, is it creditworthy? Second, if the borrower does not pay, does the structure of the transaction and its contract terms place the creditor in the best position possible to avoid or mitigate the loss? Terms of this kind include, for example, an acceleration clause which enables the creditor to sue on the entire debt if the debtor fails to pay the installment currently due; provisions entitling the creditor to receive financial statements and to conduct inspections at periodic intervals allow the creditor to monitor the debtor's business affairs and to anticipate unstable or deteriorating conditions; a clause that defines "default" broadly gives the creditor the power to commence collection activity in response to specified acts or circumstances, short of nonpayment of the debt; provision for collection costs, late payment charges, and attorneys' fees gives the creditor the right to reimbursement for expenses that are otherwise not normally recoverable.

This is not an exhaustive list, but these examples show that the contract terms are often very helpful to a creditor in policing the transaction or pursuing the debt. Of course, as important as they are, contract rights against the debtor can never guarantee success. No matter how carefully the contract is drafted, the debtor's financial troubles may be so severe and demands on the debtor's resources so intense that the mere contractual undertakings by the debtor are worthless. For this reason, the creditor may insist on protection that is not totally dependent on the debtor's ability to pay. This protection takes the form of *security*.

The two forms of contractual security in common use are *suretyship* or guarantee, and *the security interest*. Under the former, a third party acceptable to the creditor undertakes to pay the debt if the debtor defaults. Obviously the security afforded by this arrangement is only as good as the financial health of the surety. The latter device is introduced in Chapter 2. The powerful rights that it gives the creditor feature prominently in the remainder of this book.

Every right or power given to the creditor to facilitate the collection of the debt comes at some cost or detriment to the debtor. For example, a creditor's right to financial reports or to inspections may be disruptive and detracts from the debtor's business autonomy; the grant of a security interest hampers free use of the debtor's property and prevents use of the property to raise funds from other sources; strict default provisions may place the debtor in breach too easily and may result in harsh forfeiture.

In deciding whether to agree to terms favorable to the creditor, the informed and rational debtor evaluates the risks and burdens imposed and decides whether the benefits of the transaction outweigh its burdens. If the debtor's decision to sacrifice rights or to curtail freedom of action is an exercise of the debtor's contractual autonomy, the agreement is usually binding.

However, pressures from a variety of sources may affect the debtor's ability to resist harsh terms. When apparent assent to such terms is exacted by illegitimate means, the law of contract has doctrines, such as *unconscionability* or *duress* (to name two), under which rights of enforcement can be cut down to reasonable proportions.

In addition, many statutes, on both the state and federal level, regulate contract terms and curtail abusive practices in consumer credit transactions. For example, the Consumer Credit Protection Act, Title XV of the U.S. Code deals with such matters as discrimination in the grant of credit, credit reporting, disclosure of information in credit agreements, the issuance of credit cards, and the advertising of credit. The CCPA and other such statutes are not discussed in this book.

§1.4 The Enforcement of Unsecured Debt — An Overview

The difference between unsecured and secured debt surely ranks among the most fundamental and far-reaching dichotomies in debtor-creditor law. Secured debt is discussed in Chapter 2. To fully appreciate the potency of security, one needs to have some idea of the difficulties that an unsecured creditor could face in trying to collect an unpaid debt.

Suppose a seller sold goods on credit to a buyer. The sales contract obliged the buyer to pay a specified price 30 days after delivery. The debt is unsecured because no contractual provision or rule of law provides for security. The goods were delivered and accepted without objection. Thirty days have passed and the debt is due, but no payment has been made by the buyer. The buyer has no complaint about the goods or grounds for withholding payment, but has simply defaulted. To be paid, the seller must take the initiative and pursue the debt.

The seller will probably begin by asking for payment. If this does not work, the seller may decide to hand the matter over to a collection agency or an attorney who will make further efforts at recovery by contacting the debtor. State and federal statutes and the common law of torts place limits on the tactics that may be used by a creditor or its collection agent or attorney in the collection of debt — particularly consumer debt. As a general principle, collection efforts must be kept within reasonable bounds and may not harass, abuse, or coerce the debtor into paying the debt. Overzealous collection activity could give rise to liability for actual and punitive damages.

If approaches to the buyer fail to produce satisfactory results, the seller may decide to resort to suit on the debt. The seller's attorney files and serves a complaint and, unless the buyer decides at this stage to dispute the debt, the case proceeds to judgment by default. Following judgment, the creditor is able to use the court's authority and public officers to enforce payment of the debt by the process of execution described in Chapter 3.

However, this enforcement procedure is subject to a significant practical limitation: Its success is dependent upon assets of the debtor being found. If the debtor has no funds, income, or other assets to seize, there is no source from which to derive money to pay the debt. As discussed in the following chapters, even if the debtor does have some property, the creditor may not be able to seize it because it may be immune from execution or subject to the superior claims of others. In addition, a debtor who is trying to evade payment of debts may have taken the trouble to conceal assets, so that they are hard to find or identify. In addition, a debtor who has failed to pay one creditor has possibly defaulted on other debts too. Several creditors may be involved in enforcement proceedings, and some may have begun the process of debt collection earlier or moved more quickly than the seller. As a result, the debtor's available property may have been seized before the seller has had the chance to execute. (Because the seller did not retain a security interest in the goods as explained in Chapter 2, full unencumbered ownership passed to the buyer on sale, and the seller has no special claim to them — they are fair game for any creditor who levies on them first.)

If the seller is unsuccessful in finding property upon which to execute, it has various investigatory procedures at its disposal to assist in trying to locate and execute upon property. (These are discussed in Chapter 3.) However, these procedures are only helpful if there are assets to uncover and if the buyer has not been wiley enough to secrete them thoroughly. If nothing is brought to light, the seller has to wait vigilantly in the hope that the buyer will eventually acquire property, whereupon further writs of execution can be issued. If not, the judgment eventually reaches the end of its term and expires unrequited.[3]

The seller's right to pursue collection efforts under state law could also come to an end if the buyer becomes bankrupt. As we shall see later, the seller becomes an unsecured creditor of the estate and typically will receive only a partial payment — or in some cases, no payment at all — and the unpaid balance of the debt will be discharged.

In short, the unsecured creditor extends credit on the faith of the debtor's willingness and ability to pay. If that faith was misplaced, the creditor has legal means to extract payment from the debtor, but employment of those means may not be successful. If the debtor does not pay voluntarily, compulsion of payment is only possible to the extent that the debtor has economic resources. An unsuccessful judgment creditor is worse off at the end of the frustrated enforcement process because the size of the unpaid debt has been swollen by unrecovered collection expenses and legal fees.

---

3. *See* Chapter 3 for more detail. Also, the subject of judicial liens is omitted from this discussion for the sake of simplicity but is discussed in Chapters 2 and 3.

2

Secured Debt and Priorities

§2.1   Definition and Terminology

§2.1.1   Definition

A secured debt differs from an unsecured debt in one important respect: The personal obligation of the debtor to pay the debt is reinforced by a right *in rem* acquired by the creditor in certain property of the debtor. This means that if the debtor fails to pay, the secured creditor may have recourse to the property to satisfy the debt. Most commonly, the debt is satisfied by the sale of the property and the application of its proceeds to the debt. In certain cases, however, the law permits the creditor to take over the property and to keep it in full settlement of the debt. A secured creditor is therefore in a much stronger position than an unsecured creditor: Not only does it have a right of action against the debtor on the debt, but it also has a claim to property of the debtor to back up that right.

This interest in property does not typically give the creditor title to the property but is characterized as a charge against it. In other words, the creditor does not acquire an ownership right in the property when the security interest is created. Rather, ownership remains with the debtor, encumbered by the creditor's interest. It is only when the debtor defaults on the debt that the creditor becomes entitled to take action to terminate the debtor's ownership and to sell the property or take transfer of it.

§2.1.2   *Terminology*

The Latin verb "to bind" is *ligare,* from which (via French) we derive our word "lien." *Lien* is frequently used as a generic term to describe all kinds of security interest. Other common terms that are often used synonymously with lien are *security interest* and *encumbrance.* (Sometimes "lien" is used more restrictively to describe only nonconsensual interests, while "security interest" is used to refer to interests created by contract, *e.g.,* such as interests under UCC Article 9 or mortgages. The context should make it clear whether the term is used in a generic or specific sense.) The holder of a lien is a *lienor* or *lienholder,* the holder of a security interest is a *secured party* and the holder of an encumbrance is an *encumbrancer.*

In addition to these general terms, different categories of lien have their own names (*e.g., statutory lien, judicial lien,* and so on) and each specific type of lien in those categories has its own label (*e.g., mechanic's lien, tax lien, judgment lien, mortgage*). In section 2.4 the different categories of lien are classified and illustrated.

The property subject to the lien is usually called *the security* or *collateral.* The Latin roots of the latter word also reflect the concept that it represents. It combines *com* ("together with") and *latus* ("a side"), suggesting that the interest in property parallels the debt.

§2.2   The Relationship between the Debt and the Collateral

§2.2.1   *The Link between the Debt and the Collateral*

The definition of *security* incorporates two elements: a debt and property. Both must exist for a lien to have any meaning. This is probably self-evident. Without property, the debt cannot be secured; similarly, the interest in the property must secure some obligation. It has no meaning as a right in the abstract.

How is property linked to the debt? Most liens are created in a specific piece, class, or collection of the debtor's property.[1] Where the lien is created by contract, the parties agree on the collateral. Where a lien is created by operation of law or by judicial process, legal rules determine what property is subjected to the lien.

As a general rule, lien rights can be created in almost every kind of property — real or personal, tangible or intangible. However, different types of

---

1. There are such things as general liens that encumber all the debtor's property. The federal tax lien is one example. However, general liens are not very common. Usually, the property to be subjected to the lien must be specifically described in the instrument that creates the lien.

liens may be confined to particular types of property. For example, an Article 9 interest can relate only to personal property or intangibles, and a judgment lien is usually confined to real property.

Although the lien and the debt are inextricably linked, they are distinguishable as two separate components of the creditor's parcel of rights: The *debt* is a personal claim against the debtor, while the *lien* is a right in the property. The relationship between these connected but distinct rights gives rise to the following consequences and attributes.

§2.2.2 *The Distinction between Personal Liability and the Charge on the Property*

In many cases, the distinction between the debt as a personal obligation and the lien as a charge on the property is not practically significant. The debtor is usually the owner of the property, and a judgment foreclosing the lien is also a judgment on the debt. However, it sometimes happens that the right to foreclose the lien on the property is separated from the right to pursue the debtor for payment of the debt.

This occurs, for example, where state law requires the creditor to make an election of remedies (*i.e.,* to choose between suing on the lien or on the debt). It could also happen where the debtor has transferred the encumbered property, so that the creditor has to sue the new owner to foreclose the lien,[2] but must sue the debtor to recover on the debt. (Normally, the creditor would only be interested in suit on the debt if the property cannot be traced or its value is insufficient to satisfy the debt). A third situation in which the debt and lien are separate occurs under certain statutes that allow a person to acquire a lien on property even without a contractual relationship between the lienholder and the owner. For example, if a subcontractor works on the improvement of real property under a contract with a prime contractor, the prime contractor is liable on the debt. Unless the prime contractor is an actual agent of the owner, no contractual privity exists between the owner and the subcontractor. Nevertheless, if the subcontractor is not paid by the prime contractor, it is entitled to file a mechanic's lien on the property. This lien can be foreclosed to satisfy the debt, even though the owner cannot be sued personally on the debt.

§2.2.3 *Noncontemporaneous Creation of the Debt and the Lien*

Although the ultimate enforcement of the lien is predicated on the existence of a debt at the time of enforcement, it is possible that the lien and the debt

---

2. As explained in sections 2.5 and 2.7, the transferee takes the property subject to the lien.

could arise at different times and could be created by separate agreements or legal events. The fact that these rights can be created separately or successively can be very useful in some types of transactions. It can also present some interesting legal problems, which will be considered later. The present purpose is to introduce this concept and to describe situations to look out for.

(1) An unsecured debt can be subsequently secured.   When it is originally created, a debt may be unsecured. At some later time, before the debt is paid, it could be changed into a secured debt. This could happen, for example, if the parties make a later contract under which the debtor grants a security interest to the creditor to secure the preexisting debt. It could also occur by nonconsensual means through the operation of a statute or the judicial process.

As long as the security is created before the time for enforcement has arrived, the debt will be enforceable as a secured debt. However, if some third party acquired rights in the property during the gap period between the creation and securing of the debt, those rights could be superior to the security interest. In addition, the delay in securing the debt could have consequences in bankruptcy.

(2) A lien can be created in property in anticipation of future indebtedness.   A prospective borrower and lender may plan a relationship under which funds or credit are to be provided by the lender in the future. Particularly when a long-term relationship is contemplated and a line of credit is to be advanced as the debtor needs it, it may be convenient for the parties to create a lien in property at the beginning of the transaction. Of course, the lien is not enforceable until advances are actually made by the creditor, but as soon as the debt arises, it will be secured by the preexisting lien. If a line of credit is provided, then each future advance will be secured by the lien. This arrangement protects the creditor to the fullest extent possible and avoids the inconvenience of creating a new security interest every time an advance is made. This type of transaction is illustrated in Example 3.

§2.2.4   After-Acquired Collateral

As was stated in section 2.2.1, a lien must attach to particular property; a lien in the abstract is meaningless. However, a lien can be created in a piece or class of property before that property has come into existence or before the debtor has acquired rights in it.

To create such a lien, the creditor completes the legal procedure to establish the lien before the debtor acquires the property, or all of the property, that will ultimately be subject to the lien. Prior to the debtor's acquisition of the property, the lien does not extend to it, of course, but as soon as it comes into the debtor's estate the lien latches onto it. The property that will fall within the lien must be clearly identified when the lien is created. The utility of liens on after-acquired collateral is illustrated in Example 3.

§2.2.5 Purchase Money Security Interests

It is common for people to borrow money or to obtain credit for the purpose of acquiring specific property. For example, the buyer of a home or a car usually pays only a portion of the price in cash and covers the balance by a bank loan or credit from the seller. When a loan or credit is given to the debtor for the express purpose of enabling the debtor to acquire particular property and the property is itself used as collateral to secure the debt, the lien is called a *purchase money security interest* (often abbreviated as "P.M.S.I.").

The link between collateral and debt is particularly striking when the debtor's acquisition of the collateral was made possible by the value given by the creditor. For this reason, strong equities favor the holder of a purchase money interest, who is sometimes given special concessions in law. For example, UCC Article 9 allows greater flexibility in the perfection of purchase money interests and enhances their priority under some circumstances. (For the most part, these rules are beyond the scope of this book.) In some situations the Bankruptcy Code treats a purchase money interest more generously. (*See, e.g.,* section 16.1.4.) Although it is important to recognize that purchase money interests sometimes receive more favorable treatment than other liens, this difference should not be exaggerated. For many purposes, they are merely one type of consensual lien, subject to the same rules that govern other liens of that kind.

§2.3 The Creation of a Lien

A lien does not arise simply because the creditor wills it into existence. It must be created by following procedures prescribed by law. Different liens are established in different ways under a wide variety of statutes, common law rules, and equitable principles. In the next section these different types of lien will be identified and explained. Although each has its own set of rules and precepts governing its creation, operation, and effect, some common principles can be stated in broad terms.

To be fully effectual, a lien must be valid not only against the debtor but against third parties as well. The process of creating a lien valid against the debtor is known as *attachment*. Expansion of that interest to make the lien binding on third parties is called *perfection*. Sometimes a single procedure is followed to achieve both attachment and perfection, but some liens require two separate legal acts to be accomplished.

The importance of a lien's validity against third parties cannot be too strongly emphasized. If the creditor's right to the property is enforceable only against the debtor, the creditor has no protection against the claims of third parties who subsequently acquire rights in the property. Such a transferee of the property will be able to acquire it free of the lien, and the creditor will be left with a suit on the debt against the defaulting debtor. However, if the right to the property is perfected, the property will remain subject to the creditor's claim, which cannot usually be extinguished by subsequent transfer.

§2.3.1 *Attachment*

For a creditor to acquire a lien in the debtor's property that is valid against the debtor, some transaction or relationship must exist from which such an interest arises. A creditor does not, merely by virtue of being owed money, receive rights in the debtor's property. The lien may attach because of the terms of a contract, because services have been performed on the property, because equity recognizes the lien, or because the use of a particular judicial process gives rise to a lien. This is discussed more fully in section 2.4. For now, it may be observed that the law that provides for the creation of each type of lien will prescribe the requirements for attachment, such as the execution of a contract in proper form, the giving of a notice following the rendition of some service, or the completion of some other act or process.

§2.3.2 *Perfection*

The rules governing perfection vary depending upon the type of lien in question. For some liens, the very act of attachment required to create a lien valid against the debtor will simultaneously perfect the lien and make the interest effective against third parties, making any additional procedure unnecessary. However, many liens do not fall under this rule and do require some additional step to be taken before the lienholder's rights will avail against third parties. This usually involves either possession and control of the property by the lienholder, or some form of recording designed to publicize the interest.

§2.3.3 *Summary*

The *attachment date* is the date on which the lien becomes enforceable against the debtor, but the *perfection date* is the date on which it becomes effective against third parties. This means that until the acts required for perfection have been completed, the lienholder is not fully protected. Although an enforceable lien exists against the debtor, it has not yet been turned into a right of universal effect. It could therefore be defeated if some third party acquires rights in the property, whether voluntarily or under compulsion of law. (This does not mean that every subsequent third party will necessarily take precedence over the unperfected lien. Some later transferees will not prevail over a prior unperfected lienholder. This is discussed in section 2.7.)

§2.4 The Different Categories of Lien

Lien classification is not simply a technical or formal exercise. It has significant substantive implications. The different categories of lien are each subject to distinct rules and produce different consequences for their holders, the debtor, and third parties. Each category of liens is made up of a number of specific liens. The liens in each category can be quite diverse in the needs they are designed to meet, the circumstances under which they arise, their procedural prerequisites and the level of protection that they bestow on the lienholder.

What follows below is not a comprehensive treatment of all the liens that may be found in each category. However, some of the more common liens are described and used as illustrations.

§2.4.1 Consensual Liens

A consensual lien is created by contract between the debtor and the creditor. The contract must be valid and enforceable under the common law of contracts, and it must also comply with the specific rules of statute or common law that govern the creation of the particular security interest. At a minimum, the contract must describe the property and contain a grant of the interest to secure the debt. Other terms may be required for validity. Apart from that, the arrangement is consensual, so the parties have discretion in formulating the detailed terms and conditions under which the lien is granted and may be enforced.

The grant of the lien is usually part of the consideration demanded by the creditor for the extension of credit. It is often found in the contract that governs the underlying debt, or is executed simultaneously with it. However, as mentioned in section 2.2.3, these two elements do not have to be contemporaneous. (Examples 1, 2, and 3 illustrate consensual liens.)

§2.4.2 Judicial Liens

Judicial liens arise out of the court proceedings initiated by the creditor for recovery of the debt. They are not dependent on a contract with the debtor but are imposed on the debtor's property as a consequence of a particular legal procedure followed in the suit. The distinction between attachment and perfection is not relevant to most judicial liens because a single act or event both creates and perfects the lien.

Some judicial liens may come into existence prior to judgment. For example, under some circumstances the plaintiff-creditor, through the process of prejudgment attachment, may be entitled to seize property of the debtor and to have the property held as security for the prospective judgment. This seizure creates an attachment lien. Other judicial liens arise only upon or after judgment. For example, the judgment itself, when properly recorded or docketed in the prescribed recording office, creates a lien on real property in the county of recording or docketing. The levy of execution on property following judgment gives rise to an execution lien on the property.

Judicial liens are essentially last-ditch affairs. They are neither planned for nor obtained at the inception of the debt. A judicial lienholder is, in fact, nothing more than a formerly unsecured creditor who has been able to exercise the right to levy on property or to docket a judgment as part of the process of enforcing the debt by judicial action. As noted in section 1.4, there is an element of luck in acquiring the status of judicial lienholder. If the debtor is in some financial trouble, competition for assets may be fierce and a creditor may find that the debtor has no lienable property left. Even if a creditor is able to obtain a judicial lien, it is not assured that the advantage of security will not be lost. If the debtor should become bankrupt shortly after the lien is obtained, the bankruptcy trustee may be able to avoid the lien as a preference. This is discussed in Chapter 16.

Judicial liens are discussed further in section 2.7, and are illustrated by the questions in that chapter.

§2.4.3   *Statutory Liens*

Many consensual and judicial liens are governed by statute. For example, UCC Article 9 applies to security interests in personal property, and the state's civil procedure code typically provides for judicial liens. However, even though these liens may be controlled or permitted by statute, they are not statutory liens. True statutory liens are not created by contract or judicial process, but arise under the terms of a statute because the legislature has determined that a creditor of that class or a debt of that type is worthy of the protection of security. Some statutory liens have antecedents in common law and are merely legislative codifications or modifications of preexisting common law liens while others are legislative innovations.

There are many different types of statutory liens, each with its own rules and requirements. However, they do typically have a number of features in common:

(1) A statutory basis.   The lien is, of course, provided for by statute (either state or federal). The statutes are very specific about the type of debt and the class of creditor that may benefit from the lien and about the identity of the property that is subject to the lien. The transaction and the creditor must fall within the protected category for the lien to be claimed and the property must be lienable under the statute.

(2) Strict procedural requirements.   Lien statutes prescribe the procedures that must be followed for creation of the lien and usually require the creditor to take certain steps to claim it. These requirements can be very exacting, and the courts normally demand careful compliance as a prerequisite to lien validity.

(3) Attachment and perfection.   Most statutory liens are subject to the general principle that some form of notice or possession is required to effectuate the lien against the debtor, and some form of control or publicity is necessary to make the lien viable against third parties who claim rights in the property. Sometimes a single act will accomplish both ends.

(4) An underlying relationship.   Even though statutory liens are not consensual, they are obviously founded in some underlying relationship between the lienholder and the person whose property is subject to the lien. In some cases this relationship may itself be contractual in nature, but contractual privity in the underlying relationship is not always a prerequisite. The lien may be based on other grounds, such as an implied agency, the breach of a statutory duty, or unjust enrichment. When conferring a statutory lien on a particular class of creditor, the legislature has made the determination that there is some equity in favor of the creditor, or some special merit to its claim, so that the law should afford the protection of security, notwithstanding that such security was never bargained for with the debtor.

There are many types of statutory liens. Two of these (the artisan's lien and the mechanic's lien) are illustrated in Example 4. Some other examples are: the lien on crops or harvests in favor of agricultural workers, fishermen, and others, to secure the value of their labor; the attorney's lien on a documentary work product, to secure professional fees; and liens in favor of the state and federal governments to secure unpaid assessed taxes. (Attorney's and artisan's liens are based in common law and are therefore common law liens in states that have not codified them.)

§2.4.4   *Common Law Liens*

Common law liens are quite similar to statutory liens in their underlying purpose and effect. They arise by operation of law, without the agreement of the debtor, to secure an otherwise unsecured obligation incurred in a particular transaction recognized at common law as worthy of protection. The difference between them is that common law liens have not been created or codified by statute but are recognized under principles of common law applied by the courts. The most familiar common law liens are very old. They apply only to personal property, and they require possession for their creation and continued validity. They arise only when possession of the personalty is obtained and expire as soon as it is lost.

Many liens that originally arose from common law have been codified and have thereby been converted to statutory form. In the process of codification, legislatures have often restricted or expanded the scope of the lien, imposed new regulations on it, or provided for perfection by filing as an alternative to the traditional possessory form. Because of this legislative activity, common law liens are less frequently encountered today than they used to be.

Some examples of traditional common law liens (to the extent that they can still be found in uncodified form) are: the artisan's lien given to a repairer of goods, to secure the price of the repairs; the attorney's lien; the lien given to landlords and innkeepers in property brought onto their premises, to secure the arrear rent or the price of board and lodging; and the lien of warehousemen and carriers on the goods stored or transported by them, to secure storage or carriage charges.

The common law lien is illustrated in Example 4.

§2.4.5   *Equitable Liens*

Like judicial liens, equitable liens derive from the judicial process, though the circumstances and the purposes of their creation are quite different. Equitable liens do not arise as an incident of collection procedures at law, but are a remedy granted by the court in the exercise of its equitable jurisdiction.

The role of the equitable lien can be illustrated by an example: An employee embezzles money from an employer and uses it as part of the purchase price of a new car. The employer sues the employee for recovery of the embezzled funds. In awarding restitution, the court may impress an equitable lien on the car to ensure that the employer will be able to recover the stolen money by seizing and selling the very item that was bought with it.

The traditional role of equity is to provide relief where available legal remedies are inadequate. Therefore, a creditor who claims equitable relief must usually show that legal remedies cannot place it in its rightful position. However, the mere fact that legal remedies are inadequate or unavailable is not necessarily enough to make a case for equitable relief. The court will balance all the equities in exercising its discretion to grant a remedy in equity. For example, a plaintiff may be entitled to a statutory lien, provided that it follows the procedure prescribed by the statute. If the plaintiff neglects to comply with the statute so that the statutory lien (a legal remedy) is lost, does it have grounds for asking the court to impress an equitable lien on the property on the basis that its legal remedy is inadequate? The answer is usually no. To grant equitable relief under these circumstances sanctions the plaintiff's failure to comply with the law and undermines the procedural requirements of the statute.

§2.5 The Effect of a Valid Lien

§2.5.1 Against the Debtor and Subsequent Transferees

A transfer of property conveys only those rights that the transferor has in the property. Therefore, a transferee acquires the debtor's property subject to any encumbrances on the debtor's ownership. This means that once the creditor has properly complied with the rules governing attachment and perfection of the lien, an interest is created in the property that is effective not only against the debtor but also against any third party who thereafter acquires an interest in the property, whether by voluntary transfer (*e.g.*, purchase) or involuntary transfer (*e.g.*, execution).

If the debtor defaults on the secured debt, the lienholder is entitled to foreclose on the lien, and the interest of any subsequent transferee is confined to whatever surplus may be left after the lien has been fully satisfied. There are exceptions to this general rule, which are dealt with in section 2.7 and in later chapters. However, the rule is widely applicable, and in most cases the perfected lienholder is fully protected from the claims of persons whose interests arose after the lien.

§2.5.2 On Preexisting Third-Party Interests in the Property

The same rule that protects the lienholder against subsequent transferees makes the lien subservient to third-party interests in the property that were perfected before the lien. These preexisting interests may be earlier perfected liens or other recorded (and sometimes unrecorded) rights that have been conveyed by the debtor or imposed on the property by law. (Section 2.7 has a more detailed discussion of the ranking of rights in property.)

Because the lien is subject to valid preexisting third-party rights in the property, a prospective lienholder should check filing records and make other appropriate inquiries before agreeing to give credit to the debtor on the strength of a security interest in property. If the lender does not investigate, it may later find that superior interests encumber all or a substantial portion of the property's value. (Of course, a nonconsensual lienholder, such as a judicial lienholder, does not have the same opportunities for planning as a person who acquires a lien by contract.)

§2.5.3 *Oversecured and Undersecured Debt*

The security afforded by collateral is only as valuable as the property itself. If the value of the property (or, the remaining value, if there are already senior claims of record) is less than the amount of the debt, a portion of the debt will be unsecured. When the property is liquidated, this unsecured balance — the *deficiency* — will be left unsatisfied. To collect it, the lienholder must undertake the uncertain collection process outlined in section 1.4.

To avoid or at least to minimize the risk of a deficiency, a prospective lienor must satisfy itself that the debtor's equity (*i.e.*, the debtor's unencumbered economic interest) in the property is worth enough to cover the debt. If the value of the debtor's equity just barely covers the debt, the lienholder has no margin of safety to accommodate possible depreciation of the property or to cover accumulation of interest or any legal fees that may be incurred in trying to collect the debt. For this reason, a careful prospective lienholder tries to ensure that the value of the collateral exceeds the debt (as well as any senior claims) by a comfortable margin. This excess of collateral value over the debt is known as an *equity cushion:* It is the debtor's surplus equity that can absorb any adverse change in the ratio of collateral to debt.

Thus, in addition to checking for preexisting interests in the proposed collateral, a careful prospective lienholder must also attempt to make a realistic appraisal of the property and an accurate prediction of likely decreases in its value. The lienholder should also take precautions — possibly by means of contract provisions, or by periodic inspections — to ensure that the property is protected from damage or destruction during the period of the lien. As stated before, these opportunities for planning are more likely to be available where the lien arises out of a contractual relationship. A nonconsensual lienholder must usually settle for whatever property is available.

§2.6   Enforcement of the Lien

The procedure for enforcing liens varies considerably depending on the type of lien involved. A comparison of the enforcement process sketched here to that for unsecured debt (described in section 1.4) shows why security is a potent right. *See* Example 1.

Liens are enforced by a process known as *foreclosure*. In the case of some liens, the lienholder must obtain a judgment of foreclosure before proceeding with enforcement. The enforcement of other liens can be initiated immediately upon default without the court's imprimatur. The matter only comes before the court if the debtor or some other interested party challenges the foreclosure. The realization of the collateral involves two steps. The first is the seizure of the property, and the second is its application to satisfaction of the debt.

§2.6.1 Seizure of the Property

Some liens (*e.g.*, a pledge, a common law artisan's lien) are perfected by possession, so that the lienholder is already in possession of the collateral when the debtor defaults. If so, no act of seizure is needed, although some form of notice may be required.

If the lienholder does not already have possession at the time of default, it must seize the collateral as a prelude to foreclosure sale. With some liens, this seizure of the property can be accomplished by the lienholder on its own, without the assistance of the court. This is known as *self-help*. In other cases (or if the debtor resists the lienholder's attempt at seizure), a court order and the employment of court officials is necessary. If litigation concerning the foreclosure is likely to take some time, the lienholder may be able to replevy the collateral pending final determination of the suit. *See* section 3.3.5.

§2.6.2 Application of the Property in Satisfaction of the Debt

Once the property is placed under the lienholder's control, the process of realizing it takes place. There are two methods of applying the property to satisfaction of the debt: *foreclosure by sale* and *strict foreclosure*. Strict foreclosure is not universally available and can only be used with regard to certain types of liens, so foreclosure by sale is more typical.

a. Foreclosure by Sale

The most common method of applying the collateral to the payment of the debt is by foreclosure sale. In the case of some liens (an Article 9 security interest, for example), the sale may be conducted by the lienholder itself, and in others the sale is handled by the sheriff or a similar court official. Normally, the sale is by public auction, but private sales by the lienholder are authorized for some liens (Article 9, for example). Whoever conducts the sale, and whatever method is allowed, sales are always subject to some form of regulation and to a set of standards to ensure that they are honest, properly conducted, and are likely to provide as reasonable a price as possible under the circumstances. These regulations usually provide for the method of advertising the sale, the notice to be given to the debtor, and the actual conduct of the sale itself.

This does not mean, however, that anyone expects the foreclosure sale to bring in a handsome return. The law is sadly resigned to the fact that foreclosure sales seldom realize the most advantageous price and that they usually attract considerably less than the value of the goods on the open market. Therefore, a sale will not be overturned on the basis that the price was too low unless a statute provides for such a protection or the court is convinced that there was something improper in the sale process.

Once the property has been sold in accordance with the prescribed procedure, the proceeds are applied to the payment of the debt, including the costs and charges of the sale. If the price realized is insufficient to cover the debt in full, a deficiency is due to the creditor by the debtor. With some liens, foreclosure operates as a waiver of the action on the debt, so that the deficiency cannot be recovered. In many cases this is not so, however, and the creditor can proceed to recover the deficiency from the debtor as an unsecured debt. If the price paid at the sale exceeds the amount of the debt, the surplus is applied to payment of the claims of any junior lienholders who are parties to the foreclosure. *See* section 2.7. If no such claimants exist, or if there is a surplus remaining after they have been paid, the balance is paid to the debtor.

One aspect of foreclosure sales that often surprises people on first encounter is that the lienholder is usually allowed to bid and buy at its own public foreclosure sale. It pays the lienholder to do this where the distress price is lower than the market price. By buying the property, the lienholder acquires the property cheaply, gives the debtor credit for the deflated sale price, and (provided that it is recoverable in law) proceeds against the debtor for the deficiency.

It does not always work out this way, of course. If the lienholder has received too much of a bargain, the court may be persuaded to overturn the sale as abusive. Even if this does not happen, the deficiency, like any other unsecured debt, may be uncollectable, so the property may be all that the lienholder ever gets.

b.   Strict Foreclosure

For some liens, strict foreclosure is available to lienholders as an alternative to foreclosure by sale. In strict foreclosure, the lienholder does not sell the property but takes transfer of it from the debtor in full satisfaction of the debt. This means that the lienholder has no right to claim a deficiency and no obligation to pay any surplus to the debtor.

Although strict foreclosure may sometimes be the same in effect as the lienholder's purchase of the property at the foreclosure sale — especially where a deficiency action is barred after sale — the two remedies are distinct. At a foreclosure sale there is always a possibility of competing bids, and a chance that a surplus may be realized. If the lien is strictly foreclosed, no bidding takes place: The lienholder simply takes the property without having to account for any surplus value. In other words, strict foreclosure is intended to balance the books. The lienholder has no claim for any deficiency and the debtor has no claim for surplus value.

It follows from this that strict foreclosure is only of interest to a lienholder who believes that the property is worth at least as much as or more than the debt. Therefore, the likely result of strict foreclosure is that the debtor forfeits surplus equity in the property that would have been returned if foreclosure had been by sale. This is why strict foreclosure is not generally favored by the law. Even when it is allowed, as it is, for example in UCC Article 9, it is subject to limitations, controls, a notice requirement, and rights of objection.

Foreclosure issues are illustrated in Examples 1 and 2.

§2.7 Priorities among Liens and Other Interests

§2.7.1 The Function of Priority Rules

It often happens that more than one lien is created in a single piece of property. For example, a homeowner may borrow money on the security of a second mortgage, or a car repairer may acquire an artisan's lien in a car that is already subject to a security interest, or a judgment creditor may acquire a judicial lien on property that is already encumbered by someone else.

When the property is valuable enough to accommodate all the liens against it as well as all legal costs and fees, ranking of the liens is not practically important. If foreclosure occurs, enough proceeds will be realized to satisfy all the liens. However, when the property is worth *less* than the total amount of liens, there must be rules to determine how the fund should be distributed between them. The law does not usually treat all liens as equal so that they share in the proceeds of the collateral pro rata. Rather, it ranks the liens, and the proceeds are applied to the full satisfaction of each lien in order of priority until the fund is exhausted.

For example, suppose collateral worth $900 has three liens on it, each securing a debt of $500. The senior lien is paid in full. The second-ranking lien receives the remaining proceeds of $400, leaving an unsecured deficiency of $100. The junior lien receives nothing and becomes an unsecured claim.

This section introduces the concept of priority and surveys the general principles applicable to the ranking of liens and interests in property. Priority is a pervasive issue in debtor/creditor law, and the themes discussed here will be raised and built upon in many later chapters on both state law and bankruptcy.

§2.7.2   *The General Rule of Priority*

The most common method of ranking is based on the chronological sequence in which the liens arose. That is, the earliest lien has first claim to the proceeds, followed by subsequent liens, in the order that they arose. This rule, known as the "first-in-time" rule, is based on the maxim "first in time is first in right." It sounds better in Latin.

The first-in-time rule derives from the general principle, introduced in section 2.5, that rights conveyed in property cannot exceed those held by the transferee. Therefore, if a debtor's property is already encumbered by a valid lien, a second and subsequent lien can only extend to the debtor's unencumbered equity in the property.

The effective date of a lien for priority purposes is usually its perfection date. This stands to reason, because it is perfection that makes the lien viable against persons other than the debtor. *See* section 2.3.2. Sometimes a statute

or the common law recognizes an exception to this general rule and allows the lien's priority to date from attachment or to backdate to the date of attachment once it is perfected. *See* Examples 6 and 7.

§2.7.3 Departures from the First-in-Time Rule for the Protection of Certain Subsequent Lienholders

Although the earlier lien is generally given priority, there are a number of situations in which it is appropriate for the law to recognize an exception to this rule. The priority accorded to a repairer of goods illustrates one of them:

Statutes granting an artisan's lien (described in section 2.4.3) commonly provide that the repairer's lien takes priority over a preexisting security interest in the goods. This variation in the first-in-time rule recognizes that the repairer has, by providing labor and materials, maintained or enhanced the value of the property. If the preexisting lien is given priority, the benefit of the repair would go to the senior lienor, whose collateral is preserved or appreciates at the expense of the unpaid repairer. Not only does this seem unfair, but it would also discourage repairers to undertake work without advance payment.

In short, although the first-in-time rule governs unless a specific exception has been recognized by statute or court decisions, such exceptions do exist. It is therefore risky to assume that the oldest lien is always senior. The law applicable to the competing interests must be consulted.

§2.7.4 Priorities between Liens and Other Interests in the Property

It has so far been assumed that both or all of the competing interests in the property are liens. It is possible, however, that a lienholder may be contending for priority with the holder of some other interest in the property, such as a co-owner or a person who claims to have purchased the property from the debtor. These priority disputes are governed by the same general rules as apply to competing liens: The interest that first took effect usually prevails. If a valid co-ownership interest existed when the lien was created, or the debtor had validly transferred the property prior to the effective date of the lien, the lien only extends to any interest that the debtor may have retained. Similarly, if the debtor conveys rights in the property after the effective date of the lien, the transferee takes subject to the lien.

As in the case of competing liens, the exceptions to this general rule are intended to protect certain parties who acquire rights in the property in good faith and in circumstances under which they are not expected to be concerned about other interests or to check public filing records. For example, a department store may have borrowed money to purchase inventory and may have secured the loan by giving the lender a security interest in the inventory. If the first-in-time rule is rigidly applied, a customer who buys goods from the department store must be concerned about the financier's priority security interest in the inventory. Even if the customer pays the store for the goods, the financier can assert its interest in them if the store defaults on its loan. The rights of the subsequent buyer would be subject to the earlier lien on the goods. Because such a rule would make consumer transactions very risky and would inhibit retail trading, the first-in-time rule is not applied in this case. Title to the goods passes to the customer free of the financier's security interest, provided that the purchase was an honest, routine transaction.

§2.7.5   A Summary of the Issues to Be Considered in Dealing with Priorities

The ranking of liens and interests becomes important when the property is not valuable enough to satisfy all the claims against it. To determine priorities, the following questions must be resolved:

(1) Are all the liens and interests valid charges against the property?   There is no point in struggling with rules of priority unless all the contending interests are valid and effective. An invalid or unenforceable claim to the property cannot have priority, even if it was purportedly created before its competitors.

Because different liens and interests in various kinds of property are authorized or regulated by different statutes or common law doctrines, it is necessary to identify the liens or interests and the nature of the property in which they are asserted. Then, the liens or interests must be evaluated under the applicable legal rules to determine whether they have been properly created and effected.

(2) What is the effective date of each lien or interest?   As noted before, any chronological system of ranking is based on the effective date of the lien or interest. The applicable law must be consulted to determine when the right is effective against the competing claims. Usually this is the perfection date, but there are exceptions to this general rule.

(3) Identify and apply the rules of ranking.   When the first two steps have been taken, it is easier to find the applicable rules of priority. In particular, if the first-in-time rule has been departed from, the governing statute or rules of common law express the different treatment to be accorded to the lien or interest in question.

EXAMPLES

1. In This Signature Shalt Thou Conquer

Grim Repo, Inc. sold goods on credit to Wendy Vendee. At the time of sale, Grim Repo had Wendy sign a security agreement that granted it a security interest in the goods to secure their purchase price. Grim Repo immediately filed a copy of the agreement in the appropriate state recording office.

A few weeks later, Wendy failed to pay an installment due under the contract. She has persisted in her default despite a demand for payment by Grim Repo.

What course of action can Grim Repo take? How do its rights differ from those of the seller in section 1.4?

2. The Twilight of the Goods

Consider the following additional facts: When Grim Repo tried to take possession of the goods after Wendy's default, it discovered that Wendy had sold them to an itinerant junk dealer for $500 cash. Wendy claims not to know the name and whereabouts of the buyer, and Grim Repo has no way of finding him.

What is Grim Repo's position now?

3. Impignoration

Pawnporker Industries, Inc. manufactures bacon and sausages, which it sells to grocery chains and wholesalers. It typically sells to its customers on credit, and it always has a large volume of outstanding accounts receivable. Finding that its receipts from customers sometimes trickle in too slowly to meet its demands for cash, Pawnporker would like to borrow money so that it can pay its expenses without having to wait for payments from its customers.

Pawnporker has successfully applied to Couchon Equity, Inc. for a loan to be secured by its customers' accounts. The security agreement provides that Couchon Equity will advance funds to Pawnporker in an amount equal to 75 percent of its current accounts receivable. As customers pay, Pawnporker is obliged to remit a percentage of its receipts to Couchon Equity to reduce the loan balance. All new accounts that are created by future sales will automatically be included in Couchon Equity's security interest. Provided that Pawnporker complies fully with the terms of the security agreement, Couchon Equity will make additional advances to Pawnporker in the future. These advances will fall within the existing security interest and will be secured by Pawnporker's accounts.

(a) Can something as nebulous as accounts serve as collateral?

(b) Is a transaction like this valid? More specifically, can parties create a security interest that covers not only existing collateral and advances, but also collateral that comes into being and advances that are made in the future?

4. Labor's Love Lost

One evening, as Alec Smart was returning home from work, he swung his car into his driveway. As was his habit, he jabbed at the button on his garage door opener as he entered the driveway at excessive speed, intending to zoom into the garage just under the rising door. Alec had executed this maneuver successfully in the past, and he enjoyed the sensation of split second timing as the car just cleared the moving door. On this occasion, he was not as agile as usual. His finger missed the button and the door did not open.

(a) Arty Zan's lien

The next day he took his crumpled car to Arty Zan, a specialist in restoring auto bodies. Arty quoted a price of $1,000 to repair the damage, and Alec accepted. Arty set to work immediately and completed the repair two days later. When Alec arrived to collect his car, Arty presented his account. Alec looked shifty, made a great show of patting his pockets, and exclaimed that he had left his checkbook at home. He promised to mail a check to Arty as soon as he returned home. Arty, who was not born yesterday, refused to release the car to Alec until he received payment of the repair charges. Is Arty justified in holding onto the car?

(b) Mac & Nick's lien

On the same day that he took his car to Arty, Alec employed Mac & Nick's Construction Co. to remove his mangled garage door, repair the door frame, and install a new door. The contract price for this work was $1,500. Mac & Nick's completed the repair and Alec gave them a check for $1,500. The check was subsequently dishonored. Mac & Nick's will now have to struggle to get their money out of Alec. Does the law give Mac & Nick's any special protection?

5. Fiscal Jerks

Buddy Beautiful bought a bodybuilding machine from Señor Lean Sweatshop on credit. He signed a contract that obliged him to pay the price of $3,000 in monthly installments over one year. (This was a simple sale on credit. The contract did not grant a security interest to Señor Lean to secure the price.)

A week later, Buddy borrowed $2,800 from his friend Izzy Touch to finance a short but glamorous beach vacation. Buddy promised Izzy that he would repay the loan as soon as he returned from his trip. This was irresponsible. Buddy earned a small salary and had no savings or means of repaying the debt.

When Buddy failed to repay Izzy as promised, Izzy became very upset. Buddy realized that their friendship would end unless he settled the debt. Buddy therefore offered the bodybuilding machine to Izzy in full satisfaction of his claim. Realizing that he would probably never see his money again,

Izzy accepted. At the time, the machine was worth about $2,700 because it was no longer brand new.

Buddy did not pay the first monthly installment due to Señor Lean. Señor Lean, who discovered that Izzy has the machine, demanded its return. Is Señor Lean entitled to the machine?

6. Unhappy Landings

Over the last five years, the following interests have been created in a piece of real property owned by Crash Land Investments, Inc., a property developer:

(a) Five years ago Crash Land granted a mortgage in the property to Foremost Finance, Inc. The mortgage was properly executed and recorded at the time of purchase.

(b) Two years ago, Crash Land granted a second mortgage on the property to Sequacious Security, Inc. The mortgage was properly executed and recorded at the time that the loan was advanced.

(c) Last year, Crash Land engaged the services of a bulldozer operator, Tertia Thirdly III, to level the land. Tertia performed the work but was not paid her fee. She therefore properly filed a mechanic's lien against the property.

(d) A few weeks after Tertia began work, and before she filed her lien, Sally Fourth obtained a judgment against Crash Land and immediately recorded the judgment by filing it in the recording office in the county in which the property is situated. The recording creates a judgment lien on the property, effective from the date of recording.

Crash Land is insolvent and cannot pay its debts. The property represents the only prospect that these four creditors have of satisfying their claims. The current value of the property has been reliably appraised at $120,000. The current balance of the debts due to the claimants is:

Foremost	$90,000
Sequacious	$45,000
Tertia	$15,000
Sally	$20,000

If the property does in fact realize $120,000, how should this be distributed?

7. Post Mortem on Example 6

Everyone except Foremost lost money in this foreclosure. Could they have done anything earlier in their transactions to prevent this from happening?

EXPLANATIONS

1. Grim Repo has a consensual security interest in the goods. Because the credit was given to Wendy to enable her to acquire the goods, the security interest in the goods is a purchase money security interest. The interest is governed by UCC Article 9. Provided that the agreement was properly executed, the security interest attached at that time. Upon recording the interest in compliance with Article 9, Grim Repo perfected it.

After Wendy's default, Grim Repo is entitled to repossess the goods. It may do so on its own, without a court order, provided that it can effect the repossession without a breach of the peace. After taking possession of the goods, Grim Repo has the right to sell them either at auction or by way of private sale. Article 9 also permits the alternative of strict foreclosure if specified conditions are satisfied. No court is involved in this stage of the procedure either, unless Wendy files a suit challenging some aspect of it. Even if Wendy is able to delay the sale by instituting court proceedings, Grim Repo will probably be able to obtain possession of the goods pending final determination of the action by applying for prejudgment replevin.

On the facts of this Example, no third party has taken transfer of the goods or levied on them to satisfy a judgment. If this had happened, Grim Repo's perfected security interest would, with a few exceptions, take precedence over any such third-party claims.

The contrast between this case and the *unsecured* seller's situation (described in section 1.4) is striking. Grim Repo's prospects of successful collection are much stronger. Not only does it have the possibility of an expedited process, but it also has a superior right to this specific property, which can be applied to the satisfaction of its claim.

2. This question makes the sobering point that not even a secured party is absolutely secure. The collateral could be destroyed or irretrievably disposed of. The right to recover it from the transferee is useless if his identity is unknown. To some extent, the holder of a security interest can take precautions against the loss of the collateral by insuring it and monitoring the debtor's activities. However, very tight control is often not feasible. Because the collateral has disappeared, Grim Repo has become an unsecured creditor and must face all the problems of one. *See* section 1.4.

If Wendy still has the $500 she received for the goods and Grim Repo can identify it as proceeds of the collateral, Grim Repo can claim a security interest in it. Under Article 9, a secured party's interest immediately attaches to proceeds generated by the disposition of the original collateral. Of course, cash is easily dissipated, and Grim Repo's chances of finding it and tracing it to the collateral are not likely to be very good.

3. (a) **Can accounts be collateral?** Unlike the goods in Examples 1 and 2, the accounts have no physical existence. They are intangible claims that

Pawnporker has against its customers. Nevertheless, they have economic value to the extent that they represent collectible funds due to the debtor in the future, and they are an asset that can be used as collateral to secure a loan to the debtor. Their intangible nature necessitates some variation in the rules governing the creation and enforcement of a consensual lien in them. These details are beyond our scope, but it is enough to note that as with goods, the interest must attach. This occurs when the agreement is executed, value is given by the secured party, and the accounts come into existence. In addition, the interest must be perfected by filing. A security interest in accounts, as well as in many other intangible assets, is subject to UCC Article 9.

(b) Can the security interest cover after-acquired collateral and future advances? As stated in sections 2.2.3 and 2.2.4, a security interest can be structured to cover after-acquired collateral and future advances. The interest is effective immediately with regard to the first advance and the current accounts. As new accounts arise, it will attach to them, and when further advances are made, they will be added to the debt secured by the collateral.

The facts of this Example illustrate why parties may wish to enter into a transaction of this type. They contemplate a continuing relationship that is much more complex than the single secured sale in Example 1. The collateral is not constant or fixed but will change over time as current accounts are paid by customers and new ones are generated by future sales. The debt will also fluctuate as payments are made, and new amounts are advanced.

Because it is inefficient for the parties to create a new security interest each time Pawnporker needs money and to file new financing statements each time new accounts are created, they have set up what is known as a *floating lien* at the beginning of the relationship. A security interest is created immediately in all the accounts of Pawnporker, both current and future, to secure both present and future advances. The description of the collateral in the agreement and the financing statement (*i.e.,* the document filed to record the interest) expressly covers after-acquired accounts.

A transaction of this kind requires careful monitoring by Couchon Equity. It must keep track of payments by Pawnporker's customers to make sure that the loan is being repaid as accounts are settled. It will not make new advances until a sufficient volume of new accounts have been generated to cover the existing loan balance plus the new advance. It will also ensure that the ratio of equity to debt stays within an acceptable margin of safety, so that there is an equity cushion to buffer its interest against reductions in collateral value resulting from uncollectable accounts or other contingencies.

This transaction may be represented diagrammatically as shown on page 30.

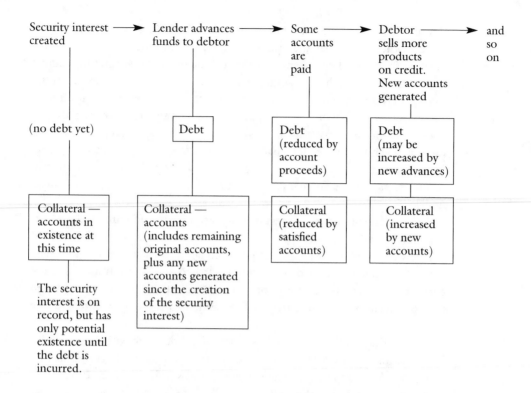

4. Arty and Mac & Nick's have both entered into contracts with Alec under which they have provided labor and materials for the repair of his property. However, neither of the repairers has been granted a consensual lien by Alec to secure the contract price.

It is quite common for states to afford such people special protection by granting them liens on the repaired property to secure the agreed price (or, in some cases, the reasonable value) of their services and supplies. The rationale for conferring lien rights on these claimants is that they have furnished performance at the request of the debtor that has conserved or enhanced his property and that it would be unfair to allow the debtor to keep that benefit without paying for it.

(a) Arty Zan's lien

Under common law, a repairer of personal property is entitled to an *artisan's lien* to secure the price or value of the repairs. Many states have codified and modernized the artisan's lien, making it a statutory lien.

Customarily, the lien is possessory. Possession is the act of publicity and control that creates and perfects the lien against the owner and third parties. The repairer must keep the repaired property until he has been paid. If he relinquishes the property, the lien lapses. Many contemporary statutes provide for filing as an alternative means of perfection, so that the lienholder can return the property without losing the lien.

Thus, by keeping the car, Arty asserts a lien in it to secure his claim for payment. He acquires this lien not because Alec granted it to him under a security agreement, and not because he has initiated court proceedings, but because the common law or a statute gives him a right to it by virtue of his relationship to the property.

(b)   Mac & Nick's lien

The lien to which Mac & Nick are entitled is known, in traditional terminology, as a *mechanic's and materialman's lien,* or in more modern formulations, as a *construction lien.* The lien is purely statutory in derivation and has no common law antecedent. It is available to any person who, at the request of the owner of real property or his actual or constructive agent, supplies labor or services (mechanic) or material (materialman) in connection with the repair or improvement of the property.

Though the rules governing mechanic's liens are particularly intricate, their essential purpose and effect is quite straightforward: If the contractor, subcontractor, or material supplier is not paid for its work or services, it is entitled to assert a lien on the real property within a specific time after the completion of its performance. The right to the lien arises in inchoate form as soon as the value is furnished by the claimant, and it must be fully perfected by notice, filing, and suit within a period prescribed by the statute.

As with the artisan's lien, the right to security is dependent not on a grant of lien rights by the owner of the property, nor on a court proceeding, but upon a qualifying relationship to the property and compliance with statutory procedures. (For a further example involving mechanic's liens, *see* Examples 6.)

5. This question is designed to determine if you are still awake.

Señor Lean is in the same position as the unsecured seller in section 1.4. It retained no interest in or ownership of the machine sold to Buddy. Title to the machine passed upon the sale, and Señor Lean was left with an unsecured debt for its price.

Izzy is also an unsecured creditor. Even though his debt arose after Señor Lean's, Buddy gave his claim preferential treatment. However, the first-in-time rule is inapplicable. It is relevant only to liens or other rights in property and not to unsecured claims. Outside of bankruptcy, the general rule is that the debtor can satisfy unsecured debts in any order that he likes and can prefer one creditor over others. Buddy's right to dispose of his property in this way is subject to one restriction: If the transfer constituted a fraud on his other creditors, they could sue to avoid it. The facts here do not furnish grounds for such an avoidance action. (*See* Chapter 4.)

Señor Lean's only remedy is to commence collection proceedings in the hope that Buddy will make an effort to pay his debt or that he has other assets that can be levied upon to satisfy it.

6. The facts of this question are represented in the diagram below.

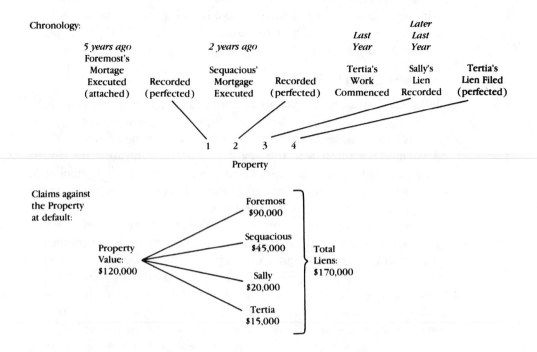

Each of the four interests asserted here must be capable of attaching to real property and must be perfected in the manner required for real property:

(a-b)   The mortgages are consensual liens. The facts state that both have been executed and recorded in accordance with the state's law governing mortgages on real property. Mortgages are normally effective upon perfection, that is, when they are recorded.

(c)   Tertia's mechanic's lien is a statutory lien. The facts state that it was properly filed only after Tertia had completed her performance. Although filing is required to perfect a mechanic's lien, the lienholder is typically permitted to file in a specified period following completion of performance. Once the filing is made, it backdates for priority purposes to the time that performance commenced. This system prevents an unnecessary flurry of filing activity at the start of the project. It also gives claimants an opportunity to file after completion of performance once it becomes apparent that there may be trouble concerning payment. Claimants are therefore able to delay filing while retaining priority status as at the date that performance commenced, provided that they accomplish the filing in the prescribed postcompletion period. By permitting this delayed filing, the statute creates the risk that a subsequent party may acquire rights in the property during the gap period, unaware of an inchoate, unpublicized superior lien. This risk is usually diminished by the observable activity on the property.

(d) The judgment lien is a judicial lien. The facts indicate that it comes into effect upon recording and extends to all the debtor's realty in the county. The recording of the judgment, rather than its grant by the court, is normally the effective date of the lien for priority purposes. (Judgment liens are discussed further in section 3.4.)

Based on these principles, Foremost's mortgage was effective first, then Sequacious's mortgage, then Tertia's lien, and, finally, Sally's judgment. Although the judgment was recorded before Tertia's lien was filed, the later filing of the lien related back to a time earlier than the recording of the judgment. Having fixed the effective dates of the interests, we can determine the distribution of the proceeds of the property by applying the first-in-time rule. (This rule applies unless the governing statute or common law doctrine provides otherwise.) This means that Foremost's mortgage of $90,000 is fully satisfied out of the fund of $120,000, leaving a balance of $30,000. This balance is applied to the payment of the mortgage debt of Sequacious, leaving a $15,000 deficiency. Tertia would have been third in line, and Sally would have been fourth, but the fund has run out and they receive nothing.

7. Sequacious, a consensual lienholder, must have known about Foremost's first mortgage when it agreed to lend money to Crash Land, secured by a second mortgage. Presumably, it realized that its interest would be junior to Foremost, but must have decided that the property was valuable enough to cover both claims. As it turned out, Sequacious misjudged.

Tertia is not a consensual lienholder, but the transaction that gave rise to her lien is contractual. She therefore also had some opportunity for planning. Had she been careful and well-informed, she would have known that she could claim a statutory lien. A search in the deeds registry would have revealed two preexisting mortgages on the property. She therefore had access to information that would have warned her that she may not be able to rely on the protection of a third-priority mechanic's lien. By performing services for Crash Land on credit, she took the risk that the property would not be valuable enough to accommodate her claim.

Although the debtor's ownership of property may have been a factor that influenced Sally to extend credit, she did not protect herself by requiring security when entering the transaction. When she obtained and recorded her judgment, she took pot luck. Her judgment lien attached to whatever property was available in the county. It was unfortunate that the property owned by the debtor was already so heavily encumbered that it had no value left. This illustrates the point made in section 2.4.2: Judicial liens are essentially last-minute rights that may arise too late to be helpful.

3

Debt Collection under State Law

§3.1 Preliminary Observations on Debt Collection by Judicial Process at State Law

The enterprise of collecting debt by court proceedings has already been introduced in section 1.4. This chapter deals more fully with the judicial procedures available to a creditor for the enforcement of a money obligation. The treatment is chronological, moving from prejudgment process to the judgment itself and then to postjudgment enforcement methods. Although most of this chapter is concerned with judicial proceedings, the last portion of the chapter, section 3.9, deals with nonjudicial collective remedies for debt collection under state law. As you proceed, bear the following points in mind:

(1) The focus here is on enforcement issues, both in the prejudgment stage of the case, and after judgment. Although this activity takes place within a civil suit, no attempt is made to deal with issues of civil procedure generally.

(2) The assumption is made for the sake of this discussion that the debtor does not defend the suit and that judgment is obtained by default. In many debt collection cases this is true: There is no dispute over the claim and the debtor simply cannot pay. However, enforcement proceedings also may be necessary in contested cases. Prejudgment remedies are available in those cases, and postjudgment collection procedures must be used if the judgment debtor fails to satisfy the judgment voluntarily.

(3) In many cases, the debts to be enforced by judicial procedures are unsecured when the suit begins. During the course of judicial

enforcement, the creditor may be able to secure the claim by obtaining a judicial lien.

(4) The procedures dealt with here are usually resorted to only after the creditor has failed to recover payment by informal means. As was discussed in section 1.4, the debtor's failure to pay may be symptomatic of more extensive financial difficulties, and other creditors may already be on the move. In addition, the spectre of bankruptcy may loom. Therefore, judicial collection proceedings are commenced in less than auspicious circumstances and must be pursued with speed and diligence if they are to have any chance of successful culmination.

(5) This is a generalized treatment of state law. Notable and sometimes dramatic variations occur from one state to another, and between state and federal courts. Where appropriate, alternative approaches are indicated, but no attempt is made to account for all the differences between jurisdictions.

The diagram on page 37 roughly traces the chronology of a debt collection case and identifies the principal issues that will be discussed.

§3.2   Executable Property and Levy

When secured claims are involved, the link between the debt and the encumbered property is crucial. *See* Chapter 2. Unsecured claims are not identified with any particular property, but their enforcement is dependent on property of the debtor being found and realized. Unless the debtor pays voluntarily, payment can only be extracted by the seizure and sale of the debtor's property to generate funds to satisfy the judgment. For this reason, the seizure and realization of the debtor's property is a recurring theme in debt collection by judicial process. Two concepts are central to this pervasive theme: executable property and levy.

§3.2.1   Executable Property

Even where the creditor's claim is undisputable and has been reduced to judgment, no enforcement can take place unless the debtor has property that can be applied to payment of the debt. Gone are the happy times when the debtor could be thrown into prison, sold into slavery, or carved up into little bits for failure to pay creditors.[1]

---

1. Imprisonment for debt was recognized by the common law both in England and America until fairly recent times. The Romans were even nastier. They allowed execution on the person of the debtor, so that he could be seized and sold *trans tiberium* (across the Tiber) into slavery. Another possibility in Roman law was for creditors to

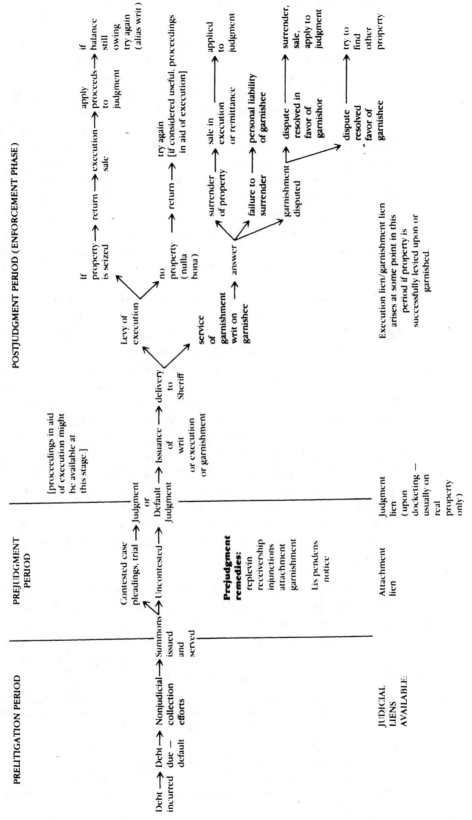

As noted in section 1.4, the debtor may have no property available for seizure, because it has already been disposed of, seized by other creditors, or encumbered by prior liens. Even if unencumbered property can be found, the creditor's ability to seize the debtor's property may be further limited: It may be immune from the claims of creditors (*i.e.*, nonexecutable).

In the absence of a specific rule to the contrary, one can generally assume that all the debtor's property, whether tangible or intangible, real or personal, is subject to the claims of creditors. However, some statutes and rules of common law provide exceptions to the general rule and make certain property nonexecutable. The reasons for protecting the property from creditors vary. They may arise from the identity and status of the debtor, the nature of the property, the nature of the claim, or some combination of these factors. The following are the most common bases for excluding property from execution:

(1) Exemptions in favor of individual debtors.   By statute, most states exempt certain property of an individual debtor from the claims of creditors. Broadly speaking, exemptions are intended to protect some of the debtor's property so that seizure by creditors does not leave the debtor destitute.

State exemption statutes vary considerably. Some simply allow the debtor to select property up to a particular value; some specifically identify classes or items of property that are protected; some prescribe both categories of exempt property and value limitations. When the worth of the exemptible asset exceeds a value limitation, the asset is only partially exempt: It is subject to execution, but the debtor is entitled to be paid the amount of the exemption out of the proceeds. The surplus is then applied to the debt.

Exemptions are discussed in greater detail in the context of bankruptcy in Chapter 13. However, it is important to note here that exemptions are claimable by the debtor in collection proceedings under state law as well as in bankruptcy. The scope of the exemptions and the procedure for claiming them are dictated by the state exemption statute.

(2) Exemptions of statutory benefits.   Apart from exemptions provided to individual debtors under the state's exemption law, other statutes may protect certain property from the claims of creditors. For example, a statute conferring a benefit or entitlement, such as a pension or disability benefits, may provide that neither the right to receive the benefit nor the benefit itself may be seized by creditors of the beneficiary.

---

divide up the body of the debtor and distribute it amongst themselves. The idea here was to terrorize the debtor's kin and friends into paying his debts.

Although imprisonment for debt has generally been abolished in the United States, some states still allow a creditor to obtain a writ of *capias ad satisfaciendum* ("body execution") under certain restricted circumstances. The right to body execution may, for example, be confined to cases where the debt arose out of willful or malicious conduct, or where the debtor is able to pay but deliberately evades payment of the judgment.

(3) Exclusions from execution based on public policy. Some assets are not executable because of various different public policies that are recognized by statute or common law. For example, if the state wishes to maintain control over the qualifications and character of those who are permitted to sell liquor, it may prohibit the assignment or transfer of liquor licenses whether by voluntary or involuntary means. Another example reflects a different public policy: Because public property serves the interest of the community, the legislature may protect it from seizure by creditors of public authorities. Therefore, the assets of a state, a local authority, or a government agency may be nonexecutable. Another common exclusion from execution protects speculative claims in property. Uncertain interests such as equitable interests in property or contingent or unliquidated claims of the debtor are often not executable. The policy behind this is the protection of the debtor's rights in inherently valuable property that is probably of little worth to the creditor. Because the rights have an uncertain value, they are likely to realize very little in an execution sale in relation to their potential worth to the debtor.

Although this is not an exhaustive list, these examples show that when property of the debtor is spoken of in the context of debt enforcement, there is always an implicit qualification that the property must be executable.

§3.2.2 Levy

The law's act of asserting control over the debtor's property on the creditor's behalf is known as levy. The procedures leading up to the act of levy are discussed in the next two chapters. The point to be made at this stage is that until the levy occurs, the debtor's property has not been subjected to the power of the law and the creditor acquires no rights in it by judicial process. The act of levy differs depending on the type of property involved. The following general rules apply:

(1) Tangible personal property. Levy is usually the sheriff's act of physically seizing the property, removing it from the debtor, and taking it into custody. In some states, if the goods are not readily removable, the sheriff may levy by taking constructive possession of them by, for example, posting a notice on the goods.

(2) Real property. Real property is levied upon not by physical seizure but by filing the writ in the real estate records.

(3) Intangible rights. Intangible rights identified in an indispensable document (*e.g.*, a negotiable instrument or a share certificate) are levied on as if they were tangible goods. Other intangible rights are levied upon by serving notice on the obligor through the process of garnishment.

(4) Identification of the property.   Sometimes a writ will specify that the sheriff must levy on specific, identified property. It is quite usual, however, for the writ to simply indicate the amount of the debtor's claim and to call upon the sheriff to find and levy upon sufficient property of the debtor to satisfy it. Therefore, when the plaintiff has not conducted an investigation before levy and has not identified executable property, the assets subjected to the levy could be selected quite randomly and fortuitously.

(5) The sheriff's return.   After completion of the levy, the sheriff submits a *return* to the court which reports the action taken and describes the property levied upon.

In summary, levy consists of the actual realization of the court's order or judgment by finding property, placing it *in custodia legis*, and removing it from the debtor's legal (and sometimes physical) control. For many purposes, the act of levy is the legally and practically crucial event in the enforcement process, because it identifies and binds particular property of the debtor to the creditor's claim. In many instances, the levy is the act that gives rise to a judicial lien in the property, thereby affording the creditor some protection against subsequent third parties.

§3.3   Judicial Prejudgment Remedies

§3.3.1   *General Principles Applicable to All Prejudgment Remedies*

Prejudgment remedies (sometimes called *provisional remedies* or *provisional process*) are forms of relief available to an eligible litigant during the period between the commencement of suit and the final judgment in the case. In sections 3.3.3 to 3.3.7, the most common of these remedies are discussed. Section 3.3.8 covers *lis pendens* which, while not a prejudgment remedy in the usual sense, provides prejudgment protection to the plaintiff in certain cases. Each of the remedies has its own characteristics, purpose, and rules; each is available on specific grounds and may be sought only by a party who qualifies for it. However, some broad principles are common to all of them.

Although under appropriate circumstances certain prejudgment remedies are available to defendants (*e.g.,* a defendant may seek an injunction to restrain some act of the plaintiff), these are primarily *plaintiffs'* remedies. They are designed to enhance the plaintiff-creditor's chances of collecting on the ultimate judgment.

By definition, prejudgment remedies are available in the phase of the case preceding the final adjudication on the merits. This gives them two important characteristics:

(1) They are ancillary in nature.   They are related to and are inextricably tied to an underlying suit initiated by the plaintiff against the defendant.

This means that the remedy cannot be sought or granted until the underlying suit has been commenced (or, in some states, is about to be commenced) and that the relief cannot survive if the underlying suit has been dismissed or terminated.

(2) Prejudgment remedies are necessarily provisional and temporary in nature. They are designed to last only until the disposition of the underlying case on its merits. Upon judgment, if the plaintiff succeeds in the action, the relief is incorporated into or superceded by the judgment and its enforcement remedies. If the plaintiff loses, the relief comes to an end. In addition, the defendant is likely to be entitled to an award of damages to compensate for loss caused by the provisional remedy which, as it turned out, was not justified.

Because prejudgment remedies are made available to a plaintiff who has not yet established a case on the merits, they have an obvious potential for harm to the defendant. The grant of the remedy deprives the defendant of property or restrains the defendant from acting before an adjudication of liability on the debt. Although the deprivation or restraint is only temporary (it remains in effect only while the case is pending), even a temporary dispossession or enjoinder can be severely damaging.

For this reason, prejudgment remedies should be carefully controlled. The statutes under which they are granted usually reflect a cautious approach to provisional relief. They require the plaintiff to make a substantive application showing reasonable prospects of success on the merits, and they impose eligibility standards, procedural safeguards, bonding requirements, and plaintiff liability for misuse of the process. Courts typically construe these statutory controls strictly and do not grant relief unless there has been proper compliance with them.

Each prejudgment remedy has its particular purpose, but as a general matter they all serve the same basic goal: to permit the plaintiff to take steps early in the case to ensure that the ultimate judgment will not be a hollow victory. A creditor faces disturbing uncertainties when initiating suit to recover an overdue debt and will often not know whether there will be any funds or assets to satisfy the debt by the time judgment is obtained. Prejudgment remedies take some of the risk out of the collection suit by allowing an eligible plaintiff to secure executable property in anticipation of a successful judgment.

§3.3.2 Due Process in Prejudgment Remedies

This section discusses federal due process standards that apply to prejudgment remedies. State constitutions are not covered here, but bear in mind that they may provide even stronger protection of due process rights.

The Fourteenth Amendment requires that a defendant receives proper notice and a meaningful hearing before being deprived of property through the grant of a prejudgment remedy. In a series of well-known cases decided between 1969 and 1975, the Supreme Court considered the due process standards applicable to prejudgment relief. *See Sniadach v. Family Finance Corp.*, 395 U.S. 337 (1969); *Fuentes v. Shevin*, 407 U.S. 67 (1972); *Mitchell v. W.T. Grant Co.*, 416 U.S. 600 (1974); and *North Georgia Finishing, Inc. v. Di-Chem, Inc.*, 419 U.S. 601 (1975). The Court revisited these standards more recently in *Connecticut v. Doehr*, 111 S. Ct. 2105 (1991).

The Court attempted to articulate the due process standards for prejudgment relief. However, it was closely divided on the issues and its membership changed during the course of the cases. As a result, the opinions tend to qualify, to distinguish, and in some respects, to contradict each other. The cases have generated much scholarly comment, and many states have made deliberate efforts to ensure that their statutes conform to the constitutional imperatives revealed or suggested by the Supreme Court. In short, the following principles appear to have been recognized:

(1) State action.   Even though a creditor seeking a prejudgment remedy may be a private person, the grant and enforcement of the remedy involves state action, so the Fourteenth Amendment is applicable.

(2) Notice and hearing.   Prejudgment remedies are not in themselves unconstitutional. The cases concern the standards for notice and hearing applicable to the prejudgment seizure of the debtor's property. The essential point of the cases is that under the Fourteenth Amendment, a debtor may not be deprived of property or property rights, albeit temporarily or provisionally, without due process. At a minimum, due process requires in most situations that the debtor be given adequate notice of the application for relief and be afforded a meaningful opportunity to be heard by a judge before it is granted.

(3) The hearing must be meaningful.   The purpose of the hearing is to establish the probable validity of the creditor's claim and to allow the debtor to challenge the application for relief before the property is seized, or the debtor's rights in property are interfered with. A pro forma hearing will not do.

(4) Ex parte proceedings.   In some circumstances, when the creditor can show that forewarning the debtor of the application will likely damage the creditor's vital interest or the public interest, an ex parte procedure is permissible. However, this must be regarded as an exceptional case and confined to situations of demonstrated urgency in which compelling reasons exist for dispensing with prior notice and hearing. As a broad principle, a court, in deciding whether to grant ex parte relief, must try to balance the debtor's right to preseizure notice and hearing against the creditor's need for immediate relief.

The statute must provide for a number of procedural safeguards in ex parte proceedings:

(a) The affidavit supporting the creditor's application cannot be conclusory and must contain substantive factual allegations that demonstrate proper grounds for ex parte relief.

(b) The application cannot be granted ministerially by a clerical official, but must be properly evaluated by a judge.

(c) The debtor must have the opportunity for a prompt postseizure hearing to challenge the grant of relief. At the hearing, the creditor bears the burden of proving a right to the remedy.

(d) The debtor is entitled to compensation if the seizure was wrongful. This right to damages must be guaranteed by a bond furnished by the creditor at the time of the application.

Ex parte relief is more likely to be justifiable when the creditor has an interest in the property, such as a lien. If no such interest exists, it will be much harder for the creditor to make a convincing case for dispensing with preseizure notice and hearing. (Ex parte proceedings are illustrated in Example 1.)

(5) Ex parte seizure of wages. It is clear that due process protection extends to all types of property, whether devoted to consumer or commercial purposes. However, some types of property are more rigorously protected than others. When the property in question is the wages of an individual, the cases strongly indicate that ex parte seizure is absolutely barred under all circumstances.

§3.3.3   Attachment

Attachment is an old remedy. Its original purpose was to compel the appearance in court of a nonresident defendant who had property within the court's jurisdiction. By taking custody of the defendant's property, the court forced him or her to submit to its power. (This is known as *quasi in rem jurisdiction*.) As the remedy developed, it acquired a second purpose: The defendant's property was seized early in the case and kept in the custody of the law so that when the plaintiff finally obtained judgment, the property was available to be executed upon.

This dual function of attachment ended in 1977 when the Supreme Court held unconstitutional the practice of seizing property as the sole basis for acquiring jurisdiction over the defendant. *Shaffer v. Heitner,* 433 U.S. 186 (1977). Jurisdiction can only be asserted constitutionally if there are at least *minimum contacts* between the forum and the litigation. Its jurisdictional function having been eliminated, attachment survives purely as a means of providing security for the plaintiff's claim where the court has jurisdiction on other grounds.

The diagram on page 44 sketches the steps that are likely to be followed in an attachment procedure. It shows both the normal procedure, in which

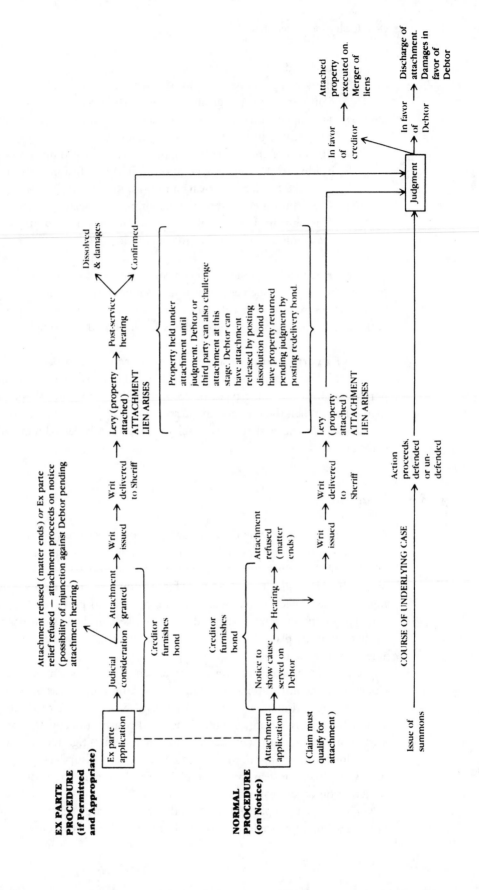

44

seizure is preceded by notice to the debtor and a hearing, and the emergency ex parte procedure.

Like other prejudgment remedies, attachment is *ancillary* to a suit on a substantive claim and cannot be sought unless such a suit is in progress. It can only be applied for after the issue of summons or, in some states, at least simultaneously with or in immediate anticipation of the commencement of suit. It is not available to all plaintiffs nor in all types of cases. For example, it is commonly confined to money claims or to certain types of money claims, such as claims arising out of an express or implied contract. Attachment may be unavailable for consumer debts, secured debts, or unliquidated debts. In some states, the plaintiff can only obtain attachment by showing special circumstances, such as evasive behavior by the debtor. Traditionally, attachment is available only in legal actions and not in equitable suits. However, equity has a procedure *(sequestration)* that serves a similar purpose

The attachment remedy presupposes that the creditor has a simple *money claim* against the debtor that is *unsecured* by and unrelated to any specific item of the debtor's property.[2] Therefore, the applicant for attachment does not need to allege a right to any particular asset, but simply asks the court to authorize the attachment of unspecified property of the debtor that is sufficient in value to cover the amount of the debt. Only executable property can be attached. Indeed, in some states attachable property is even more restricted than executable property, so that certain types of property cannot be attached even though they may be executed upon after judgment.

Attachment is perceived as a harsh remedy. Courts therefore tend to take statutory limitations seriously and *construe attachment statutes strictly*. The plaintiff must comply exactly with the prescribed procedures and must clearly be eligible for the remedy. An eligible creditor applies for attachment by filing a notice of motion supported by an affidavit. The affidavit must not only demonstrate grounds for attachment, but must also show a prima facie underlying claim on the merits. This requirement protects the debtor as fully as possible from unjustifiable attachment.

When applying for attachment, the creditor must post a *bond* indemnifying the debtor for damages for wrongful attachment. The amount of the bond may be dictated by statute or left to the court's discretion. Statutes commonly prescribe the qualifications for sureties and allow the debtor to challenge the sufficiency of the bond. The bond requirement is another important protection for the debtor, because it guarantees the payment of compensation if the attachment is overturned or the plaintiff fails to obtain judgment in the suit.

Where there are no grounds for ex parte relief, the application is served on the debtor with a notice to show cause why attachment should not be

---

2. When the creditor does allege a right to or interest in a particular item of property and requires its delivery, other prejudgment remedies, such as replevin (discussed in section 3.3.5) are appropriate.

granted. A *hearing* is held on the appointed date, at which the debtor has an opportunity to contest the application. If the creditor establishes a right to attachment, the court authorizes a writ. It is issued and delivered to the sheriff or an equivalent official, who levies on the debtor's executable property as outlined in section 3.2.2. After levy, the sheriff submits a return to the clerk of the court. If the sheriff is unable to find executable property, the plaintiff's attempt at attachment has been unsuccessful, and a nulla bona return is submitted. If, on subsequent investigation, the plaintiff discovers executable property, a further attempt at levy can be made.

Only the debtor's property can be attached. If the creditor causes *property of a third party* to be levied upon, the third party can challenge the attachment and obtain damages for conversion. Because the sheriff is also potentially liable for damages for wrongful attachment, the plaintiff is usually required to provide an indemnity bond to the sheriff before levy is attempted.

Once levy is accomplished, an *attachment lien* arises in the property. This judicial lien secures the formerly unsecured debt until judgment is obtained and execution can be effected on the property. (Example 2 illustrates the attachment lien.)

Normally, attachment remains in effect until judgment is obtained. However, the debtor is usually able to have the property returned or the attachment released by posting a bond supported by a qualified surety. Two types of bond are commonly recognized. A *redelivery bond* is an undertaking by the debtor to redeliver the property or its value if the creditor ultimately obtains judgment. The bond releases the property to the debtor but does not terminate the attachment or the creditor's attachment lien.

The other type of bond, a *dissolution* or *discharging bond,* also undertakes to pay if the creditor obtains judgment. It differs from the redelivery bond in that it completely releases the property from the attachment and extinguishes the attachment lien. The bond substitutes for the property as security.

Quite apart from the debtor's ability to reacquire the property by posting an appropriate bond, the debtor also has the right to move for discharge of the attachment for cause — for example, if the creditor fails to prosecute the suit to judgment. Discharge of the attachment for cause entitles the debtor to damages for wrongful attachment.

Once the creditor obtains judgment, the undischarged attachment converts into an *execution*. This means that a new writ is issued and delivered to the sheriff, who formally levies again on the attached property, conducts an execution sale, and applies the proceeds to satisfaction of the judgment debt. Execution procedure is described more fully in section 3.5.

§3.3.4 Prejudgment Garnishment

The essential similarity between prejudgment garnishment and attachment is that they serve the same basic goal of enabling the creditor to secure the ultimate judgment by seizing property of the debtor early in the case. The fundamental difference between them is that attachment is used to seize property in the control of the debtor or to levy on real property by an act of recording, while garnishment is used to levy on the debtor's tangible personal property in the possession of a third party or to levy on an intangible obligation owed to the debtor. In other words, prejudgment garnishment is the proper remedy when levy involves a third party, either as possessor of the debtor's personal property or as obligor on an intangible right of the debtor's. Garnishment has procedures designed to protect the rights of this third party, to compel the third party's compliance with the writ, and to ensure that the debtor is given notice of the levy and an opportunity to oppose it.

In many states, prejudgment garnishment is just a variation of the attachment procedure, adjusted to accommodate the presence of the third party. Where this is so, the two remedies have the same rules and procedures except for those relating to the levy and response to the writ. In other states, the remedies are more distinct. In some jurisdictions garnishment is treated as a separate action, with the garnishing creditor as plaintiff and the third party as defendant.

Where garnishment is just a variation of the attachment procedure, once the court has authorized the writ, the creditor (the garnishor) has a *writ of garnishment* issued and delivered to the sheriff. The writ is served on the garnishee and a copy of it is served on the debtor. It calls on the garnishee to file an answer within a prescribed time and describes any obligation owed to the debtor or any of the debtor's property in the garnishee's possession. This notice of garnishment, in addition to the earlier notice of application, gives the debtor the opportunity to claim any available exemptions or make any appropriate challenges.

Upon receipt of the writ, the garnishee must *answer* it. He may simply acknowledge owing a mature obligation to the debtor or having possession of property of the debtor and turn over the property or make payment to the sheriff. However, he may decline to pay or surrender anything to the sheriff, either because he has no debt to or property of the debtor, or because he has the right, as against the debtor, to withhold the property or payment. As the garnishee is only obliged to surrender or pay what is due to the debtor at the time of the writ, any rights good against the debtor may be asserted as an excuse to payment or delivery under the writ. If the creditor disputes the answer, the garnishee's rights are adjudicated by a summary procedure.

Whatever the basis of the answer, the garnishee is obliged to respond to the writ and answer it truthfully. Failure to do so or to surrender the garnishable asset to the sheriff renders the garnishee personally liable to the garnishor for any loss suffered. Furthermore, willful disregard of the writ may result in sanctions for contempt of court.

In most jurisdictions the *levy* of a writ of garnishment creates a lien in the garnished property equivalent to the attachment lien discussed in section 3.3.3. Once the property is taken into the custody of the law, it is retained, as in the case of attachment, until the final judgment in the underlying action. The rules governing the postseizure stage of the proceedings are usually the same as those for attachment. The diagram on page 49 sketches the sequence of prejudgment garnishment procedure and compares it to attachment.

Because an individual debtor's salary, wages, or other *earnings* are so central to the debtor's survival, their garnishment is restricted in a number of ways. As was noted in section 3.3.2, the Supreme Court has indicated that the ex parte prejudgment garnishment of personal earnings may not be constitutionally permissible. In some states, prejudgment garnishment of an individual's earnings is prohibited, while in others the bar on wage garnishment extends to the postjudgment period as well.

Even where garnishment of earnings is allowed, the *Consumer Credit Protection Act*, 15 U.S.C. §§1671 *et seq.*, limits the portion of an individual's earnings that may be garnished. These restrictions apply to both prejudgment and postjudgment garnishment. Some states have enacted legislation with even stricter limits than the federal statute. In addition to these limitations, the state's exemption statute and statutes conferring pensions or other benefits often protect earnings or income from seizure by creditors.

§3.3.5   Prejudgment Replevin or Claim and Delivery

Prejudgment replevin (also called *claim and delivery*) is somewhat similar to attachment. Both remedies allow the creditor to seize the debtor's property prior to judgment so that it can be held secure pending the final resolution of the case. The essential difference between them is that attachment is available in an action on an unsecured money claim, while prejudgment replevin is available to a creditor who sues for possession of specific property.

Prejudgment replevin is a provisional remedy derived from the common law action of replevin. *Replevin* is a possessory action at law for the recovery of specific tangible personal property that has been wrongfully taken and detained or lawfully taken but thereafter wrongfully detained by the defendant. In its prejudgment version, it is only available to a plaintiff who has a right to immediate possession of specific property, and it can only be sought when the principal action includes a claim of possession of the property in question. The principal suit may be the action of replevin itself or some other possessory action. For example, a secured party under UCC Article 9 must sue to recover possession of the collateral if it cannot be obtained from the defaulting debtor by self-help. (*See* section 2.5.) This suit qualifies as a possessory

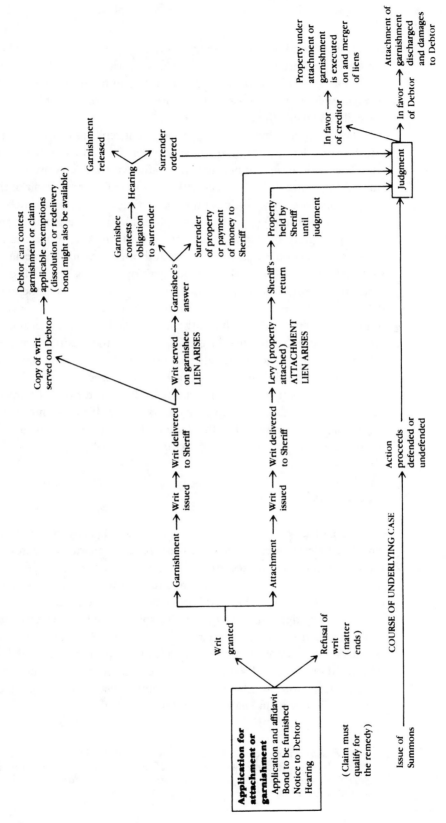

49

action, which entitles the secured party to seek prejudgment replevin. If the remedy is granted, the secured party is given possession of the collateral immediately, and holds it pending the final determination of the case. In this way, the secured party is assured that the debtor cannot harm or dispose of the collateral while the case is proceeding.

The procedure for obtaining prejudgment replevin is similar to that for attachment. The creditor makes an application after initiating the underlying suit. The application is supported by an affidavit that demonstrates, among other things, that the debtor is entitled to immediate possession of the specific personal property. Notice of the application is served on the debtor, and a hearing is held unless the state has a procedure for emergency ex parte relief. Any ex parte procedure must comply with the due process safeguards discussed in section 3.3.2. If the court authorizes a writ of replevin, it is issued and delivered to the sheriff who levies on the property. Unlike attachment, the sheriff does not retain the property while the case is pending, but delivers it to the creditor. As custodian of the property, the creditor is obliged to protect and preserve it. This duty is guaranteed by a surety bond.

Apart from the fact that the creditor, and not the sheriff, keeps the property during the course of the case, the postseizure rights and obligations of the parties are much like those in attachment proceedings. Also, like attachment, prejudgment replevin is provisional: The creditor must ultimately obtain judgment in the underlying possessory action. If the creditor fails to do so, the property is restored to the debtor who is entitled to damages for the wrongful seizure and retention of the property.

§3.3.6   Receivership

Although it has been codified in many states, receivership is an equitable remedy. When a party with an interest in an asset or estate demonstrates that the property is in need of protection, preservation, or orderly liquidation, a court of equity has the discretion to appoint a receiver to take control of the property, to administer it, and to deal with it as the court directs.

As a prejudgment remedy,[3] receivership is used to preserve property pending litigation. Like attachment, it removes property from the clutches of the defendant. However, receivership allows the property to be actively administered or conserved to prevent its deterioration or to maintain its value. It is therefore more appropriate than attachment where the property requires administration or maintenance while it is in legal custody.

---

3. Receivership is not necessarily confined to the prejudgment phase of a case. A receiver may be appointed after judgment to realize specific property, to protect it, or to prepare it for execution. Also, receivership still serves a limited role as a liquidation procedure at state law.

Like other prejudgment remedies, receivership is ancillary to a principal action. Because receivership dispossesses the debtor of property pending resolution of the case on its merits, the procedural rules and safeguards are similar to those for attachment. Grounds for the appointment of a receiver must be shown, including a probability of success on the underlying action and a likelihood that the property will suffer harm if it is not placed under the control of an impartial administrator.

Once seizure has been effected, the property is entrusted to the receiver, who is also required to post a bond guaranteeing the proper administration of the property. The powers and duties of the receiver are defined in the court order. The receiver is an officer of the court and must report and account to it.

§3.3.7 Injunctions

Courts of equity have the discretion to issue injunctions to restrain or compel action that is likely to cause irreparable harm to the applicant. The injunction is a widely used remedy that is not confined to debt collection or to the prejudgment period. When used in a pending suit, the injunction's role is to forestall conduct of the debtor that threatens to undermine the creditor's ability to enforce the ultimate judgment. For example, a creditor who has reasonable grounds to believe that the debtor is about to conceal or dispose of executable assets can seek to enjoin that prejudicial activity.

Because an injunction does not result in removal of property from the debtor, its protective power is weaker than the other prejudgment remedies. Its effectiveness depends on the debtor's obedience to the court order. A debtor who disregards the injunction is subject to civil and criminal sanctions for contempt of court, but the punishment of the debtor or a monetary award to compensate for disobedience are no help to the creditor if the debtor has no means of satisfying the judgment.

To obtain an injunction, the creditor makes an application on notice. An ex parte temporary restraining order may be available if the creditor can demonstrate urgency and can show that the injunction will be ineffectual if it is not issued immediately. An ex parte restraint is effective for only a brief period and must be followed shortly by an application, with notice and hearing, for a provisional injunction.

As in the case of other prejudgment remedies, the application for an injunction must be supported by an affidavit that demonstrates grounds for relief. The affidavit must establish a probability of success in the underlying action and a likelihood of irreparable harm if the injunction is not granted. The debtor may oppose the creditor's application. If the injunction is issued and later turns out to have been unjustified, the debtor has a claim for damages for wrongful enjoinder.

§3.3.8 *Lis Pendens*

The doctrine of *lis pendens* is not a prejudgment remedy; properly speaking, but it does provide some protection to a creditor in the prejudgment phase of litigation concerning rights to real property.

When a suit is in progress in which title, possession, or other rights in real property are at issue, the creditor may file a notice of pendency in the appropriate recording office (usually the deeds registry). The notice sets out the names of the parties, the description of the property, and the nature of the suit. Once the notice is filed, any person who acquires rights in the property from the debtor takes subject to the court's final disposition of the case. If the court ultimately grants judgment against the debtor, that judgment binds the transferee as well. The filing operates as constructive notice of the pending litigation and is effective even if the transferee did not check the filing records and had no actual knowledge of the pending suit.

Unlike an injunction, lis pendens does not prohibit the debtor from disposing of the property. It is also unlike attachment: Although the filing of the notice may seem the same as filing an attachment lien on real property, the notice does *not* create a lien. Rather, its effect is to warn third parties at large that the debtor's rights in the property are in dispute and that any interest transferred by the debtor is an uncertain one.

Another distinction between lis pendens and the prejudgment remedies discussed above is that the creditor does not need court authorization to file the notice. Provided that the doctrine applies to the case, the notice may be filed without application to court.

§3.4   The Judgment and Its Enforcement

§3.4.1 *Judgment by Default or Confession*

The *judgment* is the court's determination that the debt is due. It is the authorization needed for enforcement of the debt, whether or not provisional relief was obtained by a prejudgment remedy. This section does not deal comprehensively with judgment issues but is concerned only with the creditor's ability to obtain judgment in the absence of a defense on the merits.

When the debtor's failure to pay is the result of a lack of funds rather than a dispute over the debt, the debtor may not defend the action or, having begun to do so, may fail to prosecute the defense. In such a case, the creditor is entitled to apply for *judgment by default*. If the debt is a liquidated contract claim and personal service has been affected, some states follow the traditional practice of allowing the clerk of the court to grant the judgment. Otherwise, judgment must be granted by the court. Normally the procedure is summary, and the judgment is granted for the relief requested in the summons provided that the uncontested allegations in the summons state a cause of action. Evidence is not normally required unless some matter has to be resolved by testimony, such as evidence to fix unliquidated damages. After the judgment has been granted, it is entered by the clerk of the court in the appropriate record. The judgment becomes effective upon entry.

A debtor who permits a judgment to be obtained by default is deemed to have acquiesced in it and cannot normally appeal it. However, under some circumstances, a debtor is able to apply for reversal of the judgment on the basis of excusable neglect or the creditor's fraud or misconduct.

Sometimes a debtor does more than simply not defend the suit; he or she *consents to judgment.* When this concession is made after default, courts usually accept it provided that it was voluntarily and knowledgeably made. However, if the debtor consents to judgment *before* default, this waiver of the right to defend the suit is treated as suspect and is likely to be disregarded. This is particularly true if the confession was executed when the debt was incurred and is contained in the instrument of debt or the contract.

A confession to judgment executed at the inception of the debt is also called a *cognovit* or a *warrant of attorney.* It has been known in the common law for centuries, but over the years its original purpose has become obsolete, and its modern function is simply as a device to enable the creditor to act as the debtor's agent in acquiescing in a judgment upon the debtor's default on the debt.

The confession's potential for abuse, its frequent exploitation by unscrupulous creditors, and its harsh effects on the debtor's due process rights have made it disreputable. It is even more pernicious when it is used in standard form contracts by creditors who are "mass contractors" with market power. As a result, confessions to judgment are heavily regulated by courts, legislatures, and government agencies. They are generally not upheld at all in consumer credit transactions. In other situations, even where they are permitted, they are carefully scrutinized to determine whether they have been voluntarily and knowledgeably given under fair circumstances. In addition, the confession may have to comply with specific and strictly enforced formal prerequisites in order to be valid.

§3.4.2 The Duration of the Judgment

After obtaining judgment, the creditor usually takes steps to enforce it as soon as possible. However, it sometimes happens that immediate execution is not possible or desirable: The debtor may have no executable assets or may persuade the creditor to defer execution pending promised voluntary payment of the judgment debt. Where enforcement of the judgment is delayed for any reason, the issue of its duration becomes relevant.

All judgments have a finite lifespan; they expire or become unenforceable after a period of years. The period varies from state to state and the rules concerning the continuing vitality of a judgment are not uniform. For example, the state's statute governing judgments may provide that the judgment last for a fixed period (say ten years) after which it expires and becomes unenforceable. The statute may allow an application to be made during the period for a renewal of the judgment to extend its effectiveness for a further span. Some statutes require periodic attempts at execution on the judgment during its lifetime, failing which the judgment becomes dormant and must be revived by motion before enforcement can be attempted. A creditor who does not obtain immediate satisfaction of the judgment must take care to follow whatever procedures are necessary to keep it alive and enforceable for its full term.

§3.4.3   The Judgment Lien

A creditor who obtains a final, liquidated money judgment in a court of general jurisdiction[4] is able to obtain a judgment lien, which is one of the judicial liens discussed in section 2.4.2. To create and perfect the lien, the creditor records the judgment in a docket maintained by the clerk of the court or in some other filing system (often, the county deeds registry) designated by state law.

Upon being docketed, the judgment creates a lien on all of the debtor's real property within the county of docketing. The lien can be extended to property situated in other counties by filing the judgment in the recording offices for real estate in those counties. In most states the lien is confined to realty, but some permit it to cover personal property as well if a filing is made in the registry where security interests in personal property are recorded. Although personal property may be subjected to the lien in some states, the remaining discussion here assumes that it applies only to real property.

Remember that a *money judgment* is the basis for the lien: The property need not have been involved in the suit or identified in advance. It is subjected to the lien simply because it is located in the county of recording. The judgment lien statute and state property law determine what interest in property are lienable. Property of which the debtor is legal owner of record surely will be subject to the lien, but lesser interests (*e.g.,* equitable interests or joint ownership rights) may not be.

The lien is subject to any preexisting third-party interests recorded in the property, such as prior recorded mortgages and liens. The judgment lien may also be junior to an earlier, unrecorded interest in the property granted by the debtor to a good faith transferee for value. This is because the judgment

---

4. The judgment of a court of limited jurisdiction may not be capable of creating a lien or may have to be recorded in a more senior court to establish a lien.

lienholder is not a consensual lienholder who has relied on real estate records in extending credit to the debtor, and so the equities may dictate that the rights of the prior unrecorded interest-holder should be protected. As a general rule, the judgment lien is superior to any interest acquired in the property after the recording of the judgment lien. This rule is also subject to some exceptions where policy dictates that a subsequent bona fide transferee should be protected from the lien.

A judgment lien does not take precedence over any exemption to which the debtor is entitled. Therefore, if a residence is owned and occupied by an individual debtor, it is protected by the debtor's homestead exemption. If the property is fully exempt, the lien cannot affect it at all. Partially exempt property is lienable only to the extent of the debtor's nonexempt equity. Examples 3 and 4 deal with priority of judgment liens.

Once the judgment lien is recorded, it attaches not only to the real property held by the debtor at the time of filing but to any property in the county acquired by the debtor in the future, as long as the lien remains in effect. The lien will similarly encompass any improvements on the debtor's property and any increases in its value or augmentation of the debtor's rights in it. The judgment lien's attachment to after-acquired property rights of the debtor is an important advantage to the creditor. If the debtor owns no executable realty at the time of judgment or has only a small equity in existing property, the creditor can wait in the hope that new property will be acquired or the value of the debtor's interest will increase. Unless the statute provides a separate period of effectiveness for the lien, it lasts as long as the judgment. A judgment lienor therefore needs to be particularly sensitive to the question of duration of the judgment discussed in section 3.4.2. (Example 4 deals with the judgment lien on after-acquired property.)

When the lien is to be enforced, the lienholder follows a foreclosure procedure to sell the property and realize its proceeds. In some states the foreclosure of a judicial lien follows a public sale procedure such as that described in section 3.5. In others, special rules are prescribed for the foreclosure of a judgment lien.

§3.4.4   The Enforcement of Judgments in Other States

After a court has granted judgment, it is enforced by the means described in the following sections. However, enforcement activity is only permissible within the territorial boundaries of the court's state. The court of one state cannot simply send forth its minions to seize property located in another. To enforce a judgment in another state, the creditor must have the judgment recognized by a court in that state, whose own officials will enforce it. Under Article IV, section 1 of the Constitution, a state must give full faith and credit to a valid final judgment of another, provided that the judgment complies with the jurisdictional requirements of the Constitution and the law of the state in which it was granted.

State law prescribes the procedure to be followed by a creditor to have the judgment of another state recognized and enforced. There is some uniformity in this procedure because many states have adopted the *Uniform Enforcement of Foreign Judgments Act.* (The word "foreign" in the title of the Act refers to judgments of other states or to federal courts, not to judgments of the courts of foreign nations. A separate uniform act, mentioned briefly below, deals with judgment from other nations.)

The Uniform Act provides for a straightforward method of registering a foreign judgment by a clerical act, with recourse to the court of the recording state only if a dispute arises concerning the registration. This is an improvement on the traditional means of enforcement, which requires the plaintiff to commence suit on the judgment in the second jurisdiction. This method remains an alternative even in states that have adopted the Uniform Act.

Judgments of the courts of foreign nations are not entitled to full faith and credit under the Constitution, and they are not subject to the same procedures or laws that govern the judgments of sister states. However, principles of international comity do favor the recognition of such judgments when the judicial process of the foreign nation satisfies standards of fairness and due process. At common law, courts in the United States have recognized and enforced the judgments of foreign courts where principles of comity and due process so dictate. This common law basis for recognition has been codified in the *Uniform Foreign Money-Judgments Recognition Act.* The courts of a state that has enacted it have discretion to recognize and enforce judgments of the courts of foreign nations if the judgment satisfies the standards mentioned above and recognition does not offend the state's public policy.

§3.5   Execution

If the debtor does not pay the judgment voluntarily, the creditor must resort to execution to enforce it. Execution is the process whereby the sheriff or an equivalent official is directed by a writ to find property of the debtor, seize it, and sell it to realize proceeds with which to pay the judgment debt. Execution is regulated by statute. Courts tend to insist upon strict compliance with the statutory requirements and to invalidate deficient executions.

Execution begins with the issuance of a writ by the clerk of the court, directing the sheriff to find and levy on property of the debtor and to report back to the clerk by a specific date (called the *return date*). In some states the creditor cannot begin execution until the expiration of a waiting period after entry of the judgment. In other states, execution can proceed immediately following entry of the judgment. The debtor can apply for a stay of execution pending appeal, but the stay is usually conditioned on the debtor furnishing a bond, which can be costly.

There is also usually an outer time limit for issuing a writ. If it is not issued within a certain time of the judgment, the judgment becomes dormant and has to be revived by motion or action.

After issuance, the writ is delivered to the sheriff, who tries to *levy* on property of the debtor, often with the creditor's active guidance. The procedure for the levy of a writ of execution is basically the same as that for a writ of attachment. (*See* sections 3.2.2 and 3.3.3.) Personal property in the debtor's possession and documents that reify intangible rights are levied upon by seizure. The sheriff normally takes the property into custody pending the sale in execution, but some states permit cumbersome property to be left in the debtor's possession and posted with a notice of execution. Real property is levied upon by recording the writ in the real estate records. Other intangibles and personal property in the possession of a third party cannot be reached by a writ of execution but must be garnished.

After levy, the sheriff files a return reporting on the action taken and describing the property that has been levied upon. If the sheriff found no property, a *nulla bona return* is submitted. The return must be made before the date specified in the writ.

As in the case of attachment, if the sheriff seizes property that belongs to a third party, the true owner is able to challenge the levy and claim damages for trespass or conversion. Some execution statutes provide an expedited procedure for adjudicating the adverse claim and having the property released from execution. Because the sheriff could be liable for any tort damages, the plaintiff must provide an indemnity when delivering the writ.

Even though real and personal property are both subject to execution, the seizure and ultimate sale of *real property* is often subject to special restrictions, which have developed as a result of the historical importance of real property[5] and remain because realty is often the debtor's most valuable asset. For example, it is common for execution statutes to require the creditor to attempt levy on personal property first and to have recourse to real property only if insufficient personal property can be seized to satisfy the judgment. Also, the sale in execution of real property is usually subject to precautionary rules.

As soon as possible after completion of the levy, the process of realization takes place. After advertising and notice to the debtor, the sheriff conducts a *sale of the property* by public auction. Execution statutes prescribe the sale procedures with varying detail with the goal of ensuring that the fairest price possible will be obtained. Notwithstanding, it is generally accepted that the value of property is depressed at forced sales of this nature, and prices seldom approximate true market value.

---

5. In early common law the writ of execution, known as *fieri facias,* was confined to chattels. Real property could not be executed upon at all. If the debtor owned land, the creditor could obtain a writ of *elegit* that could reach a limited portion of the revenues from the land over a defined period of time.

The proceeds realized, less costs of execution, are remitted to the creditor in satisfaction of the judgment. If insufficient funds are generated to pay the judgment in full, the creditor may begin the process of execution again by issuing a further writ and attempting another levy and sale. If the sale proceeds exceed the debt and costs, the surplus goes in order of priority to any junior judgment creditors who participated in the sale. Any remaining surplus is paid to the debtor.

As mentioned earlier, if real property is sold in execution, the statute may afford special protection to the debtor. These protective mechanisms may be available only when the debtor's residence is being sold and may not apply to other realty. For example, the statute may require an appraisal of the property before sale and will not permit the sale at a price that is less than a defined percentage of the appraised value. Some states provide for an automatic confirmation hearing at which the court must review and confirm the sale before it is final. If there has been some irregularity in the proceedings, or if the price is unconscionably low, the court can refuse confirmation.

Even after the sale, the property is not necessarily lost to the debtor. It is common for execution statutes to allow the debtor[6] to *redeem* real property sold in execution. The redemption must be effected within a fixed period after the sale by the payment of the redemption value of the property to the purchaser. This statutory right of redemption after the sale differs from the equity of redemption in mortgage foreclosure, which is available only up to the time of sale.

The redemption price is the price paid by the purchaser at the sale; it is adjusted upwards to include interest and to reimburse the purchaser for any costs and expenditures on the property, and adjusted downwards to give the debtor credit for the economic value of fruits and revenues received by the purchaser.

The right of redemption enables the debtor to reacquire the property at the approximate distress price, so it helps a debtor who is able to raise the necessary funds before the redemption period expires. Of course, it is not of great practical value to many debtors who have no hope of finding the cash needed for redemption. The disadvantage of statutory redemption is that the purchaser acquires uncertain title at the time of the sale. This makes purchase at execution unattractive to some potential buyers, and it further depresses the prices at such sales. As a result, some states have abolished or curtailed the right of postsale redemption.

An *execution lien* attaches by operation of law to any property levied upon. Like the other liens discussed in this chapter and the last, it falls within the general category of judicial liens. The effective date of the lien differs from one state to another. The date of levy seems to be the most prevalent

---

6. The right of statutory redemption may also be given to lienholders whose liens are junior to that of the execution creditor. It is therefore possible that there are two or more persons who are entitled to redeem. Multiple redemptions are not dealt with here. Even if a lienholder does redeem, the debtor has the ultimate redemption right and can redeem from the lienholder.

alternative, but some states have selected the date of delivery of the writ to the sheriff or some other point in the process.

The purpose of the lien is to protect the creditor while the sale is pending. Because the sale is supposed to proceed expeditiously after levy, the lien is intended to be of fairly short duration and to last only as long as necessary to cover the property until realization by sale. It is not a long-term security interest, and it expires if the sale is not held within the period prescribed by the statute or, if no period is provided, within a reasonable time.

When several creditors have executed on the same property, or when there are competing interests in the property, the liens and interests must be ranked in accordance with rules of priority. The first-in-time rule applies unless there is specific provision to the contrary. If an execution creditor has a preexisting lien (*e.g.,* an attachment lien, judgment lien, or consensual lien), the execution lien merges with the earlier one and backdates for priority purposes.

§3.6 Garnishment

Postjudgment garnishment is an execution procedure used to levy on personal property of the debtor in the possession of someone else, or on an intangible obligation due to the debtor. Although in some states, postjudgment garnishment is a separate suit against the garnishee, it is more commonly just a variety of execution procedure with some variations to account for the protection of the garnishee's rights and to ensure that the debtor is notified of the garnishment so that he can assert any exemptions in the property. It is, therefore, very much like the prejudgment remedy described in section 3.3.4.

The debtor's rights of due process require that he is given notice of the garnishment that sets out his exemption rights, and must also have an opportunity to challenge the garnishment. A statute that does not provide for such notice and a hearing either before or promptly after the garnishment does not meet constitutional standards. The fact that the debtor received notice of the suit itself does not satisfy this notice requirement.

Upon delivery of the writ of garnishment to the sheriff, the levy follows the same course as the prejudgment procedure. The garnishee is obliged to answer the writ and must surrender the property or state grounds for not doing so. If the creditor does not accept those grounds, a hearing is held. If the debt is not due or the property is not returnable at the time of the writ, it must be paid or surrendered to the appropriate court official on the date that it becomes due. In many states a garnishment lien arises on levy. Also, the garnishee is personally liable for disposition of the property in contravention of the writ.

Upon payment of a garnished debt to the clerk of the court or the sheriff, the funds are remitted to the creditor to the extent necessary to satisfy the judgment. Property surrendered by the garnishee to the sheriff (whether voluntarily or after the court has conducted the hearing and ordered surrender) is sold in execution in the same way as property levied on by a writ of execution.

§3.7   Proceedings in Aid of Execution

A creditor whose attempt at execution ended with a nulla bona return may be unconvinced that the debtor truly has no executable property. The creditor may try to conduct some investigations by checking real estate records or pursuing other sources of information. In addition, two generally recognized types of judicial proceeding may be used by a disappointed execution creditor to gain information from the debtor about the existence and whereabouts of executable assets.

The older, more cumbersome procedure is the *creditors' bill in equity* — a distinct, ancillary action grounded (as are all equitable suits) on the creditor's allegation that its remedies at law for the enforcement of the debt are exhausted or inadequate. This means that the creditor must either have received a nulla bona return or must be able to show that it would be a fruitless waste of time to attempt levy.

The creditors' bill can be used to achieve a number of different goals. For example, the creditor may ask for an order compelling the debtor or other persons with knowledge of the debtor's affairs to submit to an examination by the creditor in court. If assets are revealed, the bill can be used to recover them from one who acquired them in fraud of creditors,[7] to enjoin their disposition, or to appoint a receiver to administer them pending execution. A creditors' bill can also be used to execute on equitable assets that cannot be reached by a writ of execution at law.

The more modern, streamlined *statutory proceedings in aid of execution* serve some or all of the ends accomplished by a creditors' bill. They are part of the original suit, rather than a separate action. The statutes provide at least for an examination or discovery procedure, but some go beyond this and authorize the court to order payments by installments, to enjoin the disposition of property, to appoint a receiver, or to take other steps to apply the property to the satisfaction of the debt. In some jurisdictions the statutory inquiry proceedings, like the creditors' bill, can only be used after a nulla bona return unless execution is shown to be futile. In others, the examination can take place before any writ has been issued.

§3.8   Bankruptcy and the State Law Collection Process

The possibility of the debtor's bankruptcy is one of the hazards that creditors face in pursuing collection efforts at state law. There is always a danger that the debtor or a group of qualified creditors will file a bankruptcy petition while other creditors are in the process of attempting to enforce their claims

---

7. Chapter 4 deals with fraudulent transfers. Most states also have a statutory procedure for avoiding fraudulent transfers which is designed to be more efficient than the creditors' bill.

through the state courts. If that should happen, the collection under state law is disrupted. All action is stayed, and advantages obtained by a creditor through attachment, judgment, or execution may be avoided. The possibility of bankruptcy could influence decisions and strategies in the collection process: It may spur a creditor into speedy action, or it may have the opposite effect of encouraging a circumspect approach, so as not to precipitate a petition.

§3.9 State Law Insolvency Proceedings

§3.9.1 Introduction to State Law Insolvency Proceedings

There are two commonly recognized processes available to a debtor under state law for the restructuring and compromise of debts: compositions (including extensions) and assignments for the benefit of creditors. This section outlines some general principals applicable to both.

The collection processes described in the preceding sections involve individual action by each creditor. Creditors act on their own and are concerned with the enforcement of their own claims. Although creditor activity may be individual, it is often not isolated — a debtor in financial difficulty is likely to have defaulted on several debts. When a number of creditors are attempting to enforce their claims, those furthest ahead in the collection process have the best chance of finding executable property.

Competition for the debtor's resources can be handled more fairly and efficiently through an arrangement for the collective management of claims. By such a *collective proceeding* (so called to distinguish it from creditors' individual pursuits of their claims), the debtor may be able to deal with creditors in an orderly way and to preserve assets that would otherwise be seized and disposed of at distress prices in an execution sale. Bankruptcy is the predominant and most powerful collective proceeding, but the composition and extension and the assignment for the benefit of creditors, provided for by state law, also facilitate the collective treatment of claims. These procedures are also sometimes called *insolvency proceedings*. Although the debtor need not be insolvent to be eligible to use these proceedings, a solvent debtor is less likely to resort to them. Insolvency is determined by one of two well-established alternative tests. Under the *balance sheet* or *bankruptcy test*, insolvency is an excess of liabilities over assets. Under the *equity test*, insolvency is the inability to pay debts as they become due.

State law insolvency proceedings have one attribute in common with bankruptcy: They are designed to enable the debtor to deal with creditors as a group to achieve an overall settlement of their claims. However, the analogy should not be exaggerated. Bankruptcy is a much more powerful and pervasive remedy. Among other things, the Bankruptcy Code confers extraordinary rights on the trustee to collect and administer the estate, and it has unique provisions for the protection of creditor interests, the control of creditor activity, and the discharge of debts. State law proceedings do not have the same compulsive strength. They fall far short of being equivalents of bankruptcy and are constitutionally barred from providing equivalent relief.[8] As a result, the proceedings under state law are less formal, simpler, and more dependent on cooperation between the debtor and creditors.

Because these state law proceedings do not give the debtor the same protection as bankruptcy, they are often a less desirable remedy. In some cases, however, bankruptcy is either not attractive to the debtor or is not feasible. There are many reasons why this may be. For example, the debtor may want to avoid the expense and formality of bankruptcy administration, or may not want the stigma of bankruptcy, or may not be eligible for bankruptcy relief.[9] Where bankruptcy is not a suitable option for the debtor, the state law procedures do at least provide some of the advantages that arise from the orderly management of debt. By surrendering assets for liquidation and distribution among creditors or by making a commitment to payment by future installments, the debtor may be able to persuade creditors that their interests are better served by cooperating in a collective proceeding rather than by attempting collection individually.

The two insolvency proceedings discussed here are *"voluntary"*: Only the debtor may bring them into effect. Although creditors may exert pressure on the debtor to make an assignment or a composition, they cannot initiate suit to force them on the debtor.

Under the common law, these insolvency proceedings are *not judicial remedies*. Unless a state has provided otherwise by statute, the debtor does not apply to court to sanction the proceeding, and the court does not supervise its performance. The court only becomes involved in the matter if a challenge or dispute arises.

§3.9.2   Compositions and Extensions

On hearing the word "composition," a normal person might think of Beethoven or Mozart scribbling down musical notes by the flickering light of a candle, or of Raphael or Tiepolo plotting out the spatial relationships between hordes of saints and seraphim. To a lawyer, the word has no such glorious connotations: It simply means *a contract*. More specifically, in modern usage a *composition* is a contract between the debtor and two or more creditors under which a partial payment of claims is promised and accepted in full settlement.

---

8. The federal bankruptcy power is discussed in section 5.2.

9. For a fuller discussion of eligibility for bankruptcy and some of the considerations that may motivate the filing of a bankruptcy petition, *see* Chapter 8.

An *extension* is a contract between the debtor and two or more creditors under which the debtor is allowed an extension of time within which to pay the debts. A single contract can include both a composition and an extension, providing for a reduction in the debt as well as an extension of the payment period. From now on, the word "composition" is used to refer to a contract with both these elements.

Compositions and extensions are sometimes called *workouts* — an unfortunate nickname that conjures up the unappetizing image of sweaty bodies, gyrating aerobically to the clamor of bad music.

Although compositions have been codified by some states (sometimes with additional statutory requirements), they are generally subject to the rules and principles of contract law. Thus, doctrines governing formation, performance, and breach all apply. Because compositions are *contractual* in nature, the specific structure of each one can be molded by the parties to meet the needs of their situation. As a contract, a composition needs *consideration* which courts hold to be present by virtue of the creditor's mutual forbearance and the debtor's undertaking to procure assent from other creditors. It is not necessary that all participating creditors sign the same contract. They may each make a separate contract with the debtor, as long as the contracts are interdependent and entered into in reliance on others being executed.

Because a composition is a contract, it is only binding on creditors who assent to it. They are not likely to agree to reduction or extension of their claims unless the debtor can persuade them that it serves their best interests to do so. This means, at a minimum, the debtor must demonstrate *genuine financial distress* and a *good faith* effort to deal with it. The distribution offered to creditors (which may be committed from future earnings or the liquidation of selected assets or both) must be enough to make it worthwhile for creditors to accept the settlement, rather than to press ahead with collection efforts. A debtor is held to a high standard of good faith in entering into a composition and must disclose financial information honestly and accurately. If creditors are misled, they have grounds for avoiding the composition.

As long as two or more creditors accept the composition, consideration problems are overcome. A debtor is therefore able to make a legally valid composition with less than all of the creditors. However, if acceptance of the composition is not widespread, it cannot achieve its desired end. Nonconsenting creditors can be expected to proceed with individual collection activity, thereby preventing preservation of the debtor's estate and discouraging more cooperative creditors from exercising forbearance. A debtor may have some flexibility in offering preferred treatment to a creditor who holds out — as long as this is fully disclosed to other creditors. However, the other creditors may not be willing to enter the composition if one of them is treated more generously.

If the composition is executed, its terms supercede the debtor's former obligations toward participating creditors. If the debtor consummates it as promised, the debtor's performance satisfies not only the composition but

also the original obligations that were subsumed in it. The consensual forgiveness of the unpaid balance of the original debt is an important advantage
of a composition, because a state cannot grant a discharge to a debtor in the
absence of creditor assent — the discharge is an incident of the bankruptcy
power conferred on Congress by the Constitution. If the debtor breaches the
composition, creditors are entitled to disregard it and to sue for the full outstanding balance of the original debt.

§3.9.3   *Assignments for the Benefit of Creditors*

An assignment for the benefit of creditors, or ABC, is a voluntary transfer of
property in trust by the debtor to another person (the assignee) with instructions to liquidate the property and to distribute its proceeds to those
creditors who have elected to participate. The purpose of the assignment is to
place the debtor's executable property in the hands of an impartial custodian
so that individual creditors cannot levy on it, permitting its orderly liquidation and distribution for the benefit of the creditor body as a whole. The
debtor transfers the property in trust to the custodian, specifying the terms
on which it is to be realized and its proceeds distributed.

Each creditor may choose whether or not to participate in an ABC.
However, unlike a composition, the ABC is not contractual in nature. The
debtor's power to make the assignment is an incident of rights of ownership,
deriving from the law of property. The ABC is a common law device, but it
has been codified and regulated by statute in some states.

Although the ABC has some analogy to a Ch. 7 bankruptcy, it is a much
weaker remedy, and falls far short of bankruptcy in the level of protection afforded the debtor and creditors. For example, it does not stay the creditors'
pursuit of any unassigned assets or shield the debtor from other collection
pressure; and it does not confer on the assignee the extensive powers wielded
by a bankruptcy trustee. Probably even more important, the ABC cannot, by
statute, operate as a discharge because a state statute conferring a discharge
of unpaid debt is an unconstitutional encroachment on the federal bankruptcy power. The constitutional problem does not arise if creditors themselves grant the discharge by agreement, but courts are wary of coerced
consent. They generally demand that the assent be truly voluntary, and not
simply imposed by a condition of participation in the ABC. In fact, many
courts consider that the inclusion of such a condition is prima facie bad faith,
and some states forbid it altogether.

An ABC is less formal than bankruptcy. In some states it requires no judicial approval or supervision at all and only comes before a court if someone
challenges or disputes some aspect of it. In other states, judicial participation
has been imposed by statute, but even there the procedure is much less involved than bankruptcy. Because an ABC lacks the force of bankruptcy, it is often

not a workable alternative for the debtor. However, for the reasons mentioned in section 3.9.1, the ABC may suit some debtors more than bankruptcy.

An ABC is meant to benefit creditors, as its name suggests. If creditors derive no advantage from it, it is simply a conveyance of property by the debtor without return consideration, having the effect of removing the property from the reach of execution. As such, it is a fraud on creditors (a *fraudulent transfer*) and avoidable. (*See* Chapter 4.) The debtor's discretion in deciding on the terms of the assignment is limited by this consideration and is subject to an overriding duty of good faith. An ABC that has the effect of frustrating and obstructing creditors rather than facilitating the evenhanded distribution of funds may be invalidated in its entirety or modified by the court.

There are a number of terms that are considered improper or, at best, questionable in an ABC. For example, ABCs usually cannot allow the debtor to retain the use or control of the property or to reserve some interest in it apart from the right to have any surplus proceeds returned; provide for the administration of the assets for an extended period; grant preferential treatment to a particular creditor;[10] stipulate that participating creditors must discharge the unpaid balance of their claims; or include less than all the debtor's executable property. In some states, these principles are based in common law. In others, statutes have been passed that codify them and may impose further restrictions.

After the instrument of assignment has been executed and the assignee has accepted the appointment, the debtor must deliver the property to the assignee. Ownership of the property passes to the assignee, who holds it in trust for the benefit of the creditors. The assignee acquires no greater rights in the property than the debtor had. Therefore, the assignee's interest in the property is subject to any valid preexisting third party rights.

On the effective date of the assignment, the property is treated as being *in custodia legis* and cannot be levied upon. The effective date of the assignment varies from one state to another: It may be the date of the instrument's delivery to the assignee, the date of the property's delivery, or the date the assignee accepted the transfer. In some states, the assignment must be recorded to become effective.

The assignee's essential task is to notify creditors, to call for claims, to realize the property, and to distribute the proceeds to those creditors who have proved claims. In addition to complying with the law governing the administration of assigned property, the assignee is bound by the terms of the assignment. The proper performance of the assignee's duties is secured by a surety bond. In some states the assignee is obliged to file an inventory, appraisals, and accounts.

---

10. Preferences are not generally forbidden under common law. Therefore, a fully disclosed preference may be permitted in some states. However, other states have changed this rule by judicial decision or statute and forbid preferences in ABCs.

On being notified of the assignment, a creditor may decide to participate in the ABC, file a claim, and receive whatever distribution is made. The creditor's participation is treated as tacit consent to any lawful conditions expressed in the deed of assignment. Alternatively, the creditor may refuse to participate. Unlike bankruptcy, an ABC does not stay collection activity, so the creditor is free to pursue efforts to recover the debt. As noted before, the creditor cannot execute on the property assigned under the ABC, so if the ABC is valid, the creditor's prospects or immediate satisfaction of its claim outside of the ABC are poor. However, if there is some flaw or fraudulent design in the ABC, the creditor may be able to avoid it, unless the flaw is one that can be corrected.

Even if the ABC is valid, the creditor may be able to use it as the basis of an involuntary bankruptcy petition, provided that the requirements of §303(b)(2) of the Bankruptcy Code are satisfied. (*See* Chapter 9.) Stated broadly, the Code gives creditors the power, under some circumstances, to override the ABC and force the debtor into bankruptcy. If the petition is granted, the assignment is terminated and the assignee must surrender the property to the trustee.

EXAMPLES

1.   Render unto Seizure

Some months ago, Abe Scond borrowed money from Surge & Caesar, Inc. Abe undertook to repay the unsecured loan in installments over a two-year period. Abe paid conscientiously at first, but his payments stopped at the beginning of last month. After Abe ignored demands for payment, Surge & Caesar commenced suit to recover the debt. Shortly after summons was issued, and before default judgment could be applied for, Surge & Caesar discovered that Abe had recently lost his job. His wife and children have just left the state for an unknown destination, taking the family car and a fully-loaded trailer. Apparently Abe still has some furniture and household goods in his rented apartment, but he has advertised an "everything-must-go" moving sale for next weekend, four days hence.

Surge & Caesar would like to seize Abe's remaining property before he sells it and disappears. Can this be done?

2.   This Land Is My Land, This Land Is Your Land . . .

Eartha Plott owns a piece of land. Two of Eartha's creditors claim interests in the land based on the following sequence of events:

(a)   On January 15, Victor Pyrrhic, one of Eartha's creditors, commenced suit against her to recover a debt.
(b)   On February 20, Lien & Hungry Loan Co., another of Eartha's creditors, commenced suit against her to recover a debt. Shortly

after issuing summons, Lien & Hungry filed and served an application for attachment. Eartha failed to appear at the attachment hearing, and the court authorized a writ that was delivered to the sheriff. On March 10 the sheriff levied on Eartha's land by properly filing the writ in the real estate records.

(c)   On March 20, Victor obtained default judgment in his suit against Eartha. On March 25, Victor docketed the judgment in the county in which the land is situated.

(d)   On April 1, Lien & Hungry obtained default judgment in its action against Eartha. Its judgment was properly docketed on April 3.

The land is worth $25,000. Victor's judgment is for $15,000, and Lien & Hungry's judgment is for $20,000.

What are the creditors' interests in Eartha's land? How should they be ranked?

3.   The Land Free-for-All of Homer LeBrave

On January 15, Satin Waite obtained a money judgment against Homer LeBrave, which she properly docketed in the county on January 30.

Lienardo da Vincit obtained a money judgment against Homer on January 20. He properly docketed the judgment in the County on January 25.

At this time, Homer owned no real property in the county. However, on February 28 he acquired title to a piece of land that he inherited from his late father.

Assume both judgments are still current and enforceable. How should they be ranked?

4.   A Plague on Both Your Houses

Homer owns two houses situated in another country. Lienardo discovered these properties by searching the real estate records. He recorded his judgment in the second county on March 1.

(a)   At the time, Homer was in the process of trying to sell one of the properties. He finally succeeded in selling it to Emptor B. Ware under a land sale contract on April 30. Emptor made a substantial down-payment and undertook to pay the balance of the price over a period of years. After Emptor had moved into the house and had paid several installments under the contract, he found out about the lien. He did not know about the lien when he purchased the property and is anxious to be reassured that he need not worry about it. Should he worry?

(b)   Homer's estranged wife and his two children lived in the other house. They occupy the house rent-free in terms of a separation agreement executed a few years ago. What are Lienardo's rights in the second house?

5. Credit Cardiac Arrest

Penny Foolish owns and operates a small retail store from which she derives a modest but steady income. Although she runs her business carefully, she is undisciplined and irresponsible as a consumer. Through her abuse of credit cards she has accumulated an unmanageable amount of debt. She has tried to juggle her affairs and to make some payment to everyone, but she has fallen into arrears on most of her debts. Some creditors have threatened collection action. Because Penny's inventory and business assets are her only valuable executable property, she fears that she will lose her business if she cannot settle her debts.

Penny has shredded her credit cards and wishes to try to make an arrangement with her creditors. What options are open to her?

6. The Cede of Abraham

Abraham ("Abie") Cede has made an ABC. Included in his assigned assets is a truck worth $10,000. The truck is subject to a valid, perfected security interest, securing a debt of $8,000.

What happens to the rights of the secured party when Abie transfers the truck to his assignee?

EXPLANATIONS

1. Surge and Caesar has initiated suit, but has not yet obtained judgment. To seize Abe's property immediately, an application for attachment must be made. The attachment procedure described in section 3.3.3 is too slow to help Surge & Caesar here: Abe's planned sale and departure will be over before the notice period has expired. Surge & Caesar's only chance to prevent the sale is to apply for an ex parte attachment order.

If state law permits emergency ex parte attachment, Surge & Caesar must make a convincing case that the remedy will be ineffective if it is delayed by notice and a hearing and that failure to take immediate action will cause it irreparable prejudice. The ex parte application must also satisfy the other due process standards set out in section 3.3.2: The application must be evaluated by a judge, Surge & Caesar must furnish a bond, and a meaningful post-seizure hearing must be held.

On the facts of this case, Surge & Caesar appears to qualify for ex parte attachment. The debt is a noncontingent, liquidated, unsecured monetary obligation arising out of contract. There is no indication that Abe has a defense to the claim on the merits. If Surge & Caesar's information is reliable, Abe is planning to liquidate his assets immediately and to disappear with the proceeds. Delay will leave Surge & Caesar with the expensive and possibly futile task of trying to find him and enforce its claim in another jurisdiction.

If Abe is likely to obey a court order, a temporary restraining order is an alternative to an ex parte attachment. It would enjoin Abe from disposing of the assets or leaving the jurisdiction pending an attachment hearing on notice. If a temporary injunction is likely to be effective, courts prefer it to an ex parte attachment because it is not as drastic. The debtor is not deprived of possession of the property without notice and a hearing.

Even if Surge & Caesar obtains an ex parte attachment order, this will not guarantee a successful conclusion to this process. The property that Abe has kept with him may be exempt or relatively valueless.

2. This question involves a priority contest between two judicial liens on Eartha's land. The sequence of events is as follows:

Jan. 15	Feb. 20	Mar. 10	Mar. 20	Mar. 25	Apr. 1	Apr. 3
Victor commenced suit	Lien & Hungry commenced suit	Lien & Hungry levied attachment	Victor obtained judgment	Victor docketed judgment	Lien & Hungry obtained judgment	Lien & Hungry docketed judgment

Victor's judgment lien became effective when his judgment was docketed in the county on March 25. Lien & Hungry's judgment lien was docketed on April 3. However, Lien & Hungry had attached the land on March 10. An attachment lien was created upon levy, which was accomplished by recording the attachment in the real estate records. When Lien & Hungry obtained its judgment lien on April 3, that lien merged with the attachment lien, so that Lien & Hungry's priority backdated to March 10.

On the basis of the first-in-time rule, Lien & Hungry's lien has priority over Victor's lien. It is a first charge against the property for the full amount of $20,000 plus costs. Victor's lien extends only to the surplus of approximately $5,000. Victor will have to seek other assets to cover his deficiency.

This Example illustrates the value of attachment. By attaching the property at the commencement of its suit, Lien & Hungry was able to secure its ultimate judgment and to take priority over Victor. By failing to attach the property, Victor lost the advantage even though he commenced suit and obtained judgment first.

Eartha is an individual, so she is entitled to any exemptions provided by state law. Because the property is unimproved land rather than Eartha's home, it is less likely to be exempt. However, the statute must be consulted to determine whether it provides a general exemption or some other exemption category that could include the land.

3. The sequence of events is as follows:

Jan. 15	Jan. 20	Jan. 25	Jan. 30	Feb. 28
Satin obtains judgment	Lienardo obtains judgment	Lienardo's judgment docketed	Satin's judgment docketed	Homer acquires property

The question states that both judgment liens were properly recorded. Irrespective of when the judgment was obtained, a judgment lien becomes effective only upon docketing. It does not backdate to the time of judgment.

If Homer had owned real property in the county when the judgments were docketed, each would have attached to the property upon docketing. Because the first-in-time rule governs priority, Lienardo's lien, effective on January 25, would have had priority over Satin's lien, which became effective on January 30. However, this property was only acquired by Homer on February 28. As explained in section 3.4.3, both liens automatically attached to the after-acquired property on February 28.

In some states, preexisting judgment liens are treated as effective on attachment to the after-acquired property. Even though they were docketed at different times, they attach simultaneously and rank equally. In other states, judgment liens or after-acquired property backdate to the time of docketing. Under such a rule, Lienardo's lien has priority.

4. **(a)** Yes. The judgment lien took effect before the property was sold to Emptor. Even if Emptor bought in good faith and without actual knowledge of the lien, the valid filing gave him constructive notice of it. The first-in-time rule applies and Emptor takes the property subject to the lien. Sometimes, though, the first-in-time rule is varied to protect a bona fide purchaser. However, Emptor's constructive notice disqualifies him from that status. He should have examined the title records.

(b) Homer's second house is probably protected by a homestead exemption. His family appear to qualify as his dependents, and the exemption statute is likely to cover property occupied by the debtor or his dependents. (A debtor can usually claim only one homestead exemption. If Homer owns the home in which he resides, he must select the one to exempt.) The exemption may immunize Homer's entire equity in the property, or it may be subject to a dollar limitation. In the latter case, Lienardo's lien attaches to the nonexempt equity.

5. Penny has a number of alternative means of trying to resolve her debt problems. She could select state law remedies such as those discussed in this chapter, or she could choose one of the forms of relief provided by the Bankruptcy Code. The advantages and drawbacks of bankruptcy will be discussed later. For the present, merely note that it is one of her options. Much more information is needed about Penny's affairs, for a judgment to be made on her most appropriate course of action. The present facts do allow the following tentative observations to be made:

First, an ABC will not fit Penny's needs. It requires the assignment and liquidation of all her executable property. Because she needs this property for her livelihood, an ABC defeats the purpose for which she seeks to approach creditors.

Second, a composition may be possible provided that Penny's creditors are amenable to it and her financial affairs are such that she can make a proposal that will satisfy them. If she can negotiate a composition she will be able to avoid dismemberment of her business and will be able to settle her debts by proportional payment over time without the need for the expense and trauma of a bankruptcy case.

If Penny's business assets are valuable enough to cover all her debts, creditors may not have an incentive to enter a composition. However, if Penny is insolvent and she proposes a reasonable plan of payment from future income, creditors may be persuaded that acceptance of her offer is more advantageous than an uncertain race for her assets. The percentage of payment on claims and the period of payment must be realistic and attractive in light of the creditors' prospects of immediate satisfaction. As noted before, the cooperation of creditors is essential to an effective composition.

Finally, if significant creditors are hostile to the idea of a composition, Penny will have to consider filing a bankruptcy petition to force them into a collective proceeding. The choice of bankruptcy relief is discussed further in Chapter 8.

6. Abie can transfer to the assignee only those rights that he himself has in the property. The truck therefore passes to the assignee subject to the security interest, which was properly perfected prior to the effective date of the assignment.[11] The secured party can assert its right to the collateral notwithstanding the assignment.

Even if Abie is not behind in his payments on the truck, the assignment of the collateral is likely to constitute a default under the security agreement. This entitles the secured party to foreclose on the truck. It may either recover the truck from the assignee or it may allow the assignee to sell the truck and to pay its secured claim as a priority charge on the proceeds. The assignee is entitled to any surplus that remains after the secured claim has been satisfied.

---

11. An assignee for the benefit of creditors is given the status of a lien creditor by UCC §9.301 and will take priority over a secured party who has not perfected its security interest at the effective date of the assignment.

4

Fraudulent Transfers

§4.1 Background — The Basis and Purpose of Fraudulent Transfer Law

The point has often been made that an unsecured creditor takes the risk that the debtor will have no executable property to satisfy a delinquent claim. If the absence of assets is the natural result of economic adversity, the creditor can do little about it. However, if the wily debtor has attempted to immunize assets from execution by concealing or illegitimately disposing of them, that is quite a different matter: The law gives the disappointed creditor some power to retrieve the property so that it can be subjected to execution.

The subterfuge of secreting or transferring assets to evade their seizure by creditors is not a modern invention. It is an old trick that unscrupulous debtors have been playing for centuries and that the law began to respond to a long time ago. American law on the subject is based on a statute that dates back to the reign of Good Queen Bess. Although the Elizabethans did not invent fraudulent transfer law (it predated that period), the codification became firmly established in English law and was received into American law by general adoption of the common law or statutory emulation.

Over the years, judicial embellishment of the original law had made it muddy, cumbersome, and nonuniform. For this reason, the National Conference of Commissioners on Uniform State Laws promulgated the *Uniform Fraudulent Conveyance Act* (UFCA) in 1918. The Act was adopted by about half the states. By the late 1970s, though, the Act had become out-of-date and wanting for revision to accommodate judicial decisions and recent developments in commercial law (such as the UCC and the new Bankruptcy Code). A revised model act, the *Uniform Fraudulent Transfers Act* (UFTA), was published in 1984. Since its promulgation, the UFTA has been adopted not only by many states that had enacted the UFCA, but also by some that had not had uniform legislation before.

Because of the existence of model legislation, this area is more uniform than others. The discussion in this chapter is based on the UFTA, and the citations are to sections of that Act.

The avoidance of fraudulent transfers is an issue in both state law and bankruptcy law. Many of the general principles discussed in this chapter are applicable to the trustee's avoidance of fraudulent transfers in a bankruptcy case. In this chapter, fraudulent transfers are treated in the context of state law. In section 16.3, these principles are reviewed in the context of bankruptcy law and significant variations are identified.

The action to avoid a fraudulent transfer is available to *unsecured* creditors. A lienholder or another person with a valid and perfected interest in property does not need fraudulent transfer law to protect those rights, since they are effective against the subsequent transferee.

There is something quite drastic about giving an unsecured creditor the power to attack a transfer by the debtor. The unsecured creditor has no rights in the debtor's property and normally should have no grounds for interfering with the debtor's use or disposition of it. It is only when a transfer constitutes an abuse of the debtor's ownership rights, having the effect of defeating the justifiable expectations of the unsecured creditor, that there is a basis for avoiding it. Therefore, fraudulent transfer law is a limitation on the debtor's usual power to dispose freely of property, which arises from the obligation to deal fairly with creditors.

§4.2   An Overview of the Avoidance Suit

Before dealing with the detailed rules of the UFTA, it is useful to illustrate circumstances that could give rise to an avoidance suit and to sketch the broad outlines of the action.

A creditor has obtained judgment against the debtor and has attempted execution. The sheriff finds no executable property, and submits a nulla bona return. The creditor investigates and discovers that the debtor recently transferred property to a relative for apparently inadequate consideration. If the creditor believes that it can establish grounds for avoidance, as discussed below, it commences suit against the transferee. The debtor may be joined in the suit, but the transferee is the essential party. The relief sought by the creditor is a judgment ordering restoration of the property to the debtor so that it can be levied upon to satisfy the judgment. As an alternative, the creditor is able to claim damages from the transferee based on the value of the asset.

Because the transferee is a stranger to the debtor/creditor relationship, the UFTA provides protection for his or her legitimate interests. Therefore, the grounds for avoidance require examination not only of the debtor's conduct and motives but also of the role played by the transferee in the transaction. If the transferee behaved honestly and gave value to the debtor, the transfer may not be avoidable despite the debtor's ill motives in making it, or the transferee may at least be compensated for the value given.

The UFTA is available to creditors of the transferee defined in §1(4) read with §1(3) to include persons with a wide variety of claims against the debtor. The UFTA distinguishes between creditors whose claims existed at the time of transfer, who are given broader rights of avoidance, and those whose claims arose afterwards, whose avoidance rights are more limited. The UFTA extends to the avoidance of transfers, defined in §1(12) read with §1(2) to include all disposition of an interest in assets. "Assets" include only property to the extent that it is non-exempt and not subject to a security interest.

The UFTA provides two different grounds for avoidance. The first is *actual fraud*, §4(a)(1), and the other is *constructive fraud*, which can take one of three different forms. §§4(a)(2) and 5(a). The grounds of avoidance are alternative, which means a creditor need only establish one of them.

§4.3 Actual Fraud

§4.3.1 Dishonest Intent

A creditor can avoid a transfer made by the debtor with actual intent to hinder, delay, or defraud any creditor. §4(a)(i). This ground of avoidance is available both to creditors whose claims existed at the time of transfer and to those whose claims arose afterwards, because all creditors should be able to respond to actual fraud. To avoid the transfer on the basis of actual fraud, the creditor must prove that the debtor made the transfer with the deliberate motive of removing the property from the reach of creditors.

§4.3.2 Proof of Fraud — Badges of Fraud

Unless a debtor has admitted dishonest intent, a creditor cannot prove fraud by direct evidence of the debtor's state of mind. Therefore, fraudulent intent is usually shown by proof of the debtor's conduct in circumstances that show a dishonest motive. Over the centuries, courts have identified typical patterns of behavior that create suspicion of fraud — these are called *badges of fraud*.

Badges of fraud are *not* presumptions. Nor do they relieve the creditor of the burden of proving actual fraud. They are simply inferences that help to establish the creditor's case. If the creditor can show that suspicious circumstances attended the disposition of property, the factfinder may draw an inference of fraud unless the debtor offers a plausible explanation to the contrary.

The term "badges of fraud" is traditional. It is not used in the UFTA. However, §4(b) recognizes the evidentiary value of inferences. It lists examples of suspicious behavior and states that such factors may be considered, together with any other circumstances, in deciding the question of fraudulent intent. The list in §4(b) is drawn from badges of fraud that have been recognized by courts. It is not intended to be definitive. The determination of fraud is a factual matter, and the conduct of the debtor must be evaluated in each case. Also, some indicia of fraud are more compelling than others, and a combination of several suspicious factors strengthens the inference.

Some of the examples selected from the list illustrate the kinds of activity or circumstances that may give rise to an inference of fraud: The transfer was to an insider or someone with close family or other connections with the debtor; the debtor sought to conceal the transfer; the transfer occurred just before litigation or in the face of other impending collection activity; the transfer was made just before a significant debt was incurred. (The use of inferences is illustrated by Examples 1 and 2).

It is the debtor's state of mind, rather than the transferee's, that is relevant. However, as discussed in section 4.6, the absence or presence of good faith on the transferee's part has an impact on the creditor's avoidance rights.

§4.4   Constructive Fraud

§4.4.1   *General Principles*

Constructive fraud is very different from actual fraud established by inference. If the facts constituting constructive fraud are established, a conclusive presumption of fraud is created, and inquiry into the debtor's state of mind is irrelevant. The word "constructive" indicates that fraud is construed as a matter of law, rather than established by evidence of a guilty mind. The policy basis for recognizing this type of presumptive fraud is that a disposition under the defined circumstances unfairly diminishes the debtor's executable estate and should not be allowed, even if it was not deliberately dishonest. Constructive fraud was recognized by courts long before the Uniform Acts, and the concept is incorporated into the UFTA. However, the statute does not use the term itself.

Constructive fraud has two basic elements: (1) the debtor did not receive reasonably equivalent value in exchange for the transfer, and (2) the debtor was in a shaky financial condition at the time of the transfer. This second element is only satisfied if the creditor can establish one of three specific factual situations at the time of transfer:

(1) The debtor was involved in or was about to engage in a business venture, and the transfer left the debtor with insufficient capital for the project (§4(a)(2)(i)); or

(2) the debtor was about to incur debts with the actual or imputed in-
     tention of not paying them when due (§4(a)(2)(ii)); or
(3) the debtor was insolvent (§5(a)). (Section 5(b) has a somewhat dif-
     ferent standard if the transfer was to an insider.)

A creditor whose claim existed at the time of the transfer may use any
one of the three forms of constructive fraud as grounds to avoid a transfer. A
creditor whose claim arose after the transfer may not rely on insolvency, but
may use either of the other two. This is because undercapitalization and intent not to pay future debts are both concerned with prospective financial difficulties arising from the transfer.

§4.4.2 *Reasonable Equivalence in Value*

Under §3(a), value is given by the transferee if the debtor receives property
in exchange for the transfer or a prior debt of the debtor is satisfied or secured. The UFTA itself does not provide a formula for determining whether
value is reasonably equivalent. This is left to the courts.

The test of reasonable equivalence would be easy if courts simply used a
mechanical formula in which economic values were compared and the quid
pro quo received by the debtor was required to be worth at least a fixed percentage of the property transferred by the debtor. However, this approach is
too rigid. After all, the test requires not simply equivalent value but *reasonably* equivalent value.

Therefore, it is not enough that the transaction was somewhat disadvantageous to the debtor. The values exchanged are highly relevant, of course
(the less that the debtor received for the transfer the greater the likelihood of
avoidance), but the entire context must be examined. The court will usually
take into account the relationship of the parties, the market environment,
and the apparent motive for the transfer. Even though constructive fraud is
not premised on actual fraudulent intent, this does not mean that suspicious
or unusual circumstances in the transfer are completely disregarded. The
context may justify the lower value of the exchange, based on legitimate market considerations, or it may suggest that the return value was not reasonably
equivalent. (*See also* section 4.5.)

It should also be noted that the value of property may be uncertain. Valuation is a factual issue on which there could be conflicting evidence. Where
value is subject to doubt, it may be more difficult to be sure that the consideration received by the debtor was deficient.

§4.4.3 *Financial Condition*

a. Insolvency

Under the *balance sheet* (or *bankruptcy*) *test,* insolvency occurs when liabilities exceed assets at fair value. As mentioned before, the term "assets" is defined in §1(2) to exclude property to the extent of any exemption or encumbrance. Section 2 of the UFTA uses the balance sheet test as the test for insolvency. However, the creditor's burden of proving insolvency is eased by a presumption in §2(b): If the creditor does not have the financial data to prove the debtor's insolvency under the balance sheet test, the creditor can prove that the debtor is not paying debts as they become due (the *equity test*). In other words, proof of insolvency under the equity test shifts to the defendant the burden of proving solvency with the balance sheet test.

Insolvency is measured at the time of the transfer. This means that the debtor may already have been insolvent when the transfer was made or may have been rendered insolvent as a result of the disposition of the transferred property.

Proof of insolvency under either test may involve difficult issues. The balance sheet test requires assets to be given fair value, and the appraisal of assets can be a contentious matter. A creditor may similarly have difficulties in trying to establish insolvency on the equity test to take advantage of the presumption in §2(b). To determine whether a debtor is not generally paying debts as they become due, the court must consider the proportion of debts that are not being paid on time, the patterns of payment or nonpayment, and the reasons for nonpayment. (The issue of proving general nonpayment also arises in connection with bankruptcy and is discussed in section 9.6.4.)

b. Undercapitalization or Intent to Incur Debts That Will Not Be Paid

As an alternative to showing insolvency, a creditor can rely on one of two other forms of financial instability. These two alternative tests move the focus from the traditional measure of financial precariousness — liabilities in excess of assets — to the relationship between the debtor's financial condition and intended future business activity. In broad terms, they allow the creditor to impugn a transfer for inadequate value if it was reckless or irresponsible in light of the debtor's prospective commercial dealings or if it would likely doom the debtor's planned venture to fairly certain failure. In some cases, the debtor's transfer under such circumstances may be tantamount to deliberate fraud, but this is a variety of constructive fraud; no deliberate intent to cheat creditors need be shown. Because these tests involve debtor action subsequent to the transfer, they may be relied on by future creditors as well as existing ones.

If insolvency can present difficult factual issues, these alternative tests can present impossible ones. In an obvious case, it may be easy to show that a debtor was undercapitalized or was incurring debts without the justifiable expectation of repaying them. However, in many situations there could be quite divergent opinions about the level of assets needed for a venture or the debtor's prospects of generating future earnings sufficient to support new debt.

§4.5   The Relationship between the Grounds of Constructive Fraud and Actual Fraud

Actual fraud and constructive fraud are doctrinally distinct, as the last two sections have shown. However, in some cases the conduct of the debtor may furnish grounds for avoidance under both of them. Where this happens, the creditor has to decide which ground is more likely to succeed and provide the best relief.

For example, in addition to being the elements of constructive fraud, insolvency and lack of reasonable return consideration are suspicious circumstances that can be used by a creditor to build a case of actual fraud. (They are included in the list of relevant considerations in §4(b).) In deciding whether to proceed under actual or constructive fraud when these factors are present, the creditor will evaluate the degree to which they are clearly demonstrable and the existence of other indicia of fraud. Sometimes other tactical considerations may influence the creditor's choice when the facts support either ground. For example, a posttransfer creditor who cannot avoid the transfer on the basis of constructive fraud can use the facts of insolvency and inadequate consideration as part of the case for actual fraud.

The intersection of actual and constructive fraud is also illustrated by the contextual approach taken in determining reasonably equivalent value. As noted in section 4.4.2, courts look at factors beyond the arithmetical comparison of values when deciding the issue of reasonable equivalence. Underhanded behavior by the debtor could influence the court to find that the quid pro quo received by the debtor was not reasonably adequate, and conversely, honest motives could justify a low price.

In short, there is a clear doctrinal distinction between actual and constructive fraud. The former is concerned with the state of the debtor's mind, while the latter relies on specific objective criteria. However, in some cases the distinction may be blurred. The grounds have some components in common, and sometimes even objective criteria must be interpreted in context.

§4.6   The Remedy of Avoidance and the Rights of the Transferee

Traditionally, the creditors' bill in equity had to be used to avoid a fraudulent transfer.[1] This cumbersome equitable suit[2] was replaced by a more efficient statutory cause of action under the UFCA. The statutory remedy has been further refined in §§7 and 8 of the UFTA. The creditor has a choice of two remedies:

(1)   recovery of the property from the transferee so that it can be subjected to levy and sold in execution, or

(2)   a money judgment against the transferee for the lesser of either the value of the property measured at the time of transfer or the amount of the debt due by the debtor.

Whichever course is selected, the court has the discretion to order prejudgment remedies or other appropriate ancillary relief.

Suit may be brought against the person who acquired the property from the debtor or against a subsequent transferee. However, the UFTA protects the rights of persons who acquired the property in good faith. Therefore, even though the debtor's conduct provides grounds for avoidance, the creditor's power to recover the property or to obtain damages from the transferee is subject to a number of limitations. The rules can be summarized as follows:

(1) A good faith transferee from the debtor who gave reasonably equivalent value for the property is fully protected.   No matter how guilty the debtor's motives were in conveying the property, the creditor cannot recover the property or damages from a transferee who gave the debtor fair equivalent value for it and acted honestly and without knowledge or reason to know of the debtor's fraudulent purpose.

(2) A transferee who acquired the property from the debtor in good faith, but for a value that was less than reasonably equivalent, receives partial protection.   Where the transferee from the debtor acted in good

1. The creditor's bill was introduced in section 3.7 in connection with proceedings in aid of execution.

2. Although the creditors' bill was an equitable remedy, the creditor's power of avoidance is legal in derivation. Therefore, prior to the creation of the statutory remedy, a suit to avoid the transfer was equitable, but a suit to recover damages from the transferee was legal. This classification may sound esoteric, but as you will see in Section 7.4.2, it can have practical significance. In *Granfinanciera S.A. v. Nordberg*, 492 U.S. 33 (1989), the U.S. Supreme Court held that the legal nature of a monetary claim against the transferee entitled the parties to a jury trial.

faith, but the value for the transfer is not reasonably equivalent, the transfer is avoidable. The creditor can recover the property or obtain a money judgment. However, the transferee is entitled to offset against that recovery the value that had been given to the debtor for the property. If the property is returned for execution, this offset is secured by a lien and must be paid to the transferee from the proceeds of the execution sale. If the creditor receives a money judgment, the transferee's liability under the judgment is reduced by the offset.

(3) A bad faith transferee from the debtor is given no protection against the creditor. A transferee who acted in bad faith by actively or passively colluding with the debtor receives no protection from avoidance. Even if the transferee gave value to the debtor for the property, that value is not deductible from the creditor's recovery. The transferee may try to obtain restitution from the debtor, but that is not likely to be a promising enterprise. Not only is the debtor in financial difficulty, but also the court may not be inclined to award restitution to one who participated in the debtor's fraud.

(4) A subsequent transferee (*i.e.*, one who did not take directly from the debtor) who acquired the property in good faith and for value is fully protected. Because the subsequent transferee did not deal with the debtor, the qualifications for immunity are somewhat lower than those for a transferee from the debtor. As long as the transferee acted in good faith, the equivalence of the value given for the property is not inquired into.

(5) A subsequent transferee, whether or not in good faith, shelters under the rights of a prior good faith transferee. A transferee who qualifies for protection from avoidance cuts off any rights that the creditor may have to recover the property. For that reason, the creditor has no right of avoidance against any later transferees.

(6) A subsequent transferee who did not act in good faith and did not derive rights through a good faith transferee has no protection. Like a bad faith transferee from the debtor, this transferee is subject to avoidance or a money judgment and has no offset for any value given for the property.

§4.7 Fraudulent Transfer Law and Leveraged Buyouts

§4.7.1 *What Is a Leveraged Buyout?*

A leveraged buyout (often referred to in abbreviated form as a LBO) is a transaction in which the purchase of shares in a corporation is financed by the corporation itself or secured by the assets of the corporation. In essence, the corporation provides funding to the buyer of its shares. The expectation is that reimbursement of the corporation will come from future profits that the buyer will make from the operation of the corporation's business.

LBOs are structured in many different ways. One method is for the corporation to allow the buyer to use its unencumbered assets to secure the purchase price of the shares. The seller may give the buyer credit for the price of the shares and secures this credit by having the corporation grant a security interest in its assets; or the corporation may borrow money secured by its assets, and then it may lend this money to the buyer as an unsecured loan; or the buyer may borrow money from a financial institution, and the corporation guarantees this debt, using its assets to secure its guarantee.

Transactions like this are intended to enable the buyer to purchase the shares by using the resources of the corporation to acquire funding that would otherwise not be accessible to the buyer. Their effect is to encumber the assets of the corporation for a debt that benefits not the corporation itself, but its buyer. If the corporation is successfully managed, this prejudice to the corporation will eventually be reversed as the buyer's profits generate funds to settle the debt and release the corporate assets from the encumbrance. However, if the business does not produce large enough profits, the debt will not be repaid, and the assets will be foreclosed upon. The risk of failure is borne not only by the corporation, but also by its unsecured creditors who have lost the protection of recourse to unencumbered assets. Stated differently, before the LBO, the prior owner of the corporation had an equity interest which was junior to the claims of unsecured creditors. Following the LBO, this equity has been paid out and replaced by senior secured debt.

Some people view LBOs as serving useful purposes, such as the facilitation of changes in corporate management, the promotion of efficiency, and the enhancement of investment opportunities. Those who feel this way are likely to be persuaded by the argument that fraudulent transfer law should not be applied to LBOs unless they are actually fraudulent. The contrary view is that LBOs are manipulative devices that result in the plunder of corporate assets and the imposition of crippling debt on a formerly viable corporation. From this perspective, fraudulent transfer law serves the useful purpose of shifting risk of the corporation's failure from the creditors to the parties who were responsible for the arrangements.

§4.7.2   The Application of Fraudulent Transfer Law to LBOs

LBOs are not per se fraudulent. However, when a corporation fails to pay its debts after an LBO, creditors may look to fraudulent transfer law to avoid the transfer made by the corporation in connection with the LBO. In the type of transaction described above, this transfer is the grant of a security interest by the corporation. (The grant of a security interest is a disposition of rights in property which meets the definition of transfer under the UFTA.) To avoid the transfer, the creditor must establish either actual or constructive fraud in accordance with the general principles discussed above.

Sometimes actual fraud is present (that is, the LBO is dishonestly used as a pretext to plunder the corporation's assets). However, in most cases, the LBO is not a sham or fraud, but a good faith attempt to finance the sale of ownership in the corporation, undertaken in the expectation that the debt assumed by the corporation will ultimately be satisfied from future profits. In such cases, the basis for attacking the LBO is constructive fraud: The grant of a security interest in the corporate assets increased its debt over its assets, rendering it insolvent. It is not relevant that the owner may have received equivalent value for the transfer. The corporation, which is the debtor, did not.

EXAMPLES

1. Awful and His Monet Are Soon Parted

Awful Artful owned a painting by Claude Monet, the famed Impressionist. The painting, worth several million dollars, was acquired by Awful some years ago when he was a successful entrepreneur. His business collapsed and he lost his fortune. He still has hordes of hungry creditors.

The Monet was his last remaining valuable asset. He treasured it passionately and could not bear the thought of its inevitable seizure by his creditors. He therefore made an agreement with his old comrade, Hyde Hastily, to trade the painting for a case of wine[3] worth $400. The two of them made an informal pact that when the time was right, Awful could reacquire the painting by giving Hyde a case of champagne. The exchange took place immediately. Awful soon consumed the wine in making numerous toasts to his creditors.

Shortly after this transaction, Gibbet Bach, one of Awful's creditors, obtained judgment, had a writ issued and attempted to find leviable property. The sheriff could find no assets, and submitted nulla bona return. This spurred Gibbet into an investigation that revealed the disposition of the painting. Gibbet wants to avoid the transfer and have the painting returned to Awful so that it can be subjected to levy. Does he have grounds for doing so?

2. Monet Is the Root of More Evil

Change the facts in Example 1 as follows:

Assume that when he was confronted with the impending seizure of his Monet, Awful Artful decided to take a different course. Instead of making

---

3. If the painting had been by Jean-Antoine Watteau, instead of Monet, this question would have been entitled "Changing Watteau into Wine." If the painting was by Mark Rothko, it would have been called "The Grapes of Rothko."

the exchange with Hyde, he decided that if he was going to lose the painting anyhow, he may as well sell it for a good price and use the proceeds to have some fun. He therefore hired an art dealer and instructed him to find a buyer. Awful told the dealer to act quickly and discreetly and to insist on a cash sale.

The dealer approached Rob Grave, an avid art collector, and told him that the Monet could be bought at a bargain price if Rob paid cash and asked no questions. Rob offered a price equivalent to 80 percent of the appraised value of the painting. The dealer communicated this offer to Awful who accepted it.

At an appointed time a few days later, the Monet was delivered to Rob in exchange for a suitcase full of crisp banknotes. Awful immediately splurged every cent of this impressive sum by renting a Mediterranean villa for the weekend, and flying out hundreds of guests for the wildest, most spectacular party in history.

Although Awful invited none of his creditors, he was foolish enough to encourage press coverage of his extravaganza. This led to a major creditor finding out about the disposition. The creditor has sued Rob for recovery of the painting. Are there grounds for the action?

EXPLANATIONS

1. This question is meant to illustrate a clear case of actual fraud. Gibbet should succeed in avoiding the transfer under UFTA §4(a)(i):

(a) **The barter of the painting is a transfer.** Section 1(12) defines "transfer" to cover all forms of disposition of assets by the debtor. The painting is an asset of Awful's under §1(2). Even though state law may give Awful an exemption in household goods, or even artwork, these exemptions are typically subject to value limitations that would make the exemption minuscule in relation to the worth of the Monet. At best, Awful may have a first claim to a small fraction of the proceeds when the painting is recovered and sold in execution.

(b) **Gibbet is a creditor under §1(4).** It sounds as if his claim was in existence at the time of transfer, but as he will be relying on actual fraud this does not really matter: Actual fraud is actionable by posttransfer creditors as well.

(c) **The grounds of actual fraud are clearly satisfied.** The transfer was made with the intent of hindering, delaying and defrauding creditors. Because Gibbet has not had the advantage of reading this fine, lucid statement of the facts, he will have to rely on whatever circumstantial evidence he can find to prove fraud. The transaction exhibits several badges of fraud which Gibbet's investigations should uncover: The transfer occurred while Awful was besieged by creditors, and shortly before Gibbet's unsuccessful levy; Awful was probably insolvent on the balance sheet test, and it certainly sounds as if he was insolvent on the equity test; the painting was his last remaining asset; he received laughably inadequate consideration for it; Hyde is a close friend; and Awful had an understanding with Hyde for the return of the painting in the future.

(d) Awful's insolvency together with the lack of reasonably equivalent consideration makes the transfer constructively fraudulent, too. However, if the evidence of actual fraud is sufficient, Gibbet does not need to rely on this ground of avoidance.

(e) Hyde collaborated with Awful in the fraudulent transfer. Because he is not a good faith transferee for reasonably equivalent value, he cannot successfully resist the avoidance suit, nor is he entitled to a lien or an offset to reimburse him for the wine.

2. Analysis of this problem can be broken up as follows:

(a) Actual fraud. Awful's disposition is motivated here, as it was in Example 1, by the desire to keep the Monet from his creditors. This case has several indicia of fraud in common with Example 1, but there are a few differences: Awful does not have a close relationship with the transferee, and the value received for the painting is much closer to being equivalent. On the other hand, Awful dissipated the proceeds of the painting with reckless abandon. There are surely enough suspicious circumstances to provide a solid case for actual fraud.

(b) Constructive fraud. Even though the facts concerning insolvency are unchanged, the consideration for the painting is much closer to its true value. (Comparative value is furnished as a fact in this question, so the difficult task of valuation is avoided.) Eighty percent of the appraised value may or may not be reasonably equivalent value in exchange for the painting. This decision should not be made solely on an arithmetical comparison, but should be determined in light of all the circumstances of the transaction. If the disposition was a fairly bargained, regular market transaction, there may be a justification for the buyer's offering and the seller accepting less than the market price. However, where the price is depressed as a result of a hasty clandestine disposition and is paid in cash, a good case can be made that 80 percent of the market value was not a reasonably equivalent exchange.

(c) The transferee's defense or offset. To be completely protected from avoidance of the transfer, Rob must qualify as a good faith purchaser for reasonably equivalent value. To receive the lesser protection of a lien or offest for the consideration paid, Rob must at least have acted in good faith. It has already been suggested that the price may not be reasonably equivalent. If this is so, the transfer will be avoided and the issue of the lien or offest arises.

There is a good argument that Rob did not act in good faith. Although there was no express collusion and the parties did not know each other, the transaction is unsavory. Rob may not have known the specifics of Awful's situation, but the suspicious circumstances of the sale should have put Rob on inquiry. Courts often attribute knowledge to one who avoids inquiry under circumstances that strongly suggest fraud. If Rob is found to have lacked good faith, he receives no offset or lien. His restitution claim against Awful is valueless because Awful has no assets.

5

The Nature, Source, and Policies of Bankruptcy Law

§5.1 What Is Bankruptcy?

When a debtor becomes bankrupt, the debt collection procedures that are otherwise applicable in the jurisdiction are replaced by a powerful and wide-ranging system of laws and procedures. Bankruptcy has a profound impact on the debtor, creditors, and most other parties that have an interest in the debtor's affairs.

Bankruptcy takes different forms and is flexible enough to provide different goals. It is therefore difficult to devise a general definition of bankruptcy that is both precise and meaningful. However, one can begin to define bankruptcy by identifying some of the distinctive characteristics that make it so different from collection remedies under state law:

(1) Bankruptcy is a remedial system provided for by federal law — more specifically, by Title 11 of the U.S. Code. (From now on, Title 11 is referred to as "the Code." When a Code section is cited, only the section symbol and number are used.)

(2) It is a collective remedy in that, with a few exceptions, it encompasses all of the debtor's assets and debts.

(3) It is designed to fulfill two functions: It affords relief to the debtor by resolving and settling current debts, while at the same time protecting creditors and guarding their interests.

(4) It is administered by a "system" consisting of specialized courts, government officials, and private persons.

This general description is expanded upon in the remainder of this chapter.

§5.2   The Federal Nature of Bankruptcy Law

§5.2.1   *The Federal Power over Bankruptcy*

State law generally governs the creation, performance, and enforcement of obligations. In most cases outside of bankruptcy the states, through their judicial systems, are responsible for providing remedies for creditors and appropriate protection for debtors. However, as soon as bankruptcy relief is sought, federal bankruptcy law is brought into effect. A new regime is established over the debtor's affairs.

Bankruptcy law is federal because the Constitution grants to Congress the power "[t]o establish . . . uniform laws on the subject of bankruptcies throughout the United States." Art. I, §8. In addition, the supremacy clause states that the laws of the United States made pursuant to the Constitution shall be the supreme law of the land and take precedence over state laws. Art. VI, cl. 2.

Although the records of the Constitutional Convention say very little about the bankruptcy power, contemporaneous writings indicate that a centralized bankruptcy law was regarded as one of the economic reforms essential to a viable union. The frustrating diversity of the debtor/creditor laws of the Confederated States was a barrier to interstate commerce. By establishing a uniform bankruptcy law, the Drafters hoped to promote commercial order and efficiency and to lessen the disruptive influence of local interests and rivalries. The need for uniformity and the nationwide enforcement of the bankruptcy remedy remain an important justification of federal bankruptcy power.

§5.2.2   *Bankruptcy Law and Nonbankruptcy Law*

The Code uses the term "nonbankruptcy law" to describe the generally prevailing law of the jurisdiction in which a bankruptcy case is filed. This includes the law of the state as well as all federal laws other than the Code. The term is rather awkward, akin to describing all colors as "nonblack." Nevertheless, it is frequently employed and serves the purpose of denoting a legal context that is wider than state law.

In the absence of bankruptcy, nonbankruptcy law is the only law applicable to the debtor-creditor relationship. When bankruptcy occurs, bankruptcy law interacts with this body of prevailing nonbankruptcy law in a complex and multifaceted way. Under the Supremacy Clause, bankruptcy law preempts state law to the extent that they are inconsistent, but because in many respects state law is *not* incompatible with bankruptcy law, it is preserved in bankruptcy and forms the basis of rights that are protected and upheld. Bankruptcy law does not preempt other inconsistent *federal* law: When bankruptcy law cannot be reconciled with other federal statutes, the court must interpret congressional intent to decide which is to prevail. (*See* Example 2.)

In the discussion of the substantive law of bankruptcy that follows, there will be many examples of the interaction between nonbankruptcy and bankruptcy law. For the present, simply note that bankruptcy brings into effect a whole legal structure that may alter or affirm rights and procedures provided by the underlying network of state common and statute law and federal law. The extent to which nonbankruptcy law is overridden is usually expressed in the particular provisions of the Code. Sometimes, where congressional intent is less clear, questions of statutory interpretation may be presented.

§5.3 Uniformity in Bankruptcy Law

If rights in bankruptcy are frequently determined with reference to nonbankruptcy law (consisting largely of applicable state law), can it ever be said that there is a uniform law of bankruptcy in the United States? Diversity in local law must inevitably produce nonuniform resolution of many identical issues in bankruptcy cases in different states. The topic of debtor's exemptions is used here to illustrate this point because the issue of uniformity in exemption law has been the subject of constitutional challenge. (Debtors' exemptions were introduced briefly in section 3.2 and are discussed in greater detail in Chapter 13.)

An exemption is a right granted to an individual debtor to protect certain types or items of property from seizure in satisfaction of debt. Exemptions are recognized in both state law and bankruptcy law. Every state has its own exemption statute, which is applicable to collection proceedings under state law. These statutes vary in the types, value, and extent of property that can be exempted. Some are much more generous to debtors than others.

When an individual debtor files a bankruptcy petition, you may expect the exemptions available to be governed by the Code rather than by state law: After all, a uniform bankruptcy law should give the same exemption rights to debtors throughout the United States. Section 522 of the Code does in fact provide for a standardized set of exemptions in bankruptcy cases. However, when it enacted the Code in 1978, Congress decided not to impose this uniform set of exemptions on states, and §522(b) gives states the option of substituting their own exemption laws for those provided in §522.[1] Many states

---

1. The decision in 1978 to permit states to make their own exemption laws applicable in bankruptcy has not put to rest the issue of uniformity in exemptions. It was again raised before the National Bankruptcy Review Commission (discussed in section 5.4.1) which recommended the elimination of the states' power to opt out of federal exemptions. Although the debate remains alive, Congress has not yet shown an interest in mandating a set of uniform federal exemptions. This is discussed further in section 13.2.

have exercised this power, so that the exemptions claimable by a bankrupt debtor in one state are likely to be quite different from those available to a debtor whose bankruptcy case has been filed in another.

Does this diversity of treatment contravene the Constitution's requirement of uniformity? This question was put to the Supreme Court shortly after the enactment of the Bankruptcy Act of 1898, which did not even offer an optional set of federal exemptions, but deferred completely to state exemption laws. In *Hanover National Bank v. Moyses,* 186 U.S. 181 (1902), the Court upheld the Act's incorporation of state exemption laws and laid down what has remained a fundamental principle governing uniformity: Absolute uniformity is not required. Uniformity is "geographical and not personal," and the requirement of uniformity is met when "the trustee takes in each state whatever would have been awardable to the creditors if the bankrupt law had not been passed." The general idea is that while a uniform law is required, local variations are tolerable, and uniformity in the detailed operation of the law is not essential.

The enactment of the present Code, with its uniform exemptions qualified by the states' right to "opt out," raised again the issue of uniformity. The exemption provisions were again challenged on the basis that by allowing states to substitute their own exemptions, Congress had failed to comply with the constitutional requirement of uniformity. The Seventh Circuit rejected that argument, based on the precedent of *Moyses. In re Sullivan,* 680 F.2d 1131 (7th Cir. 1982), *cert. denied,* 459 U.S. 992 (1983). We are thus left with the rather ill-defined guideline that while the uniformity of bankruptcy law is a constitutionally-mandated goal of bankruptcy legislation, it need not be perfect; there is some room to accommodate the divergent provisions of state law. The test is not whether bankruptcy law will lead to the same outcome in every state, but whether the superstructure of bankruptcy law is evenly imposed.

Though this example concerns uniformity in exemption laws, this is just one illustration of the diversity that one should expect to find in bankruptcy law. Other variations in prevailing nonbankruptcy law affect the outcome of many important issues to be settled in the bankruptcy case, including the extent and validity of liens, the legitimacy of creditors' claims, and the estate's right to property. In short, nonbankruptcy law has a profound impact on the bankruptcy case, and the requirement of uniformity should not be taken too literally.

Uniformity is affected by another, possibly more obvious, factor. Quite apart from diversity in underlying nonbankruptcy law, the Code itself is subject to differing and sometimes conflicting interpretations in different circuits of the federal court system. Except where the Supreme Court has resolved these divergent interpretations, one must expect some lack of uniformity in the interpretation and application of the Code. Of course, this routine matter affects all federal legislation and is not confined to bankruptcy law.

§5.4 The Statutory Source of Bankruptcy Law

§5.4.1 *Federal Bankruptcy Legislation*

The current code, 11 U.S.C. §§101 *et seq.,* was enacted as the *Bankruptcy Reform Act* in 1978, and has been amended several times since then, as detailed below. It is the fifth bankruptcy statute enacted by Congress. The first three were passed at various times in the nineteenth century, but none of them lasted very long, and for much of that century there was no federal bankruptcy law, leaving debtor-creditor relations to be governed only by state law. In 1898, Congress passed the *Bankruptcy Act,* which turned out to be the first durable bankruptcy statute. It lasted, with much amendment and judicial embellishments, until it was replaced in 1978 by the current Code. By the end of the 1960s, it had become clear that the old Act was outdated and had been patched up too much by amendments, judicial decisions, and procedural rules promulgated by the courts. Congress, therefore, appointed a commission in 1970 to study the bankruptcy law and to recommend a new comprehensive statute. The commission's report and proposed statute, released in 1973, drew on the traditions established under the old Act, and preserved many of its rules and principles. However, it also made many significant changes to substantive law and procedure. The report was controversial, leading to much debate and the passage of different bills in each house of Congress. Ultimately, differences were resolved in compromise, and the 1978 Code was enacted. Some of the compromises were uneasy, and never finally settled the differences that underlay them. Disputes continue to arise about them, and lead to debate about further reform.

Since its enactment in 1978, the Code has been amended several times. In addition to occasional piecemeal changes to individual sections, it has been subjected to three wide-ranging amending statutes. The first, passed in 1984, was principally concerned with trying to overcome constitutional problems relating to bankruptcy court jurisdiction. (*See* section 7.3.) The second, passed in 1986, made a number of small amendments, introduced a new form of debt adjustment for family farmers, and established a nationwide U.S. Trustee system.

The third, the Bankruptcy Reform Act of 1994, began its progress through Congress in 1992. It originated as a fairly comprehensive and extensive revision of the Code, but it was pared down to a less ambitious undertaking when it became apparent that its more controversial aspects would not pass. A compromise bill was drafted too late in the session to be acted upon, but it was revived the following year and enacted. With its controversial elements abandoned, the 1994 statute is quite tame. It deals with a variety of discrete problems that had arisen in the application and interpretation of the Code. These various changes affect both consumer and business bankruptcies, and they are noted in later chapters where pertinent to the topic under discussion.

The more complex and contentious issues were left for further investigation and deliberation of a *National Bankruptcy Review Commission* established under the Act. The Commission's charge was to study issues that had arisen under the Code, to solicit and evaluate the views of interested parties, and to submit a report and recommendation within two years. In giving the Commission its mandate, Congress made it clear that it was generally satisfied with the overall structure and operation of the bankruptcy system, and did not want proposals for radical structural change. The scope of the Commission's work was to suggest measured reform rather than a fundamental change in the system.

The Commission conducted extensive hearings and submitted its report in 1997. In some areas, all the commissioners saw the need for reform and were unanimous in their recommendations. For example, they all agreed that there was a need to improve the efficiency of business bankruptcies, including an accelerated process for small businesses; that Ch. 12 of the Code (explained in section 5.4.2) should become permanent; and that bankruptcy judges should be appointed under Article 3 of the U.S. Constitution. (This issue is discussed in section 7.3). The commissioners also agreed on several structural reforms relating to appeals, bankruptcy procedure, and the collection of bankruptcy data. However, the commissioners were sharply divided on some important issues, on which they submitted a majority and dissenting report.

The most explosive issue that divided the commissioners concerned the approach to be taken to the bankruptcy of individuals (largely consumers, but also small businesses in the form of sole proprietorships.) This controversy arises out of the undisputed fact that individual bankruptcy filings in the United States are astoundingly high and have tended to increase every year. This is a cause of concern for most people, but there is great controversy about the reason for this phenomenon. Some see the primary cause as a deterioration in the moral norm that debts should be paid and the corresponding stigma of bankruptcy, combined with an increase in irresponsible consumer spending. Others place principal blame on the consumer credit industry for the way that it seduces consumers to apply for credit and lends to those who cannot repay. In this view, reforms may be more effective if aimed at lending practices. The argument has also been made that it is essential to have a bankruptcy system in this country that is sympathetic to debtors. This is because bankruptcy functions as a social safety net in the United States (which, unlike Europe, does not have a comprehensive welfare system) by creating a haven for individuals who are overwhelmed by debt resulting from unemployment, medical expenses, or other calamities.

Five of the nine commissioners proposed a relatively mild set of changes designed to improve the process applicable to and the rate of payment in individual bankruptcies, and to curb some abuses. The other four commissioners felt that these proposals were inadequate, and that the system needed much more rigorous reform. In their dissenting report, they expressed the view that the Code allows individual debtors to discharge debt too easily, even where they are earning enough to make a greater effort at repayment. They argued for reforms that would make it much more difficult for an individual debtor to escape her debts by going through the Ch. 7 liquidation process if the debtor earned an income that would adequately support a larger recovery for creditors under Ch. 13. (The purpose and scope of these two Code Chapters is discussed further below, and is explained more fully in section 8.2.) The report engendered a fierce reaction from corporations and organizations whose interests were at stake. As a broad generalization, the consumer credit industry agreed with the dissenting view and urged tough reforms, while consumer groups, labor unions, and other organizations representing various consumer and small business constituencies and advocating for vulnerable segments of society favored the approach of the majority of the Commission. Both sides received vociferous support from academics, practitioners, and politicians. Arguments raged over a host of issues, reflecting disagreement ranging from the basic question of whether the system really was being abused or was permitting significant evasion of debt, to who was to blame for that state of affairs and the proper response to correct it.

Congress began work on a bankruptcy reform bill immediately after the Commission submitted its report, leading to the introduction of a bill in 1998. This was the first of many unsuccessful attempts to enact reform legislation over the next five years. In each session of Congress since then, legislation has been attempted, but has not passed. Although there were variations in different sessions, the typical course was that different bills would be passed in the House and Senate, a conference committee would be established, and, for one reason or another, the session would end without final action. On one occasion in 2001, Congress did succeed in enacting a bill, but it was vetoed by former president Clinton. As this is being written in 2003, a reform bill is again pending in Congress, but it is not clear if it will reach the stage of becoming law.

The various bills proposed in each House of Congress over the last few years have differed in a number of respects. However, they have been quite similar in their key aspects. (In fact, bills introduced in recent sessions have largely been reintroductions of versions that were substantially supported in prior sessions.) One thing is clear: the proposed bills have all deviated considerably from what the majority of the Commission proposed. They have disregarded some of its recommendations and have contained a number of important provisions that are contrary to the recommendations. On the issue of individual bankruptcy — the most controversial aspect of the bills and the issue that has most profoundly contributed to the difficulty in passing them — the majority in both Houses of Congress has sided with the dissenting Commissioners. The bills operate on the assumption that current bankruptcy law is too lenient on individual debtors, and that it must be changed to place more pressure on them to repay a greater percentage of their debt and to become more responsible in their financial affairs. To achieve this end, the bills would make it much more difficult for debtors to enter Ch. 7, and would confine many debtors to Ch. 13 for bankruptcy relief. The bills also contain other restrictions on bankruptcy relief. For example, they require debtors to undergo financial counseling and restrict the scope of the bankruptcy discharge. These proposed reforms will be mentioned in greater detail in the appropriate places in the remainder of the book.

§5.4.2   *The Structure and Organization of the Code*

The Code is a large statute, and a few moments spent in taking note of its structure can save much fruitless searching in the wrong places. As originally enacted in 1978, the Code had eight odd-numbered chapters running from 1 to 15. In 1986, Ch. 12, which provides for debt adjustment for family farmers, was added, and Ch. 15, which dealt with the U.S. Trustee program, was repealed and replaced by new provisions in Title 28 of the U.S. Code. Therefore, in its present form the Code consists of eight chapters: 1, 3, 5, 7, 9, 11, 12, and 13. Ch. 12 was not permanently enacted. It has a sunset clause and must be re-enacted periodically. Although the 1994 Bankruptcy Reform Commission recommended the permanent enactment of Ch. 12, Congress has not done this so far. The pending Bankruptcy Reform Bill would make Ch. 12 permanent.

The chapters of the Code fall into two broad categories. The first three (Chs. 1, 3, and 5) contain general provisions that are meant to apply to all bankruptcy cases under consideration unless they are irrelevant on the facts or some overriding provision in the specific governing chapter applies instead.

The remainder of the Code consists of five chapters devoted to separate and different forms of bankruptcy. Namely, Ch. 7 covers liquidation; Ch. 9 applies only to municipal bankruptcies; Ch. 11 applies to reorganizations; Ch. 12 may be used only by debtors who qualify as "family farmers," and Ch. 13 deals with the adjustment of debt by individual debtors with relatively small levels of debt.

When a bankruptcy petition is filed, one (and *only* one) of these chapters is selected and applicable. (Conversion from one chapter to another is possible, and is discussed later. However, even when conversion occurs, only one of the specific chapters is applicable at a time.) The provisions of the specific chapter will govern the case (together with the general chapters) and the sections found in the other specific chapters will not be of force unless they are expressly incorporated by the governing chapter. It is important to remember this because the temptation to generalize some of the sections in a specific chapter can be strong.

§5.4.3   *The Bankruptcy Rules*

The Code deals with the substantive law of bankruptcy. While it prescribes procedures in broad terms, it does not set out rules of procedure in detailed form. These rules have been promulgated by the Supreme Court in the exercise of its power under 28 U.S.C. §2075. They are intended to effectuate the provisions of the Code and are meant to supplement rather than contradict it. The rules may not alter substantive rights under the Code, and in the case of conflict the Code prevails.

In addition to the bankruptcy rules, the Federal Rules of Civil Procedure are relevant to bankruptcy practice to the extent that the rules incorporate them or do not provide for a contrary procedure. Of importance to local practitioners is Bankruptcy Rule 9029, which allows each district court to make its own local rules provided that they are not inconsistent with the Bankruptcy Rules.

§5.4.4 Other Federal Statutes Applicable in Bankruptcy

While the Code is quite comprehensive, other federal statutes have a direct bearing on bankruptcy. Title 28 of the U.S. Code has a number of important provisions relating to the bankruptcy system: Ch. 6 (§§151 to 158) deals with the appointment, duties, and functions of bankruptcy judges; Ch. 39 (§§581 to 589a) provides for the U.S. Trustee system; Ch. 85 (§1334) governs bankruptcy jurisdiction; and Ch. 87 (§§1408 to 1412) deals with matters of venue. These statutes are considered in Chapter 7.

In addition to title 28, there are other provisions scattered through the U.S. Code that might have relevance in a bankruptcy case. For example, 18 U.S.C. §§151-155 deals with crimes of dishonesty and embezzlement committed during the course of a bankruptcy case.

§5.5 The Policies of Bankruptcy Law

§5.5.1 Introduction

Because it is important to understand the policies that underlie substantive bankruptcy law, this section introduces and briefly explains the most pervasive policies and premises of bankruptcy law. The purpose here is to offer a broad perspective on policy themes, on a general and abstract level. As specific doctrines and rules are dealt with in later chapters, these policy themes will be raised again and applied in a more concrete context.

Described here as policies are the ideals of bankruptcy law — the normative or moral values that the rules of law seek to attain. In large part, this description of policy is based on what Congress itself has identified in legislative history as the goals and aspirations of the Code and on pronouncements of policy made by courts in opinions. It should be noted, however, that modern scholarship is marked by sharp and sometimes strident debate on what bankruptcy policy is or should be. This debate has both a normative aspect (that is, it addresses what bankruptcy policy should be) and a practical or empirical aspect (that is, it seeks to describe how the law actually operates.) Possibly the greatest divide is between those who believe the principal purpose of bankruptcy is to provide a procedure to deal as efficiently as possible with economic adversity (so that its fundamental goal is to maximize the return to creditors with minimal interference with their entitlements under nonbankruptcy law), and those who believe bankruptcy law serves wider social policy that takes into account and affords protection to vulnerable debtors, workers, and the community as a whole. Often, this debate centers on the question of whether bankruptcy may legitimately serve a redistributive function — whether its essential purpose is to ensure, as far as possible, the protection of those who dealt with the debtor prior to bankruptcy, or whether it may properly subject those rights to ameliorate the hardship caused to the debtor and others by financial adversity.

As a general matter, those that emphasize the goal of maximizing creditor returns are associated with the "Law and Economics" movement. Their arguments place considerable faith in the operation of the free market and consider the system that interferes with the free market as little as possible as optimal. In short, they focus heavily on what they perceive as economically efficient, market-based outcomes. Those that advocate a broader view of the legitimate goals of bankruptcy contend that economic efficiency should not be an overriding value, but that bankruptcy must provide a social safety net. Scholars who take this position are sometimes called "traditionalists." These opposing views have ramifications in all aspects of bankruptcy law and range from questions of the proper range of discretion exercised by bankruptcy courts to all substantive aspects of bankruptcy law.

Of course, this is a simplified capsule of a multifaceted debate that does not reflect all the nuances of many reams of writing and that does not take account of other strains that emerge from scholarly discourse. Academic debate aside, it is probably fair to say that the traditionalist view more accurately reflects the way in which Congress and most courts tend to see bankruptcy policy. Therefore, the policy concerns identified below are concerned both with the operation of an efficient system protecting creditor's rights under nonbankruptcy law and with the achievement of social goals. For this reason, the interaction of the policies is complex. Sometimes they pull in opposite directions and must be reconciled or prioritized. Harder still is the problem of determining whether or not the Code's provisions effectively achieve their goals. In recent years there has been a growing interest in empirical research on this question. Some of the studies suggest that motivating or deterrent rules in the Code may not be having the desired effect. One must also remember that Congress, in writing or amending bankruptcy laws, is routinely lobbied by various groups and individuals who advocate rules that best protect their own interests or those of their constituents. These interest groups can influence legislation in a way that prevents it from faithfully and single-mindedly serving the goals identified here. This overview of policy, therefore, reflects the ideals but not necessarily the realities of bankruptcy law.

The term *bankruptcy policy* is used here to mean the policy goals to be fulfilled by the Code itself. Of course, bankruptcy policy does not exist in a vacuum. It arises from and reflects deeper general norms concerning what is good or bad, right or wrong, in economic relationships. Also, the pursuit of bankruptcy relief often raises wider issues of public policy. The policies that motivated other statutes or rules of common law may clash with those to be achieved by the Code. It is therefore often necessary for bankruptcy policies to be weighed against and reconciled with countervailing policies of nonbankruptcy law.

The policy themes identified in this section are not completely self-contained. As you will see when you read them, they overlap in many respects.

§5.5.2 *The Goals and Policies of Bankruptcy*

a. The Remedial Nature of Bankruptcy

Bankruptcy is remedial in nature. Often, bankruptcy relief is sought only after the debtor's economic affairs have deteriorated to the point of collapse. For this reason, the aims of bankruptcy are necessarily modest. It is not designed to give parties their full entitlement under nonbankruptcy law. Rather, its purpose is to manage financial distress and to do the best job possible of preserving what can be saved.

b. The Protection of Debtor and Creditor Interests

In its original conception, bankruptcy was purely a creditor's remedy. In the time of Henry VIII,[2] bankruptcy law existed exclusively for the benefit of creditors, who were enabled thereby to seize all of the property of a trader who was delinquent in the payment of debts. (In early law, only traders were subject to bankruptcy.) Bankruptcy entitled the creditors not only to the liquidation of assets, but also to the imprisonment of the debtor until the remaining balance of the debts was paid. As the debtor was confined in prison and could not work, friends and relatives had to find the money to settle these debts if they wished to liberate the debtor.

As English law developed, it became more sympathetic to the plight of an honest debtor who could not afford to pay creditors in full. The concept of releasing a debtor from prison and discharging the unsatisfied balance of debt began to be reflected in statutes from the early eighteenth century.

---

2. King Hal is better known, of course, for his contribution to the law of domestic relations.

However, until well into the nineteenth century, both in English and American law, bankruptcy continued largely to be a creditor's remedy: degrading and ruinous to the debtor, frequently involving imprisonment, and offering little reason for the debtor to relish the prospects of a bankruptcy petition.

Today, the idea that bankruptcy serves two purposes — creditor protection and debtor relief — is well-established. It helps creditors by providing an evenhanded and controlled environment for the settlement of the debtor's affairs and the distribution of available assets. At the same time, it provides a haven for the straitened debtor, affording relief from the pressures of financial failure. As with other policies, this balance between debtor and creditor interests is an ideal. It is probably impossible to devise a set of rules that will achieve the best balance between the debtor and creditors in every case. Debtors and creditors are very diverse groups, and a rule that works fairly in some situations may have less desirable results in others. To the extent that the rules can be flexible enough to accommodate variations in interests, they are likely to better achieve this goal. However, the law must necessarily work at some level of generality, which may result in a less than perfect balance in some situations.

This dual purpose of bankruptcy is reflected in the fact that both voluntary and involuntary petitions are provided for by the Code, and it is also manifested in many of the rules and principles governing the management of the estate, the treatment of claims, and the rights of the debtor. The goal of trying to achieve an equitable balance between debtor and creditor interests, and of trying to protect both, is also part of the rationale for the next three policy themes.

c. The Collective and Evenhanded Treatment of Creditors

The mandatory collective nature of the bankruptcy remedy is often identified as one of its most important hallmarks. Upon the filing of a bankruptcy petition, creditors are compelled to halt that self-centered individual collection action which inevitably leads to the unequal division of the debtor's assets.[3] All of the debtor's existing assets are placed in the custody of the law, and payments made out of turn on the eve of bankruptcy must be returned. A disinterested administrator (the trustee in bankruptcy) then becomes responsible for the realization of funds and their orderly distribution to creditors.

Because the value of the estate is usually less than the total debts, most creditors are not paid in full, but they at least share equitably in the fund. This does not necessarily mean that all creditors are paid the same. Creditors who

---

3. This assumes, of course, that most debtors have more than one creditor, so there is a "collectivity" to be administered. Although this is generally true, it is not a requirement for bankruptcy relief that a debtor have several creditors. If the debtor has only one significant debt, bankruptcy is not needed to halt competition for the debtor's assets and this policy goal is not implicated. However, even where the debtor has a single significant creditor, the other goals of bankruptcy may be achieved by filing a petition.

have liens or security interests in property of the debtor are entitled to preferential treatment by virtue of their security interests. Others are ranked in
order of priority in accordance with the rules of bankruptcy law and their
rights under prevailing nonbankruptcy law. However, differentiation between creditors is thus based on the strength of their legal rights, rather than
on their speed in initiating collection procedures.

d. The Preservation of the Estate

Bankruptcy's protection of creditors goes beyond equitable and orderly distribution. The trustee in bankruptcy is given substantial powers to investigate
the debtor's affairs, to recover dispositions of property in fraud of creditors,
to reveal hidden assets, and to resolve the affairs of the debtor in a way that
best enhances the value of the estate. In addition, bankruptcy is intended to
put an end to activities of the debtor that are detrimental to the creditors or
that are likely to diminish or denude the estate. In essence, bankruptcy is supposed to be advantageous to creditors not only because it protects them from
each other's action but also because it provides mechanisms, usually otherwise unavailable, for the preservation of the estate.

Preservation of the estate obviously benefits the creditors, particularly in
a liquidation case where the assets are realized to create a fund for distribution. However, the preservation of assets often helps the debtor as well. In reorganization and debt adjustment cases, the debtor often seeks to keep assets
while funding distributions from future income. Bankruptcy protects the estate while the debtor's plan of rehabilitation is formulated and consummated.
In this respect, preservation of the estate is part of the fresh start policy discussed in the next section.

Quite apart from creditors and the debtor, preservation of the estate of
a business debtor can achieve wider social goals. If a viable but financially distressed business can be rehabilitated, the benefits of rehabilitation may extend to employees of the business, the community in which the business
operates, and customers reliant on the business.

e. The Debtor's "Fresh Start"

The goal of long-term rehabilitation of the debtor is commonly referred to as
the "fresh start" policy. Provided that the debtor has complied with the
Code's requirements and has surrendered executable assets or sufficient future income for distribution to creditors, the debtor is entitled to a new beginning, unburdened by the unpaid balance of prebankruptcy debts.

The notion that a bankrupt should be given a fresh start is relatively new
in the history of the common law. It is nevertheless firmly established in mod-

ern law and is a central policy of bankruptcy. It is intended not only to serve the interests of the debtor but also the public good: A rehabilitated individual debtor may become self-sufficient once again, rather than a public charge. The rehabilitation of a corporate or business debtor may preserve jobs and add to the general well-being of the economy. Of course, it is not invariably true that a debtor's fresh start will further the public good. For example, an individual debtor may fail to learn from the bankruptcy and may simply slide again into debt; or, where a business is failing, attempting to save it may ultimately be less economically advantageous than selling its assets to a more effective user. Furthermore, the debtor's fresh start comes at the expense of its creditors, who are forced to forgive a portion of the debt to which they would otherwise have been entitled. In addition to the direct effect that this has on the creditors themselves, the discharge of debt adds to the cost of giving credit and, therefore, affects the market as a whole. That is, borrowers in general are likely to pay more for their credit because lenders factor into their interest rates the predicted percentage of loans that will be uncollectible because of bankruptcies.

Given these countervailing concerns, it is the ongoing task of bankruptcy law to seek and maintain the proper balance between creditors' right to payment and debtors' need for a fresh start. Many complex factors go into this balance, and the point at which the balance should be struck is a matter of continuing controversy. The ideal point of equilibrium is to provide wide enough relief to maintain a safety net for unfortunate individual debtors and a means of salvaging viable business debtors, while at the same time protecting creditors from debtors who would use the law to evade payment of their debts or to shield dishonest or irresponsible conduct. Congress, therefore, tries to set the availability and extent of the debtor's fresh start at a level that creates an optimal balance between these considerations. Some feel that it has erred on the side of debtors, while others think that the balance too strongly favors creditors.

The fresh start policy is apparent in many provisions of the Code, but it is particularly manifest in the individual debtor's exemptions, the debtor's discharge, the limitations on property to be included in the estate, and in the policy favoring rehabilitation bankruptcy. Although the debtor's fresh start is an important goal of bankruptcy law, this does not mean that all debtors are unqualifiedly entitled to a fresh start. For example, a corporation in liquidation receives no rebirth following bankruptcy, and (as suggested above) other debtors may be denied a fresh start wholly or in part as a penalty for dishonest and uncooperative behavior.

f. Minimal Interference with Nonbankruptcy Rights

Bankruptcy has a strong impact on creditors and other persons involved in contractual relations with the debtor. Inevitably, many persons who expected the payment of money or some performance from the debtor will be disappointed as a result of the bankruptcy. Although this is a necessary incident of bankruptcy, the policy of the Code is to interfere as little as possible with nonbankruptcy rights and with legitimate expectations under nonbankruptcy law. Generally, the treatment of such rights under the Code is intended to affect them only as much as necessary to further the aims of the bankruptcy remedy.

g. Efficient Administration

None of the goals of bankruptcy law can be properly achieved if the system for administering the law is inadequate. The policy of efficient and constitutionally proper implementation of the bankruptcy remedy is a vital one. Many provisions in the Code deal with the structure and operation of this system, and others are designed to achieve the goal of efficient implementation and to deflect the efforts of those who would try to abuse the system. Efficient administration is an ongoing concern for judges, the United States Trustee (whose role is described in section 6.3), and Congress. The 1994 Bankruptcy Reform Commission and the bills proposed in Congress since its report have attempted to tackle the task of making bankruptcy procedure more efficient by streamlining cumbersome procedures and ensuring that debtors are not simply processed by the system, but also have an opportunity to receive counseling and information that will help them consummate rehabilitation. Even in the absence of legislation reforming the system to make it more efficient, many courts and U.S. Trustees regularly seek to work within the structure of existing law to implement procedures that allow cases to be disposed of more speedily, to enable courts to clear their dockets of cases that are hopeless, and to provide counseling to debtors.

h. The Preference for Reorganization and Debt Adjustment

In a sense, the preference for rehabilitation is not really a goal in itself, but rather is one of the mechanisms through which the fundamental goals of bankruptcy may best be achieved. Congress has decided that reorganization and debt adjustment, provided for in Chs. 11, 12, and 13, are more likely than liquidation under Ch. 7 to achieve the fundamental goals of protecting creditor interests and allowing the debtor a fresh start. For this reason, the Code has a number of provisions that are designed to encourage debtors to select rehabilitation bankruptcy rather than liquidation.[4] The goal of encouraging rehabilitation over liquidation continues to be the source of much

---

4. The differences between these forms of bankruptcy are explored in section 8.2.

controversy, especially where it involves the issue of how firmly debtors should be pressed into choosing rehabilitation.

As noted in section 5.4.1 (and discussed more fully in section 9.7), the issue of controlling an individual debtor's choice between liquidation under Ch. 7 and rehabilitation under Ch.13 has been the most controversial aspect of the reform legislation pending in Congress over the last few years. The argument behind the proposed legislation is that many individual debtors take the easy route of liquidation where they could pay off more of their debt by making payments over a period of years under Ch. 13. Opponents of the bill consider that the proposed legislation is too rigid and cumbersome, and that existing law, as properly administered by bankruptcy judges exercising sound discretion, is more flexible and adequate to the task of curbing abuse.

i.   Some Other Policy Concerns

The general policies discussed above may not entirely address or may conflict with policies concerning the collection of taxes, the protection of the debtor's employees or consumer clients, the debtor's responsibility for the environment, the debtor's familial support obligations, or other important contractual or legal relationships. This list could go on indefinitely; the point is that a debtor may have relationships or obligations that are not easily resolved by the application of a unitary bankruptcy policy. The broad goals of bankruptcy must therefore be both measured against and reconciled with other public policies.

In addition, all of the above policies flow into the wider concern about keeping the economy healthy, regulating the use of credit, and encouraging productive use of capital and savings. (Indeed, there has been much concern expressed through the years about the possible negative effects of the excessive use of credit and the large volume of bankruptcy filings.) In considering amendments to the Code, Congress is, therefore, often mindful of the positive or negative possible impact that the change in law may have on patterns of behavior exhibited by debtors and creditors.

EXAMPLES

1.   Caveat Preemptor

Congressman Sonny Favorite has received many complaints from his constituents concerning the homestead exemption provided for in the law of his state. The state allows a very modest homestead exemption, which usually covers only a small portion of the equity owned by debtors in their homes. Furthermore, the state has exercised its power under §522(b) and has declared its exemptions to be applicable in bankruptcy.

A number of constituents have lost their homes after filing bankruptcy. A homeowners' committee has tried unsuccessfully to convince the state legislature to provide a more generous exemption. The committee has now asked Congressman Favorite to sneak through a provision (perhaps tucked away in the next appropriations bill or some other gargantuan legislative compilation) that overrides state law and provides for a more substantial homestead exemption in bankruptcy.

Should Congressman Favorite bother?

2.   A Custom Fit

Under a federal customs statute passed in the late 1980s, a special license is required for the importation of certain goods. A limited number of licenses are granted under the statute. The statute allows the holder of a license to sell it to an approved buyer, but it provides that the license will be revoked automatically on the bankruptcy of the holder. Because the licenses are scarce, they are very valuable.

A license holder has recently filed a bankruptcy petition, and a controversy has arisen between the bankruptcy trustee and the federal agency that issues the licenses. The agency points to the forfeiture provision in the licensing statute and argues that no rights to the license pass to the estate. The trustee relies on §§541(a)(1) and (c) (considered more fully in Chapter 12) and claims the license as property of the estate.

How can one determine which of these conflicting provisions will control? What policies are relevant to resolving this conflict?

3.   The Fizzled Wizzkid

This is the story of Bratford Binge who was trapped, at a tender age, in the mighty credit machine. In college, Bratford was described as a boy wonder. He was the youngest summa cum laude to graduate from a prestigious business school. As a result, he had no trouble landing a glorious job at a grotesque salary with a large financial institution.

Bratford had been trained to believe that only the best was good enough for him. This perception was much encouraged by merchants and issuers of credit cards who, having ascertained from their computers that he was a fine new prospect, vied with each other to extend their coveted facilities to him. Bratford accepted every invitation to spend: An expensive apartment, a new car, the finest garments, lavish entertainment, and weekend frolics became his at a stroke of a pen.

In a few months Bratford's accumulated debt had grown so large that he has no prospect of paying it out of his generous salary. In fact, he cannot even keep current with the fractional monthly installments required on his accounts. In spite of all his spending, Bratford has acquired few assets. Those that he owns, such as his car and his furniture, are subject to security interests. Bratford is in fact insolvent.

Should Bratford be able to file a bankruptcy petition so that he can enjoy the advantages of the Code's fresh start policy?

4.   Nothing Will Come of Nothing

Precious Little, Inc. has filed a petition for liquidation under Ch. 7. It is badly insolvent. Its debts amount to $750,000 and the total value of its assets is $20,000. Its business has declined badly in the last couple of years and its revenue is insufficient to cover its operating expenses. How does this significant disproportion between its assets and liabilities and inadequate revenue affect the achievement of the goals of bankruptcy law in this case?

EXPLANATIONS

1. The exemptions available to a debtor in collection proceedings under state law are determined by the state. However, as part of its power to provide bankruptcy relief, Congress may enact a completely different set of exemptions to take effect in bankruptcy. Therefore, as long as the proposed homestead exemption is made applicable to individual debtors everywhere (and not only to the debtors in Congressman Favorite's state), it would be a legitimate exercise of the federal bankruptcy power.

The Congressman will have a political problem, rather than a legal one. As mentioned in section 5.3, a long tradition of deference to state exemption policy is reflected in the "opt out" provision of §522(b). Congressman Favorite would no doubt have a difficult job trying to find support for his proposed amendment. This has been demonstrated time and again, most recently in Congress' decision not to adopt the Bankruptcy Reform Commission's recommendation to eliminate the states' opt-out right in favor of a standardized set of mandatory federal exemptions. (The legislation currently pending does, however, propose to exercise some control over the homestead exemption by placing a dollar limit on it in bankruptcy. This is an effort to deal with states — unlike Congressman Favorite's state — that are too generous with homestead exemptions and allow the debtor an exemption in the full amount of the equity in his home, unlimited in value.)

2. The point was made in section 5.2.2 that federal bankruptcy law preempts conflicting state law. When the conflicting nonbankruptcy law is federal, it is not appropriate to talk of preemption. Rather, the contradictory statutes must be reconciled by the process of statutory interpretation. The court must decide which provision was intended by Congress to be controlling.

In anticipation of a fuller study of §541 later, even a superficial reading of §§541(a)(1) and (c) shows that Congress did intend those provisions governing property of the estate to be of some considerable force. Section 541(a)(1) brings into the estate all legal and equitable interests in property held by the debtor at the commencement of the case. Section 541(c) overrides any provision in nonbankruptcy law (that is, both state and federal law) that restricts the transfer of the debtor's property interest or that effects a forfeiture of it upon bankruptcy. This is a strong expression of congressional intent to make the Code the controlling statute.

Of course, we do not know what the licensing statute says. (It's fictional, so you can't look it up.) Ideally, if Congress did intend the customs statute to take precedence over the Code, it should have said so expressly. In the absence of such clear overriding language, a court will have to glean legislative intent by interpretation of the language of the statute, any legislative history, and enunciated or apparent policy goals. One of the canons of interpretation that may help in close cases is that Congress is supposed to remember what its earlier legislation said, so that a provision in a later statute is assumed to take precedence over an earlier conflicting statute. On the basis of this rule, the argument could be made that the later customs statute was intended to create an exception to the earlier Code provision.

Although interpretation necessarily requires a careful reading of the statutory language and the application of canons of interpretation, it must go beyond this and take into account the policy goals of the statutes. By examining and weighing underlying policies, the court is more likely to develop a clear view of legislative intent.

The principal purpose of §541 is to transfer to the estate all the debtor's rights in property at the time of the petition. This property will generate the fund for distribution in a Ch. 7 case or will form the basis for determining the distribution in a rehabilitation case. Therefore, by passing ownership of the debtor's property to the estate, the Code effects the policies of collecting and evenhandedly distributing the executable property of the debtor. It also allows the trustee to assume control of and preserve even that property that may later be transferred back to the debtor as exempt or released to a person who holds a valid interest in it. These policies would be frustrated if a private party or the government, by providing for forfeiture of rights on bankruptcy, could prevent transfer of the property to the estate. Hence, §541 makes such forfeiture provisions ineffective.

However, bankruptcy is intended to interfere with nonbankruptcy rights only to the extent necessary to advance the goals of bankruptcy law. This policy is a counterweight to the goals referred to above, and it must at least give the court pause in deciding to disregard the forfeiture provision. It is possible that the reasons for restricting transfer of the license are important enough to take precedence over the policy of avoiding obstructions to transfer of the debtor's property to the estate. Because the policy behind the customs statute is not articulated in the question, this issue cannot be pursued further. It is merely intended as an illustration of the way in which countervailing bankruptcy policies must be reconciled with each other and with public policies underlying other laws that are involved in the bankruptcy case.

3. Bratford is a reckless spendthrift who has brought his misfortune upon himself by profligacy. Some would blame Bratford for his behavior (and he is thus a poster boy for the tougher individual bankruptcy provisions in pending reform legislation). Others would point their fingers at the consumer credit industry which they accuse of having fostered, or at least aided and abetted Bratford's irresponsible use of credit.

It is a longstanding policy of bankruptcy law that relief is intended to help the honest debtor who has encountered serious financial difficulty. Bankruptcy is not supposed to enable rogues and miscreants to evade payment of their debts. (It is probably a little unkind to describe Bratford in these terms. He is more correctly characterized as a spoiled twit. Obviously, one could think of worse debtors than Bratford.) This does not mean that a rogue should never be placed in bankruptcy. Sometimes the bankruptcy of a dishonest or manipulative debtor serves the best interests of creditors — and bankruptcy is a creditor's remedy too. It does mean, however, that when bankruptcy has the effect of allowing a dishonest debtor to take advantage of creditors, it should be denied to the debtor, or if more appropriate, it should be permitted only on terms that avoid the manipulation.

To draw the line between a deserving and undeserving debtor requires a moral judgment which is not always self-evident or easy to make. Nevertheless, many provisions in the Code require the court to take into account the debtor's good faith or sincerity in determining the availability and form of relief. Sometimes an undeserving debtor may be denied relief altogether, and sometimes limits may be imposed on the advantages to be obtained by the debtor.

Another policy is suggested by the facts of this problem: The Code generally favors rehabilitation over liquidation, on the theory that creditors are usually likely to do better under a plan of payment. Because Bratford earns a good salary but has few executable assets, his creditors will be likely to receive a larger distribution if Bratford commits a portion of his income over a period of years. Therefore, there are provisions in the Code intended to encourage him to file under Ch. 11 or 13 rather than Ch. 7. If he does not take advantage of these provisions, it is possible, under some circumstances, that his failure to do so will be found to be an abuse of the Code. (Thus, we return to the good faith issue.) As noted before, the pending bankruptcy reform legislation would greatly strengthen the provisions that are currently in place to restrict people like Bratford from filing under Ch. 7. Instead of leaving it to the court to decide, on balance, whether Bratford should be allowed to file under Ch. 7, the proposed legislation would impose a means test on Bratford so that he could not obtain Ch. 7 relief if he could afford to support a payment plan under Ch. 13. The choice of relief and the restrictions on it are discussed in sections 8.2 and 8.3.

4. The goals and policies of bankruptcy law can only be fully satisfied where the estate is at least large enough to achieve all its purposes. Financial resources are needed to rehabilitate a business, and where, as here, the debtor has insufficient assets and no source of adequate future income, the Code's policy of providing a fresh start to the corporation and favoring its rehabilitation cannot be achieved. Where there is no means of funding a rehabilitation, it is simply not an option. This leaves the alternative of liquidation, but even here the paucity of assets means that the bankruptcy cannot fully satisfy all its desired ends. It can ensure that creditors are treated evenhandedly (so that the race for remaining assets can be stopped and any preferential payments made shortly before the filing can be recovered for the benefit of the estate as a whole), but the small pool of assets is likely to be expended fully or in substantial part on the costs of liquidating the bankrupt estate. This means that unsecured creditors will either receive no distribution at all or will receive a minimal payment on their claims.

It is one of the sad realities of bankruptcy that many estates are just too small to afford any significant distribution to unsecured creditors. In fact, figures collected by the Executive Office of the U.S. Trustees indicate that in just over half the cases administered in bankruptcy, creditors receive no distribution. The costs of administering an estate are paid as a first priority before any of the other unsecured creditors can receive anything, and these costs can be large. They include not only the trustee's compensation, but also any fees that must be paid to professionals (such as attorneys or accountants) engaged by the estate, and the costs of caring for and disposing of the estate's property. It does not take much to eat up a small estate, leaving it devoid of assets for funding a distribution. Of course, the policy of efficient and cost-effective administration dictates that the trustee's management of the estate should not be disproportionately expensive or wasteful, and the trustee has a duty to try to keep costs down as much as possible.

6

Participants in the Bankruptcy Case

§6.1   The Bankruptcy Court

The bankruptcy court, presided over by a bankruptcy judge, is the court most directly and intimately involved with the bankruptcy case from its inception to its final closing. Routinely, it deals as court of first instance with all matters that require judicial supervision, determination, or approval during the course of the case.

However, the constitutional stature of the bankruptcy court is awkward. It is not an independent, autonomous arm of the federal judiciary but is statutorily described as a "unit" of the U.S. district court. Its powers arise as a result of reference from the district court, and it exercises its judicial function subject to the ultimate control of that court. The jurisdiction of the bankruptcy court is discussed more fully in Chapter 7.

§6.2   The Trustee

It has long been recognized in bankruptcy law that when a debtor becomes bankrupt, an impartial person must be appointed to represent the collective interest of creditors, to control and administer the bankrupt estate, and to make distributions on claims. This person has been known by different names over time — "commissioner," "assignee," and most recently, "trustee." The *trustee* is a central figure in the bankruptcy case, whose role encompasses not only management of the estate but extensive powers to investigate the debtor's affairs, to enforce the rights of the estate, and to participate in litigation involving the estate's interests.

A trustee is required in all bankruptcy cases except for those under Ch. 11. Even in Ch. 11 cases, trustees are sometimes appointed when impartial control of the estate is necessary. In cases under Chs. 7 and 11, the Code authorizes the election of a trustee by creditors. In all other cases, and in Chs. 7 and 11 cases where creditors do not exercise the right of election, the trustee is appointed by the U.S. Trustee from a panel established by the U.S. Trustee, consisting of qualified persons who have applied to serve.

The Code itself says very little about the qualifications of a trustee. Section 321 simply states the general requirement of residency and competence. However, in terms of 28 U.S.C. §586(d), the Attorney General is required to prescribe qualifications for membership on the trustee panels, which include honesty, impartiality, professional qualifications (such as a law degree or a CPA), and requirements of general competence and experience.

In addition to qualifying for appointment or election, a trustee must also "qualify," as that term is used in §322, by posting a bond in an amount set by the U.S. Trustee to guarantee the faithful performance of the trustee's duties.

The duties of a trustee in a *Ch. 7 case* are set out in general terms in §704. In essence, the trustee's principal function is to liquidate and distribute the bankrupt estate. This primarily involves the collection of property of the estate, its realization, and its distribution to creditors. While this process may involve some interim administration of property to preserve its value, the trustee is not normally involved in the long-term management of the assets or operation of a business. The goal is to liquidate the estate as expeditiously as possible.

In pursuing this general goal, the trustee performs a number of specific duties discussed in succeeding chapters, such as investigating the debtor's affairs, employing professionals, recovering voidable dispositions, examining and contesting claims, litigating over estate interests, and making recommendations to the court on questions such as the debtor's discharge.

The permanent trustee only takes office at the meeting of creditors. Therefore, §701 provides for the appointment of an interim trustee by the U.S. Trustee. In voluntary cases, the interim trustee is appointed promptly after the filing of the petition, while in involuntary cases, the interim trustee is appointed only after the court has granted the involuntary petition. However, the court is empowered by §303(g) to order the earlier appointment if it is shown that the estate needs immediate protection. Unless creditors choose to elect a trustee at the creditors' meeting, the interim trustee becomes the permanent trustee.

Debt adjustment cases under Chs. 12 and 13 also require a trustee whose powers and duties are set out generally in §§1202 and 1302. As explained more fully in section 8.2, these cases differ from a liquidation case under Ch. 7 because their goal is not to liquidate the debtor's estate, but to revest all or part of the estate in the debtor upon confirmation of a plan of payment. Thus, the central role of the trustee is not the realization of property of the estate. The trustee is more concerned with other functions such as investigating the debtor's affairs, examining and contesting claims, recovering voidable dispositions, making recommendations on the debtor's plan, and ensuring its implementation. If the Ch. 13 debtor has a business at the time of bankruptcy, the debtor continues to operate it under the supervision of the trustee. A Ch. 12 debtor continues to conduct farming operations under the trustee's supervision. (The role of the Ch. 12 debtor in possession is narrower than that in a Ch. 11 case, because the Ch. 12 debtor in possession does not assume all the functions of the trustee, but operates under the trustee's supervision.)

The process of trustee selection is also different in debt adjustment cases. Unlike Ch. 7, Chs. 12 and 13 provide for the immediate appointment of a permanent trustee by the U.S. Trustee. There is no interim appointment and no provision for creditor election. In some regions, a trustee is appointed for each case, but in others, where the volume of cases warrants it, the U.S. Trustee is empowered by 28 U.S.C. §586(b) to appoint one or more standing trustees who serve as trustees for all Ch. 12 and Ch. 13 cases in the region. As in the case of persons appointed to the panel of trustees, the standing trustees must meet qualifications prescribed by the Attorney General.

In a *reorganization case under Ch. 11,* the usual practice is not to appoint a trustee. Instead, the debtor exercises the trustee's function as *debtor in possession,* subject to the oversight of the court and creditors' committees. Unless the context indicates otherwise, the word "trustee" includes the debtor in possession whenever it is used in Code provisions relating to a Ch. 11 case. Because a reorganization, like a debt adjustment, is designed not to liquidate but to restructure and rehabilitate the debtor, the duties of the debtor in possession focus on the operation of the business of the estate and the creation and consummation of the Ch. 11 plan. In addition, the debtor in possession performs many other trustee functions, such as collecting estate property, challenging claims, and employing professionals. Some of the trustee's duties, such as investigation of the debtor's affairs and supervision of the debtor's activities, cannot be exercised by a debtor in possession. In a Ch. 11 case those functions are exercised by the creditors' committee.

Although the appointment of a trustee is not the norm in a Ch. 11 case, the court does have the authority to appoint a trustee for cause, or where necessary to protect the rights of creditors or other interest holders. This appointment is made under §1104 upon application of a party in interest or the U.S. Trustee, and follows notice and a hearing. Cause for the appointment includes dishonesty or incompetence by the debtor in possession. Prior to 1994, there was no provision for electing a trustee in Ch. 11 cases. This was changed by the Bankruptcy Reform Act of 1994. Section 1104(b) permits a party in interest (which includes a creditor, equity interest holder, the debtor in possession and the U.S. Trustee) to request the election of a trustee within 30 days of the court ordering the appointment of a trustee. If a timely request is made, the U.S. Trustee must convene a meeting of creditors at which the election takes place under the same procedure as in a Ch. 7 case. In the absence of a timely request, the U.S. Trustee makes the appointment in consultation with creditors and interest holders, and subject to the court's approval. Whether elected or appointed by the U.S. Trustee, the trustee must be a disinterested person and must be eligible under §321. The appointment can be terminated and the debtor returned to possession, on the application of a party in interest. §1105.

The appointment of a trustee displaces the debtor in possession as manager of the estate. If there are not grounds for such severe action, but some investigation of the debtor's management or conduct is appropriate, the court may appoint an *examiner* under §1104(b). This appointment also requires an application by the U.S. Trustee or a party in interest, followed by notice and a hearing. In estates of a specified size, the examiner must be appointed if the application is made. Otherwise, appointment is ordered only if the court finds this to be in the best interests of creditors and interest holders.

Trustee's fees are governed by §§326 and 330. The general rule is that a trustee is entitled to reasonable compensation for services, based on the nature of the services, the time spent, and the market rate for those services. The reasonable fee is determined by the court, and must fall within the range set by §§330 and 326. Section 330 provides for a minimum fee for trustees, and §326 prescribes maximum limits on the fee, based on the value of the distribution from the estate. The minimum payment to and limitations on the fees of standing trustees are set by 28 U.S.C. §586(e). The trustee's fee is an expense of administering the estate, which is given first priority for payment out of the funds of the estate. (Priorities are discussed in Chapter 19.)

§6.3   The U.S. Trustee

The office of U.S. Trustee is relatively new. It was established experimentally in selected districts in 1978, and was made permanent in 1986. The entire country is now divided into regions, and a U.S. Trustee is appointed to each region by the Attorney General. The powers and duties of the U.S. Trustee are set out in 28 U.S.C. §§581–589a, as well as in various provisions of the Code itself.

The U.S. Trustee is a public official whose general responsibility is to ensure that the public interest is being properly served in the administration of bankruptcy cases. In addition to appointing trustees, the U.S. Trustee is responsible for supervising their work to ensure that estates are being competently and honestly administered. The U.S. Trustee also has extensive duties, enumerated in 28 U.S.C. §586, concerning other aspects of the bankruptcy case: monitoring plans under Chs. 11, 12, and 13; ensuring that debtors are properly filing fees, schedules, and reports; watching for debtor abuse and other illicit behavior; and assisting the U.S. Attorney in prosecuting crimes committed in the course of a bankruptcy case. The U.S. Trustee is also empowered in a number of Code sections to participate in litigation and other proceedings arising in the bankruptcy case, and may, for example, examine the debtor (§343), recommend dismissal of a case (§707), or object to a discharge (§727(c)).

While the bankruptcy court is responsible for the judicial supervision of the case, the U.S. Trustee's concern is administrative oversight. The U.S. Trustee is not an officer of the bankruptcy court, but an independent official who exercises those supervisory and administrative functions that cannot and should not be performed by the bankruptcy court itself. Also, as noted above, the U.S. Trustee can appear before the court as a party in various proceedings in the case.

The relationship between the U.S. Trustee and the court is best explained by reference to the reasons for the office's creation. Under the old Act, the bankruptcy court itself was responsible for the functions now exercised by the U.S. Trustee. It appointed trustees, participated in the debtor's examination, and closely watched the administration of the case. This system was widely criticized because the court's administrative functions intruded on its judicial role, and its close supervisory relationship with the trustee — a regular litigant in the case — compromised its impartiality. By placing these administrative and monitoring functions with the U.S. Trustee, Congress allows the court to confine itself to its proper judicial role while ensuring that a close extrajudicial check is maintained on the activities of the trustee and the debtor.

§6.4   The Debtor

The statutory name for the person whose estate is administered in bankruptcy is the *debtor*. This label was adopted by the Bankruptcy Reform Act in preference over the traditional noun *bankrupt*. Most persons, whether individuals or incorporated entities, can be debtors under the Code. There are some restrictions and limitations on eligibility for relief under the different Code chapters, which are discussed in Chapter 8. Much attention is given in the remainder of this book to the duties, rights, and activities of the debtor, but here the debtor's role in the case will be introduced by sketching some broad themes.

In a liquidation case under Ch. 7, the *debtor's role* tends to be relatively passive. The trustee is responsible for administering and liquidating the estate and making a distribution to creditors. The debtor's principal contribution to the administration of the estate is in furnishing information, cooperating with the trustee, and surrendering property. In reorganization and debt adjustment cases, the debtor participates more actively in the estate. As noted in section 6.2, the debtor's involvement is heaviest in the typical Ch. 11 case, where, as debtor in possession, it is responsible for the administration of the estate, the conduct of the estate's business, and the development of a plan of rehabilitation. In cases under Ch. 13, the trustee administers the estate and handles claims, but the debtor works with the trustee in formulating and consummating the plan. If the debtor had a business at the time of bankruptcy, he or she continues to run it under the trustee's oversight. The role of the Ch. 12 debtor falls between those of debtors under Chs. 11 and 13. Like Ch. 11, Ch. 12 recognizes the status of the debtor in possession and leaves the conduct of the farming operation in the hands of the debtor. However, the trustee fulfills many of the functions of a trustee under Ch. 13, supervises the debtor's business activities, and deals with the debtor in the formulation and performance of the plan of rehabilitation.

The debtor has a general obligation to act in *good faith* and not to abuse the spirit of the Code. This obligation ties into the policy, discussed in section 5.5.2, that dishonest debtors should not be allowed to pervert the goals of bankruptcy law. The debtor's obligation of good faith is manifested in many different provisions of the Code. For example, §707 permits the dismissal of an abusive Ch. 7 petition by a consumer debtor, §§727 and 523 punish certain types of dishonest or uncooperative behavior by allowing the court to refuse or restrict the debtor's discharge, and §§1129(a), 1225(a) and 1325(a) make a debtor's good faith a prerequisite for plan confirmation. In addition, criminal penalties are provided in 18 U.S.C. §152 for various fraudulent acts committed during the course of bankruptcy.

Although the above discussion has focused primarily on the debtor's duties and obligations, the *debtor's rights* should not be overlooked. Most of these rights stem from the policy that bankruptcy should provide a fresh start to the debtor. The individual debtor's right to exemptions and the discharge are just two examples. In addition, the Code provides many other protections to the debtor, such as limiting the availability of the involuntary petition and automatically staying all actions against the debtor upon the filing of the petition.

Many debtors are corporate entities having stockholders or other interest holders. These persons, called *equity security holders* in the Code, are obviously affected by the case because their ownership interest in the debtor is at stake. In a liquidation, they are likely to lose their investment. Unless the debtor's assets exceed its liabilities, creditor claims will consume the entire estate. However, in a Ch. 11 reorganization, they have some chance of retaining equity in the debtor if an acceptable plan or reorganization can be formulated and confirmed. Therefore, in a Ch. 11 case they have a right of participation and may be represented by a committee that functions like a creditor's committee.

§6.5   Creditors and Creditors' Committees

Creditor is defined in §101(10) to include any entity who has a provable claim against the estate. *Entity* is defined in §101(15) to include almost every kind of legal person, and *claim* is defined very broadly in §101(5) to cover all legal or equitable rights to payment, even if they are unliquidated, unmatured, contingent, or disputed. It is clear from these definitions that although creditors are brought together in bankruptcy's collective proceeding, they are a very diverse group with claims of different levels of certainty arising from a wide variety of transactions or relationships with the debtor or the estate. Furthermore, claims do not all have the same rank. With some exceptions, secured claims have the same status in bankruptcy as they have in nonbankruptcy law and are entitled to full payment from the proceeds of the collateral. In addition, the Code provides an order of priority for unsecured claims so that certain categories of claims are given preference over others.

It was stated in section 6.2 that the trustee represents the collective interest of creditors. By recovering and preserving property of the estate, the trustee helps ensure that the distribution paid to creditors is as large as possible. However, although the trustee must act in the best interests of the creditor body as a whole, this does not mean that the trustee is the partisan representative of the creditors. Frequently, the interests of the estate are opposed to those of an individual creditor or group of creditors, who are adversaries of the trustee. Litigation between the trustee and specific creditors is common.

When the debtor in possession acts as trustee in a Ch. 11 case, the debtor assumes fiduciary responsibilities. However, it requires an unusually charitable view of human nature to believe that a debtor in possession is likely to be as solicitous of creditor interests as an independent trustee would be. To ensure that creditor interests are properly safeguarded in a Ch. 11 case, the Code provides for the appointment of creditor committees.[1] Under §1102, the U.S. Trustee must appoint at least one committee of creditors holding unsecured claims. More than one committee can be appointed either if the U.S. Trustee deems it appropriate for the adequate representation of creditors or if a party in interest so requests.

The general duties of the committees are set out in §1103. They may employ legal counsel or other consultants, confer with the debtor in possession in the administration of the estate, conduct investigations into the debtor's financial affairs, participate in plan formation, and generally represent the interests of their constituent creditors. Ch. 11 usually involves negotiation between the debtor and creditors and between different creditor groups. The committees play a significant role in this respect as well. In short, the idea behind the creditors' committees is that they are representative bodies that safeguard the interests of the class of creditors they represent, not only in general oversight of the debtor but also in the negotiations that lead to the formulation of a plan.

---

1. Creditor committees can also be appointed in Ch. 7 cases, but they are not very common.

The value of a creditors' committee is dependent on the committee taking an active role in the case. Recent studies have shown that in smaller Ch. 11 bankruptcies, creditors often do not have a large enough stake in the outcome of the case to participate vigorously or at all in the committee. As a result, creditors' committees often do not serve the vital monitoring and adversarial function they were intended to have. To remedy this problem, some U.S. Trustees have begun to adopt a more proactive role where it is apparent that the committees are not effective. The Bankruptcy Reform Commission recognized the problem of ineffective committees and recommended a greater supervisory role for the U.S. Trustee, which Congress has adopted in the pending reform legislation.

§6.6   Attorneys and Other Professional Consultants

Many of the above parties are represented by attorneys. In addition, they may require the services of other professionals (*e.g.*, an accountant) for advice on the complexities of the case. These professional relationships are mostly governed by generally applicable rules of law and ethical canons. However, some provisions in the Code affect attorneys for the debtor, creditor, and trustee. For example, §329 gives the court policing power over certain fees of the debtor's attorney, §327(c) allows the debtor's attorney to be appointed to represent the estate in certain matters, §§503(3) and (4) allow creditors to claim their legal fees for an involuntary petition and certain other matters to be claimed from the estate as an administrative expense, and §1107(b) allows a creditor's attorney to act for the creditors' committee under certain circumstances.

If the estate requires the services of an attorney or other professionals, the trustee is authorized by §327(a) (with court approval) to engage such services. The reasonable fee due for the services rendered, if approved by the court, is treated as an administrative expense of the estate. Sections 327 to 330 and §503 govern the appointment and fees of attorneys and other professionals used by the estate. Trustees are often accountants or lawyers, and under §327(d) the court may authorize the trustee to perform professional services for the estate in that capacity. If the professional work is distinct from and in excess of the normal functions of a trustee, §328(b) allows the court to authorize additional compensation for it.

§6.7   Other Participants

In the preceding sections, the principal participants in a bankruptcy case have been introduced. However, every debtor is different; depending on the debtor's activities, interests, and affairs, there may be a variety of other persons who are not necessarily creditors, but whose rights are at stake in the case. For example, the debtor may be a party to unperformed (*i.e.,* executory) contracts that may be assumed or rejected by the estate; most debtors have debtors of their own who become debtors of the estate; some debtors have dependents; some have sureties or other co-obligors. Also, bankruptcy may attract the interest of a public agency. For example, the Securities and Exchange Commission may be concerned with, and is entitled to be heard in, a Ch. 11 case.

§6.8 Issues of Professional Ethics

"None but the brave deserves the fee."
DRYDEN

An attorney who is appointed trustee in a bankruptcy case, or one who represents the estate, the debtor, or some other party in interest, must be careful to comply with both the canons of professional ethics and the provisions of the Code concerning the representation of parties. Although this section cannot cover all the ethical issues that could arise in connection with a bankruptcy matter, it provides a sampling of some of the ethical concerns that may confront an attorney in a bankruptcy case.

An ethical question that often arises in bankruptcy representation involves the avoidance of actual or apparent conflicts of interest. For example, the Model Code of Professional Responsibility requires an attorney to avoid situations in which representation of a client would be impaired or compromised by some countervailing interest that the attorney may have (Canon 5). In addition, the Code itself addresses the question of conflicts of interest. Section 327(a) requires that an attorney representing the estate be disinterested (as defined in §101(14)) and hold or represent no interest adverse to the estate. A similar requirement of disinterest can be found in §327(e), governing the use by the estate of the debtor's attorney, and §1103(b), concerning representation of a creditors' committee. An attorney who acts as trustee is bound by fiduciary responsibilities to be impartial and independent (*see* section 6.2).

Section 327(a) requires that the professional neither holds nor represents an interest adverse to the estate. An attorney *holds* an interest adverse to the estate if she has some personal interest (such as a prepetition claim against the debtor) that may undermine her duty of loyalty and independence. She *represents* an interest adverse to the estate if she acts for a client (such as a creditor of the estate or a stockholder of the debtor) whose interests actually or potentially conflict with those of the estate. Since the court must approve the appointment of an attorney under §327(a), it is the court, not the attorney herself, who must make the ultimate decision on whether a disqualifying conflict of interest exists. To enable the court to make a proper determination, the attorney seeking appointment has the duty to disclose all relevant information. Failure to make disclosure of pertinent information is a serious breach of good faith that could subject the attorney to disciplinary proceedings and also result in forfeiture of fees under §328(c). The same is true of an attorney appointed to represent a creditors' committee under §1103. (Rule 2014 requires the application for authorization to disclose all the attorney's connections with interested parties so that the court is informed at the time of application of any possible conflicts.)

An actual conflict leaves no question that the attorney should be disqualified, but the court has more discretion in deciding whether a potential conflict is serious and inevitable enough to merit disqualification. The mere appearance of conflict, which does not result in any actual or potential conflict is usually not a basis for disqualification, but in some cases, the court may feel that the appearance of impropriety is serious enough that to permit the attorney to act for the estate would undermine confidence in the bankruptcy system. The requirement of lack of adverse interest and disinterestedness in §327(a) is broad and strict. It does not appear to contain a qualification that the conflict of interest must be material. (By contrast, the general category of "disinterested person" included in the definition of that term in §101(14)(E) does require a materially adverse interest.) Because the impartiality of the estate's legal representative is crucial to the faithful administration of the estate and the credibility of the bankruptcy system, courts are generally inclined to apply the standard strictly, and not to inquire whether the conflict is of sufficient magnitude to be likely to influence the attorney's judgment or conduct. However, there are cases in which the court has been willing to disregard conflicts of such a trivial nature that they are unlikely to have any impact on the attorney's behavior.[2]

The following examples illustrate situations in which ethical concerns may be raised by the representation of a party in bankruptcy proceedings.

EXAMPLES

1.   Keeping a Firm's Grip

Luce Canons, P.C., a firm of attorneys, performed some legal work for Down & Out Enterprises, Inc., for which a fee of $5,000 was charged. Down & Out has not paid the fee, and it has now filed a Chapter 11 petition.

---

2. The National Bankruptcy Review Commission recommended modifying the disinterestedness standard so that an attorney would not be disqualified from representing a Ch. 11 estate merely because she has an insubstantial unsecured claim against or equity interest in the debtor. Congress accepted this recommendation by including a provision to this effect in the pending reform bill.

Down & Out, as debtor in possession, has asked Luce Canons to represent it in a lawsuit to recover a debt due to the estate.

Should Luce Canons accept the case?

2. Et Tu, Brute?

Hiram Gunn used to be the attorney for Erstwhile Enterprises, Inc. Hiram represented Erstwhile for many years and had handled all its legal work, so he is thoroughly familiar with its affairs. A few years ago, Hiram and Erstwhile became embroiled in a fee dispute that led to the termination of their relationship.

Erstwhile recently filed a Ch. 11 petition. Hiram has been asked by a creditors' committee to represent it in the bankruptcy case.

Should Hiram agree to do so?

3. Mal[fee]sance

Bill A. Billhours had long been the attorney for Adverse Investments, Inc., a corporation of which his friend Able Skimmer was president and principal stockholder. When Adverse Investments filed a Ch. 11 petition, it applied under §327(a) for the court to approve Bill as its attorney. Bill disclosed that he had been Adverse Investments' legal advisor prior to its bankruptcy, but failed to mention that he had also legally represented Able in his personal affairs for many years. The court approved Bill's appointment, and he set to work conscientiously and vigorously representing the estate in negotiations aimed at developing a plan of reorganization. The negotiations broke down when creditors discovered that Able had made several transfers of funds from Adverse Investments to himself and family members shortly before the petition was filed. The creditors' committee successfully applied to oust the debtor in possession from control of the estate and to replace it with a trustee. The trustee terminated Bill's employment and hired her own counsel. She is now investigating whether Able's transfers of corporate assets were fraudulent.

   (a)   Bill has applied to court for compensation for the services that he rendered to the estate from the time of his appointment until his dismissal. It is conceded that he performed good-quality legal work for the estate during his tenure as its counsel, and no one contends that he participated in or even knew about Able's transfers of corporate property. Notwithstanding, the trustee objects to Bill receiving any payment of his fees. Is this a sound objection?

   (b)   Quite apart from the issue of whether Bill is entitled to his fees, consider his responsibilities with regard to the trustee's investigation of the improper conduct of Able and Adverse Investments. Is the information obtained by Bill during his investigation of Adverse protected by the attorney-client privilege?

4. Down and Out

The law firm of Filenow & Palater handles a large volume of consumer bankruptcies. Many of its clients cannot afford to pay the fee for bankruptcy representation in advance, so the firm often accepts a down payment on its fee and permits its client to pay the balance in monthly installments in the period following the petition. The firm has the client sign post-dated checks which are then banked as they become due. Is this a good practice?

EXPLANATIONS

1. Of course, if Luce Canons decides that he wishes to represent the estate, he cannot simply accept the case on his own. Court approval is required for his appointment under §327(a). In the application for approval, he must disclose to the court the fact that he is an unsecured creditor of the estate. The court will not approve his appointment unless he qualifies as a disinterested person who does not hold an interest adverse to the estate. One of the requirements to qualify as a disinterested person, as defined in §101(14) is that the person is not a creditor. (See §101(14)(A).) This would seem to settle the matter, because Luce is owed $5,000 by the estate for unpaid prepetition services. Several courts have disposed of this issue in those simple terms. However, other courts have been less wedded to the literal language of §101(14)(A), and have held that the mere fact that the attorney has a claim against the estate should not automatically disqualify him. The case must be examined to decide if there is an actual conflict between the attorney's interest as a creditor, and the estate's interests that he will represent in the task to be accomplished on behalf of the estate. For example, if the attorney is retained to represent the estate in recovering a voidable preference paid to another creditor, it would seem that the attorney's interest is congruent with rather than opposed to that of the estate. By contrast, the potential for adverse interests is strong if the attorney's role is to represent the estate in negotiating a plan of reorganization with creditors.

Note that the bar to representation in §101(14)(A) only applies if the attorney is actually a creditor in a Ch. 11 case. Section 1107(b) makes it clear that an attorney is not disqualified simply because he represented the debtor before bankruptcy. However, that prior representation could give rise to an actual or potential conflict in some circumstances, so it must be disclosed to the court and evaluated.

2. The ethical barrier to Hiram's representation of the creditors' committee is not really a conflict of interest. After all, Hiram has not been Erstwhile's attorney for years. Rather, Canons 4 and 9 of the Model Code of Professional Responsibility preclude Hiram from accepting this appointment.

Canon 4 forbids an attorney from divulging the confidences of a client. During the course of their attorney-client relationship, Hiram was privy to details of Erstwhile's affairs. Hiram cannot represent Erstwhile's creditors without violating the trust and confidence inherent in the former relationship. *In re Kujawa*, 112 B.R. 968 (Bankr. E.D. Mo. 1990), is a particularly startling example of an attorney's violation of confidence. The law firm represented the debtor for about two years. It represented him in several lawsuits, counseled him on bankruptcy issues, and had intimate knowledge of his affairs. A few months after doing legal work for the debtor, the law firm represented some of his creditors in a petition to place him into involuntary bankruptcy. When those creditors retained other counsel, the firm represented another group of creditors who sought to intervene in the case. The firm also filed as an intervening creditor on its own behalf for unpaid fees owed by the debtor. The court granted the debtor's motion to disqualify the firm and ordered the firm to pay the debtor's costs and attorney's fees relating to the motion.

Even if Hiram argues that he has no information about Erstwhile's affairs that can be used to its detriment, Canon 9 prohibits an attorney from acting in a way that creates the appearance of impropriety. Hiram's efforts on the part of the creditors would surely create a sense of suspicion and would justify Erstwhile in feeling wronged. *See e.g., In re Global Video Communications Corp.*, 19 Bankr. Ct. Dec. (CCR) 1311 (Bankr. M.D. Fla. 1989); *In re Davenport Communications Ltd.*, 19 Bankr. Ct. Dec. (CCR) 1980 (Bankr. S.D. Iowa 1990).

3. **(a)** The objection is sound, and the court may well decide to deny all compensation to Bill under §328(c), even though he did not participate in or know about Able's possible fraud, and notwithstanding that his work for the estate was competent. The disallowance of compensation is a punishment for the improper conduct of working for the estate while holding or representing an adverse interest. The trustee need not show that the conflict of interest actually did detract from the quality of representation, or that the estate suffered some tangible loss as a result of it.

The facts of this example are loosely based on *Rome v. Braunstein*, 19 F.3d 54 (1st Cir. 1994), in which the attorney for a corporation filed a Ch. 11 petition on its behalf and successfully applied to be appointed as counsel for the debtor in possession. At the time of appointment, he failed to disclose that he had represented the owner of the debtor corporation prior to the petition. He continued to represent the owner (and also his secretary) during the course of the bankruptcy, and never disclosed this either. During the Ch. 11 case, it became apparent that the owner had looted the corporation before the petition had been filed, and the creditors successfully applied to replace the debtor in possession (controlled by the owner, of course) by a trustee. The trustee replaced the attorney and the case was then converted to Ch. 7. When the attorney applied for compensation for the services he had rendered to the estate prior to his dismissal, the court refused his application, and this was affirmed on appeal.

There was no indication that the attorney collaborated in or knew of the owner's dishonesty, but the court said that this was not the point. As soon as an attorney becomes aware of any facts that may give rise to possible conflicts — whether they exist at the time of appointment or arise subsequently — he has the duty to make immediate, candid, and complete disclosure of them so that the court can determine whether the attorney is disqualified from representing the estate. Even if he did not in fact act contrary to the interests of the estate, and he did perform valuable work, the attorney clearly put himself in the position in which his loyalty was weakened and he would be tempted to give tainted advice — whether or not it is possible to identify any specific impact the conflict may have had on the interests of the estate. (Also, remember that quite apart from the sanction under §328, an attorney who fails to avoid a conflict of interest is subject to disciplinary action by the bar.)

(b) This question raises an ancillary issue: When a trustee is appointed and proceeds to investigate possible improprieties by the debtor's management, is the debtor's attorney precluded by attorney-client privilege from furnishing information that he obtained during the course of representing the debtor? In *In re Blinder Robinson & Co., Inc.*, 123 B.R. 900 (Bankr. D. Colo. 1991), the court resolved this question by finding that the trustee succeeded to the debtor's right to waive the attorney-client privilege. The court reasoned that if this were not so, the management of the debtor would control the privilege and could frustrate the trustee's investigation and shield itself from the trustee's efforts to find misappropriated assets.

4. Many attorneys require payment of fees in advance before filing a bankruptcy petition on behalf of a consumer client. However, as in the case here, some debtors just do not have the means to pay the fee in a lump sum in advance. The problem with the installment plan used by Filenow & Palater is that their claim for the fee becomes a prepetition debt as soon as the petition is filed. As such, it is subject to the stay, so that if the client does not pay, the attorney is barred from taking action to collect it, whether in the form of banking the checks or making demands or requests for payment. (The stay is discussed in Chapter 10.) It is also dischargeable, so to the extent that it is not paid out of the estate, it becomes uncollectible following the bankruptcy. (The discharge is discussed in Chapter 22.) Apart from that, some courts have held that this type of credit arrangement, by making the attorney an unsecured creditor as well as the debtor's counsel, creates a conflict of interest which disqualifies the attorney from representing the debtor.

This approach was taken in *In re Martin*, 197 B.R. 120 (Bankr. D. Colo. 1996). The attorney made a fee arrangement under which the debtor had paid a deposit and gave the attorney post-dated checks for the balance, payable after the petition had been filed. When the attorney properly disclosed the fee arrangement to the court (so there was no nondisclosure problem as in Example 3), the U.S. Trustee objected to it. The court upheld the objection under §329 on the basis that the fee arrangement creates a conflict of interest by making the attorney an unsecured creditor for his fee. Since the claim is dischargeable, the attorney has a disincentive to advise the debtor frankly that his own claim is uncollectible. The court acknowledged that its ruling made it more difficult for indigent debtors to secure representation, and recognized that this concern had motivated some courts to find a way around the problem by finding such fee arrangements nondischargeable. However, the court considered that approach to be wrong because the fees are a clearly prepetition debt, not excepted from the discharge under the Code. Absent a legislative solution, the court found no basis on which an attorney can perform prepetition legal work on credit. (Note that advance payment is required only for that legal work done up to the time of the petition. Fees for postpetition representation are not a dischargeable prepetition debt.)

A contrary approach was taken in *In re Hines,* 147 F.3d 1185 (9th Cir. 1998), in which the court analyzed the possible objections to every kind of fee arrangement that a debtor might make with her attorney, and concluded that none of them were entirely invulnerable to attack. Even the option of advance payment, as suggested by cases like *Martin,* could be impugned by claiming that the debtor's contractual right to legal services becomes property of the estate, subject to liquidation by the trustee. The court considered the situation to be untenable because it creates serious obstacles to the legal representation of debtors, and felt that in the absence of legislative action, courts had the responsibility to ensure that the bankruptcy system continued to function. The court, therefore, held that a prepetition debt for legal services, payable in installments by means of postdated checks, was neither subject to the stay nor dischargeable, and hence did not create a conflict of interest.

7

Bankruptcy Jurisdiction, the Powers of the Bankruptcy Court, and Sovereign Immunity

§7.1 Introduction

Section 5.2 explained why Congress, rather than the states, is responsible for enacting bankruptcy law. It follows that bankruptcy matters fall within the realm of the federal courts. Jurisdiction over bankruptcy is conferred on the federal district courts by 28 U.S.C. §1334, while 28 U.S.C. §157 provides for the referral of bankruptcy matters from district courts to bankruptcy courts. Section 7.2 deals with §1344 and its grant of jurisdiction to district courts, and section 7.3 discusses the way in which that power is passed on to bankruptcy courts.

§7.2 District Court Jurisdiction over Bankruptcy

A court is competent to adjudicate a case only if it has both personal and subject matter jurisdiction. In other words, the parties must be legitimately within the court's power and the case must concern a controversy that is justiciable by the court.

§7.2.1   Personal Jurisdiction

Personal jurisdiction in bankruptcy cases is not expressly addressed by 28 U.S.C. §1334. However, courts have held that the reach of the Code is nationwide, and the bankruptcy jurisdiction of the federal district courts extends to all persons who are present within the territorial boundaries of the United States. Therefore, the usual jurisdictional concept of minimum contacts does not apply in a bankruptcy case. As long as the court has subject matter jurisdiction, a party to a proceeding or suit in a bankruptcy court cannot challenge jurisdiction on the basis that minimum contacts are lacking between the transaction or property in issue and the forum. The question of which federal district is the most appropriate for the case is a question of venue. *See* section 9.2.

§7.2.2   Subject Matter Jurisdiction

The federal district courts are granted jurisdiction over five categories of proceeding by 28 U.S.C. §1334. In the first two, the jurisdiction is exclusive — that is, no other court may entertain proceedings in these categories. The second three confer nonexclusive jurisdiction on the district courts, so that some other court also has the power to adjudicate these matters. The diagram below sketches the five categories, which are explained below.

Bankruptcy Jurisdiction Under 28 U.S.C. §1334

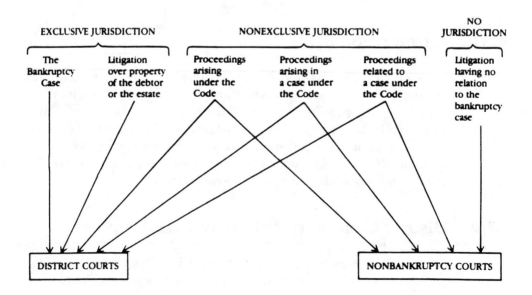

a.   Exclusive Jurisdiction

The district court has original and exclusive jurisdiction over the actual bankruptcy case itself under §1334(a). This is a narrow category, interpreted to include only the petition and its adjudication. No other court may hear and determine a bankruptcy petition.

Under §1334(e), once a bankruptcy case has been filed, the district court has exclusive jurisdiction over the debtor's property as at the commencement of the case, wherever situated, and also over property of the estate. This provision brings the property under the control of the court upon commencement of the case, even though some other court previously had jurisdiction over it.

b.   Nonexclusive Jurisdiction

Section 1334(b) grants the district court original but nonexclusive jurisdiction over three types of civil proceeding. (*Civil proceedings* include all litigated civil matters, whether suits or motions.)

(1)   *Civil proceedings "arising under title 11."* This category covers bankruptcy litigation other than the actual case itself. For a proceeding to arise under the Code, it must involve the adjudication of rights and obligations provided in the Code. In essence, the cause of action must be created by the Code, or it must involve an issue that is so linked to the Code that the issue either would not have arisen or it would have been decided differently in the absence of the Code.

(2)   *Civil proceedings "arising in" a case under title 11.* The scope of this category is rather obscure. It seems to be an intermediate classification which contemplates proceedings that, while not necessarily dependent on provisions of the Code for their existence, are somewhat more connected to it than related proceedings. In essence, this category seems to cover proceedings that are likely to arise only in a bankruptcy case. In other words, the litigation would not exist had the bankruptcy case not been filed. Some types of "arising in" litigation are obvious and straightforward. Disputes that are intimately involved with the administration of the estate, such as those concerning the allowance of claims, or the approval of a loan to the estate, would not come about outside of bankruptcy. However, there are other types of disputes that would not have arisen in the absence of bankruptcy, but which are not as tied up with, and may have no impact on the estate. For example, in *In re A.H. Robbins Co.*, 86 F.3d 364 (4th Cir. 1996), *cert. denied*, 117 S. Ct. 1183 (1996), the court held that a dispute between

attorneys over the distribution of fees from a trust created under a Ch. 11 plan did arise in the bankruptcy case because the trust would never have existed in the absence of bankruptcy. This conclusion was reached even though the dispute between the attorneys really had no conceivable impact on the estate. Such an expansive interpretation of "arising in" jurisdiction could bring into the bankruptcy court matters that are really quite tangential to the bankruptcy. Fortunately, nothing turns on distinguishing this category from the others in regard to district court jurisdiction under §1334(b), so it can be ignored for present purposes. (It comes up again in the discussion of abstention in section 7.7.3.)

(3) *Civil proceedings "related to" a case under title 11.* Although these proceedings have a relationship to the bankruptcy case, they are furthest from its central core. They involve litigation that has some relationship to the bankruptcy case, but which arises out of rights and issues of nonbankruptcy law. In the absence of bankruptcy, these disputes would be heard by another court. However, because bankruptcy has occurred, the dispute affects the estate and the district court acquires nonexclusive jurisdiction to deal with it.

Related litigation falls into one of two categories. The first, and least problematical, type of related matter is one that involves a cause of action that could have been brought by or against the debtor under nonbankruptcy law, but which has passed to the estate from the debtor to become a *claim of or against the estate.* In this type of controversy, the estate is actually a party to the litigation, so there is little trouble in identifying the matter as related to the bankruptcy case. The second category of related proceeding has generated much more difficulty. Cases in this category concern litigation in which the *estate is not involved* — it is *between other parties* — but the outcome of the litigation *could have some impact on the estate.* In these types of cases a broad view of relationship would enable one to trace some connection to the bankruptcy case, even where the litigation's actual impact on or importance to the estate is marginal. Because the scope of related litigation would be too broad if the test were simply to find some point of relationship between the third-party litigation and the case, most courts require something more. They have struggled to devise a test that distinguishes truly related litigation — over which jurisdiction is appropriate — from that which is tangential and of little actual or potential significance to the estate — which should not give rise to a claim of bankruptcy jurisdiction.

The most influential formulation of the test is that enunciated in *Pacor, Inc. v. Higgins,* 743 F.2d 984, 994 (3d Cir. 1984): A civil proceeding is related to the bankruptcy case only if its outcome could *conceivably have any effect on the estate* — if its disposition could alter the *rights, liability, freedom of action or options* of, or have an impact on the *handling or administration* of the estate. This test has been adopted by several other courts of appeal and was referred to with approval by the Supreme Court in *Celotex Corp. v. Edwards*, 514 U.S. 300 (1995). However, although the test is widely followed, there is still some uncertainty as to its application. Some courts see conceivable impact more narrowly than others. The tendency, however, is to not take the concept of conceivable impact too literally for fear that a broad conception of relatedness would expand the jurisdiction of the bankruptcy forum beyond proper limits. Therefore, a matter should not be found to be related merely because it might have some speculative or remote possible consequence to the bankruptcy case. The appropriate scope of related jurisdiction, where the case does not involve the estate as a party, should be confined to litigation that has a direct and demonstrable legal or economic impact on the estate, so that it affects the debtor's or estate's freedom of action, the administration of the estate, or the distribution to creditors. See, for example, *Zerand-Bernal Group, Inc. v. Cox*, 23 F.3d 159 (7th Cir. 1994), *In re Fedpak Systems*, 80 F.3d 207 (7th Cir. 1995).

The *Zerand-Bernal* case offers a good example of third-party litigation that cannot be regarded as related to the bankruptcy case: Zerand-Bernal bought the debtor's assets from the estate which was then distributed and the debtor's business was closed. Sometime later, a person injured by a machine sold by the debtor prior to its bankruptcy sued Zerand-Bernal on a theory of successor liability. Zerand-Bernal sought to reopen the bankruptcy case for the purpose of obtaining an injunction against the suit. The court of appeals affirmed the bankruptcy court's finding that it had no jurisdiction. The court noted that in a broad sense, the litigation could be described as related because it arose from the sale of estate assets, but it was not related within the meaning of §1334(b) because the estate no longer existed, and the suit could not affect the estate or the distribution to creditors.

Because the three categories of litigation in §1334(b) all fall within the original nonexclusive jurisdiction of the district court, the distinctions between them are not significant for the purpose of determining district court jurisdiction. Provided that the case does fall within one of the three categories, the District Court has jurisdiction over it. However, the distinction between matters arising under the Code and related matters *is* important to *bankruptcy court* jurisdiction. *See* section 7.3. *See also* Example 1, which is an exercise in distinguishing the categories of proceeding covered by §1334.

§7.2.3   *The Purpose of §1334*

By conferring exclusive jurisdiction on the district court over the case and over the debtor's and estate's property, §§1334(a) and (e) ensure that the bankruptcy remedy may be granted only by federal courts, which are also given control over the economic resources of the estate. The court's nonexclusive jurisdiction is more complicated and needs some explanation.

Prior to the enactment of the Bankruptcy Reform Act in 1978, there had been much litigation over the scope of bankruptcy jurisdiction: Did it cover only the actual bankruptcy case itself or did it extend to issues of nonbankruptcy law that were in some way related to the bankruptcy case? Congress decided to resolve this question in favor of a broad grant of jurisdiction to the bankruptcy forum, so that it could deal not only with the central bankruptcy case but also with related litigation that had an impact on the bankruptcy case or on the estate. The grant of jurisdiction in §1334(b) over civil proceedings arising in or related to the case reflects this choice. (Section 1334(b) was not the original provision enacted in 1978, but is a successor to it.)

The advantage of allowing related matters to be brought before the bankruptcy forum is convenience and efficiency: A single court is able to dispose of all controversies that are intertwined with the bankruptcy case or affect the rights and obligations of the estate. The disadvantage of this broad grant of jurisdiction is that it comes at the expense of other courts (typically, state courts) that are the usual arbiters of nonbankruptcy law and are best qualified to pronounce on it. Of course, as discussed in section 7.2.2, the mere grant of jurisdiction over related matters does not resolve the issue entirely. In close cases, it can be difficult to tell if particular litigation does in fact qualify as related. (*See also* Example 2.) Also, even if the matter is properly related, it may still be appropriate for the bankruptcy forum to refuse to hear the matter, and to defer to the other court. This is discussed in section 7.7.

§7.3   The Exercise of Bankruptcy Jurisdiction by Bankruptcy Courts

As stated earlier, although §1334 grants jurisdiction to district courts, this jurisdiction is actually exercised by bankruptcy courts in the overwhelming majority of cases. If bankruptcy judges were appointed in the same way as district court judges, with life tenure under Article III of the Constitution, they would simply be able to exercise the jurisdiction conferred by §1334, and there would be no basis for challenging their power to do so. This would clearly be the most efficient way in which to establish the bankruptcy system. This was recognized both by the commission whose work led to enactment of the 1978 Code and by the recent National Bankruptcy Review Commission. However, the political obstacles to granting this status to bankruptcy judges have so far been insuperable. As a result bankruptcy courts occupy a rather awkward position in the federal court system and essentially derive their power through the district courts. The present state of bankruptcy court jurisdiction can only be understood in light of historical developments. This section therefore begins with a brief historical introduction.

§7.3.1 *Jurisdiction Prior to 1978*

The Bankruptcy Act of 1898 vested jurisdiction over bankruptcy in the federal district courts. The district courts did not hear the bankruptcy cases themselves but appointed referees for set terms to deal with them. These referees were the predecessors of the contemporary bankruptcy courts. Their power was limited. They exercised only what was known as *summary jurisdiction,* which encompassed three categories of proceeding: Those relating to administration of the estate, those relating to estate property in the actual or constructive possession of the debtor at the time of bankruptcy, and those in respect of which the party who was not the debtor had consented to the court's exercise of jurisdiction. The existence of possession or consent was particularly troublesome because the courts recognized the concepts of constructive possession and implied consent. As a result, possession or consent could be inferred even when they did not really exist. This led to much uncertainty and litigation.

If a proceeding did not fall within the bankruptcy court's summary jurisdiction, it had to be tried in the court that had *plenary jurisdiction.* This might be the federal district court, a state court, or a federal district court in another district. Under this system, bankruptcy courts could not hear matters related to the case, even though convenience and efficiency called for their disposition in the court that was dealing with the bankruptcy case. Related litigation was dispersed, and a trustee often had to bring or defend suits in a number of different courts. Not only was this inefficient, but it also led to wasteful and time-consuming litigation on jurisdictional issues. The confusion and expense generated by the distinction between summary and plenary jurisdiction was regarded as a serious flaw in the bankruptcy system, and reform of the jurisdictional scheme was identified as an important goal of the 1978 Act.

§7.3.2 *The Bankruptcy Reform Act of 1978*

Bankruptcy court jurisdiction was one of the controversial issues in the bankruptcy reform process. The solution adopted by the Bankruptcy Reform Act of 1978 was a compromise between conflicting viewpoints. The goal of the new legislation was to expand the jurisdiction of the bankruptcy court and to make its functions more judicial and less administrative than they had been under the 1898 Act. To achieve this end, the 1978 Act sought to abolish the distinction between summary and plenary jurisdiction together with its artificial concepts of constructive possession and implied consent. The new bankruptcy courts were given broad jurisdiction to deal with not only the bankruptcy case and ancillary litigation but also with all matters that were related to the bankruptcy case. That is, the jurisdiction of the bankruptcy court extended to all those categories of proceeding currently identified in §1334. The power of the new courts included both summary and plenary jurisdiction, as those terms were understood in prior law.

Jurisdiction of this breadth can only be exercised by a judge appointed with tenure and salary protection under Article III of the Constitution. Many people recognized this at the time that the 1978 Act was passed, and advocated granting Article III status to bankruptcy judges. However, there was considerable resistance to this proposal, and the opponents of Article III status prevailed. The 1978 Act provided for the appointment of bankruptcy judges for set terms as adjuncts of the district court. In an attempt to avoid the constitutional problems of conferring extensive jurisdiction on nontenured judges, Congress granted bankruptcy jurisdiction to the district courts and, in the same statutory provision, legislatively delegated this jurisdiction to the bankruptcy courts. In other words, the district courts were used as a conduit for empowering bankruptcy courts to exercise expanded jurisdiction.

The expedient did not work. A relatively short time after passage of the 1978 Act, the Supreme Court toppled the statute's jurisdictional structure. In *Northern Pipeline Constr. Co. v. Marathon Pipe Line Co.*, 458 U.S. 50 (1982) the party who had been sued by the estate in bankruptcy court on a contract claim related to the bankruptcy case challenged the bankruptcy court's jurisdiction over the case. A plurality of the Supreme Court held that the bankruptcy court had no jurisdiction to adjudicate the contract suit. The essence of the plurality opinion is that Congress violated the separation of powers doctrine and the principle of judicial independence by conferring extended jurisdiction on a judge who did not have security of tenure and salary protection under Article III of the Constitution. The Court held that the channelling of jurisdiction through the district court by legislative delegation did not overcome the constitutional objection.

In expounding on the permissible range of adjudication that Congress may constitutionally confer on a non-Article III judge, the court distinguished between *public rights* — those that arise between the government and others — and *private rights* — those that involve the liability of one private party to another. In enacting the Code, Congress created a regulatory scheme for the restructuring of debtor-creditor relations, and thereby brought into existence rights that would not exist in the absence of bankruptcy law. Such rights, which owe their existence purely to Congressional action, fall into the classification of public rights and, because Congress created them, Congress may assign power to a nontenured judge to adjudicate them. However, rights that exist outside of the Code, and are not solely created by Congress, are private rights and Congress has no constitutional authority to assign their adjudication to a non-Article III judge.

The court returned to this public rights doctrine in *Granfinanciera, S.A. v. Nordberg*, 491 U.S. 33 (1989). It stated that Congress only has the constitutional power to allocate adjudication of a right to a non-Article III judge where the issue to be resolved either involves a public right between the government and others or involves private rights inextricably tied up with a federal regulatory program that virtually occupies the field. That is, the doctrine permits a non-Article III judge to adjudicate private rights provided that the private rights are so intertwined with the program that they take on the character of a public right. While the public rights doctrine exhibits some considerable degree of mushiness, its basic point is that a nontenured bankruptcy judge does have power to adjudicate bankruptcy rights purely created by the Code, and has some limited power beyond that to dispose of nonbankruptcy rights that are inextricably linked to the administration of bankruptcy cases. As may be expected, the greatest difficulty and uncertainty is encountered in trying to gauge the scope of this second category.

§7.3.3 1984 Reforms

The effect of the *Marathon* decision was stayed for a time to enable Congress to resolve the problem. The controversy about whether bankruptcy judges should be appointed under Article III arose again, and while it raged, the stay expired. For a time the bankruptcy system operated under emergency rules promulgated by each circuit, under which the district court maintained jurisdiction over bankruptcy cases and the bankruptcy court operated under referrals from the district court. With regard to those matters that arose directly from the Code itself, the bankruptcy court could render judgments and orders, but with regard to related matters, the bankruptcy court would make recommendations to the district court which would itself make the final determination.

The emergency rules were controversial, and their constitutionality was challenged. However, the rules were upheld by various Courts of Appeal, and remained in effect until 1984, when Congress finally passed the *Bankruptcy Amendments and Federal Judgeship Act*. This statute created the current jurisdictional system found in Title 28 U.S.C.

Congress decided against the option of giving bankruptcy judges Article III status. Instead, the 1984 amendment continues to provide for their appointment for fixed terms (14 years), subject to termination for cause such as incompetence or misconduct. The constitutional problem is dealt with by limiting the bankruptcy judges' power to decide matters and making them subject to the control and supervision of the district court. In many respects, the 1984 amendment is based on the system set up under the Emergency Rules, and it has affinities to the old referee system. It does make improvements over the referee system, however, because it consolidates jurisdiction and reduces the scattered litigation that plagued bankruptcy cases under the 1898 Act. However, because the bankruptcy court cannot constitutionally exercise this consolidated jurisdiction, the district court must play a broader role than was intended when the 1978 reforms were devised.

§7.3.4   New Proposals for Change

The National Bankruptcy Review Commission studied the jurisdictional scheme established in 1984 and recommended that bankruptcy judges be given Article III status. The Commission report contemplated a transitional period during which current judges would serve out their 14-year terms (with the right to apply for appointment under Article III if they chose), and new appointments would be under Article III. Its recommendation is based on two principal concerns. First, the constitutionality of the present system is still not beyond doubt because it has not yet been finally passed upon by the Supreme Court. Second, the jurisdictional limitations on bankruptcy courts create unnecessary complexity and continue to generate needless litigation and delay, and can be used as a basis for strategies for delay. Congress has not adopted the Commission's recommendation in the pending reform bill.

§7.3.5   An Overview of the Current System

The diagram on page 129 represents the way in which bankruptcy jurisdiction is channelled to the bankruptcy court through the district court.
  The system works as follows:

(1) *The grant of jurisdiction to the district court.* Jurisdiction over bankruptcy is conferred on the district court by §1334, as discussed in section 7.2. This jurisdiction covers the bankruptcy case itself as well as matters arising under the Code and relating to the case.

(2) *District court referral to the bankruptcy court.* The district court refers these matters to the bankruptcy court, which is described in 28 U.S.C. §151 as a "unit" of the district court. The process of referral, the relationship between the district court and its bankruptcy "unit," and the exercise of power by the bankruptcy court is dealt with in 28 U.S.C. §157. Section 157(a) allows each district court to make a blanket referral of all bankruptcy matters to the bankruptcy court. Thus, the district court does not make

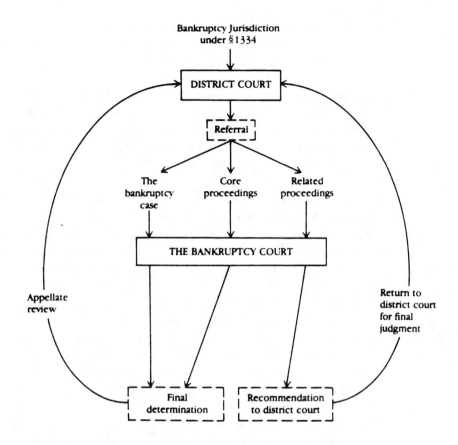

case-by-case referrals; all bankruptcy litigation commences as a matter of course in the bankruptcy court.

(3) *District court control.* Under §157(d), the district court retains ultimate control over all bankruptcy cases. If cause is shown it may, either on its own motion or on the motion of a party, withdraw any case or portion of a case from the bankruptcy court. If a case involves both issues of bankruptcy law and some other federal law regulating interstate commerce (*e.g.*, an antitrust issue), the district court must withdraw the proceeding on the timely motion of a party.

(4) *Final adjudication.* The final disposition of bankruptcy litigation depends on the nature of the rights in issue. Because bankruptcy judges do not have Article III status, the bankruptcy court cannot finally adjudicate all matters brought before it. It is empowered to make a final judgment or order in matters concerning rights that arise out of the Code itself. Under *Marathon*, Congress may provide for the determination of these rights by a nontenured judge, because Congress itself created the rights. However, the bankruptcy court may not render a final judgment in matters that are

135

merely related to the bankruptcy case but require the resolution of nonbankruptcy rights. Congress cannot entrust the disposition of these cases to a nontenured judge.

To accommodate this distinction, §157(b) differentiates *the bankruptcy case and core proceedings,* which may be finally adjudicated by the bankruptcy court, and *non-core proceedings,* in which the bankruptcy court's judgment takes the form of a recommendation to the district court that is then responsible for rendering final judgment.

1.   The case and core proceedings "arising under" the Code or "arising in a case" under the Code.   Section 157(b) allows the bankruptcy court to hear, determine, and enter orders in "all cases under title 11 and all core proceedings arising under title 11, or arising in a case under title 11." This means that the general referral by the district court enables the bankruptcy court to hear and decide the bankruptcy case as well as core bankruptcy proceedings. The role of the district court in these matters is generally limited to appellate review. §§157(b)(1) and 158.

A core proceeding under §157 corresponds to proceedings "arising under" or "arising in a case under" the Code, over which bankruptcy jurisdiction is conferred on the district court by §1334(b). A core proceeding has been defined as one that " . . . invokes a substantive right provided by title 11 or . . . that, by its nature, could arise only in the context of a bankruptcy case." This test was enunciated in *In re Wood,* 825 F.2d 90, 97 (5th Cir. 1987), and has been followed in later cases. *See, e.g., Barnett v. Stern,* 909 F.2d 973, 981 (7th Cir. 1990); *In re Wolverine Radio Co.,* 930 F.2d 1132, 1144 (6th Cir. 1991). The essential issue under this test is whether the proceedings are inextricably linked to a substantive right or obligation that owes its existence to the Code.

If the right in issue owes its existence to the Code, the litigation over it is a core proceeding "arising under" the Code. However, even if the right in issue does not owe its existence to (that is, is not created by) the Code, the proceedings involving it could qualify as core proceedings "arising in" the case if they concern an essential part of the administration of the estate. For example, in *In re Ben Cooper, Inc.,* 896 F.2d 1394 (2d Cir. 1990), *reinstated on remand,* 924 F.2d 36 (2d Cir. 1991) the proceeding in question was litigation to determine the validity of an insurance policy taken out by the estate to protect estate property as required by the Ch. 11 plan. The issue between the estate, as insured, and the insurer over the validity of the policy involved the question of whether a misrepresentation by the debtor in possession voided the policy — purely a matter of nonbankruptcy insurance and contract law. Nevertheless, the court found this to be a core proceeding "arising in" the case because the insurance contract was entered into postpetition for the purpose of protecting estate property, and was therefore essentially tied up with the administration of the estate. (The court distinguished this situation from that in *Marathon*, which involved a dispute over a contract entered into by the debtor prepetition.)

Section 157(b)(2) sets out a nondefinitive list of core proceedings. This list is a guide, but it is not entirely reliable. Litigation is only a core proceeding if it satisfies the test stated above. Congress cannot simply declare something to be a core proceeding and confer jurisdiction on the bankruptcy court over it: If a matter does not legitimately qualify as a core proceeding, its designation as such in §157(b)(2) is wrong and the provision can be struck down as unconstitutional. In *Granfinanciera, S.A. v. Nordberg*, 492 U.S. 33 (1989), the Supreme Court went behind Congress' categorizations in §157(b)(2) and determined, based on the substance of the proceeding, that a suit to avoid a fraudulent transfer, although included in §157(b)(2) as a core proceeding, did not in fact so qualify.

2.   Non-core proceedings.   If a matter is not a core proceeding but is related to the bankruptcy case, the bankruptcy judge may hear it but cannot enter an order. The judge must make a finding and submit a recommendation to the district court, which must enter the final judgment after considering the bankruptcy court's recommendation and reviewing de novo any matters to which a party has objected. §157(c)(1). This process allows the related litigation to be conducted before the bankruptcy court, but preserves a level of district court control intended to be sufficient to satisfy the constitutional limits on bankruptcy court jurisdiction. Under §157(c)(2), the district court may refer a related proceeding to the bankruptcy court for final disposition provided that all parties to the proceeding consent. Some courts have held that consent to this expanded jurisdiction of the bankruptcy court must be expressly given and cannot be inferred from a failure to object or from some other conduct. However, there is authority upholding implied consent to judgment by the bankruptcy court in related non-core proceedings. *See e.g., In re Johnson*, 960 F.2d 396, 403 (4th Cir. 1992).

§7.3.6   A Summary of the Operation of §157 and Its Constitutionality

In summary, §1334 confers bankruptcy jurisdiction on the district court and §157 empowers that court to refer its bankruptcy powers to the bankruptcy court. Although the district court makes a general referral of all bankruptcy matters to the bankruptcy court, it retains final say over all proceedings beyond the bankruptcy case and its core. The bankruptcy court can only make a final adjudication outside the core with the specific referral from the district court and the consent (and possibly only the express consent) of the parties. The district court is able to withdraw its reference in any matter. In *Home Insurance Co. v. Cooper & Cooper, Ltd.*, 889 F.2d 746, 749–750 (7th Cir. 1989), the court emphasized that the district court must actually exercise the control given to it by §157. It cannot abdicate its statutory role and act merely as an appellate court.

Notwithstanding the restriction on their power, bankruptcy courts do generally exercise wide influence over all bankruptcy matters, even those that require the final imprimatur of the district court. Busy district courts are not usually inclined to meddle unduly with the specialist bankruptcy courts. It is nevertheless unfortunate that the current system has a layer of complexity that detracts from the streamlining originally contemplated by the 1978 reforms. This complexity is motivated not by a belief that this is the optimal way to administer bankruptcy litigation but by the political difficulty of creating new Article III judges. In addition to the structural inelegance of the system, it has constitutional imperfections that have not been fully resolved. *Marathon* and *Granfinanciera* cast doubt on Congress' determination of what constitutes core proceedings, leaving the scope of the bankruptcy court's jurisdiction in a state of uncertainty.

Courts have now been operating under this patch-up for about 20 years. Although there has always been doubt about its constitutional viability, no direct challenge has made its way to the U.S. Supreme Court. In the interim, courts have made the system work as well as it can. By appointing bankruptcy judges under Article III, as the Bankruptcy Reform Commission recommended, Congress would be able to eliminate the uncertainty and complexity generated by the current jurisdictional structure. At this point, there is no indication that it is ready to take this step.

§7.4   The Jury Trial in Bankruptcy

§7.4.1   *An Outline of the Problem*

The Seventh Amendment preserves the right to trial by jury in suits at common law. It is well-accepted that the words "suits at common law" refer only to actions in law, for which juries were traditionally available, and which would have been tried by jury at the time of the enactment of the Seventh Amendment. It does not include proceedings in equity, which had never been tried by jury. Where the cause of action in issue did not exist at the time that the Seventh Amendment was enacted, but was created afterwards, the right to a jury trial is determined by examining its inherent nature and its analogy to forms of relief that did exist at that time. Bankruptcy relief is equitable, not legal, in its origins, and it is therefore clear that the Constitution does not guarantee a jury trial for the bankruptcy case itself. Nor is a jury trial available for those core proceedings that are purely an aspect of the equitable remedy of bankruptcy, or for those proceedings involving nonbankruptcy rights or remedies, whether core or related to the case, that are equitable in nature. However, where a proceeding arising in or related to the case involves a legal right or remedy, the parties are entitled to a jury trial.

Prior to 1978, jury trials were not available in cases falling within the referee's summary jurisdiction, but were available in cases that fell under the district courts' plenary jurisdiction, provided that the claim in question was legal in nature. Congress acknowledged and essentially continued this practice when it enacted the Code by providing in 28 U.S.C. §1480 that the Code does not affect any right that a party may have to a jury trial in the bankruptcy or related proceedings. That is, §1480 simply preserved the right to a jury trial, as it existed in law at the time of enactment of the Code.

As explained in section 7.3.2, Congress had intended, in the Code as enacted in 1978, that the bankruptcy court would fully dispose of all matters related to the bankruptcy under a legislatively delegated power of adjudication, and that any jury trial would simply be conducted in the bankruptcy court. However, when *Marathon* declared this scheme to be unconstitutional, it also called into question the bankruptcy court's power to conduct jury trials. (*Marathon* did not actually say that bankruptcy judges may not conduct jury trials, but the holding that bankruptcy courts could not exercise full adjudicative power over nonbankruptcy rights created uncertainty over their power to conduct jury trials involving such rights.) When it passed the 1984 amendments in response to *Marathon,* Congress made a half-hearted attempt to deal with this problem. It enacted the obscure 28 U.S.C. §1411 which apparently (but not clearly) repealed §1480 and stated that the Code does not affect any right to jury trial with regard to personal injury or wrongful death tort claims. Under 28 U.S.C. §157(b)(5) claims of this kind are excluded from the general referral of proceedings under §157(a), and are required to be heard by the district court. Therefore, the effect of §1411 was simply to do nothing more than recognize the right to jury trial in these two classes of case that would have to be tried in the district court. It did nothing to clarify what would happen in other proceedings in which the Constitution guarantees a jury trial. This led some to believe that §1480 had been repealed and that jury trials were not available in bankruptcy except in personal injury and wrongful death suits. Others believe that §1480 was not repealed and that in all situations not covered by those two enumerated classes, the court must permit a jury trial if the party would be entitled to it in nonbankruptcy law. (That is, a jury trial is available under either §1480 or §1411.) The issue of whether such trials could be conducted by the bankruptcy court was also unclear, particularly in non-core matters, in which the resolution reached in the bankruptcy court has the mere status of a recommendation to the district court. A jury decision in the bankruptcy court in such a situation would offend the normal principles of judicial deference to the factfinder, and may violate the Seventh Amendment's command that a court of the United States not re-examine a fact tried by a jury, other than in accordance with the rules of common law.

Therefore, Marathon and the 1984 amendments left uncertainty in the law on two issues: First, in which kinds of proceedings was a party entitled to a jury trial? Second, where the right to a jury trial existed, did the bankruptcy court have the power to conduct it? The first issue — in which type of proceedings is a jury trial available — was addressed by the Supreme Court in *Granfinanciera, S.A. v. Nordberg*, 492 U.S. 33 (1989). The court, however, expressly declined to deal with the second question — whether a bankruptcy court can conduct the jury trial.

§7.4.2   Proceedings in Which a Party Is Entitled to a Jury Trial

Granfinanciera involved a suit by the trustee to avoid a fraudulent transfer. The court of appeals had held that there was no right to a jury trial in such a suit because it is equitable in origin, and Congress had recognized and reinforced its equitable nature by including it in the list of core proceedings in §157(b)(2)(H). The Supreme Court reversed. It acknowledged that Congress can create public rights by statute and assign them to a non-tenured judge for decision without a jury, but Congress may not deprive parties of a jury trial where the cause of action involves a private right in respect of which the Seventh Amendment guarantees a jury trial. The classification into private and public rights depends on the nature and derivation of the right, and Congress cannot simply alter this classification by declaring a private right to be a core proceeding in §157. Although the restructuring of debtor-creditor relations is a public right, and the suit to avoid the fraudulent transfer is brought by the trustee in the bankruptcy proceedings, the suit itself is quintessentially common law in its derivation, and long-established as a creditor's suit outside of bankruptcy law. Furthermore, an examination of the history of fraudulent transfer law makes it clear that during the eighteenth century, a creditors' remedy to seek repayment of money fraudulently transferred by a debtor would not typically be heard by a court of equity, but would be treated as an action at law. (The dissenting justices questioned this reading of traditional practice and suggested that the historical record is uncertain. In any event, the court addressed only a monetary claim, not a suit to recover specific property, which is more likely to be classified as equitable.) The court therefore held that the suit involved private rights and qualifies as a suit at common law for which the Seventh Amendment guarantees a jury trial. The court confined its decision to cases in which the transferee had not, prior to the suit, filed a proof of claim against the estate. Had the transferee done so, the trustee's subsequent suit to avoid the transfer could be regarded as part of the claim allowance process, and thereby become so integral to the restructuring of debtor-creditor relations as to form part of the equitable core of bankruptcy.

In essence, the import of the decision is that in light of the Seventh Amendment, a jury trial is unavailable in only three situations:

(1) Where the claim is actually equitable in origin — that is, where, under traditional principles of the common law, the claim would be classified as arising in equity, not law.

(2) Where the claim is solely a creature of the Code, so that it qualifies as based on a public right and does not implicate a private right, and Congress has assigned the adjudication of the right to a nontenured judge who does not hold jury trials.

(3) Where the party seeking the jury trial has, in essence, waived it by filing a claim against the estate, and thereby submitting to the bankruptcy court's equitable jurisdiction to restructure the debtor-creditor relationship.

The third ground, while merely dictum in *Granfinanciera*, was revisited by the Supreme Court in *Langenkamp v. Culp*, 498 U.S. 42 (1990), in which the creditor had proved a claim against the estate, and the trustee then sued the creditor to avoid a preferential transfer made by the debtor to the creditor prior to the petition. Although *Granfinanciera* had involved a suit to avoid a fraudulent transfer the court had indicated in dictum that a suit to avoid a preference is also legal in nature. In *Langenkamp*, the court reaffirmed this. It noted that had the trustee initiated the preference suit against a creditor-transferee who had not filed a claim, the case would have been a legal claim to recover the transfer, and the creditor would have been entitled to a jury trial. However, the creditor lost this right by filing a claim, because the avoidance suit then became part of the process of claim allowance and disallowance. This is an integral part of the process of restructuring the debtor-creditor relationship which is triable in equity.

If a creditor can be held to have waived the right to a jury trial merely by filing a proof of claim and submitting to the court's equitable power, it seems to follow that the debtor, by filing the bankruptcy petition, must also be taken to waive the right to a jury trial in any proceedings in the case. Some courts have taken this view. However, in *Germain v. Connecticut National Bank*, 988 F.2d 1993 (2d Cir. 1993), the court found this waiver to be qualified and not absolute. It applies to proceedings that are part of the process of allowing or disallowing claims, which is equitable in nature. It does not cover proceedings that lie outside of that range. The proceeding in issue in *Germain* was a suit by the trustee against a bank on a theory of lender liability, which the court found to be legal in nature and subject to the right to a jury trial.

§7.4.3 The Power of Bankruptcy Courts to Conduct Jury Trials

Because in *Granfinanciera*, the Supreme Court left open the issue of whether a bankruptcy judge may conduct a jury trial, this question has been a matter of controversy. In *In re Ben Cooper, Inc.*, 896 F.2d 36 (2d Cir. 1990), *reinstated on remand,* 924 F.2d. 36 (2d Cir. 1991) the court held that a bankruptcy judge can conduct jury trials in core proceedings. This is because the bankruptcy court's determination in core proceedings is not purely a recommendation to the district court, but a final disposition, reviewable only under the normal process of appeal. Therefore the constitutional hurdle that exists in non-core proceedings — the Seventh Amendment's bar on re-examination of the jury verdict by the district court — is not implicated where a jury trial is conducted in a core proceeding. Other courts of appeal have disagreed on the basis that there is no clear grant of such power by statute, even in core proceedings, and it should not be implied given the constitutional ambiguity of the bankruptcy court's jurisdiction. The Supreme Court was given the opportunity to decide this issue in the *Ben Cooper* case, because a petition for certiorari was filed on the jury issue. However, the court denied the petition. There is general agreement that a bankruptcy court may not conduct a jury trial in non-core proceedings because the finding of the bankruptcy court is a mere recommendation to the district court, and the jury determination would not be subject to the same deference as it receives in normal appellate review.

In the Bankruptcy Reform Act of 1994 Congress tinkered with this issue without trying to resolve it definitively. It enacted 28 U.S.C. 157(e) which empowers the bankruptcy judge to conduct a jury trial provided that the district court specifically designates the bankruptcy judge to conduct that trial, and all the parties consent. This is a statutory recognition of the easiest case for arguing that the court's exercise of power is constitutional. Given the constitutional uncertainties about the bankruptcy court's power to deal with matters involving private rights, this is probably the best that Congress can do, short of changing the entire system by giving Article III status to bankruptcy judges.

§7.5   The Injunctive, Contempt, and Sanctioning Powers of the Bankruptcy Court

Section 105(a) confers general authority on the court to ". . . issue any order, process, or judgment that is necessary or appropriate to carry out the provisions of this title," and to act sua sponte, where necessary, to take action to enforce its orders or to prevent abuse of process. Three of the significant powers encompassed by this general provision are the court's power to issue injunctions, to deal with contempt of court, and to sanction improper conduct in relation to the case.

§7.5.1   *Injunctions*

The two most important forms of injunction in a bankruptcy case are routine, self-executing bars to action that are not expressly ordered by the court, but arise as a matter of law — that is, automatically — at certain stages of the proceedings. The first is the automatic stay under §362 which takes effect immediately upon the filing of the bankruptcy petition, and enjoins all action to collect debts due by the debtor, or to seize or dispose of the debtor's property. (*See* Chapters 10 and 11.) The second is the injunction on actions to collect a discharged debt, which goes into effect under §524(a)(2) as an incident of the discharge. (*See* Chapter 22.) As important as these two injunctions are, they are of limited scope: They are concerned only with action to collect property or money from the estate or the debtor. It frequently happens that other conduct must be restrained to ensure that the case proceeds as desired or the estate is not harmed. For example, it may be necessary to forbid creditor action against a third party guarantor, or to prevent obstructive or harassing action against a person associated with the debtor. The court's general equitable power under §105(a) gives it authority to issue injunctions of this type. The injunction can only be issued if the court has jurisdiction generally over the matter in issue, which means that the proceedings in which the injunction is issued must arise under the Code, or in a case arising in or related to a case under the Code.

The Supreme Court considered the bankruptcy courts' general injunctive power in *Celotex Corp. v. Edwards*, 514 U.S. 300 (1995). A tort claimant had won a judgment against Celotex, the debtor, in a federal district court in Texas (which is in the Fifth Circuit). The debtor had appealed and posted a supersedeas bond. The debtor gave the surety a security interest in certain funds as collateral for the bond. The creditors won the appeal, and the debtor then filed for bankruptcy under Ch. 11 in Florida (which is in the Eleventh Circuit). When the creditors sought to execute on the bond against the surety, the Florida bankruptcy court issued an injunction against enforcement of the bond. The bankruptcy court granted the injunction on the basis that enforcement of the bond, while against the surety and not against the estate directly, would harm the debtor's prospects of successful reorganization. This was because the surety would be able to realize on its collateral for reimbursement if it was called on to pay under the bond. A tussle then developed between the bankruptcy court, which sought to assert its injunction, and the courts of the Fifth Circuit in which execution of the bond had been authorized. The court of appeals for the Fifth Circuit adopted the view that the injunction was improper and therefore not binding on the creditors because enforcement of the bond would have no impact on the estate.

The issue in the case was whether the creditors could ignore the injunction and proceed with enforcement of the bond. Normally, an enjoined party must obey an injunction, even if erroneous, until such time as it is reversed on appeal. The only time that a party can disobey an injunction and then raise its invalidity as a defense in ensuing contempt proceedings is where the injunction is so patently beyond the court's jurisdiction that it has only a frivolous pretense to validity. As the proper exercise of jurisdiction was a key element of the issue of whether the injunction could be disregarded, the Supreme Court had to decide if the bankruptcy court did have jurisdiction to issue the injunction. It found that the litigation between the creditors and the surety was sufficiently related to the case under the *Pacor* test to confer related jurisdiction on the court. Execution on the bond would trigger the surety's right to claim the estate property in which it had the security interest and this, in turn, would upset the debtor's prospects of being able to rehabilitate itself under Ch. 11. Therefore, the Supreme Court held that obedience to the injunction was required, and the creditors could not disregard it, and later attack its jurisdictional grounds in subsequent contempt proceedings.

As the suit on the bond was a related case, and not a core proceeding, it raised the question of whether the bankruptcy court could itself issue the injunction, instead of submitting its findings and recommendation to the district court, which must issue the final order under 28 U.S.C. §157(c)(1). The dissent considered that the latter would have been the correct procedure, and an order by the bankruptcy court on its own was patently lacking validity. The majority disagreed because it found the injunction to be merely an interlocutory order, not a final order as contemplated under §157(c)(1).

§7.5.2   Contempt of Court

A court enforces obedience to its orders and respect for its processes by the power to sanction violations of its orders or disrespectful conduct. Contempt sanctions fall into two principal categories: Civil and Criminal. Civil contempt itself is divided into two types. *Compensatory civil contempt* is simply a money judgment to compensate the plaintiff for loss caused by the defendant's disobedience to the order. *Coercive civil contempt* takes the form of a fine or imprisonment imposed for the purpose of persuading the party to comply with an order. Its coercive purpose means that the sanction is imposed only as long as the disobedience continues. Once the party stops resisting the order, the fine ceases to accrue, or the imprisonment ends. (For example, the court may fine the violator $100 per day until the violation ceases, or may order the violator imprisoned until he comes into compliance.)

Criminal contempt is, like other criminal sanctions, a punishment for wrongful conduct. Its goal is not to amend the violator's conduct, but to impose a penalty on him for having committed the violation. For this reason it normally takes the form of a set fine or prison term, without the option of bringing the punishment to an end by ceasing the improper behavior.

Because of the jurisdictional limitations on bankruptcy courts, the extent of their power to deal with contempt is unclear. The 1978 Code did not impose any limits on the bankruptcy court's civil contempt powers, but it did restrict its power to punish for criminal contempt. This restriction was set out in 28 U.S.C. 1481 (repealed in 1984) under which the court could not use imprisonment as a punishment, and could only impose a fine for contempt committed in its presence. When §1481 was repealed in 1984, all reference to contempt power disappeared from the Code.

In the absence of statutory authority, courts generally find the power to sanction civil contempt to be inherent in the powers conferred on the court in §105(a). The bankruptcy court's power to impose penalties for criminal contempt is less clear. Some courts have found a criminal contempt power, but others have not, based on the reasoning that the imposition of criminal sanctions implicates the right to a jury trial and other procedural safeguards that are not adequately assured by an Article I court. (For example, see *In re Dyer*, 322 F.3d 1178 (9th Cir. 2003).) *Dyer* shows that the distinction between civil and criminal contempt is not always obvious. The bankruptcy court had made an award for compensatory civil contempt that included substantial punitive damages. The Court of Appeals held that a civil contempt order that imposes a significant penalty takes on the nature of criminal contempt and exceeds the court's power under §105(a).

§7.5.3   *Sanctions for Improper Conduct*

Under Bankruptcy Rule 9011, a bankruptcy court has the power to impose monetary sanctions on an attorney or party who, in pleadings or other documents submitted to the court, has made a representation that is frivolous or otherwise for an improper purpose, or has made unwarranted legal claims or factual allegations that have no evidentiary support. *In re Rainbow Magazine*, 77 F.3d 278 (9th Cir. 1996) held that even if the improper conduct is not covered by Rule 9011 (say, for example, it does not involve the submission of a document to the court), the bankruptcy court has the inherent power under §105(a) to sanction conduct that is vexatious or disobedient. The court's power to deal with matters of decorum and respect are part of the power granted by Congress in §105(a) to carry out the provisions of the Code.

§7.6   Appeals from the Bankruptcy Court

§7.6.1   *The Appellate Structure in General*

In related proceedings, where the bankruptcy court's determination is merely a proposed finding of fact and conclusion of law, the district court makes the final order or judgment. Under 28 U.S.C. §157(c)(1), this process of necessity involves review of the bankruptcy court decision by the district court, and the district court's final determination is subject to appeal to the court of appeals and then to the Supreme Court in the usual way. In core proceedings (or in related proceedings where the district court, with the consent of the parties, has referred the matter to the bankruptcy court for final determination under §157(c)(2)), the decision of the bankruptcy court is appealable under §158 to the district court or, if the circuit has established a bankruptcy appellate panel and the requirements set out below are satisfied, to the panel. (The bankruptcy appellate panel, consisting of three bankruptcy judges, substitutes for the district court as the court of first review.) From there it is appealable in the usual way to the court of appeals and the Supreme Court.

Therefore when a bankruptcy court decides a case, even where that decision is a final order or judgment within the court's jurisdiction over core proceedings, there is an initial (and extra) layer of appeal, either to the district court — a trial judge sitting alone, or to a panel of three judges of equal rank to the bankruptcy court. The National Bankruptcy Review Commission questioned the utility of subjecting parties to this extra layer of appeal. It argued that this could add cost to the proceedings where the parties decide to proceed to the next level of appeal. Also, because neither the decision of the district court or BAP is binding precedent, appeals at this level merely bind the parties, and add little to the development of the law. The Commission therefore recommended that this first level of appeal should be eliminated, with appeals going directly from the bankruptcy court to the court of appeals. The current reform bill does not propose any alteration to the appellate structure.

§7.6.2   Bankruptcy Appellate Panels

One of the innovations of the 1978 Code was to authorize the judicial council of each circuit to establish a bankruptcy appellate panel (abbreviated as BAP), consisting of three bankruptcy judges, to substitute for the district court as an appellate tribunal of first instance. The idea was to lift some of the workload from the district courts and to create a specialist appellate panel which would have great expertise in bankruptcy matters. The Code made it voluntary for the circuits to establish these courts, and only two — the First and Ninth Circuits — took advantage of this power. The First Circuit abolished its BAP after the *Marathon* decision because it believed that it would violate the Constitution to have only non-tenured judges involved with the case up to the first appellate level. However, the Ninth Circuit did not share this concern, and it has maintained its BAP, which has generally been regarded as a successful and valuable court. (The Supreme Court has not considered the Constitutionality of BAPs, so this issue has never been finally resolved.)

Because the Ninth Circuit experience was positive, Congress decided in 1994 to press the other circuits into using such panels. It therefore amended §158(b) to require the establishment of a BAP in every circuit unless the circuit's judicial council finds that there are insufficient judicial resources available in the circuit, or the establishment of the panel would result in undue delay or in increased cost to the parties in bankruptcy cases. The determination to have or not to have a BAP is capable of reconsideration by the judicial council at periodic intervals. It is also possible for two or more circuits to establish joint BAPs. Since 1994 several circuits have created BAPs.

Even where a circuit has a BAP, §158 imposes two restrictions on the panel's power to hear appeals. If either precondition is not satisfied, the appeal must go to the district court instead: First, under §158(b)(1) and (c)(1) all the parties to the suit must consent to the submission of the appeal to the BAP. Second under §158(b)(6) the majority of district judges in the district must have voted to authorize the BAP to hear appeals from that district. That is, the district court judges, by declining to vote to authorize appeals to the BAP in their district, can in effect veto the establishment of a BAP insofar as their district is concerned.

As noted earlier, the BAP is composed of bankruptcy judges from within the circuit. It would not be appropriate for a member of the panel to participate in deciding an appeal from the district in which she normally sits as a trial judge. Therefore, §158(b)(5) forbids any member of the panel from hearing an appeal originating from a case in her own district.

Because BAPs are made up of panels of bankruptcy judges, the constitutional infirmities of bankruptcy courts must inevitably raise questions about the powers of the BAPs. However, as a BAP hears appeals only when the district courts have authorized them and the parties have consented, constitutional issues generally do not arise. The precedential weight of decisions of the BAPs has been controversial. It is not clear if their decisions have any precedential value at all, or if they do, whether they bind bankruptcy courts only in the district from which the appeal originated, or in the circuit as a whole. Some bankruptcy courts within a BAP's circuit have considered themselves bound by all BAP decisions, but others have not. The precedential weight of BAP decisions on district courts or courts of appeal is even more dubious. It seems inconceivable that a senior Article III judge, who reviews and hears appeals from the very judges on the BAP panel, could be bound by their decision. The National Bankruptcy Review Commission noted the unsatisfactory consequences of appellate courts whose precedential value is unclear.

§7.7 Abstention

§7.7.1 Introduction

Where a court does have jurisdiction over a matter, it may decide to forgo that jurisdiction by abstaining from hearing the matter. The nature and effect of the court's abstention depends on whether the court's jurisdiction is exclusive or nonexclusive. If it has exclusive jurisdiction, no other court can hear the matter, so abstention is equivalent to dismissal (or if a temporary abstention, suspension) of the case. This form of abstention is governed by §305. If the court has nonexclusive jurisdiction, abstention leaves it open for another court to hear the case. The purpose of this kind of abstention, governed by 28 U.S.C. §1334(c), is to defer to that other court.

§7.7.2   Abstention under §305 of the Code

Section 305 concerns the bankruptcy court's abstention from the bankruptcy case. Because the bankruptcy court has exclusive jurisdiction over the case, abstention under §305 does not result in the case being taken up by another court: There is no other court in the United States with jurisdiction to hear a bankruptcy petition. Thus, the effect of abstention under §305 is the dismissal of the case or, if the court abstains temporarily, its suspension. Notice and a hearing must precede the court's decision to abstain.

There are two bases for the court's abstention under §305. The first is a general equitable ground — dismissal or suspension of the case would better serve the interests of creditors and the debtor. (For example, the court may dismiss or suspend an involuntary case initiated by uncooperative creditors because the debtor and other creditors are working together to achieve a composition.)

The second is more specific. The court may dismiss or suspend the case in deference to bankruptcy or equivalent insolvency proceedings pending in a court of a foreign country, provided that the foreign law has safeguards and protections for all parties reasonably equivalent to those provided by the Code, and reasons of efficiency and international comity favor abstention in favor of the foreign court.

§7.7.3   Abstention under 28 U.S.C. §1334(c)

As discussed in section 7.2, 28 U.S.C. §1334(b) gives the district court wide nonexclusive jurisdiction over proceedings arising under the Code or arising in or related to the bankruptcy case. This jurisdiction is then referred by the district court to the bankruptcy court. Although the court possesses this broad jurisdiction, it is not always appropriate to exercise it. Sometimes the best interests of justice dictate that related proceedings be dealt with by the state court that has concurrent jurisdiction over them. This is particularly true where the proceedings had already begun in state court before the bankruptcy was filed. Abstention under §1334(c) permits, and in some cases *requires*, the district court to defer to the state court where it is the most appropriate forum. Although §1334(c) mentions only the district court, motions to abstain are dealt with by the bankruptcy court under the general referral from the district court.

Section 1334(c) provides for two forms of abstention: *permissive absten-tion* under §1334(c)(1) and *mandatory abstention* under §1334(c)(2). Each has its own grounds:

1. Permissive abstention. In a core proceeding, a court is permitted to abstain in favor of a state court where it considers that abstention is in the interest of justice, or in the interest of comity with state courts or respect for state law.

In some core proceedings, there is no state court with jurisdiction to hear the matter because the right being adjudicated is provided by the Code. However, recall that core proceedings include matters that could only arise in the context of a bankruptcy case. These proceedings can involve issues of state law, and at the edges, they can be difficult to distinguish from related proceedings. For example, in *In re Southmark Corp.*, 163 F.3d 925 (5th Cir. 1999), the proceeding in issue involved adjudication of a malpractice claim made by the debtor in possession against accountants hired by the estate to investigate prepetition investment transactions. Although state law governed the malpractice claim, the court held it to be a core proceeding because it was generated in the course of administering the estate and could therefore, by its very nature, arise only in the context of bankruptcy. The state law basis of the claim was not dispositive, and the bankruptcy court's control over profes-sionals hired by the estate is a crucial aspect of bankruptcy administration, having a direct bearing on the distribution of the estate. In addition, the accountants' advice directly affected the assets of the estate because it influ-enced the estate's decision on asset recovery.

2. Mandatory abstention. The court is obliged to abstain when the following requirements are satisfied:

(a) A timely motion for abstention is made by a party to the proceed-ing in question.

(b) The proceeding is based on a state law claim or cause of action.

(c) The proceeding is related to the bankruptcy case, but does not arise under the Code or in the bankruptcy case. (In other words, manda-tory abstention is only required in related matters. The distinction between these categories is set out in section 7.2.)

(d) The jurisdiction of the district court is based solely on §1334. That is, there are no grounds for federal jurisdiction independent of bankruptcy (*e.g.*, diversity jurisdiction).

(e) The dominant view is that action must already have commenced in the appropriate state court. However, some courts interpret §1334 (c)(2) to apply, even if action has not yet commenced, provided that it clearly will be instituted.

(f)   The action can be timely adjudicated in the state court.

If the court determines that all these requirements are met, it must abstain from the matter. If all the requirements are not satisfied, abstention is not mandatory, but the court may nevertheless exercise its discretion to abstain under §1334(c)(1).

§7.8   Removal and Remand under 28 U.S.C. §1452

Removal may be thought of as the opposite of abstention. When a court abstains, it forgoes its jurisdiction in favor of another court. When a matter is removed, it is transferred from another court and taken up in the bankruptcy forum.

After a bankruptcy petition has been filed, a party to a related civil proceeding that is pending in another court may remove that proceeding to the bankruptcy court under §1452(a). (Again, the section refers only to the district court, but removal is to the bankruptcy court under the general referral.) A matter cannot be removed to the bankruptcy court unless it falls within the court's jurisdiction under §1334. Section 1452(a) expressly confines removal to civil matters and forbids removal of cases before the U.S. Tax Court and cases by a governmental unit to enforce its police or regulatory power.

Upon removal, the bankruptcy court is seized of the matter and can deal with it in the same way as it deals with other cases. However, the court may not necessarily keep the case after removal. Section 1452(b) allows the court to remand it back to the original court on any equitable ground. Also, the grounds for abstention in §1334(c) are applicable, so the court can abstain from a matter that is removed to it, thereby returning it to the original court. Remand may be requested by a party who objects to the removal, or may be decided upon by the court sua sponte.

§7.9   Sovereign Immunity

§7.9.1   Background and the General Principle of Sovereign Immunity

The doctrine of sovereign immunity stems from the common law principle that the monarch could not commit a wrong, and the crown could not be sued without consent in own courts by its own subjects. The concept of sovereign immunity entered American law as a basic principle of common law, precluding suit by a citizen against either state or federal government in state or federal court unless the government in question has consented to the suit, has waived the immunity, or has abrogated it by statute. With regard to federal courts, the principle of sovereign immunity was embodied in the Eleventh Amendment to the U.S. Constitution, which provides that "The judicial power of the United States shall not be construed to extend to any suit in law or equity, commenced or prosecuted against one of the United States, by citizens of another state, or by citizens or subjects of a foreign state." Although the express language of the Eleventh Amendment does not mention suits against a state by its own citizens, or suits based on federal causes of action in state courts, it is established by Supreme Court precedent that it encompasses such suits as well.

The doctrine of sovereign immunity has many complex aspects to it, but we are concerned here only with its impact on the power of bankruptcy courts (and other federal courts in bankruptcy cases) to deal with claims and suits by the debtor or the estate against either a state or the federal government. Even in this limited range, the ramifications of sovereign immunity in bankruptcy are hugely complex and nuanced. This note attempts to do no more than outline the basic principles and offer a sense of some of the complicated questions courts have had to resolve. The Bankruptcy Act of 1898 had no provision relating to the sovereign immunity of state or federal governments. This meant that bankruptcy courts were hampered in their ability to dispose of claims that the estate had against government agencies, or to render orders binding on those agencies, because the agencies could not be subjected to suit without their consent. This was inefficient and contrary to the bankruptcy goals of collective and evenhanded treatment of creditors and the debtor's fresh start. Congress therefore attempted to remedy the problem by enacting §106 in the 1978 Code.

Section 106 covers three distinct situations. First, §106(a) seeks to abrogate the sovereign immunity of governmental units, making them subject to the bankruptcy process where they have claims against the debtor or the estate has claims against them. (A "governmental unit" is widely defined in §101(27) to include a variety of foreign and domestic governmental entities. For present purposes, it encompasses both the federal and state governments, including their agencies and departments.) The essential point of §106(a) is to get rid of the sovereign immunity doctrine by abolishing it legislatively with regard to most central aspects of the bankruptcy case. Second, §106(b) codifies a principle, long recognized by judicial precedent prior to its enactment, that a state or federal governmental unit, by proving a claim against the estate, waives sovereign immunity in relation to matters arising out of that claim. This principle arises from the well-established rule that a governmental unit may waive sovereign immunity by consenting to suit, either expressly or by implication, or by initiating action in a court, thereby subjecting itself to the court's jurisdiction. Third, §106(c) provides for the setoff of claims by and against a governmental unit.

§7.9.2   *The Statutory Abrogation of Sovereign Immunity under §106(a)*

As you read this discussion of §106(a), bear in mind that it is of greatest importance where a state or federal government has not proved a claim in the estate.[1] If the governmental unit has proved a claim in the estate, §106(b) or (c) will apply and may obviate the problem of immunity that would otherwise have to be dealt with under §106(a).

As enacted in 1978, the predecessor of §106(a) (then numbered §106(c)) provided, in essence, that if a governmental unit was a creditor, it would be treated like other creditors and would be subject to all the Code provisions and all court determinations applicable to creditors generally. In this way, the Code was intended to abrogate the sovereign immunity of both the state and federal governments. At the time it was believed that Congress had the power, acting pursuant to its authority to enact uniform bankruptcy law under Article I of the U.S. Constitution, to abrogate both federal and state sovereign immunity in bankruptcy cases.

For Congress to abrogate sovereign immunity effectively, the statute must satisfy two tests. First, the intent to abrogate immunity must be clearly and unequivocally expressed. Second, Congress must be acting within its constitutional power in enacting the abrogation. In 1989 the U.S. Supreme court held that §106 failed the first test in that it did not adequately express clear Congressional intent to abrogate sovereign immunity. Congress was able to amend the statute to cure this problem, which it did in 1994. A short while later, in 1996, the U.S. Supreme court dealt a more profound blow to §106 by indicating that there were fundamental problems with the second test—Congress exceeded its power in its attempt to legislate a wide abrogation of sovereign immunity.

In *Hoffman v. Connecticut Dept. of Income Maintenance*, 492 U.S. 96 (1989), the court held that the original version of §106(a) (former §106(c)) did not adequately express Congressional intent to abrogate sovereign immunity. In response, Congress amended §106 in 1994 to articulate the abrogation unequivocally. It eliminated the vague language that said that

---

1. Proof of claim is discussed in Section 19.4. In essence, it is the submission of a claim in the estate by a creditor that will allow that creditor to participate in any distribution from the estate. There are a number of reasons why a governmental unit may not prove a claim in the estate. For example, the government may not be a creditor of the estate, but may instead owe the estate money or some obligation. Even if the government is a creditor, there are a number of reasons why it may not file a claim. For example, in a Ch. 11 case it is not usually required to file a claim to be included as a creditor in the estate. In a Ch. 7 or 13 case, where it must file a claim to participate in the distribution from the estate, it may choose not to file a claim because there is no prospect of distribution, or because the government does not wish to compromise its immunity.

government units were to be treated as creditors, notwithstanding any assertion of sovereign immunity, and substituted the current §106(a)(1) that specifically abrogates sovereign immunity as to governmental units with regard to proceedings under numerous listed provisions of the Code. The list of sections includes most proceedings that arise under the Code, and are integral to the bankruptcy case and to the bankruptcy court's power to deal with rights and obligations created by the Code. Section 106(a)(2) authorizes the court to hear and determine any issue under those sections in proceedings involving a governmental unit, and §106(a)(3) permits the court to issue orders and judgments against a governmental unit. As noted earlier, §106(a) is intended to apply to any action to enforce the estate or debtor's rights under the enumerated sections, irrespective of whether the governmental unit is a creditor of the debtor or has filed a claim in the estate.

As mentioned above, when §106 was enacted, Congress believed that it had the power to abrogate the sovereign immunity of both the federal government and state governments by virtue of its power over bankruptcy under Article I. However, this impression was dispelled by the U.S. Supreme Court in *Seminole Tribe of Florida v. Florida*, 517 U.S. 44 (1996). The case did not involve bankruptcy, but concerned Congress' power to regulate commerce with the Indian tribes (the Indian Commerce Clause), another power granted to Congress under Article I. The court held that Congress did not have the power under the Indian Commerce Clause to abrogate the states' sovereign immunity. Passages in both the majority and dissenting opinions in *Seminole Tribe* indicate that the Supreme Court considered that its decision would cover other powers granted to Congress under Article I. Shortly after deciding *Seminole Tribe*, the Supreme Court again signaled that this is indeed what it had in mind. In *In re Merchants Grain, Inc.*, 59 F.3d 630 (7th Cir. 1995), the Seventh Circuit Court of Appeals held that §106(a) was a valid abrogation of state immunity. On appeal, the Supreme Court vacated the judgment without comment and remanded the case for reconsideration in light of *Seminole Tribe*. (*In re Merchants Grain, Inc.*, 59 F.3d 630 (7th Cir. 1995), *vacated sub. nom. Ohio Agricultural Commodity Depositors Fund v. Mahern*, 517 U.S. 1130 (1996).) Since *Seminole Tribe*, most courts, including several courts of appeal, have accepted that the Supreme Court's holding applies equally to all Article I powers, including the power to enact bankruptcy law. However, a minority of courts, including the Sixth Circuit Court of Appeals in *In re Hood*, 319 F.3d 755 (6th Cir. 2003), have disagreed, and have held that *Seminole Tribe* is not applicable to the bankruptcy power in Article I and therefore does not affect §106(a). Their reasoning, based on an analysis of Constitutional history, is that there is an important distinction between the bankruptcy power in Article I and the Indian Commerce Clause: When the states agreed to confer power on Congress to enact a uniform law of bankruptcy, they ceded their sovereign immunity with regard to litigation arising out of bankruptcy law.

Therefore, in the view of most courts, *Seminole Tribe* invalidated the abrogation of sovereign immunity in §106(a) as against states insofar as it infringes their Eleventh Amendment protection from suit. It must be stressed that the problem arising from *Seminole Tribe* applies only to state government. Congress clearly does have the power to abrogate the sovereign immunity of the federal government, so §106(a) is effective in relation to proceedings against a unit of the federal government. (See Example 3(a).) In addition, the Eleventh Amendment covers only states, so it does not immunize local and municipal governments from suit, provided that the suit does not implicate the state or its resources. That is, a local government is not protected by the Eleventh Amendment if it is autonomous and not merely an agent of the state, and the suit does not create any state responsibility under the order or judgment.

Even with regard to state governments, the precise impact of *Seminole Tribe* on §106(a) is uncertain, and many courts have held that state governments are not entirely impervious to the orders and processes covered by the section. As a general matter, states are subject to bankruptcy law by virtue of the Supremacy Clause (U.S. Const. art VI, cl.2.) and are bound to take cognizance of bankruptcy proceedings except to the extent that the Eleventh Amendment shields them from the power of the federal courts. The Eleventh Amendment refers only to "suits in law or equity," so if an order or judgment of a federal court in a bankruptcy matter does not amount to a legal or equitable suit against a state, the state is not immune from it. Courts have struggled with the scope of what is meant by a "suit." *In re NVR LP*, 189 F.3d 442 (4th Cir. 1999), provides guidance on the distinction, based on the court's survey of extensive judicial precedent. A suit involves the commencement of litigation against the state, in which the plaintiff seeks to obtain something to which he has a legal right. The state must be named as a defendant and must be served with a process that mandates it to appear in court. However, if legal proceedings merely implicate the state's rights, but do not require it to participate in the litigation (even though it may have the right to join the action), the proceedings do not qualify as a suit.

It is quite easy to identify a matter as a suit if the complaint or process summons the state to court to defend a claim for a money judgment against the state. However, even if no money judgment is claimed, a proceeding nevertheless qualifies as a suit if the process obliges, rather than invites, the state to appear in court. This distinction is crucial because in the course of a bankruptcy case, the court may issue many orders that are required for the orderly management and disposition of the estate and that emanate from the court's jurisdiction over the bankruptcy case. These orders are not directed against a particular creditor, but they inevitably must effect the rights of creditors. Creditors have standing to participate in hearings relating to these orders, but they are not compelled to do so. These orders do not constitute suits against a creditor state, so the state is not immune from the legal effects of such orders. A few examples illustrate this type of order: The bankruptcy petition itself is not a suit against a creditor state. Although the petition will impact the state's right to recover the debt, it is not directed against the state, and the state is not compelled to appear in court to defend against it. In a case under Ch. 11 or 13, the court makes an order confirming a plan, which binds creditors generally. (Plan confirmation is discussed in Chapters 20 and 21.) However, this does not qualify as a suit because creditors are not required to appear in court. The same is true of a court order granting the debtor a discharge. (Discharge is discussed in Chapter 22.) In addition to orders of this kind, a state is also bound by the consequences of bankruptcy that occur automatically, without the need for a court order. For example, the collection rights of a creditor state are affected by the automatic stay that arises as soon as the petition is filed, but the stay is not a suit because it does not involve the filing of any process against the state. (The stay is discussed in Chapter 10).

By contrast, there are a number of proceedings in a bankruptcy case that are directed against a particular creditor, and that take the form of adversarial proceedings (whether by motion or suit) against that creditor. If the creditor in question is a state, such proceedings are barred by the state's sovereign immunity. For example, payments made by the debtor to a state just before bankruptcy may qualify as avoidable preferences (discussed in Chapter 16). A proceeding instituted by the trustee against the state to recover the preference is directed specifically against the state and seeks a judgment against the state, so it is a suit. Similarly, if the trustee contends that the state owes money or property to the estate, a proceeding to obtain the money or property is a suit.

This distinction is coherent up to a point, but it presents a difficult conundrum: Some bankruptcy processes are not suits, so they are not precluded by sovereign immunity and they bind the state. However, if the state disregards them, any effort to compel the state to comply with them must be made by a court process directed against the state that does constitute a suit subject to the Eleventh Amendment. As a result, the actual enforcement of any order or process against a non-consenting state is problematical. For example, even though the state is bound by the automatic stay, if it ignores the stay the debtor or trustee cannot commence a proceeding against the state to order compliance or to hold it liable for damages. Similarly, if the state disregards the discharge, the debtor cannot commence suit to enjoin the violation or hold the state liable for damages. Courts have struggled with this incongruity since *Seminole Tribe*. In many cases, the end result is that the court is hamstrung in enforcing its order unless the state has itself initiated a suit to collect the debt or to enforce the debtor's or estate's duty affected by the order. (See Example 3(b).) Once the state itself invokes the jurisdiction of the court, the bar of sovereign immunity falls away with regard to any defense or counterclaim to the state's suit. For example, in *Texas v. Walker*, 142 F.3d 813 (5th Cir. 1998), the debtor obtained a discharge in a Ch. 7 case. After the case was closed, the state sued him for a debt that was arguably covered by the discharge. When he raised the discharge as a defense, the state contended that as it never filed a proof of claim in the bankruptcy case, it was not bound by the discharge by virtue of its sovereign immunity. The court held that the discharge order in the prior bankruptcy case was not a suit against the state because it did not involve any process directed against the state or compelling it to appear in court. Therefore, sovereign immunity did not apply to the discharge order, which had a binding effect on the state. The debtor could not have sued the state to enforce the order, but as the state had initiated suit to collect the debt, the debtor could raise the discharge as a defense to that suit. (Although the court held that the discharge could be asserted as a defense, there was some question of whether the debt in question may have been excluded from the discharge, so the case was remanded for final determination on that issue.)

In some situations, the difficulty of enforcing a bankruptcy court order against a state may be ameliorated by a doctrine established in an early U.S. Supreme Court case, *Ex parte Young*, 209 U.S. 123 (1908). The doctrine distinguishes suits against the government from suits against a state official to enjoin continuing violations of federal law. The doctrine holds that although the state itself is immune from suit, that immunity does not extend to a state official who is acting in violation of federal law. Because a state cannot authorize its officers to violate federal law, the official is deemed to be acting on his own and sovereign immunity is not implicated. The *Ex Parte Young* doctrine only allows injunctions to restrain prospective conduct. It can therefore be used by a bankruptcy court to enjoin certain prospective actions by state officials, such as actions in violation of the automatic stay or activity in disregard of the discharge. However, because the doctrine can only be used where there is a state official acting in continuing violation of federal law, and the only remedy that it contemplates is injunctive relief, it has its limits. It is not even clear that the *Ex Parte Young* doctrine survived *Seminole Tribe* because a passage in *Seminole Tribe* hints that Congress, in enacting the Code, may have eliminated remedies not contained in the Code's remedial scheme. However, several courts have applied the doctrine in the years since *Seminole Tribe*. (For a discussion of these cases, see *In re Claxton*, 273 B.R. 174 (Bankr. N.D. Ill. 2002). See also Example 3(b).)

§7.9.3 *Waiver of Sovereign Immunity by Consent and by the Filing of a Proof of Claim under §106(b)*

Seminole Tribe was concerned with the abrogation of state sovereign immunity by Congress. Congressional abrogation of immunity by statute must be distinguished from waiver of immunity by the governmental unit that is party to the proceedings. It is a well-established principle that even where Congress cannot itself legislate to abrogate sovereign immunity, a state government can waive sovereign immunity by consenting to suit. (The same is true of the federal government in areas not covered by the abrogation in §106(a), which, as noted above, is valid as regards units of the federal government.) If this waiver is voluntary and expressed clearly and unequivocally, no constitutional problem arises. The government has given up its immunity and cannot invoke the Eleventh Amendment. However, the case is more difficult if the government action falls short of clear and express consent and must be inferred from conduct. Courts formerly recognized a doctrine of constructive waiver, under which a government could be taken to have waived immunity by participating in a federal program or federally regulated activity, or even by engaging in interstate commerce. However, in *College Savings Bank v. Florida Prepaid Postsecondary Education Expense Board*, 527 U.S. 666 (1999), (a case involving trademark legislation, not bankruptcy law) the court rejected the constructive waiver doctrine. A constructive waiver (in essence, a waiver deemed as a matter of law) is not dependent on the state's voluntary decision to waive its immunity, but is based on Congress' decision to infer waiver from a state's decision (albeit voluntary) to engage in certain activity. This comes too close to the involuntary abrogation that Congress unsuccessfully attempted in §106(a). Therefore, a waiver must be actually established on the facts. However, this does not mean that the waiver has to be express. Long-established caselaw recognizes that a waiver can be implied.

The most common form of implied waiver arises out of a governmental unit's voluntary invocation of the jurisdiction of the federal court. Therefore, if a governmental unit institutes suit in federal court, it implicitly waives sovereign immunity with regard to any claims that the estate may have against it arising out of the same transaction or occurrence on which the government's suit is based. Such counterclaims are called "compulsory counterclaims" in the Federal Rules of Civil Procedure. In the bankruptcy context, long before the enactment of the Code, it had been established by the U.S. Supreme Court that a governmental unit invokes the jurisdiction of the bankruptcy court if it files a proof of claim in a bankrupt estate. This constitutes an implied waiver of sovereign immunity with regard to any claims or defenses pertaining to the allowance of its claim. This principle forms the basis of §106(b), which states that "a governmental unit that has filed a proof of claim in the case is deemed to have waived sovereign immunity with respect to a claim against such governmental unit that is property of the estate and that arose out of the same transaction or occurrence out of which the claim of such governmental unit arose."

Because Congress anticipated that §106(a) would apply to proceedings under all the specified Code sections, it intended §106(b) to be relevant only where the matter in question was not covered by §106(a). That is, it was intended to be used where the claim against the government did not qualify for statutory abrogation, but arose from a transaction or event in respect of which the governmental unit had submitted to the bankruptcy court's power by proving a claim. Because *Seminole Tribe* gutted §106(a) in relation to state government, §106(b) assumes greater importance with regard to state governmental units. It is usually the only basis for avoiding a state assertion of immunity. However, because the federal government is subject to abrogation under §106(a), subsection (b) is needed only for those suits and proceedings against the federal government that are not covered by the Code sections enumerated in §106(a).

It seems clear, even in light of *Seminole Tribe*, that if a governmental unit proves a claim in the estate, it is taken to waive sovereign immunity with regard to any compulsory counterclaim by the estate that arises from the same transaction as its claim. However, the possible range of §106(b), and especially the meaning of the word "deemed," is circumscribed by *Seminole Tribe* and *College Savings Bank*. Because Congress does not have the power to abrogate state immunity or to recognize a constructive waiver, it cannot "deem" a proof of claim to constitute a waiver of anything beyond the narrow range of a compulsory counterclaim. Therefore, §106(b) is constitutional only to the extent that it is narrowly construed to include only those proceedings against the state that qualify as compulsory counterclaims. (See *In re Jackson*, 184 F.3d 1046 (9th Cir. 1999); *Arecibo Community Health Care v. Commonwealth of Puerto Rico*, 270 F.3d 17 (1st Cir. 2001). In *Arecibo*, the First Circuit Court of Appeals initially held that §106(b) was unconstitutional because it constituted a constructive waiver. However, on rehearing, the court reversed itself and held that §106(b) is constitutional because it gives rise only to a partial waiver. By proving a claim the state avails itself of the jurisdiction of the court only to the extent of any counterclaims by the estate arising out of the same transaction or occurrence.)

Some cases have further limited the constitutionally permissible scope of §106(b) by confining its validity to claims against the very government agency that filed the proof of claim so that the estate cannot assert a counterclaim based on a debt due by another agency of the same government. Some courts have limited §106(b) to defensive counterclaims (that is, those that merely raise a defense to payment by the estate, reducing or eliminating the estate's debt to the government). These courts hold that §106(b) cannot be used to allow a money recovery by the estate where the debt owed by the state exceeds the estate's debt to the state. Other courts (for example, *Arecibo*, above) have disagreed, holding that as long as the counterclaim does qualify as a compulsory counterclaim, it may extend to affirmative recovery.

The waiver recognized by §106(b) ameliorates the sovereign immunity doctrine to some extent by subjecting a creditor state to the power of the bankruptcy court in many cases. However, §106(b) has obvious limits. It does not help where the creditor state chooses not to prove a claim in the estate, which it may decline to do if it values its immunity more than the prospective payment that it may derive from the bankruptcy. Even if it does prove a claim, the waiver relates only to counterclaims that arise from the same transaction or occurrence as the claim. (See Example 3(c).)

§7.9.4 Setoff of Claims by and against a Governmental Unit under §106(c)

Section 106(c) provides that any claim that the estate may have against a governmental unit may be offset against a claim that the governmental unit has against the state. Under general principles of law, where two parties are mutually indebted, the debts may be set off against each other so that no payment exchanges hands except to the extent that one of the debts is larger than the other. Setoff rights arise in bankruptcy where a creditor of the estate is also a debtor of the estate. As a general rule, provided that the creation of the mutual debts is legitimate, the Code recognizes setoff rights under state law and permits a creditor to deduct the full amount of his debt to the estate from his claim. The setoff rights of creditors are dealt with in §553, which is discussed in section 16.2.

Where a government is the creditor, the setoff right is complicated by the state's sovereign immunity. If the estate is barred from enforcing its claim against the government, this could mean that the government could assert its claim against the estate, but cannot be made to pay its debt to the estate. The simple purpose of §106(c) is to overcome this obstacle to setoff by providing that an assertion of sovereign immunity does not preclude the setoff between the government's claim and a claim that is property of the estate. Although §106(c) does not express the prerequisite that the government prove a claim against the estate, this is a condition of the setoff. Unlike counterclaims under §106(b), the government debt set off under §106(c) need not arise from the same transaction or occurrence as the government's claim. Section 106(c) does not contemplate affirmative recovery by the estate. That is, the right of setoff is confined to the reduction of the government's claim. If the estate's claim against the government is larger than the government's claim, the estate cannot obtain an affirmative recovery under §106(c). Because §106(c) does not implicate a suit against a state, but is confined to reduction of the debt due by the estate to a state, it does not give rise to constitutional problems. The operation of setoff under §106(c) is illustrated by *In re Microage Corp.* 288 B.R. 842 (Bankr. D. Ariz. 2003). The state proved a claim against the estate for taxes. During the course of the claim allowance process, the estate claimed a tax refund under a different and unrelated program set up by the state. As a result, the estate's refund claim did not qualify as a counterclaim arising out of the same transaction or occurrence as required by §106(b). However, the court held that this did not bar setoff under §106(c) because the estate simply sought to reduce the debt to the state and did not claim an affirmative recovery. (See Example 3(c).)

EXAMPLES

1. Forum Follows Function

Julie Dixon resides in State *A*, where she owns and operates a retail store. Her business has done poorly over the last couple of years and she has fallen behind on her payments to creditors. Her credit has been cut off, and she does not have the cash to buy any more inventory. A number of Julie's creditors have decided to file a petition to place her in involuntary Ch. 7 bankruptcy.

Each of the controversies described below has arisen or will arise either in connection with the bankruptcy case itself or in relation to Julie's affairs. Consider whether or not the federal district court in State *A* (referred to in this Example as "the court") has jurisdiction over each of them in terms of §§1334(a), (b), or (d). (Do not consider bankruptcy court jurisdiction under §157. This is dealt with in Example 2.)

(a) Does the court have jurisdiction to hear the petition and to grant an order adjudicating Julie bankrupt?

(b) About a year before her bankruptcy, Julie purchased some new display cases on credit for her store and gave the seller a security interest in the display cases to secure their price. Because she defaulted on the installments, the seller repossessed the display cases a few weeks prior to the filing of the petition. The seller scheduled a foreclosure sale, but was prevented from proceeding with it because the filing of the bankruptcy petition automatically stays all actions by creditors to enforce a lien against property of the estate or the debtor. Under §362, the creditor may apply to court for relief from this stay if grounds for relief are present. (*See* Chapters 10 and 11.) Does the court have jurisdiction to hear and determine the application for relief from stay?

(c) A few weeks before the petition was filed, Julie, sensing the impending onslaught, repaid to her brother an unsecured loan of $5,000. Although the loan was not yet repayable, Julie was concerned that if she did not repay it immediately, her other creditors would pounce on her assets and leave her insufficient funds to settle her brother's loan. This preferential transfer is avoidable by Julie's trustee under §547. (*See* Chapter 16.) Does the court have jurisdiction over the trustee's avoidance suit against Julie's brother?

(d) Prior to bankruptcy, Julie bought some inventory from one of her suppliers. When the inventory was delivered, Julie protested that it was defective and demanded a price reduction. The supplier refused. At the time of Julie's bankruptcy, this dispute has still not been resolved. The supplier has proved a claim for the sale price of the goods, and the trustee has objected to it. Does the court have jurisdiction to resolve this dispute?

(e) A few months before bankruptcy, Julie obtained a loan from a finance company. Because the finance company was concerned about her credit, it insisted that she find a surety to guarantee her debt. Julie's sister undertook the suretyship obligation. When Julie became bankrupt, the finance company decided to sue the surety for payment of the debt. Does the court have jurisdiction to deal with the suit between the finance company and the surety?

(f) About a year before Julie's bankruptcy, one of her employees was involved in a collision while making a delivery for her in his own car. The driver of the other vehicle was badly injured and is claiming substantial damages from Julie's employee. Julie's employee is insured, and his insurer is handling the claim on his behalf. There is a dispute about which of the drivers is to blame for the collision. If Julie's employee is found to be at fault, there is a chance that his liability to the other driver will exceed his insurance coverage, and that the other driver will seek to claim the balance from the estate on the theory that the injury was caused by the employee in the course of his employment. Does the court have jurisdiction to hear the suit between the injured driver and Julie's employee?

(g) Shortly before bankruptcy, Julie had sold goods to a buyer who resides in State X, located some 2,000 miles from State A. The transaction was conducted through the mail, and the buyer has never set foot in State A. The buyer mailed a check to Julie in payment for the goods, but the check bounced. Does the court have jurisdiction to deal with the trustee's suit against the buyer on the check?

(h) A year or so before her bankruptcy, Julie bought a computer on credit. The seller retained a security interest in it to secure the unpaid balance of the price. The security interest is valid and unavoidable, and the debt to the seller exceeds the value of the computer. The trustee therefore abandoned it to the seller under §554. (As discussed in section 12.4, §554 permits the trustee to abandon estate property if the debtor has no equity in it and the property is of no value to the estate.)

After recovering the computer from the trustee, the seller refurbished it and fraudulently sold it as new. Upon discovering this, the buyer demanded cancellation of the sale and return of the price. Does the court have jurisdiction over the suit between the buyer and seller?

2. Esprit de Core

Decide whether the controversies described in Example 1 are core or noncore proceedings. In answering the question, consider the general guidelines identified in section 7.3.6 as well as the nonexhaustive list provided by §157(b)(2). For convenience, the proceedings referred to in Example 1 are summarized here:

(a) The bankruptcy petition.
(b) The secured party's application for relief from stay.
(c) The trustee's suit to avoid a preferential transfer.
(d) A seller's claim for sale price of goods, challenged by the trustee on the grounds that the goods were defective.

(e) A creditor's suit against a debtor's surety.

(f) The tort claim against Julie's employee.

(g) The trustee's suit against the drawer of a dishonored check drawn in favor of the debtor.

(h) A suit between the buyer of a computer and the seller, to whom the computer had been abandoned by the estate.

3. Immune Deficiency

Sophie Wren filed a Ch. 7 bankruptcy petition. In her schedule of liabilities, she listed back taxes due to the federal government. Although (as you will see in sections 19.6.4 and 22.5.4) certain tax debts are given priority and are non-dischargeable, these back taxes were owed for a period for some years before bankruptcy, and they were too old to qualify for priority or for exclusion from the discharge. Another debt listed in Sophie's schedule was a debt of $10,000 owing to the state Department of Economic Development for licence and permit fees, incurred in connection with a failed land development project in which Sophie had been engaged. Both these claims were general unsecured claims. There were no funds in Sophie's Ch. 7 estate to pay general unsecured claims. During the course of the Ch. 7 case, the court granted Sophie a discharge.

(a) The I.R.S., realizing that the estate would make no distribution to general unsecured creditors, did not prove a claim in Sophie's Ch. 7 case. Shortly after the case was closed, the I.R.S. wrote a letter to Sophie demanding payment of the back taxes. Sophie moved to reopen the bankruptcy case and filed suit against the I.R.S., seeking an order enjoining the I.R.S. from seeking to collect them. May the I.R.S. resist the suit on the grounds of sovereign immunity?

(b) Like the I.R.S., the state Department of Economic Development did not prove a claim in Sophie's Ch. 7 case. After the case was closed, it wrote to her, demanding payment of the licence and permit fees. May Sophie obtain an injunction from the bankruptcy court, prohibiting the state Department of Economic Development from attempting to collect the debt?

(c) Change the facts relating to the state's claim as follows: A month before her bankruptcy, Sophie's car was involved in a collision with a van owned by the state Department of Forestry. The van was driven by an employee of the forestry department on official business, and it is clear that the accident was caused by his negligence. The cost of repairing Sophie's car is $4,000. At the time of her bankruptcy, she had claimed the cost of repair from the state, but the state had not yet responded to her claim.

The state Department of Economic Development proved a claim in the estate for $10,000 in respect of the licence and permit fees. The trustee would like to recover the tort claim of $4,000 from the state. If the state refuses to pay the tort claim, will the trustee's enforcement rights be affected by sovereign immunity?

EXPLANATIONS

1. **(a)** The petition, the consequent hearing, and the order for relief are the "case under Title 11" (*i.e.*, the bankruptcy case) over which the court has exclusive jurisdiction under §1334(a).

(b) Even though this application for relief from stay is intimately connected with the bankruptcy case, it is not the "case under Title 11" referred to in §1334(a). However, it is a "civil proceeding arising under Title 11" over which the court has jurisdiction in terms of §1334(b).

In the clearest case, a matter arises under title 11 when the proceeding in question arises from the provisions of the Code itself and the right asserted owes its existence to the Code. In other words, if the proceedings would not exist under nonbankruptcy law and there would be no cause of action in the absence of the Code, they arise under it. A proceeding may arguably also arise under the Code and qualify as a core proceeding if it involves an issue so linked to the Code that the provisions of the Code are determinative of it, and the issue would not have arisen or would have been decided on a different basis under nonbankruptcy law. Such proceedings are called *core proceedings*. See Section 7.3.5.

Note that §1334(b) gives the court original but not exclusive jurisdiction over these matters arising under the Code, so it seems to contemplate that some of them might be entertained by other courts. Nevertheless, it is hard to imagine that matters so intimately connected with the bankruptcy case could or should be dealt with in other courts. This issue is not likely to come up very often, because other courts would not normally be motivated to adjudicate such matters and, in any event, §1334 does not confer jurisdiction on them to do so — it merely provides for the district court's bankruptcy jurisdiction.

(c) The trustee's right to avoid the transfer owes its existence to §547. However, the avoidance suit requires the determination of rights created by nonbankruptcy law. Therefore, even though the suit does arise under the Code, the presence of nonbankruptcy issues places it in the category of related proceedings. This makes no difference to the applicability of §1334(b), which covers both categories. However, it does have an impact on bankruptcy court jurisdiction under §157, as discussed in section 7.3.

(d) The dispute in this question involves issues of state law: the rights of a seller and buyer under UCC Article 2. Had Julie not become bankrupt, the case would have been resolved in a state court. However, as she is bankrupt, the seller must claim against her estate, and the trustee succeeds to her defense. The outcome of the case will have an impact on the estate, because it will affect the size of the seller's claim against the estate.

Although the claim and objection procedure are provided for by the Code, the substantive rights do not arise under the Code. Rather, they are related to the bankruptcy case. Such related proceedings also fall within the court's jurisdiction under §1334(b). As in question (c), it makes no difference for the purpose of district court jurisdiction whether the litigation arises under the Code or is related to the case because both categories are covered by §1334(b). However, this difference is significant with regard to the bankruptcy court's jurisdiction over them, as discussed in section 7.3.

Where the impact on the estate is as clear as this — the related litigation actually involves the estate — the outcome binds it and affects the distribution to creditors. There is, therefore, no difficulty in seeing that the litigation is related to the bankruptcy case. However, matters are considerably more difficult where the impact of the proceeding is less direct and obvious — as discussed in questions (e) and (f).

(e) Like the sales dispute in question (d), the suit between the finance company and the surety involves issues of state law that exist in the absence of bankruptcy and would normally be resolved by a state court. Therefore the suit against the surety certainly does not arise under the Code. The question is whether the suit is related to the bankruptcy case so that the court has jurisdiction over it. The fact that the estate is not a party to the suit is a strong indicator that the suit is not related to the bankruptcy case. However, this is not conclusive. Even though the estate is not a party, a suit between outsiders can have enough connection with and impact on the estate to be related to the bankruptcy case.

Where the litigation does not involve the estate directly, the widely accepted test, annunciated in *Pacor, Inc.* and approved in general terms by the Supreme Court in *Celotex Corp.* (both cases are cited in section 7.2.2) is that the outcome of the proceeding must have some conceivable effect on the bankruptcy case, altering the rights, liabilities, freedom of action, or options of the debtor, or affecting the handling or administration of the estate. Although some courts have been willing to think of conceivable impact in broad terms, the prevailing view is to require a convincing demonstration that the litigation will likely have a direct, non-speculative, and measurable legal or economic consequence on the estate. This impact is a factual question to be determined by analyzing the effect of the litigation.

If the finance company wins the suit and is paid by the surety, the impact on the estate is a substitution of creditors. The finance company falls away as a creditor, and the surety, who has a right of recourse against the debtor, becomes a creditor in the estate. If this is all that happens, there is no real impact on the estate. Its liabilities are unaltered. However, the litigation between the surety and finance company could do more than simply determine the identity of the creditor. The case could determine the validity of the debt or could fix the amount of the claim. If so, the impact on the estate could be significant.

Therefore, if the extent and validity of the debt is in issue in the case, the litigation would surely satisfy the test of relatedness — its outcome would have a measurable and preclusive effect on the estate's liability to the surety. In *In re Brentano's* 27 B.R. 90 (Bankr. S.D.N.Y. 1983) the court found that an action between a creditor and surety had enough of a relationship to the bankruptcy case to fall within the court's jurisdiction. This view was cited with approval in *Pacor Inc.*

In re Canion, 196 F.3d 579 (5th Cir. 1999), provides another interesting illustration of litigation that has a conceivable effect on the bankruptcy case. Before the debtor filed a Ch. 7 petition, the creditor obtained judgment against him for breach of contract. A short time after the petition, the creditor sued a number of associates of the debtor in the bankruptcy court, alleging that they had conspired with the debtor before bankruptcy to secrete assets and to frustrate the creditor's collection efforts. The suit was based on various theories, including tort, fraudulent transfer, and equitable piercing. After the creditor lost the case in bankruptcy court, he asserted that the judgment was of no effect because the bankruptcy court lacked jurisdiction. (Although it may seem odd that the creditor would be able to challenge the jurisdiction of a court in which he chose to commence suit, the court of appeals noted the subject matter jurisdiction of the court is so fundamental that it can be challenged even under these circumstances and at this stage.) The creditor argued that his suits against the debtor's associates were not related to the bankruptcy because even if he obtained judgment against and was paid by the associates, they would simply subrogate to his claim against the debtor. The effect would be nothing more that a substitution of creditors, which would not impact the estate. The court disagreed. Subrogation is an equitable remedy, and a court of equity may decline to allow it to persons who have themselves behaved inequitably by colluding with the debtor to secrete assets and impair the creditor's collection efforts. Therefore, if the creditor could collect from the associates, they may not be able to assert claims against the debtor. As a result, the effect of the suit against the associates could be to reduce the estate's debt. Because the litigation could have the conceivable effect of reducing the estate's liability to the creditor, it is a related matter.

(f) This situation is similar to that in question (e) in that any litigation between the third parties — the other driver and the employee — could have a conceivable impact on the estate: If the employee is found to have been negligent and his insurance does not cover the full extent of his liability, the injured driver may assert a claim against the estate. However, the likelihood of impact is more remote than in question (e). In that question, the estate's obligation to reimburse the surety is clearly established as an incident of the suretyship obligation. By contrast, the estate's possible exposure to liability in this case is contingent, not only on the employee being found to have been negligent, but also on his insurance coverage (and his own assets) being inadequate, and the plaintiff establishing a basis for employer liability in tort law. This connection may be too speculative to satisfy the stricter reading of *Pacor, Inc.* In fact, *Pacor, Inc.* itself involved an indemnity claim which the court found to be insufficiently related to the bankruptcy case because the disposition of the litigation would not have bound the estate as potential indemnitor and it was not even clear that the estate would be legally obliged to indemnify for the loss.

(g) The drawer of the check is the debtor's debtor. He resides in State *X*, remote from State *A* in which the court sits. In addition, many essential elements of the transaction occurred in State *X*. Nevertheless, the court's jurisdiction to hear the action on the check is not dependent upon the defendant's presence in State *A* nor on any concept of minimum contacts. Instead, it arises out of §1334, and the court has jurisdiction over this action because it arises in or is related to the bankruptcy case. *See In re Whippany Paper Board, Inc.,* 15 B.R. 312 (Bankr. N.J. 1981).

Although the check is property of the estate under §541 (see Chapter 12), the court's jurisdiction over the check derives from §1334(b). Its jurisdiction does not arise from §1334(e), which cannot be used as an alternative basis of jurisdiction. Section 1334(e) applies only to disputes that relate to the debtor's or estate's rights in property. There is no issue in this case concerning the estate's right to the check. The estate's claim is simply for payment of money due in terms of the check.

(h) This controversy is very remote from the bankruptcy case. The computer has been abandoned and the dispute between the seller and the new buyer has no relevance to the estate. The matter is not related to the bankruptcy case as required by §1334(b). The court has no jurisdiction over it.

For some examples of cases that have found nonbankruptcy litigation to be unrelated to the bankruptcy case and outside the court's jurisdiction, see *In re Hall's Motor Transit Co.,* 889 F.2d 520 (3d Cir. 1989) (where real property sold by the estate was rezoned after sale, the court had no jurisdiction to adjudicate the dispute between the buyer and the local authority concerning the zoning, because the dispute had no impact on the bankruptcy case); *In re Alexander,* 13 Bankr. Ct. Dec. (CCR) 47 (Bankr. N. Dak. 1985) (the court had no jurisdiction over a priority suit between two secured parties relating to property abandoned to the debtor as exempt); *National City Bank v. Coopers & Lybrand,* 802 F.2d 990 (8th Cir. 1986) (the court had no jurisdiction to hear a creditor's malpractice suit against accountants based upon work done in connection with a bankrupt company). In each of these cases, there is some relationship between the litigation and the bankruptcy case, but it is not strong enough to justify an exercise of jurisdiction by the court. The outcome will have no discernable impact on the case.

2. **(a)** The bankruptcy petition is the case under title 11. It may be heard and finally disposed of by the bankruptcy court under §157(b)(1).

(b) The application for relief from stay is specifically identified in §157(b)(2)(G) as a core proceeding. It is correctly so listed. Because the stay is created by the Code and the proceedings would not exist in the absence of the Code, Congress has the power to permit them to be finally adjudicated by a nontenured judge. The bankruptcy court can make a final order reviewable by the district court only on appeal.

(c) The trustee's suit to avoid the transfer is also specifically listed as a core proceeding in §157(b)(2)(F). However, this is one of the areas in which Congress may have overstepped its authority in identifying core proceedings in §157(b)(2). If a matter is not directly related to the adjudication of rights granted by the Code, Congress cannot, simply by listing it, make it a core proceeding.

The avoidance of preferential transfers is dealt with in Chapter 16. As explained there, the power to avoid preferences is conferred on the trustee by the Code and does not exist outside of bankruptcy. On this basis, there is some argument for treating it as a core proceeding. However, the avoidance power is also tied up with the rights of the transferee under nonbankruptcy law, and litigation concerning the avoidance of a preferential transfer involves adjudication of these private rights. This may take the avoidance suit out of the core.

This issue was raised by the Supreme Court in relation to a fraudulent transfer in *Granfinanciera, S.A. v. Nordberg*, 491 U.S. 33 (1989). The Court was not directly concerned with the legitimacy of the listings in §157(2). The focus of the case was whether the defendant was entitled to a jury trial in a trustee's suit to avoid a fraudulent transfer. Although §157(b)(2)(h) treats the avoidance of a fraudulent transfer as a core proceeding, and although the trustee was asserting the avoidance power provided by §548, the court characterized the avoidance suit as a matter of private right — a quintessentially common law suit clearly within the protection of Article III.

Should the same analysis apply to a suit to avoid a preferential transfer? There is an important difference between suits to avoid fraudulent transfers, which have been available to creditors outside of bankruptcy for centuries, and suits to avoid preferential transfers, which are inherently a bankruptcy remedy, and could therefore be treated as solely a creature of the Code. (Even prior to the enactment of a uniform bankruptcy law, preference suits were always connected to some sort of bankruptcy process, and, unlike fraudulent transfer suits, were never available as a general creditors' suit. They serve the bankruptcy goal of evenhanded treatment of creditors, which is not an aim of nonbankruptcy law.) This would suggest that although Congress erred in including suits to avoid fraudulent transfers in §157(b)(2), it was correct in characterizing preference avoidance suits as within the core — after all, such suits could not exist outside of bankruptcy.

Granfinanciera and *Langenkamp v. Culp*, 498 U.S. 42 (1990) make it clear that a suit to avoid a preference is a legal claim which would give rise to a right to a jury trial. However, characterizing it as legal, rather than equitable, is not tantamount to saying that it is thereby necessarily non-core. Although many core proceedings are equitable, it is possible to have a core proceeding that is legal in nature. Therefore, the determination of whether the suit falls within the core of bankruptcy has to be decided on the "public rights" analysis expounded by the Supreme Court. It is not clear how a preference suit should be classified. As intimated earlier, the trustee's right to avoid a preference is based on a combination of Code and nonbankruptcy principles, and the adjudication of the latter are an integral part of the avoidance suit. However, this, of itself, does not conclusively mean that the matter is non-core. If the source of the right is the Code, it seems appropriate to treat the matter as a core proceeding, even though nonbankruptcy law is implicated in its resolution. (Further examples of suits involving a combination of bankruptcy and nonbankruptcy rights are discussed in question (d).)

(d) The seller's claim for the price of the goods is a claim against the estate. The seller's submission of a proof of claim, the trustee's objection, and the allowance or disallowance of the claim are part of the bankruptcy process and listed as a core proceeding in §157(b)(2)(B). However, the substantive rights of the parties must be determined under state law. Does the recourse to state law remove this dispute from the core? Section 157(b)(3) states specifically that the mere fact that the resolution of a matter is affected by state law does not exclude it from the core. However, as in question (c), one cannot rely too heavily on §157 because it is unconstitutional to the extent that it mischaracterizes proceedings as core.

Irrespective of what §157 says, does this litigation satisfy the test for determining core proceedings? The fact that state law must be resorted to does not inevitably mean that a matter is non-core, provided that it involves a substantive right that could only arise in a bankruptcy case. That is, the focus should be more on the source of the cause of action, not on the substantive law implicated in resolving it. Notwithstanding, the involvement of state law questions makes categorization less certain. This may be illustrated by two cases decided in the Second Circuit after *Granfinanciera*: In *In re Manville Forest Products Corp.*, 896 F.2d 1384 (2d Cir. 1990), a suit challenging a claim was found to be a core proceeding even though it involved adjudication of the contract between the debtor and the creditor. The court reasoned that the creditor's proof of claim brought the claim within the core of bankruptcy, even though litigation on the contract would otherwise have been a related proceeding. In *In re Ben Cooper, Inc.*, 896 F.2d 1394 (2d Cir. 1990), *reinstated on remand*, 924 F.2d 36 (2d Cir. 1991), the court found that a dispute concerning a postpetition insurance policy taken out by the estate was a core proceeding. Although litigation on an insurance contract would normally be a related proceeding, the fact that the policy was taken out by the estate after bankruptcy to protect estate property brought it into the core. The court followed *Ben Cooper*'s reasoning in *In re Agri-Concrete Products, Inc.*, 153 B.R. 673 (Bankr. M.D. Pa. 1993). The debtor in possession sued the party to a postpetition contract for breach. The court held this to be a core proceeding. Although a suit on a prepetition contract would surely not be a core proceeding, a postpetition contract does not fall within the scope of *Marathon*. Such a contract is entered into by the trustee or debtor in possession as an officer of the bankruptcy court, and the contract is integral to the administration of the estate. (See also *In re Southmark*, discussed in section 7.7.3.)

If nothing else, these cases indicate that the characterization of proceedings is a difficult task that is not capable of being resolved by the simple test of whether or not rights under state law are at issue.

(e) In Explanation 1 (e), the suit against the surety was treated as falling within the district court's jurisdiction over related proceedings. This is not a core proceeding because it does not involve the enforcement of any right conferred by the Code. Even though the bankruptcy court may hear the action and make a determination, the bankruptcy court's findings of fact and conclusions of law must be submitted to the district court under §157(c)(1), and the district court will enter judgment after considering the bankruptcy court's proposed disposition.

(f) If the tort suit qualifies for bankruptcy jurisdiction at all, it would be a related proceeding in the same way as the suit against the surety in Question (e). However, as Explanation 1(f) indicates, the connection to the bankruptcy case may be too remote for the litigation between the injured driver and the employee to be treated as related.

(g) In this case the trustee is a party to the suit and is acting pursuant to the duty to collect estate property. Nevertheless, the trustee's suit on the check is not a core proceeding. The substantive and central right that is being enforced here is the debtor's right to payment on the check. This right is not conferred by the Code but by state law, even if its enforcement is undertaken for the benefit of the estate. It is thus a related non-core proceeding. In *Marathon*, the court found an analogous contract suit to be beyond the bankruptcy court's core jurisdiction. *See also In re P&P Oilfield Equipment, Inc.*, 71 B.R. 621. (Bankr. D. Colo. 1987), in which the court held that the trustee's suit to recover the price of the goods sold was a non-core proceeding. Some courts have taken a different view. For example, in *In re Total Transportation*, 87 B.R. 658 (Bankr. D. Minn. 1988), the court held that the trustee's suit to collect a matured prepetition contract debt should not be treated as a contract suit, but as a trustee's suit to recover property of the estate under §542, which is included as one of the enumerated core proceedings in 28 U.S.C. §157(b)(2)(E).

(h) In Explanation 1(h), the suit between the seller and buyer of the computer did not qualify as a related matter for jurisdictional purposes. Obviously, if it does not fall within the district court's bankruptcy jurisdiction under §1334, the question of whether or not it is a core proceeding cannot even arise.

3. **(a)** Congress clearly does have the power to abrogate the sovereign immunity of the federal government. One of the sections included in the list in §106(a) is §524, which provides that the discharge operates as an injunction against any further efforts to collect the debt. As an agency of the federal government, the I.R.S. is subject to the abrogation of sovereign immunity in

§106(a), and cannot raise immunity to resist Sophie's suit to declare the debt discharged and to restrain collection efforts.

(b) Most courts agree that Congress' attempt to abrogate the states' sovereign immunity in §106(a) is unconstitutional and invalid. Therefore, although a state may be subject to an order, such as a discharge order, issued by the bankruptcy court under the Code, the debtor cannot sue the state to enforce the order. This incongruity is well described in *In re Claxton*, 273 B.R. 174 (Bankr. N.D. Ill. 2002). The court points out, however, that the debtor does have possible avenues for relief. One would be to assert the discharge in state court. Although there is some question of whether state sovereign immunity permits a person to take the initiative to vindicate federally created rights, even in state court, the opportunity to raise the discharge defensively should be available if the state ever sues Sophie for the taxes.

Apart from this, the *Ex Parte Young* doctrine may allow Sophie to pursue her injunction claim in the bankruptcy court. The doctrine allows a private citizen to enjoin a state official from engaging in conduct that violates federal law. The theory behind the doctrine is that a state cannot authorize its officials to violate federal law, so the conduct is deemed to be that of the official alone and is therefore not protected by sovereign immunity. The injunction must name the official, not the state, as defendant, and it must relate to future conduct. The doctrine does not allow any compensation for past wrongs. There is some question about whether *Seminole Tribe* undermined the *Ex Parte Young* doctrine. However, as *In re Claxton* points out, several courts, including some courts of appeal, have applied it to injunctions to enforce a discharge order and to prevent state officials from trying to collect discharged taxes.

(c) The claim arising out of the collision belongs to the trustee. It was a legal interest of the debtor at the time of the petition, and therefore (as you will see in section 12.2.1) it became property of the estate upon commencement of the case. In the absence of a proof of claim by the state, the trustee would be barred by sovereign immunity from suing the state on the claim. However, the state Department of Economic Development has filed a claim in the estate for Sophie's unpaid taxes, so §106(b) or (c) might apply.

Once the state has proved a claim in the estate, §106(b) deems the state to have waived sovereign immunity with respect to any claim against it by the estate that is property of the estate and that arises out of the same transaction or occurrence as the state's claim. Section 106(b) is generally regarded as constitutional, provided that the "deemed" waiver is confined counterclaims that have a logical connection to the claim and qualify as compulsory counterclaims. The claim for damage is caused by the collision but it does not arise out of the same transaction or occurrence as the claim. It is therefore not covered by §106(b), as that section has been narrowly construed since *Seminole Tribe*. (Even if it had qualified as a compulsory counterclaim, some courts would not consider it to be encompassed within §106(b) because it is not against the same state agency.)

Although the state's proof of claim does not result in a waiver under §106(b), the estate's tort claim can be asserted as a setoff under §106(c), which is not confined to compulsory counterclaims against the same state agency. The setoff can only be used defensively and cannot result in affirmative recovery from the state. Because the estate's claim is $4,000 and the state's claim is $10,000, this problem does not arise because the setoff will merely reduce the state's claim to $6,000.

8

Debtor Eligibility and the Different Forms of Bankruptcy Relief

§8.1   Introduction

The distinction between liquidation under Ch. 7 and rehabilitation under Chs. 11, 12, or 13 was introduced in section 5.5.2 and is taken up again here and examined from the perspective of a debtor who is about to file a bankruptcy petition. This chapter is concerned with the eligibility of different debtors for four types of bankruptcy relief, the factors that may influence a debtor in selecting between alternative forms of relief, and the possibility of postpetition conversion from one form of relief to another.

§8.2   An Overview of the Distinction between Liquidation and Rehabilitation

§8.2.1   *Liquidation*

Liquidation under Ch. 7 is bankruptcy in its oldest traditional sense — the direct descendant of the creditors' remedy of old, described in section 5.5.2. Its aim is the surrender and dissolution of the debtor's executable estate for the purpose of generating a fund to be applied to the payment of creditors. After the debtor has become bankrupt, a trustee is appointed who has responsibility for collecting the debtor's nonexempt unencumbered assets, turning them into liquid form by converting them to cash, and making a distribution to creditors who have proved claims in the estate. The fund is paid out to creditors in the Code's order of priority. Because it is common for Ch. 7 debtors to be insolvent, most creditors, particularly those who hold non-priority unsecured claims, receive only a pro rata payment of their claims. Often, the pro rata distribution is no more than a small fraction of the claim, and in quite a high percentage of cases, the estate has so few assets that after the costs of administration are paid, there are no funds left to pay unsecured creditors any distribution at all. The unpaid balance is usually discharged when the debtor is an individual. A corporate debtor does not receive a discharge under Ch. 7: Once it has been liquidated, it becomes defunct. This lack of discharge does not usually help creditors, who have no prospect of recovering the unpaid balance of their claims from a corporate shell. However, the existence of the undischarged debts prevents trafficking in shell corporations.

§8.2.2   *Rehabilitation Bankruptcy*

Ch. 11, 12, and 13 each have their own rules and principles, which are discussed more fully in Chapters 20 and 21. However, they share a common purpose that distinguishes them from Ch. 7. Their general goal is not to liquidate the debtor's assets[1] but to provide the debtor the opportunity of preserving all or part of the prepetition estate in return for a commitment (formulated in a plan of rehabilitation) to make specified payments to creditors over a period of time. The level of payment required by the Code is too complex for discussion at this point and is left for Chapters 20 and 21. As a general yardstick, one can say that the premise of the Code is that the value received by creditors under the plan must at least be equal to the present value of what creditors would have received if the debtor had been liquidated under Ch. 7. Of course, this is regarded as the minimum. The goal is that creditors will, in fact, do better than they would have in a liquidation.

Rehabilitation under Chs. 11, 12, or 13 is only a viable alternative to liquidation if the debtor has some reasonable prospect of honoring the commitments made in the plan. As a requirement of having the plan confirmed by the court, the debtor must be able to show that it is feasible and that there is likely to be a stream of income or other sources of funding or property to support the plan. Once the plan has been confirmed by the court, it becomes the blueprint for the debtor's rehabilitation. During the period that the debtor is in bankruptcy, that is, from the filing of the petition until the ultimate

---

1. It is possible for a debtor's estate to be liquidated under these chapters. In fact, Ch. 11 expressly recognizes this possibility. However, this discussion focuses on the principal goals of rehabilitation bankruptcy and is not concerned with liquidation plans.

consummation of the plan, creditors are held at bay and the debtor has the opportunity to restructure business operations or to reorder financial affairs with the goal of achieving financial health. If the debtor fails to consummate the plan, the debtor might end up in liquidation. Alternatively, the case might be dismissed so that the creditors' collection rights under state law are restored.

The discharge of prepetition debts is an important element of bankruptcy. Both individuals and corporations can receive a discharge in rehabilitation bankruptcy. The discharge rules vary. *See* Chapter 22. For the present, the following general principle can be stated: *Discharge is intended to be the reward of a successful plan of rehabilitation.* It was noted in section 5.5.2 that the Code has a general preference for rehabilitation bankruptcy and provides various incentives to encourage debtors to choose it over liquidation. Some of these incentives will be considered in section 8.5 in the discussion of choice of relief and in Examples 1 and 2.

§8.2.3 A Practical Perspective on the Distinction between Liquidation and Rehabilitation

Although it is possible to draw a fairly clear line between liquidation and rehabilitation based on the premises and the provisions of the Code, it is important to remember that matters become much muddier as the Code is applied in actual cases. Some of this lack of precision will become apparent later, as we take a closer look at the various specific aspects of the different types of bankruptcy, but a general observation may be helpful at the start. Although some cases do proceed exactly along the lines of a pure liquidation (that is, all the estate's assets are realized and the proceeds distributed) or a full rehabilitation (that is, the plan is completely and successfully consummated, leaving the debtor rehabilitated and creditors better off than they would have been had liquidation occurred), things are often not that tidy. For example, an individual Ch. 7 debtor has various means of avoiding the liquidation of all her property, primarily because of exemptions, but also because when the property is subject to a security interest, it may be possible for the debtor to make an arrangement with the secured creditor to keep the property in exchange for a commitment to keep paying installments due on the contract. Likewise, a rehabilitation plan under Ch. 11 or 13 may provide for the partial liquidation of assets as a means of deriving the resources needed to fund the plan. Furthermore, rehabilitation is usually a long-term process, dependent on predictions of future economic conditions, the debtor's abilities, and the cooperation of creditors or other persons (such as an employer, a lender, or investor) whose help is needed in the debtor's revival. Even if the plan is not unrealistically optimistic to begin with, economic conditions may be less than desired, the debtor may just not have the ability to do what is needed, or the anticipated cooperation may not be forthcoming. This may lead to the failure of the rehabilitation attempt and ultimate liquidation. In the end, creditors may be worse off than they would have been had liquidation taken place immediately.

§8.3   Different Types of Debtor

Before discussing eligibility for relief, it is useful to identify the different types of natural or legal persons that may become debtors under the Code and to draw some distinctions between them.

§8.3.1   *Individuals, Partnerships, and Corporations*

A debtor is a "person or municipality concerning which a case under this title has been commenced." §101(13). "Person" includes an individual, partnership, and corporation, but not a governmental unit. §101(41). "Corporation" includes a variety of juristic persons, both incorporated and unincorporated. §101(9). "Individual" is not statutorily defined. It means a real, honest to goodness, living, breathing, warm-blooded mammal of the species homo sapiens. "Partnership" is also not defined in the Code and must be determined with reference to state law. (The Code recognizes a partnership as an entity distinct from the individual partners and contemplates the possibility that a partnership may be a debtor even if the partners are not.)

The Code therefore recognizes four general categories of debtor: *Individuals, partnerships, corporations,* and *municipalities.* The distinction between the groups is often important because many provisions of the Code, and indeed some chapters of the Code in their entirety, exclude one or more of them. It is useful to remember this, and to be attentive to whether a particular Code section speaks generally of "the debtor" or is restricted to a more narrow category, such as "individual debtor."

This book does not deal with municipal bankruptcy nor with the specific rules applicable to partnership bankruptcy; the two principal types of debtors discussed here are *individuals* and *corporations.* The distinction between them is pervasive, because the impact of bankruptcy on a corporation is bound to differ in many respects from that on an individual. Sometimes these differences are purely factual, reflecting the different scope and nature of corporate and individual economic operations. However, they sometimes arise from Code provisions that reflect a policy of conferring rights on one type of debtor but not on the other. For example, exemptions are intended to save the individual debtor from penury, so they are made available to individuals but not corporations.

§8.3.2   Consumer and Business Debtors

It is easy to draw the distinction between individual and corporate debtors, because corporations are distinct legal entities in nonbankruptcy law and the Code itself recognizes this. It expressly provides for different treatment of individuals and corporations in several respects. By contrast, the Code itself does not as clearly articulate the difference between consumer and business debtors. The only definition pertinent to the distinction is §101(8), which describes a "consumer debt" as one "incurred by an individual primarily for a personal, family or household purpose." From this it is clear that one should not simply equate individual and consumer debtors: An individual is not a consumer debtor unless the bulk of his or her debt is incurred in the course of domestic consumption. Where an individual debtor owns a business as a sole proprietorship, his debts will likely be a combination of consumer and business debts.

For many purposes, it is not legally significant to differentiate between consumer or business debtors because most provisions of the Code apply equally in the bankruptcy of both. When the Code intends to provide a special rule for one or the other, it does so expressly (*e.g.,* §707(b), which concerns dismissal for substantial abuse, is confined to consumer debtors).

Notwithstanding, the distinction between consumer and business debtors is functionally significant and pervasive because the property, obligations, and affairs of a consumer are likely to be quite different from those of a business. This creates factual differences between these two types of bankruptcy so that provisions of the Code relevant to the one often just do not come into issue in the other. The importance of this factual difference is accentuated by the distinct policy concerns that dominate each type. Business bankruptcies tend to implicate larger concerns of economic welfare, such as productivity, market stability, and employee protection, while consumer bankruptcies often highlight social policies such as the prevention of homelessness, the protection of the common person and her dependents, and the social ills of the abuse of credit. It should be stressed, however, that this distinction is likely to be more obvious where the business is a legal entity distinct from its owners (such as a corporation), and has operations of some size. At the margins, the difference between business and consumer bankruptcies is less functionally significant. For example, the stereotypical consumer debtor is a person who earns his income from employment and spends most of it on living expenses or on buying goods and services for personal use. However, if the same debtor is self-employed, his purchases, loans, and credit card debt may commingle household and business transactions.

Because of these very different factual contexts and policy concerns, it is common for consumer and business bankruptcy to be seen as quite distinct legal regimes. This dichotomy is reflected not only in specialization by practitioners, but also in the way that some books, articles, and law school courses are organized. Although it is important to keep this in mind, it is also necessary to recognize that many provisions of the Code do not differentiate between consumers and businesses, and are potentially applicable to both.

A similar practical distinction could be drawn within the category of business bankruptcy itself. Substantial factual differences exist between the bankruptcy of small businesses (especially those that are not organized as corporations) and large corporate debtors. Up to a point, the Code recognizes this distinction by providing a few alternative procedures that may be more suitable for, or, in some cases, are only available to business debtors of one kind or the other. (These are noted in Chapter 21.) However, here again, many provisions of the Code are equally applicable to both and may potentially apply to either.

While this book does often point to the difference between consumers, small businesses, and large corporations, it is not so organized as to treat each category as a self-contained subject. Rather, because they do have so many rules and principles in common, the preferred approach here is to focus on substantive topics, and to point out, where appropriate, that certain rules and procedures are likely to be more relevant to some types of debtors than to others.

§8.3.3   Family Farmers

Ch. 12 of the Code is exclusively devoted to *family farmers*. The term describes a farming operation conducted by a family, either in their capacity as natural persons or in the form of a family-held corporation.

In 1986, following a period of great economic hardship suffered by farmers, Congress enacted Ch. 12 of the Code. Ch. 12 is largely based on Ch. 13, but it includes some elements of Ch. 11 and some special provisions designed to make it suitable for smaller, family-owned operations. Only a debtor who qualifies as a family farmer may choose to file for relief under Ch. 12, but a family farmer is not confined to Ch. 12 and may seek relief under any other applicable Chapter.

When it was originally enacted, Ch. 12 had a sunset clause: Unless Congress took further action, it would have been automatically repealed in 1993. Congress extended it temporarily in 1993 and has continued to enact short-term extensions ever since. Although Ch. 12 is regarded as successful and the National Bankruptcy Review Commission recommended its permanent enactment, Congress has not yet made it a permanent chapter of the Code. The pending bankruptcy reform legislation does contain a provision to enact Ch. 12 permanently.

§8.4   Debtor Eligibility

Section 109 states who may be a debtor under the Code. The section has a broad rule dealing with eligibility for bankruptcy generally and a set of more specific rules that govern eligibility for each type of bankruptcy relief under Chs. 7 through 13. A debtor must meet both the general prerequisites and those for the specific chapter under which relief is sought. Section 109 is sometimes described as providing *threshold qualifications:* Qualification under §109 is necessary for the debtor to be entitled to relief. However, even if the debtor is eligible, other provisions in the Code may preclude relief. For example, a debtor may be eligible for Ch. 13 but may not be able to satisfy the further requirements for plan confirmation. Also, for example, the debtor may be eligible for some forms of relief under a voluntary petition but may not be compelled into that chapter by an involuntary petition.

§8.4.1   *The General Qualifications*

Section 109(a) sets out the general qualification for bankruptcy relief. It covers almost everyone who is resident, domiciled, conducts business, or owns property in the United States: individuals, partnerships, corporations, and municipalities. There are no other general qualifications. The debtor does not have to show grounds for seeking relief such as insolvency or creditor pressure. (Note, however, that creditors who file a petition for involuntary bankruptcy do have to establish grounds for relief, as discussed in section 9.6.)

Section 109(g) imposes a temporary limitation on general eligibility to prevent abusive successive filings by individuals and family farmers. If the individual debtor or family farmer has had a case dismissed because of uncooperative or disobedient behavior, or voluntarily dismissed the case following a creditor's application for relief from stay, the debtor may not become a debtor under the Code for a period of 180 days after the dismissal.

This rule is intended to make it difficult for a debtor to file consecutive petitions for the purpose of obstructing creditors' collection efforts at state law by interrupting them with the automatic stay. Courts differ on the exact scope of §109(g)(2), which denies eligibility to an individual or family farmer for 180 days after he requested and obtained voluntary dismissal of a case following the filing of a motion for relief from stay. Some courts take the section at its face meaning, interpret the word "following" to mean "after," and apply it mechanically, so that the debtor is barred from filing for bankruptcy simply if voluntary dismissal occurred subsequent to the filing of a motion for relief from stay. Other courts, while they agree with this meaning, have used different theories to overcome the harsh effects of literal application of the statutory language. Some hold that they have the discretion to permit a second filing within the 180 days following dismissal if the circumstances would make denial of bankruptcy relief unfair or absurd; other courts treat "following" to mean "as a result of," so that if there is not a causal link between the motion for relief and the debtor's voluntary dismissal, the debtor is not barred by §109(g)(2) from seeking relief within 180 days of the dismissal; others have recognized a good faith exception to §109(g)(2). On this approach, the section would not be applicable if the motion for relief from stay was filed and then withdrawn or denied before the debtor sought dismissal. These different interpretations (as well as a another that I will not mention because it seems to make no sense at all) were discussed and evaluated in *In re Richardson*, 217 B.R. 479 (Bankr. M.D. La. 1998), in which the court concluded that the clear language of §109(g) indicates that Congress intended to impose a simple standard for barring serial filings, and that the test is simply one of sequence—the section comes into effect whenever a motion for voluntary dismissal is made after a motion for relief from stay. By asserting discretion to apply the section, or by trying to evaluate cause and effect, a court undermines the purpose of the section and weakens its effectiveness in curbing abusive serial filings.

While we are on the subject of plain meaning, it should be noted that there is one respect in which applying the literal meaning of §109(g) would have a peculiar result. By providing that no such individual or family farmer "may be a debtor" under the Code, it suggests that they are impervious to involuntary petitions during that 180-day period as well. This cannot be the intended result, considering that the rule is aimed at debtor abuse and should not deprive creditors of their involuntary bankruptcy remedy.

§8.4.2   *Eligibility for Relief under Each of the Separate Chapters*

In addition to the general qualifications, each Chapter has its own eligibility requirements, set out in §§109(b) through (f). These qualifications are summarized below, and some of them are considered in Examples 1 and 2.

(1) **Ch. 7 (§109(b)).**   At present, Ch. 7 relief is widely available. Anyone who may be a debtor under the Code may be a debtor under Ch. 7 except for railroads, insurance companies, and banks, banking, and savings institutions. (The financial failure of these types of businesses is dealt with by other statutes.) A debtor may be placed in Ch. 7 bankruptcy voluntarily or involuntarily.

Although Ch. 7 eligibility is broad under existing law, it would be significantly pared down if the pending bankruptcy reform bill is ever enacted. The bill, like its unsuccessful predecessors over the last few years, would impose a means test on debtors who seek to file under Ch. 7. If an individual debtor earns an income above a set level and has a certain amount of net income, the debtor would be deemed to be able to afford to undertake a Ch. 13

payment plan, and would be precluded from filing for relief under Ch. 7. The proper scope of the means test, and the very idea of imposing such a test, is controversial. (The controversy is explained in section 5.4.1 and the impact of the proposed test is discussed in section 9.7.)

(2) Ch. 9. (§109(c)). Ch. 9 relief is confined to municipalities. It is not dealt with in this book.

(3) Ch. 11. (§109(d)). The eligibility requirements for Ch. 11 are the same as those for Ch. 7, except that railroads may file under Ch. 11 and stockbrokers and commodity brokers may not. Stockbrokers and commodity brokers are required to file under special provisions of Ch. 7 designed to protect customers' accounts. A debtor may be placed in Ch. 11 voluntarily or involuntarily.

(4) Ch. 12. (§109(f)). Only a family farmer with regular annual income may file a Ch. 12 petition. A debtor may not be placed in Ch. 12 involuntarily. The meaning of "family farmer with regular annual income" is defined in §§101(18) and (19). The definition of "family farmer" in §101(18) is complex. In essence it covers an individual or individual and spouse who conduct a farming operation, or a family farming operation organized as a privately held corporation or partnership. In addition to qualifications concerning source of income for an individual (and shareholding and assets for a corporation), the debtor must meet debt limits both with regard to the total indebtedness and its source. The general purpose of the qualifications is to confine Ch. 12 to relatively small individual or family-owned farming operations having debts and income substantially related to the farming activity. Section 101(19) defines "regular annual income" to mean that the farmer's annual income is sufficiently stable and regular to enable payments to be made under a Ch. 12 plan. Income is measured on an annual basis because farming is cyclical and may not generate regular income for shorter periods. *See also* §101(2) (the definition of "farmer") and §101(21) ("farming operation").

(5) Ch. 13. (§109(e)). Only an individual with regular income whose debt falls within the limits of §109(e) may be a debtor under Ch. 13. A debtor may not be placed in Ch. 13 involuntarily. Section 109(e) sets out three distinct requirements for eligibility. First, the debtor must be an individual; second, he must have regular income; and third, his total debt at the time of filing must not exceed the prescribed limit.

An "individual with regular income" is defined in §101(30) to mean an "individual whose income is sufficiently stable and regular to enable such individual to make payments under a plan under chapter 13..." Section 109(e) does not state the date on which the regular income requirement must be measured. The date of filing is pertinent, but the court may consider this issue prospectively, so that even if the debtor does not have regular income at the time of filing, he will be eligible if he has a good prospect of regular income when the time for payments under the plan arrives. If the debtor has a job and earns a periodic wage or salary, there is little difficulty in establishing that he has a stable and regular income. This is true even if he is an at-will employee who could be fired at any time. However, where the debtor's earnings come from a less conventional or predictable source, there could be a dispute over his eligibility for Ch. 13. For example, in *In re Baird*, 228 B.R. 324 (Bankr. M.D. Fla. 1999) the debtor was employed when he filed his Ch. 13 petition. About nine months after filing (but before his plan was confirmed) he lost his job. About three weeks after that, he suffered a stroke. Although he was no longer able to make payments called for by the plan,[2] his son continued to pay the payments due under the plan. A creditor moved to dismiss the case on the grounds that the debtor had no regular income. (Therefore, this case illustrates a situation in which the challenge to the debtor's eligibility was made some time after filing, but before the plan had been confirmed.) The court found that the son's voluntary payments qualified as stable and regular income. It reasoned that the eligibility requirements of §109(e) should be interpreted broadly to take account of diverse and non-traditional sources of income. The creditor argued that the son's payments could not be regular and stable income because they were purely voluntary and he could stop paying at any time. The court responded that the mere fact that payments could cease at any time does not disqualify them. After all, the same is true of a debtor's salary under an at-will employment contract, and salary would not be disqualified as regular and stable income just because the debtor has no guarantee of continued employment.

Ch. 13 is available only to debtors with relatively small estates. Section 109(e) sets out the maximum amount of noncontingent, liquidated secured debt and of noncontingent, liquidated, unsecured debt that a debtor may owe to be eligible for Ch. 13 relief. If either the secured or the unsecured debt exceeds the amount listed for that category, the debtor may not obtain Ch. 13 relief, and must choose between Chs. 7 and 11.

Under the 1978 Code, the dollar amounts of the maximum indebtedness were stated in set figures that could be changed only by legislative amendment. (They were $100,000 for unsecured debt and $350,000 for secured.) The Bankruptcy Reform Act of 1994 increased these amounts to $250,000 and $750,000 respectively. It was apparent that in the approximately 15 years that it took Congress to get around to amend §109(e) to

---

2. Under §1326, a Ch. 13 debtor must begin making payments 30 days after filing the petition. Therefore, payments under the plan begin even before confirmation of the plan.

increase these amounts, inflation had the effect of excluding from eligibility estates which, in real terms, would have been contemplated under the original figures to be small enough to qualify for Ch. 13. To prevent this kind of problem in the future, the 1994 amendments added §104(b) to the Code, which delegates to the Judicial Conference of the United States the task of updating these amounts (as well as others elsewhere in the Code) at three-year intervals, based on changes in the Consumer Price Index. The new amounts apply to cases filed after the effective date of the adjustment. The first such update was promulgated effective April 1, 1998. Since then, there has been another update in April 2001 and there will be a further update on April 1, 2004. In cases commenced in the three years following April 1, 2001, a debtor may file for Ch. 13 relief only if her noncontingent, liquidated unsecured debt is less than $290,525, and her noncontingent, liquidated secured debt is less than $871,550. (As you can see, the disadvantage of this system is that the formerly neat, rounded figures are now replaced by odd sums that are hard to remember and more vigorously challenge one's arithmetical skills. Well, at least they dropped the cents.)

A debtor and spouse may file a joint Ch. 13 petition, but their combined debts must be within the limits set for an individual. An individual who is otherwise qualified for Ch. 13, but is a stockbroker or commodity broker, cannot file under Ch. 13. Under §101(3), an individual has regular income if the income is sufficiently stable and regular to enable payments to be made under the Ch. 13 plan.

§8.5   Choice of Relief

When a debtor is eligible for relief under more than one chapter of the Code, the debtor must decide which form of relief is most appropriate. In most cases, the choice is between liquidation or some form of rehabilitation. However, some debtors may qualify for more than one of the rehabilitation chapters and must decide not only between liquidation or rehabilitation but also between the advantages and drawbacks of the different applicable types of rehabilitation. A full understanding of the factors that influence choice of relief can only come after a thorough study of bankruptcy law, so a detailed discussion of this issue is premature at this stage. Some of the issues that influence the choice of relief are introduced in Examples 1 and 2. An overview of the differences between Chs. 7, 11, 12, and 13 is set out in the appendix. Look through it before considering the questions. It provides comparison between the chapters, suggests the advantages and disadvantages of each, and provides some ideas on what considerations may influence choice of relief.

The question of whether an individual debtor should have the right to choose freely between Ch. 7 liquidation and Ch. 13 rehabilitation is very controversial at present. Many people, including, predictably, the consumer finance industry, but also, it seems, a substantial faction of Congress is concerned that Ch. 7 has become a vehicle used by debtors to obtain release from debt with little or no sacrifice or effort at repayment. Even in good economic times, the number of personal bankruptcy filings is huge and continues to grow. The concern is often expressed that part of the reason for this is that too many individuals use credit irresponsibly and then find it too easy to employ the bankruptcy system to shirk the payment of their debts. There has been much debate over changing the law to make it harder for debtors to choose bankruptcy under Ch. 7 if they have enough income to support a Ch. 13 plan. Advocates for this change contend that a significant number of debtors who could afford to pay a sizeable portion of their debt under a Ch. 13 plan opt instead to take the easy way out by filing under Ch. 7, liquidating their few nonexempt assets, and discharging their debts with no effort at repayment. They argue that debtors with sufficient earnings to afford payments under a Ch. 13 plan should be denied the choice of liquidation under Ch. 7.

Others feel that the perceived abuse of Ch. 7 is greatly exaggerated, and is based on the self-serving studies and arguments of credit card companies and other lenders, who are seeking to increase their profits by squeezing a few more dollars out of distressed debtors. Furthermore, they feel that to the extent that an increase in bankruptcies is caused by irresponsible use of credit, a large share of the fault lies with lenders who indiscriminately issue credit cards and encourage spending. They should not be rewarded by a change of the law in their favor. Opponents of restricting the availability of Ch. 7 fear that such restrictions would deny effective bankruptcy relief to debtors who are in genuine financial distress (in many cases caused by factors over which they have no control) and struggling to survive.

As noted in section 5.4.1 (and discussed more specifically in section 9.7), four dissenting members of the National Bankruptcy Review Commission submitted a separate report in which they recommended restricting an individual debtor's choice between Chs. 7 and 13. They suggested a means test that would measure the debtor's ability to make future payment under a Ch. 13 plan and preclude the debtor from filing for relief under Ch. 7 if his means were adequate to support such a plan. This recommendation attracted enough support in Congress to form the basis of provisions prescribing a means test in the various bills introduced in successive sessions of Congress since 1998, including the currently pending bill.

§8.6   Conversion from One Chapter to Another

The selection of relief under a particular chapter is not irreversible. The debtor and other parties in interest are able, subject to certain restrictions, to apply to court to convert a case under one chapter into a case under another.

For example, a debtor may have filed a petition for relief under Ch. 13. During the course of the case, it may become apparent to the debtor that the choice was not the best one, or circumstances may have changed to alter the prospects of successful debt adjustment. The debtor is able to convert the case into a case under another chapter, such as a liquidation under Ch. 7. Similarly, the creditors may be able to show that the debtor's Ch. 13 case is abusive or has little chance of successful consummation. Instead of applying for dismissal of the case, they may decide to seek conversion of the case into a Ch. 7 liquidation. A debtor also has the right to convert a case initiated by an involuntary petition. For example, if creditors have filed a petition for involuntary relief under Ch. 7, the debtor may convert the case to Ch. 13, thereby avoiding liquidation in favor of debt adjustment. The rules relating to conversion are rather intricate; the general principles are as follows:

(1) Each chapter of the Code has its own rules and limitations relating to conversion. Sections 706, 1112, 1208, and 1307 govern conversion from Chs. 7, 11, 12, and 13, respectively.

(2) A case cannot be converted to a particular chapter unless the debtor is eligible for relief under that chapter. Therefore, the eligibility requirements (discussed in section 8.4.2) apply to conversions as they do to the original petition.

(3) Conversion may occur in both voluntary and involuntary cases and at the behest of the debtor, a creditor, the trustee, or another party in interest. The debtor is treated more liberally than other parties in converting from one chapter to another: In some cases the debtor has an absolute right to convert to any eligible chapter, while in others conversion requires court authorization. There are also some specified instances in which the debtor's ability to convert is restricted. *See, e.g.,* §706(a) and §1112(a).

   If the conversion is sought by a party other than the debtor, the court can only order the conversion after notice and a hearing and upon a showing of cause. The restrictions applicable to an involuntary petition, discussed in Chapter 9, apply to conversion as well: If a creditor could not have filed an involuntary petition to place the debtor in bankruptcy under a particular chapter, the case cannot be converted to that chapter without the debtor's consent. (For example, a creditor cannot file an involuntary petition under Chs. 12 or 13, and cannot move for conversion to those chapters either.)

(4) As explained in sections 9.4 and 9.6, the dates of the filing of the petition and the order for relief are significant for many purposes. When a case is converted, the date of conversion is treated like the filing of a new case for some purposes but not for others. Section 348 sets out the rules concerning the impact of conversion and

indicates which incidents of bankruptcy are treated as arising on the conversion date and which of them continue to be measured from the original petition or order for relief.

(5) With some limitations, a case can be converted from one chapter to another at any time during the course of the bankruptcy proceeding. Conversion is not confined to the initial stages of the case.

EXAMPLES

1. Farm Fatale

Yokel Yummy's Family Farm Foods, Inc. manufactures and markets frozen microwaveable breakfasts. It has a factory on the outskirts of the city in which it processes fresh dairy products cultivated on its own farm and combines them with the most delectable chemicals and other additives to produce a variety of tasty breakfast dishes. These products are then packaged in generous amounts of plastic and inserted into brightly colored, eye-catching boxes. There is a solid market for instant breakfasts, and Yokel Yummy's has done quite well ever since it began operations some time ago. Its profits had risen gradually over the years.

Last year it suffered a series of calamities. Its stock of egg-laying poultry was decimated by a virulent disease. A short time later, its workers went on strike and the factory was shut down for over three months before the labor dispute was settled. The final blow occurred a few months after that: Some packages of food contained bacteria that made consumers seriously ill, resulting in lawsuits claiming millions of dollars in damages.

The poultry and labor crises have drained Yokel Yummy's resources, and its potential liability to its poisoned customers is frightening. In addition, adverse publicity has badly damaged sales of its product. Yokel Yummy's has not been able to keep current on the payment of its debts, and many of its loans are in default.

Yokel Yummy's has decided to seek bankruptcy relief.

(a) Is it eligible for bankruptcy, and if so, under which chapters?

(b) What factors should be taken into account by Yokel Yummy's in choosing between the chapters for which it is eligible?

(c) What impact would it have on your answers to (a) and (b) if the debtor was not Yokel Yummy's Family Farm Foods, Inc., but rather Mr. Yokel Yummy, doing business as a sole proprietor under the trade name "Yokel Yummy's Family Farm Foods"?

2. Allegro Con Brio

Viva Voce is a soprano who has gained international renown for her large voice and awesome temper. She used to be a great prima donna, but now, in her twilight years, she earns her living by making guest appearances, usually for one or two performances, at various provincial opera productions. In a typical season, she may sing in as many as twenty cities. The season usually lasts from September to May. During the rest of the year, she does some teaching and a few concerts. This year, her earnings were $90,000. Last year, her income was $110,000, and the year before $75,000.

Viva does not have many assets. She owns a house, valued at $250,000, subject to a mortgage of $120,000; a car worth $15,000, subject to a security interest of $10,000; and an assortment of household goods and other personal property worth approximately $80,000. In addition to the two above-mentioned secured debts, Viva owes unsecured debts in a total amount of $45,000.

A few months ago, Viva was rehearsing for a performance in a small city, quite remote from the cultural mainstream. The conductor of the orchestra was a nervous, plodding man of limited musical insight. When he spoiled Viva's famous mad scene by employing the wrong tempo, Viva lost her temper: She grabbed his baton and chased him around the concert hall, beating him on the head with it while heaping the vilest and most slanderous abuse upon him.

The conductor sued Viva for $1 million damages. The trial of the tort action has just begun, and Viva could feel the hostility of the jury as the story of her excessive rage unfolded. Sure that the conductor will win the case she decided to seek refuge under the Bankruptcy Code.

(a) For which chapters is Viva eligible?

(b) What factors should Viva take into account in choosing between those chapters for which she is eligible?

EXPLANATIONS

1. **(a) Eligibility for relief.** Yokel Yummy's is clearly eligible for relief under Chs. 7 and 11 because none of the exclusions in §§109(b) or (d) are applicable. As noted before, these two chapters of the Code are the most universally available. Yokel Yummy's, a corporation, may not be a debtor under Ch. 13, which is confined to individuals. §109(e). Ch. 12 is available to corporations provided they qualify as family farmers with regular annual income (§109(f)). To qualify as a family farmer, Yokel Yummy's must not only be owned by a family, but it must also meet the detailed requirements in §§101(18) through (21). The facts are not sufficient to conclude that the corporation satisfies these eligibility requirements.

(b) Choice of relief. Assuming that Yokel Yummy's is not eligible for Ch. 12, it is left with a choice between Chs. 7 and Ch. 11. What factors will be taken into account in making the choice? In essence, the decision to be made by the debtor is whether its financial difficulties are such that it is not feasible to restructure the business operation and deal with its liabilities. If there is no prospect of reorganization, Ch. 7 is the appropriate choice. It will result in cessation of the corporation's business, the realization of its assets, and the distribution of the proceeds to creditors. The corporation will not be rehabilitated and it will become defunct.

On the other hand, if there is a prospect that the corporation's business can become viable again after reorganization, Ch. 11 is an attractive alternative. It gives the debtor a great deal of flexibility in reordering its affairs. After filing the petition, the debtor negotiates with creditors in an attempt to formulate a plan of reorganization that will allow it to continue in business while compromising its debts and restructuring its operations. Among other things, it may sell off unprofitable or unwanted assets or operations, reject or restructure its contractual relationships, resolve unliquidated, contingent, and disputed claims, and alter the terms of its secured obligations. The debtor usually remains in control of its business as a debtor in possession and is entrusted with administration of the estate. If the debtor is able to have a plan confirmed and can consummate it, it will ultimately emerge from bankruptcy in a leaner and more efficient form, so that it can continue to delight the consuming public with its toothsome breakfast treats.

Although the facts of this question are not detailed enough for a full analysis of Yokel Yummy's prospects of effective reorganization, there are some hints that Ch. 11 may be feasible. The corporation's financial problems have been caused by a series of setbacks, rather than by marketing or management difficulties (although the calamities may, of course, be attributable to lapses in management). Some ugly products liability claims have to be disposed of, but if the corporation is able to deal with this issue and restore consumer trust, its business could revive and become profitable again.

(c) On this variation of the facts, the business is not a corporation, legally distinct from its owners (shareholders), but simply the individual debtor himself, Yokel Yummy, doing business in his individual capacity under a trade name. Therefore, if the debtor elects to rehabilitate instead of liquidate, he may not be confined to a choice between Chs. 7 and 11, as in Explanation (a), but may be able to choose Ch. 13 instead of Ch. 11. Although Ch. 13 is commonly associated with consumer bankruptcies, it is not confined to consumer cases and is available to any individual debtor who satisfies its other eligibility requirements. In fact, many small businesses are conducted as sole proprietorships, and it is quite common to find Ch. 13 debtors who aim not only to deal with household and personal debt, but also handle business debt and attempt to save a business.

The question does not give us enough information to determine if Yokel's income from the business is likely to be stable and regular. We are also not told how much debt he has. Apparently his potential tort liability is huge and would surely put him over the limitation on unsecured debt. However, until the tort claimants have obtained judgment against him, the tort debts are not liquidated and would not be counted for eligibility purposes under

§109(e). If Yokel does not qualify for Ch. 13 relief, either because he cannot show stable and regular income or because his debt is too high, he would be confined to Ch. 11 for rehabilitation relief. If he is eligible for Ch. 13 relief, he would have to decide whether Ch. 13 or Ch. 11 is more suitable to his circumstances. Section 8.5 noted that it is beyond our present scope to consider all the factors that a debtor must weigh in deciding to file under Ch. 11 or 13. (The appendix will give you some idea of the main advantages and disadvantages of each.) As a general matter, Ch. 13 is much simpler and more streamlined, so it is often the best choice for a small business debtor who is eligible for it. However, Ch.11 gives the debtor more control over the estate and allows greater flexibility.

As regards the choice between rehabilitation (under either Ch. 11 or 13) and Ch. 7 liquidation, many of the same considerations apply as those outlined in Explanation (b). However, unlike a corporation, Yokel Yummy will survive Ch. 7. (As regards an individual debtor, "liquidation" is not really used in the same sense as, say, Josef Stalin may have used it.) Nevertheless, Ch. 7 will result in the liquidation of Yokel's business assets and the termination of his business, so if he believes that there is a chance of rehabilitating the business, Ch. 13 is the better alternative.

2. (a) Eligibility for relief   Like Yokel Yummy's, Viva is eligible for relief under both Chs. 7 and 11, because none of the exclusions in §§109(b) or (d) apply to her. Ch. 11 is not confined to corporations, even though it tends to be associated with corporate reorganization.

Viva is also eligible for Ch. 13 if she meets its prerequisites: She must be an individual with regular income, having noncontingent liquidated unsecured debts of less than $290,525 and noncontingent liquidated secured debts of less than $871,550. (These figures apply if she filed after the 2001 update, and will increase again for cases filed after April 1, 2004.)

(1) An individual with regular income.   Section 101(30) defines an "individual with regular income" as one whose income is sufficiently stable and regular to enable payments to be made under the Ch. 13 plan. Over a three-year period, Viva's income ranged from a low of $75,000 to a high of $110,000. She does not have a steady job, but enters into short-term employment contracts each year. Although the Code does not require a person to be a regular wage earner to qualify for Ch. 13, it does require some predictability in income so that performance under the plan is reasonably assured. When a debtor is in Viva's position, the court must assess the likelihood of a reliable source of income, based on all of her circumstances: for example, her ability to budget irregular earnings, the likelihood of her being able to secure future performance engagements, and the amount she needs to maintain herself. In short, while the stability of Viva's income is an issue, she is not necessarily disqualified because of its irregularity as long as the facts show sufficient reliability to support a plan.

(2) The debt limitations.   Viva satisfies the debt limitations. Her secured debt (the mortgage and the security interest in the car) totals $130,000, which is well within the $871,550 limit. Her unsecured debt is $45,000 plus a potential liability to the conductor of $1 million. The debt to the conductor is not counted in determining Viva's eligibility for Ch. 13 relief because it is unliquidated. (Note: Do not confuse the issue of excluding a debt for eligibility purposes from the issue of allowing the debt as a claim against the estate. Once Viva has filed her Ch. 13 petition, the conductor will prove a claim that will either be admitted or objected to and resolved by negotiation or litigation.) The debt is unliquidated because its amount cannot be computed arithmetically from settled facts, such as a contract term or other known figures. The conductor's claim can only be determined following a trial and judgment or a settlement agreement. The conductor's claim is disputed, but that would not have excluded it from the debt calculation. Also, even though the debt is dependent on a jury finding that Viva is liable to the conductor in tort, that does not make the debt contingent. A contingent debt is one that is conditional upon a future uncertain event occurring. The tortious conduct creating the debt has already occurred. The jury determination is a process of factfinding, not a legal contingency in the sense that the term is used in law. (Some courts have taken a different view and have treated disputed debts as unliquidated or contingent.)

The fact that the conductor's claim is unliquidated explains why it may be advantageous to Viva to file now, rather than to wait until the tort action is over. If judgment is given in favor of the conductor for an amount of $245,525 or more, Viva will no longer be eligible for Ch. 13 relief.

(b)   Viva's choice of relief.   Many factors will influence Viva's choice between Chs. 7, 11, and 13. Various considerations are identified in general terms here. They will be discussed in greater detail in later chapters.

(1)   Chs. 11 and 13 will allow Viva to keep her assets and to formulate a plan providing for the payment of claims from future income. In a Ch. 7 case, Viva's assets will be liquidated. Although she is entitled to exemptions, the exemptions may not be large enough to cover her full equity in the assets, in which case she will lose her property and will receive cash from the proceeds in payment of her exemptions. Ch. 7 allows Viva to retain property through redemption or a reaffirmation agreement, but debtors are often not able to take advantage of these procedures because of lack of funds or creditor resistance.

With regard to the secured debts, Chs. 11 and 13 give the debtor the opportunity to maintain payments to the secured party and to cure defaults in prebankruptcy installments. The debtor is even able to modify the terms of some contracts to provide for an extended payment period. (However, the right to modify does not extend to the home mortgage.)

(2)   The extent of the discharge varies depending on the chapter chosen. Ch. 13 offers the debtor a much more generous discharge than Chs. 7

and 11. In Viva's case this is relevant. Arguably, the conductor's claim arises from willful and malicious injury. It is dischargeable in Ch. 13 but not in Chs. 7 or 11.

   (3)   Viva's financial commitment will be greater in Chs. 11 and 13 than in Ch. 7. In a Ch. 7 case, the distribution to creditors is made from the proceeds of the debtor's nonexempt assets. She does not have to pay anything further into the estate. In Chs. 11 and 13 the debtor has to make a commitment of payment from future income over a period of years. This means that in exchange for being allowed to keep her assets, Viva will sacrifice a portion of her future income for some time. Furthermore, the level of payment required of her is fixed at certain minimum levels by Chs. 11 and 13. Various factors go into the determination of the total amount that the debtor must pay under the plan. In general terms, the distribution to be received by creditors must at least equal what they would have received had the estate been liquidated, adjusted upward to compensate them for having to accept payment over time. In addition, other factors can operate to increase this amount further. For example, priority claims require full payment in Chs. 11 and 13, which is not required in Ch. 7; Ch. 13 requires the debtor to commit all her disposable income to the plan, even if that means that creditors receive more than they would have been paid in a Ch. 7 liquidation; Ch. 11 has complex voting and acceptance procedures that allow creditors to put pressure on the debtor to increase her level of commitment. As noted in section 5.5.2, it is the expectation and premise of the Code that creditors will do better under Chs. 11 and 13 than they would have done under Ch. 7.

   (4)   Viva's choice could also be affected by the relative speed of disposition of the different types of relief. Because Ch. 7 involves liquidation and distribution as soon as possible, the bankruptcy administration usually comes to an end much earlier than a case under Ch. 11 or 13, which involves a pay-out period that extends over some years.

   (5)   The above distinctions focus primarily on the choice between Ch. 7 on the one hand and Chs. 11 and 13 on the other. As between Chs. 11 and 13 themselves, the choice is usually dictated by the extent and complexity of the debtor's estate. As the eligibility discussion indicates, some debtors are obliged to use Ch. 11 for rehabilitation simply because Ch. 13 is not available. In Viva's case, for example, if the conductor's suit had reached the stage of judgment and he had been awarded damages of more than $224,250, that liquidated claim would have pushed her over the debt limit.

   Ch. 13 is usually more appropriate than Ch. 11 for an eligible debtor with straightforward financial affairs. It is simpler and has less procedures and safeguards that have to be complied with. A trustee is appointed, so the debtor plays a less active role in administering the estate. Creditors, too, have lesser rights of involvement. In addition, Ch. 13 has some advantages over Ch. 11. Its discharge is broader, and it protects cosigners on any consumer debts incurred by the debtor. Notwithstanding this, in some cases a debtor who is eligible for Ch. 13 may nevertheless decide to file under Ch. 11 because it provides more flexibility and allows the debtor more control over the estate.

(6) A debtor who is eligible for relief under more than one chapter has the discretion to select the most advantageous relief. However, this discretion is not unbridled. When a debtor's choice of relief is motivated by bad faith or an intent to abuse the spirit of the Code, the court may refuse the relief and dismiss the case. The issue of the debtor's good faith in choosing between alternative types of relief is raised in several contexts later. It is merely noted here as a qualification to the discussion on Viva's rights. One issue that may arise on the facts of this case is whether it would be bad faith for Viva to file a Ch. 13 petition so that she can discharge her liability for her intentional tort, which would not be dischargeable in Ch. 7. As a general rule, the answer is no. This issue is discussed in more detail in sections 20.6 and 22.8. (As noted in section 8.5, the pending bankruptcy reform legislation would amend the Code to change the flexibility available to debtors like Viva by precluding Ch. 7 relief where the debtor does not meet a means test.)

9

The Commencement
of the Bankruptcy Case

§9.1   Introduction

The commencement of the bankruptcy case is governed by §§301 to 303. The cardinal distinction made in those sections is between voluntary and involuntary petitions. As was noted in section 5.5.2, the voluntary petition is of comparatively recent vintage. For a long period of its history, bankruptcy was strictly a creditor remedy against a debtor, rather than a debtor's refuge. Today, voluntary petitions make up the vast bulk of bankruptcy filings, and it is common to hear of a beleaguered debtor "seeking the protection" of or "declaring" bankruptcy.

This chapter covers voluntary and involuntary petitions and proceedings associated with the initial phase of the bankruptcy case. For the sake of simplicity, the Ch. 7 case involving an individual debtor is used as the model for this discussion. With some variations, bankruptcy under the other chapters follows a similar path in the initial stages. The chart on page 170 traces the sequence of routine core proceedings in a Ch. 7 case. The time periods are as stated in the Rules, but most can be extended by the court.

§9.2   Venue

Section 7.2 explained that 28 U.S.C. §1334 grants jurisdiction over bankruptcy to district courts generally. 28 U.S.C. §§1408, 1409, and 1412 deal with the question of which federal district is the most appropriate geographical locale for the disposition of the proceedings. As with other sections of title 28, these provisions refer only to the district court. Once venue is

Rough Skeleton Showing the Sequence of a Ch. 7 Case

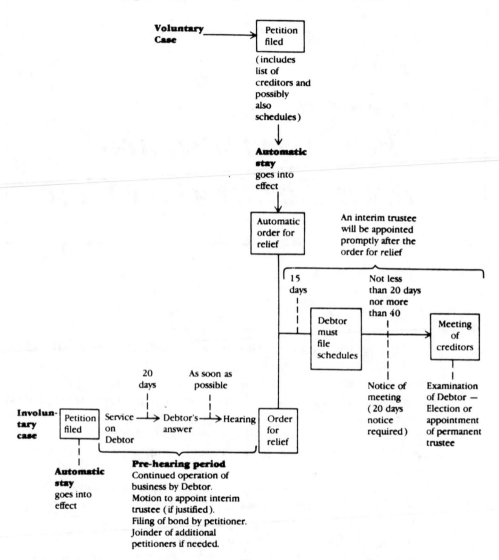

determined, the bankruptcy courts in that federal district deal with the proceedings under the general referral from the district court. Venue rules curtail the petitioner's or plaintiff's freedom to choose a geographic location for the bankruptcy case or other proceedings. They are designed to prevent forum shopping and to make it difficult for a person to initiate proceedings in an unsuitable place that is awkward or inconvenient for other parties in interest. This does not mean that the correct venue is always convenient for everyone. The appropriate location could be distant from the situs of a transaction or property or from the home base of a party. However, restrictions on venue give the courts some control over the choice of federal district by the debtor, petitioning creditors in an involuntary case, or plaintiffs in related cases.

The venue rules are not discussed here in detail. As a general matter, the proper venue of the bankruptcy case is determined by the debtor's location (defined in §1408 by alternative tests) for the 180 days before the petition. Under §1409, the venue of the case itself is also usually the proper venue for proceedings ancillary to the case, but the section recognizes exceptions to this rule in defined circumstances under which another venue is more appropriate.

§9.3   The Voluntary Case

When an attorney is consulted by a client who needs bankruptcy relief, the first task is to obtain information about the client's affairs. Detailed knowledge is required for the accurate completion of the schedules that must be filed with or shortly after the petition. In addition, the attorney needs a comprehensive understanding of the debtor's economic history and current financial position in order to fulfill the role of counseling the debtor on choice of relief, identifying potential problems, and planning the appropriate course of action to be taken in the case. For example (without attempting to be definitive), the attorney needs to have information about the debtor's location to determine venue, and to have full details about the debtor's financial history, assets and liabilities, business affairs, pending lawsuits, disposition of assets, income, and future plans and desires.

Once all this information is gathered, the case is commenced by filing a petition. (Ideally, an attorney should not file a petition until she has all the pertinent information and can assess the impact of filing and anticipate potential problems. However, reliable information is not always available. In addition, sometimes the need to file immediately means having to proceed without complete information.) In a voluntary case, the filing of the petition operates automatically as an *order for relief,* that is, as an order placing the debtor in bankruptcy. The form of the petition is simple. It does not even look like a pleading, because it has been designed so it can easily be completed by checking boxes, and can be computer-generated. In essence, it provides information about the debtor, contains minimal assertions establishing venue and eligibility for relief and identifies the chapter under which relief is sought. A consumer debtor must acknowledge understanding the choice of relief, and this acknowledgment must be certified by the debtor's attorney. The debtor's signature of the petition certifies the accuracy of the allegations in the petition and constitutes an assertion, under Rule 9011, that the petition is filed in good faith and not for abusive purposes.

The supporting documents, filed with or shortly after the petition, include a list or schedule of liabilities, with the identity of creditors so that the clerk can notify them of the filing; a schedule of property; a schedule of claims, properly categorized into secured and unsecured classes, and identified as to whether they are contingent, liquidated or disputed; a claim of exemptions; a schedule of income and expenses; a schedule of executory contracts; a summary of the debtor's financial history and current financial position; and a statement of intent by the debtor with regard to the proposed surrender of encumbered property, or its retention by reaffirmation or redemption, or the avoidance of any liens on it.

§9.4   The Voluntary Petition As an Order for Relief

In an involuntary case, the debtor does not become bankrupt until a hearing is held and the court gives judgment granting the creditors' petition. *See* section 9.6. This judgment is referred to in the Code as the *order for relief.* In a voluntary case, there is no formal adjudication of bankruptcy. In terms of §301, the filing of the petition automatically places the debtor in bankruptcy. In other words, in a voluntary case, the filing of the petition itself constitutes the order for relief.

Many provisions in the Code specify that certain consequences come into effect on the filing of the petition. Others specify that the date of the order for relief is the relevant date for particular purposes. It is important to remember that in voluntary cases, the filing and the order for relief are the same date, while in involuntary cases they are different. For example, §701 requires an interim trustee to be appointed after the order for relief. This means that the trustee is appointed immediately after the petition in a voluntary case but is only appointed after the hearing and adjudication of bankruptcy in an involuntary case. (Even in an involuntary case, a creditor can apply to court for the appointment of a trustee before the order for relief. The creditor must show cause, such as grounds to believe that the debtor will mismanage the estate in the interim period.) By contrast, §362 provides that the automatic stay comes into effect upon filing of the petition. Therefore, in both voluntary and involuntary cases, it takes effect at the commencement of the case.

§9.5   Joint Cases, Jointly Administered Cases, and Consolidation

§9.5.1   *Joint Cases*

If spouses own assets and owe obligations jointly, the bankruptcy of only one of the spouses does not provide full relief to the family as an economic unit: The nonbankrupt spouse remains liable on joint debts. Therefore, both spouses may need to file for bankruptcy. They may file separate petitions but are permitted by §302 to file a *joint case.* This saves costs, because the joint debtors pay a single filing fee and a single set of administrative costs. Joint filing does not mean that the estates of the spouses are combined. The court has the discretion under §302 to allow them to be consolidated or to require them to be kept separate. The considerations that affect the decision to consolidate or separate the estates are noted below. A joint petition can only be filed voluntarily. Creditors cannot file an involuntary petition against spouses jointly. In an involuntary case, the creditors of each spouse must file a petition against the spouse that is their debtor. Often spouses are joint debtors, so these would be the same creditors.

Section 302 is applicable only to spouses. There is no provision in the Code for a joint case to be filed by debtors other than spouses, no matter how closely related they may be. (A partnership is treated as a separate entity under the Code, so a partnership petition is not a joint petition.) Therefore, for example, it is not possible for affiliated corporations or for a corporation and its owner, or for a partnership and its individual partners to file a joint petition. Even though the insolvency of a corporation may result in the insolvency of its owner (so that both must file bankruptcy), these two entities must file separate petitions.

The Code does not define "spouses," but the apparent intent and plain meaning of §302 is to confine the availability of joint petitions to those who are legally married. It is, therefore, a matter of state law as to whether the debtors qualify as spouses. For example, in *In re Allen,* 186 B.R. 769 (Bankr. N.D. Ga. 1995), the court refused to allow a homosexual couple to file a joint petition, even though they had gone through a form of marriage ceremony and were cohabiting. The court said that there is no federal test of marriage, and since their union was not recognized as a marriage under applicable state law, they could not be treated as spouses for bankruptcy purposes.

§9.5.2 Joint Administration

Even though closely related debtors, other than spouses, cannot file a joint petition, the court is able to order the joint administration of their cases. Joint administration keeps the estates separate so that each has its own assets and liabilities but places the estates under the administration of the same trustee, thereby cutting down administrative costs and allowing for the more convenient disposition of the cases. Joint administration is therefore an administrative device to save costs and allow for the more efficient handling of the separate estates. It is provided for in Rule 1015(b).

§9.5.3 Consolidation of Cases

(a) **Procedural Consolidation.** Rule 1015(a) provides for the procedural consolidation of cases where two petitions have been filed in the same court involving the same debtor. This might occur, for example, where two sets of creditors have both filed involuntary petitions against the same debtor. The rule permits the court to combine the cases. As only one debtor is involved, procedural consolidation is distinct from the other situations described here.

(b)   Substantive Consolidation.   In addition to the above type of procedural consolidation, the court also has the power as a court of equity to consolidate cases against separate debtors. This is called substantive consolidation. Substantive consolidation is not provided for in the Code, but is a judicially devised remedy based on the courts' equitable discretion. Where spouses or other closely related debtors are each placed in bankruptcy — whether under a joint petition or separate petitions — the court can combine their estates so that assets are pooled and creditors of each become creditors of the general estate.

Substantive consolidation has consequences much more profound than those of joint administration, and it can have a significant impact on the rights of creditors. Creditors of the estate with the higher asset-to-debt ratio will receive less if the estate is consolidated with a poorer one. For this reason, substantive consolidation is not routinely permitted even if the debtors are closely affiliated. It is usually appropriate only when the affairs of the debtors are so entangled that it is difficult to separate their assets and liabilities, and creditors had generally dealt with the debtors as a single economic unit without relying on their distinct identity. This may occur where spouses have commingled their property and most of the debts incurred by each spouse relate to family or household transactions. It may also happen where an individual has run a corporation in a way that it is difficult to unscramble the corporate and individual assets.

A court is not likely to use its equity powers to order substantive consolidation unless the case satisfies two criteria: First, the estates must be in fact intertwined — the debtors must have acted in a way that has blurred their distinct identities, so that their assets are commingled and it is difficult to sort out which transactions should be ascribed to each. Second, the equities in favor of treating the debtors as a unit must outweigh those of keeping the estates separate. In resolving this second criterion, the court must balance the economic prejudice that some creditors will suffer if the estates are not consolidated against the harm that the debtors and other creditors will suffer if it is. The court must take into account, not only the manner in which the debtors conducted their affairs, but also the relative reliance interests of those creditors who did not realize that the debtors were distinct, and those who understood the debtors to be separate entities and dealt with them on that basis. There is a link between substantive consolidation and the equitable remedy of piercing the corporate veil, in which a court disregards the separate identity of the corporate entity and its shareholder. While the doctrines are conceptually related, they are distinct. For a fuller discussion of the factors to be taken into account and the considerations to be weighed in deciding whether the estates of debtors should be substantively consolidated, *see In re Augie/Restivo Baking Co., Ltd.*, 860 F.2d 515 (2d Cir. 1988); *In re Giller*, 962 F.2d 796 (8th Cir. 1992); *In re Reider*, 31 F.3d 1102 (11th Cir. 1994).

§9.6 Involuntary Cases

§9.6.1 *Introduction*

Involuntary cases make up quite a small percentage of the bankruptcy filings each year, which shows how far the emphasis has moved from bankruptcy as a creditors' remedy. Section 303, which governs involuntary cases, has many restrictions and limitations, making involuntary relief available only in a narrow range of circumstances.

To obtain an involuntary order for relief, petitioners must satisfy two distinct sets of requirements. First, the qualifications for filing prescribed by §§303(a), (b), and (c) must be met. Thereafter, at the hearing of the involuntary case, the petitioners must establish grounds for relief under §303(h).

Creditors who petition for involuntary bankruptcy take a risk, especially if they are not sure of their qualification or grounds, or if they have some ulterior motive for filing. Section 303(i) authorizes the court to award costs and attorney's fees to the debtor if the petition is dismissed other than by the consent of all petitioners and the debtor. In addition, if the petition was filed in bad faith, the court can award compensatory damages to the debtor and, if the bad faith filing was egregious enough, punitive damages. *In re John Richards Home Building Co., LLC*, 291 B.R. 727 (Bankr. E.D. Mich. 2003) is a dramatic illustration. The petitioner's claim arose out of a contract under which the debtor was to build a $3 million home for the petitioner. During the course of construction, the parties became involved in a dispute. The petitioner filed a suit against the debtor in state court. The debtor defended the suit and counterclaimed. Shortly after commencing the suit in state court, the petitioner filed the involuntary bankruptcy petition. He knew that the debtor strongly disputed his claim and filed the petition out of spite to punish the debtor and intimidate it into paying the claim. He threatened and cajoled other creditors to join the petition, and even went so far as to hire a public relations firm to publicize the fact that he had filed it. The court found that the petition had harmed the debtor's business reputation and had caused its work to dry up. It awarded the debtor costs and attorneys fees as well as $4.1 million in compensatory damages and $2 million in punitive damages.

§9.6.2 *Qualifications for Filing under §§303(a), (b), and (c)*

An involuntary petition is permitted only if the following qualifications are satisfied:

(1) The debtor must be subject to involuntary bankruptcy. Most debtors can be subjected to an involuntary petition, but §303(b) forbids the filing of an involuntary case against a noncommercial (essentially, charitable) corporation or a farmer. All farmers, not only those who qualify for the narrower category of "family farmer," are immune from involuntary bankruptcy. ("Farmer" is defined in §101(20).)

(2) Section 303(a) confines involuntary petitions to cases under Chs. 7 and 11. A debtor cannot be placed involuntarily into bankruptcy under Chs. 12 or 13.

(3) Section 303(b)(1) requires that the petitioner or petitioners hold noncontingent, undisputed unsecured claims aggregating at least $11,625. A claim is only to be treated as disputed if it is subject to a bona fide dispute. The term "bona fide" suggests a subjective test—that the debtor have an honest belief in the basis for disputing the debt. However, several courts have adopted a stricter objective test and require either that there is a genuine issue of material fact as to the debtor's liability or a meritorious legal argument against liability. See, for example, *In re BDC 56 LLC*, 330 F.3d 111 (2nd Cir. 2003). To qualify as a dispute, the debtor's contentions must relate to the claim itself and cannot simply be a counterclaim arising out of a different transaction. In *In re Seko Investment, Inc.*, 156 F.3d 1005 (9th Cir. 1998) the court distinguished a counterclaim arising from the same transaction as the claim—which would make the claim disputed for the purposes of §303(b)(1)—from a counterclaim arising out of a different transaction, which would not. However the court recognized that although the unrelated counterclaim would not render the debt disputed, the amount of the counterclaim should be deducted from the petitioner's claim when calculating the dollar amount of the claim for the purposes of the monetary qualification in §303(b)(1).

As originally enacted in 1978, the qualifying amount for petitioners was $5,000. The Bankruptcy Reform Act of 1994 doubled it and also provided in §104, as with other monetary amounts, that it would be reviewed and changed at three-year intervals based on the Consumer Price Index. The periodic changes do not require Congressional action, but have been delegated to the Judicial Conference of the United States.[1] The amount of $11,625 was established by the administrative adjustment under §104 in 2001, and applies to cases filed in the three years beginning on April 1, 2001. It will be adjusted again in 2004.

---

1. *See* section 8.4.2, in which the dollar adjustments are explained more fully in relation to Ch. 13 eligibility requirements.

This requirement means that if the petition is filed by a single creditor (as is permissible in circumstances explained in 4 below), that creditor must have a noncontingent, undisputed unsecured claim of at least $11,625 against the debtor. If the petitioner's claim is partially secured (*i.e.*, the collateral is worth less than the debt), the deficiency must be at least $11,625. If more than one creditor petitions, the combined value of the petitioners' noncontingent undisputed unsecured claims must be at least $11,625. (Example 1 illustrates the petitioners' minimum claim qualifications.)

(4)   The number of petitioners required for an involuntary petition depends on the size of the creditor body. In simple terms, if the debtor has 12 or more creditors, at least three must join in the petition. If the debtor has eleven or fewer creditors, only one petitioner is needed. The petitioners must, of course, satisfy the claim requirements described in 3 above.

Where three creditors are required, they must be three separate, independent entities. Section 303(b)(1) does not prohibit related creditors (for example, a shareholder in a corporation and the corporation itself, or a parent corporation and its subsidiary) from being co-petitioners. However, courts have recognized that the purpose of the three-petitioner rule is undermined if one of the petitioners controls another or manipulates matters to gain the required number of petitioners. Therefore, courts go behind the apparent separate identity of petitioners if one of them is not really independent, but is controlled by another, or if one of the petitioners has assigned part of its claim to another person to create an additional petitioner. Where petitioners are related, it is a question of fact whether they are so closely connected that they should not be treated as separate petitioners.

Control is often a crucial factor in deciding if the petitioners, although separate legal entities, should be treated as factually separate. Therefore, if related corporations share the same board of directors and management, a court is likely to look very carefully at whether they should be counted as separate petitioners under §303(b)(1). However, all the facts must be taken into account, and even if the petitioners do share the same boards and management, they may legitimately be treated as distinct. For example, in *In re Sims*, 994 F.2d 210 (5th Cir. 1993), the three petitioners were affiliated corporations. They all had the same officers, but they operated in different regions and maintained separate bank accounts. The debtor's indebtedness to each petitioner arose out of different transactions entered into between the debtor and that petitioner. The court found the petitioners to be separate entities for purposes of §303(b)(1). Although they were related, they operated as separate corporations and had strictly honored the corporate form regarding assets, taxes, and intercorporate dealings. They had each transacted with the debtor as separate corporations, and had not manipulated the debts so as to evade the three-creditor rule. The court recognized that the relationship between creditors might be a motivating factor in the decision to participate in the petition, but that relationship should not preclude them from being counted as separate petitioners if they were each genuine creditors who were both legally and factually separate. (The analysis here is analogous to that conducted by courts under the equitable doctrine of piercing the corporate veil, and is similarly confined to situations in which legal separateness should be disregarded because the entities have acted inequitably to mislead or manipulate.)

If three creditors are needed, their status as creditors and the amount of their claims are measured as at the date of the petition. In *In re Faberge Restaurant of Florida*, 222 B.R. 385 (Bankr. E.D. Fla. 1997), the debtor tried to defeat an involuntary petition by paying the claim of one of the petitioning creditors after the petition had been filed. This did not work. The court said that the number of creditors is measured at the date of the filing of the petition, and the debtor cannot trump the petition by seeking to eliminate one of the debts postpetition.

The petitioners need not all be involved in the petition from the outset. Section 303(c) permits a qualified creditor to join in the petition at any time before the case is dismissed or relief is ordered. Therefore, if a single petitioner files, believing the debtor to have less than 12 creditors, and it later appears that there are more, the petitioner can solicit additional petitioners. Section 303(c) appears to impose a lesser requirement on a joining creditor than §303(b) imposes on a creditor who initially files the petition, because §303(c) disqualifies only to creditors with noncontingent claims, and says nothing about disputed claims. In *In re Kujawa*, 112 B.R. 968 (Bankr. E.D. Mo. 1990), the court said this was merely an oversight, and that the claim of a joining creditor cannot be subject to a bona fide dispute.

Not all creditors are counted in deciding whether or not the debtor has 12 or more creditors. Section 303(b) provides a formula for deciding who is to be excluded from the count. The statutory language must be looked at quite carefully to pick up all the excluded categories: §303(b)(2) says that the petition may be filed by a single petitioner "if there are fewer than 12 *such holders*" excluding any employee or insider of the debtor, or any recipient of a voidable transfer. On the express language of §303(b)(2), one can readily identify three types of claimants that are excluded from the count: (a) employees of the debtor, (b) insiders of the debtor, (c) recipients of voidable transfers. In addition, the italicized language refers back to the preceding subsection, §303(b)(1), which provides an additional two categories for exclusion: (d) holders of contingent claims, and (e) holders of claims subject to a bona fide dispute.

Regarding the last qualification, a useful illustration of the counting of claimants under §303 can be found in *In re Skye Marketing Corp.*, 8 Bank. Ct. Dec. (CCR) 100 (Bankr. E.D.N.Y. 1981): By excluding an insider, voidable claims, and contingent claims, the debtor's list of 24 creditors was reduced to less than 12, so that a petition by a single creditor was competent.

By contrast, in *Atlas Machine and Iron Works v. Bethlehem Steel Corp.*, 986 F.2d 709 (4th Cir. 1993), the creditor sought to exclude about 60 of the debtor's 66 creditors on the grounds that the debts to them were not over-due, and hence must be regarded as disputed. The argument was that if those creditor's had sued for the debts before they fell due, the debtor could have disputed them. The court rejected this argument, observing that a dispute for the purpose of excluding the debt from the court must involve a merito-rious existing conflict. Because the petition had been filed by a single credi-tor, and the creditor did not satisfy the burden of showing that the debtor had less than 12 creditors as counted under the standards of §303(b), the pe-tition was dismissed.

The purpose of the three-petitioner rule is to protect the debtor from in-voluntary bankruptcy at the instance of a single creditor who cannot muster support for the petition. However, the rule is confined to estates having twelve or more claimants because it could be difficult to find three partici-pants within a very small creditor pool. Usually, insiders, employees, and re-cipients of avoidable transfers have a stake in keeping the debtor out of bankruptcy, and they are regarded as unlikely to join in a petition. This is why they are disregarded in determining the number of creditors. (Example 2 il-lustrates the counting of claimants under §303(b)(2).)

The policy of protecting a debtor from single-creditor action in a small estate cannot be thwarted by trafficking in claims. Therefore, if the estate does have 12 or more creditors, it is clearly not legitimate for a single would-be petitioner (or two petitioners) to create the required number of petition-ers by splitting an existing claim and assigning part of it to a friendly third party. Similarly, if petitioners are so closely interconnected that they are in truth alter egos of each other, they should not be treated as separate entities for the purpose of making up the necessary number of petitioning parties. However, this does not mean that the petitioners have to be completely un-related. Affiliated entities may properly join in filing a petition provided that they are each capable of making an independent decision to file (that is, one of them is not controlled for this purpose by the other) and each is genuinely owed a separate debt by the debtor. (This is illustrated by Example 3(a).)

§9.6.3 Procedures from the Filing of the Petition to the Order for Relief

The involuntary petition identifies the petitioners, alleges compliance with requirements of §303(b), states facts supporting venue, and asserts that the debtor is a person against whom relief may be sought. The petition must also allege one of the two grounds for involuntary relief set out in §303(h). After the petition is filed, the clerk of the court issues a summons and the summons and petition are served on the debtor. If the debtor wishes to controvert the case, it must file an answer within 20 days of the service. In the answer, the debtor may raise any applicable defense, whether arising from nonbankruptcy law (*i.e.*, a substantive defense to the claim of a petitioning creditor) or from the Code (*e.g.*, the petitioner's failure to satisfy the requirements of §303).

However, some challenges to the petition, such as those concerning jurisdiction or venue or based on the contention that the petition fails to state a cause of action, are more appropriately raised in a motion to dismiss the petition, which must be filed in the 20-day period for answering the petition. In some circumstances, a motion for abstention under §305 (discussed in section 9.3) may be the debtor's best response to the petition. In challenging the petition, the debtor may demand a bond under §303(e) to secure any costs or damages that may be awarded on dismissal of the petition.

Because there is some period of delay between the filing of the petition and the grant of the order for relief, §303(f) permits the debtor to continue the operation of a business and to deal with property during the period between the petition and the order for relief. However, if a creditor is able to show that the debtor is likely to mismanage property or harm the estate by this activity, it is entitled to apply to court under §303(g) for the appointment of an interim trustee to take over the debtor's affairs. The order can only be granted following notice to the debtor and a hearing.

If the debtor does not controvert the petition, the court is required by §303 to grant the order for relief. Even though the section does not say so expressly, the court obviously has the discretion to review the petition before granting the order to ensure that an adequate case for relief appears on its face. If the debtor does answer the petition, there must be a trial on the issues raised by the pleadings, and the petitioners must establish one of the two grounds for involuntary bankruptcy set out in §303(h).

§9.6.4   The Grounds for Relief

If the debtor controverts the petition, §303(h) permits an order for relief to be granted only if the petitioners are able to establish one of two alternative grounds for relief:

(1)   The debtor is generally not paying debts as they become due, unless such debts are the subject of a bona fide dispute; or

(2)   Within 120 days before the filing of the petition, a custodian was appointed or took possession of the debtor's property. This requirement is not satisfied if the custodian was appointed to take possession of less than substantially all the debtor's property for the purpose of lien enforcement.

The grounds for relief serve an important function in contested involuntary cases: They constitute a justification for forcing an unwilling debtor into bankruptcy and limit the power of creditors to obtain bankruptcy relief. It is not enough for creditors to show merely that the debtor owes them money and has not paid. By demonstrating one of the two grounds of relief, they also show that the debtor's financial problems are more general. The two situations that constitute grounds of relief are indicative of broad financial instability in the debtor's affairs.

The requirement that creditors establish grounds for relief has a long tradition in bankruptcy law. Prior to 1978, the petitioners had to establish that the debtor had committed one of several "acts of bankruptcy" that included making fraudulent or preferential transfers, admitting inability to pay, or making an assignment for the benefit of creditors. The grounds in §303(h) replace these acts of bankruptcy by substituting circumstances regarded as directly relevant to the debtor's financial condition. The two grounds are alternative. Only one need be established by the petitioners.

a. General Nonpayment of Due Debts (§303(h)(1))

Section 303(h)(1) requires a general pattern of nonpayment of undisputed mature debts during the period immediately preceding the petition. The general failure to pay due debts is known as *equity insolvency*. (*See* sections 3.9.1 and 4.4.3.) Insolvency on the equity test is a good barometer of the debtor's financial difficulty, and easier for creditors to prove than insolvency on the *balance sheet* test (an excess of liabilities over assets). Because wide default on debts is a manifestation of financial distress, concerned creditors are given the ability to place the debtor in involuntary bankruptcy so that they can prevent deterioration of the estate and a race for assets by creditors.

In deciding whether a debtor is generally not paying due debts, courts are obviously influenced by the percentage of debts in default, both in number and value. The more widespread the default and the larger the proportionate value of overdue debt, the more likely that general nonpayment will be found. However, courts also look beyond the bare figures and take into account such factors as the relative importance of the unpaid debts, the length of time that they are overdue, the extent to which the size of overdue payments has increased over a period of time, the degree of irresponsibility shown by the debtor, and other factors that tend to demonstrate that the debtor's position is precarious enough to justify involuntary relief. *See, e.g., In re CLE Corp.,* 59 B.R. 579 (Bankr. N.D. Ga. 1986); *In re Westside Community Hospital Inc.,* 112 B.R. 243 (Bankr. N.D. Ill. 1990). Examples 3 and 4 deal with the test of general nonpayment of debts.)

The requirement that unpaid debts not be subject to a bona fide dispute means that if the debtor's reason for not paying the debt is a legitimate factual or legal dispute with the creditor, the debt may not be taken into account in deciding whether the debtor is generally not paying debts when due. Courts generally apply the same objective test here as they do when considering whether a petitioner's claim is the subject of a bona fide dispute for purposes of qualifying the petitioners: There must be a *prima facie* meritorious defense. Thus, "bona fide" is not wide enough to cover an honest but misguided dispute by the debtor. *See, e.g., In re Rimell,* 946 F.2d 1363 (8th Cir. 1991).

Where a debtor has only one creditor, default on that debt inevitably constitutes universal default. Nevertheless, some courts have refused to grant involuntary relief where the debtor has only one creditor on the basis that the nonpayment of a single debt is contrary to the concept of general nonpayment. An exception is made to this rule where there is evidence of fraud by the debtor. In *In re Concrete Pumping Service, Inc.,* 943 F.2d 627 (6th Cir. 1991), the court questioned the propriety of precluding the use of §303(h)(1) in a single-creditor case. It considered that general nonpayment should be found where there is default on the debtor's only debt, and the totality of the circumstances justifies relief.

b.   The Appointment of a Custodian within 120 Days Prior to the Petition (§303(h)(2))

Who is this mysterious custodian? If the debtor hires a janitor to take care of property, can the creditors pounce? The answer is found in §101(11), which defines *custodian* to mean a receiver or trustee appointed under nonbankruptcy law or an assignee for the benefit of creditors. The appointment could result from a voluntary arrangement initiated by the debtor or from a court order in a nonbankruptcy case. Custodial proceedings are usually used by or against insolvent debtors. Therefore this ground, like the first one, is premised on a manifestation of the debtor's insolvency. By filing an involuntary petition, concerned creditors are able to take the debtor's estate out of the state law trusteeship and bring it under the aegis of the Code. However, they must act within 120 days of the appointment or taking of possession. Section 303(h)(2) is expressly not available when the appointment of the custodian is for the purpose of enforcing a lien against less than substantially all of the debtor's property.

§9.6.5   *The Effect and Consequences of the Order for Relief in an Involuntary Case*

If the petitioners are able to establish grounds for relief at the hearing, or if the case is uncontroverted and the petition shows grounds for relief, the court grants the order for relief under Ch. 7 or Ch. 11. The order for relief is the judgment placing the debtor in bankruptcy. Its effect is explained in section 9.4. Following the order for relief, the debtor must file the schedules discussed in section 9.3. The time period for filing them is the same as in a voluntary case but is measured from the order for relief rather than the petition date. Unless an interim trustee was appointed for cause earlier in the proceedings, the interim trustee is appointed after the order for relief.

§9.7   Dismissal of a Bankruptcy Case

The debtor's right to dismiss an involuntary case was mentioned in section 9.6.3. This note more generally surveys the possibility of dismissal of the case by the debtor, a creditor, or another party in interest. Dismissal may not always be the best form of relief for a party that wishes to stop or change the course of a bankruptcy case. An application for abstention or conversion may sometimes be a more desirable alternative. (Abstention and conversion are discussed in sections 7.7.2 and 8.6.) The issues involved in dismissal can be intricate. This survey deals only with a broad description of its scope and purpose.

Each chapter of the Code has its own section governing dismissal: §§707, 1112, 1208, and 1307. Dismissal terminates the bankruptcy case: The debtor and the estate are released from bankruptcy and the creditors' collection rights at state law are no longer stayed. Section 349 lists the effects of dismissal. There are myriad reasons why a debtor, creditor, or other party in interest may seek dismissal of a case, and depending on the circumstances, dismissal may serve or run counter to the interests of different parties. There are three different situations in which the case may be dismissed:

(1) Voluntary dismissal by the petitioner.   A debtor who has filed a voluntary case may, in effect, seek to "withdraw" the petition by requesting dismissal. In a Ch. 7 or 11 case the debtor must show cause for dismissal, and the case can be dismissed only after notice of a hearing. *See* §§707(a) and 1112(b). In Chs. 12 and 13, the debtor has an absolute right to dismiss unless the case has previously been converted from Ch. 7, 11, or (in a Ch. 13 case) from Ch. 12. *See* §§1208 and 1307).

Petitioners in an involuntary case may also decide to withdraw their case. Section 303(j) requires that such a voluntary dismissal be preceded by notice to all creditors and a hearing. If the debtor does not consent to the dismissal, the petitioners could be liable for costs or damages under §303(i). As noted in section 9.6.1, costs and fees may be awarded even if the petition was filed in good faith. If the petition was filed in bad faith, the court may also award compensatory, and even punitive, damages to the debtor.

(2) Dismissal for cause by a party other than the petitioner.   Dismissal for cause is available under all chapters of the Code. The motion to dismiss must be heard by the court after notice. As discussed in section 9.6.3, the debtor may move to dismiss an involuntary petition on the grounds that there is a defect in the case or that it has not been properly prosecuted. Also, a creditor or other party in interest may move to dismiss the debtor's voluntary case for cause. Cause may consist of any one of a variety of reasons. Each of the sections dealing with dismissal sets out a nonexclusive list of some of these reasons which, in the case of a voluntary petition, include various types of dilatory or uncooperative behavior by the debtor.

(3) Dismissal by the court on grounds of lack of cooperation, abuse of process, or bad faith.   Various provisions of the Code empower the court or the U.S. Trustee to dismiss the case on specific or general grounds of improper conduct by the debtor. For example, §§707(a)(3), 1112(e), and 1307(c)(9) allow the U.S. Trustee to move for dismissal if the debtor in a voluntary case fails timely to file the information and schedules required under §521. In addition to these specific provisions, the court's equitable power under §105(a) allows it, on the motion of a party in interest or *sua sponte*, to dismiss a case in appropriate circumstances.

(4) Dismissal of a Ch. 7 case on grounds of substantial abuse. §707(b) allows the court or the U.S. Trustee to dismiss a case by an individual consumer debtor if the grant of relief would be a substantial abuse of Ch. 7. Dismissal for substantial abuse has become a significant monitoring device in Ch. 7 consumer cases.

Dismissal for substantial abuse under §707(b) was introduced into the Code by the 1984 amendments. Prior to that, any dismissal of a Ch. 7 case had to fit into the "for cause" requirement of §707(a). Its enactment was intended to curb the rising number of consumer bankruptcies filed by debtors who were using Ch. 7 as an easy way out of financial difficulty. The general purpose of §707(b) is to effectuate the policy of withholding bankruptcy relief from an undeserving debtor. However, the section is not universally applicable and is modest in its reach. It has a presumption in favor of granting relief, which gives the debtor the benefit of any doubt; it can only be raised by the court or the U.S. Trustee; finally, it is restricted to Ch. 7 cases filed by an individual whose debts are primarily consumer debts. Section 707(b) has given rise to a number of difficult issues, and courts disagree about its reach and scope. The most taxing issues under §707(b) are as follows:

What are consumer debts? "Consumer debt" is defined in §101(8) as one incurred by an individual primarily for personal, family, or household purposes. Therefore, to apply §707(b) the court must determine which of the individual debtor's debts are in fact consumer debts, and must then decide if those debts predominate in the case. Not every debt incurred by an individual who is not in business automatically qualifies as a consumer debt. It is the purpose of the expenditure that counts. Some courts use a test of profit motive: Therefore, if a householder and wage-earner decides to borrow money to fix up his home before selling it, this is not a consumer debt, but it would be a consumer debt if his purpose in doing the renovations is to enable him to increase his enjoyment of his home. Similarly, a debt that is not incurred with the intent of achieving some personal desire — for example, a tort debt incurred by negligently damaging property in a car accident — is not a consumer debt. (As this last illustration shows, a debt is not classified as a consumer debt just because it was not incurred for business or profit purposes. Some debts are neither business nor consumer debts.)

When does an estate consist primarily of consumer debts? Where a debtor has both consumer and other debts, §707(b) can only be used if the claims in the estate arise primarily from obligations incurred by the debtor for personal or household purposes. This means that it is not necessary that the debtor has only consumer debts, but they must predominate. This restriction reflects Congress' focus on controlling abusive filings in consumer bankruptcies. Where consumer debts form the bulk of the estate in both number and value, it is easy to determine that they predominate. However, where they form the majority of the debt in one, but not the other, of these, the question is more difficult (but the total value of the consumer debt should surely be a more useful indicator than the number of debts). Courts tend to avoid any rigid, mechanical formula to decide if consumer debt forms the primary part of the debtor's obligations, but look at a combination of number and amount in light of the total circumstances of the case. Given the Code's intent to confine §707(b) to cases primarily involving consumer credit, the proper search is for the underlying nature and pattern of the debtor's affairs.

Standing to raise §707(b). Section 707(b) states expressly that only the court or U.S. Trustee may use it, and that dismissal on grounds of substantial abuse cannot be ordered "at the request or suggestion of any party in interest." It is not clear how literally this language should be taken: A party other than the U.S. Trustee definitely cannot make a motion for dismissal under §707(b), but the wording of the section can also be interpreted to mean that a party cannot even *approach* the U.S. Trustee for the purpose of persuading that official to seek dismissal. In *In re Clark,* 927 F.2d 793 (4th Cir. 1991), the court rejected this interpretation and held that the U.S. Trustee is permitted to make a motion to dismiss at the suggestion of a party in interest. The court reasoned that this does not contravene the purpose of §707(b), which was meant to shield the debtor from partisan motions to dismiss for substantial abuse. Furthermore, the court felt that to hold otherwise would discourage creditors from reporting abusive behavior to the U.S. Trustee.

What constitutes substantial abuse? Substantial abuse is not defined in the Code, so courts have some discretion in formulating its meaning. In general terms, the inquiry is whether the filing constitutes an abuse of the spirit of Ch. 7, which is intended to aid an honest but unfortunate debtor. Influential factors include the debtor's apparent purpose in seeking relief, the cause of the debtor's financial trouble (whether resulting from misfortune or irresponsible spending), and the appropriateness of Ch. 7 relief. This last factor has given courts trouble: If the debtor can afford to support a Ch. 13 plan that provides for larger payments to creditors, Ch. 7 liquidation could constitute an unfair attempt to evade debts as cheaply as possible — yet Congress has given debtors the right to choose relief. This issue is examined in Example 4.

Does §707(b) work? Pending reform legislation. Section 5.4.1 surveys the report of the National Bankruptcy Review commission in 1997 and the progress of subsequent legislative reform efforts. As mentioned there, the issue of whether to restrict individual debtors from seeking relief under Ch. 7 has been the most divisive aspect of the report and of the reform bills introduced in Congress in each of the years following the report. The idea of restricting the debtor's choice between Ch. 7 and 13 is not new. Both when the Code was enacted in 1978, and again when §707(b) was added in 1984, there were proposals to require debtors with the means to support a Ch. 13 plan to use Ch. 13 instead of Ch. 7. However, Congress did not choose that route, and instead passed the milder "substantial abuse" standard, restricting its use to the U.S. Trustee and the court, and subjecting it to a presumption in favor of granting the relief requested by the debtor.

However, the proponents of a tougher test have never given up the fight. They urged the Commission to strengthen §707(b), but the majority of the Commission was not persuaded and did not recommend significant change. The dissenting commissioners did see merit in a more draconian approach, particularly in light of annual increases in the number of individual bankruptcies and a perception that too many debtors used Ch. 7 as an easy way out of their debts. The dissent felt that §707(b) was not strong enough, relied too heavily on the discretion of the judge, and was not sufficiently effective in precluding Ch. 7 relief where an individual debtor could afford to support a Ch. 13 payment plan. The dissenting commissioners recommended that the substantial abuse standard in §707(b) be replaced with a more rigorous and exacting means test, that the presumption in favor of the debtor be eliminated, that the section no longer be restricted to debtors whose debt is primarily consumer debt, and that use of the section no longer be confined to the U.S. Trustee or the court. This idea gained significant support in Congress, and it has been featured in the successive reform bills introduced since 1998, including the bill currently pending in Congress

The gist of the proposed reform legislation (which differs somewhat, depending on which of the many versions of the bill one examines) is that §707(b) would still provide for the dismissal of the case on grounds of abuse. However, ability to pay under a Ch. 13 plan would become much more central to the determination of abuse. The section would make a fundamental distinction between debtors who earn more or less that the national median family income for a family of the debtor's size. A debtor who earns less than the median would be treated much the same as under current law, and would have a relatively unrestricted choice between Chs. 7 and 13, subject to the general ground of dismissal for abuse. However, a debtor whose income exceeds the national median would have to satisfy a prescribed means test. This test would be based on a complex formula. In essence, it would compare the debtor's prospective monthly income over the next five years to his reasonable living expenses (based not on his actual budget, but on a formulation promulgated by the I.R.S. to determine how much must be paid by a delinquent taxpayer on overdue taxes, combined with provisions in the Code itself), plus the administrative costs of a Ch. 13 case and his payments on secured and priority debts. If the debtor's income exceeds this expense by a defined percentage, abuse would be presumed. (In other words, if, based on the statutory formula, the debtor has sufficient income to pay a defined percentage of general unsecured debt over a five-year period under a Ch. 13 plan, his filing under Ch. 7 would be presumed abusive, and would have to be dismissed unless he can show special circumstances to rebut the presumption.) The proposed means test would essentially remove the discretion that is now exercised by courts to make determinations on a case-by-case basis, and would confine them to a much more definite formula. It would preserve some small amount of judicial discretion by creating a "safe harbor" that would allow the court not to dismiss the case if it finds that there are special circumstances that would make it impossible for the debtor to pay under Ch. 13.

If this proposed legislation passes, it will have a massive, but as yet unknown impact on individual bankruptcies. Quite apart from any adverse effect on vulnerable and honest debtors, which is feared by opponents and dismissed by proponents, the intricate formula of the means test will surely add to the complexity of individual Ch. 7 cases.

§9.8 The Creditors' Meeting

After the order for relief, the U.S. Trustee must convene a meeting of creditors under §341. The meeting is held in all cases, whether under Ch. 7, 11, 12, or 13. Rule 2003 requires the meeting to take place between 20 and 40 days after the order for relief in a Ch. 7 or 11 case (the periods are slightly different in Ch. 12 and 13 cases), subject to some leeway for the court to set a different time. Under Rule 2002, the clerk of the court must give creditors at least 20 days notice of the meeting.

Section 341 requires the U.S. Trustee to preside at the creditors' meeting. The bankruptcy judge is not involved and is in fact barred from attending by §341(c).[2] The principal purpose of the meeting is the examination of the debtor under §343 by creditors, the trustee, or the U.S. Trustee. A debtor who fails to appear or to answer truthfully can be penalized by

---

2. Prior to 1978, the judge did preside at the meeting. This function was terminated and placed in the hands of the U.S. Trustee as part of the reforms designed to eliminate the court's administrative functions. *See* section 6.3.

dismissal of the voluntary petition, denial of the discharge, or even criminal charges if perjury or fraud are involved. Rule 2004 governs the content and scope of the examination, which may range over the debtor's financial affairs, conduct, and other matters relevant to the administration of the estate or the discharge. In addition to examining the debtor, creditors in a Ch. 7 case may elect a trustee or a creditors' committee at the meeting. As noted in sections 6.2 and 6.5, this power is not frequently exercised.

EXAMPLES

1.   The Unwholley Trinity

Cookie Crumbles owns and operates a bakery. In the last few months she has missed payments to creditors, and some of them have commenced collection proceedings. A group of five creditors, wishing to prevent a race for Cookie's executable assets, have met and agreed to seek legal advice about filing an involuntary bankruptcy petition. The five creditors are a produce supplier that is owed $4,000; a finance company that is owed $13,000 on a loan, secured by a perfected security interest in equipment with a present value of $12,000; a bank to which Cookie is obligated under a suretyship agreement in terms of which Cookie guaranteed the $20,000 debt of a corporation of which she is a shareholder; an advertising agency that is owed $15,000 for services rendered, which Cookie refuses to pay because she contends that the agency made a number of serious mistakes in the advertising campaign; and a seller of equipment that is owed $5,000. Under the sale agreement, this debt falls due for payment next month.

Are the creditors qualified to file a petition?

2.   The Baker's Dozen

Another of Cookie Crumbles' creditors is U.O. Dough Co., Inc., which has an unsecured noncontingent, undisputed claim of $14,000. U.O. Dough Co. has filed an involuntary petition against Cookie. In her answer to the petition Cookie has alleged that she has 18 creditors who are identified as follows: U.O. Dough Co; the five creditors listed in Example 1; two employees who are owed arrear wages; Cookie's mother, who lent her money to help her pay some bills; six more trade and general creditors; two more secured creditors; and a utility company that is owed less than $50 for last month's services.

Should U.O. Dough Co. find another two creditors to join in the petition?

3.   Once More unto the Breaches, Dear Friends

Assume that Cookie does have more than 11 creditors. U.O. Dough Co., Inc. was able to find two other creditors to join in the petition. The petition was filed and Cookie opposed it, requiring the petitioners to establish grounds for relief under §303(h). Cookie's total debt is $300,000. She has defaulted on 11 of her 18 debts over the last few months. The total value of her overdue debts, including the $15,000 disputed debt to the advertising agency, is $180,000.

Can the petitioners establish grounds for relief?

4. Seven's Deadly Sin

Desiree Moore has recently filed a Ch. 7 petition. Her schedule of assets and liabilities shows that she has three secured debts totaling $300,000 and 15 unsecured debts totaling $90,000. Her largest secured debt, constituting 60 percent of her total secured indebtedness, is a loan for the purchase of investment property, secured by the property itself. The other two secured debts, making up the remaining 40 percent, are a home mortgage and a purchase money interest on an expensive luxury car. Of her unsecured debts, 14 are for credit purchases of consumer goods and services. These make up 50 percent of her total unsecured debt. The other half of her unsecured debt consists of a single debt for attorney's fees incurred in litigation concerning her investment activities.

Desiree's schedule of income and expenditures reflects a net monthly salary of $4,000. She shows monthly expenses of exactly the same amount. Her expenses include mortgage and car payments, food, clothing, golf club dues, private school fees for her child, and opera and theatre subscriptions. Desiree's statement of intent indicates that she plans to negotiate reaffirmation agreements with the mortgagee and car financier, so that she can keep these assets by maintaining the payments for them out of her postpetition income. These two secured creditors will therefore ultimately receive the full benefit of their bargains. The third secured creditor will also be paid in full because its collateral is worth as much as the debt. Unsecured general creditors will receive a minuscule distribution from Desiree's estate. This is because Desiree has very little unencumbered nonexempt property. At most, its liquidation value is $5,000.

The U.S. Trustee argues that Desiree's Ch. 7 filing is a substantial abuse of the Code and has moved for dismissal of the case under §707(b). Should the motion be granted?

5. Detaxification

Tex E. Vader has just filed a Ch. 7 petition. His largest debts are owed to the federal and state governments for arrear income taxes on his salary and overdue property taxes on his home. Although part of this indebtedness is a nondischargeable priority claim (as will be discussed in Ch. 22), the greater portion of it does not qualify for priority treatment and will be discharged in the Ch. 7 case. These tax debts constitute about 70 percent of the claims against the estate. The rest are for consumer loans and credit cards. Tex earns a good income and could afford to pay a significant part of his dischargeable debt under a Ch. 13 plan. He has filed a Ch. 7 petition because, as he has told many people, "I worked hard for that money and need it more than the government does."

Should Tex's petition be dismissed for substantial abuse?

EXPLANATIONS

1. The total number of Cookie's creditors is not stated. If she has 12 or more, 3 creditors must join in the petition. If she has 11 or less, only 1 petitioner is required. In either event, the creditors in the group *cannot* satisfy the requirements of §303(b) because none of them, singly or in combination, hold noncontingent, undisputed unsecured claims against Cookie of at least $11,625. (As noted earlier, this is the figure promulgated in the 2001 adjustments under §104.)

The produce supplier is only owed $4,000 and by itself does not qualify. The finance company's $13,000 claim is secured to the extent of $12,000. Only the unsecured deficiency of $1,000 may be counted for the purpose of qualifying it as a petitioner. The bank's claim on the suretyship is contingent. Suretyship obligations are conditional upon a future uncertain event: the default of the principal debtor. The facts do not indicate that this has occurred. The advertising agency's claim is disputed. The dispute must be bona fide. Cookie must have a legitimate, good faith defense to the claim based on a meritorious legal argument or a genuine issue of material fact. The test for a bona fide dispute requires both subjective honesty and an objective basis in fact or law. The facts suggest that there may indeed be a genuine dispute over this claim. If the advertising agency joins in the petition, Cookie must raise the dispute in her answer, and the court will decide the question in a summary fashion for the purposes of ruling on the petition. Although the equipment seller's claim is not yet due, this does not bar its participation in the petition. Maturity of the debt is not a requirement of §303(b).

Thus, the only qualified petitioners are the produce supplier ($4,000), the finance company (unsecured deficiency of $1,000), and the equipment seller ($5,000). Their combined claims add up to $10,000 and fall short of the value requirement by $1,625.

2. The issue here is whether Cookie has 12 or more creditors, so that three petitioners are required under §303(b). In counting the number of claim-holders for the purpose of determining whether there are fewer than 12, employees, insiders, and transferees of avoidable transfers are excluded by the express terms of §303(b)(2). In addition, §303(b)(2) says that there must be fewer than 12 "such holders." The "such" refers to the claimants described in §303(b)(1), whose claims must be noncontingent and undisputed. Thus, in addition to the three express exclusions, §303(b)(2) also excludes from the count all holders of contingent or bona fide disputed claims. *See In re Skye Marketing Corp.*, 8 Bankr. Ct. Dec. (CCR) 100 (Bankr. E.D.N.Y. 1981).

It has already been stated in the analysis of Example 1 that the bank's claim is contingent and the advertising agency's claim is subject to a dispute that is apparently bona fide. In addition, the claims of the two employees and Cookie's mother are excluded. (Cookie's mother is an insider as defined in §101(31).) It is also possible that the utility claim may be excluded. Some courts have not counted claims of small value on the theory that debts of trivial value should not be used to exaggerate the size of the creditor body. *See, e.g., In re Rassi*, 10 Bankr. Cr. Dec. (CCR) 385 (7th Cir. 1983). The facts indicate that three secured creditors are included in the count. Although the secured portion of a claim cannot be used to satisfy the claim value requirement for petitioners in §303(b)(1), secured claimants are not excluded from the creditor count. The reference to "such holders" in §303(b)(2) relates back only to the requirements of noncontingency and lack of bona fide dispute in §303(b)(1).

Even if all these six claimants are excluded, the creditor body still numbers 12, and U.O. Dough Co. must find two cohorts. Under §303(c), they may join at any time prior to the case being dismissed or relief ordered. Because U.O. Dough Co.'s debt exceeds the $11,625 minimum qualification, it need not be concerned about the size of the other petitioner's claims. U.O. Dough Co. must find genuine preexisting creditors. It may not try to evade the requirements of §303(b) by assigning portions of its claims to associates or cooperative third parties for the purpose of creating three claimants out of one. This is barred by caselaw and by Rule 1003.

If U.O. Dough Co. cannot find two more petitioners, the petition will be dismissed. Section 303(i) gives the court authority to grant costs or a reasonable attorney's fee to the debtor. If the filing was made in bad faith (say, for example, U.O. Dough Co. knew that there were more than twelve creditors and that it had no reasonable prospect of finding copetitioners), the court may also award compensatory and punitive damages.

3. The second ground in §303(h) does not apply. No custodian had been appointed or took possession of Cookie's property. Relief must therefore be based on the fact that Cookie is not paying her debts as they become due. The express language of §303(h)(1) excludes bona fide disputed debts from the determination of general nonpayment. Therefore, provided that Cookie's dispute over the advertising agency's debt has genuine merit, it must not be treated as an unpaid debt. This means that Cookie is in default on ten debts totaling $165,000 — just over half her debts in number and value.

As stated in section 9.6.4, the number of overdue debts and the percentage of debt overdue are important factors to be taken into account in deciding whether there is general nonpayment of debts. However, courts also evaluate the nature and importance of the defaulted debts as well as the circumstances of the default, to try to obtain a sense of whether the pattern of nonpayment manifests serious financial distress. The facts in this case show that Cookie has fallen behind quite badly on her debt payments. Although this is a strong indicator of equity insolvency, not enough information is furnished to permit full consideration of the issue. Her defaults appear to be relatively recent, and there may be factors that suggest that this is a temporary liquidity problem rather than a true case of equity insolvency.

4. Section 707(b) is only applicable to an individual whose debts are primarily consumer debts. Section 101(8) defines consumer debts as those incurred primarily for personal, family, or household purposes. Although consumer debts are often thought of as being incurred in relation to consumable goods and services, courts generally read the definition in §101(8) more broadly to cover debt used to acquire capital assets, provided that these assets are used for personal or household purposes. In *In re Price*, 280 B.R. 499 (9th Cir. B.A.P. 2002) the court, following *In re Kelley* below, held that a debt incurred to buy a home and secured by a home mortgage is a consumer debt. Thus, if the motive of a transaction was the generation of income, the indebtedness arising from it is not a consumer debt. Only two of Desiree's debts have a business purpose — the secured claim for the purchase of the investment property and the attorney's fee. This means that two out of three secured debts, constituting 40 percent in value of total secured debt, and 14 out of 15 unsecured debts, constituting 50 percent in value of the total unsecured debt, are consumer debts. If the secured and unsecured debts are looked at in combination, 16 of 18 of her debts, constituting 42 percent of her total debt in value are consumer debts: They are a majority of her debts in number, but a minority in amount.

In deciding whether an individual's debts are primarily consumer debts, courts tend to focus on the value but also take number into account. *See, e.g., In re Booth*, 858 F.2d 1051 (5th Cir. 1988); *In re Kelley*, 841 F.2d 908 (9th Cir. 1988). In Desiree's case, these factors pull in opposite directions. Because value is more meaningful than number, an argument can be made for giving it more weight. However, that would preclude use of §707(b). A court that sees the need to judge the debtor's good faith under §707(b) surely has the flexibility, in a case where the overwhelming number of debts are consumer debts and their proportion in amount is close to half, to find that the debts are primarily consumer debts.

Having made that determination, the court must consider whether the Ch. 7 filing is a substantial abuse of the Code. In essence, Desiree's purpose is to keep her relatively high income for herself, maintaining a privileged standard of living, while her general creditors have to be satisfied with a meager distribution from her small estate. She plans to discharge her debts with a minimal sacrifice. If she filed under Ch. 13 instead, cut down on her living expenses, and committed her disposable income to payments under a plan, her creditors would receive a more substantial payment over time.

There is some controversy over the use of §707(b) to dismiss a Ch. 7 petition on the principal ground that the debtor has the means to pay more under Ch. 13. The argument against using it in these circumstances is that the Code does not state that Ch. 7 relief is available only to debtors who cannot afford to perform a Ch. 13 plan. In fact, when it was enacted in 1984, the "substantial abuse" standard in §707(b) was chosen by Congress over a proposed express rule to that effect.[3] The argument in favor of using §707(b) to refuse Ch. 7 relief to a debtor who can afford large payments under Ch. 13 is that §707(b) does not disqualify this as a principal consideration. Furthermore, creditors are treated unfairly when a debtor with a good future income can insulate it from creditors by surrendering current assets of relatively modest value. Some cases have treated the debtor's ability to pay more under a Ch. 13 plan as a sufficient ground, on its own, for finding substantial abuse. See In re Walton, 866 F.2d 981 (8th Cir. 1989); U.S. Trustee v. Harris, 960 F.2d 74 (8th Cir. 1992). Other courts, while regarding this as an important, even a primary, factor, require a finding of substantial abuse to be made under all the circumstances of the case. On this "totality of the circumstances" approach, other indicia of bad faith, such as irresponsible spending, intentional prepetition wrongdoing, or underhand dealings with creditors, are also taken into account. See, e.g., In re Kelley, supra; In re Krohn, 886 F.2d 123 (6th Cir. 1989); In re Green, 934 F.2d 568 (4th Cir. 1991); In re Lamanna, 153 F.3d 1 (1st Cir. 1998).

No indication of this kind of behavior is present in Desiree's case, but her proposed level of postpetition spending in relation to the size of the distribution to creditors surely offends the spirit of the Code. Some courts would go to great pains to make sure that she does not get away with such behavior. If her case is dismissed, she must face her creditors' actions in state court or seek relief under Ch. 13.

5. If the tax debts are consumer debts, the issue in this case would be the same as in Example 4: Whether it is, in itself, a substantial abuse of Ch. 7 for a debtor to file under that Chapter with the deliberate intention of escaping debt that she could afford to pay more fully in Ch. 13. However, before reaching that issue, it must be determined if income tax debts due by an individual on his salary and property taxes on his home do indeed qualify as consumer debts. If they do, §707(b) is clearly applicable. If not, there is at least a question (as discussed in Example 4) of whether her debts are primarily consumer debts.

---

3. As noted in section 9.7, the pending bankruptcy reform legislation would, if it passes, completely reverse this approach, and would make ability to support a Ch. 13 plan the principal and express basis for finding an abuse of Ch. 7.

Although a debtor may use most or all of his salary for household and domestic purposes, courts have generally held that income taxes are not consumer debts. A common explanation for this is that an income tax debt is not incurred as part of the process of consumption, but is involuntarily imposed on the taxpayer by the government for the public welfare. This was the court's basis for denying the U.S. Trustee's motion for dismissal in *In re Brashers*, 216 B.R. 59 (Bankr. N.D. Okl. 1998). The involuntary nature of the debt was the determinative factor in *Brashers*, and the court said that this compulsive quality of the debt made it inappropriate to apply the usual inquiry into the debtor's purpose in incurring the debt — the concept of debtor intent becomes tenuous where the liability is imposed on him by law. Where income taxes are concerned, the classification of the debt as nonconsumer is justified on the more general test of profit motive: It is the generation of income, not its expenditure, that creates the tax liability, so the debt truly is incurred in the production of income and is hence not a consumer debt. It makes no difference that the fruits of the income are then used for personal or household purposes. Classifying a tax debt as nonconsumer also seems to be consonant with the Code's underlying purpose of confining §707(b) to cases principally involving claims arising out of consumer credit transactions.

The property tax claim is not as easy to classify as the income tax claims because it is not really expended in a profit-seeking venture (even if there is some prospect that the home may ultimately be sold at a profit) and is more closely tied to ownership of the debtor's home and to consumption.[4] Nevertheless, on the test in *Brashers*, it would not be counted either. In *In re Stovall*, 209 B.R. 849 (Bankr. E.D. Va. 1997) the court reached the same result, for the same reason, in connection with a debt for a personal property tax. (The case did not involve §707(b), but was concerned with the codebtor stay under §1301(a) which also applies only to consumer debts.) The court held that the amount owing for personal property tax (a sales tax due on a car that the debtor had bought) was not a consumer debt because it was an obligation imposed on the debtor for the public welfare, and was not "incurred" by the debtor as contemplated by §101(8). The court noted that it was not a business debt, but the definition of consumer debts did not simply include all debts without a business motive. A debt could be neither a business nor a consumer debt. See also *In re Westberry*, 215 F.3d 589 (6th Cir. 2000).

As Tex's obligations are not primarily consumer in nature, §707(b) cannot be used. However, this does not mean that the court is powerless to dismiss the case. Section 707(a) allows the court to dismiss a case on general grounds

---

4. As noted in Explanation 4, most courts hold that debts relating to the acquisition and upkeep of real property — including payments on a home mortgage — are consumer debts, even though a home is not commonly thought of as consumer *goods*, and despite the fact that there is some indication in the legislative history of §707(b) that home mortgages were not intended to be included in determining if the debtor's obligations were primarily consumer debts.

of cause, and this subsection may include cause arising out of the debtor's bad faith or abusive conduct in cases other than those covered by §707(b). However, it is not entirely clear if §707(a) can be used for this purpose because its language creates an interpretational difficulty. It states that a court may dismiss a case only for cause, including unreasonable delay by the debtor, failure to pay fees, and failure to file required schedules. The list is clearly non-exclusive because §707(a) states that cause includes the specified matters. However, the enumerated situations that give rise to cause all consist of failure to comply with procedural requirements. This has led some courts to hold that the specific reference to only procedural noncompliance means that any other unspecified bases for cause must also be procedural in nature, and do not extend to more general grounds of bad faith or abuse. This approach was taken in *In re Padilla*, 222 F.3d 1184 (9th Cir. 2000). The court said that unlike Chs. 11 and 13, Ch. 7 does not contemplate an ongoing relationship between the debtor and creditors under a plan, and therefore does not have an express general requirement of good faith, as is found in the plan confirmation standards in Chs. 11 and 13. As a result, the debtor's absence of good faith in filing cannot, on its own, be a ground for dismissal under §707(a).

Even if §707(a) does not furnish a basis for dismissal, there is another possibility where the case does not fit within §707(b). The court has the discretion, within its general equitable powers conferred by §105(a), to make any order necessary or appropriate to carry out the provisions of the Code, including an order of dismissal if the debtor has been guilty of abuse of process. This was recognized in *In re Kestell*, 99 F. 3d 146 (4th Cir. 1996). The debtor filed for Ch. 7 relief for the sole purpose of evading payment of the nondischargeable portion of debts due to his ex-wife under a divorce judgment. (He had in fact indicated the intention to reaffirm his other debts, and had declared that he did not want his ex-wife to get anything.) He also failed to disclose and turn over certain assets. The court held that the divorce judgment was a consumer debt and that, in the totality of the circumstances, the debtor's conduct constituted a substantial abuse under §707(b). However, it also noted that even had the obligation to the ex-wife had not been a consumer debt, the debtor's conduct was an abuse of process which would have warranted an order of dismissal under §105(a). The debtor was motivated, not by a desire to achieve an equitable distribution among creditors and a fresh start, but to avoid paying his ex-wife.

The behavior of the debtor in *Kestell* is far worse than Tex's, and it is not clear that abuse of process would be constituted merely because Tex is using Ch. 7 to discharge more of his debt than he would be able to do in Ch. 13. Nor is it clear that the test of abuse of process is exactly equivalent to substantial abuse. Nevertheless, §105(a) is worth remembering as an alternative for cases that do not fall into §707(b).

10

The Automatic Stay

§10.1 Introduction

Since time immemorial, dogs have responded to the command "stay" by resting on their behinds and forgoing intended activity. While no scholarly commentator has traced the origins of the bankruptcy stay to this tradition, the link is striking. The stay does for the debtor and the estate what its canine equivalent does for the neighbor's cat: protection from harassment, pursuit, and dismemberment. In simple terms, the automatic stay is an injunction that arises by operation of law immediately upon the commencement of the bankruptcy case. It is described as automatic because the act of filing the bankruptcy petition is all that is required to bring it into effect. No application for the injunction is made, and no court order is needed.

The stay is provided for in §362. Its effect is to impose a wide-ranging prohibition on all activity outside the bankruptcy forum to collect prepetition debts from the debtor or to assert or enforce claims against the debtor's prepetition property or estate property. The range of the stay, delineated by §§362(a) and (b), is examined in section 10.4. Before studying the details of those provisions, it is helpful to outline the purpose, nature, and scope of the stay.

§10.2 The Purpose of the Automatic Stay

The automatic stay is a very important incident of bankruptcy. It is essential to the accomplishment of its two central goals: the debtor's fresh start and the evenhanded treatment of creditors. By halting individual collection activity by creditors, the stay prevents depletion of the debtor's assets and preserves them for surrender to the trustee or retention by the debtor in possession. Creditors can no longer seek advantage by pressing on with enforcement measures; they are compelled to channel their claims through the bankruptcy process. In addition to preserving the estate, the stay gives the debtor sanctuary from creditor pressure so that orderly liquidation can be arranged or a plan formulated for the debtor's rehabilitation.

The stay is also vital to the bankruptcy court's power to deal effectively with the case and related litigation. By stopping enforcement proceedings in other courts, it allows the bankruptcy court to exercise its jurisdiction and to assume the central role described in Chapter 7. Henceforth, all litigation relating to the case must be brought before the bankruptcy court and will be resolved there, unless the court itself permits continuation of the proceedings elsewhere by abstaining or granting relief from the stay.

The freezing of all collection activity benefits the creditor body as a whole by preserving the estate for evenhanded distribution. However, the interests of creditors in general often run counter to the interests of a particular creditor whose collection efforts are frustrated by the stay. Usually the creditor can do no more than accept the inevitability of the stay, prove a claim in the estate, and await a proportionate distribution. However, in some situations a creditor whose enforcement efforts are impeded by the stay may be able to demonstrate grounds for lifting it so that the enforcement process can continue. The circumstances under which relief from stay may be granted are discussed in Chapter 11.

§10.3   The Nature and Scope of the Stay

As stated before, the stay is an automatic injunction barring a broad range of action against the debtor and the property of the debtor and the estate. The nature and scope of the stay can be best understood if the following general principles are kept in mind:

(1)   *The stay is binding on all entities.*   "Entities" is defined in §101(15) to include individuals, corporate entities of all kinds, and governmental units.

(2)   *The stay comes into effect upon the filing of the petition.*   This holds true for both voluntary and involuntary cases. In an involuntary case, therefore, the stay precedes the order for relief and operates much like a preliminary injunction prior to the adjudication of bankruptcy.

(3)   *The stay remains in effect for the duration of the case.*   When the debtor receives a discharge, creditors' attempts to collect discharged debts are permanently enjoined. Therefore, for many creditors the advent of the stay forever ends collection efforts under nonbankruptcy law. (Qualifications to this broad observation are discussed in section 10.5 and Chapter 11.)

(4)   *The stay applies in all forms of bankruptcy.*   However, because there are significant differences between liquidation and the different forms of

rehabilitation, the impact of the stay is likely to vary depending on the type of relief sought. For example, because Ch. 7 is intended to provide for the expeditious liquidation of the estate, the stay is likely to focus on preservation of property and the protection of the debtor for the relatively short period during which the estate is collected, realized, and distributed. By contrast, a debtor under Ch. 11 is engaged in plan formulation, negotiations, the operation of a business, and the use of estate assets. The debtor's ability to keep creditors at bay during this process of restructuring is vital to the success of the effort at rehabilitation, but creditors assume a greater risk of loss while the debtor uses estate property and works on reorganization. If the attempt at rehabilitation fails, the delay in enforcement of rights caused by the stay could have resulted in irreparable damage to a creditor. *See* Chapter 11.

(5) *The effectiveness of the stay does not depend on creditors' notice of the filing.* The stay binds them as soon as the petition is filed, even if they only find out about it later. Therefore, a creditor cannot seek to retain an advantage gained by violating the stay on the grounds that it had no knowledge of the bankruptcy when committing the contravention. Some courts have characterized acts in violation of the stay as voidable, so that the trustee or the debtor must apply to court to have the act set aside. Other courts — the majority, it seems — treat acts in violation of the stay as null and void, so that no affirmative steps need be taken to avoid them. *See* section 10.7 and Example 1.

Although innocent violations of the stay are ineffective, deliberate violations can have even more serious consequences. In addition to losing any advantage gained by the violation, a willful transgressor is liable to the debtor for any actual damages suffered and, if the disobedience is egregious, for punitive damages too. The violator may also be held in contempt of court. *See* section 10.7 and Example 1.

(6) *The stay does not preclude action in the bankruptcy court.* Creditors and other parties in interest may institute proceedings in the bankruptcy court itself concerning matters that are otherwise subject to the stay.

(7) *The stay is not an end in itself.* It does not determine the validity of claims or dispose of them. It simply suspends action on the claim outside of the bankruptcy process. In due course the claim will be asserted against the estate and will be dealt with in the claim procedure. Any issues concerning the claim will be adjudicated by the bankruptcy court itself or will be resolved in another forum following relief from stay.

(8) *Although the stay is comprehensive, it does not cover every conceivable activity.* When the stay does not apply to a particular action but it is in the best interests of the estate to restrain that action, §105 gives the court the power to issue an injunction. The injunction under §105 is not automatic and must be issued by the court following an application on notice and a hearing. The applicant for the injunction must demonstrate good cause for the grant of relief.

§10.4   The Range of the Stay: §§362(a) and (b)

Sections 362(a) and (b) set out what activity is stayed and what is not. Section 362(a) prescribes eight different categories of activity that must stop when the petition is filed, and §362(b) lists a number of specific types of activity that are not stayed. If a particular act is not mentioned in either subsection, and §362(a) cannot be interpreted to encompass it, the act is not subject to the stay. To prevent it from occurring, the debtor or trustee must convince the court to use its injunctive powers under §105. Some of the activities included and excluded from the stay are illustrated by Examples 1 and 2.

§10.4.1   Activity Included in the Stay — §362(a)

The different types of activity stayed by §362(a) can be classified into three broad categories:

(1) Activity against the debtor.   The stay prohibits all activity against the debtor relating to the collection of claims that arose before the commencement of the bankruptcy case. This includes the commencement or continuation of judicial or administrative proceedings to adjudicate or enforce the claim as well as private nonjudicial action (such as correspondence, personal contact, or exercise of a right of set off) aimed at recovering the debt. This activity against the debtor is forbidden by §§362(a)(1), (2), (6), (7), and (8).

The stay of actions against the debtor applies only to prepetition claims. After the petition has been filed, the debtor's fresh start begins. Postpetition transactions by the debtor do not give rise to claims against the estate but are the debtor's own responsibility. They can be enforced against the debtor through the normal collection methods of nonbankruptcy law.

(2) Activity against property of the debtor.   Section 362(a)(5) prohibits any steps to create, perfect, or enforce a lien against property of the debtor to secure a prepetition claim. This provision protects the debtor's property — as distinct from estate property — from the claims of prepetition creditors. The distinction between estate property and the debtor's property is explained in Chapter 12. For the present, it is sufficient to note that the filing of the petition creates a bankruptcy estate that consists primarily of property in which the debtor had an interest at the time of the filing. Property acquired by the debtor after the petition, as well as certain property released to the debtor from the estate, falls into the new fresh-start estate of the debtor. Section 362(a)(5) forbids prepetition creditors from seeking to satisfy their claims by attempting to establish or enforce liens against the debtor's fresh-start property. The stay covers only prepetition debts. A postpetition creditor has full rights of enforcement against the debtor's property.

(3) Activity against property of the estate. As stated above, a bankruptcy estate is created upon the filing of the petition. The preservation of estate property and the evenhanded treatment of creditors call for a wide-ranging stay on all postpetition activity to remove property from the estate or to establish or enforce an interest in it. The stay of action against estate property is wider than the stay protecting the debtor and property of the debtor, in that it applies to both prepetition and postpetition claims. A postpetition creditor of the debtor has no claim to property of the estate and has no right to try to reach estate property. However, the estate itself may incur obligations. The stay prevents creditors of the estate from taking action to assert their claims against estate property outside of the normal claim procedures.

The stay of activity against property of the estate is provided for in §§362(a)(2), (3), and (4). These provisions cover the enforcement of prepetition judgments as well as acts to obtain possession of property of or from the estate, to exercise control over estate property, or to establish or enforce a lien against estate property.

§10.4.2 Activity Excluded from the Stay — §362(b)

This note does not summarize all the exclusions from the stay in §362(b). Some of them are very specific and technical and relate to particular types of debtors or narrow classes of regulated transactions. The more general exclusions fall into two broad groups:

(1) The stay does not affect certain specified activities that do not involve the collection of debt but are concerned with the enforcement by governmental units of noncommercial responsibilities of the debtor. For example, the stay does not apply to criminal proceedings against the debtor (§362(b)(1)) or to proceedings by governmental units to enforce police or regulatory powers (§§362(b)(4)). It is a question of fact whether a particular governmental activity falls within one of the exclusions from the stay, so the purpose and effect of the action must be examined. These exclusions can be found in Examples 2(f) and (h).

(2) The stay does not affect certain specified actions taken by a creditor under nonbankruptcy law to perfect or consolidate rights against the debtor or the estate. The rationale for these exceptions is that they are merely legal procedures that the creditor is entitled to take under nonbankruptcy law to validate a legitimate claim. For example, under §362(b)(3) a creditor may perform acts to perfect or to maintain or continue perfection if that action is recognized by §§546 or 547 as binding on the estate (this is illustrated by Example 2(g)) or may comply with the procedures required by

UCC Article 3 for the presentment, notice, and protesting of a negotiable instrument (§362(b)(11)).

As noted earlier, in addition to the exceptions that fit into the above two categories, §362(b) contains a variety of particular exceptions that apply to stated acts in relation to specific types of transactions. A glance down the list in the subsection will give you an idea of the kinds of activity involved — for example, certain setoffs by commodity brokers and others, certain actions by government to assess or determine tax liability, the eviction of a tenant where the lease of nonresidential property had expired prepetition, and so on. Most of these exceptions have been recognized because Congress was persuaded that the interests of the debtor and creditors in general would not be harmed by permitting the identified action to continue without leave of the court, or that the rights are important enough to permit continued enforcement without interruption from the stay. Although we will not identify and discuss each of these specific exceptions, there is one that should be noted because it is significant in cases in which an individual debtor has support obligations.

The impact of bankruptcy on the dependents of an individual debtor is a matter of ongoing concern. This is particularly so where the dependents are also creditors because the debtor has support obligations to them under a prior agreement or court order. To prevent a debtor from using bankruptcy to evade these support obligations, the Bankruptcy Reform Act of 1994 enacted a number of provisions giving these debts special treatment, including higher priority, exclusion from the operation of the exemptions, non-avoidability of a lien securing them, and nondischargeability. (These aspects of the Act will be dealt with in the appropriate places later.) In addition, a new exception to the stay was created. Under §362(b)(2), the stay does not bar the commencement of an action or proceeding to establish paternity, to establish or modify an order for alimony maintenance or support, or to collect such debts from property that is not property of the estate (that is, from the debtor's own property).

Only those transactions that are listed in §362(b) are excluded from the stay. Therefore, if §362(a) covers a particular activity and it does not fall within one of the exclusions of §362(b), it is subject to the stay.

§10.5   Termination of the Stay

The stay of a particular activity may be lifted by the court following an application for relief from stay under §362(d). This is discussed in Chapter 11. Apart from that, §362(c) provides for termination of the stay in the normal course of the bankruptcy proceedings. It treats the stay of acts against estate property differently from the stay of other acts.

Under §362(c)(1), the stay of acts against estate property continues until the property is no longer property of the estate. Property may be released by the estate for different reasons. For example, the trustee may sell it in the course of liquidation; it may be abandoned to a claimant because neither the debtor nor the estate has any equity in it; it may be abandoned to the debtor as exempt. Section 362(c)(1) is of limited effect. It does not authorize proceedings against the property following release by the estate, but merely makes the stay inapplicable to the extent that it was grounded on the fact that the estate had an interest in the property. Although it is no longer property of the estate, it may still be protected from the stay on some other ground. For example, if property is abandoned to the debtor as exempt, it still cannot be subjected to the claims of prepetition creditors, who remain bound by the stay of actions against the debtor and the debtor's property (*see* Example 2(b)). However, a postpetition creditor of the debtor could perfect a security interest in it or seize it in execution, because postpetition claims are not affected by the stay of acts against the debtor or the debtor's property.

The stay of all acts other than acts against property of the estate continues in effect under §362(c)(2) until the case is closed or dismissed or a discharge is granted or denied, whichever occurs first. This provision sounds broader than it is. If a debt is discharged, the creditor is permanently enjoined from collecting it under §524(a)(2), so the stay is succeeded by the postdischarge injunction. In such a case, the termination of the stay is no cause for celebration by the creditor. However, if the stay terminates as a result of dismissal of the case, the expiry of the stay entitles creditors to continue collection activity under nonbankruptcy law. Similarly, if a debt is excluded from the discharge or if the debtor is denied a discharge altogether (*see* Chapter 22), enforcement of the nondischarged debt or debts may proceed.

§10.6 The Effect of the Stay on Limitation Periods — §108

Under nonbankruptcy law, creditors' claims are subject to statutes of limitation. Because the stay halts lawsuits and collection efforts, a creditor may be prevented from initiating suit within the time required by nonbankruptcy law. If the bankruptcy case is not dismissed and the claim is settled and discharged in the course of bankruptcy, the postpetition expiry of the limitation period is irrelevant. The creditor will have no occasion to commence proceedings in another court.

However, if the bankruptcy case is dismissed, the stay is lifted, or the debt is excluded from the discharge, the creditor's right to continue nonbankruptcy enforcement proceedings revives. The stay does not toll the limitation period entirely. However, §108(c) gives the creditor an opportunity to commence suit after termination of the stay. It provides, in essence, that if the claim is subject to a limitation period (including not only a statute of limitations but also a period fixed by court order or contract) and that period had not expired before the petition was filed, it will not expire until the time fixed by nonbankruptcy law or 30 days after notice of the termination or expiry of the stay, whichever is later. In other words, if, when the creditor is notified of termination of the stay, the nonbankruptcy limitation period had not expired and has more than 30 days to run, suit must be commenced in the remaining limitation period. However, if the period expired during the stay or will expire within 30 days of notice of termination, the creditor has 30 days following notice to commence suit.

It must be stressed that the creditor's right to commence suit after the stay under §108 only applies when the stay is terminated by dismissal of the case or a grant of relief from stay and the debt in question has not been discharged. If the stay ends simply because the case has been concluded and the debt is discharged, the post discharge injunction of §524 precludes any further enforcement action.

§10.7   The Effect of Violating the Stay

The stay binds creditors as soon as the petition is filed, whether or not they have knowledge of it, and any act in violation of the stay, whether innocent or deliberate, is ineffective to give the actor any advantage. Apparent legal rights acquired in violation of the stay are a nullity, and the creditor is obliged to restore any money or property (or its value). There is some difference of view on the legal effect of an act in violation of the stay. Some courts regard an act in violation of the stay as *voidable,* so that it remains effective unless the debtor or trustee moves in bankruptcy court to have it set aside. *See, e.g., Sikes v. Global Marine, Inc.,* 881 F.2d 176 (5th Cir. 1989); *In re Siciliano,* 13 F.3d 748 (3rd Cir. 1994). However, the majority view is to treat the act as *void,* so that the actor gains no legal advantage from it, even if no motion for avoidance is made. *See, e.g., Ellis v. Consolidated Diesel Electric Corp.,* 894 F.2d 371 (10th Cir. 1990); *In re Schwartz,* 954 F.2d 569 (9th Cir. 1992); *Jones v. Cain,* 804 A.2d 322 (D.C. Ct. of App. 2002). The latter approach gives the stay greater potency.

If the violation of the stay is innocent, its impact is limited to ineffectiveness of the act, as stated above. However, a deliberate violation has further consequences:

(1) Attorneys' fees, costs, compensatory and punitive damages. Section 362(h) renders a wilful violator liable for actual damages suffered by an individual as a result of the violation. For a violation to be wilful, the action must be motivated by a specific intent to violate the stay. Once a creditor has notice of, knows, or has reason to know of the bankruptcy filing, any deliberate act in violation of the stay is wilful. (See *Patton v. Shade*, 263 B.R. 861 (C.D. Ill. 2001).) It is no defense for the creditor to claim that the action was taken in a good faith belief that it was not subject to the stay. In *In re Kaneb*, 196 F.3d 265 (1st Cir. 1999) the mortgagee's file contained an unsigned order for relief from stay. When the file was forwarded to its attorney, he erroneously thought that relief had been granted and proceeded to foreclose the mortgage. The court held that the violation was wilful despite the creditor's attorney's belief that the mortgage was no longer subject to the stay.

Damages include actual (compensatory) damages, costs and attorneys' fees and, in appropriate circumstances, punitive damages. Punitive damages are only appropriate where the violation is not merely deliberate, but motivated by malice or are otherwise particularly egregious. Some courts have held that compensatory damages might include damages for mental distress in appropriate circumstances. For example, in *In re Kaneb* (above) the court allowed damages for mental anguish where the debtor was an elderly widower who lived in a condominium complex in Florida. He suffered distress when neighbors shunned him after notices of foreclosure came to their attention. Many courts are wary of awarding mental distress damages too readily. *Patton* (above) refused them in the absence of medical evidence establishing that the debtor suffered more than humiliation or annoyance. *Aiello v. Providian Financial Corp.* 239 F.3d 876 (7th Cir. 2001) was not willing to recognize mental distress damages at all unless the creditor's collection activity amounted to tortious conduct. The creditor had violated the automatic stay by making a somewhat aggressive attempt to persuade the debtor to reaffirm the debt, but the court said that the conduct did not amount to tortious coercion or extortion. The court said that §362(h) is aimed at financial protection, not peace of mind, and was not meant to compensate the debtor for the transient distress of dealing with the creditor's improper approach.

By using the word "individual" rather than "debtor," §362(h) intends to provide the remedy not only to the debtor, but to any individual who can establish economic loss as a result of the violation. Some courts have held that "individual," as it is used in §362(h), should not be interpreted in the usual sense to mean a natural person, but should extend to all entities, including artificial persons, so that a corporate debtor can also claim damages for a wilful violation of the stay. *In re APF Co.*, 264 B.R. 344 (Bankr. D. Del. 2001) discusses court of appeals authority for this approach. Other courts have disagreed. For example, in *In re Just Brakes Corporate Systems, Inc.*, 108 F.3d 881 (8th Cir. 1997), the court held that this interpretation violates the plain meaning of the word, as it is used consistently in the Code.

Furthermore, given that the subsection was enacted in 1984 as part of a package of amendments relating to consumers, to broaden its meaning is also contrary to apparent legislative intent. Courts that find §362(h) inapplicable where the debtor is an artificial person recognize that the court nevertheless has the power, under §105(a), to award compensatory damages to a corporate debtor for violation of the stay. However, an award of punitive damages may be beyond the bankruptcy court's general equitable jurisdiction.

(2) Contempt of court.   Although the stay arises automatically and is not an express court order, it is treated as such, and deliberate disobedience to it constitutes contempt of court. Therefore, whether or not damages are awardable under §362(h), a deliberate violation of the stay could expose the violator to sanctions for contempt of court. Given the uncertainties in the jurisdiction of the bankruptcy court (discussed in Chapter 7), there remains some question over the existence and extent of the bankruptcy court's power to sanction contempt.

Most courts accept that under the general authority to issue orders and judgments conferred on them by §105(a), bankruptcy courts do have the power to impose civil contempt sanctions. See, for example, *In re Walters,* 868 F.2d. 665 (4th Cir. 1989); *In re Norris,* 192 B.R. 863 (Bankr. W.D. La. 1995); *In re Dyer,* 322 F.3d 1178 (9th Cir. 2003). These may take the form of a compensatory order (which would be very much like the compensatory damages awarded under §362(h), and, therefore, not appropriate in addition to such damages), or a coercive order, designed to compel compliance by imposing a conditional punishment on the violator, to be terminated when he ceases the violation.

The bankruptcy court's power to impose criminal sanctions for contempt (that is, to punish the violator for having intentionally disregarded the stay) is less clear. In *In re Dyer* (above) the court said that §105(a) confers powers on the court only to the extent necessary to enforce the provisions of the Code, which can usually be accomplished by civil contempt sanctions. In addition, punitive sanctions raise due process concerns (such as the right to a jury trial) for which Article 1 courts are not equipped. The court noted that a bankruptcy court's inability to impose punishment for criminal contempt is not inconsistent with its power to grant punitive damages under §362(h). If the person seeking relief for the violation is an individual who qualifies for protection under §362(h), the Code authorizes punitive damages. However, if the person claiming relief is not covered by §362(h), such as the trustee, the only sanction available is under §105(a), which does not allow for punitive sanctions. Of course, the bankruptcy court is a unit of the district court, so even if the bankruptcy court has no power to impose criminal contempt sanctions, the district court can do so. (See section 7.5.2 for further discussion of the bankruptcy court's contempt power.)

EXAMPLES

1. Mutiny for the Bounty

Hinda DeLay defaulted on a loan from Blitzkrieg Bank. The bank commenced a collection suit, obtained default judgment, and issued a writ of execution. On June 1, the sheriff levied on nonexempt personal property owned by Hinda. Under state law, a lien arose in the property upon levy. An execution sale is scheduled for June 15. On June 14, Blitzkrieg received notice from the clerk of the bankruptcy court, informing it that Hinda had filed a voluntary Ch. 7 petition on May 31. Because the collection suit was so close to its conclusion, the bank decided that it made sense to proceed with the sale, thereby avoiding the need to become involved in Hinda's bankruptcy proceedings. Was that a good decision?

2. To Owe Is Human, To Forestall, Divine

The following questions concern the activities of various creditors of Justin Tyme, who filed a voluntary Ch. 7 petition on July 1 of this year. Consider whether the action described in each question is affected by the automatic stay. Consider both the inclusions in §362(a) and the exceptions in §362(b).

(a) Last year, Justin's brother obtained a short-term loan from a finance company, and Justin guaranteed the debt as surety. The due date of the loan is July 15. Justin's brother did not pay it and has no assets. On July 20, the finance company wrote a letter to Justin telling him that his obligation as surety had become due and requested payment. Does the letter violate the stay?

(b) Last year, Justin borrowed money from his bank. When he failed to repay the loan on its due date in February, the bank commenced suit to recover the amount of the loan. The bank obtained judgment at the end of June, just prior to the petition. After the petition had been filed, the bank wished to execute on its judgment. There are two vehicles parked outside Justin's home. One is an old car, abandoned to Justin by the trustee because it is exempt, and the other is a motorbike purchased by Justin from his postpetition income. Can the bank execute on either of these assets?

(c) At the time that Justin became bankrupt, he was in possession of a safe deposit box at his bank. A few weeks before bankruptcy, Justin's aunt asked him to put her jewelry in his safe deposit box for safekeeping while she was on vacation. Justin deposited it in the box and gave his aunt a duplicate key to the box so that she could remove the jewelry when she wanted it. May the aunt remove her jewelry from the box on her return from vacation in July?

(d) Justin owes a large prepetition debt to a clothing store. The store's manager had become increasingly frustrated at Justin's failure to pay the debt. When he heard of Justin's bankruptcy, the manager was enraged. He sent an employee to picket Justin's home. The employee marched up and down outside Justin's residence for several hours with a large sign reading "Justin Tyme does not pay his debts." Is this a violation of the stay? If so, can Justin recover damages?

(e) Some months before his bankruptcy, Justin was playing pool in a bar. He became involved in a dispute with one of the other players, and Justin attacked him viciously, beating him with this pool cue. After this incident, the barkeeper told Justin never to return to his premises again. Shortly after the attack, the state initiated a criminal prosecution against Justin. In addition, when Justin tried to enter the bar again, the owner of the bar commenced proceedings in state court to enjoin him from entering or loitering about the property. (This is known as a disbarment proceeding.) At the time that Justin filed his bankruptcy petition, these two proceedings were pending. How will the stay affect them?

(f) Two months prior to Justin's bankruptcy, a contractor completed an alteration to Justin's home. The contractor has not been paid. Under the state's mechanic's lien law, the contractor is entitled to a lien on the property to secure the price of the work. Under the statute, the lien attaches to the property with priority effective from the date of commencement of the work, provided that the claimant files a lien claim in the deeds registry within three months of completion. The claimant is required to commence action to foreclose the lien within six months of filing the claim. The contractor had not filed a lien claim by July 1, the petition date. Does the stay prevent the contractor from filing the lien and commencing suit in the periods prescribed by the state statute?

(g) For several months before his bankruptcy, Justin neglected to have his garbage hauled away. It has accumulated in piles in the front yard of his house. In June, the city health department warned Justin that if he did not have the garbage removed, action would be taken against him. Justin ignored the warning. Not only has he failed to clean up the existing garbage, but he continues to add new refuse to the heap.

On July 5, the city initiated suit in municipal court to enjoin further dumping and to compel Justin to remove the existing garbage. In the event that Justin fails to obey the cleanup order, the city asks the court for authority to clean up Justin's yard itself and to charge Justin for the cleanup costs. Was the city allowed to commence this proceeding? If the municipal court grants the order, can it be enforced?

(h) At the time of the petition, Justin had a savings account with a balance of $5,000 at his credit union. He also owed the credit union a balance of $8,000 on a loan. Under nonbankruptcy law, where two persons are mutually indebted, the debts may be set off against each other. That is, either party may deduct the amount due to him before paying what he owes the other. An account in a bank (or a credit union) is a debt due by the bank to its customer. Therefore, if the customer also owes money to the bank or credit union, it can refuse to permit withdrawal from the customer's account, and can set off the monies in the account against what the customer owes. Section 553 gives full effect to a setoff right in bankruptcy, and treats the debt as secured. (Setoff is discussed in section 16.2).

When Justin's credit union becomes aware of the bankruptcy of a customer who owes it money, its routine procedure is to place a "hold" on the customer's account. It does this because customers have been known to make hasty withdrawals from accounts, thereby defeating the credit union's right to claim the setoff in the bankruptcy case. On July 5 the credit union heard of Justin's bankruptcy and it immediately imposed the hold on Justin's account. Justin discovered this on July 7 when he tried to withdraw the funds and close the account. He claims that the credit union has violated the stay. Is he correct?

EXPLANATIONS

1. No. The stay took effect on May 31 upon the filing of Hinda's petition. Any action taken subsequent to that is a violation of the stay. As noted in section 10.7, the majority view is that an act in violation of the stay is void, so any advantage obtained by the creditor is a nullity.

The levy on June 1 violated §362(a)(2), which forbids enforcement of a prepetition judgment against the debtor or property of the estate. The levy also violates §362(a)(1), which bars the continuation of judicial proceedings against the debtor, and §362(a)(4), which prohibits any act to create, perfect, or enforce a lien against property of the estate. (The levy creates a judicial lien and Hinda's property became property of the estate under §541 on the date of the petition.) The fact that Blitzkrieg did not know of the bankruptcy filing when it levied on June 1 does not validate the levy. The stay is effective whether or not the creditor knew of it. Blitzkrieg's execution lien is a nullity and the property or its proceeds must be returned to the estate.

By continuing with the sale in execution after acquiring knowledge of Hinda's bankruptcy, Blitzkrieg compounded its violation of the stay and became a willful transgressor. As discussed in section 10.7, this could lead to liability beyond the restoration of the property or its value to the estate. Section 362(h) renders a willful violator liable for actual damages suffered by an individual as a result of the violation. As Hinda is an individual debtor, this section is applicable here. In addition to compensatory damages, the award includes costs, attorney's fees, and in appropriate cases, punitive damages. As an alternative, Blitzkreig could be liable for contempt of court under §105(a). There is no indication on the facts that Hinda suffered any loss as a result of the sale of the property, which was nonexempt and had become property of the estate by that time.

Blitzkrieg should, therefore, not have ignored the notice of Hinda's bankruptcy. By proceeding, it gained no advantage and could attract liability beyond the duty of having to disgorge its benefit. No doubt it is frustrating for a creditor to be deprived of the fruits of its collection action so close to its successful conclusion, but the purpose of the stay is to prevent depletion of the estate by one creditor at the expense of the creditor body as a whole. The correct response would have been for Blitzkrieg to surrender the property to the trustee and to prove a claim in the estate for its unpaid debt. This claim will ultimately be paid at the rate payable to claims of that rank — general unsecured claims. It should be noted that even if the petition had been filed after June 1 (when Blitzkrieg obtained its lien), the advantage gained by the execution would be avoided. It would have been a preferential transfer, avoidable by the trustee under §547. *See* Chapter 15.

2. **(a)** Section 362(a)(6) prohibits acts to collect, assess, or recover a prepetition claim from the debtor. Even a polite request for payment is a violation of the stay. It is not clear if the finance company knew about Justin's bankruptcy when it sent the letter. If it had no notice, knowledge, or reason to know of the stay, the letter will not result in liability under §§362(h) or 105(a).

The stay only covers the collection of prepetition debts. The suretyship contract, while executed prior to the petition, is subject to a contingency — Justin's brother's default — that occurred only after the petition was filed. Notwithstanding, the debt itself is prepetition. The execution of the suretyship contract, rather than the removal of the contingency, is the event that determines the date on which the debt arose.

(b) The bank is an unsecured judgment creditor. By levying on the two assets, it hopes to satisfy its claim rather than wait in line for a pro rata distribution from the estate. Obviously this cannot be tolerated. The car has been abandoned to Justin, so it is no longer property of the estate and is not subject to the stay on actions against estate property under §§362(a)(2), (3), and (4). However, that does not help the bank. The car is now the debtor's property, and levy is stayed by §362(a)(1), which forbids the continuation of process to recover a prepetition claim against the debtor. The bike was never estate property, but levy against it is likewise stayed by §362(a)(1). Alternatively, §362(a)(5) applies: As the levy would create a judicial lien on the bike and car, it violates the bar on action to create a lien on the debtor's property to secure a prepetition claim.

(c) This question emphasizes the broad language of §362(a)(3), which stays not only acts to obtain possession of or to exercise control over property of the estate but also to obtain possession of property from the estate. In other words, the stay operates not only to protect property that belongs to the estate but also property of third parties over which the estate has acquired control.

As explained in Chapter 12, the jewelry is not property of the estate because Justin has no beneficial interest in it and holds it only for safekeeping. In due course, once the aunt's ownership is established, the trustee will release it to her. In the interim, however, the trustee has acquired control of the safe deposit box and its contents, and the stay prohibits attempts to interfere with that control. Justin's aunt must go through the proper channels to obtain release of the property by the trustee, subject to oversight by the court. In this way, the stay protects the integrity of the trustee's supervision over and custody of property that was in the debtor's possession at the time of the petition until such time as its proper disposition can be determined.

(d) The facts of this question are not entirely the product of an outlandish professorial mind. They are inspired by an actual case: *In re Sechuan City, Inc.,* 18 Bankr. Ct. Dec. (CCR) 1177 (Bankr. E.D. Pa. 1989). In that case the debtor operated a restaurant in hotel premises under a lease arrangement with the hotel. After the debtor filed a bankruptcy petition, the hotel management had signs posted at hotel entrances stating, among other things, that the restaurant did not pay its bills and had dishonored its obligations. The court found that the conduct of the hotel was intended to shame or coerce the debtor into paying a prepetition debt and was therefore an act to collect a debt in violation of §362(a)(6). To be barred by the stay, the creditor's behavior must be aimed at putting pressure on the debtor to pay the debt. Behavior that is merely annoying is not forbidden by the stay. Of course, the inference can easily be drawn that any harassment of the debtor is motivated by a desire to coerce payment.

In *Sechuan City,* the hotel had argued that its signs were protected by the First Amendment's guarantee of free speech. The court rejected this argument because the signs were intended to further the selfish ends of the hotel, rather than to make a statement concerning public affairs. The First Amendment cannot be used to shield a violation of the stay.

Because the creditor's actions are willful, damages may be awarded under §362(h). In *Sechuan City* the debtor was awarded actual damages on the basis that the signs had discouraged patronage of its business and had resulted in financial loss. The debtor must show actual injury to receive damages under §362(h). Unlike the restaurant, Justin has not suffered interference with his capacity to earn. A creative attorney may be able to develop an argument for injury on some tort theory, but this seems to be rather a tenuous case for actual damages. Punitive damages could be awarded for egregious conduct. It could be that this activity may cross that threshold. However, courts often refuse to allow punitive damages unless actual damages are proven. Even if Justin is upset by the picketing, he should not be able to claim emotional distress damage, as discussed in section 10.7.

(e) The criminal case against Justin is not stayed. Section 362(b)(1) excludes from the stay the commencement or continuation of a criminal action or proceeding against the debtor. The reason for this exclusion is that bankruptcy should not intrude upon the operation of the state's criminal law system. On these facts, there is no question that the criminal proceedings are not subject to the stay because they clearly have no relationship to the collection of a debt. However, sometimes criminal proceedings may have the effect of (and may be motivated by the desire to) persuade or coerce the debtor to pay money to or for the benefit of the victim. For example, a person who received a bad check from a debtor may initiate criminal proceedings in the hope of extracting payment from the debtor, or a court may suspend a sentence on condition that the debtor makes monetary restitution to the victim.

Where debt collection motives are intertwined with criminal proceedings, there have been cases that have held that such proceedings should not be covered by the exception in §362(b)(1), but should be subject to the stay. However, the better view seems to be that a bankruptcy court should not interfere with the prosecution of criminal cases, no matter what the underlying motive or effect of the criminal prosecution may be. This approach was adopted by an en banc decision of the court of appeals in *In re Gruntz*, 202 F.3d 1074 (9th Cir. 2000). The debtor had been convicted and sentenced to imprisonment for failure to pay child support. He claimed that the criminal proceedings were a violation of the stay because their purpose was to collect a debt. The court said that §362(b)(1) unambiguously excludes criminal prosecutions from the stay and reflects a strong policy of not having federal courts interfere with criminal proceedings in state court. Federal courts should not be examining criminal proceedings to try to divine if the underlying basis of the prosecution is debt collection. Criminal prosecution is on behalf of all citizens of the state, not on behalf of an individual creditor. The public prosecutor's decision to pursue criminal charges is an independent determination made by the government, irrespective of what the victim's motive may be.

The suit for the injunction is an action against the debtor that was commenced before the petition. It is therefore stayed by §362(a)(1). However, it neither seeks to coerce payment of a debt from Justin nor does it affect his property or property of the estate. Because the goals of bankruptcy are not furthered by the stay of the enjoined proceedings, the barkeeper may argue that §362(a) should not apply. A safer course would be to abide by the stay but to apply to the bankruptcy court for relief so that the action can continue.

(f) Justin's home became the property of the estate upon the filing of the petition. In the absence of an exception in §362(b), any attempt to perfect the lien by filing offends both §362(a)(4) and §362(a)(6). Commencement of the foreclosure suit is barred by §362(a)(1).

However, §362(b)(3) *does* provide an exception to the stay for perfection of the lien. It provides that the stay does not apply to any act to perfect or to maintain or continue perfection of an interest in property to the extent that the trustee's rights and powers are subject to such perfection under §546(b). (Section 546(b) is explained more fully in section 15.3.1.) In simple terms, it recognizes the effectiveness against the estate of a provision of nonbankruptcy law that permits perfection of an interest to backdate upon completion of the act of perfection. In the context of this case, §546(b)(1)(A) upholds the rule of state law that allows the builder to perfect the mechanic's lien by filing within three months of completion, thereby acquiring a lien effective as from the date of commencement of the work. Section 362(b)(3) excludes the act of perfection from the stay, so that it can be accomplished within the portion of the statutory period that remains unexpired after the petition has been filed. Perfection by filing is affected by the normal procedure prescribed by state law. However, if seizure of the property or commencement of suit is required to complete perfection, §546(b)(2)(A) requires that this act is substituted for by giving notice to the trustee.

Thus, the builder is able to proceed with the lien filing as if no bankruptcy petition has taken place. Instead of commencing suit six months thereafter, he must give the trustee notice under §546(b) within that period. By following these procedures, the builder is able to acquire a valid lien on the property which will give him a secured claim against the estate. If §§546(b) and 362(b)(3) did not validate the builder's right under nonbankruptcy law to file the lien and commence suit in the stated periods, the advent of bankruptcy before the builder had taken the action would have defeated his statutory lien. Congress has made the policy decision not to interfere with a state's statutory scheme to protect lienholders with an extended perfection period.

(g) The stay under §362(a) applies to all entities, including governmental units. However, §362(b)(4) excludes from the stay the commencement or continuation of an action or proceeding by a governmental unit to enforce its police or regulatory power, and it permits the enforcement of a judgment other than a money judgment obtained for the purpose of exercising that power. The gist of this subsection is: Despite the stay, the government may proceed to the stage of judgment in any action to enforce its police or regulatory power. If the judgment is not monetary in nature, enforcement proceedings may continue beyond the judgment; if the judgment is for money, the proceedings must end at the point of judgment and further enforcement is stayed, as it would be with other monetary claims.

The city health department is a governmental unit as defined in §101(27). The disposal of waste is undoubtedly within the city's police or regulatory power. Therefore, the commencement and continuation of the proceedings in municipal court, up to the stage of enforcement of the judgment, is excluded from the stay under §362(b)(4).

Not every kind of action or proceeding by a governmental unit is an exercise of police or regulatory power. Governments often engage in commercial transactions. In this role their claims are no different from those of private creditors and are subject to the stay. The question of whether the government is acting as a regulator or commercial creditor is one of fact, to be determined by examining the nature of the transaction or relationship, its purpose and its underlying policy motivation. The fact that proceedings may ultimately result in a money judgment does not necessarily disqualify the proceedings as regulatory. Often, a monetary assessment is needed to penalize violations of policy or to effect a regulatory purpose. For example, in *In re Commonwealth Companies, Inc.*, 913 F.2d 518 (8th Cir. 1990), a civil fraud action brought by the United States under the False Claims Act was held to be regulatory and excluded from the stay under §362(b)(4). The court found that the goal of the suit was not merely to recover compensation for fraud, but also to penalize it and to deter such conduct by others. By contrast, in *In re Corporation de Servicios Medicos Hospitalarios de Fajardo,* 805 F.2d 440 (1st Cir. 1986), the Puerto Rican Department of Health was held not to be entitled to rely on §362(b)(4) to continue with an action arising out of a contract with the debtor to operate hospital services.

In *Commonwealth Companies,* the court, in excepting the suit from the stay, made it clear that once a money judgment was obtained, the enforcement of that judgment is stayed. The exception to the stay in §362(b)(4) only permits enforcement of nonmonetary judgments.

In Justin's case, the city's suit aims to enjoin Justin's violation of the law and to compel him to cure his prior noncompliance, or to pay the city for doing so. The judgment is both a prohibitory injunction forbidding future violations of the law and a mandatory injunction compelling rectification of a prior breach of the law. The bar on future violations is not a money judgment and is excluded from the stay under §362(b)(4). However, the cleanup order is a money judgment that requires the estate to spend money in doing the work itself or to pay the city to do it. The cleanup order is therefore not excluded from the stay under §362(b)(4), and the city cannot proceed beyond the judgment to enforce it unless it applies for and receives relief from stay.

These issues do not typically arise in the bankruptcy of slothful suburbanites, but they have come up in cases involving corporate or business debtors who have offended important government regulations in the area of pollution control, labor relations, consumer protection, and trade practices. *See, e.g., Penn Terra Ltd. v. Department of Environmental Resources,* 733 F.2d 267 (3d Cir. 1984) (concerning the enforcement of environmental regulations) and *N.L.R.B. v. P.I.E. Nationwide, Inc.,* 923 F.2d 506, 511-512 (7th Cir. 1991) (concerning proceedings before the NLRB).

(h) We will concentrate on the stay issue and ignore, for the present, the fact that Justin himself had no right to try to take the funds out of his account which is now estate property. Section 553 preserves and gives secured status to the credit union's right to set off the monies in the account against Justin's debt to it. The effect of this is that the credit union has a secured claim of $5,000 and an unsecured claim for the remaining $3,000 of the loan. However, the credit union is stayed by §362(a)(7) from exercising its right of setoff. That is, although it will ultimately have the right to claim the setoff, it cannot simply help itself to the funds in the savings account. It must seek the permission of the court to do so by applying for relief from stay. As noted in the question, however, the problem is that if it cannot freeze the account pending the court's authorization to exercise the setoff right, it cannot protect itself from the loss of its security by the customer's improper withdrawal. Some courts dealing with this issue recognized this dilemma, but others were unsympathetic and held that the bank could not act on its own to place a freeze on the account. Its only choice was to apply as quickly as possible for relief from stay, and hope that the customer did not beat it to the funds before relief was granted.

The Supreme Court removed this window of vulnerability by holding, in *Citizens Bank of Maryland v. Strumpf,* 516 U.S. 16 (1995) that the placing of a temporary administrative hold on a bank account while the bank applies for relief from stay is not, in itself, a violation of §362(a)(7). The court reasoned that by temporarily freezing the account, the bank is not actually exercising the right of setoff by permanently removing the funds from the account. It is merely suspending payment of its debt to its customer. To refuse to recognize its power to do this would eviscerate its right to claim a setoff, which is preserved in bankruptcy by §553. It is also inconsistent with §542(b) which requires a party to pay a debt due to the estate only when it is due and payable. The court also rejected the debtor's argument that the hold violated two other provisions of §362(a). It did not violate §362(a)(3) because the hold was not an act to obtain possession of or control over estate property. From the bank's perspective, the account was not property, but merely a debt to the estate. Nor did it violate §362(a)(6) which precludes the creditor from attempting to recover a claim from the debtor. *Strumpf* makes it clear that it applies only where the hold is temporary, so the creditor must move diligently to obtain relief from stay. The consequence of delay is illustrated by *In re Wicks,* 215 B.R. 316 (E.D.N.Y. 1997). The debtor's credit union placed a hold on the account upon learning of the bankruptcy and did nothing about applying for relief from stay until the debtor initiated proceedings, four months later, to obtain damages for violation of the stay. The court said that because the credit union had shown no intent to move diligently for relief from stay, the hold could not be regarded as temporary, within the contemplation of *Strumpf,* and it must therefore be taken to be an actual attempt to exercise the right of setoff in violation of §362(a)(7).

11

Relief from Stay and Adequate Protection

§11.1   Introduction

Chapter 10 described the breadth and impact of the stay and showed how it prevents activity to recover or secure prepetition debts or to assert interests in property of the estate. Sometimes the claimant's right to continue the stayed activity outweighs the interest of the estate or the debtor in suspending it. To enable the court to safeguard the rights of claimants in such circumstances, §§362(d)-(g) provide a procedure under which the court can grant relief from stay if the claimant establishes grounds for it. Section 362(d), the central provision, sets out the forms and grounds for relief, while §§362(e), (f), and (g) deal with ancillary procedural and evidentiary matters.

Because the stay is so wide-ranging and affects so many types of activity, applications for relief from stay are common. Although they are often made almost immediately after the petition has been filed, they could arise at any time during the case. If the court grants relief, the order benefits only the party who applied for it and covers only the activity in issue in the application. With regard to all other persons and all other matters, the stay remains in effect.

§11.2   The Procedure for Relief from Stay

A party who wishes to obtain relief from stay must file a motion requesting relief. Section 362(d) requires the court to grant relief after notice and a hearing if grounds for relief are shown. Under §102(1), the phrase "after notice and a hearing" means that appropriate notice must be given, but that a hearing need only be held if a party in interest requests it. The application is a "contested matter" (that is, a proceeding on motion rather than a trial) and is governed by Rules 4001 and 9014.

Other procedural and evidentiary matters are provided for in §§362(e), (f), and (g). Section 362(e) is intended to encourage speedy disposition of applications for relief from stay of acts against property of the estate, and provides for the automatic grant of relief 30 days after the application unless the court acts on it and orders continuation of the stay. The court is given some leeway in postponing the final determination of the application by making a preliminary order but §362(e) was amended in 1994 to curtail this discretion. The section formerly required the final hearing to be commenced within 30 days of the preliminary hearing. However, it often happened that the final determination, while begun in time, could still result in serious delay before it was ultimately resolved. Section 362(e) now provides that the final hearing must be concluded within 30 days of the preliminary hearing unless the parties consent to an extension or unless the court extends it for a specific time based on compelling circumstances. Section 362(f) permits the court to grant emergency relief following an ex parte application where the interest of the party seeking relief will be irreparably harmed if relief is not given immediately and there is no time for notice and a hearing. Section 362(g) deals with the burden of proof in applications for relief from stay. Because the burden is allocated differently on constituent elements of the grounds for relief, it is more conveniently discussed in section 11.4.

§11.3   Forms of Relief

Section 362(d) sets out four alternative forms of relief from stay: *Termination, annulment, modification,* or *conditioning*. This allows the court flexibility in providing relief that is most appropriate to the circumstances.

Termination of the stay is the lifting of the stay so that the applicant can commence or resume the suspended activity. Termination ends the stay only from the time of the order, so it does not validate prior acts in violation of the stay.

Annulment terminates the stay retroactively, so that the stay is treated as if it was never in effect; prior acts in violation of the stay become valid. Annulment is therefore regarded as an extraordinary remedy and is usually used only in exceptional circumstances (*e.g.,* when the debtor has abused the system and the applicant's actions were in good faith and not in willful violation of the stay).

Modification of the stay is appropriate when the court decides to permit some activity but not to allow the applicant full rights to proceed with the enforcement of the claim. For example, the court may modify the stay by allowing the applicant to continue with litigation to the point of judgment,

Relief from Stay — Alternative Dispositions

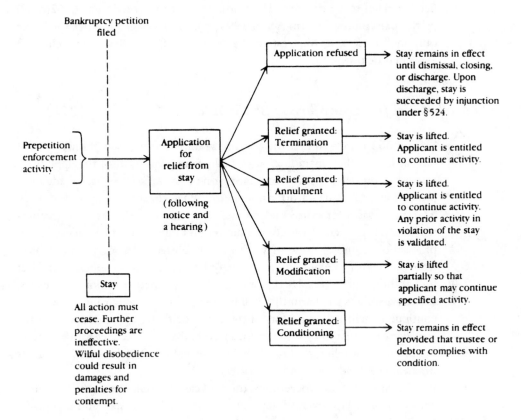

but not to proceed with enforcement of the judgment. Modification is a form of partial or limited relief.

If the court *conditions* the stay, it leaves the stay in effect, subject to the debtor or trustee satisfying some condition. For example, if the application for relief is based upon the grounds that the claimant's interest in property is deteriorating, the court may allow the stay to continue in effect on condition that the trustee takes steps to halt the deterioration or to compensate for it.

The diagram above summarizes the different dispositions of an application for relief from stay.

§11.4   Grounds for Relief

Section 362(d) sets out three separate grounds for relief from stay. The first, in §362(d)(1), is the broad ground, and is available as a basis for relief from the stay of any action described in §362(a) whether an act against the debtor, or against property of the debtor or the estate. The second, in §362(d)(2), is a narrower ground that applies only to the stay of acts against property. The two grounds are independent of each other. Only one of them need be satisfied for relief to be granted. The third, added to the section as §362(d)(3) by the Bankruptcy Reform Act of 1994, is a special basis for relief applicable only in "single asset real estate" cases. Each of these bases for relief are explained below.

§11.4.1   Relief from Stay for Cause (§362(d)(1))

Section 362(d)(1) requires the court to grant relief from stay if the applicant has cause for relief, including lack of adequate protection of the applicant's interest in property. Apart from stating one basis for cause (lack of adequate protection), §362(d)(1) does not specify what constitutes cause for relief. The other bases for cause under §362(d)(1) are as varied as circumstances may dictate. It is left to the court's discretion to grant relief whenever appropriate. For example, cause may arise from abusive behavior by the debtor, from the debtor's default under a plan, or because it is more efficient or fairer for another court to resolve the case. In deciding whether or not cause exists, the court weighs the harm that will be suffered by the applicant if the stay is continued against the interests of the estate or the debtor protected by the stay. For cases that discuss the various factors that may be relevant to a showing of cause for relief, *see In re Robbins,* 964 F.2d 342 (4th Cir. 1992); *In re Mazzeo,* 167 F.3d 139 (2nd Cir. 1999).

In most motion proceedings, the applicant for relief bears the burden of proving cause. However, in applications for relief from stay §362(g) places the burden of proving lack of cause on the party opposing relief (*i.e.,* the debtor or trustee). Thus, the applicant must allege cause and make out a prima facie case that cause exists, but the burden of nonpersuasion falls on the opposing party. The burden is allocated in this way because the stay is a form of injunction. As it is automatic, the trustee or the debtor do not have to apply for it and are initially relieved of the burden of establishing grounds for it. This places them in a better position than the normal applicant for an injunction, who must show grounds for relief. Therefore, once the continuation of the stay is challenged, the debtor or trustee must take up the burden of justifying its remaining in effect.

§11.4.2   Relief from Stay of Acts against Property on the Ground That the Debtor Has No Equity in the Property and the Property Is Not Necessary to an Effective Reorganization (§362(d)(2))

It is worth stressing again that §362(d)(2) applies *only* to the stay of acts against property and cannot be used to obtain relief from stay of acts against the debtor. Where acts against property are in issue, this ground is an alternative to relief for cause under §362(d)(1). Section 362(d)(2) has two conditions that both must be satisfied for relief to be granted: The debtor has no equity in the property and it is not necessary for an effective reorganization. In essence, the basis for relief is that neither the debtor nor the estate will obtain an economic advantage by keeping the property, so the applicant's right to enforce its claim to the property should not be further suspended.

Under §362(g), the applicant for relief bears the burden of proving that the debtor has no equity in the property, and the party opposing relief bears the burden on all other issues. This means that the applicant must establish that the value of the property does not exceed existing valid encumbrances. The applicant must allege and make a prima facie showing of the other elements of §362(d)(2), but the burden of nonpersuasion falls on the party opposing relief.

a. The Debtor's Lack of Equity in the Property (§362(d)(2)(A))

The *debtor's equity* is the value in the property in excess of all encumbrances on it. If there is an exemption in the property or it has revested in the debtor under a plan, this equity is wholly or partially owned by the debtor. Otherwise it is property of the estate. Thus, reference to the debtor's equity in property in §362(d)(2) includes both the debtor's and the estate's interests in the property.

The existence and extent of the debtor's equity is determined by valuation of the property. The Code's general policy on valuation is expressed in §506 concerning the valuation of secured claims: The court should try to place a realistic value on the property in light of the purpose of the valuation and the property's proposed use or disposition. (For example, if the property will be disposed of on the market by a private sale, market value should be used rather than foreclosure value.) Valuation is usually established by expert testimony. When the parties' witnesses disagree, the court must resolve the conflict by assessing the reliability, credibility, and relevance of their valuations. The court may accept one of the appraisals or make a determination of value based on the evidence taken as a whole. For examples of actual cases involving valuation issues in an application for relief from stay, *see In re Castle Ranch of Ramona*, 3 B.R. 45 (Bankr. S.D. Cal. 1980); *In re Sutton*, 904 F.2d 327 (5th Cir. 1990). *See also* Examples 1 and 2.

If the debtor is found to have equity in the property, relief from stay cannot be granted under §362(d)(2) because one of its two elements is not satisfied. Further inquiry into the role of the property in an effective reorganization is not necessary. However, if no equity exists, the second element of §362(d)(2) becomes relevant.

b.   The Property Is Not Necessary to an Effective Reorganization (§362(d)(2)(B))

In a Ch. 7 case, no reorganization is contemplated so the property cannot be necessary to an effective reorganization. Therefore, in a Ch. 7 case the second test is satisfied as a matter of course: If the debtor has no equity in the property, relief from stay should be granted.

Reorganization is the principal goal of Ch. 11, and §362(d)(2)(B) was drafted with Ch. 11 cases in mind. (Its applicability to cases under Chs. 12 and 13 is discussed below.) In a Ch. 11 case, the debtor usually attempts to operate its business while formulating and effectuating a plan to restructure its debts and reorganize its operations. Therefore, if property is a necessary component of the debtor's business operations, depriving the debtor of the ability to use the property will damage its chances of overcoming its financial difficulties. For this reason, the fact that the debtor has no equity in the property is not enough to warrant relief from stay unless, in addition, the property does not advance the debtor's attempt at successful reorganization. Because §362(d)(2)(B) requires that the property be necessary to an "effective" reorganization, it is not enough for the debtor to show merely that the property will be used in its reorganization. The debtor must also establish that the proposed reorganization is feasible. This prediction can be difficult to make. While not addressing the issue in depth, the Supreme Court indicated a broad guideline by dictum in *United Savings Association of Texas v. Timbers of Inwood Forest Associates,* 484 U.S. 365 (1988): The debtor must show that there is a reasonable prospect of successful reorganization within a reasonable time.

Usually, the earlier in the case that the application for relief is made, the harder it is to make an accurate prediction of the debtor's prospects of successful reorganization. Therefore, courts tend to adopt a more lenient test when the application for relief is made early in the case. Even when there is doubt about the debtor's chances of successful reorganization, if some prospect for success exists, the court is likely to refuse relief from stay. However, if the reorganization has been limping along for some time and no longer looks promising, the court may be more readily persuaded that the reorganization is unlikely to be effective. For example, in *In re Sun Valley Ranches,* 823 F.2d 1373 (9th Cir. 1987), the application for relief was made after the debtor had been in Ch. 11 bankruptcy for three years, during which time it had suffered losses and the property had declined in value. It also had become clear that the debtor could not pay the amount proposed in the plan. The court lifted the stay. See also *In re Bowman,* 253 B.R. 233 (9th Cir. B.A.P. 2000). For further illustrations of the application of §362(d)(2)(B), *see* Examples 1 and 2.

Because §362(d)(2)(B) uses the word "reorganization," there has been some question about whether it applies only in Ch. 11 cases or also in cases under Chs. 12 or 13. This is because Ch. 11 is officially entitled "reorganization," while Chs. 12 and 13 are headed "debt adjustment." If it does not apply under Chs. 12 and 13, then the effect of §362(d)(2) would be the same as in Ch. 7: Once the debtor has no equity in the property, relief from stay must be granted. Although some courts have taken this view, the more favored interpretation is to read "reorganization" broadly to include rehabilitation under Chs. 12 and 13. Thus, one should treat §362(d)(2)(B) as requiring that the property is not necessary to the debtor's fresh start, whether the debtor is in business or is a consumer who may need the property for personal rehabilitation, and irrespective of whether the case has been filed under Ch. 11, 12, or 13. (*See* Example 2.)

§11.4.3 Single Asset Real Estate Cases

Section 362(d)(3) was added in 1994 to deal with complaints by mortgage holders that the stay was being abused in "single asset real estate" cases — that is, in cases involving a debtor whose only business was the ownership of a single piece of income-producing real estate. The problem encountered was that when the property market suffered a downturn, some of these debtors ran into difficulty in paying their mortgages. Although economic conditions meant that they had no realistic prospects of reorganizing until the market improved, they would file for relief under Ch. 11 just to hold off foreclosure as long as they possibly could. Some of these cases could have been and were disposed of on the basis of relief from stay for cause under §362(d)(1), but Congress decided to address the problem more directly by enacting subsection (d)(3).

Section 362(d)(3) applies only to a "single asset real estate" case, which is defined in §101(51B) to be a case in which the debtor derives substantially all of its gross income from the rental of a single piece of real property which is, essentially, either used as commercial premises or as an apartment complex larger than four units. The definition has a debt ceiling which confines it to cases in which the debtor's mortgages and liens on the property do not exceed $4 million. Section 362(d)(3) can, therefore, only be used by a mortgage holder as a basis for relief from stay in relatively small estates.

As indicated earlier, §362(d)(3) is designed for use by a mortgagee of the property that constitutes the debtor's dominant asset. It is a ground for relief completely independent of and separate from the grounds in §362(d)(1) and (2), which remain available as alternative bases for relief. In essence, its purpose is to prevent dilatory behavior by putting pressure on the debtor to devise a workable plan within 90 days of the order for relief or, if this has not been possible, at least to make payments of interest at the market rate to mortgage holders. If the debtor does neither of these things, the mortgagee may obtain relief from stay 90 days after the order for relief.

§11.5   Lack of Adequate Protection As Cause for Relief from Stay under §362(d)(1)

§11.5.1   *The Interests Entitled to Adequate Protection*

As stated earlier, the lack of adequate protection is the only cause for relief from stay that is expressly mentioned in §362(d)(1). The concept of adequate protection plays a significant role in applications for relief from stay and also arises in connection with the trustee's dealings with encumbered estate property.[1]

Section 362(d)(1) permits relief from stay when the applicant's interest in property lacks adequate protection. Adequate protection is only available to holders of interests in property of the estate or the debtor and cannot be sought by unsecured creditors. Section 362(d)(1) is thus confined to claimants such as secured creditors, lessors who have leased property to the debtor, coowners of the debtor's property, and others with a valid interest in property. The existence of such a valid interest in property is determined with reference to nonbankruptcy law. In the remainder of the discussion, the secured claim is used to exemplify an interest for which adequate protection is sought.

§11.5.2   *The Circumstances under Which the Need for Adequate Protection Arises*

When the petition is filed, the debtor's property becomes property of the estate under §541. Because all the debtor's legal and equitable interests in property fall within the estate, property of the estate includes property that is subject to liens or security interests. Provided that these encumbrances are valid under nonbankruptcy law and do not have qualities that make them avoidable in bankruptcy, they remain effective against the estate. At the appropriate time, the secured creditor is entitled to be paid out the full value of the secured claim (whether in a lump sum or by installments under a plan) or to have the property abandoned so that it can be foreclosed upon. In the interim, the stay prevents the secured creditor from taking any action to enforce the interest.

The stay creates a risk for the secured creditor. In the absence of the stay it could have foreclosed on the property immediately upon the debtor's default and applied the proceeds to satisfaction of its claim. Because the stay prevents immediate foreclosure, the creditor faces the risk that its collateral may decline in value while the stay is in effect, so that if the property eventually has to be realized, it may generate fewer proceeds. If the collateral value drops below the amount of the debt, the reduction in value eats away the

---

1. Adequate protection is raised again in Chapter 17.

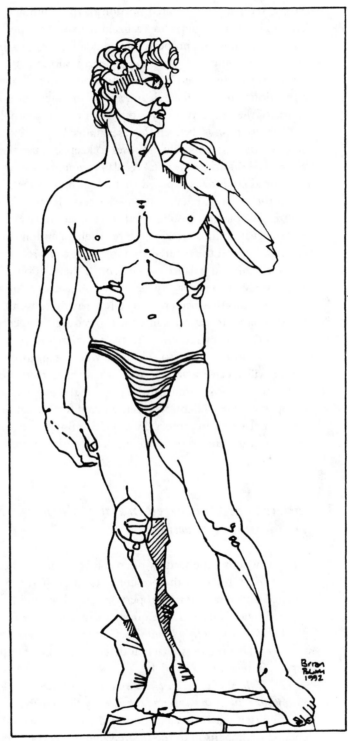

ADEQUATE PROTECTION

security, reducing the secured portion of the claim and increasing the deficiency. This risk of delay in realization exists irrespective of whether the trustee is holding the property for liquidation under Ch. 7 or the estate or debtor is retaining and using the property pursuant to a plan of rehabilitation. However, because Ch. 7 cases typically aim at fairly prompt liquidation or abandonment of collateral, and the estate does not normally make extensive use of the property, delay is often not a serious problem.

The situation is different in cases under Chs. 11, 12, and 13, where the debtor or the estate usually proposes to keep and use the property while the claim is paid off under the plan. As plan payments can extend over some time, the secured creditor is exposed to a much more substantial risk of devaluation. If the debtor's rehabilitation is successful, the risk of loss does not materialize: The plan is consummated and the secured claim is eventually paid in full. However, if the debtor's attempt at rehabilitation fails, the estate ends up in liquidation and the secured creditor is left to its recourse against the property for the unpaid balance of the debt. If the relationship between the debt and the value of the property has changed adversely during the period of the stay, the creditor has been prejudiced by having to wait.

Adequate protection is intended to reduce the secured creditor's risk of loss from the stay by requiring the trustee to maintain the value of the collateral relative to the debt, so that if or when realization occurs, the secured creditor will receive as much as it would have recovered upon immediate foreclosure. If the secured claim is jeopardized by a likely change in the ratio of property value to debt, the secured creditor has cause for relief from stay unless the trustee can protect the claim from such deterioration by providing a means of offsetting it or bolstering the security interest.

§11.5.3   Factors to Be Considered in Determining the Need for Adequate Protection

To decide whether the security interest is adequately protected, a comparison must be made between the present ratio of property value to debt and the predicted future ratio if the property is to be kept and used or disposed of as proposed by the estate. Three questions must be asked:

(1) *If the stay is lifted and foreclosure proceeds, what is the claimant likely to receive?* This requires a factual determination of the present value of the property in relation to the debt.

(2) *If the stay is left in effect and the estate deals with the property as proposed, what is likely to happen to the value of the property in relation to the debt?* This inquiry involves a calculation of the rate of increase or decrease of the debt and a comparison to the future value of the collateral. To predict future

value, account must be taken of such factors as appreciation or depreciation of market value, deterioration of the property through use, hazards to the property, and insurance coverage.

(3) *What is the likelihood of successful rehabilitation?* In a Ch. 7 case, the first two inquiries are sufficient to determine the need for adequate protection because the only issue is whether delay in liquidation will prejudice the secured claim. In rehabilitation cases, this third inquiry must be pursued. If there is a good chance that the debtor's plan will be consummated, the risk of eventual liquidation of the property under adverse circumstances is diminished. Therefore, if the debtor's prospects of recovery seem good, the lower probability of liquidation may offset some uncertainty about the future debt-collateral ratio.

As these factors indicate, the need for adequate protection is a factual issue that involves reliance on opinions and evidence concerning not only present value but also a prognostication of future value and an assessment of the efficacy of the debtor's rehabilitation efforts. This factual determination can be difficult, particularly where conflicting testimony is offered by the parties.

The following simple example illustrates the process of comparison: Say that the debtor owes $100,000 to the secured creditor that is secured by a lien on a piece of machinery with a present value of $100,000. If foreclosure took place immediately, the secured claim would be paid in full (less the foreclosure costs, which are ignored here for the sake of simplicity). If the stay remains in effect and the estate uses the machine during the course of its rehabilitation efforts, the machine will depreciate by 20 percent per annum. If the rehabilitation fails in a year's time, and the machine is then realized, the secured claim will be worth only $80,000. Unless it is anticipated that the debt will also be reduced by at least $20,000 during this period, the interest is not adequately protected. Relief from stay should be granted unless the trustee can provide a means of fully offsetting this depreciation. *See* section 11.5.4.

By contrast, say that the present value of the machine is $150,000 and the debt is $100,000. The claim is oversecured. If the predicted depreciation is 20 percent, the claim will still be oversecured in a year's time irrespective of how much is paid on the claim, and the claimant will still receive full payment if liquidation occurs at that stage. Thus, the interest is adequately protected, and there is no cause for relief from stay. (Once again, complicating factors such as the accural of interest and foreclosure costs are disregarded here.) This second example illustrates that the existence and size of an *equity cushion* — that is, a surplus of debtor equity in the property over the secured claim[2] — is often important in adequate protection cases. If the property is valuable enough to provide a buffer of encumbered equity to accommodate

---

2. *See* section 2.5.3 for a further explanation of this term.

likely depreciation, the secured claim is protected. Of course, the question of whether such an equity cushion exists and how large it should be to assure protection can be difficult to resolve. For a useful example of a case concerning this issue, *see In re Alyucan Interstate Corp.*, 12 B.R. 803 (Bankr. D. Vt. 1981). *See also* Example 2.

It must be stressed that the secured creditor is only entitled to protection of the present value of its interest and cannot demand an improvement in its position. For example, if the debt is $100,000, the present value of the collateral is $90,000 and depreciation is predicted to be 20 percent per annum, adequate protection requires maintenance of the %₁₀th's secured claim. It does not entitle the undersecured creditor to make up the $10,000 deficiency.

§11.5.4   *The Means and Method of Furnishing Adequate Protection*

Section 362(d)(1) merely refers to adequate protection without indicating what it is. There is in fact no definition of the term in the Code. However, §361 provides three examples of how adequate protection may be furnished. Section 361 is not intended to be exclusive: Any means by which the trustee can assure protection of the claimant's interest can be tendered as adequate protection.

The three methods of providing adequate protection suggested by §361 are:

(1) Cash payments (§361(1)).   If the estate has sufficient income, it can make cash payments to the claimant to reduce the debt and maintain the ratio between the claim and the property value.

(2) Additional collateral (§361(2)).   If there is unencumbered property in the estate, the trustee can provide adequate protection by granting a lien on additional property or replacing the existing lien with a lien on property of greater value.

(3) A grant of an "indubitable equivalent" (§361(3)).   The third suggested form of adequate protection is the most general. Section 361(3) authorizes the trustee to propose adequate protection by giving the claimant any form of relief that will result in realization of the "indubitable equivalent" of the claimant's interest in property. This quaint term, standing in sharp contrast to the otherwise pedestrian statutory prose, was lifted from an opinion by Learned Hand, who knew how to turn a phrase. The formulation really sets a standard for measuring the protection, rather than suggesting a means of providing it. It requires the court to decide whether a means of protection proposed by the trustee ensures that the claimant will certainly receive no less than the value of its property interest.

Section 361(3) expressly excludes the grant of an administrative expense priority as a means of providing adequate protection. Congress felt that such a grant is too uncertain a means of protection, because the estate may not have sufficient assets to pay administrative expenses in full. (Administrative expenses are a first priority unsecured claim, so they are paid before all other unsecured creditors. *Priorities* are discussed in section 19.6.)

As stated in section 11.4.1, the trustee, as the party opposing relief from stay, bears the burden of proving that the interest is adequately protected. If the trustee believes that the interest is not at risk, he or she will seek to prove that nothing need be done to bolster it. If it seems that adequate protection is lacking, the trustee has the initiative of offering corrective measures of the kind suggested in §361. The court then determines whether or not the interest is adequately protected and grants relief from stay if it is not. *See, e.g., In re Blehm Land & Cattle Co.,* 859 F.2d 137 (10th Cir. 1988). Relief need not take the form of an immediate lifting of the stay. If the court determines that adequate protection is lacking and that any measures proposed by the trustee are insufficient to cure the problem, it can condition the stay on the trustee taking specified action to protect the interest. It is also possible for the trustee and claimant to settle the adequate protection issue by agreeing to the form of protection to be provided. Such an agreement can be made an order of the court.

§11.5.5 *Variations in the Means of Furnishing Adequate Protection in Ch. 12 Cases*

Section 361 does not apply to cases under Ch. 12. Section 1205 provides its own list of ways in which adequate protection may be furnished in a Ch. 12 case. In some respects, §1205 is the same as §361; §§1205(b)(1) and (2) are identical to §§361(1) and (2), except for a change in wording that expressly describes the interest to be protected as the value of the property securing the claim or the ownership interest in property. This express language was included to make it clear that the interest to be protected did not include the lost opportunity costs of an undersecured creditor. At the time of enactment in 1986, decisions by Courts of Appeal included these lost opportunity costs as part of the interest to be protected under §361. Sections 1205(b)(1) and (2) overruled this interpretation for Ch. 12 cases. In 1988 the Supreme Court overruled the Courts of Appeals and held that §§361 and 362 do *not* protect lost opportunity (*see* Example 4). Therefore, the difference in wording between §§1205(b)(1) and (2) and §§361(1) and (2) no longer represents a difference in substance.

Section 1205(b)(4) has the same effect as §361(3), except that it substitutes more specific language for the vaguer test of indubitable equivalence. Section 1205(b)(3) includes a third specific example of a means of providing adequate protection by the payment of reasonable market rent for the use of farmland.

§11.5.6   The Failure of Adequate Protection: Superpriority under §507(b)

As stated in section 11.5.3, the determination that the interest is adequately protected is based on evidence of present value and predicted future value. This evidence is speculative and could be wrong. If realization of the property eventually becomes necessary, it may turn out that deterioration of the property-debt ratio was worse than anticipated, so that the interest was not adequately protected.

Section 507(b) is intended to provide relief to the secured creditor under these circumstances. It states that if the trustee provided adequate protection to a claimant, and the protection turns out to be inadequate, the shortfall is treated as a priority claim that ranks at the top of the administrative expense priority category. This places the claim for the shortfall resulting from the misjudgment of adequate protection in a position senior to all other priority claims in §507 — it is given *superpriority*. As long as the estate owns unencumbered property to generate a fund for the payment of unsecured creditors, this fund will be used to satisfy the shortfall before any of the other priority and general unsecured creditors are paid. The superpriority therefore enhances the claimant's chances of full recovery.

Section 507(b) is not clearly drafted. Not only does it send the reader on a wild goose chase by a cryptic reference to §507(a)(1), but it also has some restrictive language that appears to confine relief to cases in which the trustee has furnished adequate protection. Literally interpreted, it does not apply when the court has refused relief from stay on the basis that adequate protection already exists without further bolstering by the trustee. (*See* Example 3.)

EXAMPLES

1.   The Better Part of Value Is Discretion

Maladroit Manufacturing Co., Inc. has filed a bankruptcy petition under Ch. 7. Among the debtor's assets is a large piece of machinery that forms an integral part of its manufacturing plant. The machine was purchased on credit from Lien Machine Inc. for $500,000 about two years prior to bankruptcy. At the time of sale, Lien Machine perfected a security interest in the machine to secure the price. The current balance on the debt is $200,000. Maladroit had defaulted in its payments prior to filing the petition, and Lien Machine had been about to foreclose on the machine when the petition was filed.

Almost immediately after the petition was filed, Lien Machine applied for relief from stay under §362(d)(2) so that it could continue its foreclosure. At the hearing of the relief application, an appraiser hired by the estate testified that the market value of the machine is $250,000. Lien Machine offered evidence by two appraisers. The one testified that the market value of the machine is $195,000. The other testified that the value of the machine, if sold by auction in a foreclosure sale, is not more than $150,000.

(a) Is Lien Machine likely to obtain relief from stay under §362(d)(2) in this Ch. 7 case?

(b) Would the answer be different if Maladroit had filed a petition under Ch. 11?

Note: Lien Machine seeks relief under §362(d)(2). This question is confined to grounds for relief under that provision and does not address the alternative ground for relief for cause under §362(d)(1).

2.   Don't Give Up the Ship

Rocky Shoal filed a Ch. 13 petition last month. His prize possession, and his only asset of economic value, is a sailboat that he uses for recreation. He bought the boat on credit from High Seize Boating Co. two years ago. Under the sales contract, he undertook to repay the loan in monthly installments over five years, and granted High Seize a security interest in the boat to secure the balance of the price. The security interest is validly perfected under state law and unavoidable.

Rocky defaulted in his payments two months before filing the petition. High Seize had initiated foreclosure proceedings that have been suspended by the automatic stay. At the time of the filing of the petition, the balance due on the loan was $30,000.

High Seize has applied for relief from stay under §362(d)(2) on the ground that Rocky has no equity in the property, and it is not necessary for an effective reorganization. As an alternative, High Seize also argues that it has cause for relief under §362(d)(1) because its interest in the boat is not adequately protected.

Both High Seize and Rocky's trustee have offered testimony on the value of the boat. The appraiser produced by High Seize places a present market value of $30,000 on the boat and predicts that it will depreciate 10 percent during the next year. The appraiser estimates that the boat would realize only $20,000 in a distress foreclosure sale. The trustee's appraiser estimates the market value of the boat to be $50,000 and its distress sale value to be $35,000. She disagrees that the boat will depreciate over the next year: Rocky has taken meticulous care of it, and the market for good used boats is vigorous.

(a) Does High Seize have grounds for relief from stay under §362(d)(2)?

(b) Does High Sieze have grounds for relief under §362(d)(1) as a result of lack of adequate protection?

3. Indecent Exposure

Assume that the court, in evaluating the evidence in High Seize's application for relief from stay, finds that the boat is indeed worth $50,000, leaving an equity cushion of $20,000. The court also determines that the value of the boat is likely to remain stable, that the boat is fully insured, and that Rocky has a good prospect of successful rehabilitation. Because the equity cushion is sufficient to accommodate interest that accrues on the claim and will also act as a buffer for any unexpected drop in market value, the court finds the interest to be adequately protected and refuses relief from stay under §362(d)(1). Because the debtor has equity in the property, relief is also refused under §362(d)(2).

Rocky's Ch. 13 plan is confirmed. Under the plan he proposes to pay High Seize its full $30,000 plus interest over a three-year period and to retain the boat, which remains subject to the lien until the plan is consummated. About a year after the plan confirmation, Rocky loses his job. He can no longer afford payments under the plan and converts the case to Ch. 7. At this time, the balance of the debt to High Seize is $22,000. The trustee attempts to liquidate the boat so that High Seize can be paid and any surplus can be placed in the estate's general fund. However, because of an economic recession, the used boat market has collapsed. The best offer received for the boat is $20,000. Because High Seize realizes that it will do no better itself, it does not object to the trustee's sale. The proceeds of the sale are paid out to High Seize. What can be done about the shortfall?

4. Opportunity Knocked

Asset Indigestion Inc. recently filed a Ch. 11 petition. Its principal asset is a piece of real property subject to a mortgage held by Linger Longingly Loan Co. At the time of the petition, the debt secured by the mortgage was $450,000. The value of the property has declined over the last few years as a result of an economic slump in the region. The experts agree that its value at the time of the petition is $425,000 and that the property market has stabilized. Although there is little prospect of prices rising in the near future, they are not likely to decline either.

Linger Longingly has applied for relief from stay on the ground that its interest lacks adequate protection. It argues that if the property were sold immediately, the proceeds of $425,000 would be realized and could be invested elsewhere to generate income. If the estate is allowed to keep the property, Linger Longingly will be delayed in realizing it, and therefore loses the opportunity of reinvestment. Should relief from stay be granted?

5.   Underdogs in the Manger

Multilien Investments, Inc., a debtor in Ch. 11, owns a piece of real property worth $5 million. It owes $4.7 million to Premier Mortgage Co. on a first mortgage, $600,000 to Secundo Security Co. on a second mortgage, and $400,000 to Trinity Finance Co. on a third mortgage. Premier has moved for relief from stay under §362(d)(2) on the ground that the debtor does not have an equity in the property and that it is not needed for an effective reorganization. The debtor opposes the motion. It is joined in its opposition by the two junior lienholders, who realize that if Premier is allowed to foreclose now, Secundo will recover only portion of its undersecured debt from the proceeds and Trinity's lien will be wiped out. They feel that if the debtor is allowed to keep the property, a predicted upward trend in the market may benefit their interests. They argue that if one just takes into account the mortgage of Premier, the party seeking relief, the debtor does have an equity of $300,000 in the property, and this should preclude Premier from getting relief under §362(d)(2). Is this a good argument?

EXPLANATIONS

1.   (a) **Is lien machine likely to obtain relief from stay in this Ch. 7 case?**   Two elements must be satisfied for relief to be granted under §362(d)(2). First, the debtor must have no equity in the property. (Because the debtor's prepetition property becomes property of the estate, the debtor's equity is in fact the estate's equity in the property.) The equity is the excess in the property's value over the amount of the debt of $200,000. Under §362(g), Lien Machine bears the burden of proving that the debtor has no equity in the property.

Without attempting to make a determination of the correct value to be used, this question raises the issue that valuation is a factual question that is often based on conflicting opinion evidence. If the evidence of the estate's appraiser is accepted, the debtor does have equity in the property; the creditor's evidence contradicts this. The court must attempt to determine a realistic valuation based on the credibility of the witnesses, the proposed use and disposition of the property, and any other relevant factors. The value fixed by the court could be different from that suggested by any of the experts. One of the issues suggested by the question is whether market value or distress sale proceeds is a more realistic figure. The machine is to be liquidated, but there may be an opportunity to sell it on the market by private sale, rather than by auction.

If the court finds that the property is worth more than $200,000, the debtor has equity in the property, and relief from stay cannot be granted under §362(d)(2). If the property is found to be worth $200,000 or less, the first element is satisfied, and the second must be determined: Because this is a Ch. 7 case, the property cannot be necessary for an effective reorganization, and this element is inevitably satisfied. Therefore, unless the debtor has equity in the property, the grounds for relief under §362(d)(2) are satisfied and the stay will be lifted.

(b) Is the answer different if Maladroit had filed under Ch. 11? The first part of the test remains the same, but the question of whether the property is necessary to an effective reorganization is now relevant. To decide this, two factors must be considered: (1) the debtor must need the property for its reorganization efforts, and (2) the debtor must have a prospect of successful reorganization. Section 362(g) places the burden on the debtor (as the party opposing the relief) to prove these matters. As this is a Ch. 11 case, the debtor in possession represents the estate.

The question indicates that the machine is an integral part of the plant, thereby suggesting that the debtor may be able to satisfy this aspect of the test. No information is given on the prospects of Maladroit's success in its effort to reorganize. However, because the application is made very early in the Ch. 11 case, the court is likely to lean in favor of giving the debtor a chance and will be less exacting in the level of proof required to show the likelihood of rehabilitation.

Even if relief from stay is refused at this stage, Lien Machine will be able to make a new application if circumstances change. Also, even though consideration of §362(d)(1) has been excluded by this question, it should be noted that any possible deterioration in the debt-collateral ratio could serve as grounds for relief under that section.

2. (a) Relief under §362(d)(2). Rocky may or may not have equity in the property, depending on the valuation fixed by the court. As in Example 1, the experts clash on the valuation issue: On High Seize's evidence, Rocky has no equity in the property, and the trustee's figures show otherwise. Also, the choice between distress liquidation value and market value has to be made based on the likely disposition of the boat. Thus, the court must not only resolve the conflict on value, but must also decide what standard of valuation is most realistic. High Seize bears the risk of nonpersuasion under §362(g).

If the debtor has no equity in the property, one of the two requirements for relief under §362(d)(2) is satisfied, and the question of whether the property is needed for an effective reorganization must be considered. Although there is some dissent on the question, §362(d)(2)(B) is generally regarded as being applicable in Ch. 13 cases, in spite of the use of the word "reorganization." In Ch. 13, the question is whether the asset is necessary for the debtor's rehabilitation — that is, whether it is needed to affect a fresh start. While one cannot be dogmatic about it (some courts are very solicitous of the Ch. 13 debtor's desire to retain property), this is apparently purely recreational property that is not used to support or shelter Rocky or to enable him to earn income. It is therefore very likely that the court will find that the property is not necessary to the debtor's "effective reorganization."

In summary, if the court determines that Rocky has no equity in the property, and also finds the property not to be necessary for an effective reorganization, relief from stay will be granted under §362(d)(2). However, even if these grounds for relief are not satisfied, High Seize may still have cause for relief under §362(d)(1) if its interest is not adequately protected.

(b) Relief for lack of adequate protection. The property interest to be protected here is High Seize's valid, perfected security interest in the boat. It cannot be emphasized too strongly that it is the interest in property, not the debt, that requires protection. If the property is worth as much or more than the debt, the interest in the property is the full amount of the debt. If the property is worth less than the debt, part of the debt is unsecured, and the right to adequate protection relates only to the portion secured by the property. Once again, the valuation of the property is an important factual issue.

To decide whether High Seize's interest is adequately protected, the present and predicted future relationship between the debt and collateral value must be compared. The process of determining current value for the purpose of §362(d)(1) is the same as it is for §362(d)(2). It must be decided whether market or liquidation value is the proper measure, and the evidence must be weighed to decide what that value is. Also, the probability and extent of future change in that value in relation to the debt must be determined.

Assume that the testimony of the trustee's appraiser is accepted, and that High Seize usually resells repossessed property on the retail market, making market value the proper measure. The market value of the boat is $50,000 and the debt is $30,000. An immediate foreclosure would yield enough to pay the secured claim in full with costs and interest, and a surplus would remain for the estate. As the trustee's appraiser predicts a stable or rising value for the boat, this position will not deteriorate. An oversecured creditor is entitled to receive interest on its claim and costs until the surplus equity is exhausted, but there is a large enough equity cushion to accommodate increase in the debt by the addition of interest and costs. In short: On the trustee's evidence, the interest is adequately protected.

High Seize's appraiser fixes the current market value at the same level as the debt — $30,000. An immediate sale would give High Seize almost full payment of its claim after deducting sale costs. However, as there is no equity cushion and the appraiser predicts a decline in the value of the boat, a delay in foreclosure will prejudice High Seize. Even though Rocky will pay off the debt over time under his plan, it is not clear that those payments will be high enough or will begin soon enough to offset the decline in collateral value. If not, relief from stay must be granted unless the trustee is able to offer additional protection under §361. This could take the form of an immediate cash payment to reduce the debt, the provision of additional collateral, or any other means of ensuring that High Seize will receive the indubitable equivalent of its interest. The facts indicate that Rocky has no other valuable property, so augmentation of the collateral may not be possible. It is not clear whether the other means are open to him.

This example illustrates two possible resolutions of the case. However, the court is not obliged to accept either of the two conflicting appraisals. It could decide a figure and rate of depreciation somewhere between those offered by the parties. The court would then decide, based on its factual finding, whether there is a sufficient equity cushion to protect the interest from deterioration. Although present and future value are very important considerations in deciding adequate protection, they are not the only factors to be taken into account. The debtor's prospects of rehabilitation are also relevant, and a strong likelihood of success may counteract some doubt in valuation. Also, because Rocky will retain and use the boat while the Ch. 13 plan is being consummated, adequate protection also requires that High Seize's interest is protected by insurance from loss or destruction of the collateral.

3. Assuming that the court's estimate of value at the time of the application was correct (it may not have been, but this will never be known), there has been a gross miscalculation of market trends. As a result, the protection of the interest was not adequate. Section 507(b) provides that if the trustee furnishes adequate protection and fails adequately to protect the claimant, the shortfall is to be given priority over all administrative expenses. (This provision is obscurely drafted, but this is its basic meaning.)

The claim for the shortfall is unsecured, but because it is given a rank at the top of administrative expenses (which are themselves a first priority claim), the shortfall has a reasonable prospect of full payment. Although the estate may be insolvent, the shortfall has first claim to whatever fund exists in the estate.

One of the problems in the language of §507(b) is that it refers only to the case in which the trustee has provided adequate protection. On the present facts, the trustee was not called on to provide any protection because the court concluded that the interest was already adequately protected. It is not clear whether §507(b) covers this situation.

4. The argument finds support in §§361 and 362. Section 362(d)(1) requires relief if the interest in property is not adequately protected, and §361(3) talks of relief that will result in the realization of the indubitable equivalent of the claimant's interest in property. If the estate retains the property, Linger Longingly will not receive interest — §506(b) only permits interest where the value of the collateral exceeds the debt. An undersecured creditor is not entitled to interest on its claim.[3] Therefore, it is true that the

---

3. The debtor's plan must provide for payment of the present value of claims, which in effect is equivalent to interest for the period of the plan. This is explained in Chapters 20 and 21. The interest referred to in §506(b) is payable in the period before confirmation and expands the size of the claim.

stay has the effect of depriving Linger Longingly of an opportunity to reinvest the proceeds of the claim and to earn interest on it. This interpretation was favored by two Courts of Appeal that held that §361 required the protection of the present value that could be derived from immediate realization of the property. As a result, the undersecured creditor was entitled to interest to offset lost reinvestment opportunity. *See In re American Mariner*, 734 F.2d 426 (9th Cir. 1984); *Grundy National Bank v. Tandem Mining Corp.*, 754 F.2d 1436 (4th Cir. 1985).

This approach was rejected by the Supreme Court in *United Savings Association of Texas v. Timbers of Inwood Forest Associates, Ltd.*, 484 U.S. 365 (1988). The Court said that the interest in property to be protected is the value of the property itself, not the right to take possession of the property and realize it. It reached this conclusion by examining §§361 and 362 in the context of the Code as a whole. One of the key points relied on by the Court was that §506 clearly does not intend an undersecured creditor to receive interest on its claim. Therefore, it conflicts with §506 to provide for the payment of interest that is lost because the property is not realized and the proceeds reinvested. In addition, if the loss of interest was a ground for adequate protection, undersecured creditors could obtain relief from stay as a matter of course under §362(d)(1).

The inability to get pendency interest places undersecured creditors in a difficult position and causes them losses where the prospects for successful reorganization are uncertain and the debtor is struggling (with attendant delay) to devise a confirmable plan. This may motivate them to look more carefully at the possibility of seeking relief either for cause (such as that the poor prospects of reorganization call into question the debtor's good faith in filing the Ch. 11 case), or on the basis of §362(d)(2). By definition, the debtor has no equity in the property where the mortgage is undersecured, and the poor prospects of success may establish that the property is not needed for an effective reorganization.

Although the third alternative ground of relief is not universally available, it may be so here because this is a single asset real estate case in which the mortgage debt fits within the debt ceiling of §101(51B). Section 362(b)(3) may, therefore, provide a basis for relief if market conditions are not such as to enable Asset Indigestion to devise a plan of rehabilitation with some speed. The facts do not indicate how much time has passed since the order for relief. The debtor has 90 days from that time to propose a plan that has a reasonable prospect of being confirmed within a reasonable time, or if that cannot be done, it must at least, from the end of the 90-day period, commence paying interest at the market rate to Linger Longingly on the value of its interest. If it fails to do either of these, Linger Longingly can obtain relief from stay.

5. Some courts have accepted this argument where junior lienholders have opposed the senior lienor's motion for relief from stay under §362(d)(2).

However, this approach is difficult to reconcile with the plain language of §362(d)(2). Although the Code does not itself define what is meant by debtor's "equity," it is generally understood to mean the debtor's (or estate's) remaining economic interest in property — the surplus owned by the debtor (or estate) — after all liens on the property have been satisfied. If there is more than one lien on the property, the debtor is entitled only to what is left after all have been satisfied. It, therefore, goes against common usage, and is not supported by any statutory language, to define "equity" for purposes of §362(d)(2) as meaning whatever is left after the senior lien is satisfied. This was the view taken in *In re Indian Palms Associates, Ltd.,* 61 F.3d. 197 (3rd Cir. 1995), which insisted on using the plain and accepted meaning of "equity." The court noted that it is appropriate to disregard junior liens for the purposes of deciding whether the senior lienholder has an equity cushion which will adequately protect its interest. The reason for this is that from the perspective of the senior lienor, it does not matter if the debtor himself, or other junior interests, are entitled to the value in the property in excess of the lien. In either event, the excess value is available to act as a cushion to the senior lien. However, just because "equity cushion" is used to describe value in the property that may not actually qualify as debtor's equity in the usual sense does not mean that a similar meaning is appropriate in §362(d)(2). The role that debtor's equity plays in that section is quite different. There, the fact that the debtor (or estate) has an economic interest in the property is one of the justifications for allowing the estate to keep it.

Of course, the finding that the debtor has no equity in the property does not end the inquiry. The next question to be decided is whether the property is necessary for an effective reorganization. The example does not provide facts to decide this.

12

Property of the Estate

§12.1   The Creation of the Bankruptcy Estate and Debtor's New Estate

Section 541(a) states that an estate is created by the commencement of the bankruptcy case. The bankrupt estate is a new legal entity, separate from the debtor. In a Ch. 7 liquidation of an individual debtor, the break between the debtor and the estate is most complete. The debtor's property, as at the date of the petition, passes to the estate. In due course, all this property (with the exception of property that is abandoned by the trustee as discussed in section 12.4) is liquidated and its proceeds distributed to creditors.

At the same time as the bankruptcy estate is created, the individual Ch. 7 debtor[1] begins to accumulate a new estate. This new estate consists of earnings and property acquired after the filing as well as property that has been released to the debtor from the estate as exempt or abandoned by the trustee has having no economic value. These postpetition assets of the debtor are the basis of his or her fresh start. As mentioned in sections 10.4.1 and 10.6, prepetition creditors cannot reach them because they are stayed from doing so pending the debtor's discharge, and are thereafter permanently enjoined from collecting prepetition debts.

The diagram on page 240 shows the flow of property into and out of the Ch. 7 estate of an individual debtor, and the birth of the debtor's postbankruptcy estate.

Section 541 applies in cases under Chs. 11, 12, and 13, as it does in Ch. 7. Like a Ch. 7 filing, a petition under any of the rehabilitation chapters creates

---

1. A corporation in liquidation cannot be rehabilitated. (*See* sections 8.2.1 and 22.1). It therefore does not acquire a new estate. When the corporation's bankrupt estate has been liquidated, the corporation ceases to operate and is ultimately de-registered.

Flow of Property in a Ch. 7 Case

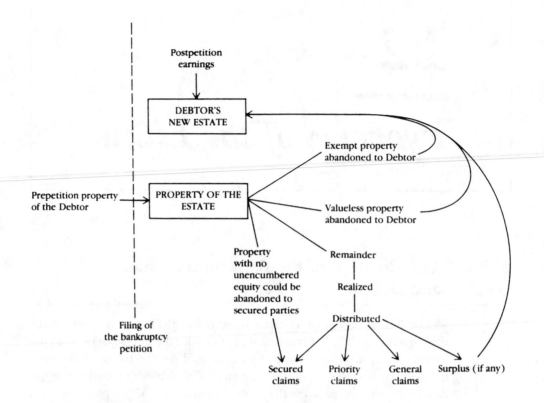

a bankruptcy estate as a legal entity separate from the debtor. However, because rehabilitation bankruptcy is aimed at preservation of the estate for the debtor rather than its liquidation, the break between the bankruptcy estate and the debtor's fresh start estate is not as complete or final. Chs. 11, 12, or 13 enable the debtor to reacquire prepetition property from the estate by committing postpetition earnings or other property or value to the payment of claims that would otherwise have been settled by the liquidation of the property. In effect, by using property or postpetition income that would not have been part of the Ch. 7 estate, the debtor is able to save property that would have been liquidated under Ch. 7. The debtor is usually able to keep and use estate property pending confirmation of the plan. Upon confirmation, all property in the estate that is not otherwise disposed of under the plan revests in the debtor. If the plan is ultimately consummated, the debtor keeps this property, which forms part of the debtor's new estate. However, if the debtor's attempt at rehabilitation fails and the case is converted to Ch. 7, the debtor's right to keep estate property ends and the property is surrendered to the trustee for liquidation.

There are differences between the treatment of property under Chs. 11, 12, and 13 that are not taken into account in the above description. One important difference is that only under Chs. 12 and 13 does property acquired by the debtor after the petition continue to enter the estate until the case is closed. This is explained in section 12.2.2. Despite such differences, the following broad outline of the relationship between the bankrupt estate and the debtor's new estate makes the essential distinction between rehabilitation and liquidation cases. The diagram below reflects the flow of property in a Ch. 13 case. Comparison with the Ch. 7 diagram illustrates the distinction.

§12.2   The Composition of the Estate

§12.2.1   *Legal and Equitable Interests of the Debtor at the Time of the Petition*

As stated in section 12.1, the bankruptcy estate is created at the commencement of the case. In both voluntary and involuntary cases, the date of filing the petition is the crucial date for determining the debtor's property interests that pass to the estate. Section 541 prescribes the composition of the estate: §541(a) states what is included in the estate, and §§541(b) and (d) make some specific exclusions from it. The broadest and most far-reaching provision is §541(a)(1), which includes in the estate "all legal or equitable interests of the

Flow of Property in a Ch. 13 Case

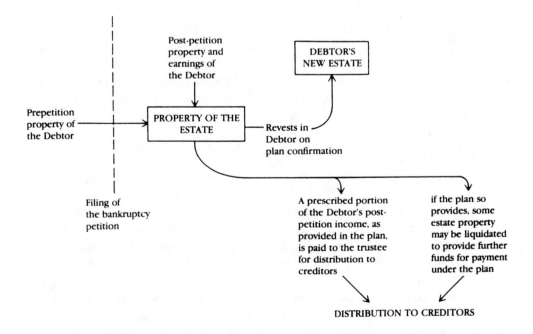

265

debtor in property as of the commencement of the case." The remaining provisions of §541(a) deal with ancillary categories of property such as community property, property recovered by the trustee in the exercise of avoidance powers, certain bequests acquired by the debtor within a prescribed time of the petition, proceeds of estate property, and property acquired by the estate itself.

Although §541(a)(1) brings into the estate all the debtor's legal and equitable property interests at the time of the petition, it does not define *what* these interests are. The question whether or not the debtor has an interest in property and the determination of the nature and extent of that interest must be resolved under nonbankruptcy law. That is, bankruptcy law provides for the estate's succession to the debtor's property rights, but nonbankruptcy law governs the issue of whether and to what extent a particular asset is the debtor's property. Example 1 illustrates some of the inclusions and exclusions of §541 in conjunction with nonbankruptcy law.

Although nonbankruptcy law is deferred to on this issue, the deference is not absolute. Section 541(c) invalidates any provision of nonbankruptcy law, as well as any condition created by contract or transfer instrument, that restricts the transfer of property rights so that they do not pass to the estate on bankruptcy. Therefore, if the debtor has a property right under nonbankruptcy law but a contract or state law declares that right nontransferrable to the estate or forfeited upon the debtor's bankruptcy, the restriction is ineffective. Section 541(c) is intended to prevent a state or a private party from circumventing §541(a).

§12.2.2 *Property Acquired after the Filing of the Petition*

Section 541 focuses primarily on the property interests held by the debtor at the time of the petition. In most cases, the debtor continues to acquire property after the petition has been filed, such as new income from employment or business, or returns from prepetition transactions, investments, or assets. It is necessary to decide whether this new property falls into the estate or is retained by the debtor as part of the new fresh start estate. The chapter under which relief is sought affects this question.

a.   Chs. 7 and 11

In a Ch. 7 liquidation and a Ch. 11 reorganization, the general rule is that all earnings and property acquired by the debtor subsequent to the filing from sources that are not related to prepetition property remain property of the debtor and do not become property of the estate. However, §§541(a)(6) and (7) include in the estate proceeds and profits of estate property and property acquired postpetition by the estate itself. In some cases, it may be difficult to decide whether property acquired after the petition belongs to the debtor or the estate. This is illustrated by Example 2.

b.   Chs. 12 and 13

In Chs. 12 and 13, the general rule is different. In terms of §§1207 and 1306, property of the Ch. 12 or 13 estate includes not only property qualifying under §541 at the time of petition but also all property (as defined in §541) acquired and all remuneration for services earned by the debtor up to the time that the case is closed, dismissed, or converted. In other words, §§1207 and 1306 provide for property and income of the debtor to continue entering the estate until the case comes to an end, either because the plan is consummated or because the debtor's plan of rehabilitation fails.

Postpetition property and earnings are included in the Ch. 12 or 13 estate so that the trustee has supervisory power over them while the debtor is performing under the plan. Because the property vests in the debtor upon confirmation of the plan, and the debtor retains possession of it, the trustee's control of the property is legal rather than physical. *See* §§1207(b), 1227, 1306(b), and 1327. The trustee does handle property that is to be distributed under the plan so that installments due by the debtor under the plan are paid to the trustee for distribution.

c.   The Effect of Conversion from Ch. 12 or Ch. 13

Because property of the Ch. 7 estate is fixed at the date of the petition while property and earnings continue to enter the Ch. 12 or 13 estate after the petition, conversion from Ch. 12 or 13 to Ch. 7 gives rise to the question of whether the converted Ch. 7 estate includes property acquired by the debtor after the petition but before the conversion.

Section 348 deals with the effect of conversion. Its general rule, in §348(a), is that although the conversion constitutes the order for relief under the chapter to which the case is converted, the original petition date remains the effective date of commencement of the case for all purposes except those specified in the section. Prior to 1994, the Code did not deal expressly with the question of whether the property of the converted Ch. 7 estate was determined as at the date of the original petition under Ch. 12 or 13, or at the later date on which the case was converted to Ch. 7. Some courts held that because the section included no express exception relating to property of the estate, the general rule of §348(a) applied, and only the property owned by the debtor at the time of the original filing entered the converted Ch. 7 estate. Other courts held that the Ch. 7 estate consisted of all the debtor's property at the date of conversion. Although there was no clear statutory basis for this finding, these courts reasoned that such an approach would create a disincentive to conversion, and would thereby further the Code's preference for reorganization.

A new §348(f) was added by The Bankruptcy Reform Act of 1994 to resolve this split where the conversion is from Ch. 13 to Ch. 7. Provided that the debtor converted to Ch. 7 in good faith, the Ch. 7 estate includes only that property of the original Ch. 13 estate that is still in the debtor's control or possession at the time of conversion. If the conversion is in bad faith, the Ch. 7 estate consists of all the property of the Ch. 13 estate (which includes property acquired by the debtor subsequent to the original petition) as of the time of conversion. Section 348(f) is confined to conversions from Ch. 13, and does not clarify what happens in a conversion from Ch. 12.

§12.3   The Trustee's Power to Compel Delivery of Property of the Estate ("Turnover")

Section 521(4) obliges the debtor to surrender all property to the trustee when the petition is filed. Under §542, any property of the debtor in the possession of other persons must be delivered to the trustee or its value accounted for; likewise, a debt due to the debtor must be paid to the trustee. The duty to deliver property to the estate (*turnover*) under §542 applies even if the estate's equity in the property is small. Section 542(a) expressly applies to all property that may be used, sold, or leased by the trustee, or that may be exempted by the debtor. The link between this turnover requirement and the automatic stay is apparent. Even a creditor with an interest in property is obliged to relinquish possession to the trustee. If the creditor wishes to recover the property so that the interest can be enforced, application must be made for relief from stay. Section 542(a) makes an exception to the duty of delivery to the trustee for property that is of inconsequential value or benefit to the estate.

If the property is in the hands of a custodian, including an assignee for the benefit of creditors or a receiver or trustee who was appointed in nonbankruptcy law to administer any property of the debtor, then §543 applies rather than §542. Section 543 requires the turnover of and accounting for all the debtor's property or its proceeds in the control of the custodian. As soon as the custodian receives knowledge of the bankruptcy, the administration of the nonbankruptcy insolvency proceedings end and no further distributions may be made. The purpose of §543 is to ensure that upon bankruptcy, the trustee supersedes any nonbankruptcy trustee of the debtor's property. The section protects certain parties to whom the custodian has incurred obligations in the course of administering the property, and it provides for compensation to be made to the custodian for services rendered.

Provisions in both §§542 and 543 protect persons who have transferred property or made payments to third parties or to the debtor in good faith and without knowledge of the bankruptcy filing. Unless those exceptions apply, if a person fails to deliver estate property voluntarily the trustee is able to compel delivery by court order. In addition, §502(d) provides for the disallowance of the entire claim of a creditor who has failed to turn over property recoverable by the trustee.

§12.4   Abandonment of Property by the Trustee

Some property that enters the estate is of no value or benefit to the estate. This may be because it is fully encumbered and is not needed for the debtor's rehabilitation, because it is fully exempt and cannot be liquidated for the benefit of creditors, because it costs more to maintain than it is worth, or simply because it has no economic value. The efficient administration of the estate and fairness to the holder of the interest in the property dictate that such property should be given up by the estate. Section 554 permits the court to authorize or order its abandonment. The initiative to abandon property may be taken by the trustee under §554(a) or applied for by a party in interest under §554(b). In either event, notice and a hearing is required. Under §102, this means that notice must be given to parties in interest, but a hearing is only held if objection is made.

To illustrate the factors that are taken into account by the trustee in deciding whether or not to abandon property, consider an asset in the estate that is subject to a perfected, unavoidable security interest securing a debt that exceeds the property's value. Because the entire proceeds of the collateral are needed to satisfy the secured claim, liquidation of the property will produce no proceeds for the estate. Therefore, in a Ch. 7 case, the retention of the property imposes an administrative burden on the estate with no corresponding advantage, and abandonment is appropriate. By contrast, as discussed in section 11.4.2, the estate's lack of equity in the property is not dispositive in a rehabilitation case. The property may be needed to enable the debtor to reorganize successfully. This is why §554 permits abandonment when there is both no value and no benefit to the estate.

While the trustee's abandonment of burdensome property is intended to benefit the estate by disposing of property that will drain the estate's resources, the right to abandon such property is not absolute and may be affected by policy considerations beyond the Code. For example, in *Midlantic National Bank v. New Jersey Department of Environmental Protection*, 474 U.S. 494 (1986), the court held that the trustee's power of abandonment does not override state laws reasonably designed to protect public health. The trustee cannot abandon polluted property to evade estate responsibility for its restoration, thereby shifting the full burden of cleanup to the public authorities.

Section 554 does not indicate to whom the property is abandoned. If the debtor has no rights in the property, it could be abandoned to the party that holds an interest in it. Because neither the estate nor the debtor has an interest in the property, it is no longer affected by the stay upon abandonment. However, if the debtor does have some right to the property, it is abandoned to the debtor; this does not release the property from the stay of enforcement of prepetition claims. Therefore, if the property is subject to a prepetition claim, the claimant must seek relief from stay to enforce it.

For example, suppose that an item of property worth $1,000 is subject to a security interest of $800, and the debtor has an exemption of $400 in the property. The estate has no interest in the property, because its value is fully covered by the secured claim and the exemption. As explained in Chapter 13, the secured claim takes priority over the exemption, so that the secured creditor's interest is $800 and the debtor's is $200. The property is abandoned to the debtor. Unless the debtor successfully negotiates a reaffirmation agreement or otherwise makes arrangements with the secured creditor to retain the property and to resume payments on the debt, the secured creditor has the right to apply for relief from stay. If the application is granted, the secured creditor forecloses on the property, receives proceeds sufficient to pay its claim in full plus costs, and pays over the surplus to the debtor.

Section 554(c) provides that at the close of the case, property that was included in the debtor's schedule but was not administered in the estate will be abandoned to the debtor. If it happens that any property is left in the estate at the end of the case, it is returned to the debtor. This situation is only likely to occur if the estate was not insolvent, so that all the property was not needed to pay claims, or if a particular item of property was worthless and unrealizable but was not abandoned to the debtor earlier in the case.

EXAMPLES

1. Coup d'Estate

At the time of filing a petition for Ch. 7 relief, an individual debtor has the various interests described below. Which of these interests become property of the estate under §541?

(a) Tort claim. A year before the petition, the debtor was injured by a negligently driven automobile. At the time of the petition, the debtor's claim against the driver had not yet been litigated. Is the tort claim property of the estate?

(b) Check. Six weeks before filing the petition, the debtor enjoyed some root canal work at the hands of Dr. Diabolo Dredge. Dr. Dredge submitted an account which the debtor passed on to her dental insurer. A week before bankruptcy, the debtor received a check from the insurer in payment of the claim. The check is payable to the debtor. At the time of the petition, the debtor had not deposited the check or paid Dr. Dredge. Is the check property of the estate? Would the answer be different if the debtor had deposited the check in her bank account prior to the bankruptcy?

(c) **Refrigerator.** About five months before bankruptcy, the debtor borrowed money from Newgate Loan Co. to finance the purchase of a refrigerator. When the funds were advanced, Newgate properly perfected a security interest in the refrigerator in accordance with state law. One month before bankruptcy, the debtor defaulted on the loan payments, and Newgate took possession of the refrigerator for the purpose of foreclosing on its security interest. By the time the petition was filed, Newgate had not yet held its foreclosure sale. Is the refrigerator property of the estate?

(d) **Furniture.** Two weeks before bankruptcy, the debtor held a garage sale at which she sold a well-worn dining room suite to Reese Cycle. Reese could not take delivery of it immediately because he needed to borrow a truck from a friend to haul it away. Nevertheless, he paid for it in cash at the time of the sale.

Before Reese managed to arrange for the truck, the debtor filed the bankruptcy petition. Is the dining room suite, which is still in the debtor's possession, property of the estate?

(e) **ERISA plan.** Some years prior to filing, the debtor began to participate in a tax-exempt retirement plan under the Employee Retirement Income Security Act (ERISA). For the purpose of meeting the statute's requirements for tax-exempt status, the plan contained an antialienation provision that precluded the assignment or alienation of benefits under the plan. The benefits under the plan have not matured. Is the debtor's retirement nest egg property of the estate?

(f) **Season tickets.** Prior to filing, the debtor subscribed to baseball season tickets. The contract under which he bought the tickets clearly states that the subscription is not transferrable. However, season subscriptions are often sold by holders, and the team does not usually challenge the sales. On this occasion, it does claim that the tickets are not property of the estate. Is it correct in its assertion?

2. Straggling Assets

Although property acquired by a Ch. 7 debtor after the petition is generally part of the debtor's new estate, §541(a) includes certain postpetition receipts in the estate if they have an appropriate connection with prepetition property. Consider whether the following postpetition acquisitions are property of the estate:

(a) **Kittens.** At the time of the petition, the debtor owned a highly pedigreed pregnant cat. The cat produced a litter three weeks after the filing. Who owns the kittens?

(b) **Postpetition income.** The debtor sold her business about 11 months before filing the petition. At the time of sale, the debtor entered into a non-competition agreement with the purchaser under which the debtor agreed, for a consideration of $100,000 per year, not to compete with the business in a specified area for a period of five years. The annual payments were to be made at the end of each of the five years. About a month after the petition, the debtor received the first payment. Is it property of the estate?

(c) **Inheritance.** Three weeks after the petition the debtor's Uncle Lucrum died, leaving her a generous bequest. What happens to the debtor's inheritance?

EXPLANATIONS

1. Sections 541 and 542 should be applied as follows:

(a) **Tort claim.** The broad language of §541 is inclusive enough to bring this unliquidated tort claim into the estate. The definition of property of the estate in §541 extends to almost every prepetition asset of the debtor, whether tangible property or intangible rights, and including unliquidated claims.

(b) **Check.** Normally, a check drawn in favor of the debtor and in her possession is property of the estate. However, the exclusion in §541(d) applies in this case. The estate does not acquire property in which the debtor holds only legal title, and not an equitable interest. This check was given to the debtor for the clear purpose of paying Dr. Dredge. The legislative history of §541 indicates that the debtor should be regarded as holding the check in constructive trust for Dr. Dredge, so that beneficial ownership does not pass to the estate.

If the check had been deposited, the same general principle applies to the fund in the debtor's bank account, provided that the claimant can trace the fund into the account in accordance with equitable tracing principles. This question illustrates how nonbankruptcy law (in this case the equitable remedy of constructive trust) is used to determine the debtor's property rights. For another example of the use of constructive trust principles, see *Reliance Insurance Co. v. Brown,* 40 B.R. 214 (W.D. Mo. 1984), in which the court allowed a victim to recover funds obtained by the debtor's fraud. A constructive trust is a remedial fiction of equity. *A fortiori,* if the debtor holds property subject to a valid express trust, the beneficiary's interest does not become estate property. *See, e.g., In re California Trade Technical Schools, Inc.,* 923 F.2d 641 (9th Cir. 1991), in which monies held in trust by the debtor school under federal student assistance programs were excluded from the estate.

(c) **Refrigerator.** The foreclosure sale has not yet taken place, and it is stayed upon the advent of bankruptcy. Even though the debtor defaulted on the loan, and foreclosure proceedings had begun prior to the petition, the debtor may still have a vestigial ownership interest under state law, consisting of the right to redeem the collateral under Article 9 and the right to any surplus sale proceeds. If the debtor still has such an ownership interest under state law, this interest passes to the estate under §541(a)(1). Newgate may apply for relief from stay so that foreclosure can proceed or, if the debt equals or exceeds the value of the refrigerator, it may seek abandonment. In any event, until such relief is granted, the estate is entitled to the refrigerator and the trustee can demand turnover under §542.

It must be stressed that the existence and extent of the debtor's right in foreclosed property is determined by state law, so if state law treats repossession of the collateral as transferring ownership to the secured creditor, there will be no property interest to pass to the estate. This happened in *In re Kalter*, 292 F.3d 1350 (11th Cir. 2002). The debtors had defaulted on loans secured by security interests in vehicles. The secured parties had repossessed the vehicles before the petitions had been filed, but had not yet sold them at the time of the debtors' bankruptcy. The court determined that under state law, ownership of collateral passed to a secured party upon repossession. Therefore, at the time of the petition, the debtors no longer had any property interest to pass to the estate.

(d) **Furniture.** To answer this question, one needs to know if the sale without delivery passed title to Reese. If it did, the suite is not property of the estate because the debtor has no interest in it. If it did not, the suite is property of the estate and Reese is left with an unsecured claim against the estate for the price paid in advance. Although §541 affects transfer of the debtor's property to the estate, nonbankruptcy law determines the nature and extent of the debtor's rights in property. In this case the applicable nonbankruptcy law is UCC Article 2, which provides for the passage of title when the goods were identified to the contract. Provided that the debtor's retention of possession was in good faith and not intended to defraud or mislead creditors, her continued possession would not preclude acquisition of title by Reese.

(e) **ERISA plan.** The fund in the retirement plan is prepetition property of the debtor that would enter the estate under §541(a)(1) unless the prohibition on transfer is effective in bankruptcy. Section 541(c)(1) generally overrides restrictions on the transfer of property under contract or nonbankruptcy law, so that such property passes to the estate in spite of the restriction. This general rule is subject to an exception: §541(c)(2) upholds in bankruptcy "[a] restriction on the transfer of a beneficial interest of the debtor in a trust that is enforceable under applicable nonbankruptcy law. . . ." Therefore, the issue to be decided is whether the pension fund with its antialienation provision qualifies as a trust for the purposes of §541(c)(2).

There had been a longstanding conflict among Courts of Appeal on this question. Some held that the plain language of §541(c)(2) applied to pension plans subject to the antialienation provisions of ERISA, so that the funds in such plans were not included in the estate. Others, relying on the legislative history of §541(c)(2), held that Congress intended the exclusion to apply only to spendthrift trusts recognized as nonexecutable under applicable state law, which may or may not include a qualified ERISA plan.

The conflict between the circuits was resolved by *Patterson v. Shumate,* 112 S. Ct. 2242 (1992), in which the Supreme Court favored the plain-meaning approach to §541(c)(2). The court said that recourse to legislative history is unnecessary, because the clear language of §541(c)(2) covers all trusts subject to restrictions on alienation enforceable under nonbankruptcy law. ERISA-qualified plans satisfy this condition. The Court considered that this plain-meaning approach was also consistent with ERISA's policy of protecting pension benefits, which outweighed the bankruptcy policy of broad inclusion in the estate. (Note that even if a pension plan does not meet ERISA qualifications, it could still qualify as a trust subject to restructions on transfer under state or other federal law. See *In re Williams,* 290 B.R. 83 (Bankr. E.D. Pa. 2003).)

(f) **Season Tickets.** The facts of this example are based on *In re Platt,* 292 B.R. 12 (Bankr. D. Mass. 2003), in which the trustee claimed that the debtor's Boston Red Sox season tickets were property of the estate. The trustee ultimately lost on an issue of proof—he could not show that the debtor actually owned the tickets in his personal capacity. However, the court said that had the trustee been able to prove this, the tickets would have become property of the estate. The non-transferability clause in the season ticket subscription contract would not have been upheld under §541(c)(1) because the team's practice was to permit transfers.

2. The postpetition acquisitions are dealt with in the following way:

(a) Kittens. The cat became property of the estate upon the debtor's bankruptcy. Although the litter was born after the petition, it is property of the estate under §541(a)(6) which includes in the estate all proceeds, product, offspring, rents or profits of or derived from estate property.

(b) Although the earnings from the non-competition agreement accrue postpetition, the agreement creating the right to the earnings was entered into prepetition. In *In re Andrews,* 80 F.3d 906 (4th Cir. 1996), the debtor argued that the payments due after bankruptcy under such an agreement are not property of the estate, but are earnings from services performed by the debtor after the commencement of the case, excluded from the estate under §541(a)(6). The debtor's reasoning was that he became entitled to the payments by refraining from competing, and this forbearance did constitute an ongoing service that he performed for the purchaser after the petition. The court disagreed, observing that it was too much of a stretch to include inaction in the concept of performance of services under §541(a)(6). Furthermore, the court reasoned that the purpose of the exclusion in §541(a)(6) was to facilitate the debtor's fresh start by separating from the estate whatever new income he may earn by post-filing endeavors. The proceeds from the non-competition agreement were not of this nature, but arose out of and were ancillary to the sale of an asset before bankruptcy. As such, the earnings derived from the debtor's prepetition activities, and were more properly viewed as proceeds of estate property.

The court analogized to *Segal v. Rochelle,* 382 U.S. 375 (1966), in which the Supreme Court held that a tax refund payable postpetition was property of the estate, and not part of the debtor's fresh-start estate. Although the right only accrued after the petition, the source of the right was taxes overpaid on prepetition earnings, rooted in the prebankruptcy past and not implicated in activities relating to the debtor's fresh start.

The dissent in *Andrews* disagreed that forbearance is not a service. It felt that only the debtor could perform the non-competition agreement, and his reward for refraining from competition in the postpetition period should be treated as earnings from the debtor's services after commencement of the case.

(c) Inheritance. Section 541(a)(5) includes in the estate any property that the debtor acquires or becomes entitled to by bequest, devise, or inheritance within 180 days after the petition, if such property would have been property of the estate if the debtor had an interest in it at the time of the petition. The inheritance is estate property.

13

Exemptions, Redemption, and Reaffirmation

§13.1   The Concept of Exemptions

Exemptions were first introduced in the explanation of executability in section 3.2.1, and have since been mentioned in a number of different contexts. For example, in section 5.3, they were used to show that uniformity in bankruptcy law has some tolerance for variety, and they were identified in sections 5.5.2 and 8.3.1 as an important component of the debtor's fresh start. Although exemptions are discussed here in connection with bankruptcy, they are also available in collection proceedings under state law. In fact, as explained in sections 5.3 and 13.2, state exemption statutes have significant force in bankruptcy.

Exemptions are only available to individual debtors. Whether under state law or in bankruptcy, the goal of exemptions is to insulate certain of the debtor's property from the claims of creditors so that the debtor is not rendered destitute by seizure or liquidation. In bankruptcy, property released to the debtor as exempt forms part of the debtor's new estate, thereby helping the debtor to gain a fresh start.

Exemptions are provided for in §522. They are claimable by individual debtors in all cases, whether under Ch. 7, 11, 12, or 13. Exemptions are used most directly in Ch. 7 cases, where fully exempt property is released and the cash value of partial exemptions is paid out from the estate to the debtor. In cases under Chs. 11, 12, and 13, estate property vests in the debtor upon confirmation of the plan, except as otherwise provided for in the plan. (*See* section 12.2.) Therefore the debtor does not directly use exemptions to reacquire estate property; instead, exemptions help the debtor because *they are deducted from the liquidation value of the estate.* This liquidation value is one of the factors taken into account in determining the minimum level of payment required for plan confirmation. (Standards for plan confirmation are explained in Chapters 20 and 21.) Exemptions are also relevant in all cases for the purpose of lien avoidance under §522(f), which is discussed in section 13.5.

§13.2   Exemptions Applicable in Bankruptcy Cases

When the Bankruptcy Reform Act was enacted in 1978, there was a difference of opinion on whether the Code should provide a standardized set of exemptions applicable to all individual debtors, irrespective of their state of domicile. Section 522 reflects a compromise between advocates of uniform bankruptcy exemptions and those who favored deference to nonbankruptcy exemption law: §522(d) provides a set of uniform bankruptcy exemptions, but §522(b)(1) empowers states to override the exemptions in §522(d). A state may enact legislation substituting the nonbankruptcy exemptions applicable in its jurisdiction for those listed in §522(d). If a state exercises its power under §522(b)(1), debtors who are domiciled in that state in the 180 days prior to bankruptcy cannot claim the exemptions listed in §522(d) but are entitled to exemptions provided by state law, together with any applicable federal nonbankruptcy exemptions. (Federal nonbankruptcy exemptions are typically found in statutes that confer benefits such as Social Security on an individual and make those benefits nonexecutable by creditors.) Because the majority of states have chosen to "opt out" of §522(d), debtors in most jurisdictions do not have a choice between bankruptcy and nonbankruptcy exemptions: They have the same exemptions in bankruptcy as are available in collection proceedings under nonbankruptcy law.

If the state in which the debtor is domiciled has not elected to substitute nonbankruptcy exemptions under §522(d), the debtor may choose to claim either the uniform exemptions in §522(d) or those allowed under nonbankruptcy law. Spouses who are joint debtors must elect the same set of exemptions. If they cannot agree, exemptions under §522(d) apply.

Although most states have chosen to make their own exemptions exclusively applicable in bankruptcy, the actual extent and nature of exemptions available to debtors filing in one state is often not dramatically different from those available to debtors in another. Many states have quite similar exemption laws, based roughly on the same model as the federal exemptions. However, there are some states which provide atypically generous exemptions (such as the homestead exemption of unlimited amount, permitted in a few states) or notably stingy exemptions. As a result, there are some states in which a debtor does significantly better or worse than the norm. This has led to some concern that the current "opt-out" approach results in discriminatory treatment of debtors based purely on their state of domicile, and that it provides an incentive for forum shopping.

As a result, the compromise of the 1978 Code has never stilled the debate between those who favor a standardized set of federal exemptions and those who prefer continued deference to state law. This issue was taken up by the National Bankruptcy Review Commission in its 1997 report. Its majority recommendation criticized the current non-uniform system as an abrogation of Congressional responsibility over the control of the bankruptcy system. It considered that deference to state law has not necessarily had the beneficial effect of making exemption laws sensitive to local economic factors and cultural values, but has been just as likely to produce quite random variations in the nature and extent of exemptions, resulting in unnecessarily generous treatment of some debtors, and insufficient protection of others. The majority report, therefore, recommended that the "opt-out" provision should be repealed and exemptions in personal property should be standardized in the Code. The Commission did suggest that some limited deference continue to be given to state law with regard to the homestead exemption — the state can set the amount of the exemption, subject to a minimum and maximum figure prescribed in the Code. The majority report also proposed changes to the set of exemptions to be provided in the Code. In particular, it favored removing the specific categories of property and replacing them with a lump-sum dollar limit so that the debtor could select any property for exemption up to the stated dollar value. This aspect of the report was criticized by the dissenting commissioners as too favorable to debtors.

In its annual attempts to enact bankruptcy reform legislation since the Commission report, Congress has not followed the Commission's recommendation to standardize exemptions in bankruptcy or to eliminate categories in favor of a lump-sum exemption amount. It has, however, tried to devise a means of dealing with the disparate treatment of the homestead exemptions in state law. A few states have a homestead exemption without a dollar limit. Many members of Congress consider residents of these states treated too generously, as they are able to exempt a significant amount of their worth by investing everything in their homes. This problem is particularly perturbing where a debtor converts non-exempt assets on the eve of bankruptcy by selling them and using the proceeds to buy a homestead, or to increase his equity in an existing home by paying down the mortgage. In some cases, debtors who contemplated filing bankruptcy, and who lived in states with a more modest homestead exemption, have sold their assets, moved to a state with an unlimited homestead exemption, and used the proceeds to buy an expensive home. The different reform bills proposed over the last few years have contained provisions to deal with this problem, but it is not clear which of them would end up in the legislation, if it passes. One or both of the following amendments might be made to current law: First, the Code would recognize the state law homestead exemption in bankruptcy, subject to a range that sets the minimum and maximum amount of the exemption allowed in bankruptcy cases. Second, the Code might increase the period during which a debtor must be resident in a state before being entitled to use that state's homestead exemption.

§13.3   The Nature of Exempt Property

Exemptions are granted at the expense of creditors, whose recourse is limited to nonexempt assets. Because exemptions detract from creditor interests, they should be limited and controlled so that they are no more generous than they need to be to accomplish their goal of preventing the debtor's impoverishment. Although exemption statutes vary considerably, many of them follow the same pattern: They specify the types or classes of property that may be claimed as exempt and impose a value limit on the exemptions. Assets that qualify for exemption are typically ordinary necessities such as household goods, the debtor's home and means of transportation, items of sentimental value, and property on which the debtor depends for a livelihood, such as tools of the trade or disability or pension payments. (*See* Example 4.)

Because so many states have exercised their right under §522(b)(1), the determination of the nature and extent of exemptions is largely in the hands of state legislatures, and the provisions of §522(d) are often inapplicable. However, §522(d) is representative of the approach adopted in many exemption statutes and serves as an example of the kinds of property and the value limitations that one might encounter. It lists several specific types of property that may be exempted, such as the debtor's homestead, items of personal and household property, tools of trade, health aids, and monetary assets necessary for the debtor's support. There is also a general exemption that the debtor may use to augment any other category or to exempt property that is not listed.

The value limits of the exemptions in §522(d) stayed constant for almost 20 years from the time that they were enacted in 1978, getting increasingly smaller in real terms as a result of inflation. They were eventually updated by the Bankruptcy Reform Act of 1994. To prevent this erosion of actual value in the future, the Act also added §104(b) to the Code, delegating to the Judicial Conference of the United States the task of adjusting the dollar amounts of the exemptions (as well as the amounts reflected in several other sections of the Code) every three years, based on the Consumer Price Index. The first such adjustment was made with effect from April 1, 1998 and the second with effect from April 1, 2001. The next adjustment will be made with effect from April 1, 2004. The adjusted amounts apply only to those cases filed after the effective date of the adjustment. Even with these inflationary adjustments, the dollar amounts of exemptions are deliberately set at a modest level. For example, the debtor's homestead exemption, as adjusted in 2001 is $17,425, and the new figure for the motor vehicle exemption is $2,775. Unless the debtor's equity in such assets is small, the exemption does not cover the debtor's entire interest in them. Where property is partially exempt, the estate is entitled to the nonexempt portion of the debtor's interest so that the property itself is not returned to the debtor. Instead, the debtor is entitled to payment of the value of the exemption from its proceeds.

§13.4   The Procedure for Claiming Exemptions

Exemptions do not automatically take effect. To claim them, the debtor must file a list of exempt property under §522(*l*). If the debtor fails to file the list, a dependent of the debtor may do so, thereby safeguarding the exemptions. The claim of exemptions is provided for in Schedule C of official form 6. Rules 1007 and 4003(a) require the schedule to be filed with the petition or within 15 days after the order for relief. Under Rule 1009, the debtor is able to amend the schedule of exemptions at any time up to the closing of the case.

The trustee or a creditor has the right to challenge the debtor's claim of exemptions. Rule 4003(b) requires objection to be filed within 30 days of the creditors' meeting. Rule 4003(c) places the burden on the objector to prove that the exemption is improperly claimed. Section 522(*l*) states that unless such an objection is made, the property is exempted as claimed. Therefore, if the trustee and creditors are not vigilant, the debtor could get away with an excessive exemption claim. In *Taylor v. Freeland & Kronz*, 503 U.S. 638 (1992), the Supreme Court held that if the creditor or trustee fails to file the objection within the 30-day period (or within such extended period as the court allows), the right to object is barred and the exemption stands, even if the debtor had no colorable basis for claiming it. It is not settled whether the court may reject an impermissible claim of exemption sua sponte before the expiry of the objection period. *See, e.g., In re Coones*, 954 F.2d 596 (10th Cir. 1992). This issue was left open in *Taylor.*

§13.5   The Debtor's Power to Avoid Certain Interests That Impair Exemptions

§13.5.1   *General Scope and Purpose of the Debtor's Avoidance Power*

As a general rule, a debtor's exemption in property does not avail against the holder of a valid consensual security interest in that property. By granting the interest, a debtor has effectively waived the right to assert the exemption against the consensual lienholder. Statutory liens are also usually immune from exemption claims. These liens are conferred by the legislature to protect persons who have enhanced or preserved the value of the property. If the debtor was allowed to assert an exemption against such a lien, the statutory protection of the lienholder would be undermined. By contrast, an exemption normally does take precedence over a judicial lien that attaches to the property. Judicial liens are acquired by the very process of seizure or judgment against which exemptions are meant to protect the property.

The purpose of §522(f)(1)(A) is to give effect to the primacy of the debtor's exemptions over judicial liens, by empowering the debtor to avoid them to the extent that they impair her exemptions. Section 522(f)(1)(B) creates a limited exception to the general rule that exemptions cannot be used to avoid consensual security interests. It extends the debtor's avoidance power to security interests of a certain type in specific classes of exempt property. This exception reflects Congress' determination that transactions of the kind identified in the subsection are predatory and should not be permitted to undermine the debtor's exemptions.

§13.5.2   *Judicial Liens*

Section 522(f)(1)(A) allows the debtor to avoid a judicial lien in exempt property to the extent that the lien impairs an exemption to which the debtor would have been entitled in the absence of the lien. With an exception relating to alimony, maintenance, and support, §522(f)(1)(A) applies to all judicial liens, whether created by prejudgment proceedings, by recording of the judgment, or by postjudgment proceedings such as execution. Also, unlike §522(f)(1)(B), it applies to all types of exempt property.

Public policy strongly disfavors the evasion of support obligations, and Congress felt that a debtor should not be able to escape his duty of maintenance and support by filing bankruptcy. As a result, the Bankruptcy Reform Act of 1994 enacted several provisions that give such obligations a special status, and prevent a debtor from using bankruptcy as a means of escaping them. We have already seen that enforcement of them is not subject to the stay (section 10.4.2), and we will discuss later that they are classified as priority claims, are not covered by the avoidance provisions of the Code, and are nondischargeable.

As part of this package of protections, §522(f)(1)(A) was amended to exclude from avoidance a judicial lien securing a debt to a spouse, former spouse, or child of the debtor for alimony, maintenance, or support. The lien must have arisen in connection with a separation or property settlement agreement, divorce decree, or other judicial or administrative determination. The protection extends only to the extent that the lien secures a debt that actually is for alimony, maintenance, or support, and it is lost if the debt is assigned. Therefore, a creditor spouse cannot prevent the avoidance of a judicial lien that secures a property settlement or some other non-support debt, simply by denominating it as a debt for alimony, maintenance, or support. The bankruptcy court must go behind the labeling of the debt in the court order or the parties' agreement, and must make an independent factual determination of whether or not the debt genuinely arose as part of the debtor's support obligation. This distinction can be a tricky one, because where spouses separate or divorce, it is not always easy to decide whether and to what extent a payment commitment constitutes a support obligation or a financial settlement. In fact, in some cases, support commitments and property settlements are very much intertwined and the distinction can be quite artificial, because the extent of the support to be paid is settled in light of other property allocations. (This issue is discussed again in sections 19.6.4 and 22.5.4 because the priority and discharge rules make the same distinction.) To ensure unavoidability of a lien on the debtor's existing property, securing a property settlement or other non-support debt, the creditor spouse must record a consensual security interest (such as a mortgage) in the property.

§13.5.3 Avoidable Nonpossessory, Nonpurchase-money Security Interests

Section 522(f)(1)(B) creates a narrow exception to the general rule that consensual liens take priority over an exemption in the collateral: The debtor may avoid a nonpossessory nonpurchase-money security interest in specified household or consumer goods, tools of trade, or professionally prescribed health aids to the extent that the security interest impairs an exemption in such property. The scope of §522(f)(1)(B) is very limited. The security interest can be avoided only if all three requirements of the section as satisfied: The secured party must not have perfected the interest by taking possession of the collateral, the loan or credit must not have been provided to enable the debtor to acquire the collateral, and the impaired exemption must relate to one of the three types of property specified. Section 522(f)(1)(B) is aimed at a particular type of transaction under which a creditor secures the debt by filing a security interest in household goods or other necessities already owned by the debtor. In many cases, the property is likely to be worth more to the debtor than its realization value, so that the threat of foreclosure gives the creditor great power over the debtor. Congress was concerned about abuses in transactions of this type, which it regarded as manipulative and unethical. It therefore subordinated them to the debtor's exemption.

The Bankruptcy Reform Act of 1994 added §522(f)(3), a limited qualification to the debtor's power to avoid a nonpossessory, nonpurchase-money lien in tools of trade where state law exemptions apply and the state either has no monetary limit on the exemption or prohibits the avoidance of consensual liens on exempt property. The subsection is obscurely drafted and its purpose unclear. Its apparent effect is to limit the amount of the debtor's avoidance under these circumstances.

§13.5.4   Avoidance "to the Extent" of Impairment

Section 522(f) does not necessarily result in the total avoidance of offending judicial liens and security interests. It permits avoidance only to the extent necessary to preserve the exemption. Therefore, if the debtor's equity in the property exceeds the exemption, the lien or security interest remains a valid charge on the nonexempt portion of the equity. For example, assume that the debtor owns a piece of equipment used as a tool of trade. The value of the equipment is $2,000. The debtor's exemption under §522(d)(6) is $1,625. If a judicial lien attached to the property securing a judgment of $600, it would impair the debtor's exemption to the extent of $225. It can therefore be avoided to that extent and becomes a secured claim for $375 and an unsecured claim of $225. If the value of the collateral is $1,625 or less, the lien is avoided entirely, and if the collateral is worth $2,225 or more, it is not avoidable at all. *See* Example 1.

§13.5.5   A State Cannot Override the Avoidance Power in its "Opt-out" Statute

As explained in section 13.2, states have the power under §522(b) to enact legislation substituting nonbankruptcy exemptions for those provided in §522(d). In conferring this power on the states, §522(b) refers only to the substitution for exemptions listed in §522(d). It does not authorize states to override any other provisions of §522. Nevertheless, courts had reached contrary results on the question of whether a state, in substituting its own exemptions under §522(b), could negate the debtor's avoidance power under §522(f) by making an exemption subject to liens that would otherwise be avoidable. This controversy was settled in *Owen v. Owen,* 500 U.S. 305 (1991), in which the Supreme Court held that the debtor may avoid a lien under §522(f) even though state law gives the lien precedence over the exemptions. The Court focused on the language of §522(f), which allows avoidance of the lien to the extent that it "impairs an exemption to which the debtor would have been entitled" under §522(b). The court reasoned that the inquiry called for by this language is not whether the lien impairs an exemption to which the debtor is actually entitled under the statute, but whether it impairs one to which the debtor would have been entitled if no lien existed.

§13.5.6   How Impairment Is Measured

Although *Owen* set the basic meaning of "impairment," it did not resolve the question of how that impairment is measured. Congress attempted to provide some guidance on this issue in the Bankruptcy Reform Act of 1994 by adding §522(f)(2). Section 522(f)(2)(A) defines "impairment" by setting out an arithmetical formula. To find the amount of impairment:

(1) Determine what the value of the debtor's interest in the property would be (that is, the equity that the debtor would have in the property) in the absence of liens.

(2) Add together:

   (a) the lien to be avoided, plus,

   (b) other liens on the property, plus,

   (c) the amount of the debtor's exemption.

(3) Compare 1 and 2. The exemption is impaired to the extent that 2 is greater than 1.

Section 522(f)(2)(B) makes it clear that (when there is more than one lien on the property) once a lien has been avoided, it is no longer taken into account in calculating the total of "other liens" for the purpose of avoiding any remaining lien. Section 522(2)(C) states that the subsection does not apply to a judgment arising out of a mortgage foreclosure.

The formula seems quite easy to work with in an uncomplicated case. However, it does raise some questions and present interpretational difficulties, under some circumstances. The following three examples show the basic operation of the formula in two easy cases and then in one more difficult one.

Say that a homestead worth $200,000 is subject to an exemption of $50,000. There is only one judicial lien of $180,000 on the property. The lien can be avoided to the extent that:

> *The total of*
> the amount of the lien itself ($180,000), plus
> other liens ($0), plus
> the exemption ($50,000)
> = $230,000
> *exceeds*
> the value that the debtor's interest would have in the property in the absence of liens ($200,000).

Therefore, the lien is avoided by $230,000 − $200,000 = $30,000. As a result, it remains a lien on the property to the extent of $150,000.

Say that the same property is subject to 2 judgment liens, the senior is for $100,000 and the junior is for $80,000. Although §522(f)(2)(A) does not say so, the avoidance must be directed at the junior avoidable lien first. (If this were not so, the avoidance of the senior lien first would elevate the junior lien in priority, because under §522(f)(2)(B), the avoided senior lien would not be taken into account in that second avoidance action.) The calculation is therefore:

(1) *First apply the calculation to the junior lien.*
The total of
the junior lien ($80,000) plus
"all other liens" — the senior lien ($100,000) plus
the exemption ($50,000)
= $230,000
exceeds
the debtor's equity interest ($200,000).

Therefore, the junior lien is avoided, by $230,000 − $200,000 = $30,000. As a result, it survives only to the extent of $50,000.

(2) *Next, apply the calculation to the senior lien.*
The total of
the senior lien ($100,000) plus
"all other liens" — the remaining unavoided portion of the junior lien ($50,000) plus
the exemption ($50,000)
= $200,000.

This is exactly equal to the debtor's unencumbered equity, and it, therefore, does not impair the exemption at all and is unavoidable.

Say that the homestead, worth $200,000 and subject to an exemption of $50,000, has three liens on it. The first is a consensual first mortgage of $70,000, perfected a year before bankruptcy. The second is a judgment lien of $80,000, recorded eight months before bankruptcy. The third is consensual second mortgage of $60,000, perfected six months before bankruptcy. If this was non-exempt property, the priority of the three interests would simply be based on the first-in-time rule. This would mean that the first mortgage would be entitled to full payment of $70,000, then the judgment lien would be entitled to full payment of $80,000. Finally, the second mortgage would be third in line. It would only be paid what is left of the value of the property, $50,000, and would have an unsecured deficiency of $10,000.

As the property is exempt, the debtor is able to use §522(f)(1)(A) to avoid the judicial lien, but not the consensual liens. (The consensual liens cannot be avoided under §522(f)(1)(B) because the homestead is not one of the exemptions protected by that subsection.) Therefore, the assumption that we made in the prior illustration, that the junior lien must be avoided first, cannot apply to the second mortgage. The avoidance is directed at the judgment lien only. The calculation is as follows:

The total of
the amount of the judgment lien ($80,000), plus

all other liens ($130,000), plus
the exemption ($50,000)
σ $260,000
exceeds
the value that the debtor's interest would have in the property in the absence of liens ($200,000).

Therefore, the judicial lien is avoided to the extent of $60,000. It becomes a secured claim of $20,000 and an unsecured claim of $60,000. The twist here is that this does not mean merely that the debtor's exemption is preserved. It also has the effect of elevating the second mortgage above the judicial lien. That is, avoidance under §522(f)(1)(A) benefits not only the debtor, but also the unavoidable consensual lien that would otherwise be junior to the judicial lien. This can be seen if we set out the distribution of the proceeds of the property: First mortgage, $70,000; second mortgage, $60,000; exemption $50,000; unavoided portion of judgment lien, $20,000. On similar facts, the court in *In re Kolich*, 328 F.3d 406 (8th Cir. 2003), found this apparent anomaly to be a little unsettling, but nevertheless consistent with the intent of Congress in enacting the formula in §522(f)(2). The bankruptcy court had excluded the junior mortgage from the calculation, thereby holding that the judgment lien did not impair the exemption. The B.A.P. reversed, and the court of appeals affirmed the B.A.P. The court of appeals reasoned that Congress deliberately included "all other liens" in the impairment formula, so there was no justification, on the plain wording of the subsection, to disregard the junior mortgage. The holder of the judgment lien argued that the literal application of the formula gave a windfall to the junior mortgagee, but the court was not persuaded. It said that Congress could have drafted the formula to exclude junior consensual lines from the calculation, but did not. This demonstrates congressional intent to treat consensual liens more favorably, even if it means that avoidance of the judicial lien would have the effect of elevating their priority.

§13.6 The Individual Debtor's Redemption Right in Ch. 7 Cases

Under §722, when property is subject to a lien that secures a dischargeable consumer debt, an individual debtor in a Ch. 7 liquidation may redeem the property from the lienholder. The property must be tangible personal property intended primarily for personal, family, or household use and it must have been either exempted or abandoned. As the above restrictions show, redemption is available only in narrow circumstances. Under §521(2) the debtor must file a statement of intention within 30 days of the petition indicating whether or not the property will be redeemed. *See* section 9.3. The redemption must be affected within 45 days of the statement of intention.

By redeeming the collateral, the debtor in effect buys it from the secured creditor for the amount of the allowed secured claim. If the value of the collateral is equal to or exceeds the debt, the debt will be fully allowed as a secured claim provided that is valid and unavoidable. To redeem, the debtor must pay the claim in full. However, if the collateral is worth less than the debt (so that the creditor is undersecured), the allowed secured claim and hence the redemption price is limited to the value of the collateral.

Section 722 requires the property to be abandoned or exempt. Unless the lien is avoidable under §522(f), the existence of an exemption does not reduce the redemption price to be paid to the lienholder. As noted in section 13.5, exemptions do not avail against liens except to the extent provided in §522(f). The requirement of abandonment or exemption relates to the existence or extent of the estate's interest in the unencumbered equity in the property. If the collateral value is exactly equal to or less than the secured debt, the estate has no interest in the property, so it is likely to be abandoned, thereby allowing the debtor to redeem it by settling the secured claim. Similarly, if the property is worth more than the debt but the equity is fully exempt, the estate has no interest in it and redemption can be affected by paying the secured claim. However, if the equity exceeds the debtor's exemption, the estate does have an interest in the property, and redemption is not possible unless the debtor first pays out the estate's interest so that the trustee will abandon the property. Following abandonment, the debtor may redeem by paying the redemption price to the secured claimant. (Example 5 illustrates this point.)

Although §722 does not state so expressly, it is generally interpreted to require the debtor to redeem in cash. Most courts have refused to allow a debtor to redeem by installments unless the secured creditor consents. This means that redemption is not practical for a debtor who has no means to raise the necessary cash after having filed bankruptcy. A debtor in that position cannot salvage encumbered property in a Ch. 7 case unless a reaffirmation agreement can be negotiated with the secured creditor.

The debtor's right to redeem is provided for only in Ch. 7 cases because redemption is not needed in Chs. 11, 12, and 13. Under those chapters, the debtor is able to retain desired property upon confirmation of a plan providing for protection of the security interest and periodic payments on the debt. The rehabilitation process under Chs. 11, 12, and 13 in fact permits the debtor to "redeem" collateral by installments under the plan. Therefore, a debtor who wishes to keep property, but cannot afford to redeem it for cash, has an incentive to choose rehabilitation rather than liquidation under Ch. 7. However, even in a Ch. 7 case, the debtor may have alternatives to redemption, as discussed in the next two sections.

§13.7 Reaffirmation

§13.7.1 *The General Principles of Reaffirmation*

A reaffirmation agreement is a contract between the debtor and a creditor under which the debtor agrees to pay a debt that would otherwise be discharged. Reaffirmation agreements are governed by §524. Sometimes the debtor may initiate negotiations for a reaffirmation agreement and sometimes the creditor may be the party that first proposes reaffirmation to the debtor. A creditor who approaches the debtor to suggest reaffirmation takes the risk that the debtor will object to the overture and claim that the creditor has violated the stay. Most (but not all) courts do not consider a mere suggestion of reaffirmation to be a per se violation of the stay, and recognize that by providing for a reaffirmation process in §524, the Code must be somewhat tolerant of creditor-initiated proposals for a reaffirmation agreement. But if the creditor's conduct is overbearing, coercive, deceptive, or harassing, a court may well find that the creditor has overstepped the mark and is using §524 as a pretext for trying to evade the strictures of the stay. As discussed in section 10.7, this could render the creditor liable for costs, fees, and damages under §362(h), or for sanctions for contempt of court under §105(a). This distinction between legitimate negotiation and disregard for the stay can be illustrated by a couple of cases. In *In re Duke*, 79 F.3d 43 (7th Cir. 1996) the creditor sent a letter to the debtor's attorney, with a copy to the debtor, offering to reinstate the debtor's credit line if he elected to reaffirm the debt. The court found that this approach did not violate the stay. There was no coercion or threat in the creditor's conduct, and the offer to reinstate the credit line was merely an incentive for reaffirming, rather than a penalty for not doing so. *In re Seelye*, 243 B.R. 701 (Bankr. N.D. Ill. 2000) grudgingly followed *In re Duke*, but took a strict approach. It regarded *In re Duke* as having created a very narrow judicial exception to the clear and absolute language of §362(a)(6), which stays "any act to collect . . . or recover" a prepetition claim from the debtor. The court confined this judicial exception to its narrowest terms and refused to apply it to dismiss the debtor's claim for damages under §362(h), where it appeared that the creditor did not notify the debtor's attorney of the proposed reaffirmation and did not send the debtor a covering letter adequately explaining the nature and effect of the reaffirmation.

Even where the debtor initiates negotiations, the creditor's reaction could be attacked as a violation of the stay. In *In re Jamo*, 283 F.3d 392 (1st Cir. 2002) the debtor, not the creditor initiated contact, offering to reaffirm a debt secured by a home mortgage. The creditor responded, declining to enter a reaffirmation agreement for the mortgage debt unless the debtor also agreed to reaffirm some unsecured debts that the debtor owed to the creditor. The court held that the creditor did not violate the stay by refusing to reaffirm except on that condition. The court noted that reaffirmation is a contract, and the creditor can refuse to make the contract unless the debtor agrees to its terms. If circumstances give the creditor bargaining leverage, and it chooses to take advantage of its superior bargaining position, this is not a violation of the stay as long as the creditor does not engage in coercive or harassing conduct.

In dealing with reaffirmation agreements, we must recognize that very different considerations apply to the reaffirmation of secured and unsecured debts. Section 524 makes no express distinction between secured and unsecured debts, and either are capable of being reaffirmed if the requirements of the section are satisfied. However, there is a very important practical difference: Where a debt is secured, the debtor's motive in entering a reaffirmation is the desire to keep the collateral, instead of losing it to liquidation and foreclosure. Reaffirmation is therefore available to the debtor as an alternative to redemption where the debtor wishes to keep the property, but cannot find the cash to settle the secured claim or otherwise does not meet the qualifications of §722. Where a debt is unsecured, the advantage to be gained by the debtor from reaffirmation is less obvious and possibly non-existent. Courts therefore approach the reaffirmation of unsecured debt with greater suspicion. After completing this discussion of general principles applicable to all reaffirmations, we will look separately at the reaffirmation of secured and unsecured debts.

Because the debtor's discharge is such an important consequence of bankruptcy, the Code places a number of restrictions on reaffirmation agreements. To be enforceable, the agreement must comply with the following conditions set out in §§524(c) and (d):

(1)   The agreement is valid only to the extent that it is enforceable in nonbankruptcy law. At common law, the debtor's promise to pay a discharged debt does not require consideration because the original consideration given by the creditor creates a "moral obligation" sufficient to support the new promise. However, statutory or common law policing doctrines such as unconscionability, fraud, and duress may make the agreement avoidable under nonbankruptcy law.

(2)   The agreement must have been made before the discharge is granted and it must be filed with the court.

(3)   The debtor may rescind the agreement at any time before the discharge is granted, or within 60 days of the agreement having been filed in the court, whichever is the later. The agreement must conspicuously express this rescission right.

(4)   The agreement must contain a clear and conspicuous statement advising the debtor that the reaffirmation is not required under the Code, under non-bankruptcy law, or under any agreement that is not itself in accord with §524(c).

(5)   If the debtor was represented by an attorney when the agreement was negotiated, the attorney must file a declaration with the agreement

stating that the debtor's consent was informed and voluntary, that the agreement does not impose an undue hardship on the debtor or a dependent, and that the attorney fully advised the debtor of the legal effect and consequences of an agreement of that kind, and of default under it. If the debtor was unrepresented at the time of negotiating the agreement and is an individual, the agreement needs court approval that is granted only if the agreement does not impose undue hardship on the debtor or a dependent and is in the debtor's best interests. (This applies only where the debt is a consumer debt, other than a consumer mortgage reaffirmation.)

(6) At the time for the individual debtor's discharge, the court holds a discharge hearing at which the debtor must be present in person. If the debtor had not been represented by an attorney at the time of negotiating the agreement, the court must use the occasion of the discharge hearing to tell the debtor that the agreement is not required by law. The court must explain its effect and must determine whether or not the agreement satisfies all the requirements described above. An amendment to §524(d) in 1994 makes it clear that this procedure is not to be followed if the debtor was legally represented in entering the agreement.

These restrictions apply only to *reaffirmation agreements*, that is, to contracts under which debtors undertake the obligation to pay the debts. Under §524(f), they do not apply when, instead of promising payment, the debtor actually makes a voluntary payment of the debt.

§13.7.2 The Reaffirmation of Secured Debt as an Alternative to Redemption

This discussion focuses on the reaffirmation of secured debt as a means of retaining the property that secures the debt. Where reaffirmation is used by a debtor to keep property that would otherwise be liquidated, the rationale for the reaffirmation is clear. As stated in section 13.6, redemption under §722 is available only in very narrow circumstances. If the property does not qualify for redemption or the debtor cannot find the cash to redeem, reaffirmation could be an alternative means of keeping collateral that would otherwise be liquidated in a Ch. 7 case. If the debtor intends to reaffirm a secured debt, the statement of intent under §521(2) must so indicate, and the debtor must perform that intent within 45 days of filing the notice.

Reaffirmation has disadvantages that redemption does not have. Because it is consensual, the debtor cannot simply reaffirm by tendering the amount of the secured debt; the debtor must negotiate with the secured creditor. The creditor has no obligation to enter a reaffirmation agreement and has little incentive to assent to such an arrangement unless it gives the creditor a benefit beyond that expected from liquidation of the property. (*See* Example 7.)

Unlike redemption, reaffirmation is not confined to Ch. 7 cases. However, because Chs. 11, 12, and 13 allow the debtor to retain property by providing for payments under a plan, the debtor does not need to use reaffirmation to keep property. In fact, if the debtor's primary goal is to prevent the liquidation of encumbered property, bankruptcy under Ch. 11, 12, or 13 may be easier and less expensive than attempting to negotiate reaffirmation agreements in a Ch. 7 case.

§13.7.3   The Reaffirmation of Unsecured Debt

Where reaffirmation is used by a debtor as a means of keeping property that would otherwise be liquidated, the rationale for the reaffirmation is clear. However, there is less obvious advantage to a debtor who reaffirms an unsecured debt. There are various reasons why a debtor may wish to pay an unenforceable unsecured debt. For example, creditor pressure, the desire not to damage a relationship, the hope for future credit, or guilt. Where there is no clear economic benefit to the debtor for the reaffirmation, the court should look even more carefully at the transaction to ensure that the requirements of §524 have been satisfied.

The reaffirmation of unsecured debt has caused much controversy lately, fueled by several cases of widespread abuse by large providers of consumer credit, which were found to have routinely bullied bankrupt customers into entering reaffirmation agreements. In many cases, these agreements were not filed with the court as required by §524. In addition, studies have shown that quite a significant number of debtors make informal reaffirmations that are never subjected to court scrutiny. The majority report of the National Bankruptcy Review Commission recommended that reaffirmation should be confined to secured debt, and no longer permitted to the extent that a debt is unsecured. This recommendation has not been adopted in the pending reform legislation. It proposes, instead, to strengthen the creditor's disclosure requirements relating to reaffirmation and to provide for more rigorous enforcement to ensure that creditors follow them.

§13.8   The Ch. 7 Debtor's Retention of the Collateral under the Original Contract — the "Ride-Through"

As noted earlier, §521(2) requires the debtor to file a statement of intention concerning the retention or surrender of property securing a consumer debt, and to state whether redemption or reaffirmation will be sought. Although §521(2) expressly provides only for surrender, redemption, or reaffirmation, some courts have held that it does not preclude other options. Based on this interpretation, they have recognized that under certain circumstances the debtor may elect to retain the collateral while continuing to pay installments to the secured party as required by the contract. This is known as a "ride-through" because the secured transaction rides through the bankruptcy without being formally administered and dealt with as part of the estate.

Not all courts recognize the "ride-through." Some, for example, *In re Edwards,* 901 F.2d 1383 (7th Cir. 1990) and *In re Johnson,* 89 F.3d 249 (5th Cir. 1996) hold that §521(2) is purely procedural — a notice provision that confers no power on the debtor to deal with collateral in any way beyond the three alternatives enumerated in the section: surrender, redemption, or reaffirmation. Other courts have been willing to accept the "ride-through" as a fourth alternative. *In re Belanger,* 962 F.2d 345 (4th Cir. 1992), one of the courts that permitted a "ride-through," imposed the following conditions for this alternative to be available to the debtor: The debt must be a secured consumer debt; the debtor must not have fallen into default in the payment of installments under the contract; and the estate must have abandoned the property as exempt or lacking in equity.

The approach in *Belanger,* in effect, allows the debtor to keep the original contract alive in spite of the bankruptcy, but it does not have the same consequences as reaffirmation. Although the lien survives the discharge and may be foreclosed if the debtor later defaults, the absence of a reaffirmation agreement means that the debtor's personal obligation on the debt is discharged. *See* section 19.6.3. While survival of the lien protects the secured claimant if the collateral maintains its value, discharge of the debtor's personal liability means that the secured claimant has no recourse if, upon default, the collateral has depreciated below the balance of the debt. Also, depreciation of the collateral could place the secured claimant in a worse position than redemption would have done, because redemption requires an immediate cash payment of the collateral's present value.

The National Bankruptcy Review Commission considered the "ride-through" to be unfair to creditors for the reason mentioned earlier: The absence of reaffirmation constitutes an involuntary modification of the transaction by discharging the debtor's personal liability, and leaving the creditor with no recourse beyond the property if the debtor later defaults. The Commission recommended amending §521(2) to expressly disallow the "ride-through" so that the debtor would have no power to resist repossession of the collateral unless he either redeems it or reaffirms the debt. Congress adopted this recommendation in the pending reform legislation.

EXAMPLES

For illustrative purposes, questions involving exemptions are based on the standardized list of exempt property in §522(d). Although §522(d) often does not apply, either because the debtor has elected nonbankruptcy exemptions or because the state has exercised its power under §522(b), these Examples raise principles that are relevant to exemption issues generally. The examples are based on the exemption amounts in §522(d), as adjusted under §104 with effect from April 1, 2001.

1. If Music Be Defeat of Lien, Play On

Blessid R. De Poor is an impoverished pianist who is struggling for recognition in the world of music. He lives in a cold garret and owns no property of value except for a concert grand piano on which he practices. Blessid needed a loan desperately, but could not satisfy the credit qualifications normally required by lenders. One day he saw an advertisement on a matchbook cover in which a philanthropic company named Fleshpound Finance Co. offered to extend easy credit to the tired, the poor, and the huddled masses yearning to breathe free. Blessid responded to the advertisement. Fleshpound agreed to lend Blessid $5,000, but insisted on collateral to secure the loan. To satisfy this demand, Blessid granted Fleshpound a security interest in his piano. The security interest was properly perfected under state law.

About a year later, Blessid filed a Ch. 7 petition. At the time of the filing, the balance of the loan is $4,000. The piano is worth $6,000.

Can Blessid avoid the security interest under §522(f)?

2. A House Divided

An individual Ch. 7 debtor owns a small house valued at $100,000, subject to a security interest of $90,000. She earns her living by housesitting for people when they travel. She usually has about ten housesitting jobs a year, which means that she lives in other people's homes for a total of about 30 weeks in a year. When she is not housesitting, she lives in her own house. Is the debtor entitled to an exemption in the house? If so, how much can she exempt? What would her exemption be if the house was not subject to a mortgage?

3. Appraise for Us Sinners, Now and at the Time of Our Debt

A firm value was given for the house in Example 2. It is the prerogative of law professors to fabricate convenient facts. Courts are not supposed to exercise the same creativity with regard to factfinding. How would the value of the homes be decided in a bankruptcy case?

4. The Importance of Being Earnest

The property in the Ch. 7 estate of Earnest Everyman is valued at $52,000. It consists of the following assets: Earnest's equity of $30,000 in his home;

furniture, appliances, household goods, and personal effects, with a total value of $16,000; a car worth $4,000; carpentry tools worth $2,000, used by Earnest in his job.

Connie Seur, another Ch. 7 debtor, is an art lover. Instead of buying a house, furniture, and other items of ordinary personal property, she has chosen to live in a cheap furnished apartment and to ride the bus. She has spent all her disposable income on artwork. As a result, her Ch. 11 estate consists of household and personal effects worth $4,000 and a collection of paintings, sculpture, ceramics, and musical recordings with a total value of $48,000.

What is the maximum that each of these debtors can exempt under §522(d)? What does the comparison of their exemptions say about the emphasis, underlying policy, and possible inequity of the Code's exemption scheme?

5. Ars Longa, Vita Brevis

Given the answer to Example 5, should Connie Seur have sold some of her *objects d'art* before filing her bankruptcy petition, and reinvested the proceeds in a cute little tract home, furnishings, a used car, and other exempt assets?

6. Diamonds Are for Eva

One of the assets in the estate of Eva Porate is a diamond ring. About a year before bankruptcy, Eva had obtained a loan from Unrequited Loan Co. and had granted Unrequited Loan Co. a valid security interest in the diamond ring to secure the loan. The proceeds of the loan were used to pay off a number of smaller consumer debts that had accumulated on high-interest credit cards.

At the time of bankruptcy, the balance of the loan is $5,000. The ring is valued at $7,150. Eva would like to redeem the ring. Can she do so? How does the answer change if the ring is valued at $4,500 or $7,500?

7. A Lacklucre Performance

Eva Porate, the debtor in Example 7, cannot raise the cash needed to redeem the ring, and the courts in her circuit do not permit redemption by installments. Eva wishes to enter into a reaffirmation agreement with Unrequited Loan Co. under which she will repay the debt in installments and keep the ring.

Eva's salary is just sufficient to support herself and a minor child. If she scrimps very hard and foregoes a few meals a week, she can put aside $200 per month to pay Unrequited Loan Co. This is $75 less per month than she was obliged to pay under the original security agreement, so she needs an extension of time to pay off the debt. Eva is willing to pay interest at the rate fixed in the original contract, and Unrequited would retain its security interest. The balance of the debt is $5,000. The ring is worth $7,150. Is Eva able to use the reaffirmation process to keep the ring?

8.   Affirm Offer

Another of Eva Porate's debts was an amount of $5,000 owed on a credit card. After the issuer of the card received notice of Eva's bankruptcy filing, it wrote a letter to her in which it noted the outstanding balance on the card and stated, "We realize that you have the right to discharge this debt in your bankruptcy case. However, before you do this, we urge you to bear in mind that bankruptcy can have a serious impact on your ability to obtain credit in the future. We therefore invite you to consider entering into the attached reaffirmation agreement. If you elect to make this agreement and you repay the outstanding balance due to us in installments as reflected therein, we will reinstate your credit card with your former credit limit. Please discuss this with your attorney, who will explain the procedure you must follow to reaffirm this debt." Has the credit card issuer done anything wrong in sending this letter?

EXPLANATIONS

1.   The piano appears to qualify as a tool of trade in which the debtor may claim an exemption of $1,750 under §522(d)(6). The question of whether property qualifies as a tool of trade involves both factual and legal determinations. The factual issue is whether the property is used by Blessid to earn his livelihood. It apparently is: Blessid uses the piano to practice his art, from which he ekes out his miserable living. The question of whether an object qualifies as a tool of trade can be subtle. In *In re Gregory*, 245 B.R. 171 (10th Cir. B.A.P. 2000) the debtor was a security guard. He was armed with a pistol at work and also owned a second pistol for shooting practice. He claimed the practice pistol as a tool of trade. The court held that although the debtor was required to have a pistol for work, this was not the pistol used for his work, and his employer did not require him to own a practice pistol. (The state had opted out under §522(b), so the court was interpreting the applicable state exemption, which is worded differently from §522(d)(6), but the case is nevertheless a good illustration of the factual determination.)

The legal issue is whether Congress intended an item of this kind to be included in the exemption covering tools of trade. Some courts interpret "implements" and "tools of trade" narrowly to include only small hand implements or devices of modest value and to exclude expensive equipment. Others adopt a more liberal approach, which includes any property used in the debtor's work and necessary to his livelihood.

Fleshpound's security interest in the piano is a nonpossessory nonpurchase-money interest, and tools of trade are one of the three categories of property covered by the avoidance provisions of §522(f)(1)(B). Blessid can avoid the security interest to the extent that it impairs his exemption. If only the tools of trade exemption in §522(d)(6) is used, the lien cannot be avoided. That exemption is limited to $1,750, and there is a $2,000 equity in the piano beyond the amount of the security interest. Thus, the interest does not impair the exemption which can be fully paid out of the equity with a surplus over for the estate.

However, §522(d)(5) gives the debtor a general exemption of $925 plus up to $8,725 of any unused amount of the homestead exemption. The debtor may apply the general exemption to any otherwise nonexempt property, or may use it to augment an existing exemption category. The facts suggest that Blessid has no homestead and no other valuable property. He could therefore use the general exemption to fully exempt the piano. In *In re McNutt*, 87 B.R. 84 (9th Cir. B.A.P. 1988), the court held that if the general exemption is combined with the tool of trade exemption, §522(f) can be used to avoid the interest to the extent that it impairs the aggregate exemption: The language of §522(f) is broad enough to encompass any exemption which the debtor is entitled to claim in property that is a tool of trade. It is not confined to the $1,750 exemption in §522(d)(6), where the property qualifies for other exemptions as well. By combining the exemptions, Blessid is able to avoid the security interest in full and to claim the piano from the estate. Fleshpound is left with an unsecured claim against the estate.

2. The debtor may claim the homestead exemption under §522(d)(1), provided that the debtor or a dependent uses the property as a residence. The value of the exemption is $17,425 but the debtor is able to increase it to $18,350 by adding the $925 general exemption provided for in §522(d)(5). This question is answered on the assumption that the general exemption has been used for another asset, so the amount of the homestead exemption is $17,425.

The general rule is that the debtor's temporary absence from the homestead, with a specific intent to return, does not prevent the debtor from claiming the exemption. Although the debtor's absences do add up to more than half a year, they are temporary and the debtor does always return to her home, which is her permanent abode.

This property is subject to a mortgage of $90,000, so the debtor's equity in the home is worth only $10,000. Unless §522(f) applies—which it clearly does not in this case—the debtor's exemption is subordinate to a valid consensual security interest in the property. By granting the mortgage, the debtor is taken to have waived the exemption as against the mortgagee. This is recognized by §522(c)(2).

Therefore, the debtor may claim an exemption in the house up to the value of the equity of $10,000. Section 522(d)(5) allows the debtor to add to the general exemption up to $8,725 worth of unused homestead exemption. Therefore, the entire unused balance of $7,425 may be used to exempt other property. Because the mortgage and the exemption consume the entire value of the house, there is no value in it for the estate, so it should be abandoned by the trustee. Had there been no mortgage on the house, the debtor would have claimed the full exemption of $17,425 and the balance of the $100,000 would have gone to the estate.

3.   Section 522(a)(2) defines value for the purposes of §522 as the fair market value of the property at the date of the petition; or when property enters the estate after the petition, at the date that the estate acquires the property. The determination of fair market value is a factual issue to be decided on all the available evidence. This can in itself be a difficult question to resolve. (Some of the difficulties in valuing property are discussed in relation to relief from stay in section 11.4.2 and in Examples 1 and 2 of Chapter 11.)

In addition, courts have had difficulty in interpreting what is meant by *fair market value* in the bankruptcy context. If the facts suggest that the property will not be sold on the open market but will be liquidated, the use of market value results in artificially high appraisal. The impact of an unrealistic appraisal could be to the advantage or disadvantage of the debtor, depending on the facts. For example, in some cases a high valuation could harm the debtor by leading to the conclusion that the equity in the property exceeds the debtor's exemption. In other cases, a low valuation could make it appear that the debtor has no equity over a security interest, so that the property is abandoned to the secured claimant, or an application for relief from stay is granted. For this reason, some courts have been influenced by liquidation value where this has seemed more realistic, in spite of the reference to market value in §522(a)(2).

4.   Each of the estates is worth $52,000, yet Earnest's exemptions are greater than Connie's. Earnest can claim exemptions in a total amount of $32,175, made up as follows:

(a)   Homestead under §522(d)(1), limited to $17,425
(b)   Household goods and personal effects under §522(d)(3), limited to $450 per item and to a maximum aggregate value of $9,300
(c)   Motor vehicle under §522(d)(2), limited to $2,775
(d)   Tools of trade under §522(d)(6), limited to $1,750
(e)   General exemption of $925 under §522(d)(5), to be applied to nonexempt property or to enhance an existing exemption category

Connie can claim the $9,300 exemption under §522(d)(3), subject to the $450 limit per item. All of Connie's property is covered by this category. In addition, Connie can select further property to exempt under the general exemption of §522(d)(5). As Connie has not used the homestead exemption, the general exemption has a limit of $9,650. Connie's total exemptions are $18,950.

Earnest, with his rather commonplace patterns of acquisition, does much better than Connie. This is characteristic of many exemption statutes, which focus on necessities that are deemed essential to the debtor's survival.

(Of course, that does not mean that the debtor will be able to keep these necessary items. If their value exceeds the exemption limit, they will be liquidated and the debtor will get no more than the exemption value in cash.) The statutory specification of exemptable property allows the legislature to control exemptions, confine them to property vital to the debtor's survival, and make it harder for debtors to abuse them. However, if an exemption statute is too rigid and too specific in its selection of exemptable property, it can lead to unfair and groundless discrimination against debtors whose needs and interests differ from the generalized preconception of the legislature. The general exemption in §522(d)(5) gives some recognition to this problem by providing a small-value elective exemption that is augmented if the debtor does not take the full homestead exemption.

The majority report of the National Bankruptcy Review Commission favored the abolition of most of the specified categories of exempt property (with the exception of the homestead and a few identified classes of personal property) and the substitution of a lump sum amount, enabling the debtor to select whatever property he might wish, up to the stated total value. The pending reform legislation does not adopt this recommendation.

5. A debtor who wishes to take full advantage of exemptions may be tempted to do some prebankruptcy planning by selling nonexempt property before filing and purchasing exempt property with the proceeds. Although this type of prepetition manipulation seems underhanded, there is support for it in the legislative history of the Code. Congress has indicated that the debtor should be able to make full use of her exemptions. In light of this, courts have recognized that the prepetition conversion of nonexempt assets into exempt property is not per se wrongful. However, they have policed this kind of activity by applying a good faith test. If the conversion is fraudulent, that is, if the debtor has behaved dishonestly or deceptively in making the conversion, the exemption could be denied. Alternatively, the court may permit the exemption to be claimed, but take the debtor's fraud into account in deciding whether to limit or deny the debtor's discharge.

The line between permissible prepetition planning and dishonest behavior is not an easy one to draw. As a general guideline, the question is whether the debtor has had to conceal the activity or otherwise mislead a creditor in order to affect the conversion. This is discussed in *In re Reed,* 700 F.2d 986 (5th Cir. 1983), and is also raised by Example 1 of Chapter 22 in the context of the discharge.

This question also suggests an ethical dilemma for the debtor's legal advisor in the prepetition period. While the attorney is obliged to inform the debtor of the right to enhance exemptions, the attorney must be careful not to collaborate in or encourage dishonest dealings by the debtor.

Although there is no statutory bar on prepetition asset conversion at present, the pending reform legislation proposes some control on it, at least insofar as the debtor's augmentation of the homestead exemption is attributable to fraudulent dispositions of non-exempt property.

6. The ring can be redeemed only if all the requirements of §722 are satisfied. All except one are clearly satisfied: Eva is an individual; the ring is tangible personal property; the ring is apparently intended primarily for personal use; the debt is a consumer debt, incurred for the purpose of settling existing credit card accounts; the debt is dischargeable. (Discharge is discussed in Chapter 22. Assume for now that none of the exclusions from discharge are applicable on the facts of this case.).

In addition to these requirements, there is one that needs fuller discussion—the property must be exempt or abandoned. The satisfaction of this requirement depends on the value of the ring in relation to the debt. If the value of the ring is $7,150, the claim is fully secured with a surplus of $1,150 that constitutes the debtor's equity in the property. The equity is exemptable by Eva under §522(d)(4), which provides for a $1,150 exemption in jewelry held for personal family or household use. Provided that Eva has claimed the ring as exempt, she may redeem the ring by paying Unrequited the amount of its secured claim of $5,000. Most courts require that the redemption price is paid in cash.

If the ring is worth $4,500, Unrequited is undersecured. Because §722 permits redemption by payment of the secured claim, the value of the collateral sets the upper limit on the redemption price. However, a further adjustment must be made in this particular case: The loan is a nonpossessory, nonpurchase-money security interest in jewelry, which is included in the category of consumer goods in §522(f)(1)(B),[1] so Eva can avoid the interest to the extent that it impairs her exemption of $1,150. Because the exemption is fully impaired, the security interest and hence the redemption price is reduced to $3,350. The remainder of the debt ($1,650) is a general unsecured claim against the estate.

If the ring is worth $6,500, the redemption price is set at the amount of the debt ($5,000) as in the first example. However, unlike the first example, the debtor's equity of $1,500 exceeds the $1,150 exemption. The estate has a $350 interest in the property, so that it is not fully exempt and will not be abandoned by the trustee. To satisfy the requirements of §722 and affect redemption, Eva must pay the estate its interest of $350 so that the trustee will abandon the property. This means that Eva must be able to raise $5,350 in cash to redeem the property.

---

1. Note that jewelry is specifically mentioned in §522(f)(1)(B), but that it is not expressly included in the household goods exemptuion in §552(d)(3). It is provided for separately in §522(d)(4). This suggests that the jewelry exemption is confined to the amount of $1,150 in §522(d)(4), and the exemption amount should not be augmented by adding an additional $450 from §522(d)(3).

7. Eva's first problem is to convince Unrequited to enter into the reaffirmation agreement. Because the collateral is worth $7,150, Unrequited's secured claim will be settled in full upon impending liquidation of the property. There is sufficient equity in the ring to cover Eva's exemption, so the lien cannot be avoided under §522(f).[2] Because Unrequited will do well on liquidation, it has little incentive to make a contract with Eva under which it accepts extended payment from a debtor with a disastrous credit record who can only afford to make the proposed payments by skipping meals.

Had the value of the ring been lower, Eva would have been in a better bargaining position. Her ability to cut down the security interest under §522(f)(1)(B) would enable her to make an offer of reaffirmation that improved the level of payment expected by Unrequited. This, combined with other factors (such as an attractive interest rate and a likelihood that the ring would not depreciate in value over the term of payment so that later foreclosure will not result in loss) could outweigh the risk of default under the reaffirmation agreement.

Even if Unrequited could be persuaded to enter into a reaffirmation agreement, the provisions of §§524(c) and (d) must be satisfied. These restrictions are intended to protect the debtor from the coerced or uninformed assumption of liability for a discharged debt. In addition to imposing requirements to ensure that the debtor acted voluntarily in entering into the reaffirmation, §524 requires an impartial review of the agreement. If Eva was represented by an attorney when negotiating the reaffirmation, the attorney must certify that the agreement is informed and voluntary and that it does not impose an undue hardship on her or her dependent. If Eva was not legally represented when negotiating the reaffirmation, the court cannot approve the agreement unless it is satisfied that it is in the debtor's best interests and does not impose an undue hardship on her or her dependent.

Reaffirmation agreements under which the debtor receives some advantage, such as the right to retain property that would otherwise be liquidated, are generally regarded as more justifiable than those that merely reaffirm unsecured debts. However, the facts indicate that Eva cannot afford the reaffirmation and that the proposed payments will impose a strain on her household budget. The ring is not a necessity, and Eva's efforts to keep it seem irresponsible. If Eva is legally represented, her attorney would be hardpressed to certify the reaffirmation as not imposing an undue hardship on her and her child. If she is not legally represented, the court would have similar difficulty

---

2. If the ring was worth more than $7,150, Eva's chances of using reaffirmation to keep the property would be further reduced because the estate would then also have an interest in the property and would have to be paid out the value of its interest. As the value of the collateral is worth exactly as much as the security interest and the exemption, Unrequited's recovery could be reduced by the costs of realizing the property. This is disregarded for the sake of simplicity.

and would in addition be likely to find that the agreement does not serve her best interests.

Where a debtor is legally represented, the attorney may be placed in an awkward position: Even though the debtor truly desires the agreement, the attorney must refuse certification if he or she believes that it imposes an undue hardship on the client or a dependent. The attorney must act conscientiously in providing the certificate. An attorney who signs the certificate without independently assessing the debtor's financial situation and ensuring that the debtor's decision is rational and supportable could be subject to sanctions. For example, in *In re Vargas*, 257 B.R. 157 (Bankr. D.N.J. 2001), the court, on finding that the attorney failed to conduct a proper undue hardship analysis, required him to disgorge his fees. To avoid having to veto the debtor's wishes, an attorney who cannot recommend reaffirmation may be allowed to withdraw and have the debtor approach the court pro se for approval. *See In re Brown*, 95 B.R. 35 (Bankr. E.D. Va. 1989).

Finally, it should be noted again that a debtor who wishes to retain property should consider filing under Ch. 13, which is designed to enable the debtor to modify the payment terms of a secured debt. It is only where, on balance, Ch. 7 liquidation is more advantageous than Ch. 13 that the process of reaffirmation of secured debt is worthwhile.

8. As discussed in section 13.7.3, a creditor who approaches the debtor to propose reaffirmation takes the risk that its action may be construed as an attempt to recover a claim against the debtor in willful violation of the automatic stay. (Section 362(a)(6).)

Most courts will not find a violation of the stay if the creditor's proposal for reaffirmation is not aggressive, coercive, or harassing. Also, it is wiser for the creditor to make the approach through the debtor's attorney, and to make sure that the debtor is fully informed about the nature and effect of the reaffirmation. Any deception or non-disclosure could cause problems for the creditor. Although the distinction between an incentive and a threat can be quite subtle, the letter in Eva's case may not overstep the mark and violate the stay. The warning of a bad credit rating could be construed as vaguely threatening, but it does not seem strong enough to be coercive. It does not really indicate that this creditor would take any action adverse to the debtor if the offer is refused. Further, as the creditor would have no obligation to extend credit to the debtor in the future, the hint that it may not do so unless the debtor reaffirms is not properly regarded as a threat.

14

The Trustee's Avoidance Powers: General Principles and Policies

§14.1   Introduction

In general terms, the avoidance powers enable the trustee to set aside certain transactions entered into by the debtor prior to the filing of the petition. (All of the Code's avoidance provisions relate to the prepetition period except for §549, which is concerned with postpetition transactions.) The avoidance powers are aimed primarily at transfers of property by the debtor, but some are also applicable to obligations assumed by the debtor. *Transfer* is defined very broadly in §101(54) to include every mode of disposing of property or an interest in it. A transfer may be voluntary or involuntary, and it may be an outright disposition of property or the grant of an encumbrance or other interest in it.

The avoidance of prepetition transfers is part of the trustee's function of collecting estate property and maximizing the estate's value. In the discussion of property of the estate in section 12.2, the general rule was expressed that property enters the estate only to the extent that the debtor has an interest in it, as determined under nonbankruptcy law. The trustee's avoidance rights qualify that general rule. By enabling the trustee to overturn certain prepetition transfers of the debtor, the Code in effect allows the estate to recover property interests that the debtor had relinquished before bankruptcy. If transactions are avoidable under the Code but irreversible by the debtor under nonbankruptcy law, the estate's property interest is in fact stronger than that held by the debtor at the time of the petition.

In addition to going beyond the debtor's rights, the trustee's avoidance powers exceed the rights of avoidance available to creditors under nonbankruptcy law. Some of these powers are unique to bankruptcy, while others have counterparts in nonbankruptcy law. However, even when nonbankruptcy law forms the basis of avoidance, the concentration of several alternative means of avoidance in the hands of the trustee, aided by legal fictions created by the Code, place the trustee in a much stronger position than any creditor could occupy outside of bankruptcy.

Each of the trustee's avoidance powers is examined in Chapters 15 and 16. This chapter introduces them generally, outlines some procedural issues and common themes, and explains their basic concept and rationale.

§14.2   The Structure of the Avoidance Provisions

Before discussing the trustee's avoidance powers, it is helpful to identify the following provisions in the Code that bear on these powers and to indicate their functions.

(1)   The trustee's power to avoid prepetition transactions is conferred by §§544, 545, 547, 548, and 553, which prescribe the transactions that are avoidable and specify prerequisites for avoidance.

(a)   §544 allows the trustee to avoid transfers and obligations that could have been avoided under nonbankruptcy law by an actual unsecured creditor or by specified hypothetical claimants.

(b)   §545 gives the trustee limited power to avoid certain kinds of statutory liens.

(c)   §547 allows the trustee to avoid preferential transfers that occurred within 90 days (or in the case of insiders, within one year) before the petition.

(d)   §548 gives the trustee the power, similar to that available to creditors under state fraudulent transfer law, to avoid fraudulent transfers and obligations that occurred within a year before the petition.

(e)   §553 allows the trustee to avoid setoffs to the extent they involve disallowed claims or arose out of certain transactions within 90 days prior to the petition.

(2)   Although §552 is not an avoidance provision strictly speaking, it does have the effect of partially avoiding floating liens[1] to the extent that they would otherwise cover collateral acquired after the petition has been filed. Under §552, a security interest in after-acquired collateral is confined to such collateral acquired up to the time of bankruptcy and proceeds of that collateral. It does not attach to property acquired by the estate or the debtor after the petition.

---

1. This type of transaction is explained in section 2.2.4.

(3)   Although it is also not an avoidance power in the same sense as the others, §558 should be included in this list. It allows the trustee to succeed to any defense that the debtor may have against any entity. Hence, if the debtor has an avoidance right under nonbankruptcy law (*e.g.,* the right to rescind a transfer on grounds of the transferee's fraud), the trustee may exercise that right for the benefit of the estate.

(4)   Section 549 permits the trustee to avoid unauthorized postpetition transfers.

(5)   Section 546 imposes limitations on the avoidance powers. It contains a statute of limitations and also subjects the trustee's avoidance rights to provisions of nonbankruptcy law that confer protection on certain transferees in specified transactions.

(6)   The effect of avoidance is governed by §§550 and 551. Section 551 allows the estate to take over the rights the defeated transferee had in estate property, so that avoidance benefits the estate rather than the holders of junior interests in the property. Section 550 provides for the recovery of property by the estate following avoidance of the transfer. Section 502(d) adds further force to the obligation to surrender property by providing for the disallowance of the claim of a transferee who fails to turn over property to the estate.

(7)   The provisions discussed here are concerned with the trustee's avoidance power. Remember, however, that the debtor has the right under §522(f) to avoid certain liens that impair exemptions. (*See* section 13.5.)

(8)   Finally, this list of relevant statutory provisions would be incomplete without a reminder that §101 must be consulted for the definition of many terms used in the avoidance sections.

§14.3   Applicability of the Avoidance Powers in Liquidation and Rehabilitation Cases

The avoidance powers are applicable in all cases under the Code, whether filed under Ch. 7, 11, 12, or 13. However, they have a somewhat different effect in rehabilitation and liquidation cases. In a case under Ch. 7 the trustee's exercise of the avoidance powers directly benefits the creditor body. Recovered property swells the value of the fund to be distributed, and the avoidance of encumbrances and obligations adjusts the share in the fund by eliminating claims against the estate or demoting claims from secured to unsecured status.

In cases under Chs. 11, 12, and 13, the link between the creditors' interest and the avoidance power is not as direct, because much (if not all) of the estate property ultimately reverts to the debtor. Therefore, the debtor may be the principal beneficiary of avoidance actions. The advantage to creditors from avoidance derives from the fact that the liquidation value of the estate sets a minimum level of payment under the plan. The recovery of property enlarges that liquidation value and thereby raises the minimum standards for confirmation of the plan. Also, as in liquidation cases, the avoidance of encumbrances or obligations eliminates secured claims or obligations of the estate, which increases the share of remaining creditors in the liquidation value of the estate.

§14.4   Exercise of the Avoidance Power by a Debtor in Possession or Other Parties

All the avoidance provisions specifically confer the avoidance power on the trustee. As noted in section 6.2, in Ch. 11 cases the debtor in possession normally exercises all the powers of a trustee. It is therefore common for the debtor in possession to represent the estate in avoidance litigation. This leads to the paradoxical result that it is frequently the very debtor who made the transfer or incurred the obligation that later seeks to avoid it. Although this anomaly has occasionally caused courts to balk at allowing avoidance by a debtor in possession, the usual approach is to recognize that the debtor in possession is really operating in a new capacity.

Avoidance rights cannot normally be exercised by anyone other than the trustee or debtor in possession. There are some narrow exceptions to this. In a Ch. 11 case, the court might authorize a creditors' committee to avoid a transfer if the debtor in possession unjustifiably fails to do so. Although the creditor's committee cannot simply take the initiative and sue, the court has the discretion to authorize suit. See *In re The V Companies*, 292 B.R. 290 (6th Cir. B.A.P. 2003); *Official Committee of Unsecured Creditors of Cybergenics Corp. v. Chinery*, 330 F.3d 548 (3rd Cir. 2003). Also, §522(h) provides for another limited exception for individual debtors. If a transfer of exempt property is avoidable and the trustee does not attempt to avoid it, the debtor may do so provided that the transfer was involuntary and the debtor did not conceal the property.

§14.5   The Avoidance Suit and the Enforcement of a Judgment of Avoidance

To seek the avoidance of a transfer or obligation, the trustee must commence suit in the bankruptcy court. The suit takes the form of an adversary proceeding — essentially, a civil lawsuit within the bankruptcy case. Avoidance suits are included in the list of core proceedings in 28 U.S.C. §§157(b)(2)(F), (H), and (K). This indicates that Congress considered them to be centrally related to the bankruptcy process and fully within the jurisdiction of the bankruptcy courts. However, as discussed in section 7.3, Congress's determination of whether or not a matter is a core proceeding is not dispositive; the Supreme Court has cast doubt on the characterization of avoidance actions as core proceedings because they involve the adjudication of rights under nonbankruptcy law.

If the avoidance action concerns an obligation incurred by or an interest in property granted by the debtor, the court's determination of avoidability results either in disallowance of the claim against the estate or in invalidation of the claim to the property. If the action is aimed at the avoidance of a transfer of property by the debtor, judgment in favor of the trustee obliges the transferee to return the property or its value to the estate. Section 550 governs the enforcement of this obligation. Section 550(a) allows the trustee to recover the property (or its value, if the court so orders) from the initial transferee who received or benefited from the transfer and from any subsequent transferee. Although this means that there may be more than one person liable for the property or its value, §550(d) makes it clear that the estate can only obtain a single satisfaction.

Section 550(b) limits the trustee's right to recover from a subsequent transferee who takes the property for value, in good faith, and without knowledge of the voidability of the transfer (*i.e.*, *a bona fide purchaser*). A bona fide purchaser is not liable to return the property or its value; any later transferee who takes in good faith is also protected from avoidance. Section 550(b) applies only to subsequent transferees and cannot be used as a defense by the person who acquired the property from the debtor.

Under §550(e), any transferee who acquired the property in good faith but who is not entitled to protection under §550(b) is given a lien on the property to secure the lesser of the net cost of any improvement made to the property after transfer (offset by profits from the property) or the increase in value resulting from the improvement. This lien is available to both the initial transferee and to any subsequent transferee who does not satisfy the requirements of §550(b), provided that the transferee acted in good faith in acquiring the property.

In many cases, the initial transferee of property is a creditor who acquired the property in satisfaction of a debt. When the transfer is avoided, the previously settled indebtedness becomes an unpaid claim once again. To encourage such transferees to surrender property to the estate following avoidance of the transfer, §502(d) provides for the disallowance of the transferee's claim against the estate unless the property is returned. In *In re Davis*, 889 F.2d 658 (5th Cir. 1989), the court observed that this provision is intended to be *coercive* rather than *punitive*: It is supposed to put pressure on the creditor to turn over the property to the estate within a reasonable time after having been ordered to do so.

§14.6 Preservation of the Transfer for the Benefit of the Estate

Section 551 states that any avoided transfer is preserved for the benefit of the estate with respect to property of the estate. This means that when the trustee avoids an interest in estate property, the estate automatically succeeds to the avoided rights in the property. This allows the trustee to assert those rights against any other interest in the property that is junior to the avoided interest. Say, for example, that there are two security interests in a piece of estate property. Both are valid under state law, and the first security interest has priority over the second. If the senior interest is avoidable in bankruptcy[2] but the junior interest is not, the trustee avoids the senior interest and is then able to assert its priority over the junior one. Were it not for §551, the avoidance of the superior interest would simply promote the junior lien, so that it becomes first in line as claimant to the proceeds of the property. Section 551 ensures that when the trustee exercises the avoidance power, it is the estate, rather than the holder of the junior interest, that benefits from the avoidance.

§14.7   The Statute of Limitations and "Reach-Back" Provisions

Two statutes of limitation pertain to the period within which the trustee must act to assert the avoidance powers.

First, §546(a) requires that actions or proceedings for avoidance be commenced at the latest before the case is closed. However, if the case takes a long time to close, the limitation period ends before then: The action must be commenced before the later of two years from the order of relief, or (provided that the first trustee is appointed or elected within that two-year period) one year from the appointment or election of the first trustee.

Second, §550(f) requires that actions or proceedings to recover property following avoidance be commenced within the earlier of one year after the transfer has been avoided or by the time that the case is closed or dismissed.

These provisions recognize that avoidance proceedings consist of two distinct stages: the action of avoidance itself and the enforcement of the judgment of avoidance by proceedings to compel turnover of the property under §550. Of course, the trustee is able to make the avoidance and turnover claims in the same suit, so that judgment on these issues is granted simultaneously.

These limitation periods must be distinguished from so-called *reach-back* provisions contained in the avoidance sections themselves. Some powers of avoidance apply only to transfers that occurred within a specific period before the petition. That is, the trustee can "reach back" only so far into the prebankruptcy period to avoid certain transfers. These periods are noted in the discussion of the different avoidance powers in Chapters 15 and 16. While the reach-back provisions prescribe the retrospective temporal range of the avoidance power, limitation periods require the trustee to initiate avoidance proceedings within a specific period during the bankruptcy case. (*See* section 15.1.3 for further discussion of this distinction.)

---

2. Section 16.1 explains how an interest could be avoidable in bankruptcy notwithstanding its validity under state law.

§14.8 The General Purpose and Goals of the Avoidance Powers

Before becoming involved in the intricacies of the avoidance powers, it is useful to identify the principal policies that motivated their enactment and that continue to influence courts in their interpretation. These broad policy themes are not served equally by all the avoidance provisions. Each section is designed to achieve specific ends with regard to particular types of transactions. However, there are common threads, and a survey of them at the outset helps create a perspective from which the detailed rules may be viewed. The themes raised here will arise again in a more concrete context in Chapters 15 and 16.

(1) **Most avoidance powers are intended to facilitate the bankruptcy goals of preservation of the estate and collective treatment of claims.** Two of the fundamental bankruptcy policies identified in section 5.5 are the preservation of the estate and collective treatment of claims, leading to the optimum distribution to creditors in the order of priority prescribed by law. These policies could not be effectively realized if the trustee was able to look no further than the remnants of the debtor's estate at the time of the filing of the petition. In many cases, the debtor's bankruptcy is preceded by a period of financial crisis in which creditors jostle for advantage by collection activity and the debtor responds to pressure by making payments to particular creditors or by disposing of property. Much activity in this period could be abnormal or contrary to regular business practices; some of it could be dishonest or manipulative.

By permitting the trustee to go back into the prebankruptcy period and to avoid dispositions made and obligations incurred irregularly or illegitimately, the Code gives the trustee's power of preservation some retrospective effect. The trustee is able, to some extent at least, to ameliorate the harm caused by disruptions prior to the filing of the petition. In addition to restoring value to the estate, the avoidance deprives the creditor of the inappropriate advantage obtained in the period preceding bankruptcy and brings the creditor into bankruptcy's collective process. The argument is also made that the avoidance powers have a preventative function that goes beyond the case at hand. If it is generally understood that certain advantages will be avoidable if the debtor becomes bankrupt, creditors may be discouraged from pursuing them, because gains will be short-lived and futile. Of course, to many creditors, the possibility of avoidance may be no disincentive at all, because the risk of having to return the avoided transfer will be outweighed by the prospect of benefit if bankruptcy does not occur in the near future.

(2) **The avoidance provisions attempt to differentiate between legitimate and illegitimate transactions.** It will become clear when the prerequisites for avoidance are discussed in Chapters 15 and 16 that the

309

avoidance powers do not extend to every prepetition transfer or obligation. They are aimed at transactions that are perceived by Congress to be irregular or illegitimate, in that they unfairly or unjustifiably diminish the estate or undermine the proper order of distribution in bankruptcy. This limitation on the avoidance powers is very important. If every prepetition transfer or obligation could be overturned, the risk of a debtor becoming bankrupt would make all credit transactions hazardous and unappealing. Furthermore, it is one of the fundamental policies of bankruptcy that rights under nonbankruptcy law should be interfered with only to the extent necessary to affect the essential goals of bankruptcy such as estate preservation and evenhanded treatment of creditors. In creating the avoidance provisions, Congress was sensitive to the tension between effecting the goals of bankruptcy and protecting legitimate rights under nonbankruptcy law. Accordingly, the avoidance provisions constantly call for the distinction to be drawn between legitimate and illegitimate transactions.

(3) The avoidance powers are frequently used to invalidate unpublicized rights.   In a sense, this point is really a subcategory of the previous one, but the issue of unpublicized rights is so pervasive and significant that it should be identified as a distinct policy concern. The *secret lien* is often identified as a prime example of unpublicized interests. In its purest form, this hideous creature is a collusive transaction between the debtor and a creditor under which the debtor grants a lien to the creditor to secure the debt but the creditor refrains from recording it with the deliberate intent of helping the debtor to mislead others into believing that the property is unencumbered. As the discussion in Chapter 2 stresses, a creditor who has acquired a lien to secure a genuine debt has very little incentive to aid a dishonest debtor by keeping it secret. The lack of perfection subordinates the lienholder to most other interests in the property and could even be avoidable by an unsecured creditor of the debtor as a fraudulent transfer. Therefore, a true secret lien is a fairly unusual phenomenon except in bogus transactions.

However, unpublicized liens and interests are quite common because lienholders sometimes fail to record their liens as a result of neglect, delay, or error. The law is generally intolerant of such unpublicized interests, even where they are not attributable to actual fraud, because the lienholder's failure to perfect creates a potential for abuse by the debtor and a danger of misplaced reliance by third parties. Therefore, as a general rule, when nonbankruptcy law requires an act of publicity to perfect a lien, failure to complete the act makes the lien avoidable unless particularly strong equities favor the lienholder.

15

The Trustee's Avoidance Powers: Unperfected Interests and Statutory Liens

§15.1 The Avoidance of Unperfected Interests under §544

§15.1.1 Introduction

The basic idea behind §544 is that the trustee should have the same avoidance rights that would be available in nonbankruptcy law to the classes of persons identified in the section. Section 544 does not create rights of avoidance that are peculiar to the bankruptcy trustee, but rather confers a status on the trustee under which avoidance rights under nonbankruptcy law may be exercised. However, the concentration of these nonbankruptcy rights in the hands of the trustee, combined with the operation of legal fictions, gives the trustee a collection of powers that are unavailable to any actual creditor under nonbankruptcy law. The two subsections of §544 are distinct and provide different avoidance powers.

§15.1.2   The Trustee's Status as a Hypothetical Lien Creditor, Execution Creditor, or Bona Fide Purchaser of Real Property under §544(a)

Section 544(a) is known as the "strong arm" clause — a nickname inherited from its predecessor in the Bankruptcy Act. It confers three hypothetical roles on the trustee: those of judicial lienholder, unsatisifed execution creditor, and bona fide purchaser of real property.

Section 544(a) expressly declares that the trustee's assumption of any of these hypothetical positions is not dependent on the existence of an actual creditor or purchaser. The trustee is not a successor to the existing rights of any person, but obtains the status as a matter of law. This means that when no actual purchaser or creditor does exist, the advent of bankruptcy brings into effect an avoidance power that was merely potential or abstract before the petition — although the rights could have been asserted in theory, there was in fact no one entitled to assert them. In this sense, although §544(a) is based on nonbankruptcy law, its legal fictions give the trustee powers that had not in fact been acquired by anyone else by the time of the petition.

Section 544(a) also states expressly that the trustee's rights of avoidance are not affected by any knowledge that the trustee or any creditor may have. This is because the trustee acts in an official capacity and occupies the applicable status hypothetically. Any knowledge that would affect the equities against a real purchaser or lien creditor should therefore not be applicable to the trustee. (*See* Example 3.)

a.   The Trustee As Hypothetical Judicial Lienholder

Section 544(a)(1) gives the trustee the power to avoid any transfer of property or any obligation incurred by the debtor that would be avoidable in non-bankruptcy law by a creditor who has a judicial lien on all the debtor's property as at the date of the petition.[1] *Judicial lien* is defined in §101(36) to mean a lien arising out of judgment, levy, or some other judicial process.

The trustee's use of §544(a)(1) is illustrated by Example 1.

---

1. The actual language of §544(a)(1) is rather more convoluted. It refers to a creditor who extends credit and gets a lien at the time of the commencement of the case. This language was intended to make it clear that the Code meant to overturn some pre-Code caselaw that is no longer of concern to us. The reference to "simple contract" merely signifies that the judicial lien to be used in the hypothesis must be an ordinary one and not one that is given special priority under nonbankruptcy law.

b.   The Trustee as a Hypothetical Unsatisfied Execution Creditor

Section 544(a)(2) gives the trustee the avoidance power that would be available in nonbankruptcy law to a creditor who obtains a nulla bona return on an execution as at the date of the petition. This provision is not much used because it only applies where state law gives a creditor special avoidance rights after a nulla bona return. This does not seem to be the case in many states.

c.   The Trustee as a Hypothetical Bona Fide Purchaser of Real Property

Section 544(a)(3) gives the trustee the avoidance power that would be available in nonbankruptcy law to a bona fide purchaser of real property from the debtor who obtained and perfected that status on the date of the petition. Like the other provisions of §544(a), this subsection is expressly not dependent upon the existence of an actual bona fide purchaser. Simply stated, §544(a)(3) employs the fiction that the trustee is a perfected bona fide purchaser of realty as of the date of the petition. If, under nonbankruptcy law, such a bona fide purchaser would take precedence over the preexisting interest in it, the trustee can avoid the debtor's transfer of that interest.

Under state law a bona fide purchaser often has more powerful rights than a judicial lienholder. This is because some unperfected interests in real property are given priority over a subsequent judicial lien in the property, but not over a later bona fide purchaser. Where interests in real property are vulnerable to avoidance, the hypothetical bona fide purchaser status therefore augments the trustee's power beyond that of a hypothetical lien creditor. The value of this hypothetical status of the trustee is illustrated by Example 3.

§15.1.3   The Trustee's Status as Successor to an Actual Unsecured Creditor under §544(b)

Section 544(b)(1) states that the trustee may avoid any transfer made or obligation incurred by the debtor that is avoidable in prevailing nonbankruptcy law by a creditor holding an allowable unsecured claim. Unlike §544(a), this subsection does not create a hypothetical status. Rather, it provides for the trustee's succession to the avoidance rights of an actual unsecured creditor. The word *unsecured* must be stressed; the trustee cannot use this provision to acquire the more powerful rights of a lienholder. Although an actual unsecured creditor must be in existence, the creditor need not have proved a claim in the estate. All the subsection requires is that the claim would be allowable if proved. The power of avoidance under §544(b)(1) is not deemed to arise on the date of the petition. Although the trustee succeeds to the avoidance right on the petition date, the effectiveness of the right against the transferee is determined as at its actual effective date, that is, the date that the real-life creditor became entitled to exercise it.

As discussed in sections 1.4 and 4.1, unless the debtor has transferred property fraudulently, unsecured creditors have very little power to avoid transactions entered into by the debtor. For this reason, §544(b)(1) is of limited use to the trustee. In fact, most of the cases decided under §544(b)(1) involve fraudulent transfers. Even when fraudulent transfers are involved, §544(b)(1) is often not needed to avoid them because §548 gives the trustee the nonderivative power to avoid fraudulent transfers. (*See* section 16.3.) Section §544(b)(1) may be helpful, however, if the state's fraudulent transfer law provides broader powers of avoidance than §548 or if it allows the trustee to reach back earlier into the prebankruptcy period than §548 does. More specifically, §548 allows the trustee to avoid fraudulent transfers made within a year before the petition, but the statute of limitations under the UFTA is four years. Therefore, if a transfer occurred, say, two years before the petition, the trustee cannot use §548. But if there is an actual creditor who has the right to avoid the transfer under the UFTA, the trustee can use §544(b) to take over that creditor's avoidance rights, on which the UFTA limitation period has not yet run. (*See* Example 2.)

Where the trustee uses §544(b), the state law statute of limitations therefore operates as an alternative reachback period. This must be distinguished from the statute of limitations under the Code, which limits the period during which the trustee must bring an avoidance suit after the bankruptcy case has been filed. For example, in *In re American Energy Trading, Inc.*, 291 B.R. 159 (Bankr. W.D. Mo. 2003), the fraudulent transfers occurred in August 1999. The Ch. 11 case was filed in September 1999, and the trustee brought the suit to avoid the transfer under §544(b) in July 2002. Under state law there was a four-year statute of limitations, which would have allowed the trustee to reach back to avoid the transfer. However, the trustee failed to bring the avoidance suit within two years of the commencement of the case, as required by §546(a), so the court dismissed the trustee's suit as time-barred.

Section 544(b)(2), added to the Code by an amendment enacted in 1998, qualifies the trustee's right to avoid a transfer by having recourse to state law under §544(b)(1). If the transfer satisfies the definition of a "charitable contribution" in §548, so that it would be exempted from avoidance as a fraudulent transfer under §548, it cannot be avoided by the trustee's use of state law either. As more fully explained in section 16.3, this amendment is intended to protect charitable organizations, particularly churches, from having to return to the estate tithes and contributions of limited amount, made by the debtor without actual intent to defraud creditors.

§15.2   The Avoidance of Statutory Liens under §545

The nature and purpose of statutory liens was discussed in section 2.4.3. Section 101(53) defines them as liens "arising solely by force of a statute on specified circumstances or conditions. . . ." The definition includes common law liens of distress for rent, and it expressly excludes consensual security interests and judicial liens even if they are provided for by statute. The bankruptcy definition comports with the general meaning of the term under nonbankruptcy law.

The trustee's power to avoid statutory liens is provided for and delimited by §545, which is narrow in its scope. As a general rule, a statutory lien that is validly obtained and perfected under nonbankruptcy law is fully effective upon the bankruptcy of the debtor and cannot be avoided unless it fits into one of three categories specified by §545:

Under §545(1), a statutory lien is avoidable if it is specially created to take effect only upon the debtor's insolvency, bankruptcy, or financial distress. By providing for a lien that arises upon the debtor's financial distress, the state turns a formerly unsecured claim into a secured one, thereby tampering with the order of priority in bankruptcy and infringing upon the federal bankruptcy power.

Under §545(2), a statutory lien is avoidable if it is not perfected or enforceable against a hypothetical bona fide purchaser who is deemed to have purchased the property on the date of commencement of the case. This subsection is similar to §544(a)(3), in that it gives the trustee the hypothetical status of a bona fide purchaser as at the petition date so that the trustee can avoid the lien if it could have been avoided under nonbankruptcy law by a bona fide purchaser of the property. Unlike §544(a)(3), it is not confined to real property.

Under §545(3), statutory liens for rent or of distress for rent are avoidable in bankruptcy. ("Distress" in this context stems from the word "distraint," which means the seizure or detention of a chattel.) This subsection invalidates landlord's liens in bankruptcy, whether created by statute or common law. The discrimination against liens for rent or distress of rent predates §545(3), and stems from the policy decision made some time ago that lessors should be treated as unsecured creditors and not be given any special rights in bankruptcy unless they have obtained a consensual security interest in the lessee's property. The traditional landlord's lien has fallen into disfavor and is not protected in bankruptcy, even if it is still recognized under state law.

The trustee's limited power to avoid statutory liens reflects the policy goals outlined in section 14.8. Most statutory liens are conferred on particular classes of creditor by state law or federal nonbankruptcy law because the legislature has determined that these claimants have a special need for protection. If the Code allowed the trustee to overturn statutory liens that were validly obtained under nonbankruptcy law, it would undermine this protection. Hence, apart from landlord's liens, statutory liens are avoidable only where they are an usurpation of the bankruptcy power or are insufficiently perfected for protection under nonbankruptcy law. Section 545 is illustrated by Example 4.

§15.3   The Effect of §546 on the Trustee's Avoidance Rights under §§544 and 545

Section 546 contains a number of different restrictions on the trustee's avoidance rights. The statute of limitations in §546(a) has already been discussed in section 14.7. Two other provisions of §546 are also relevant to the trustee's avoidance powers under §§544 and 545.

§15.3.1   *The Preservation of Nonbankruptcy Backdating Rules by §546(b)*

The operation of §546(b) (introduced in the context of the automatic stay — *see* Example 1(f) of Chapter 10) effectuates rules of nonbankruptcy law that provide a grace period to a lienholder within which to perfect its interest in property. If nonbankruptcy law has a generally applicable rule that permits perfection of an interest to backdate, the trustee's powers of avoidance are subject to the rule. Therefore, if the interest is unperfected at the date of the petition but the period prescribed by nonbankruptcy law for perfection has not yet expired, the holder of the interest may perform the act of perfection at any time before the expiry of the applicable period. Upon perfection, the interest backdates to the earlier effective date prescribed by nonbankruptcy law. The requirement that the backdating must be "generally applicable" means that the law authorizing the backdating must apply generally to the lien or interest in question and cannot be geared to the debtor's bankruptcy or insolvency. Example 4 provides a further illustration of the application of §546(b).

§15.3.2   *The Preservation of the Seller's Reclamation Rights by §546(c)*

As stated in section 1.2, an unsecured seller of goods has no special interest in the goods once title has passed to the buyer. If the buyer fails to pay, the seller is in the position of a general unsecured creditor. A limited exception to this rule is recognized under common law and by UCC §2.702. Under common law, a buyer is deemed to make an implied representation of solvency when purchasing goods; if the buyer was insolvent upon receiving the goods, and the seller was unaware of this, the seller may rescind the contract and reclaim the goods on grounds of fraud. UCC §2.702 codifies this right, although in qualified form: If a buyer receives goods on credit while insolvent, and the seller did not know of the insolvency at the time, the seller may demand return of the goods within ten days of their receipt by the buyer. If the buyer had made a written misrepresentation of solvency to the seller within three months before delivery, the ten-day limit does not apply.[2] The seller's reclamation right is subject to the rights of a bona fide purchaser from the buyer.

Section 546(c) subjects the trustee's right of avoidance to any right of reclamation available to a seller under statute or common law. As in the UCC, demand must be made within ten days of the debtor's receipt of the goods. Under an amendment to §546(c)(1), added in 1994, this ten-day period is extended to twenty days if the bankruptcy filing occurs within the ten-day period.

There are a number of limitations to the seller's reclamation rights under §546 which are not found in UCC §2.702: It requires the sale to have been in the ordinary course of the seller's business, it makes no allowance for the extension of the ten-day reclamation period when there has been a written misrepresentation of insolvency, and it requires a written demand for reclamation. In addition, the definition of insolvency in bankruptcy is stricter than under the UCC. The Code generally requires the balance sheet test to be used, whereas the UCC permits insolvency to be established on either the balance sheet or equity test. Even if these additional requirements are satisfied, the court has the discretion to refuse reclamation and to give the seller an administrative expense priority or a lien instead. The operation of §546(c) is illustrated by Example 5.

EXAMPLES

1. Reach Back and Touch Someone

Rock Bottom has just filed a voluntary petition under Ch. 7. About a year ago he borrowed money from Confidential Credit Corp. and secured the loan by granting Confidential a security interest in equipment used in his business. A security agreement and financing statement were properly executed by the parties, but Confidential neglected to record the interest because of a clerical oversight. This error was only discovered after Rock had become bankrupt. Rock still owes a substantial balance on his loan.

Can the trustee in Rock's estate use §544 to avoid Confidential's security interest?

---

2. In 2003, the American Law Institute and the National Conference of Commissioners on Uniform State Laws approved a revision of UCC Article 2. The revisions will be submitted to state legislatures for enactment. The revised UCC §2.702 removes the ten-day limit for the demand, and replaces it with a reasonable time after the buyer's receipt of the goods. The revision also removes the qualification relating to the buyer's misrepresentation.

2.   The Invasion of the Booty Snatcher

Rock Bottom had been in financial difficulty for some years before his bankruptcy. Eighteen months before his petition, when threatened by impending judgments in collection suits, he transferred a valuable antique desk to a friend. Although the desk was worth $15,000, Rock gave it to his friend as a gift, subject to the understanding that the friend would donate it back when Rock's financial position became less hazardous.

A creditor with an unsecured claim of $1,000 allowable against Rock's estate would have had the right to avoid the disposition of the desk under the state's fraudulent transfer law, but never exercised that right.

(a)   Can the trustee take over the creditor's avoidance right under §544?

(b)   If so, to what extent can the transfer of the desk be avoided?

(c)   If the trustee avoids the transfer and recovers the desk, is the creditor whose rights were assumed entitled to any priority in the proceeds of the desk?

3.   Manny Fest's Destiny

(a)   Manny Fest bought a condominium from No Con Do, Inc., a property developer. The parties executed a contract of sale in terms of which Manny paid a down payment and obliged himself to pay the balance of the price in monthly installments. The sale should have been recorded, but it was not.

Manny moved into the condominium immediately after the contract was signed. He remained in possession of the property, and continued to pay his monthly installments. About a year after he bought the condominium, No Con Do, Inc. filed a voluntary Ch. 7 petition.

Can the trustee avoid Manny's equitable interest in the condominium under §544?

(b)   Change the facts in (a) as follows: Manny Fest paid the down payment but never occupied the condominium. He had purchased it as an investment and left its management as a rental unit in the hands of No Con Do, Inc. No Con Do, Inc. subsequently filed a Ch. 11 petition and, acting in its capacity as debtor in possession, seeks to avoid Manny's interest under §544(a)(3).

Should it succeed?

4.   Hell Hath No Fury Like a Workman Scorn'd

Ownerous Investments, Inc. filed a Ch. 7 petition on July 1. During the previous May it had entered into a contract with Jerry Bilt, a building contractor, to execute an alteration to a building that it owned. Jerry began work in early May and completed the job near the end of June. Although Jerry was to be paid in full on completion of the work, Ownerous failed to pay him. Jerry had taken no action to enforce his claim by the time Ownerous filed its petition.

Under the state's mechanic's lien statute, Jerry is entitled to a lien to secure his claim. He is not obliged to take any action to create the lien at the time of commencing work. The statute gives him three months following completion of the work in which to file a claim of lien. He must then institute action to foreclose the lien within six months of filing the claim. Provided that the claim is filed and suit is commenced within the prescribed periods, the lien is effective from the date on which construction commenced What is the status of Jerry's claim against the estate?

5. Red's Sale in the Sunset

Red Alert was about to move from his suburban home to a downtown apartment. Just before he made the decision to move, he had bought an expensive propane barbecue and meat smoker. Because this gadget is unsuited to the cloistered life of a high-rise dweller, he decided to sell it. On June 25 he sold it to Pearl Loin, a coworker. The parties agreed that Pearl would take delivery of the barbecue on that day and would pay for it at the end of the month. On June 28, a group of Pearl's creditors filed an involuntary bankruptcy petition against her. On June 30, Pearl told Red of this, and informed him that she could not pay for the barbecue. Red demanded its return, and Pearl referred him to her trustee. Should the trustee accede to Red's demand?

EXPLANATIONS

1. Quite inadvertently, Confidential's loan to Rock was much more confidential than anticipated. It failed to publicize its interest by filing, and thereby became the holder of a dreaded secret lien. As mentioned in section 14.8, there is a general policy against the enforcement of unrecorded interests in bankruptcy as well as under nonbankruptcy law because unrecorded interests are potentially prejudicial to third parties who may deal with the debtor in reliance on the appearance that no encumbrance exists. With some exceptions, this policy precludes enforcement of the unpublicized interest, even if the failure to record was not deliberate and no actual third party was misled by the lack of recording.

The unperfected interest is avoidable under §544(a)(1), which gives the trustee the hypothetical status of an ordinary judicial lienholder who acquired a lien on all Rock's lienable property (including the business equipment) on the date of the petition. This status enables the trustee to avoid Confidential's unperfected interest, because applicable nonbankruptcy law — in this case, UCC §9.317 — gives a judicial lien priority over a security interest that was unperfected at the time that the lien arose. The effect of avoidance is to leave Confidential with a general unsecured claim against the estate.

Section 544(a)(1) can only be used when the interest remains unperfected at the time of the petition. Had Confidential realized its error and perfected the interest before the petition was filed, the interest could not have been avoided under §544(a). However, the last-minute filing created a preference avoidable under §547, discussed in section 16.1 and in Example 3 of Chapter 16.

2. The facts in this Example illustrate the trustee's succession to the rights of an actual creditor under §544(b).

(a) Although §548 also empowers the trustee to avoid fraudulent transfers, it cannot be used in this case because it reaches back only one year before the petition date. By taking over the creditor's avoidance power under nonbankruptcy law, the trustee is subject to the statute of limitations applicable to the creditor's suit, which is likely to be longer than 18 months. For example, it is four years under the UFTA. This allows the trustee to reach back four years to avoid transfers in that time. (Note, however, as explained in section 15.1.3, the trustee must bring the suit within two years of the order for relief as required by §546(a).) It is not necessary that the creditor has proved a claim in the estate, provided that the claim is an allowable unsecured claim. The facts indicate that it is. Under the principles discussed in section 4.3, the actual creditor could have avoided the transfer, and the trustee can therefore do likewise.

(b) It is clear that if the creditor had exercised the avoidance rights under state law, the transfer could have been avoided only to the extent necessary to satisfy the claim, that is, $1,000. However, if the trustee uses §544(b) to succeed to the rights of the creditor, an old doctrine, derived from *Moore v. Bay*, 284 U.S. 4 (1931), extends the trustee's avoidance power to the entire transfer. The legislative history of §544(b) indicates that Congress intended the *Moore v. Bay* doctrine to continue to apply under the Code. For a recent case that applies the doctrine, *see In re DLC, Ltd.*, 295 B.R. 593 (8th Cir. B.A.P., 2003).

(c) In addition to the doctrine mentioned above, *Moore v. Bay* spawned another principle: If the trustee recovers a transfer by using the rights of an actual creditor under §544(b), the transferred property is returned for the benefit of the estate as a whole. The creditor whose rights were used is entitled to no special treatment and has a nonpriority unsecured claim against the estate. (*DLC, Ltd.*, above, recognizes this principle as well.)

3. **(a)** To decide whether the trustee can avoid Manny's interest under §544, one needs to establish what that interest is and how it would fare against the various real or hypothetical adversaries provided for in §544. These questions must be resolved with reference to nonbankruptcy law. Assume (as is likely to be true in many states) that the rules of nonbankruptcy law are as follows: A written but unrecorded purchase of realty makes the purchaser an equitable owner of the property. This equitable ownership interest is superior to a subsequent judicial lienholder and unsatisfied execution creditor, but it does not take priority over a bona fide purchaser of the property from No Con Do, Inc. This distinction is based on the general expectation that judgment creditors do not typically rely on filing records, but a bona fide purchaser is likely to do so. However, the protection of the bona fide purchaser is subject to an exception: If the equitable owner is in clear and open possession of the property, his occupation serves as constructive knowledge of his interest to any subsequent purchaser. This imputed knowledge precludes the subsequent purchaser from attaining the status of bona fide purchaser, even in the absence of actual knowledge of Manny's interest.

Under these rules of state law, the trustee cannot avoid Manny's interest by assuming any of the roles provided in §544. The actual or hypothetical creditor interests are inferior to the unrecorded equitable ownership, and Manny's open possession of the property would defeat the claim of one who would otherwise have qualified as a bona fide purchaser. This result is not changed by the provision in §544(a) that the avoidance power may be exercised regardless of any knowledge of the trustee or of any creditor. This applies only to any actual knowledge, not constructive knowledge of the trustee. The rights of the estate should not be affected by what the trustee or a creditor might know because the trustee is merely an official representing the estate, not an actual participant in the transaction whose knowledge may affect the equities of the case. However, constructive knowledge is a legal fiction imputed to a person irrespective of what he actually knows, for the purpose of protecting an earlier equitable interest that has achieved a level of publicity sufficient to be treated as quasi-perfection. For this reason, it should bind the trustee as hypothetical occupant of the status, in the same way as it would bind an actual party. This was the conclusion reached in *McCannon v. Marston,* 679 F.2d 13 (3d Cir. 1982).

(b) Because Manny is no longer in open possession of the condominium, constructive knowledge of his equitable ownership would not be imputed to a subsequent purchaser of the property. The trustee can therefore avoid the interest under §544(a)(3). This result follows in a straightforward way from the conclusions in (a). However, the factual variation raises another issue: Is it appropriate to allow the debtor in possession to exercise the trustee's avoidance power when the debtor itself sold the property to Manny, managed it for him, and had intimate knowledge of his rights? This seems to stretch the statutory disregard for the trustee's knowledge beyond all decent limits.

Some courts have refused to allow a debtor in possession to use §544(a)(3) to avoid an unrecorded interest arising out of a transaction in which it participated prior to the time that it became bankrupt. However, most courts permit a debtor in possession to use §544(a)(3) on the reasoning that when a debtor becomes a debtor in possession, it acts in a new capacity as representative of the estate. The avoidance of the transfer does not merely further its own interests, but the interests of creditors as well. *See, e.g., In re Eads,* 69 B.R. 730 (Bank. 9th Cir. 1986), *aff'd in part sub nom. In re Probasco,* 839 F.2d 1352 (9th Cir. 1988); *In re Sandy Ridge Oil Co.,* 807 F.2d 1332 (7th Cir. 1986).

4. Statutory liens are generally upheld in bankruptcy provided that they are valid and perfected under nonbankruptcy law. This principle is reflected in §545(2), which allows the trustee to avoid a statutory lien only if it would be avoidable by a bona fide purchaser of the property as at the time of bankruptcy. As in §544(a), the hypothetical status in §545(2) requires reference to the nonbankruptcy law governing the lien. The mechanic's lien statute protects Jerry from a bona fide purchaser of the property provided that he complies with the requirements for perfection within the statutory time limits. The statute backdates Jerry's lien, so that if someone had purchased the property from Ownerous on the petition date, the purchaser's interest would have been junior to the inchoate construction lien, provided that Jerry thereafter made the lien filing in the prescribed three-month period and commenced suit to foreclose the lien within six months from the recording date.

The advent of bankruptcy before the end of the statutory perfection period does not detract from Jerry's right to complete the perfection requirements. Section 546(b) preserves the backdating rules of nonbankruptcy law as long as they are generally applicable and are not created to take effect only upon the debtor's insolvency or bankruptcy. However, §546(b) changes the procedure to be followed to complete perfection. The filing of the claim of lien takes place as normal under state law and is excluded from the stay by §362(b)(3). (*See* Example 1(f) of Chapter 10.) However, instead of commencing the foreclosure suit thereafter, Jerry must give notice to the trustee within the period prescribed by the state statute for the commencement of suit.

This example shows that the policy against unrecorded interests is not absolute. Jerry has a "secret" lien on the property for some months. A prospective purchaser may or may not be alerted to the possibility of such a lien by observing any construction work on the property, but this may not be apparent, especially after construction. Sometimes effective protection of the unrecorded interest holder outweighs the need to protect persons who subsequently deal with the debtor. In fact, some statutory liens do not require recording at all, but arise automatically and avail against all subsequent purchasers of the property. Such liens are protected in bankruptcy under §545. This is illustrated by *In re Loretto Winery Ltd.,* 898 F.2d 715 (9th Cir. 1990), in which an automatically perfected, unpublicized statutory lien in favor of grape growers was held to be unavoidable in bankruptcy because it was effective against a bona fide purchaser under §545(2). The court acknowledged the policy against secret liens, but pointed out that it was a general policy, not a rigid rule, and held it must take second place to a clear state policy of giving strong protection to agricultural workers by granting them an automatic lien in the product of their labor.

5. Outside of bankruptcy, Red is entitled to reclaim the goods under UCC §2.702 if he can show that Pearl was insolvent when she received the barbecue and he only discovered this afterward. He has made a demand for the barbecue within ten days of its receipt by Pearl.[3] Section 546(c) recognizes the seller's reclamation right in the buyer's bankruptcy, but it imposes requirements beyond those of the UCC. One of these requirements is that the goods were sold in the ordinary course of the seller's business. Protection is therefore confined to merchant sellers and does not extend to casual sales like the present one. Red does not qualify for reclamation under §546(c). Although this disposes of Red's claim to the goods, it should also be noted that his demand was oral. While an oral demand is adequate under the UCC, §546(c) requires it to be in writing.

Section 546(c) does not itself avoid the seller's reclamation right. Section 546 is concerned with limitations on the trustee's avoidance power and is therefore expressed in positive terms — it says that a reclamation right that meets its requirements is unavoidable by the trustee. As Red's right does not satisfy §546(c), it can be avoided provided that it falls within one of the avoidance provisions of the Code. The trustee can avoid it under §544(a)(1) if, under state law, the seller's reclamation right is not effective against a subsequent judicial lienholder. If not, the argument could be made that the right is avoidable under §545(1) because it is, in effect, a statutory lien effective upon insolvency. The difficulty with this argument is that some courts have found the seller's reclamation right not to be a statutory lien.

---

3. As mentioned in section 15.3.2, revised UCC §2.702 substitues a reasonable time for the ten-day period. However, in bankruptcy, the seller is still subject to the ten-day limit (extended to 20 days if the petition is filed within the ten-day period) provided in §546(c).

16

The Avoidance of Preferences, Setoff, Fraudulent Transfers, and Postpetition Transfers

§16.1 Preferential Transfers under §547

§16.1.1 Introduction

Section 547 is a frequently used provision that generates volumes of caselaw. Although it ties into nonbankruptcy law, it is unlike §544 in that it does not base the trustee's avoidance power on the nonbankruptcy rights of actual or hypothetical parties. It goes beyond rights recognized in nonbankruptcy law and allows the avoidance of transfers that are fully effective outside of bankruptcy. This is because nonbankruptcy law generally permits the preferential treatment of a creditor (*e.g., compare* section 3.9.3 on assignments for the benefit of creditors) but preferences are contrary to the goals and policies of bankruptcy.

Section 547 permits the avoidance of transfers in the 90 days (or, in the case of insiders, one year) before the petition that give the creditor an advantage to which it is not entitled in bankruptcy. It does not allow the trustee to impugn *every* transfer to creditors in this period — only those that satisfy all its elements. The basic purpose of these elements is to identify transfers that illegitimately prefer the creditor and that thereby undermine the collective process of bankruptcy and offend the bankruptcy goals of evenhanded treatment of creditors and preservation of the estate.

Section 547 is aimed at creditors who have previously given consideration to the debtor for the transfer. Therefore, unlike §548 or state fraudulent transfer law, it is not concerned with the recovery of dispositions for inadequate value. Nor is it concerned with the state of mind of the debtor or the transferee. It has no requirement of bad faith, knowledge, or deliberate advantage-taking. In fact, the grounds for avoidance under §547 are entirely objective: If the transaction has the external attributes set out in §547, it is avoidable.[1]

Section 547 has two operative subsections: §547(b) confers the power of avoidance on the trustee, listing five elements that must be satisfied for the transfer to be avoidable. If any *one* of these elements is not satisfied, the transfer cannot be avoided. Section 547(c) contains exceptions to the trustee's avoidance power. Even if a transfer meets all the requirements of §547(b), it cannot be avoided to the extent that it fits within one of the exceptions in §547(c). It must be stressed that §547(c) only becomes relevant if all the elements of §547(b) are satisfied. If they are not, the transfer is unavoidable, and recourse to §547(c) is not necessary.

The remaining subsections of §547 are ancillary to §§547(b) and (c). Section 547(a) supplements the definitions in §101 by defining some terms that are not included in the general definition section. Section 547(e) is also definitional in a sense, in that it sets out a formula for determining when a transfer takes place. This determination can be crucial in avoidance suits, and it is explained in section 16.1.3. Sections 547(f) and (g) are concerned with the burden of proof in avoidance suits. Section 547(g) requires the trustee to prove all the elements of avoidance under §547(b), but this burden is alleviated in part by §547(f), which rebuttably presumes the debtor's insolvency in the 90 days preceding the petition. Under §547(g), the transferee must prove the grounds for nonavoidability if it invokes one of the exceptions in §547(c).

Section 547(d) concerns certain transfers to sureties to secure reimbursement for a bond to dissolve an avoidable judicial lien. This provision is not discussed here.

§16.1.2   The Elements of §547(b)

To be avoidable under §547(b), the transfer must satisfy every one of the following requirements:

---

1. Preference rules have not always been as objective as they are under §547. Under the Bankruptcy Act, the trustee had to show that the transferee had reasonable cause to believe that the debtor was insolvent at the time of transfer. This standard survived partially in the 1978 Bankruptcy Reform Act, but was eliminated entirely in 1984.

(1) There must have been a transfer of an interest in property of the debtor to or for the benefit of a creditor (§547(b)(1)). The transfer is the transmission of value from the debtor to the creditor, either directly or in an indirect way, so as to confer a benefit on the creditor. *Transfer* is defined in §101(54) in very broad terms to cover a wide variety of dispositions. (*See, e.g.,* Example 7.) *Creditor* is defined in §101(10) to mean the holder of a prepetition claim against the debtor. *Claim,* in turn, is given a wide-ranging definition in §101(5).

(2) The transfer must have been for or on account of an antecedent debt (§547(b)(2)). *Debt* is defined in §101(2) to mean liability on a claim that, as mentioned above, is comprehensively defined in §101(5). Although the Code defines debt, it offers little guidance on the meaning of *antecedent,* except for the apparently tautologous language in subsection (b)(2): ". . . owed by the debtor before such transfer was made." The intent is clear: If the debt arose before the transfer was made, it is antecedent. This is true even if the period of time between the two sides of the exchange is very short. (If there is only a short delay between the creation of the debt and the transfer, one of the exceptions in §547(c) will probably apply, as discussed in section 16.1.4. However, for the purposes of satisfying §547(b), all the trustee needs to establish is that the debt arose at some time before the transfer was made.)

The Code does not provide rules for determining when the debt came into being. The question of when the debt arose — that is, when the debtor became legally obligated to the creditor — must be determined under nonbankruptcy law. The creation of the debt must not be confused with the due date for payment of the debt. The time that the debt arises (*e.g.,* liability comes into existence) may be much earlier than the time that this liability is fixed, mature, and unconditionally payable.

(3) The debtor must have been insolvent at the time of the transfer (§547(b)(3)). *Insolvent* is defined in §101(32), which uses the balance sheet test (liabilities exceed assets at fair valuation) rather than the equity test (not generally paying debts as they fall due) to determine insolvency. Because the value of both assets and liabilities must be established to determine insolvency, difficult valuation issues can arise. This is illustrated in *In re Trans World Airlines, Inc.,* 134 F.3d 188 (3rd Cir. 1998), in which the court had to decide if the debtor had been insolvent at the time transfers had been made. Because liquidation was not imminent at that time, the court said that the reference to fair valuation in the insolvency definition in §101(32) required that the debtor's assets be valued as if the business was a going concern and the assets were being sold on the market without pressure to dispose of them quickly. Although the reference to fair valuation in the section qualified only assets and not liabilities, liabilities must also be calculated as if the business was a going concern, and not discounted to take into account that the debtor may not remain in business.

Because §547(f) presumes the debtor to have been insolvent during the 90 days before the petition, the trustee's burden of proving this element is eased. The presumption is not conclusive and may be rebutted by the transferee.

(4) The transfer must have occurred within the prepetition avoidance period (§547(b)(4)).   The avoidance period is 90 days before the filing of the petition, unless the transferee is an insider as defined in §101(31), in which case it is one year before the petition. It is not clear if one should count the 90 days backwards from the bankruptcy date (which seems the most sensible approach, and accords best with the language of §547) or forward from the transfer date (as the language of Rule 9006 seems to suggest). In most cases, this would not be a crucial issue, but it could be determinative where the transfer is on the borderline of the period.

Because the reachback period is one year where the transfer was to an *insider,* the question of whether a person qualifies as an insider is crucial where a transfer occurred more than 90 days before the petition, but within a year of it. Section 101(31) lists a number of persons who qualify as insiders, but it states that the definition "includes" such people. This is taken to mean that it is non-exclusive, and even if a person has a relationship to the debtor that is not specifically mentioned in §101(31), that person could qualify as an insider if her connection to the debtor during the period of the transfer was intimate and influential enough to have enabled her to obtain privileged treatment. For example, in *In re McIver,* 177 B.R. 366 (Bankr. N.D. Fla. 1995) the debtor's live-in companion was held to be an insider. Although §101(31) refers only to relatives of an individual (defined in §101(45) as individuals related by affinity or consanguinity within the third degree), the court felt that the relationship between the debtor and transferee was a bond equivalent to affinity.

For the one-year reachback period to apply, the actual target of the avoidance suit must be an insider. Prior to 1994, some courts had held that if a transfer to a non-insider actually benefitted an insider (say, for example, because the insider had guaranteed the debt, and the payment, therefore, released him from his contingent liability), then the one-year period could be applied to avoid the transfer to the non-insider. This approach was known as the *Deprizio* rule, after the leading case espousing the principle, *In re V.N. Deprizio Construction Co.,* 874 F.2d 1186 (7th Cir. 1989). The Bankruptcy Reform Act of 1994 overruled this approach by enacting §550(c), which makes it clear that even if a transfer made between 90 days and one year before bankruptcy could be avoided against the insider, the trustee cannot recover the property transferred or its value from a non-insider.

(5) The transfer must have improved the creditor's position (§547(b)(5)).   The transfer must have enabled the transferee to receive more than it would have received if the transfer had not been made and the debt had been paid at the appropriate rate under a Ch. 7 distribution. This element, sometimes called the *improvement-in-position test,* is the heart of §547(b). Its basic purpose is to test whether the prebankruptcy transfer gave the creditor a higher level of payment on its claim than it has the right to receive. It is this attribute of the transfer that makes the creditor's advantage illegitimate and undermines bankruptcy's collective process.

Irrespective of whether the case had been filed under Ch. 7, 11, 12, or 13, the test requires a hypothetical Ch. 7 liquidation to be calculated. A comparison must then be made between the total payment that the transferee would receive if the transfer is left intact and the total payment that it would receive if the transfer was restored to the estate and the transferee proved a claim in the estate for the debt that had been reduced or eliminated by the transfer. If the first figure is higher than the second, the improvement in position test is satisfied. The operation of the test is illustrated in Examples 1, 2, 4, and 7.

§16.1.3 The Timing of the Transfer

The timing of the transfer is crucially important for a number of purposes. For example, the date of the transfer must be known to decide if it falls within the avoidance period, if it was for an antecedent debt, or if the debtor was insolvent when it was made. Section 547(e) provides the formula for determining the date of the transfer. In broad terms, §547(e) treats the transfer as having occurred on the date on which it became effective between the parties under nonbankruptcy law. However, if, under nonbankruptcy law, some act is required to perfect the transfer (*e.g.,* the filing of a financing statement to perfect the transfer of a security interest in the debtor's property), the transfer will occur only on the date of perfection, unless the act of perfection is completed within ten days of the transfer taking effect. (Examples 1, 3, and 4 address timing issues.)

Section 547(e)(3) provides a further qualification. It states that for the purposes of the section, a transfer is not made until the debtor has acquired rights in the property transferred. This means that even if the act of perfection (such as the public filing) occurs within ten days of the transfer taking effect, the timing of the transfer is delayed if the debtor has not yet acquired an interest in the property. That is, the ten-day rule does not apply to property that the debtor does not own at the time of perfection, even though he may anticipate acquiring it in the future. The date of transfer is delayed until he actually does acquire the property. The significance of this is illustrated by *In re Morehead*, 249 F.3d 445 (6th Cir. 2001). The creditor obtained judgment against the debtor in 1995 and served a continuing wage garnishment on the debtor's employer in 1997, under which the employer automatically deducted the garnished amount from the debtor's wages in each future month. The debtor filed his Ch. 7 petition in November 1997. The issue was whether the wage garnishments during the 90 days before bankruptcy were avoidable preferences. The bankruptcy court held that they were not because, under state law, the creditor obtained a perfected garnishment lien on all the garnished wages as soon as it served the garnishment order on the employer in 1997. The court of appeals reversed on the basis of §547(e)(3): Even though the transfer was perfected outside the 90-day period, the debtor did not acquire rights to the wages until he earned them. (The court rejected the theory, adopted by other courts, that once garnishment occurs, the debtor loses the right to the portion of his wages that have been garnished.)

Because the timing of the transfer is often dependent on the date it was perfected, the meaning of "perfection" is important. Section 547(e)(1) defines perfection for the purposes of §547 with reference to nonbankruptcy law. In the case of real property, perfection is complete as soon as a subsequent bona fide purchaser "cannot" acquire a superior interest in the property, and perfection of all other property is complete as soon as an ordinary judicial lienor "cannot" acquire superior rights. In the usual situation, this means that perfection will only occur under nonbankruptcy law from the time that the act required for perfection (for example, filing the proper document in the correct records office) is accomplished. However, with regard to certain types of interest, nonbankruptcy law permits the effective date of the interest to *backdate* to some specified earlier time. (For examples of backdating see Example 6 of Chapter 2, Example 5 of Chapter 15, and section 3.5.) As noted in section 15.3.1, §546 generally recognizes and preserves these backdating rules in bankruptcy. However, the Supreme Court held in *Fidelity Financial Services v. Fink*, 118 S. Ct. 651 (1998), that the same rule does not apply in §547(e), because the language of that section indicates that "perfection" is used there in a different sense. In §546, it is used to mean the legal conclusion that the interest is perfected, but in §547(e) it is used to mean the act necessary to effect that perfection. The court found this meaning to be apparent from the fact that §547(e) says that perfection occurs when a creditor on a simple contract "cannot acquire" a superior judicial lien. The court reasoned that a creditor *can* acquire a superior judicial lien at any time during that gap period, even though that lien would lose priority to the transferee if the transferee thereafter performed the act of perfection that would give it retrospective effect. Unless and until that act is performed, the judicial lienholder "can" acquire a superior lien, and it is only when the act of perfection is complete, that it "cannot" any longer achieve priority. For this reason, §547(e)(1) must be interpreted to date perfection only from the time that the final act of perfection, and not from any earlier date to which it would relate back under state law. (This issue is discussed further in Example 4.)

§16.1.4 Exceptions to Avoidance under §547(c)

Section 547(c) provides eight exceptions to the trustee's avoidance power under §547(b). As stated before, the correct sequence of analysis is to determine first if the transfer is avoidable under §547(b). If it is not, there is no occasion to use §547(c); if it is, §547(c) should be consulted to determine if any of the exceptions apply. Once the trustee has established that the transfer is avoidable, the burden shifts to the transferee under §547(g) to prove that an exception is applicable.

The structure of separating the avoidance power and the exceptions is an innovation of the 1978 Code. Prior law did not expressly recognize exceptions, but often reached similar results through a combination of a stricter test for avoidance and judicially created qualifications. The exceptions in §547(c) serve much the same purpose as the cases under prior law: They refine and qualify the avoidance power to distinguish legitimate ordinary-course business dealings from last-minute preferences. In this way, the Code preserves transactions that are technically preferential because they satisfy all the elements of §547(b) but do not truly confer an inappropriate advantage on the recipient. This abstract observation is more clearly demonstrated in the discussion of the specific exceptions.

All the exceptions apart from §§547(c)(6) and (8) preclude avoidance of the transfer only "to the extent that" it is covered by the exception. It is therefore possible for a transfer to be *partially* avoidable. The eight exceptions are as follows:

(1) A substantially contemporaneous exchange for new value (§547(c)(1)). Although it satisfies all the requirements for avoidance under §547(b), a transfer may not be avoided to the extent that it was intended by both parties to be a substantially contemporaneous exchange for new value given to the debtor. *New value* is defined in §547(a)(2) to mean money, goods, services, or new credit, and can also include the release of property previously transferred by the debtor, provided that the original transaction is unavoidable.

The essential feature of this exception is that the transferee gives something new of economic worth to the debtor as an immediate exchange for the transfer. The exception is not needed if the creditor's consideration (the "debt") is exactly simultaneous with or follows the debtor's transfer to the creditor, because the debt would not then be antecedent for purposes of §547(b). However, if the creditor's consideration precedes the debtor's transfer even by a short time, the debt is antecedent. When the parties intended a contemporaneous exchange and the delay is in fact inconsequential, §547(c)(1) prevents avoidance of the transfer on a technicality. No rigid time period is prescribed in §547(c)(1), and the question of substantial contemporaneity must be decided under all the circumstances of the transaction.

The legislative history of §547(c)(1) indicates that Congress had check transactions in mind in enacting this exception: When a debtor writes a check in payment of, say, goods or services, the parties may think of the exchange as a cash transaction, but the delay in presenting and paying the check means that the debtor in fact owes a debt for a short period and the payment of the check is a transfer for that debt. Provided that the parties genuinely intended a contemporaneous exchange and the transfer of funds takes place routinely, §547(c)(1) makes the transfer unavoidable.

Although a check transaction exemplifies the application of §547(c)(1), it is not the only situation in which the exception can be used. For example, it has been held to apply when a creditor released a lien on the debtor's property in exchange for payment of the debt. Even though the debt itself was not new value, the release of the lien was. *In re Robinson Bros. Drilling, Inc.*, 877 F.2d 32 (10th Cir. 1989). Similarly, when a debtor paid the creditor in settlement of a disputed debt, the settlement of the dispute was treated as new value, even though the creation of the original debt was earlier in time. *Lewis v. Deithorn*, 893 F.2d 648 (3d Cir. 1980).

When a secured party fails to perfect its interest in the ten-day grace period, some courts hold that the transaction cannot qualify as substantially contemporaneous, even if the parties really did intend the transfer to be contemporaneous, and the delay was inadvertent or caused by oversight. They reason that Congress has made it clear, by providing for a ten-day grace period §547(e)(2)(A), that a delay of more than ten days cannot be substantially contemporaneous. *See,* for example, *In re Holder*, 892 F.2d 29 (4th Cir. 1989). Other courts take a less rigid approach and are willing to look at all the circumstances to decide if a delay, even if more than ten days, might qualify for the exception. For example, in *In re Dorholt*, 224 F.3d 871 (8th Cir. 2000), the creditor did not file until 16 days after making the loan. The parties had intended an immediate filing, but it was delayed as a result of an oversight by the service bureau hired by the secured party to make its recordings. The court said that "substantially contemporaneous" is a flexible term and there is no justification for creating a per se rule by importing into §547(c)(1) the ten-day limit of §547(e)(2)(A). To decide if a transfer is substantially contemporaneous, the court should look at all the circumstances, including the length of the delay, the reason for it, the nature of the transaction, the intent of the parties, the risk of misleading others, and the equities of the case. The court considered that the situation in the case was exactly the type of transaction that §547(c)(1) was designed to protect.

The protection of contemporaneous exchanges is consistent with the policies underlying the avoidance of preferences. Such transactions are not last-minute attempts to thwart the order of distribution in bankruptcy, but tend to be regular commercial transactions. For this reason, the transferee's legitimate expectations under nonbankruptcy law outweigh the estate's interest in disturbing the transfer.

(2) Ordinary course payments (§547(c)(2)). Section 547(c)(2) excepts a transfer from avoidance to the extent that it satisfies three requirements: First, it must have been the payment of a debt incurred by the debtor in the ordinary course of business or financial affairs of both the debtor and the transferee. Second, the payment must have been made in the ordinary course of business or financial affairs of both the debtor and the transferee. Third, the payment must have been made in accordance with ordinary business terms.

As originally enacted in 1978, §547(c)(2) also required that the payment must have been made within 45 days of the debt. Although this 45-day requirement was eliminated in 1984, some courts still applied it until the Supreme Court put a stop to the approach in *Union Bank v. Wolas,* 112 S. Ct. 527 (1991), in which the Court held that neither the wording of §547(c)(2) nor its legislative history precluded its application to long-term debt. *See* Example 5.

The word "ordinary" is used three times in §547(c)(2). This triple incantation shows that Congress was serious about confining the exception to situations in which both the debt and its payment were exceedingly routine. Note that it is not enough that the debt and payment were made in the ordinary course. In addition, the terms on which the payment was made must be such as would normally be present in a transaction of that kind, in light of both the debtor's practice and the industry norm. It is a question of fact, to be decided under all the circumstances of the case, whether a debt was incurred and paid in the ordinary course. The test in §547(c)(2) has both a subjective and an objective element that involves inquiry into both the actual business practices of the debtor and the normal practices and standards prevailing in the trade or locality. *See In re Fred Hawes Organization, Inc.,* 957 F.2d 239, 243-245 (6th Cir. 1992), *In re Roblin Industries, Inc.,* 78 F.3d 30 (2nd Cir. 1996). The court adopted a particularly flexible approach in *In re Jan Weilert RV, Inc.,* 315 F.3d 1192, *as amended,* 326 F.3d 1028 (9th Cir. 2003). The court said that in looking at the trade context to decide on "ordinary business terms," the court must focus on similarly situated parties. This means that the court should not just take into account the usual payment practices between the parties and in the trade, but that it should also consider the usual way of dealing with a business in financial distress. The court considered that payment patterns should not be treated as outside the ordinary course of business unless the transaction is so aberrant that it goes beyond the usual means of dealing with a financially shaky debtor.

Section 547(c)(2) is meant to prevent the avoidance of normal prebankruptcy transfers that conform to the debtor's pattern of dealing. Such transactions create legitimate expectations in the transferee and do not constitute the type of last-minute transfers that are associated with a creditor's scramble for advantage on the eve of bankruptcy. *See In re Fulghum Construction Corp.,* 872 F.2d 739, 743 (6th Cir. 1989). The National Bankruptcy Review

Commission recommended that this goal of protecting legitimate, routine transactions would be adequately served by making the objective and subjective inquiries alternative. That is, the transfer should be unavoidable either if it conforms to the debtor's ordinary practices or if it complies with usual industry practice. This recommendation was adopted in the pending reform legislation.

Many different types of transactions are covered by the exception. For example, it protects regular trade purchases by a business debtor on short-term credit and payments made by a consumer debtor for monthly expenses such as utilities or services. (Many small-value consumer transfers are also excepted from avoidance by §547(c)(6). In addition, since the decision in *Wolas*, it is clear that the exception also extends to regular periodic payments made on a long-term debt incurred in the ordinary course of the debtor's and creditor's affairs. *See* Example 5. In the absence of this exception, many such payments would be avoidable under §547(b) as transfers for an antecedent debt during the 90-day prepetition period.

(3) Purchase money security interests (§547(c)(3)). A purchase money security interest is one granted by the debtor to secure a loan or credit used to acquire the very collateral subject to the interest. (*See* section 2.2.5.) An interest qualifies as a purchase money interest for the purposes of §547(c)(3) to the extent that it secures new value given by the transferee to the debtor at or after the execution of a security agreement describing the collateral, and the new value is both intended to be used and is in fact used to acquire the collateral. The rationale for making an exception for purchase money interests is that the holder of the interest has enabled the debtor to obtain the property that secures the debt.

Section 547(c)(3) does not absolutely except purchase money interests from avoidance. It merely creates a limited protection to the secured party by providing a special grace period for perfection: The interest is unavoidable provided that it is perfected within twenty days from the date on which the debtor received possession of the collateral. (It used to be ten days, but was increased to twenty days in 1994 to better fit in with the period most widely recognized under state law.) This differs from the general grace period for perfection under §547(e), which is ten days from the date on which the interest took effect under state law. (*See* section 16.1.3.) Therefore, if a purchase money security interest would otherwise be avoidable because it was perfected beyond the period required by §547(e), it is saved from avoidance if the debtor received possession of the property after the effective date of the transfer and perfection occurred within twenty days of that later date.

It is important to understand the limited scope of §547(c)(3). It merely creates an alternative grace period for perfection that could save the purchase money interest from avoidance if it would otherwise be treated as a transfer for an antecedent debt or a transfer within the 90-day period by virtue of the operation of §547(e). (*See* Example 3.)

If a state provides a longer grace period than the 20 days allowed under §547(c)(3), the Supreme Court has held in *Fidelity Financial Services v. Fink,* 118 S. Ct. 651 (1998) that the 20-day period overrides the longer period permitted outside of bankruptcy. The court found that the word "perfected" as used in §547(c)(3)(B) has the same meaning as in §547(e), so that the act of perfection itself must be accomplished within the 20-day grace period, no matter what retrospective effect state law may provide for the act. The facts of *Fink* illustrate the issue: Fidelity financed the debtor's purchase of a new car. Under Missouri law, a purchase-money lender has 30 days from the debtor's taking of possession of the goods to file its security interest, and if it files within that period, its perfection backdates to the date on which the interest attached. Fidelity did file its interest within the 30 days allowed by state law, but after the 20 days allowed by §547(c)(3)(B). Under state law, the interest backdated in priority to the date of attachment, which was well within the 20-day period. The court said that this was not good enough — the act of perfection must occur within the 20-day period. Quite apart from the semantical argument mentioned in section 16.1.3, the court found support for its reading of the sections in Congress' apparent purpose when it extended the grace period to 20 days in 1994 — to make the grace period uniform and to conform with the period used in most states. To recognize a longer grace period in the few states that permit it makes the 1994 amendment pointless.

(4) The "net result" exception (§547(c)(4)). If, after receiving an avoidable transfer, the creditor gives to the debtor new value that is not itself secured or paid for by a new transfer, the otherwise avoidable transfer cannot be avoided to the extent of the new value. This exception in §547(c)(4) is known as the *net result rule.* The name, which was inherited from its predecessor section under the Bankruptcy Act, is a little deceptive because §547(c)(4) does not net out all transfers to and from the debtor in the 90-day period. It applies only to value given to the debtor after the preferential transfer.

The justification for the net result rule is that a creditor who extended new credit or other value to the debtor after payment of an older obligation was probably motivated by that payment to deal further with the debtor. If, upon bankruptcy, the earlier payment is reversed, the creditor's reliance is defeated. The earlier payment would have to be returned and a claim made against the estate for both the old debt and the new one. Apart from being unfair to the creditor, a rule like this would discourage persons from dealing with a debtor in financial difficulty, because they would not be able to rely on the payment of earlier obligations as a basis for extending new credit. *See In re New York City Shoes, Inc.,* 880 F.2d 679, 680 (3d Cir. 1989). In addition, it could be argued that the later value, in effect, returns the preference to the estate, thereby reversing its prejudicial effect. The operation of §547(c)(4) is illustrated by Example 6.

The scope of §547(c)(4) is narrow, and the protection given to creditors who deal with the debtor is quite restricted. Payments are protected only to the extent that new value is given after the payment without a corresponding new transfer by the debtor. The question of what constitutes new value involves an inquiry similar to that under §547(c)(1), and the definition of new value in §547(a)(2) applies here as well. For §547(c)(4) to be applicable, the value given must constitute a new benefit to the estate, which replenishes it after the transfer. *See In re Jet Florida Systems, Inc.,* 841 F.2d 1082 (11th Cir. 1988).

In re Armstrong, 291 F.3d 517 (8th Cir. 2002), provides an interesting illustration of what constitutes new value for the benefit of the estate. The debtor was an attorney who enjoyed an expensive lifestyle by embezzling clients' funds and engaging in fraudulent investment schemes. He turned to gambling in an attempt to recover the funds. He applied for and was granted a $50,000 line of credit from Hurrah's casino in Mississippi. The casino allowed him to sign markers and agreed to hold them for 30 days before presenting them to the debtor's bank for payment. The debtor managed to reach his credit limit in two days. Thirty days later, the casino deposited the first batch of markers and was paid. (The debtor did not have money in the bank when they were presented, but he managed to procure funds by fraudulently obtaining a loan to cover the markers.) The debtor returned to the casino for another try. His luck did not improve and he again ended up having signed markers to the full extent of his limit of $50,000. He was insolvent during this entire period. This time he did not pay the markers and filed a bankruptcy petition. The payment of $50,000 to the casino occurred in the 90-day period, and the trustee sought to avoid it as a preference. The casino argued that the transfer fell within §547(c)(4) because the new line of credit that it gave to the debtor qualified as new value following the transfer. The court disagreed. It held that the credit was not new value as contemplated by §547(a)(2) because it was not money's worth in services. The new credit did not replenish the estate, but diminished it by encouraging the debtor to dig himself even deeper into the hole that he had made for himself. (The casino also argued various other exceptions, none of which worked. One of the more striking ones was a theory, under §547(c)(2), that this gambling splurge, for the purpose of replacing funds that the debtor had obtained by theft and fraud, was in the debtor's ordinary course of business.)

(5) Floating liens in inventory and receivables (§547(c)(5)). Floating liens were introduced in section 2.2.4. In this type of transaction, the security interest secures all advances made by the secured party in the future and automatically attaches to all new collateral (typically accounts or inventory) acquired by the debtor in the future. The parties contemplate that the secured party will advance funds to the debtor when inventory or accounts come into existence. As the inventory is sold or the accounts are paid, the loan will be reduced by the proceeds. When a further batch of inventory is acquired or accounts are generated, the secured party will again make an advance in proportion to the value of the new collateral. In this way, the relationship between the debt and the collateral is kept stable.

If the debtor becomes bankrupt in the course of such a continuing secured transaction, many transfers are likely to have been made to the secured party in the 90 days before bankruptcy. Every payment and every acquisition of new collateral would qualify as a transfer. To examine each one of these transfers for the purpose of determining avoidability would be an exhausting task because the total figures for each month may represent numerous transactions. Furthermore, such a painstaking examination of the multitude of transfers under the floating lien could unfairly undermine the secured party's reliance on the routine activity in its continuing relationship with the debtor.

To solve these problems, §547(c)(5) presents a simplified test for determining whether and to what extent the aggregation of all the transfers in the 90-day period should be avoided as a preference. The language of this section is convoluted, but the concept is quite straightforward: When a floating lien arrangement in accounts or inventory has been validly created (note that the section applies *only* to these two types of commercial collateral), each separate transaction in the 90-day period does not have to be examined. The transfers to the secured party are unavoidable except to the extent that all the transfers in the 90-day period caused a reduction in the shortfall between collateral and debt (*i.e.,* in the deficiency) to the prejudice of unsecured creditors in the estate. If the secured party is an insider, the prebankruptcy period is, as usual, one year. If the transaction is first brought into effect within the applicable prebankruptcy period, the reduction of the shortfall must be measured from the time that new value was first given.

Therefore, the focus of §547(c)(5) is not on the *individual* transfers in the prebankruptcy period but on the transferee's *overall improvement in position* over the prebankruptcy period. If the collateral was worth less than the debt at the beginning of that period and transfers to the transferee during the period had the effect of eliminating or reducing that shortfall as at the date of the petition, the transfers are avoidable to the extent that they made up the shortfall.[2] Although the two-point comparison can involve complex issues, such as valuation questions, it greatly simplifies what could be a very arduous examination of each transfer in an ongoing relationship that involves many individual transfers. It therefore assists a creditor who has been keeping an eye on the debtor's business and making sure that the value of the collateral never drops below the debt. For example, in *In re Smith's Home Furnishings, Inc.,* 265 F.3d 959 (9th Cir. 2001), the secured party had financed the

---

2. Note that §547(c)(5) is concerned only with transfers within the prebankruptcy period. Under §552(a), acquisitions of collateral after the petition are excluded from the floating lien and are estate property. Proceeds of prepetition collateral generally belong to the secured party, even if they are received postpetition, provided that nonbankruptcy law recognizes an interest in such proceeds, and the transfer of the proceeds is not otherwise avoidable. §522(b).

debtor's inventory through a floating lien. When the debtor began operating at a loss in 1995, the secured party reduced its line of credit and required a substantial paydown of the debt. In the 90 days before bankruptcy, the debtor paid about $12 million to reduce the debt. On bankruptcy, the remaining inventory was released to the secured party, who liquidated it. The trustee sought to recover the $12 million as a preference. Even though the secured party had required the debtor to make substantial payments on the loan in the 90-day period, the court held that the transfers were saved by §547(c)(5) because the trustee could not discharge his burden of showing that the creditor had been undersecured as at the 90-day date.

In determining the transferee's improvement in position, transfers are not counted to the extent that they did not reduce the value of the estate to the prejudice of unsecured creditors. Therefore, for example, if the collateral is inventory that appreciated in value due to market conditions, or if it is accounts that turned out to be more collectable than originally supposed, this augmentation of the value of the collateral could reduce any shortfall without harming the estate.

In summary, §547(c)(5) is applied by taking the following steps:

(a) *Determine the first date for comparison.*   This is 90 days before the petition for a noninsider, a year for an insider, or the date of the first advance, if that occurred after the start of the applicable prebankruptcy period.

(b) *Determine the amount of the debt and value the collateral on this first date.*   If the secured party is undersecured (*i.e.*, the collateral is worth less than the debt), calculate the shortfall.

(c) *Determine the amount of the debt and the value of the collateral on the date of filing the petition.*   Calculate any shortfall.

(d) *Compare the shortfall on the two dates.*   There is a voidable preference to the extent that the shortfall has been reduced, provided that the reduction has reduced the value of the estate to the prejudice of other creditors.

Like the other exceptions to avoidance, §547(c)(5) is designed to protect legitimate, routine transactions that do not enable the creditor to obtain an impermissible advantage on the eve of bankruptcy. A holder of a floating lien who monitors the debtor's dealings with the collateral is able to reduce the risk of a shortfall. However, a lienholder who permits the debt to become undersecured takes the risk that any attempt to redress the deficiency by payment or new collateral could fall within the prebankruptcy period and be avoidable. Because the prebankruptcy avoidance period can only be ascertained once the petition has been filed, the lienholder will not know when it has begun until after the attempt at bolstering the interest has been made. Therefore, a careful lienholder should treat every day as the potential comparison date, and try to ensure that no shortfall ever occurs.

Because §547(c)(5) requires a comparison of debt-collateral ratios at two points, valuation of the collateral at each stage is often an important issue on which the trustee and transferee may disagree. The extent of avoidance is enhanced by a lower value on the comparison date and a higher value on the bankruptcy date, and is reduced by contrary trend. (But bear in mind that valuation, on its own, is not the sole determinative factor. As noted above, to the extent that an increase in value results from an increase in market price or other facts not to the prejudice of creditors, there is no transfer.) As always, valuation is a factual issue to be determined under the circumstances of each case.

Before evidence can be received on value, the standard of valuation must be determined. Valuation of accounts could be based on their face value, collection value (the amount actually paid by customers), market value (the amount for which the accounts could be sold in a factoring transaction), book value (the amount at which they would be valued in accordance with accepted accounting practices), or contract value (the value placed on the accounts by the parties themselves when entering the transaction). Similarly, inventory could be valued based on its retail, wholesale, liquidation, or going-concern value. In deciding on the standard for valuation, the court must try to make a realistic assessment of the use or disposition of the collateral. Whatever standard of value is chosen, it must be applied to both the comparison date and the bankruptcy date.

(6) Statutory liens (§547(c)(6)). Section 547(c)(6) simply provides that statutory liens must be dealt with under §545 and they are beyond the scope of §547. If a statutory lien is unavoidable under §545, the trustee cannot try to avoid it under §547, even if it arose in the prebankruptcy period and satisfies all the elements of §547(b).

(7) Payments of debts for alimony, maintenance, and child support (§547(c)(7)). As part of the package of amendments to protect the support claims of spouses and children of a debtor, (*see, e.g.,* sections 10.4.2 and 13.5), the Bankruptcy Reform Act of 1994 added this new exception to avoidance. Although a payment may satisfy all the elements of §547(b), it is unavoidable to the extent that it was a bona fide payment of a debt to a spouse, former spouse, or child for alimony, maintenance, or support. To qualify for this exception, the debt must have the same characteristics that qualify it for special treatment in other sections of the Code (such as exemption from the stay, priority, and nondischargeability). That is, it is protected from avoidance only to the extent that:

(a) It was a bona fide payment made in satisfaction of a genuine support obligation, and is not a payment of some other kind of debt (such as a property settlement). The nature of the debt must be determined as a question of fact, irrespective of how it may have been labeled.

(b)   The obligation arose from a separation or property settlement agreement or from an order of a court or other proper adjudicative or administrative body.

(c)   The debt had not been assigned voluntarily or by operation of law.

(8) Small-value transfers for consumer debts (§547(c)(8)).   When the debtor is an individual whose debts are primarily consumer debts, §547(c)(8) excludes from avoidance transactions in which the total value of property transferred is less than $600. This exception was added to the Code by the 1984 amendments to prevent the recovery of small preferences in consumer bankruptcies. The National Bankruptcy Review Commission recommended that a minimum cutoff should also be enacted in non-consumer cases, and it has proposed that a transfer should not be avoidable in a non-consumer case unless the aggregate of transfers to the creditor exceeds $5,000.

§16.2   Setoff under §553

As a general principle of law, the debts of two persons who are mutually indebted may be set off against each other. To the extent of the smaller debt, they cancel each other out, and the only payment that need change hands is the remaining balance of the larger debt. For setoff to operate, the debts must be mutual: This means that each party is both a creditor and a debtor of the other in the same capacity. (For example, *A* is indebted to *B* in her personal capacity. *B* is indebted to *A* in *A*'s capacity as trustee for a trust. *A* cannot offset her personal debt to *B* against *B*'s debt to *A* as trustee. Mutual indebtedness is raised in Example 8.) In addition, both debts must be valid and enforceable. The debts need not have arisen out of the same transaction.

When one of the mutually indebted parties becomes bankrupt, the other party's exercise of the right of setoff under nonbankruptcy law results in full payment of the debt due from the bankrupt debtor to the extent that it is covered by the other debt. Such a transaction could satisfy all the elements of §547(b). For example, say that the debtor became indebted to the creditor for $1,000 four months before bankruptcy. Two months later, the debtor performed services for the creditor in an unrelated transaction for a fee of $1,000. Setoff simply cancels each debt. If the debtor was insolvent at the time of setoff, the transaction satisfies all of the five elements of §547(b). It is a transfer to a creditor on account of an antecedent debt, made while the debtor was insolvent, during the 90-day prebankruptcy period. The setoff prefers the creditor in position because it results in full payment of the debt. Had there been no setoff, the creditor would have had to pay the estate the $1,000 owed to the debtor and would have proved a claim for the $1,000 owed by the debtor. This claim would have been paid at the rate of distribution payable to general unsecured creditors. None of the exceptions in §547(c) apply.

Notwithstanding its potentially preferential effect, a right of setoff valid under nonbankruptcy law is generally upheld in bankruptcy provided that it does not fall within the limited grounds of avoidance under §553. A valid right of setoff may be exercised at any time up to the petition, and may also be asserted thereafter following relief from stay. (Setoff is subject to the stay under §362(a)(7) and cannot be exercised postpetition without relief being obtained.) In fact, it has been held that the right of setoff even survives the debtor's discharge, so that if the debtor or estate sues to recover a debt, the defendant may raise the setoff notwithstanding discharge of the defendant's claim. See *In re De Laurentiis Entertainment Group, Inc.*, 963 F.2d 1269 (9th Cir. 1992). In reaching this conclusion, the court found that the strong language in §553 protecting the right of setoff and the historical deference given to setoff rights in bankruptcy overrides the discharge provisions in §§1141 and 524(a)(2). See also *In re Bare*, 284 B.R. 870 (Bankr. N.D. Ill. 2002).

The limitations on setoff in §553 are designed to prevent abuses and to ensure that a creditor does not try to manipulate setoff rights to obtain an inappropriate advantage. The right of setoff may not be exercised by a creditor to the extent that any one of the following conditions are satisfied:

(1) The creditor's claim has been disallowed as a claim against the estate (§553(a)(1)).

(2) The creditor has acquired the claim by transfer from another entity either during the 90-day prebankruptcy period while the debtor was insolvent or after the commencement of the case (§553(a)(2)). As in §547, there is a presumption of insolvency during the 90-day prebankruptcy period (§553(c)). This exception is aimed at transactions in which a debtor of the estate takes over the claim of a creditor of the estate so that the debt and claim can be offset. Such a transaction would enable a creditor to receive full value for its claim by selling it to a person indebted to the estate, thereby gaining a preference. At the same time, the estate is prejudiced because its claim (payable in full) is set off against its debt (payable at the rate of bankruptcy distribution).

(3) The debt due from the creditor was incurred during the 90-day prebankruptcy period, while the debtor was insolvent, and for the purpose of obtaining a right of setoff against the claim owed to the creditor (§553(a)(3)).

(4) The setoff has enabled the creditor to improve its position in a manner forbidden by §553(b). The *improvement in position test* uses a two-point comparison similar in concept to that in §547(c)(5), but with different rules. Stated in the simplest terms (and without its qualifications and refinements), the test is intended to prevent a creditor from using setoff in the 90 days before bankruptcy in order to recover more of its claim than it could have

recovered if the mutual debts had been set off 90 days before the petition. The test requires measurement of the amount (if any) by which the creditor's claim exceeds its debt to the debtor on the 90-day date and on the date of setoff. If the *insufficiency* in the setoff — that is, the amount of the creditor's claim in excess of the debtor's claim — is reduced between the 90-day date and the setoff date, the offset is recoverable by the trustee to the extent of that reduction.

The policy of protecting the right of setoff is a longstanding one. It runs counter to bankruptcy's general aim of evenhanded treatment of creditors because a creditor with a right of setoff is given more favorable treatment than one who received payment of the debt during the prebankruptcy preference period. This is partly justified by the fact that a genuine setoff is less likely to be a last-minute transfer designed to disturb the normal order of distribution. However, the principal reason for giving special treatment to the right of setoff is that it has traditionally been perceived as akin to a security interest — the mutual debt secures each party against the other's nonpayment. The following cases describe the right of setoff in bankruptcy: *In re De Laurentiss Entertainment Group, Inc.*, 963 F.2d 1269 (9th Cir. 1992); *In re Davidovich*, 901 F.2d 1533 (10th Cir. 1990); *Durham v. SMI Industries*, 882 F.2d 881 (4th Cir. 1989); *In re United Sciences of America, Inc.*, 893 F.2d 729 (5th Cir. 1990); *In re Elcona Homes Corp.*, 863 F.2d 483 (7th Cir. 1988). *See also* Example 8.

§16.3   Fraudulent Transfers under §548

The trustee may avoid fraudulent transfers in the prepetition period either by using state fraudulent transfer law, which is accessible to the trustee under §544(b) (*see* section 15.1.3), or by employing the Code's own avoidance provision in §548. Section 548 is based on the UFCA (the predecessor to the UFTA) and therefore has many similarities to the uniform state law. *See* Chapter 4. The following surveys the differences and similarities between §548 and the UFTA:

(1) One of the most important differences between the UFTA and §548 is their temporal range: §548 allows the trustee to avoid transfers that occurred within one year of bankruptcy, and the UFTA generally allows creditors a period of four years from the transfer in which to commence an avoidance suit.[3] As noted in

---

3. As explained in section 14.7 and section 15.1.3, the one-year period in §548 is a reach-back period: It specifies the period of vulnerability of the transfer. It is not a statute of limitations (a period within which the trustee must act to avoid the transfer). The statute of limitations is provided in §546(a). The four-year period under the UFTA is a statute of limitations, but it operates as a reachback period for purposes of avoidance. Thus, the trustee can reach back four years to avoid the transfer, but must commence suit within the limitations period under §546(a).

section 15.1.3, if the transfer occurred more than a year before the petition, the trustee may be able to avoid it by using state law under §544(b), even though it cannot be avoided under §548.

(2) Because §548 is used by a trustee in bankruptcy rather than by an individual creditor, it does not have provisions distinguishing existing and future creditors like those found in the UFTA. Also, the avoidance remedy itself is different. Section 548 does not have the remedial alternatives of the UFTA, but it is subject to the general rules (outlined in section 14.5) governing the return of avoided transfers to the estate.

(3) The UFTA contains detailed provisions for the protection of good faith transferees for value and subsequent transferees. A similar set of protections is provided in §548(c), which grants lien rights in favor of a good faith transferee for value, and in §550, which protects good faith subsequent transferees. (*See* section 14.5.)

(4) The UFTA lists badges of fraud, but §548 does not. However, the list of the badges of fraud in the UFTA is merely a codification of long-recognized inferences which are used by the courts in deciding the question of actual fraud under §548.

(5) The definition of insolvency is similar in the UFTA and the Code, but under the UFTA equity insolvency creates a presumption of insolvency.

(6) There are some striking similarities in language between §548 and the UFTA, in part because §548 was based on the UFCA, the predecessor to the UFTA, and in part because the UFTA was drafted under the Code and adopted some of its language. The influence of the Code can be particularly felt in the definition of terms such as "insider," "creditor," and "transfer," and in the determination of the effective date of the transfer. The congruence in the statutes in defining the concepts of actual and constructive fraud reveals their common heritage from the UFCA.

See Example 7, which presents an issue of constructive fraud under §548.

It is not clear if the transfer of exemptable property qualifies as a fraudulent transfer. Some courts have held that if the property is exemptable, its transfer does not harm creditors and should not be avoidable. Others (the majority, it seems) say that the fact that the debtor could have claimed the property as exempt should not be taken into account. For example, *Tavenner v. Smoot*, 257 F.3d 401 (4th Cir. 2001), followed this approach. The court based its reasoning on two factors. First, §522(g) contemplates the avoidance of transfers of property that could have been exempted. The subsection penalizes the debtor who made a deliberately fraudulent transfer by only allowing her to assert the exemption after recovery of the property if the transfer was involuntary and she did not conceal the property. Second, the court noted that property is not inherently exempt, and the debtor has to claim it as exempt in her schedules. If she fails to claim an exemption, the property remains in the estate for the benefit of creditors.

Section 548(a)(2) specifically provides that a charitable contribution to a qualified religious or charitable entity or organization is not to be treated as a transfer for less than a reasonable equivalent value provided that the contribution does not exceed 15 percent of the debtor's gross annual income for the year in which it was given, or if in excess of that percentage, the contribution was consistent with the debtor's practices in making such contributions. Section 548(d)(3) defines "charitable contribution" and "qualified religious or charitable entity" with reference to the definitions used for tax-deduction purposes, but it adds the further restrictions that the debtor must be an individual and the donation must be cash or a financial instrument. Because the exception relates only to constructive fraud (a transfer made by the debtor while insolvent, for less than reasonably equivalent value), it does not shield a transfer made with fraudulent intent to a charity or religious organization.

These provisions were added to §548 in 1998. Although they cover both charities and religious organizations, Congress was primarily concerned about protecting churches from having to return tithes and contributions upon the debtor's bankruptcy. (Prior to 1998, courts were divided on whether such donations could be avoided as constructively fraudulent. The uncertainty was exacerbated in 1997 by the Supreme Court overturning a more general statute, the Religious Freedom Restoration Act of 1993.) By preventing the avoidance of gifts to charities and churches, §548(a)(2) allows an insolvent debtor to continue to be generous at the expense of creditors. The generosity could be quite spectacular because the 15 percent limit applies only to the contribution in issue, not to the total of contributions that the debtor may make. In addition, the limit can be exceeded if the debtor has a history of making greater contributions. This inequity can be ameliorated by interpreting §548(a)(2) narrowly. For example, in *In re Zohdi*, 234 B.R. 371 (Bankr. M.D. La. 1999) the court, noting that §548(a)(2) does not exclude contributions "to the extent of" the 15 percent, held that if the contribution exceeded the 15 percent and does not fit in with the debtor's prior practices, the entire contribution, not just the excess over 15 percent, must be avoided.

§16.4   Postpetition Transfers under §549

The avoidance powers discussed up to now concern prepetition transfers. Section 549 gives the trustee the power to recoup estate property that has been transferred without authority *after* the petition has been filed. It is conceptually quite different from the other avoidance provisions: Its aim is not the reversal of prepetition harm, but the preservation of property of the estate. The central basis for avoidance under §549 is lack of authority to make the disposition. Therefore, if after the case has been commenced the debtor makes an unauthorized transfer of estate property to settle a prepetition debt, the trustee does not need to establish the elements of §547 to avoid the transfer, but simply relies on lack of authority under §549.

Section 549(a) allows the trustee to avoid postpetition transfers that are not authorized by the Code itself or by the court and to avoid transfers that are authorized only under §§303(f) and 542(c). The reference to the two other Code sections requires explanation:

Section 303(f) allows a debtor in an involuntary case to continue to operate its business and to use or dispose of estate property until the order for relief is granted. However, once the order for relief is granted and a trustee is appointed, the trustee can use §549(a)(2)(A) to overturn any transfers made by the debtor unless they were approved by the court or they satisfy the requirements of §549(b). Section 549(b) validates transfers during the gap period to the extent that the transferee gave something new of economic value in exchange for the transfer, whether or not the transferee knew of the bankruptcy.

Section 542 requires entities who have property of the estate or who owe debts to the debtor to turn over the property or to pay the debts to the estate. Section 542(c) protects an entity who, acting in good faith and without actual knowledge or notice of the commencement of the case, transfers the property or pays the debt to someone other than the trustee. The transfer is treated as fully effective for the purpose of discharging the transferor's obligations to the debtor, and the transferor is not liable to the estate as a result of the inadvertent disposition. Although the good faith transferor is protected by §542(c), the person who receives the payment or the property is not covered by that section. Section 549(a)(2)(A) makes that transferee vulnerable to attack by the trustee. For example, immediately after a petition is filed, and before the trustee takes control of the estate, the debtor draws a check in favor of a creditor. Upon presentment, the bank pays the check in good faith and without notice or knowledge of the filing. Section 542(c) excuses the bank from liability to the estate for the improper payment of funds that had become property of the estate. However, this protection does not extend to the payee of the check, who has received an unauthorized postpetition transfer avoidable under §549(a).

In addition to these avoidance powers, §549 contains two other provisions. First, §549(c) requires a copy or notice of the petition to be recorded with the title records pertaining to real property in the estate. If a bona fide purchaser (*i.e.,* one who purchases the property for fair equivalent value, in good faith, and without knowledge of the bankruptcy) purchases the property under an unauthorized sale from the debtor, and that interest is perfected prior to the recording of the notice of bankruptcy, the transfer may not be avoided. If less than equivalent value was given, but the purchaser otherwise meets the standards of bona fide purchaser and the transfer was perfected before notice of the bankruptcy was recorded, the transfer is avoidable but the purchaser acquires a lien on the property to secure reimbursement of the value given.

The second provision is §549(d), which is a statute of limitations governing the avoidance of postpetition transfers. The trustee must commence avoidance proceedings before the earlier of two years after the transfer or the time that the case is closed or dismissed.

EXAMPLES

1. Pried before the Fall

On January 1, Binow & Palater, Inc. sold and delivered goods to Gloria Transit Co., Inc. The price of the goods, $2,000, was to be paid within 30 days of delivery. Gloria Transit failed to pay on due date, February 1. After making demands for payment, Binow & Palater received a check for $2,000 from Gloria Transit on March 30. The check was deposited immediately and was paid by Gloria Transit's bank on April 5.

On July 1, Gloria Transit filed a voluntary Ch. 7 petition. After secured and priority claims are paid, the fund remaining in the estate will be enough to pay ten percent of unsecured general claims. Has there been a transfer avoidable under §547(b)?

2. Pleasures of the Flush

On January 1, Gloria Transit Co., Inc. bought some other goods on credit from Prudential Purveyors, Inc. At the time of the sale, Prudential retained a security interest in the goods that was properly perfected by filing under UCC Article 9 on January 20. The price of the goods was $2,000. Gloria Transit was obliged to pay for the goods in two installments due at the end of February and March. It failed to make the payments on due date. Upon being threatened with foreclosure, it paid half the debt ($1,000) on April 10. No further payments were made, and Gloria Transit filed its Ch. 7 petition on July 1.

If the collateral is worth $2,500 at the time of the petition, can the trustee avoid the payment of $1,000? What difference would it make if the collateral was worth $1,500 or $2,000?

3. Ten-Day Mercies

On February 15, Gloria Transit Co., Inc. borrowed money from D. Laid Security, Inc. to purchase a piece of equipment. On that day, the parties executed a security agreement under which Gloria Transit gave a security interest in the equipment to D. Laid Security. D. Laid Security immediately remitted the loan funds to the supplier of the equipment, which delivered the equipment to Gloria Transit on the same day.

D. Laid Security normally perfects its secured transactions immediately. However, because of an oversight, no filing was made at the time of the agreement. The omission was discovered during a routine audit in May, and the filing was made on May 3.

Gloria Transit filed its bankruptcy petition on July 1. Is there an avoidable transfer here?

4.   Backdating beyond the Reachback

In January, a customer of Gloria Transit Co., Inc. commenced suit against it for damages arising out of a breach of contract. On January 15, the plaintiff obtained an order of attachment, and on January 20 it levied on a piece of equipment owned by Gloria Transit. On June 1, the plaintiff obtained judgment against Gloria Transit. On June 10, it levied execution on the equipment that had been held in the sheriff's custody under the writ of attachment. A sale in execution was scheduled for July 3. On July 1, before the sale could take place, Gloria Transit filed its bankruptcy petition.

Has there been a transfer avoidable under §547(b)?

5.   The Long and Short of It

On February 15, Annie C. Dent borrowed $5,000 from Fallshort Finance Co. for the purpose of paying for some orthodontic treatment for her son. To secure the loan, Annie executed a security agreement granting Fallshort Finance a security interest in an Oriental carpet that had been appraised at $6,000. Fallshort Finance filed a financing statement in proper form on February 20. Unknown to both parties, the carpet had been incorrectly appraised, and its true value was only $2,500. This fact was not discovered until Annie's trustee had the carpet reappraised after her bankruptcy.

In terms of the loan agreement, Annie was obliged to repay her debt to Fallshort Finance at the rate of $200 per month. She paid on time in the months of March, April, and May, and then defaulted, leaving a balance of $4,400 plus interest due to Fallshort Finance. Before Fallshort Finance could proceed to foreclose on its security interest, Annie filed her bankruptcy petition on July 1.

Are any of the transfers to Fallshort Finance avoidable under §547(b)? Will any exception in §547(c) protect such transfers from avoidance?

6.   The Fool's Last Measure of Devotion

(a) In February Chico N. DeMail borrowed $5,000 from his friend, Annette Result, promising to repay the loan in a month. When he failed to pay on due date, Annette began to nag him, and eventually threatened never to speak to him again unless he repaid her. Eventually, on May 15, Chico sent Annette payment of the $5,000 together with a thoughtful gift and a sugary note apologizing for the delay. Unknown to Annette, Chico was insolvent at this time.

On June 1, Chico called on Annette with a hard luck story and a plea for another loan. Being softhearted, Annette loaned him $3,000, which he promised to repay in two weeks. As before, Chico failed to repay the loan on its due date and still owned the money to Annette when he filed a voluntary Ch. 7 petition on July 1. Shortly thereafter, Chico's trustee in bankruptcy demanded that Annette pay to the estate the $5,000 received from Chico on May 15.

Is the trustee justified in making this demand?

(b) Assume that, as before, Chico sent a check to Annette on May 15. However, he did not wait until June 1 to ask her for another loan. Instead, he called her on May 17 with his hard luck story. He told her that since his earlier payment to her had depleted his bank account, he now desperately needed $3,000 to pay overdue rent and avoid eviction. Being softhearted, Annette made the loan to him on May 17. At this point, Chico's $5,000 check had not yet cleared. It was eventually paid by his bank to Annette's bank on May 19. How do these new facts change the analysis of Example 6(a)?

7. The Taming of the Shrewd

Several years ago, Erstwhile Enterprises, Inc. purchased a plot of land as an investment. To finance the purchase, it borrowed money from Promised Land Co. and granted a mortgage on the property to Promised Land to secure the loan. The mortgage was properly recorded at the time. After suffering losses on its investments for some years, Erstwhile Enterprises became insolvent and could no longer raise the funds to pay its debts. In January of this year it ceased payment of installments due on its mortgage. Promised Land commenced suit, obtained judgment, and foreclosed on the property. After complying fully with statutory notice and advertising requirements, Promised Land held a foreclosure sale on April 15. The sale was conducted in all respects in accordance with the law.

Shrewd Investment Co., a land speculator, attended the sale. Because bidding was light, it managed to buy the property for $30,000. At the time its fair market value was $50,000. The proceeds of the foreclosure sale were paid to Promised Land by the sheriff. They were just sufficient to settle the balance owing under the mortgage plus the costs of foreclosure.

Erstwhile Enterprises filed a bankruptcy petition on July 1. Can the foreclosure sale be avoided?

8. Debt and Taxes

Two years ago, Mutual Obligation Co., Inc. entered into a contract with the U.S. Air Force in which it undertook to construct buildings on an air base. It breached the contract and became liable to pay damages to the Air Force. The Air Force sued to recover the damages and the parties settled the suit a few months ago. In terms of the settlement, Mutual agreed to pay the Air Force $500,000. Last month, Mutual obtained a judgment in a case that had been pending in the U.S. Tax Court, obliging the Internal Revenue Service to refund $300,000 in overpaid federal taxes. Mutual had been struggling financially for some time, and it has now filed a petition under Chapter 7. It is badly insolvent, can no longer conduct its business, and will be liquidated. At the date of filing, it had not paid the damages due to the Air Force and has not received a refund of its overpaid taxes from the I.R.S.

Immediately after the filing, the government applied for relief from stay so that it could offset the tax refund of $300,000 due to Mutual against the $500,000 damages due by Mutual. It would then prove an unsecured claim of $200,000 against the estate. The trustee has challenged the government's claim of setoff on the grounds that Mutual's claim is against the I.R.S., not the Air Force, that Mutual and the Air Force are not mutually indebted. In the alternative, the trustee argues that even if the indebtedness was mutual, the setoff right is avoidable because it arose within 90 days of bankruptcy. Are these good arguments?

EXPLANATIONS

1. The chronology of the transaction is as follows:

				90-day period		
Jan 1	Feb. 1	Feb./Mar.	Mar. 30	Apr. 2	Apr. 5	July 1
Goods sold on credit and delivered	Payment due	Demands made	Check received		Check paid	Bankruptcy filing

The first question to ask is whether the transfer is avoidable under §547(b). It does satisfy all five of the requirements for avoidance. First, the payment is a transfer to the creditor. When payment is made by check, it is not the delivery of the check, but its payment by the drawee bank that constitutes the transfer. This was settled by *Barnhill v. Johnson,* 112 S. Ct. 1386 (1992), in which the Court, following general principles of nonbankruptcy law, held that transfer only occurs for the purposes of §547(b) when the check is paid by the bank. The check itself is not a transfer of property but is merely an order to the bank, calling on it to pay the holder on presentment. Therefore, until payment is actually made, no property passes from the debtor to the payee.[4]

Second, the transfer is on account of an antecedent debt. In a sale of goods, the debt of the buyer normally arises when the goods are delivered. *See In re Energy Co-Op, Inc.,* 832 F.2d 997 (7th Cir. 1987). Thus, the debt was created on January 1 and is antecedent to the transfer on April 15.

Third, Gloria Transit is presumed to have been insolvent at the time of the transfer. The facts do not indicate whether Gloria Transit was insolvent at the time of the transfer. Under §101(32), insolvency is determined on the basis of the balance sheet test. The presumption of insolvency in §547(f) eases the trustee's burden of proving this element.

Fourth, the transfer occurred within the prepetition avoidance period. Because Binow & Palater is not an insider of Gloria Transit Co., the preference period is 90 days before the petition. Counted back from the bankruptcy date, the 90-day period begins on April 2. As payment of the check on April 5 is the transfer, it is within the 90-day period.

Fifth, the transfer improves the position of Binow & Palater. The improvement-in-position test requires a comparison to be made between the total amount Binow & Palater would receive in a Ch. 7 distribution if the transfer had not been made, and the total satisfaction it receives (combining the transfer and the Ch. 7 distribution on any balance of its claim) if the transfer is left undisturbed. If the transfer is not avoided, Binow & Palater is paid in full; if it is avoided, Binow & Palater, as a general unsecured creditor, will receive approximately ten percent of its claim. (The percentage will be slightly over the ten percent stated in the facts because the fund available to unsecured creditors will be increased by the value of the returned transfer.) Hence, the transfer has improved the position of Binow & Palater. Section 547(b)(5) is almost always satisfied when the transfer has been made to a general unsecured (or partially secured) creditor and the estate has insufficient

---

4. *Barnhill* focused on the question of whether delivery or payment of the check constituted the transfer for the purposes of §547(b). The Court expressly confined its opinion to §547(b) and left open the issue of whether a different rule should apply where the date of transfer must be determined for the purpose of establishing an exception under §547(c). There is substantial lower court authority that the date of delivery, rather than the date of payment, should be determinative where the transferee seeks to show that a transfer was substantially contemporaneous under §547(c)(1), or is made in the ordinary course of business under §547(c)(2), or constitutes a post-transfer payment of new value to the debtor under §547(c)(4). The Supreme Court acknowledged that the policy of protecting regular commercial practices could justify a different rule under these subsections.

funds to pay general unsecured creditors in full. Any portion of the debt that is satisfied by a prebankruptcy transfer is paid at a higher rate than it would be in bankruptcy.

Having determined that §547(b) is satisfied, one must now consider if one of the exceptions in §547(c) applies. None of them do. Most are not even remotely relevant, but §§547(c)(1) and (2) merit some discussion. Section 547(c)(1) does not save the transaction because the transfer is not a substantially contemporaneous exchange for new value. Although §547(c)(1) was drafted with check transactions in mind, the kind of exchange contemplated was the immediate delivery of a check in payment of the goods or services. In the present case, the parties intended a credit transaction. Section 547(c)(2) protects ordinary course transactions and covers regular payments on ordinary debts. In the present case, the debt may have been incurred in the ordinary course of business, but the payment was not routine or regular. It was overdue, and followed some pressure by the creditor. This is not the kind of payment that should be excepted from avoidance under §547(c)(2).

2. Chronological diagram:

Jan. 1	Jan. 20	Apr. 2	Apr. 10	July 1
Sale and creation of security interest	Perfection of security interest	90-day date	Overdue partial payment of $1,000	Bankruptcy filing

Unlike Binow & Palater in Example 1, Prudential has a perfected secured claim. (Although the creation of a security interest is expressly included in the definition of transfer in §101(54), that transfer is not within the preference period, and its avoidance is not in issue.) The payment of $1,000 on April 10 is also a transfer. It satisfies the first four requirements of §547(b) (*see* the analysis in the Explanation to Example 1). However, the fact that Prudential has a secured claim affects the improvement-in-position test of §547(b)(5).

If the collateral is worth $2,500 on the date of the petition, the payment to Prudential did not enable it to do better than it would have done in the absence of the transfer: Prior to the transfer it had a secured claim of $2,000 which would have been paid in full from the proceeds of the collateral. The transfer reduces the claim to $1,000, which would still be paid in full, with a large surplus left over for the estate. Either way, Prudential is paid in full. Because one of the requirements of §547(b) is not satisfied, the transfer is unavoidable. This shows that a valid security interest, perfected before the 90-day preference period, fully protects the creditor, provided that the collateral is sufficiently valuable to accommodate the entire debt. (Example 3 deals with the creation of a security interest within the 90-day period.)

If the collateral is worth only $1,500 at the time of the petition, the improvement-in-position analysis changes. The transfer reduced the debt to $1,000, so that it became fully covered by the collateral. Without the transfer, the debt would have been undersecured with a deficiency of $500. As the deficiency would have been paid as a general unsecured claim, Prudential would not receive full payment unless the estate has sufficient funds to pay general unsecured claims in full. Thus, by eliminating the deficiency, the transfer improved Prudential's position and is avoidable. None of the exceptions in §547(c) apply. As a result, Prudential is obliged to return the $1,000 to the estate and to prove a claim for its secured debt of $1,500 and its unsecured debt of $500. (By agreement between the parties, Prudential may be permitted to keep the $1,000 and to set it off against the secured claim, leaving it with a secured claim of $500 and an unsecured claim of $500.)

If the collateral is worth $2,000, the result seems to be the same as it was in the first example: The transfer did not improve Prudential's position, because the secured claim would have been paid in full out of the collateral even in the absence of the transfer. However, the exact equivalence of the debt and collateral does change the answer: A secured claimant is entitled to interest, legal costs and attorney's fees under §506(b), to the extent of any surplus value in the collateral. See sections 19.5 and 19.6.3. Without the transfer, there would be no such surplus, so no interest, costs, and fees could be claimed. However, payment of the $1,000 creates a surplus by reducing the debt in relation to the collateral value. The right to interest, costs, and fees improves Prudential's position and makes the transfer avoidable. This demonstrates that a secured creditor does well to ensure that an equity cushion exists in the collateral so that payments on the debt are fully protected.

3. Chronological diagram:

February 15	April 2	May 3	July 1
Security agreement executed. Collateral acquired by Debtor.	90 day date	Perfection	Bankruptcy filing

The facts mention no payments to D. Laid Security, so the only transfer in issue is the grant of the security interest which, as stated before, constitutes a transfer under §101(54). Although D. Laid Security discovered its error before the petition was filed, thereby preventing avoidance of its interest under §544(a),[5] the perfection in the 90-day period could make the transfer avoid-

_____

5. See section 15.1.2 and Example 1 of Chapter 15.

able under §547(b). The crucial issue is the date of the transfer: If it occurred at the time of execution of the security agreement, it is outside of the 90-day period and is contemporaneous with the debt. However, if it occurred when the interest was perfected, it falls within the 90-day period and is some considerable time after the creation of the debt.

Section 547(e)(2) sets out the rules for fixing the date of the transfer:

(1) The transfer normally takes effect for bankruptcy purposes on its effective date as between the parties under nonbankruptcy law.

(2) If an act of perfection is required by nonbankruptcy law, that act must be completed within ten days of the effective date as between the parties. If so, the effective date remains the date of the transfer for bankruptcy purposes. If perfection is delayed beyond the ten-day period, the date of perfection becomes the transfer date. (Under §547(e)(1), a transfer of real property is perfected when a bona fide purchaser of the property from the debtor cannot acquire an interest in the property superior to the transferee. A transfer of personal property is perfected when it is effective against an ordinary judicial lienholder.)

(3) If the transfer has not been perfected by the time the petition is filed, the transfer is deemed to have occurred immediately before the filing of the petition. However, if the ten-day period for perfection has not yet expired when the petition is filed, the transferee may complete the act of perfection within the 10-day period, in which case the transfer occurs on the date that it took effect between the parties.

Under UCC Article 9, a security interest takes effect between the parties (*attaches*) when the security agreement is signed, the debtor has rights in the collateral, and value is given by the secured party. This happened on February 15 when the agreement was executed, D. Laid Security advanced money to the seller, and the equipment was delivered to Gloria Transit. The perfection of the interest occurred on May 3 when the proper filing was made. Because the perfection is more than ten days after the date on which the transfer took effect as between the parties, the transfer is deemed to have occurred on the perfection date. This places the transfer in the 90-day period, and it removes it in time from the debt, thereby making the debt antecedent. Therefore, assuming that the presumption of insolvency cannot be rebutted, the elements of §547(b) are satisfied — there is a transfer to D. Laid Security on account of an antecedent debt within the 90-day period. Because D. Laid Security would be a general unsecured creditor in the absence of the transfer (its unperfected interest would be avoided under §544), the transfer does improve its position unless the estate is solvent and can pay all creditors in full. The 10-day grace period in §547(e), like the avoidance power in §544, is a manifestation of the policy against unrecorded interests. By placing the security interest in jeopardy if there is a delay in perfection beyond the fairly short period of 10 days, it encourages secured parties to record their interests expeditiously.

As the perfected security interest is avoidable under §547(b), it is appropriate to consider whether any exceptions in §547(c) are applicable. None of them help D. Laid Security. Section 547(c)(1) is not likely to save the transfer. As noted in section 16.1.4, some courts will not even consider a delay of more than ten days as substantially contemporaneous. Even those courts that are willing to adopt a more flexible test where delay is inadvertent are unlikely to find a delay of nearly three months substantially contemporaneous. Section 547(c)(3) also does not save the transfer. Even though the interest was a purchase money security interest, the special grace period for perfection, measured 20 days from the debtor's receipt of possession of the collateral, does not extend the time for perfection on the present facts. As it happened, the delivery of the collateral to the debtor coincided with the effective date of the transfer. Sadly for D. Laid Security, the old adage, "a stretch in time saves Article Nine," does not apply here.

4. Chronological diagram:

January 15	January 20	April 2	June 1	June 10	July 1
Attachment authorized	Attachment writ levied	90-day date	Judgment	Execution levied	Bankruptcy filing
	attachment lien			execution lien	

As discussed in section 3.3.3, attachment gives rise to an inchoate lien that is effective on the date of the levy of the writ of attachment. When execution is ultimately levied after judgment, the execution lien merges with the earlier attachment lien and backdates for priority purposes to the date of the levy of attachment. Therefore, although the execution lien is a transfer[6] within the 90-day period, the prior attachment lien has already secured the debt so that the execution lien does not prefer the lienholder in position. Section 547(b)(5) is not satisfied, and the lien is unavoidable.

Although the execution lien backdates in priority, this example does not raise the issue dealt with by the Supreme Court in *Fidelity Financial Services, Inc. v. Fink,* 118 S. Ct. 651 (1998). As discussed in section 16.1.3, the court held that "perfection," as used in §§547(e)(1)(B) and (c)(3)(B), means the act of perfection, not its retrospective priority date. For this reason, if a transfer was perfected outside the grace period allowed by those sections, the perfection cannot be backdated to fit within the grace period, even if nonbankruptcy law permits such backdating for priority purposes. In the present case, we are not concerned with trying to backdate the perfection of the

---

6. The definition of transfer in §101(54) includes involuntary dispositions.

execution lien under §547(e) so as to avoid the problem of a transfer for a noncontemporaneous debt, nor is a purchase-money grace period involved under §547(c)(3). Even if we concede that the execution lien is a transfer for an antecedent nonpurchase-money debt, it is simply unavoidable because the creditor is already secured by the attachment lien, and execution within the period of currency of the attachment lien gives the creditor no new advantage that prefers it in position. True, the attachment lien is inchoate in the sense that it would lapse if the creditor failed to levy execution within the prescribed time after judgment, but the lapse of an existing lien because of inaction is not the same as the retrospective creation of a potential lien, which does not become effective unless action is taken within the prescribed time.

5. There have been four transfers to Fallshort Finance in this case: the grant of the security interest and the three payments. The security interest and the first payment are outside the 90-day period and are not in issue. The payments for April and May are avoidable under §547(b) because they satisfy all the elements of that subsection. (Example 2 explains why the payment to an undersecured creditor satisfies the improvement-in-position test.)

The payments were not contemporaneous exchanges for new value, so §547(c)(1) is not applicable. However, §547(c)(2) may be, in that the payments were regularly scheduled installments due under the loan agreement. The loan in the present case is a long-term debt. Courts had split on the question of whether §547(c)(2) applies to monthly payments on long-term loans. Some courts, relying on an historical analysis of §547(c)(2), had held that Congress intended it to be applicable only to routine short-term credit transactions that are substantially contemporaneous. However, in *Union Bank v. Wolas*, 112 S. Ct. 527 (1991), the Supreme Court held that §547(c)(2) is equally applicable to both short-term and long-term debts. The plain wording of the section does not distinguish them, and there is nothing in the legislative history to compel a contrary conclusion. The test is thus not whether the payment relates to a current expense, but whether the underlying transaction itself and the payment were ordinary course transactions.

In the present case, the loan was incurred by Annie for the purpose of paying for her son's orthodonture. The fact that Annie probably does not often borrow large sums of money for dental work does not itself preclude the loan from being an ordinary course transaction, as long as it fitted in with her ordinary patterns of domestic expenditure and can be considered a normal transaction for one in her position. Fallshort Finance must also have been acting in the ordinary course of business in making the loan to her. If this test is satisfied, and the monthly payments also qualify as ordinary course, regular payments (which they do), they are protected from avoidance.

6. **(a)** If it were not for §547(c)(4), the trustee would be entitled to demand return of the payment of $5,000 because it satisfies all the elements of a preference under §547(b). Annette would be obliged to return the money and prove a claim against the estate for the two loans totaling $8,000.

However, §547(c)(4) makes the transfer to Annette unavoidable to the extent that, after the transfer, Annette gave new value to Chico without receiving a new transfer in exchange for it. After being paid the $5,000, Annette made a second loan of $3,000 value must be offset against the $5,000 preference, making only $2,000 of the payment avoidable. Annette may therefore keep $3,000 of the payment, but must return $2,000 to the estate and prove a claim for $5,000.

(b) The new issue raised by this change in the facts concerns the timing of the transfer from Chico to Annette — the repayment of the loan of $5,000. For §547(c)(4) to apply, the new value (Annette's second loan of $3,000) must be given after Chico's otherwise avoidable transfer. While there was no question that the transfer preceded the new value in Example (a), the change of facts makes this an issue here. If the delivery of the check was the transfer, the new value was given after it, and the answer would be the same as in Example (a) — the transfer is excepted from avoidance to the extent of $3,000. However, if payment of the check by Chico's bank is the transfer, the $3,000 loan was made before the transfer and the exception in §547(c)(4) is inapplicable. This would mean that the payment of $5,000 would be avoidable in full and Annette would have nothing more than an unsecured claim for both loans — $8,000.

It was stated in Example 1 that the Supreme Court held in *Barnhill v. Johnson,* 112 S. Ct. 1386 (1992) that when payment is made by check, the transfer occurs, for the purpose of §547(b), when the check is paid, not when it is delivered. The court made it clear that its decision was confined to §547(b), and that different considerations may apply in determining the point of transfer in connection with the exceptions under §547(c). Since *Barnhill* was decided, lower courts have indeed found that the goals of §§547(c)(1), (2), and (4) are best served by treating the delivery of the check, and not its payment, as the transfer. *In re Lee,* 108 F.3d 239 (9th Cir. 1996) and *In re Tennessee Chem. Co.,* 112 F.3d 234 (6th Cir. 1997) are cases that adopted this position with regard to §547(c)(4). The courts reasoned that the delivery of the check is more appropriately treated as the transfer for the purposes of §547(c)(4) because such a rule best protects the creditor's reliance and the debtor's chances of rehabilitation. That is, where a creditor immediately gives new value to the debtor in reliance on a check payment, before the check has cleared, this reliance should be protected. This rule also helps advance the debtor's chances of overcoming his financial difficulty by encouraging creditors not to cut him off and cease furnishing credit to him. (These cases involved business debtors, so the policy of enhancing the debtor's prospects of staying in business is more strongly implicated. However, even in a consumer transaction such as the present, there is social worth in protecting the transferee's reliance and encouraging dealings with the debtor.)

Note, however, that the transferee cannot blindly and indefinitely rely on the delivery of a check: In *Lee* the check delivered was in fact never paid and was ultimately replaced by a cashier's check. The court held that the date of delivery of the check should only be treated as the transfer if the check does in fact clear within ten days of delivery. If it does not, the payment is the transfer. The court therefore found that as the check had never been paid, and had been replaced by a cashier's check, the later cashier's check delivered after the new value had been given, must be treated as the transfer.

7.   The foreclosure sale is a transfer of the debtor's property. It is expressly included in the definition of "transfer" in §101(54).[7] The foreclosure sale in fact constitutes two transfers: the payment of the sale proceeds to Promised Land and the conveyance of the property to Shrewd Investment. The transfer to Promised Land was on account of an antecedent debt and was made while the debtor was insolvent within the 90-day prebankruptcy period. However, Promised Land is a fully secured claimant. It received from the sale no more than the value of its perfected secured claim, and did no better than it would have done in a Ch. 7 distribution if the transfer had not been made. Therefore the improvement-in-position test is not satisfied, and the transfer is not avoidable under §547.

The transfer to Shrewd Investment is not a preferential transfer to a creditor, and is therefore not avoidable under §547. However, because the sale occurred within a year of the bankruptcy filing, it is vulnerable under §548. It is not suggested that the debtor, Erstwhile Enterprises, was guilty of actual fraud in this involuntary disposition. However, it was insolvent, so that if the foreclosure proceeds are less than reasonably equivalent value, the grounds of constructive fraud in §548(2) are satisfied. Courts had been divided on the question of whether a low price received at a foreclosure sale should be treated as inadequate value. Some, following *Durrett v. Washington National Insurance Co.*, 621 F.2d 201 (5th Cir. 1980), held that a foreclosure sale at less than fair market value was constructively fraudulent. (In dictum, the *Durrett* court suggested a benchmark of 70 percent of fair market value as the minimal acceptable price at a foreclosure sale. This standard had been followed by courts that took the *Durrett* approach.) Others, adopting the approach of *In re Madrid*, 21 B.R. 424 (Bankr. 9th Cir. 1982),[8] held

---

7. Section 101(54) was amended in 1984 to include foreclosures. The amendment overrules *In re Madrid*, 725 F.2d 1197 (9th Cir. 1984), in which the court held that the foreclosure could not be a transfer, because the original mortgage transferred the interest to the mortgagee. Subsequent to the amendment, the Ninth Circuit acknowledged in *In re Ehring*, 900 F.2d 184 (9th Cir. 1990), that this decision is no longer good law.

8. This aspect of the opinion by the Bankruptcy Appellate Panel was not considered by the Court of Appeals in the opinion cited in note 7, and was not affected by the amendment to §101(54) in 1984.

that a foreclosure sale was not a constructively fraudulent disposition of the debtor's property even if the distress price was well below market value, provided that the sale was regularly conducted and noncollusive. In other words, if the sale had been lawfully and honestly conducted, the price was presumptively adequate.

These divergent approaches emphasized different interests. *Durrett* allowed valuable property to be returned to the estate, while *Madrid* safeguarded the interests of a buyer at a lawful, noncollusive foreclosure sale. In *In re Bundles*, 856 F.2d 815 (7th Cir. 1988), a third, median approach was adopted which required a factual evaluation of each case to decide whether, under all the circumstances, the admittedly low price obtained at the distress sale was sufficient. While the conduct of the sale and the normal market value of the property were relevant elements in the inquiry, neither was dispositive.

These disparate approaches were finally resolved by the Supreme Court, at least insofar as foreclosure sales are concerned, in *BFP v. Resolution Trust Corp.*, 114 S. Ct. 1757 (1994). The court sided with the *Madrid* approach, and ruled that as long as the foreclosure sale is conducted in compliance with state law, the proceeds received from the sale are conclusively deemed to be reasonably equivalent value. The majority reasoned that as distress sales are seldom at market price, §548 could not be intended to allow courts to use a market standard of any kind to evaluate the price received at a foreclosure sale. The court found this interpretation to be supported by Congress' choice of wording in §548, which uses "reasonably equivalent value," and not "fair market value" as the basis of measuring adequacy of consideration for the purposes of §548. The dissenting Justices were receptive to the argument that even if market value is not used, "reasonably equivalent value" suggests than an inquiry could still be made into whether the price was a reasonable distress price. However, the majority rejected the idea of any kind of evaluation of the equivalence of the foreclosure price, and established a clear rule that the only relevant inquiry is whether the sale complied with state law.

BFP is expressly confined to foreclosure sales. Although its reasoning could persuade lower courts to adopt a similar rule in other distress sales, the case does not settle the divergence of views among Courts of Appeal in cases other than foreclosure. As the proceeding under which Shrewd Investment acquired the property is a foreclosure sale, *BFP* governs, and as the sale fully complied with state law, it cannot be avoided as a fraudulent transfer.

8. Before Mutual obtained the tax court judgment, the Air Force had an unsecured claim of $500,000 against it. If the government cannot offset the debt to the estate for the tax refund against the Air Force's claim against the estate, it will have to pay the full $300,000 to the estate, and will prove its general unsecured claim of $500,000. Because the estate is badly insolvent, it may receive nothing or only a small fraction of its claim. However, if it can set off the debts, it could keep the $300,000 that would otherwise have been payable to the estate and apply it to the payment of its claim, which would be treated as secured to the extent of the $300,000. Only the balance of $200,000 would be an unsecured claim. Given the insolvency of the estate, the setoff would surely improve the government's position.

Under nonbankruptcy law, setoff can only be used when the parties are mutually indebted. It may sound as if this requirement is not satisfied here because Mutual's debt is owed to the Air Force, but it is the I.R.S., not the Air Force, that is indebted to Mutual. However, the real creditor is the U.S. Government, and the Air Force and I.R.S. are simply agencies of the creditor. They are not separate entities. In *In re HAL, Inc.*, 122 F.3d 851 (9th Cir. 1997), the court permitted the setoff of debts owed by the debtor to some federal agencies against debts due to the debtor by others. It held that for the purposes of setoff, all agencies of the federal government must be treated as parts of a single governmental unit — a unitary creditor — and that a debt due to one agency of this unit can be offset by a debt owed by another. (The same principle would apply to agencies of the government of a single state, but obviously would not apply when agencies of different states or state and federal governments are involved.)

This conclusion makes sense as a matter of principle, because all these agencies derive their funding and authority from a centralized source, and do not operate autonomously. It has some support in the language of §553, read with the definitions in §101, but there is an ambiguity in §101(27) which could also justify a contrary argument: Section 553 refers to the setoff right of a "creditor," which is defined in §101(10) to be an entity with a claim against the debtor. "Entity" is in turn defined in §101(15) to include a governmental unit, which is defined in §101(27) to include the United States, states, and other local and regional authorities, as well as their departments, agencies, and instrumentalities. *HAL* read this as meaning that the U.S. Government, including its agencies and constituent parts, must be deemed an indivisible governmental unit, but a glance at that section will demonstrate that it could just as easily be read to mean that each constituent part qualifies as a "governmental unit" on its own.

Once the issue of mutual indebtedness is resolved, we must look at §553 to see if any of its grounds for avoidance are satisfied. They are not. Contrary to the trustee's argument, there is no bar to setoff merely because the mutual debt was created within the 90 days before bankruptcy. For the setoff to be avoidable, the setoff must be tainted in one of the ways specified in §553, which involve a defect in the claim itself or conduct by the creditor designed to create an improper improvement in position in the 90 days before bankruptcy.

17

The Trustee's Power to Deal with Estate Property and to Obtain Credit

§17.1 Introduction

Sections 363 and 364 are concerned with two central administrative functions of the trustee: The power to deal with estate property and to enter into credit transactions on behalf of the estate. Both sections are part of Ch. 3, which is applicable in all cases whether under Ch. 7, 11, 12, or 13. Of course, the powers are not equally relevant in every case, nor are they used in the same way or to the same extent in different types of bankruptcy. As a general matter, the trustee's sale of estate property is likely to predominate in Ch. 7 cases, whereas the ability to lease and use property and to obtain credit is likely to play a more significant role in rehabilitation cases. Also, the powers are likely to be used more extensively in business bankruptcies than in consumer cases.

Sections 363 and 364 are meant to enable the trustee to conduct the affairs of the estate to best advantage, whether that involves liquidation or the conduct of the debtor's business or affairs. In Ch. 11 (and to some extent in Ch. 12) this role, like other trustee functions, is exercised by the debtor in possession who is not likely to approach estate administration with the same impartiality as a disinterested trustee. Therefore, the conduct of the estate's

361

affairs by a debtor in possession is likely to attract closer monitoring by creditors and the court.

Both §§363 and 364 distinguish between actions that are and are not in the ordinary course of the debtor's business. The trustee has wider discretion to enter into ordinary course transactions and normally conducts such activity routinely without special permission of the court. However, extraordinary activity can only be undertaken with court authority, obtained after notice and a hearing. (As stated before, *notice and a hearing* is defined in §102 to mean that parties in interest must receive notice, but that a hearing need not be held unless a party in interest requests it.)

§17.2   The Use, Sale, or Lease of Estate Property under §363

§17.2.1   *The Distinction between Ordinary and Extraordinary Transactions*

Section 363 provides authority for the trustee's dealings with estate property, sets out some general principles governing the exercise of this power, and places limits on the trustee's discretion for the protection of creditors and other parties whose interests may be affected by the trustee's activities. Section 363 encompasses a wide range of activity, from the disposition of estate assets to the operation of equipment, the use of resources and premises, and the routine conduct of daily operations.

As noted in the introduction, §363 makes a fundamental distinction between transactions in the ordinary course of business, which may be conducted within the trustee's discretion, and those outside the ordinary course, which require notice to interested parties and, where requested, a hearing and court approval. The basic idea behind this distinction is that the trustee should be able to maintain routine business operations with a minimum of interference but should not be permitted to enter extraordinary transactions without giving notice to creditors and other interested parties and, if need be, justifying the transaction to the court.

The trustee may only enter into ordinary course transactions without notice and a hearing under §363 if the debtor had been engaged in business at the time of the petition and the postpetition conduct of business operations is generally allowed in the chapter under which the petition has been filed. Section 363(c)(1) is expressly premised on the trustee's underlying statutory authorization to operate the debtor's business under §§721, 1108, 1203, 1204, or 1304. In rehabilitation cases, if the debtor had a business at the time of the petition, authority to continue its operation is the norm.

Sections 1108, 1203, 1204, and 1304 allow the trustee to continue business activities unless the court orders otherwise. Therefore, in rehabilitation cases, the trustee may continue the debtor's ordinary business operations under §363(c)(1) without notice or court approval unless such activity has been curtailed by court order. (The exception to this rule, for cash collateral, is discussed in section 17.2.5.)

In liquidation cases the opposite is true. Because Ch. 7 is aimed at the expeditious liquidation of the estate, the continuation of the debtor's business is not normally contemplated. Section 721 requires court approval for any business activity by the trustee, and stipulates that such approval should be granted only for a limited time and only upon a showing that further business operations are in the best interests of the estate and consistent with orderly liquidation. In a Ch. 7 case, therefore, there can be no ordinary course business activity without notice and a hearing under §363(c)(1) unless the conduct of the business has first been authorized by the court under §721.

In short, unless the debtor conducted business at the time of the petition and the continuation of the business is permitted under the Chapter governing the petition, notice and a hearing is required for any use, sale, or lease of estate property, whether or not in the ordinary course of business. If the continuation of ordinary business operations is authorized, ordinary course transactions may proceed at the trustee's discretion, but any transaction involving the extraordinary use, sale, or lease of estate property must be preceded by notice and a hearing. (*See* Example 1.)

To know if notice must be given, the trustee must decide if a transaction fits within the scope of ordinary business operations. In some situations this is not a difficult question to resolve. For example, if the debtor's business is the retail sales of goods, a routine sale of inventory to a customer is obviously in the ordinary course of business, but the sale of all the debtor's inventory or the disposition of one of its branches is not. In cases where there is doubt, the determination of the ordinary or extraordinary character of the transaction is a factual question to be resolved under all the circumstances of the case. Courts have developed a two-prong test for deciding if a transaction is in the ordinary course of the debtor's business. One focus of the test, sometimes called the *vertical dimension,* is on the reasonable expectations of parties in interest. The other, sometimes called the *horizontal dimension,* looks more broadly at the commercial context in which the debtor's business is operated. The purpose of the inquiry is to ascertain whether parties in interest could reasonably have anticipated a transaction of this type, given the range and scope of the debtor's business and the normal practices in the business environment in which the debtor participates. If not, the transaction is outside the ordinary course of the debtor's business, and interested parties must be informed of it and given an opportunity to demand a hearing. *See In re Dant & Russel, Inc.,* 853 F.2d 700 (9th Cir. 1988). *See also* Example 1.

§17.2.2   *The Approval of Transactions outside the Ordinary Course of Business under §363(b)(1)*

If the use, sale, or lease of property is outside the ordinary course of business, the court must determine whether it should be approved under §363(b)(1). The standard for approval is that the transaction serves the best interests of the estate and furthers the legitimate ends of the bankruptcy. This is a factual determination, to be made in the context of the case as a whole. Say that a Ch. 11 debtor in possession proposes to sell an estate asset during the period prior to plan confirmation. In deciding if the sale should be approved, the court is likely to take a number of factors into account. For example, it will assess whether the transaction is advantageous to the estate. The sale may be desirable because it earns a good profit, brings in vital cash, or disposes of burdensome or unprofitable property. It will also decide whether the transaction is compatible with the larger scheme of rehabilitation envisioned for the estate and whether the transaction is likely to further or hamper the debtor's rehabilitation strategy. Even if the transaction does seem to further the estate's interests, the court may not approve the sale under §363 if it is better to defer the sale so it can be dealt with in the plan. Section 363 is used for extraordinary dealings with estate property prior to the confirmation of the plan. If there is no need for immediate action, it is usually better for the transaction to be included in the plan and subjected to the scrutiny of the confirmation process, which contains safeguards more stringent than those available under §363.[1] The same consideration may apply if the transaction is so complex that it cannot realistically be called a sale or lease of property. Examples 1(e) and 2 illustrate the factors to be considered by a court in approving sales outside the ordinary course of business.

§17.2.3   *The Protection of Interests in Property That Is to Be Used, Sold, or Leased*

Sales at low prices and disadvantageous use or lease of estate property diminishes the value of the estate. Unsecured creditors may therefore object to transactions that appear to be undesirable. Secured creditors or other persons who have an interest in estate property usually have an even more immediate stake in preventing the sale, use, or lease of the property in which they have an

---

1. These safeguards are explained in Chapter 21. They include the publication of a disclosure statement detailing plan provisions, voting on the plan by creditors, and compliance with statutory confirmation requirements. The notice and hearing process in §363(b)(1) does not provide safeguards of equal strength.

interest. Section 363 has a number of provisions designed to protect these interests in estate property. In terms of §363(d), the trustee's power to deal with property must be consistent with any relief from stay granted under §363. In addition, the holder of the interest in estate property may seek adequate protection under §363(e) if the proposed use or disposition of the property jeopardizes that party's interest in it. The right to adequate protection applies to all proposed transactions under §363, whether or not they are in the ordinary course of business and irrespective of the nature of the property. Under §363(o), the party who claims adequate protection bears the burden of proving the interest, but the trustee must prove that the interest is adequately protected. The factors that are evaluated by the court in deciding if adequate protection exists (such as the presence of an equity cushion and the debtor's prospects of successful reorganization) are the same as those discussed in connection with relief from stay, as are the standards for evaluating the adequacy of any additional protection offered by the trustee under §361. As in the case of relief from stay, the court has discretion in selecting an appropriate remedy. Section 363 allows the court to permit or prohibit the use, sale, or lease of collateral absolutely or subject to conditions. Apart from the protection of interests in property generally, §363 has special rules to preserve cash collateral, discussed below.

Sections 363(f) through (k) impose restrictions and qualifications on the trustee's power to sell property of which the estate is a co-owner or which is subject to a lien or interest held by another. Like §363(e) on adequate protection, most of these provisions apply to both extraordinary sales and to sales in the ordinary course of business. In essence, they permit the sale of property free and clear of interests, or the sale of both the estate's and the other party's undivided interests only under specified conditions. If such a sale occurs, the holder of the interest is paid out the value of the interest from the sale proceeds. In some situations, the co-owner must be given a right of first refusal to purchase the property at the proposed sale price. When property is sold outside the ordinary course of business under §363(b), the holder of a lien in the property is entitled to bid at the sale, and if the lienholder purchases the property, to offset its claim against the purchase price.

§17.2.4   Insolvency or Bankruptcy Clauses in Prepetition Contracts or Nonbankruptcy Law

In dealing with property of the estate, section 11.2.1 indicated that §541(c) invalidates *ipso facto clauses* — provisions in contracts or nonbankruptcy law that restrict transfer or provide for the forfeiture of property rights on bankruptcy — so that private parties or states cannot circumvent bankruptcy law by making the debtor's property interests nonassignable to the trustee.

Similar considerations exist with regard to the trustee's power to use, sell, or lease property. To prevent states or private parties from negating the trustee's power to deal with property under §363, §363(*l*) disregards contractual or statutory provisions that provide for the forfeiture or modification of the debtor's property rights upon insolvency or bankruptcy.

§17.2.5   *Restrictions on Dealing with Cash Collateral*

Section 363 treats cash collateral differently from other property of the estate. The essential difference is that cash collateral may not be dealt with by the trustee, even in the ordinary course of business, unless the holder of the interest in that collateral consents or the court authorizes the transaction after notice and a hearing. *Cash collateral* is defined in §363(a) to mean cash or a cash equivalent that is subject to an interest held by someone other than the estate. The most common form that this interest takes is a security interest in the cash collateral, either as original collateral or as proceeds of original collateral. Of course, the security interest must be valid under nonbankruptcy law, and if the cash collateral is proceeds of original collateral, the security interest must validly extend to such proceeds under nonbankruptcy law. Quite a wide range of property is considered to be the equivalent of cash under §363(a). The definition includes not only banknotes and bank accounts, but also various kinds of negotiable or readily transferrable commercial paper such as negotiable instruments, documents, and securities. These are treated as cash equivalents because they can be liquidated easily by being sold to purchasers who take free of the rights of the secured party. Example 3 illustrates different types of cash collateral.

The liquid nature of cash and cash equivalents explains the stricter approach in §363 to the trustee's dealings with cash collateral. Because the debtor's business needs cash to operate, it is very tempting for the estate to spend these assets, thereby dissipating them in the ongoing conduct of the business. A creditor who has a security interest in such assets is therefore in much greater danger than other secured creditors of having its collateral frittered away in the payment of daily business expenses. For this reason, §363(c)(2) freezes the use of cash collateral even when this normally would be in the ordinary course of running the business, until the trustee either obtains permission from the interest holder or authority from the court to deal with it. In addition, §363(c)(4) obliges the trustee to keep cash collateral separate and to account for it, unless the creditor or court dispenses with this requirement. Sections 363(d) and (e) make it clear that the authorization to deal with cash collateral is subject to any relief from stay that has been granted and is conditional upon adequate protection of the interest.

§17.3   Postpetition Credit under §364

§17.3.1   *The Rationale of §364*

Section 364 deals with credit given to the estate after the petition has been filed. In these transactions the estate is the debtor, and is liable for payment of the debt. (Such estate debts qualify as administrative expenses with top priority for payment.) A Ch. 7 estate does not usually need to borrow money. However, a debtor that is undergoing rehabilitation and is attempting to operate and reorganize its business often requires credit to support its operations. In some cases, financing is vital to the debtor's survival and successful reorganization. To obtain credit, the debtor needs to convince the prospective financer that it has good prospects of rehabilitation. In addition, because of the risk that the debtor will not overcome its financial difficulties, the postpetition lender is likely to require some security or an assurance of priority if the debt is not repaid. Section 364 assists the trustee in obtaining postpetition credit by providing the means for securing or otherwise protecting financial transactions entered into by the estate.

Like the ordinary use, sale, or lease of estate property, the routine creation of postpetition unsecured debt is within the discretion of the trustee. However, credit transactions outside the ordinary course of business and the creation of secured debt must be authorized by the court following notice and a hearing. The assumption of new debt by the estate is potentially detrimental to existing unsecured creditors. If the reorganization ultimately fails, new creditors with secured or priority claims will consume assets or funds that would have been available to pay the prepetition claims. Thus, postpetition financing creates a dilemma: If the debtor obtains new credit, its chances of successful rehabilitation are improved, and prepetition unsecured creditors have a chance to receive a higher level of payment than they would have received in liquidation. However, if new credit is obtained and the debtor fails in the end, the estate's assets will have been further encumbered, the expenses of administration will have increased, and the source of funds formerly available to unsecured creditors will have been reduced or eliminated. Because prepetition creditors bear a large part of the risk of failure, courts are usually careful to try and protect their interests when called upon to approve a postpetition credit transaction. Fully secured prepetition creditors are not as vulnerable as unsecured creditors because their claims are protected by their liens. However, proposed postpetition financing can, under some circumstances, affect the security of a prepetition secured creditor. If this is a possibility, the prepetition creditor can demand adequate protection as a precondition to the court approving the financing.

§17.3.2   *The Credit Arrangements Permitted by §364*

Section 364 is based on the policy that the trustee should be required to find the least onerous financing available. For example, if unsecured credit is available, it is to be preferred to secured credit. If secured credit is necessary, unencumbered property should be used as collateral rather than property subject to an existing interest. This policy is expressed in the hierarchical organization of the section. It proves for the possibility of four different levels of credit transaction that are progressively more burdensome for the estate, and makes it clear that credit on more stringent terms should not be approved unless easier terms are unavailable.

The four levels of transaction are as follows:

(1) Unsecured debt incurred in the ordinary course of business (§364(a)).   If continuation of the debtor's business is authorized under §§721, 1108, 1203, 1204, or 1304, the trustee has the power to obtain unsecured credit in the ordinary course of business. The debts so incurred are given the priority of an administrative expense, so that they will be paid before all other unsecured claims. (*See* section 19.6.) This provision is similar in concept to §363(c)(1), which was discussed in section 17.2.1. Unless the court orders otherwise, these routine credit transactions do not require notice or a hearing. The test for deciding whether or not a transaction is in the ordinary course of business is the same as that applicable to the use, sale, or lease of estate property.

(2) Unsecured debt outside the ordinary course of business (§364(b)).   If the unsecured credit transaction does not fall within the normal course of the debtor's business (or if there is no authority to operate a business under the applicable chapter of the Code), the trustee must obtain court permission, following notice and a hearing, to incur the unsecured credit. The approved credit is given administrative expense priority. The general grounds for approving the credit transaction are similar to those for approving the use, sale, or lease of estate property outside the ordinary course of business: The court must be satisfied that the transaction is on fair and reasonable terms, that it is likely to further the interests of the estate, and that it will not impose an unjustifiable burden or risk on parties in interest.

(3) Secured or superpriority credit (§364(c)).   If the trustee cannot obtain unsecured credit allowable as an administrative expense, §364(c) allows the court, after notice and a hearing, to approve security or special priority for the debt. Section 364(c) provides the court with three alternatives: It may authorize *superpriority* for the debt, placing it ahead of administrative expenses so that it is paid in preference over all priority and general unsecured claims, or it may allow the trustee to secure the debt by a lien on unencumbered property or by a junior lien on encumbered property. *See* Example 5. The court is not confined to any one of the alternatives and can approve a transaction that combines them. In addition to determining that unsecured credit is unavailable, the court takes into account the same factors as those identified for §364(b), in deciding whether to approve a transaction under §364(c).

(4) Credit secured by a senior or equal lien on encumbered property (§364(d)). The credit terms in the prior categories do not infringe upon the rights of existing secured claimants. Only if the credit is unobtainable by any other means and the need for it is demonstrated by the trustee can the court (after notice and a hearing) approve credit that is secured by a lien senior or equal to an existing lien on estate property.

The grant of such a lien endangers the valid preexisting security interest in the property and the holder's legitimate expectation of full satisfaction of its secured claim. It therefore should only be approved in compelling circumstances. Section 364(d) also requires the existing interest to be adequately protected. The trustee has the burden of proving adequate protection. Again, the principles discussed in section 11.5 apply here: If there is not sufficient value in the property to accommodate both the old lien and the new one, with a comfortable equity cushion for the old lien, the trustee cannot obtain approval for the new lien unless adequate protection is provided by new collateral, payment to reduce the debt, or some other means.

§17.3.3 Cross-Collateralization

Because a bankrupt debtor is usually a poor credit risk, it may be unable to entice a new lender to extend credit. It may therefore approach an existing creditor for further advances. Because the existing creditor has a stake in the debtor's rehabilitation, it has some incentive to provide new financing if it believes that the debtor's reorganization may be successful as a result. The creditor has an even stronger incentive to provide postpetition financing if its prepetition claim is unsecured or undersecured, and the debtor is willing to provide collateral to secure both the new credit and the unsecured prepetition credit. Such an arrangement is known as *cross-collateralization*. In short, it is the provision of postpetition credit to the estate on condition that the collateral securing the new credit also covers the unsecured or undersecured prepetition claim. For cross-collateralization to benefit the lender, there must be a present or anticipated excess equity in the collateral beyond the amount of the new debt. For example, suppose a creditor is owed a prepetition debt of $5 million, secured by collateral worth $4 million. The creditor agrees to make a new postpetition loan of $2 million to the debtor to enable it to reorganize. As a condition of this postpetition loan, the creditor demands a security interest in unencumbered property of the estate worth $3 million, which will secure both the postpetition loan and the prepetition debt. If this arrangement is authorized by the court, the creditor not only secures the new financing, but also bolsters the security for its prepetition debt and eliminates its unsecured deficiency. In essence, the creditor uses its bargaining power in negotiating postpetition financing to improve the position of its undersecured prepetition debt at the expense of other unsecured creditors. This offends the bankruptcy policy of evenhanded treatment.

It is not clear whether cross-collateralization is permissible. Some bankruptcy courts have allowed it, albeit reluctantly, when the debtor in possession can show that the business will not survive without the proposed financing, the estate cannot obtain better financing, the proposed lender will not agree to better terms, and the transaction is in the best interests of the estate and creditors. *See In re Vanguard Diversified*, 31 B.R. 364 (Bankr. E.D.N.Y. 1983). Other courts, including the only Court of Appeals to address the issue directly, have held that a court may not sanction a postpetition financing scheme involving cross-collateralization. In *In re Saybrook Mfg. Co., Inc.*, 963 F.2d 1490 (11th Cir. 1992), the court noted that §364 authorizes only the granting of liens for postpetition loans and gives the court no power to extend the lien to a prepetition debt. Although bankruptcy courts do have general equitable powers to adjust claims to avoid unfairness, this does not entitle them to authorize the preferential treatment of a claim in contravention of the Code's priority scheme and the fundamental policy of evenhanded treatment of creditors.

§17.3.4   Protection on Appeal

A party in interest may appeal the court's approval of postpetition credit. If the estate needs the advance urgently, the delay resulting from an appeal could be damaging. Therefore, provided that the court has not stayed action pending appeal, §364(e) allows the parties to proceed with the transaction immediately after approval, notwithstanding appeal. As long as the creditor has acted in good faith, the debt and its supporting lien or priority authorized by the court remains valid and enforceable even if the approval is reversed or modified on appeal. The mere fact that the creditor knows that an appeal is pending does not constitute bad faith.

EXAMPLES

1.   All in a Good Course

Carrion Business, Inc., which operates a chain of three retail stores, has recently filed a voluntary Ch. 11 petition. Are the following proposed transactions within the ordinary course of the debtor's business?

(a) The debtor keeps the stores open and continues selling inventory to customers.

(b) The debtor proposes to conduct a mammoth clearance sale at which it plans to sell all its slow-moving inventory at greatly reduced prices, to reduce stock and improve its cash flow.

(c) The debtor proposes to use the cash generated by its sale of inventory to pay salaries, rent for its premises, and other operating expenses.

(d) One of the debtor's three stores has never made a profit. The debtor enters into an agreement with one of its competitors under which it proposes to sell the unprofitable store to the competitor for cash.

(e) The debtor has filed the petition under Ch. 7 rather than Ch. 11. The trustee wishes to keep the stores open for a few months and to continue selling inventory to customers to liquidate the inventory at its retail value.

2. The Pleasure of Their Company

Joyful Trifles, Inc. is a long-established manufacturer of teddy bears and other warm, fuzzy toys. When the computer age dawned, Joyful Trifles began stuffing its fluffy creatures with electronic innards that enabled them to growl, jabber, and converse. The electronic components are manufactured by Sound Bytes, Inc., a profitable and financially stable company in which Joyful Trifles is the majority shareholder. These shares are Joyful Trifle's most valuable asset.

Despite this innovation, Joyful Trifles made losses for several years. Joyful Trifles has filed a Ch. 11 petition in an attempt to restructure its business. While it was attempting to formulate its plan of reorganization, it received an offer for the purchase of its shares in Sound Bytes, Inc. The prospective buyer has offered a very good price for the shares, provided that the sale can be executed speedily. Because it needs the money badly, Joyful Trifles wishes to accept the offer. Upon being notified of the proposed sale, some creditors have objected. What factors should the court take into account in deciding whether or not to approve the sale?

3. Shackled Shekels

Fiscal Jam Co., Inc. has just filed a petition under Ch. 11. The debtor operates a berry farm, makes its produce into jam, and sells the finished product to supermarkets. Fiscal Jam owns its farm, a cannery, and a warehouse building. It does not need the entire warehouse for its own product, and leases a portion of the building to a tenant.

At the time of filing the petition, Fiscal Jam's estate included the following property:

(a) The debtor's inventory of jam, subject to a security interest in favor of a lender.

(b) Proceeds of the sale of jam, received prior to the bankruptcy filing and deposited in a special proceeds account, as required by the security agreement between the debtor and the inventory financer.

(c) Proceeds of the sale of jam, received after the bankruptcy filing and deposited in the special account.

(d) Accounts receivable, representing debts due to the debtor by its customers for jam sold on credit.

(e) Undeposited checks received from customers in payment of jam sold.

(f) Rent paid by the tenant of the warehouse and deposited in the debtor's general bank account. The warehouse is encumbered by a mortgage that was granted by the debtor to the bank that originally loaned it money to purchase the property.

(g) Other funds in the general bank account, derived from sources other than sales of inventory and rent. The bank in which this account is maintained had made a loan to the debtor prior to the petition, and the loan remains unpaid.

Which of these assets satisfy the definition of cash collateral?

4. Sweet Liberty of Land

A few years ago, Phil Adelphos and his sister Phobia bought a piece of property as an investment. They hold title as co-owners with undivided half-shares. When they bought the property, they financed its price with a loan from Rigor Mortgage Co., which recorded a mortgage on the property to secure the debt.

Phil as now filed a Ch. 7 petition. His trustee has tried unsuccessfully to sell Phil's half-interest in the property, subject to the mortgage. Although no one wishes to buy Phil's encumbered half-interest, the trustee has found someone who is willing to purchase the entire property free of all encumbrances. The price offered is sufficient to pay off the mortgage, leaving a substantial equity to be divided between the estate and Phobia. Can the trustee accept the offer?

5. Damned with Faint Appraisal

Last year, Receding Airlines, Inc. filed a Ch. 11 petition. Shortly thereafter, one of its secured creditors, Mayday, Mayday & Co., applied for relief from stay on the grounds that its collateral (some equipment owned by the debtor) was not adequately protected. In response to the application, the debtor augmented the collateral by including some additional equipment. The court found that the increase in collateral adequately protected Mayday's interest, and it refused relief from stay. A few months ago, the court approved a loan to the estate from Mortimer Post, Inc. and authorized its payment in priority over all administrative expenses, as provided for in §364(c)(1).

Receding Airline's attempt at reorganization has failed and the company is in liquidation. It now appears that the additional collateral given to Mayday was not enough to offset depreciation. Although it was fully secured at the time that it applied for relief from stay, its collateral now falls short of its debt by $200,000. The balance due to Mortimer Post on its loan is $2 million.

After secured claims are paid, the fund remaining in the estate for distribution to all creditors is $1.5 million. How will this fund be distributed?

EXPLANATIONS

1. (a) **The continued operation of the retail business.** The routine operation of the debtor's stores is clearly in the ordinary course of its business. Unless the court has ordered otherwise, this activity is authorized by §1108 and encompassed within §363(c)(1). The sale of inventory to customers may proceed without notice and a hearing. This comports with the goals of Ch. 11, which is intended to enable the debtor to try to reorganize and revitalize its business. Unless there is some good reason to restrict the debtor's normal income-producing endeavors, the debtor should be able to get on with its business without the disruption and inefficiency of notifying interested parties of its routine activities and seeking court approval in the event of objection.

(b) **The mammoth clearance sale.** This venture is not as obviously in the ordinary course of business as the day-to-day dealings with retail customers. To decide whether a transaction is in the ordinary course of business, one must consider the reasonable expectations of parties in interest in light of the commercial context in which the debtor operates. If the transaction is one that can reasonably be anticipated as part of the debtor's normal business operations, it is an ordinary course transaction. The facts are not sufficient for a definitive answer. However, if periodic clearance sales are part of the debtor's business practice, and such sales are not inconsistent with expected activity in the debtor's trade, this may qualify as an ordinary course transaction. In addition, the degree of markdown, the inventory included in the sale and the period of the sale must not be dramatically different from usual.

(c) **The use of proceeds of inventory to pay business expenses.** Provided that the payments are not abnormal or accelerated, the payment of business expenses is an ordinary course transaction. *See, e.g., In re James A. Phillips, Inc.,* 29 B.R. 391 (S.D.N.Y. 1983). The facts do not state whether the inventory was subject to a security interest. If it was, the funds generated by the sale of inventory is cash collateral, and it cannot be used even to pay ordinary course business expenses without notice and a hearing or the consent of the secured party.

(d) **The sale of the unprofitable store.** It may, indeed, be a good idea for the debtor to dispose of the unprofitable store as part of its Ch. 11 reorganization. However, this is not an ordinary course transaction and it must at a minimum be done with notice and an opportunity for a hearing under §363(b). Even this procedure may not be appropriate. Unless there is a good reason to authorize the sale under §363 because, for example, the debtor needs to dispose of the store without delay, it is more appropriate for the debtor to provide for the sale in the plan of reorganization so that it is subject to the safeguards of the plan confirmation process.

(e) **The operation of the stores by a Ch. 7 trustee.** Even though the operation of the stores is in the ordinary course of the debtor's business, §363(c)(1) only allows the trustee to conduct the business of the debtor without notice and a hearing if continued operation is authorized in the chapter under which the bankruptcy is filed. In Ch. 7 cases, §721 allows the short-term operation of the business only if the court authorizes it as being in the best interests of the estate and consistent with orderly liquidation. Therefore, in a Ch. 7 case, the trustee may not continue running the stores, even in the ordinary course of business, unless the court has given permission to keep the stores open for a limited period in order to realize the most advantageous price for the inventory.

2.   This question is inspired by *In re Lionel Corp.*, 722 F.2d 1063 (2d Cir. 1983). Like Joyful Trifles, Lionel Corp.'s most valuable asset was stock that it owned in a profitable corporation that manufactured electronic components for its toys. In the *Lionel* case, the proposed sale was motivated not by an attractive offer to buy the shares but by pressure exerted by major creditors to sell the shares for the purpose of realizing a substantial cash fund. The proposed sale was objected to by stockholders in the debtor and by the SEC (which is also an interested party in Ch. 11 cases involving public corporations).

In reversing the approval of the sale by the lower courts, the Court of Appeals explored the issue of whether the sale of a major asset should be permitted under §363, rather than included in the plan and made subject to the safeguards of the confirmation process. In deciding this question, the court must be concerned not only with the merits of the transaction (*i.e.,* whether it is advantageous, represents good business judgment, and will further the ends of successful reorganization) but also with its timing. Earlier case law refused to authorize preconfirmation sales of major assets unless the debtor had shown an emergency situation (*e.g.,* if an immediate sale does not take place, serious harm would be suffered by the estate because the asset would perish or depreciate). *Lionel* rejected this standard as too rigid, and applied a test of *articulated business justification,* under which the court must decide if, in all the circumstances of the case, an immediate sale is based on a reasonable business judgment and is likely to be in the best interests of the estate. Some of the questions to be asked in making this determination are: Is the proposed sale on such attractive terms that they are not likely to be repeated if the sale is not executed? Is the asset likely to depreciate or appreciate? Will the management of the asset constitute a drain on the resources of the estate? Is the sale of the asset at this stage consistent with the debtor's plans for rehabilitation? *See also Stephens Industries, Inc. v. McClung*, 789 F.2d 386 (6th Cir. 1986), in which the court permitted the sale under §363 of all the assets of the debtor, a radio station, including its FCC license. The estate no longer had the capacity to keep its radio station operational and risked revocation of its license for going off the air. The immediate sale was therefore necessary to prevent loss of the license which was the estate's most valuable asset. In effect, the sale amounted to the liquidation of the estate, which is not an appropriate use of §363 except in the most pressing circumstances.

Although the facts of this problem are not detailed enough to provide answers to all these questions, they seem to be somewhere between *Lionel* and *Stephens Industries*. They do not suggest a dire emergency like that in *Stephens Industries* but they do suggest some business justification — an advantageous price — that was absent in *Lionel*. (In *Lionel* the creditors wanted the sale because it would have generated proceeds to pay their claims. However, there was no good business reason to sell the shares in the electronics company at that time: They were not depreciating, the price was not adequate, and no emergency required disposition.)

3. The classification of the collateral is as follows:

(a) The inventory, although readily disposable property, is not cash collateral. It is neither commercial paper nor a cash equivalent as required by §363(a). Therefore, because the debtor is authorized to continue its business under §1108, sales of inventory in the ordinary course of business may continue without notice and a hearing under §363(c)(1).

(b) The funds in the special bank account are identified as proceeds of inventory. The inventory is subject to a security interest. UCC Article 9, which governs such security interests, automatically extends the interest to identifiable proceeds received by the debtor in exchange for the original collateral. Hence, the funds in the special account are cash collateral under §363(a). They cannot be used by the debtor unless court authority or creditor consent is given under §363(2).

(c) The only difference between these proceeds and those described in question (b) is that these were received after the petition was filed. Postpetition proceeds of estate property are included in the estate. §541(a)(6). In terms of §552(b), they are subject to the security interest because they are proceeds of prepetition collateral under a valid prepetition interest that extends to proceeds under nonbankruptcy law. In defining cash collateral, §363(a) expressly includes postpetition proceeds in which a security interest is recognized by §552(b). Therefore, like the funds deposited in the special account before commencement of the case, these identifiable cash proceeds of inventory, received after the filing of the petition, are cash collateral.

(d) Like the inventory in question (a), these accounts are not commercial paper or cash equivalents. They are simply intangible claims that the debtor has against its customers. They do not fall within the definition of cash collateral. However, the accounts are identifiable proceeds of original collateral in which the security interest continues under §552(b). When the accounts are paid, the payments are likewise identifiable proceeds and will be cash collateral.

(e) The checks are negotiable instruments under UCC Article 3, and are cash collateral under §363(a).

(f) Rent earned by the estate from a lease of real property also becomes property of the estate under §541. Prior to 1994, §§552(b) and 363(a) simply treated rents and profits of property in the same way as they dealt with the proceeds of collateral: If the rent fell within the perfected interest of the mortgage under state law, the mortgagee's interest was recognized in bankruptcy law and the rent was cash collateral. However, rent earned from mortgaged property did present a particular difficulty that had not arisen in connection with the proceeds or product of other collateral, because some courts refused to find a valid interest in rent proceeds unless the mortgagee had taken specific steps under nonbankruptcy law to perfect its right to such rent proceeds. To eliminate this conflict, the Bankruptcy Reform Act of 1994 added §552(b)(2), which makes it clear that as long as the security agreement itself extends the security interest to cover rent earned from the property, the rent is to be treated in bankruptcy as proceeds under the security interest and hence as cash collateral, irrespective of whether any further act of perfection is required or was taken under nonbankruptcy law. (Section 552(b)(2) also covers another matter that was subject to different judicial interpretations prior to 1994: Some courts had treated amounts due on the hire of hotel rooms as accounts receivable, rather than rent, so that they could not qualify as cash collateral within the security interest of the mortgagee of the hotel property. Section 552(b)(2) makes it clear that they are to be treated as proceeds of that security interest.)

(g) These funds are not proceeds of original collateral. However, because the debtor is indebted to the bank, and the bank has a right of setoff against the account, the funds are treated as collateral of the bank to the extent of its unpaid claim. (*See* §553, discussed in section 16.2.) A deposit account is included in the definition of cash collateral in §363(a). This question illustrates one of the ways in which an original interest in cash collateral may arise.

4. This question merely introduces §§363(f), (h), (i), and (j). It is not a comprehensive treatment of those subsections, which are full of difficult issues. The facts suggest that the estate will benefit from the sale of both Phil's and Phobia's shares, free of the mortgage. Under appropriate circumstances, §363 gives the trustee the power to sell not only the debtor's interest but the other interests as well, using the proceeds of the sale to pay them out and keeping the balance for the estate.

The sale free of Rigor Mortgage's interest is governed by §363(f), which permits such a sale only if one of five conditions is satisfied. There is some doubt about the scope and meaning of certain of these requirements, but this is the gist of the subsection: The sale free and clear of the mortgage can be effected with the consent of Rigor Mortgage. In the absence of such consent, it can only occur if the mortgage's validity is in genuine dispute; nonbankruptcy law provides a means of sale free and clear of the mortgage; the mortgagee can be compelled by litigation to accept money satisfaction; or the sale price of the property exceeds the aggregate value of all liens on the property. Notwithstanding the existence of any one of these grounds, there remains the general requirement under §363(e) that adequate protection of Rigor Mortgage's interest be provided. If the property does qualify for sale free and clear of the mortgage, Rigor Mortgage's interest will attach to or will be paid out in full from the proceeds.

Phobia's share of the property may be sold only if all four of the conditions in §363(h) are satisfied: Partition is impracticable; the sale of the estate's interest alone would realize significantly less; the benefit to the estate outweighs the detriment to Phobia; and the property is not used for the production or supply of electrical energy or gas. In addition, §363(i) gives Phobia the right of first refusal at the sale price, and §363(k) requires the trustee to pay over to Phobia her share of the sale proceeds.

5. Section 11.5.6 and Example 3 of Chapter 11 deal with Mayday's situation. If adequate protection is provided, and it later turns out to have been inadequate to protect the interest, the shortfall is given *superpriority* by §507(b). It takes precedence over administrative expenses, which are themselves the highest priority claims to be paid out of the estate after secured claims have been settled.

However, Mortimer Post's claim has also been given superpriority under §364(c)(1). Because the fund available for distribution cannot settle both claims, they must be ranked. A comparison of the wording §§507(b) and 364(c)(1) reveals that while §507(b) gives Mayday's claim "priority over every other claim allowable under [§507(a)(1),]" §364(c)(1) gives Mortimer Post's claim "priority over any or all administrative expenses of the kind specified in . . . §507(b)." In other words, Mortimer Post's claim is placed above all administrative expenses, including Mayday's superpriority claim. Therefore, if a claim under §507(b) has superpriority, a claim under §364(c)(1) is one step better, and can be described as having "ultrapriority" (or, if you prefer, "hyperpriority" or "summapriority").

The fund of $1.5 million is therefore paid to Mortimer Post, which has an unsatisfied balance of $500,000 on its claim. Mayday receives no payment at all on its deficiency of $200,000, so the backup to its adequate protection failed. In addition, unsecured creditors of the estate, both priority and general, have borne the risk of the debtor's failure, because the payment of the postpetition loan has consumed the entire fund and left nothing for the payment of claims.

18

Executory Contracts and Unexpired Leases

§18.1   Introduction

The trustee's duties and powers in dealing with executory contracts and unexpired leases are set out in §365 — a long, confusing section, full of detail, subtleties, and gaps. It consists of general provisions as well as subsections that relate to particular types of contract, including, amongst others, leases of nonresidential real property, shopping centers, airport premises, and nonconsumer personal property. For the most part, these specific subsections are confined to the transactions that they identify, but they sometimes create interpretational questions in the general provisions, because it is not always clear if the rules that they express are confined to the transactions identified, or are merely rules of general application expressed in relation to the transaction in question, but existing in unarticulated form elsewhere.

The complexity and confusion generated by §365 was acknowledged by the National Bankruptcy Reform Commission in its 1997 report, in which it recommended that the section be redrafted to focus more clearly on its concept and to get rid of cumbersome constructs and terminology. (This is discussed briefly in sections 18.2 and 18.3.) The pending bankruptcy reform legislation does not attempt a significant revision of §365.

Although §365 is complex, the goal of this chapter is to focus on basic principles. The essential goal of §365 is similar to that of §§363 and 364: to empower the trustee to take best advantage of the rights and assets of the estate while affording some protection to the countervailing interests held by other parties. Many of the provisions of §365 attempt to balance the good of the estate against the other party's right to receive the benefit of its bargain.

Being part of Ch. 3, §365 applies in all forms of bankruptcy, but its operation and importance in each case depends on the nature of the debtor's prepetition affairs and the form of bankruptcy relief sought. Although §365 is often most significant in Ch. 11 cases, because Ch. 11 debtors often have many outstanding contractual relationships, one should fully expect to find it arising in bankruptcies under other chapters as well. When §365 is used in a Ch. 11 case, the usual rule applies that the trustee's function is exercised by the debtor in possession unless the court orders the appointment of a trustee for cause. In most situations, the court must approve the assumption or rejection of an executory contract. The estate is obliged to notify the other contracting party of its election, and the other party has the opportunity to object to the proposed action.

§18.2   The Meaning of "Executory Contract" and "Unexpired Lease"

The Code does not define *executory contract* and *unexpired lease*. The standard definition of executory contract is based on the meaning given to that term (as used in the Bankruptcy Act) in a 1973 law review article by Professor Countryman: A contract is *executory* if the obligations of both parties are so far unperformed that the failure of either to perform would be a material breach. In other words, a contract only qualifies as executory for bankruptcy purposes if, at the time of bankruptcy, both parties had material obligations outstanding. If either had fully or substantially performed, the contract is no longer executory and should not be dealt with under §365. Similarly, if the contract had terminated prior to bankruptcy, either because its term had ended or because one of the parties rightfully canceled it, it is not executory.

Although the Countryman definition is approved in the legislative history of §365 and is frequently quoted by courts, there is a trend toward a more *functional approach* that looks not only at the materiality of the unperformed portion of the contract, but also takes into account the materiality of the contract and the impact on the estate of allowing the trustee to assume or reject the contract. This approach is motivated by the concern that a rigid test of materiality, that examines only the contractual significance of outstanding mutual performances, may make some contracts unassumable because one side has substantially performed. As the principal goal of assumption or rejection of an executory contract is to benefit the estate, a court should consider not merely if there has been substantial performance, but also what effect the determination of executoriness will have on the estate, the interests of creditors, and the debtor's prospect of rehabilitation. This thinking is expressed, for example, in *In re Riodizio, Inc.*, 204 B.R. 417 (Bankr. S.D.N.Y. 1997). (*See* Example 1.)

In its 1997 report, the National Bankruptcy Review Commission recognized that the flexible test has created confusion and uncertainty in the definition of an executory contract. The Commission recommended at least a statutory clarification of the definition. However, the recommendation went beyond that to suggest that the very concept of executory contracts should be changed, so the focus is less on the question of whether a contract is executory and more on the question of whether it is in the estate's interests to perform or breach a contract. As noted in section 18.1, the pending reform legislation does not contain fundamental changes to §365.

Section 365 refers not only to executory contracts, but also to *unexpired leases*. This is redundant because an unexpired lease is nothing more than a variety of executory contract. However, this special mention does reflect the section's preoccupation with leases, as discussed below. Some types of leases are subject to special rules, but except to the extent that these specific rules are provided for in various subsections of §365, contracts of lease are governed by the same general rules and principles that apply to other executory contracts, and no statutory distinction is made between them. In recognition of this, and for the sake of brevity, the term "executory contracts" is used from now on to include unexpired leases unless the context indicates otherwise.

§18.3 The Problem of Special Treatment of Selected Transactions

As mentioned earlier, there are several kinds of transactions that are dealt with specifically in §365. Sections 365(b)(3) and (h)(1)(C) deal only with leases of premises in shopping centers; §§365(c)(4) and (d)(5) through (9) apply only to leases of aircraft terminals or gates; §§365(d)(3) and (4) apply only to leases of nonresidential real property; §365(d)(10) applies only to leases of nonconsumer personal property (such as leases of equipment and other goods used for business); §§365(h)(2), (i), and (j) deal only with contracts under which the debtor is the seller of a timeshare interest; §365(n) deals solely with licenses of intellectual property; and §365(o) applies only to commitments by the debtor to a federal depository institution. Except to the extent indicated in the specific sections, the transactions singled out for special treatment are subject, not only to the particular rules set out in the pertinent subsection, but also the more general rules applicable to all contracts.

The special treatment of certain types of transaction is generally justified on the basis that they present particular or unique problems and issues. For example, nonresidential realty leases and equipment leases typically involve long-term obligations with substantial economic value. Because the estate's power to assume or reject them could have a significant impact, not only on the estate's prospect of rehabilitation, but also on the economic well-being of the nondebtor, special protection of the nondebtor party may be appropriate.

However, it must also be recognized that successful lobbying plays a role in the enactment of industry-specific rules, at a cost to the policy of evenhanded treatment.

In its 1997 report, the National Bankruptcy Review Commission identified two problems that these special provisions have caused. First, they make the section unmanageably complex, and second, they can result in interpretational difficulties when it comes to determining the treatment to be accorded to executory contracts that are not subject to special rules. The most common problem here is that in some cases a subsection governing a particular type of contract expresses a rule that is not unequivocally intended to be applicable only to the contract in question. This leaves doubt about whether Congress has merely expressed the general rule that would in any event arise by implication elsewhere in §365, or if the expression of the rule in the specific subsection is meant, by negative implication, to exclude that rule in subsections that are silent on the issue. Although the Commission stopped short of recommending the repeal of the transaction-specific rules, it did suggest that a rationalization and streamlining of §365 may make it less necessary to have them.

§18.4   The Estate's Right to Assume or Reject Executory Contracts

In making provision for executory contracts, the Code distinguishes bilateral contractual relationships from unilateral contract rights. If one party to a contract has fully or substantially performed, all that remains is the other party's claim for counter performance. Therefore, if the debtor had fully performed its contractual obligations by the time of bankruptcy, the outstanding performance due by the other party is simply a right of the debtor's which becomes property of the estate under §541. Conversely, if the other party has fully performed, the debtor's remaining obligation gives rise to a prepetition claim, to be proved in the estate and paid at whatever rate of distribution is due to claims of that class.

However, when material performance is due on both sides at the time of the petition, so that the contract qualifies as executory, the Code recognizes this not simply as a set of claims by and against the estate, but as a live relationship between the debtor and the other party. Section 365 gives the trustee the option of honoring this relationship or repudiating it. If the trustee elects to keep the relationship in existence, the estate assumes the contract, thereby adopting it so that it becomes the estate's contract. The estate is entitled to receive the other party's performance and is liable for the obligations undertaken by the debtor. The performance due by the estate qualifies as an administrative expense and is thus entitled to priority under §507(a)(1). *See* section 19.6.4.

The trustee's election to reject the contract constitutes a breach that is treated by §365(g)(1) as a prepetition breach by the debtor. The other party to the contract becomes a creditor (it is specifically included in the definition of "creditor" in §101(10)(B)), and its claim for damages for breach of contract is classed by §502(g) as a general unsecured prepetition claim. It is paid in the bankruptcy distribution at whatever fractional rate is due to such claims. Some claimants do even worse than this: §§502(b)(6) and (7) limit damage claims for the unexpired period of realty leases and employment contracts so that the rejection of these long-term contracts does not result in excessive claims against the general fund of the estate. Because the estate pays damages at the reduced rate payable to unsecured claims, the estate is able to commit a more profitable breach than the debtor would have been able to do outside of bankruptcy.

If the estate first assumes a contract and later rejects it, the rejection is the estate's breach and the other party's damages are treated as an administrative expense under §365(g)(2). These damages are measured at the time of rejection or, if a rehabilitation case was converted to Ch. 7 between assumption and rejection, at the time of conversion.

In deciding whether to assume or reject the contract, the trustee tries to serve the best interests of the estate. If the contract is advantageous and profitable or if, in a rehabilitation case, it advances the debtor's plans for economic recovery, the trustee should assume it. Conversely, if the contract is not on favorable terms, the estate could do better by using its resources elsewhere, or the contract imposes an unacceptable burden or risk on the estate, the trustee should reject it. It should be noted, however, that the trustee does not have absolute discretion to adopt an opportunistic approach to the contract. As indicated below, courts sometimes refuse to approve a rejection unless it is clear that performance would place an undue burden on the estate.

§18.5 The Procedure and Standards for Assumption or Rejection

Section 365(d)(1) requires the trustee in a Ch. 7 case to assume or reject the contract within 60 days of the order for relief or in such extended period as the court may for cause allow. If action is not taken by the end of that period, the contract is deemed to have been rejected. In cases under the other chapters, unless the contract is a nonresidential realty lease, the trustee may make the decision to assume or reject at any time up to confirmation of the plan. Upon application of the other party to the contract, the court can require the trustee to make an earlier decision.

In all cases, leases of nonresidential real property must be assumed or rejected within 60 days of the order for relief unless the court extends that period for cause. These leases are given special treatment under a group of provisions added to §365 by amendment in 1984. Commercial real estate leases can involve large, expensive premises, and the 1984 amendments were designed to require more speedy action by the trustee so that the lessor is not subjected to uncertainty for an extended period.

An affirmative decision to assume or reject must be approved by the court following a motion by the trustee on notice. However, if the contract is deemed rejected because of the trustee's failure to act within the prescribed period, the rejection is automatic and does not require court approval.

The most widely accepted standard for the court's approval of the trustee's decision to assume or reject is the *business judgment rule*. The court will not interfere with the trustee's decision if it was based on a good faith, reasonable business judgment that appears beneficial to the estate. *See* Example 2. When the trustee seeks to reject a contract, some courts have imposed a stricter test under which rejection will not be approved unless assumption of the contract would be unduly burdensome to the estate. The debtor's general obligation of good faith is relevant in this context, and may justify disapproval of rejection if the bankruptcy filing was primarily motivated by a desire to use the rejection power to escape an unwanted contract. *See* Example 4.

§18.6   Interim Performance

In many cases, performance may be suspended on both sides pending the trustee's decision to assume or reject. However, some contracts may involve continuing performance by the other party in the period before the decision is made and there is nothing in §365 that allows the nondebtor party to withhold performance pending the estate's decision to assume or reject the contract. For example, the estate may retain possession of leased property during this period. If the contract is ultimately rejected, the general rule is that the other party is entitled to compensation, payable as an administrative expense, for the reasonable value of any benefit received. Reasonable value may be less than the contract rate, and it is only payable to the extent that the estate was actually enriched. Therefore, for example, if the estate retained residential premises but did not use them, no compensation is payable.

Section 365(d)(3) makes an exception to this general rule for nonresidential realty leases: The estate is obliged to perform the debtor's lease obligations at the full contract rate during the period before rejection whether or not the estate derived any economic benefit from the premises. The Bankruptcy Reform Act of 1994 added §365(d)(10) which extends similar protection to lessors of nonconsumer personal property (that is, leases of goods such as equipment used for business purposes). While the basic concept is the same, the subsections differ in their detailed wording in two respects:

(1) §365(d)(3) obliges the estate to render full and timely contractual performance to the nonresidential realty lessor immediately from the time of

the order for relief, while §365(d)(10) requires that the estate performs obligations to a nonconsumer personal property lessor "first arising from or after 60 days from the order for relief." Although one cannot divine a clear meaning from this incoherent language, it seems that where a commercial personal property lease is concerned, the trustee is given 60 days' leeway before performance must begin. Section 365(d)(10) gives the court the discretion (after notice and a hearing) to issue an order changing this if the equities so dictate.

(2) While the protection given to a nonresidential real property lessor under §365(d)(3) applies in all forms of bankruptcy, §365(d)(10) protects the personal property lessor only in a Ch. 11 case.

§18.7   The Assumption of Contracts in Default

To assume a contract that is in default, the trustee must comply with §365(b)(1) by curing the default, compensating for any loss caused by it, and giving the party adequate assurance of future performance under the contract. The question of whether there has been a default is determined with reference to the contract terms and nonbankruptcy law.

Under §365(b)(2) two types of default need not be cured:

(1) If the default is simply the violation of an ipso facto clause (explained in section 18.11), the default really cannot be cured without the debtor dismissing the bankruptcy case and becoming solvent. It would, therefore, be an absurdity to demand such cure, and §365(b)(2) does not require it.

(2) If the default consists of the failure to pay a penalty rate or it consists of some nonmonetary default (for example, the debtor's failure to keep a business open during the hours specified in the contract), cure of that default is not needed for assumption.

Section 365(b)(3) goes to some length in expressing what is required for adequate assurance of performance in connection with leases of premises in shopping centers,[1] but it does not otherwise offer guidance on what assurances of cure, compensation, or future performance are adequate. It is left to the court to evaluate the trustee's proposals for rectifying the breach and assuring future performance. The concept of adequate assurance of future performance is taken from UCC §2.609, which entitles a party to a sales agreement to demand such assurances when there are grounds for insecurity about the other party's ability

---

1. See Example 3. According to the legislative history of §363(b)(3), shopping centers are singled out for special attention because the owners of these temples of commerce need assurance not only of future rental payment but of the planned tenant diversity so essential to the successful operation of shopping complexes. The maintenance of tenant mix also protects the interests of other retailers in the center by ensuring that the lessor is not precluded from honoring its commitment to them concerning the type of other businesses to be operated in the building.

to perform. Both under the UCC and in §365(b)(1)(c), assurance is provided by showing that resources are likely to be available for the discharge of the contractual obligations and performance appears to be commercially feasible. (There is some conceptual affinity between adequate assurance of performance and adequate protection, in that they both aim to reduce the risk to the other party of the estate's continuing commercial activity.)

§18.8   Nonassumable Contracts

Section 365(c) denotes three types of executory contracts that may not be assumed. The bar on assumption arises as a mater of law and does not depend on the existence or absence of a clause in the contract forbidding or restricting assignment.

§18.8.1   *Contracts That Are Not Assignable in Nonbankruptcy Law*

In the absence of consent by the other party, §365(c)(1) prevents the assumption of a contract if applicable law (that is, nonbankruptcy law) excuses the other party from accepting performance from or rendering performance to someone other than the debtor or the debtor in possession. Section 365(c)(1) therefore respects rights of nontransferability under nonbankruptcy law and enables the other party to resist assumption by the estate if transfer of the contract could have been prevented outside of bankruptcy. It is a general rule of contract law that contractual rights and duties can be transferred. (The transfer of rights is called *assignment,* and the transfer of duties, *delegation.*) However, the common law recognizes exceptions to this rule. For example, if the contract contemplates personal performance by a party, that party cannot delegate the duty to perform. Similarly, rights to performance cannot be assigned if this would reduce the other party's expectation of proper counter-performance. In addition to rules of contract law, other policies may motivate statutory prohibition on the transfer of certain contractual rights and duties. For example, contracts with the government can usually not be transferred by the other party.

The reference in the section to laws that excuse the nondebtor party from accepting performance from or rendering it to an "entity other than the debtor or debtor in possession" (with no mention of the trustee), raises the question of whether the estate's assumption rights are different depending on whether it is represented by a debtor in possession or a trustee. Some cases have held that they are not. If nonbankruptcy law bars the assignment of the contract to a hypothetical third party, it cannot be assumed by the estate, whether administered by a trustee or a debtor in possession. The reasoning of these courts is that the debtor in possession is a different legal entity from the debtor. This approach is called the "hypothetical test" because it focuses not on whether the party to perform the contract (that is, the debtor in possession) is functionally the same as the debtor, but asks instead whether a hypothetical third party would be allowed to take over the contract. For cases that adopt this approach, see *In re West Electronics, Inc.,* 852 F.2d 79 (3d Cir. 1988); *In re Catapult Entertainment, Inc.,* 165 F.3d 747 (9th Cir. 1999). Other cases have disagreed. For example, in *In re G.P. Express Airlines, Inc.,* 200 B.R. 222 (Bankr. D. Neb. 1996), the court reasoned that although the debtor in possession is a legal entity distinct from the debtor for all other purposes, it is functionally the same entity as the debtor where the performance of the contract is concerned. Therefore, if the debtor in possession will perform the contract itself, and does not intend to assign it, it is artificial to refuse assumption merely because the contract could not be assigned to a hypothetical third party. See also *Institute Pasteur v. Cambridge Biotech Corp.,* 104 F.3d 489 (1st Cir. 1997).

§18.8.2 Loan and Financing Transactions

Section 365(c)(2) forbids the trustee from assuming a contract to make a loan, to extend other debt financing or financial accommodations to the debtor, or to issue a security of the debtor. Limited in its scope, it does not cover all credit transactions but is confined to loan and financing contracts. Therefore, for example, it does not include many types of transactions in which the debtor is given credit, such as leases or credit sales of goods or services. Courts construe §365(c)(2) strictly and refuse to extend it to contracts whose primary purpose is not the provision of a loan or financing. For example, in *In re Thomas B. Hamilton Co. Inc.,* 969 F.2d 1013 (11th Cir. 1992), the debtor in possession, a merchant, wished to assume a contract under which a bank purchased credit card sales drafts generated by the debtor's sales to its customers. The bank argued that the contract was nonassumable because it extended financial accommodations to the debtor — the bank credited the purchase price of the drafts to the debtor subject to a charge-back if a customer disputed the charge. The court held that §365(c)(2) did not apply because, although some extension of credit was involved in the relationship, its primary purpose was to enable the debtor to enter into credit card sales to its customers. Hence, the contract was held to be assumable. The court reached the same conclusion in *In re VAL Corp.,* 293 B.R. 183 (Bankr. N.D. Ill. 2003), in relation to a credit card processing agreement between the debtor (United Airlines) and a bank. The court noted that the general approach to §362(c)(2) is to interpret it narrowly so as to confine it to the narrow range of transactions that it identifies.

It may seem at first glance that §362(c)(2) is merely a more specific application of the general ground for nonassumption in §362(c)(1). After all, in most financing contracts, the identity and creditworthiness of the debtor are material elements that could excuse the nondebtor party from accepting transfer of the contract under §365(c)(1). However, §365(c)(2) is a stricter provision than §365(c)(1): While nonassumable contracts may be assumed under §365(c)(1) with the consent of the other party, §365(c)(2) makes no exception for assumption by consent. In *In re Sun Runner Marine, Inc.*, 945 F.2d 1089 (9th Cir. 1991), the court held that the lender's consent cannot override the prohibition on assumption in §365(c)(2) because its purpose is to protect the interests of all creditors in the estate. Such an assumption is tantamount to postpetition credit under §364 and must be subjected to the protective procedures of that section. (*See* Example 2.)

§18.8.3   *Terminated Leases of Nonresidential Real Property*

Under §365(c)(3), the estate may not assume a lease of nonresidential real property that had been terminated under nonbankruptcy law prior to the order for relief. (*See* Example 3.) This subsection was added in 1984 as part of the group of provisions (mentioned earlier) that were designed to protect the rights of lessors of nonresidential realty. It seems unnecessary, because any lease or contract that had been validly terminated prior to the order for relief is no longer executory and should not be assumable. In fact, §365(c)(3) is mischievous: By expressing the rule only in regard to nonresidential realty leases, it could give rise to the inference that other contracts are assumable despite valid prepetition termination.

§18.9   Bankruptcy Termination or Ipso Facto Clauses

A provision in a contract that allows the nondebtor to declare default or to terminate the contract on the grounds of the insolvency, financial condition, or bankruptcy of the debtor (a *bankruptcy termination* or *ipso facto clause*) is ineffective in bankruptcy. The disregard of such clauses and provisions of nonbankruptcy law has already been discussed in connection with property of the estate (section 12.2.1), the avoidance of statutory liens (section 15.2), and the trustee's power to deal with estate property (section 17.2.4). These provisions reflect the general policy of preventing states or private parties from undermining the bankruptcy process through laws or contractual terms that are designed to take effect on bankruptcy.

Section 365 refers to ipso facto provisions four times: §365(b)(2) does not require cure of a breach of an ipso facto clause in a contract: §365(c)(1) makes such contract terms ineffective in deciding whether contract rights are transferable under nonbankruptcy law; §365(e)(1) prevents termination or modification of an executory contract after the petition on grounds of an ipso facto clause in the contract or in nonbankruptcy law; §365(f)(3) prevents termination or modification under such a clause or provision of nonbankruptcy law when the trustee assigns an executory contract after assuming it. Note that §§365(b)(2) and 365(c)(1) apply only to contractual clauses, while §§365(e)(1) and 365(f)(3) cover provisions of nonbankruptcy law as well.[2] The bar on enforcing ipso facto termination rights comes into effect once the petition has been filed. If the other party validly exercised the termination right prior to bankruptcy, based on the debtor's insolvency or financial condition at that time, the termination is effective to end the contract so that it is no longer executory when the bankruptcy case is commenced.

§18.10 Postpetition Termination by the Other Party on Grounds Other Than an Ipso Facto Clause

A contract may provide grounds for termination other than the bankruptcy or financial condition of the debtor. If valid in nonbankruptcy law, termination rights not based on an ipso facto clause are effective against the estate.[3] Also, some contracts (*e.g.,* leases) create obligations that continue until the expiry of a set term. If the contract can be validly terminated after the commencement of the case, the other party has the right to take the necessary steps to bring it to an end. However, because the debtor's contract rights are property of the estate, the other party must, in most cases, apply for relief from stay before exercising termination rights. *See In re Carroll,* 903 F.2d 1266 (9th Cir. 1990). There is a narrow exception to this rule: When the term of a nonresidential realty lease ends before bankruptcy or afterwards, the lease ceases to be property of the estate under §541(b)(2), and the lessor's postpetition action to retake possession of the premises is excepted from the automatic stay by §362(b)(10). The exclusion from property of the estate and the stay apply only where term of the lease has expired. If termination is based on other grounds, the lease is subject to the same rules as other contracts.

---

2. At first glance, §§365(e)(1) and (f)(3) may seem to conflict with §365(c)(1), which generally upholds rules of nonbankruptcy law that preclude the transfer of contractual rights and obligations. However, the rules of nonassignability upheld in §365(c)(1) are general rules of law, while the ipso facto provisions in §§365(e)(1) and (f)(3) are geared to take effect only on bankruptcy. *See also* section 18.13.

3. Remember, however, that §365(b) permits the estate to cure defaults, so termination on grounds of default is subject to the estate's right to cure.

§18.11   Problems of Rejection in Partially Executed Contracts

If a contract is entirely executory, rejection is a clean break: Contractual rights and obligations terminate on both sides, save for the nondebtor party's unsecured prepetition claim for damages. However, the nondebtor party may have begun performance prior to the debtor's bankruptcy and may be fairly regarded as having earned rights under the contract by the time of the petition. Are these earned or vested rights terminated upon rejection, or does rejection cancel only rights to future performance?

In a few select situations, §365 protects vested contractual rights and confines the effect of rejection to the estate's prospective performance. If the debtor is the lessor of real property, §365(h) allows the lessee to elect either to treat the rejection as a termination of the lease or to remain in possession of the property until the end of the lease term. If the lessee chooses to continue in occupation, the lessee retains all its rights under the lease, such as those relating to the due dates for rent and other payments, the right to occupy and use the premises, and to sublet them. This is now expressly stated by §365(h)(1)(A)(ii), which was added by the Bankruptcy Reform Act of 1994 to make it clear that the lessee retains full rights and not (as some cases had held) merely the right to possession. However, even though all the lessee's rights remain intact, this does not mean that the estate is compelled to render services called for by the lease. It is relieved from performing any of its future obligations as lessor such as the provision of services and the maintenance of the premises. The lessee's obligation to pay rent continues, but it may offset against the rent any damages suffered as a result of the nonperformance of the lessor's duties. Similar protection is made available by §365(i) to a possessory vendee who purchased real property from the debtor under an installment sale. (*See* Example 1.) Under §§365(h)(2) and (i), a timeshare purchaser is given the same rights as a lessee or vendee depending on whether the purchaser has completed its purchase, or has merely taken possession of the interest under a contract in which the purchase has not been completed. When the debtor is the licensor of a right to intellectual property, §365(n) allows the licensee to elect to treat the rejected contract as terminated, or to retain its existing rights for the contract term, subject to qualifications that are not explored here. In each one of these situations, rejection terminates the estate's burden of continuing performance under the contract but treats fundamental contract rights as having vested in the other party, so that they are not lost upon rejection unless that party chooses to treat the relationship as at an end.

The fact that Congress has provided specifically for these transactions creates uncertainty with regard to all other contracts in which substantial rights have been earned by the nondebtor party prior to the petition.

Application of the *expressio unius* rule of statutory construction suggests that rejection of other contracts terminates all rights under them, leaving the other party with nothing but an unsecured prepetition claim for damages. However, a better approach seems to be for the court to interpret the contract to ascertain whether it is severable into executed and executory portions. If so, rejection can be confined to the executory portion of the contract, leaving vested rights in effect. This seems to have been the approach in *Leasing Services Corp. v. First Tennessee Bank*, 826 F.2d 434 (6th Cir. 1987). That case was distinguished and not followed in *In re Register*, 95 B.R. 73 (Bankr. M.D. Tenn. 1989).

§18.12 Rejection of Collective Bargaining Agreements in Ch. 11 Cases

A collective bargaining agreement is an executory contract, and it can therefore be assumed or rejected under §365. However, a strong national policy favors protecting workers from unfair labor practices and enforcing collective bargaining agreements. This policy must be balanced against the bankruptcy policy of allowing the estate to reject burdensome contracts in its attempt at rehabilitation.

In 1984, the Supreme Court dealt with the rejection of collective bargaining agreements in *N.R.L.B. v. Bildisco*, 465 U.S. 513 (1984). It upheld the trustee's power to reject these agreements, and enunciated a test for approving rejection that differs from the business judgment test and the burdensome test (outlined in section 18.5). Under this test, the rejection may only be approved if the trustee shows that the collective bargaining agreement burdens the estate and the court is satisfied, after weighing all the circumstances, that the equities favor rejection. The Court also held that the trustee could unilaterally reject or modify the agreement with immediate effect, before obtaining the court's approval.

Congress enacted §1113 in 1984 in reaction to *Bildisco*. It continues to permit a Ch. 11 debtor to reject or assume a collective bargaining agreement, but it provides a procedure for negotiation that must precede a rejection and imposes an obligation on the debtor and the union representatives to attempt to agree to a modification before the debtor applies to court for rejection. Section 1113 codifies the *Bildisco* requirement that the court should not approve rejection unless the balance of the equities favors it. *In re American Provision Co.*, 44 B.R. 907 (Bankr. D. Minn. 1984), and *In re Mile Hi Metal Systems, Inc.*, 899 F.2d 887 (10th Cir. 1990), explain the process to be followed under §1113.

§18.13 Assignment

Up to this point, the discussion has been based on the premise that the estate will perform the contract after assumption. However, the trustee may be unwilling or unable to take on the burden of performance even though the contract is advantageous. In this situation, it may be in the best interests of the estate for the trustee to assume the contract and then to sell it to someone else. The buyer of the contract takes an assignment of it (including both the assignment of the debtor's rights and a delegation of its duties) and the estate is able to realize the value of the debtor's contractual rights without incurring the obligation to perform.

If the contract is of a kind that would have been assignable by the debtor outside of bankruptcy, there is no reason why the trustee, as successor to the debtor, should not enjoy the same right. Section 365(f) embodies this principle by permitting the trustee to assign an assumed contract, on condition that the assignee provides adequate assurance of future performance. The trustee must assume the contract first, which means that all the limitations on and qualifications for assumption apply as discussed above. The further requirement that the assignee furnishes adequate assurance of future performance is intended to protect the other party from being forced into a contractural relationship with someone who is financially unstable or otherwise unlikely to provide a performance that conforms to the contract. This is important, because the other party has no recourse against the estate if the assignee breaches. Upon assignment, §365(k) relieves the estate of all liability for postassignment breaches.

As stated in section 18.8, §365(c)(1) prohibits assumption (and consequent assignment) of a contract by the trustee if, irrespective of the contract terms, applicable law excuses the nondebtor party from accepting performance from or rendering it to a person other than the debtor. Section 365(f)(1) is expressly made subject to §365(c), yet it appears to contradict §365(c) by making a contract assignable notwithstanding a provision in the contract or in applicable law that prohibits assignment. Clearly, both subsections override contractual antiassignment clauses, but §365(c) appears to uphold antiassignment rules of nonbankruptcy law while §365(f) appears to render them ineffective.

Courts have had trouble reconciling these provisions. Although there are a number of cases that offer somewhat differing approaches to the question of how they are to be read consistently, courts do in fact succeed in accommodating the conflicting language of the two sections. In broad terms, without attempting to account for the more subtle distinctions between the cases, one can say that the difference between the sections lies in the distinction between the general and the particular. Section 365(f) invalidates contractual antiassignment clauses, and also overrides nonbankruptcy laws that generally uphold antiassignment clauses in contracts, or generally prohibit the assignment of contract rights. By contrast, section 365(c) gives effect to nonbankruptcy law that makes certain specific types of contract unassignable, whether or not the contract contains an antiassignment clause. Therefore, in short, although §365(f) generally renders ineffective antiassignment clauses and nonbankruptcy laws that preclude assignment, this disregard of non-bankruptcy law is not absolute. It is qualified by §365(c) when the rule of nonbankruptcy law is designed to protect the legitimate expectations of the nondebtor party in circumstances where the transfer of a particular type of contract would damage those expectations. If you would like to read the discussion of this issue in some of the cases, *see,* for example, *In re Pioneer Ford Sales, Inc.,* 729 F.2d 27 (1st Cir. 1984); *In re Magness,* 972 F.2d 689 (6th Cir. 1992); *In re Claremont Acquisition Corp.,* 186 B.R. 977 (C.D. Cal. 1995); *In re CLFC, Inc.,* 89 F.3d 673 (9th Cir. 1996). *See also* Example 5.

EXAMPLES

1. Range on the Home

Alice N. Vendorland sold a house to Wendy Vendee under a land sale contract. In terms of the contract, Wendy is obliged to pay the price of the land in installments over several years. Wendy occupied the property immediately after execution of the contract. Alice has no duty under the contract to maintain the property or perform other services. Her only outstanding obligation is to transfer title to the property when all payments have been made.

Alice has become bankrupt. The contract still has a few years to run before Wendy is due to complete her payments. The property has appreciated since the sale, and Alice's trustee wishes to reject the contract so that the property can be recovered by the estate and resold at a higher price.

(a) Is this contract executory?

(b) If so, can the trustee reacquire the property by rejecting the contract?

2. The House That Jack Billed

Jack Pott owned some land on which he decided to build a house. He entered into a construction financing contract with Fairweather Funding, Inc., under which Fairweather agreed to lend him funds to pay for the building. The contract provided for advances to be made in the form of direct payments to the contractor as work progressed. Fairweather recorded a mortgage on the property at the time of the contract to secure the advances to be made. Jack then contracted with Housebound, Inc. for construction of the house.

After the house had been half built and Fairweather had advanced about half of the loan, Jack filed a Ch. 11 petition. Property values have appreciated, and if the house is completed, the property can be sold for a good profit. Jack, as debtor in possession, would like to assume the contracts so that he can finish the house. May he do so?

3.   A Shopping Maul

Jack Pott, whose Ch. 11 case was referred to in Example 2, operates a business as a tinker. He occupies leased premises in a small building on the town's commercial strip. The building consists of three retail units. The other two are occupied by a tailor and candlestick maker.

In the months before Jack's petition, he had fallen into arrears in his rental payments. The lessor served a notice of termination on him a few days before the bankruptcy petition was filed. Notwithstanding, he remains in occupation of the premises and hopes to stay there until the lease term expires in several years' time. As part of his reorganization, he hopes to diversify his business to improve its profitability. In addition to mending pots, he plans to sell new ovenware and kitchen equipment.

Jack has just received a notice of eviction from the lessor, informing him that if he has not vacated the premises by midnight, he will be forcibly ejected. Can Jack resist the eviction and keep the premises?

4.   Good Try, Sweet Prince

Martin A. Idle is an actor. He recently contracted with a public broadcasting station to perform the role of Hamlet in a television production of that play. Shortly before filming was to begin, Martin received an irresistible offer to play the principal heartthrob in a prime-time soap opera, which would give him national exposure, fame, and fortune. He cannot work on both productions at the same time.

Martin filed a Ch. 11 petition and, as debtor in possession, he immediately rejected the contract with the public broadcasting station so that he can accept the offer of the other contract. Can he do this?

5.   A False Assumption

Sandy Trapp is a member of a country club. To avoid congestion on its golf course, the club distinguishes general membership from golf membership and restricts golf privileges to a strictly limited number of people. Golf membership has been fully subscribed for decades, and new admissions can only occur when existing members leave. As a result, golf privileges are prized, and people who desire them have to wait for years. To ensure an equitable and orderly succession to vacancies, the club maintains a waiting list and fills openings in golf membership in order of seniority.

Sandy holds a coveted golf membership. He has filed a Ch. 7 petition. His trustee has discovered that several people who are not near the top of the list are eager to buy Sandy's membership and are willing to bid against each other for it. The trustee realizes that the sale of the membership will bring substantial funds into the estate. The trustee seeks to assume Sandy's golf membership and to sell (assign) it to the highest bidder. The country club objects.

May the trustee assume and assign Sandy's golf membership?

EXPLANATIONS

1. **(a)** The standard traditional test for deciding whether a contract is executory is that there are material unperformed obligations on both sides. In this contract, Wendy still has to pay the balance of the purchase price and probably has other obligations as well concerning the maintenance and protection of the property. Her outstanding performance is surely material. Alice's only remaining obligation is to transfer title to the property when payment is complete. Although some courts have held this to be a material unperformed obligation, others (*e.g., In re Streets & Beard Farm Partnership,* 882 F.2d 233 (7th Cir. 1989)) have said that the transfer of title is a legal formality that is not significant enough to make the contract executory. This difference of opinion shows that the materiality of an outstanding performance is a matter of contract interpretation on which courts can differ.

Because a focus on nothing more than the materiality of the outstanding obligations can be very rigid, some courts have moved away from the traditional test in favor of a more flexible "functional approach." This continues to take the materiality of outstanding obligations into account, but treats this as a guideline rather than a firm test, and also examines the nature of the contract and the impact on the estate of classifying it as executed or executory.

It has been argued that a land sale contract should not be treated as an executory contract at all because it is analogous to a credit sale of the property secured by a mortgage and should therefore be regarded simply as a secured claim by or against the estate and not be dealt with under §365. Some courts have accepted this argument, and others have not. In *In re Terrell,* 892 F.2d 469 (6th Cir. 1989), the court, while conceding the merit of the analogy, pointed out that the transactions are legally quite distinct and should not be treated alike in the absence of Code authority. Whatever approach is taken, if the contract is executory, it must be dealt with under §365. If not, the contract rights are property of the estate.

(b) If the contract is executory, it falls within the special rule in §365(i) for the protection of a possessory purchaser of real property. Even if the trustee rejects the contract, Wendy is entitled to remain in possession of it and to complete her purchase under the terms of the contract. Therefore, in the present case the characterization of the contract as executory does not enable the trustee to reacquire the property. (If the contract was not covered by §365(i), the question raised in section 18.11 would have arisen: Could the estate terminate all Wendy's contract rights by rejection, thereby reacquiring the property for resale at a better price and leaving Wendy with a claim for damages to be paid at the rate payable to unsecured prepetition creditors? To avoid the harshness of such a result, the court might sever the contract into executed and executory portions, so as to give rejection prospective effect only. In other words, the court could reach the same result as that prescribed expressly by §365(i).)

2. Both contracts are unquestionably executory. The estate cannot assume the financing contract; it clearly falls within the exception to assumption in §365(c)(2). As the contract cannot be assumed, Fairweather cannot be compelled to provide further funds. The advances already made are a secured prepetition claim against the estate. Section 365(c)(2) does not authorize assumption, even with the consent of Fairweather. However, if the property has in fact appreciated so that Fairweather is assured of the full benefit of its bargain, Jack may be able to persuade it to provide the remaining funds under a new credit agreement negotiated and approved in terms of §364.

The construction contract is assumable, but if the estate cannot obtain the needed financing it may not be able to perform its obligations to Housebound. There apparently has not been a default in the contract, so Housebound is not entitled to adequate assurance of performance under §365(b). However, to obtain court approval of the assumption on the business judgment standard, Jack must how that the estate has the means to perform its obligations under the contract and that assumption is likely to benefit the estate. Ultimate benefit to the estate can be established by evidence of appreciating value, but unless the construction financing is still available, Jack may not be able to demonstrate a source of funding for progress payments under the contract. (In assuming the contract, the estate cannot modify its terms, so Jack cannot force Housebound to defer payment until the property is sold.)

3. Even if the lessor has grounds for resisting assumption of the lease and evicting Jack, the notice of eviction and threat of forcible dispossession is a violation of the automatic stay. Before trying to enforce any rights that it may have, the lessor must apply to court for relief from stay. (The exception to the stay under §362(b)(10) does not apply. It only covers termination by expiry of the lease term.)

If the lease was validly terminated prior to the order for relief, it cannot be assumed. Because this is a lease of nonresidential real property, §365(c)(3) expressly so provides. The facts merely state that the lessor served a notice of termination on Jack before the bankruptcy petition was filed. It is not clear if this constituted a complete and valid act of termination. This question must be resolved with reference to the terms of the lease and applicable nonbankruptcy law. State law may require court proceedings to complete the termination, or it may give the lessee a cure period or require other procedures and safeguards for termination. *See In re Windmill Farms, Inc.,* 841 F.2d 1467 (9th Cir. 1988), in which the state antiforfeiture statute was held to be available to trustee.

If the lessor had validly completed termination procedures by the time of the petition, the lease cannot be assumed and the lessor may recover the premises following relief from stay. If not, the lease may be assumed. Although this is a Ch. 11 case, the period for assumption for a nonresidential realty lease is 60 days. §365(d)(4). Pending assumption, the estate must continue to perform the debtor's obligations under the lease in terms of §365(d)(3). Under §365(b), the default in the lease must be cured by payment of the outstanding arrears, compensation must be paid for any financial loss suffered by the lessor, and adequate assurance of future performance must be given. Adequate assurance generally requires a showing by the estate that it has a reasonable prospect of rendering its performance under the contract. When a shopping center lease is involved, adequate assurance is defined more specifically in §365(b)(3) to include not only a showing that the estate has a reasonable prospect of making rental payments but also that all conditions of tenancy (including such terms as use or exclusivity provisions) will be honored and that the assumption will not disrupt any tenant mix in the center. Jack's proposed change in retail operations would have to be tested against these standards.

It is not clear if the building qualifies as a shopping center. The term "shopping center" is not defined in the Code, but the legislative history of §365 and the case law indicate that a shopping center is more than just a building that houses a group of retail tenants. It has attributes such as a planned tenant mix to ensure that stores complement rather than compete with each other; common areas and common services such as parking lots and mall areas; regulations governing business hours; and lease terms that contain restrictions and guarantees reflecting this sense of community. *See In re Joshua Slocum Ltd.,* 922 F.2d 1081 (3d Cir. 1990). Although the facts are not detailed enough for a conclusion, it is possible that this three-unit building on a commercial strip does not satisfy the test for a shopping center.

4. Martin, in his capacity as debtor in possession, is using §365 to reject the *Hamlet* contract so that he can accept the offer, in his personal capacity, to star in the soap opera. The issue is whether Martin can use §365 to relieve himself of the unwanted contract so that he can enrich his "fresh start" estate by taking advantage of an opportunity for untold post-bankruptcy riches.

This Example is based on *In re Carrere,* 64 B.R. 156 (Bankr. C.D. Cal. 1986), in which a soap opera star filed a Ch. 11 petition for the purpose of rejecting an existing contract to appear in one such thespian delight so that she could take the opportunity of participating in a better one. The court refused to approve the rejection. It reasoned that in a Ch. 11 or 7 case, post-petition earnings are excluded from the estate under §541(a)(6). This, combined with the rule of §365(c)(1) that personal service contracts are nonassumable, deprives the trustee or debtor in possession of standing to reject a contract for personal services of the debtor. The purpose of §365 is to benefit the estate, not to help the debtor increase future income. (The court noted that this analysis would not work very well in a Ch. 13 case because postpetition earnings are part of the estate, but suggested that the equities would favor the same result under Ch. 13.)

A contrary approach was taken in *In re Taylor*, 913 F.2d 102 (3d Cir. 1990). That case also involved an entertainer (a musician) who sought to reject a recording contract in his Ch. 11 case. The court said that even though a personal services contract cannot be assumed by the estate, and earnings from postpetition personal services are not property of the estate, it is a nonsequitur to say that the estate cannot reject the contract: There is no restriction in §365 on the rejection of personal service contracts, and no requirement that a contract be property of the estate in order for it to be rejected. The court addressed the *Carrere* opinion and distinguished it on the basis that the debtor in that case has filed the petition for the purpose of evading the contract, rather than to take advantage of the rehabilitation goals of Ch. 11. By contrast, the debtor in *Taylor* was in need of relief from financial adversity.

A similar resolution was reached in *All Blacks B.V. v. Gruntruck*, 199 B.R. 970 (W.D. Wash. 1996), in which the court found that as the petition was filed in good faith, the question of whether it was property of the estate was not relevant to the trustee's decision to reject it. *In re Brown*, 211 B.R. 183 (Bankr. E.D. Pa. 1997) went even further, applying nothing more than the business judgment test to decide if rejection was proper.

When the bankruptcy filing has not been abusive, the decision in the latter three cases furthers the fresh start policy of bankruptcy law, and the more technical view taken by *Carrere* seems to make a rather artificial distinction between the benefit to the Ch. 11 estate and the debtor's postpetition estate. However, when the filing is a manipulation of bankruptcy law to achieve an ulterior purpose, the court is justified on grounds of bad faith and as a matter of equity to disapprove the rejection. That's show biz!

5. This question is a simplified version of the facts in *In re Magness*, 972 F.2d 689 (6th Cir. 1992), cited in section 18.13. In that case, the court characterized the debtor's golf membership as an executory contract in which both parties had material outstanding obligations: the debtor's payment of dues and the club's provision of golfing facilities. The court's central focus was the reconciliation of §362(c)(1), which upholds rules of nonbankruptcy law excusing the nondebtor party from accepting the assignment and assumption of a contract, and §362(f)(1) which overrides antiassignment provisions in contracts and nonbankruptcy law. The court held that while §362(f) sets out the general rule disregarding barriers to assignment in bankruptcy, §362(c) recognizes an exception to this rule where the assignment of the contract in question would have an adverse impact on the rights of the nondebtor party, and nonbankruptcy law protects those rights by permitting the nondebtor party to refuse assignment.

The court found that assignment of the golf membership would adversely affect the club's maintenance of an orderly method of filling golf vacancies, and would force it into a breach of its obligations to members on the waiting list. State law upholds reasonable rules developed by voluntary associations and hence would excuse the club from accepting the assignment of a golf club membership. Therefore, the court concluded, §362(c)(1) precludes the trustee's assumption and assignment of the debtor's golf membership without the club's consent.

19

Claims against the Estate

§19.1 Introduction

The subject of creditor claims and their ranking has arisen frequently in earlier chapters. This chapter focuses more systematically on the rules and principles governing the assertion of claims against the estate and the distribution of estate funds or property to creditors. It begins with an explanation of the different types of claim that may be proved against the estate. It then surveys the process of claim submission and allowance, and examines the ranking of claims.

§19.2 What Is a Claim?

§19.2.1 The Definition of "Claim"

Section 101(5) defines *claim* very broadly to include any secured or unsecured right to payment arising in law or equity. The claim need not be fixed, settled, and due at the time of the petition, but it may be unliquidated, contingent, unmatured, or disputed. To qualify as a claim, the obligation must give rise to a right to payment. A non-monetary right (such as an injunction that merely mandates or restrains some conduct of the debtor without any alternative for a monetary remedy) is not a claim. Of course, many injunctions and other judicial and administrative orders do provide for a payment alternative because they might permit recourse to compensation if the debtor fails to obey the order.

The question of whether an obligation of the debtor represents a right to payment, thereby qualifying as a claim, has important consequences. If the obligation is not a claim, the obligee has no right to participate in the bankruptcy distribution, and the obligation is not discharged in bankruptcy. The significance of determining whether an obligation is a claim is illustrated by Examples 2 and 3 and is discussed further in the context of the discharge in section 22.2.

§19.2.2 Unliquidated, Contingent, Unmatured, and Disputed Claims

Section 101(5) expressly includes unliquidated, contingent, unmatured, and disputed claims. A claim is *unliquidated* if its amount is not fixed and certain and cannot be calculated arithmetically from known data. For example, a tort claim arises upon commission of the tort, but is unliquidated until determined by adjudication or settlement. A claim is *contingent* if the debtor's liability is conditional upon the happening of a future uncertain event. The possibility of this contingency occurring is in the actual or presumed contemplation of the parties when their relationship is created. For example, when a surety guarantees the debt of the principal debtor, the surety's debt comes into existence upon execution of the suretyship, but liability on the debt only arises if the principal debtor defaults. (*See also* Examples 2 and 3.) A claim is *unmatured* until the time for payment comes about. For example, when goods are purchased on 30-days' credit, the debt is created on delivery of the goods, but it only matures at the end of the 30-day credit period. (Because the passage of 30 days is not an uncertain event, the debt cannot be considered contingent.) A claim is *disputed* if the debtor challenges the existence or extent of liability. The fact that a debt is disputed does not, in itself, make the debt unliquidated or contingent if the underlying debt itself is of fixed amount and unconditional.

A debt that is subject to one or more of these barriers to enforcement at the time of the petition is nevertheless a claim against the estate. During the course of the case, the issue or issues affecting enforcement will be resolved by negotiation or litigation: Disputes will be settled or adjudicated, and a value will be placed on unliquidated or contingent claims, as discussed in section 19.3. Bankruptcy inevitably alters contractual due dates for unmatured debts. Some may be accelerated, especially in liquidation cases, while others may be extended in terms of a plan of rehabilitation.

§19.2.3 Prepetition and Postpetition Debts

Although the claim may not yet be enforceable at the time of the petition, it must, in most cases, have come into existence before bankruptcy. As a general rule, only prepetition debts of the debtor are claims against the estate. Debts incurred by the debtor after the petition are charges against the debtor's fresh start estate. However, some postpetition debts *are* treated as claims against the estate. The most important category of postpetition claims are those arising from the administration of the estate or the conduct of its business. Some examples of such claims are mentioned in section 19.6.4, and were also encountered in sections 17.3.2 (claims for postpetition credit under §364) and 18.4 (claims for performance due by the estate under an executory contract assumed under §365). Claims for administrative expenses are given priority, as discussed in section 19.6.4, provided that they were incurred with proper authority. The other classes of postpetition claims against the estate are not really postpetition claims in the full sense. Although they arise after the petition, they are in fact linked to a prepetition transaction. For example, the rejection of an executory contract occurs after the petition, but it gives rise to a claim deemed by §365(g)(1) to have arisen prepetition. Similarly, a claim created by the avoidance of a transfer is deemed to be a prepetition claim by §502(h).

There are two situations, applicable only in Ch. 13 cases, where the debtor's personal postpetition debts may be included as claims against the estate. In the first, §1305(a)(1) permits governmental units to prove claims in the estate for postpetition taxes owing by the debtor.

In the second situation, §1305(a)(2) enables a proof of claim to be filed in the estate by a person who has extended credit to the debtor in a postpetition consumer transaction for the debtor's purchase of "property or services necessary for the debtor's performance under the plan." The property or services must be essentials such as medical treatment or the repair of vital property, and they must relate to the debtor's personal or domestic affairs, not to business activity. The creditor does not have to prove this postpetition claim against the estate. It has the option of treating the debt as a nondischargeable claim against the debtor's fresh start estate and collecting it from the debtor personally. However, the claim may be hard to collect. The debtor may have little cash to spare after making payments to the trustee under the plan, and the creditor cannot enforce the debt against estate property until the close of the case, by virtue of the stay under §362(a)(3). Therefore, the creditor may elect to prove the claim in the estate to ensure payment under the plan. The drawback to the creditor is that if the debtor obtained prior approval of the transaction from the trustee, or such approval was impractical, any balance of the debt unpaid in the Ch. 13 distribution is discharged by §1328(d). The creditor is barred from proving a claim in the estate if the creditor knew or should have known that the debtor could have obtained the trustee's advance approval and failed to do so.

§19.2.4   Claims against the Debtor's Property

When one thinks of prepetition claims against the estate, one usually assumes these are debts on which the debtor was personally liable at the time of bankruptcy. In most cases this assumption is correct, but §102(2) extends "claim" to cover not only the debtor's personal obligations but also claims against the debtor's property. It is possible that a right to payment constitutes a charge on property of the debtor even though the debtor has no personal liability on it. This may happen, for example, when a secured party holds a nonrecourse security interest in the debtor's property. (That is, the secured party's claim is limited to the collateral, and the debtor is not responsible for any deficiency.) It could also occur with some statutory liens, such as mechanic's liens, which attach to real property even though the work was ordered by the prime contractor rather than the owner. Because the lienholder and owner have no contractual relationship, the owner has no personal debt to the lienholder. However, if the claim is not paid, the lienholder is entitled to foreclose on the property to recover payment.[1] Section 102(2) makes it clear that such claims against the debtor's property are to be treated as claims in bankruptcy.

§19.3   The Estimation of Contingent and Unliquidated Claims

In the normal course of events outside of bankruptcy, liability on an unliquidated or contingent claim is settled with the passage of time. An unliquidated debt will be made certain by negotiation or litigation, and a contingent debt will either become due or fall away, depending upon whether or not the future contingency occurs. In bankruptcy it is not always possible to allow the resolution of contingent or unliquidated liability to take its normal course, because the process of resolution may hold up the bankruptcy case. Therefore, §502(c) requires contingent or unliquidated claims to be estimated where necessary to prevent undue delay in the administration of the estate.

In some situations, the estimation can be provisional — for example, when an immediate determination of the claim is needed to fix the claimant's voting rights in a Ch. 11 case, but final resolution of the claim by normal means is likely to occur as the bankruptcy case proceeds. In other situations, when the prospect of timely resolution is poor, estimation may have to be a final determination that fixes the claimant's distribution from the estate.

If estimation is required, §502(c) leaves it to the court to decide on the most efficient and reliable means of making the estimation. This may involve a truncated trial, arbitration, a summary evaluation by the court, or authorization of appraisal or negotiation. The goal is to make as accurate an estimate

---

1. For a further example of a situation in which a claim exists against property of the estate without corresponding personal liability of the debtor, see Example 4 of Chapter 20. That question deals with the treatment of a mortgage in a Ch. 13 case after the underlying debt has been discharged in an earlier Ch. 7 case.

as possible while keeping delay to a minimum. To liquidate an unliquidated claim, the court evaluates testimony on the debt or loss. The fixing of a contingent claim can be more awkward, because a contingent claim by its nature depends on the occurrence of an uncertain future event. Even if the amount of the contingent claim is certain (*i.e.*, it is liquidated), the ultimate liability could be for the full debt or nothing, depending upon whether or not the event occurs. The court has to decide on the probability of the event occurring and must try to value the contingent claimant's chance of having a realized claim against the estate. If the contingent claim is also unliquidated, the uncertainty is greater still, and the court must resolve both the probability of actualization and the extent of the debt. (Example 2 raises some of the difficult issues concerning contingent claims.)

§19.4   The Proof and Allowance of Claims

A proof of claim is the creditor's formal submission of a claim against the estate. Following the debtor's submission of the list of creditors, the clerk notifies them of the bankruptcy and calls for the submission of claims. (If it is clear that the estate is too insolvent to make any distribution to unsecured claims, the clerk informs them to save them the trouble of proving claims.) In a Ch. 11 case, a creditor need not prove a claim unless its claim is listed as disputed, contingent, or unliquidated, or the claim is unlisted and the creditor otherwise comes to know of the bankruptcy. In cases under all other chapters, unsecured creditors must prove claims to be included in the distribution. Unless there are good grounds for excusing the delay, claims must be filed by the date specified (the "bar date") to be allowed.

Because a secured claim encumbers specific property of the estate, a secured claimant need not prove a claim to protect the lien. Even though the debtor's personal liability is discharged in bankruptcy, the lien (that is, the right in the property) survives the discharge. This principle is codified in §506(d), which states the general rule that a lien is void to the extent that it secures a claim that is not allowed. It then goes on, in §506(d)(2), to except a claim that was not allowed only because it was not proved. An undersecured creditor must prove a claim to receive a distribution on its deficiency.

Section 502 deals with the allowance of claims. Once a claim is proved, it is allowed automatically unless a party in interest files a timely objection to it.

Sections 502(b), (d), and (e) set out the grounds for disallowing the claim. Most of the grounds apply only to the extent that the claim falls within their terms, so it is possible for a claim to be reduced, rather than completely disallowed. The ground in §502(b)(1) — that the claim is unenforceable against the debtor and the debtor's property under an agreement or applicable law — is the most general one, and allows objections on the merits of the claim under nonbankruptcy law. The other grounds are much more specific (but are not covered here); two of them, mentioned in previous chapters, serve as examples: §§502(b)(6) and (7), limit damages claimable by lessors and employees whose contracts have been rejected (*see* section 18.9) and §502(d) bars claims by a transferee who has failed to return property to the estate after the transfer has been avoided (*see* section 14.5). The disallowance of claims for unmatured interest under §502(b)(2) is considered in section 19.5. Even after a claim has been allowed or disallowed, §502(j) permits it to be reconsidered for cause, so that the objector or the claimant can apply for a new ruling if new evidence, fraud of the other party, or other grounds exist for reopening the matter.

As a general rule, claims in a Ch. 7 case are paid near the end of the bankruptcy proceedings, after claims have been determined and assets liquidated. In rehabilitation cases, most payments begin after confirmation of the plan, and continue over time as provided for in the plan but payments could be made earlier if appropriate. (For example, administrative expenses are often paid for when incurred, and payments to a secured party may be needed to ensure adequate protection.)

§19.5   Interest on Claims

Section 502(b)(2) disallows claims for unmatured interest (*i.e.*, interest on the debt that had not yet been earned when the petition was filed). This may sound like accrual and unusual punishment, but it makes no sense to pay interest on claims when the fund in the estate is insufficient to pay full principal due to creditors. In fact, the bar on the payment of interest is not absolute: It has three significant qualifications.

First, interest is payable on fully secured claims to the extent that the value of the collateral exceeds the secured debt. Section 506(b) (discussed in section 19.6.3) permits a secured claimant to recover postpetition interest as long as there is an equity cushion in the collateral against which it can be charged. Once accumulated interest has consumed this surplus equity, the right to interest ceases.

Second, §726(a)(5) does in fact allow interest to be paid on unsecured claims to the extent that funds are left over after principal has been fully paid to all claimants. Because interest is a low-ranking claim, it is only paid where the estate is solvent. Section 726 is part of Ch. 7 and therefore not directly applicable in other forms of bankruptcy. However, as discussed in Chapters 20 and 21, rights to distribution in Ch. 7 form a yardstick for confirmation of rehabilitation plans, so an entitlement to interest in Ch. 7 does have an effect on the rights of creditors in other chapters.

Third, postpetition interest must not be confused with "present value" payments under plans of rehabilitation. As explained in Chapters 20 and 21, a plan under Ch. 11, 12, or 13 must propose to pay creditors at least the present value of what they would have received if the estate had been administered and distributed under Ch. 7. Because the plan provides for payment over time, this present value is calculated by increasing the amount payable on the claim to compensate for the delay in payment. Although this compensation is analogous to interest, it is not covered by the bar on interest in §502. In rehabilitation cases, §502 is essentially confined to the period between the petition and confirmation of the plan.

§19.6 Claim Classification and Priorities

§19.6.1 General Principles

The dichotomy between secured and unsecured claims is thoroughly familiar by now. In summary, secured claims are satisfied by the collateral or its proceeds. If there is more than one lien on a piece of property, the secured claims are ranked in accordance with priority prescribed by nonbankruptcy law, as discussed in Chapter 2. In bankruptcy, ranking is not confined to secured claims: Unsecured claims are also divided into different priority categories. At the top of the list are superpriority claims. Thereafter, §507(a) lists nine priority classes in descending order. They are followed by general unsecured claims, which are in turn followed by low priority categories such as unmatured interest on unsecured claims.

The ranking of claims is the same in all forms of bankruptcy, whether under Ch. 7, 11, 12, or 13, but the rules governing the treatment of claims in Ch. 7 are different from those applicable in other chapters. In a Ch. 7 case, the fund realized from the liquidation of estate property is applied in turn to each class of priority claims in order of rank. A senior class must be paid in full before the next class is entitled to any distribution. The fund travels down the hierarchy until it is exhausted. If the fund is insufficient to pay all claims in a class in full, it is shared pro rata in that class. Because most bankrupt estates are insolvent, the fund is seldom large enough to cover all claims. Often, the insolvency is so severe that only claims in the top priority class or classes receive payment. Because general unsecured claims are fairly low in the order of priority, it is quite usual for them to receive only minimal payment or no payment at all from an insolvent estate.

The standards for plan confirmation in Chs. 11, 12, and 13 require all §507 priority claims to be paid in full unless holders of the claims agree to the contrary. Therefore, the ranking of different classes of priority claims does not have the same significance in rehabilitation cases as it has in Ch. 7. If the plan does not propose to pay them in full, it cannot be confirmed. However, this does not mean that the priority ranking of claims is unimportant in a rehabilitation case. As explained in section 20.7.2, the rate of distribution under Ch. 7 has an impact on the question of whether full payment is made at face value or present value. Even if the plan provides for full payment of priority claims and it is confirmed, the ranking of priority claims could later become directly relevant if the rehabilitation fails and the debtor is ultimately liquidated.

The existence of priority claims has a further impact on a rehabilitation case, in that it affects the minimum payment required for unsecured claims. As explained further in Chapters 20 and 21, the amount that would have been paid on unsecured claims, if the debtor had been liquidated, is used as one of the yardsticks to decide if the plan may be confirmed: General unsecured claims must receive at least as much under the plan as the present value of what they would have received in a Ch. 7 liquidation. This means that if priority claims would have consumed all or a significant portion of the fund if the debtor had been liquidated, the minimum payment required for unsecured claims in the plan is correspondingly lessened.

§19.6.2   The Order of Distribution

The table on page 409 summarizes the order of distribution. The different categories of claim are explained thereafter. (*See also* Example 5.) Secured and priority claims are governed by §§506 and 507, respectively. The order of distribution for general unsecured claims and lower-ranking orders is provided for in §726, which, as noted earlier, only applies to Ch. 7 cases, but is indirectly applicable in other cases.

§19.6.3   Secured Claims

a.   The Definition and Nature of Secured Claims

The nature and effect of security has been given much attention in prior chapters. In summary, a lien that is valid under nonbankruptcy law and unavoidable under the Code is fully effective in bankruptcy, and is satisfied in full to the extent of the value of the collateral. (Nowhere in the Code is this expressly stated; it must be inferred from provisions such as §§506 and 361, taken in conjunction with general principles of nonbankruptcy law.) Although the lienholder's right to foreclose is subject to the automatic stay, and the estate may retain the collateral in furtherance of its efforts at rehabilitation, the lienholder is entitled to adequate protection of its interest and to ultimate full payment of its secured claim. Priority between competing liens in the same property is determined under the principles of nonbankruptcy law.

Section 506(a) defines a *secured claim* as an allowed claim that is secured by a lien on property in which the estate has an interest, or an allowed claim that is

The Order of Distribution in Bankruptcy

A. SECURED CLAIMS

Fully secured debts ———— secured claim ———— Paid in full plus interest and costs (to extent of equity cushion)

Partially secured debts ———— secured portion ———— Paid in full to extent of collateral

————— deficiency ————— General unsecured claim

B. ULTRAPRIORITY CLAIMS — $364(c)(1)

C. PRIORITY CLAIMS

(1) Administrative Expenses
1st rank — superpriority claims under $507(b)
2nd rank — other admin. expenses under $503

(2) Ordinary course business expenses in gap period between filing and order for relief, in involuntary cases

(3) Wages and salaries (limited)*

(4) Employee benefits (limited)*

(5) Grain producers and fishermen — claims against processor or storehouse (limited)*

(6) Deposits for consumer goods or services (limited)*

(7) Alimony, maintenance, and support due to the spouse, ex-spouse, or child of the debtor

(8) Various taxes (limited)*

(9) Claims arising out of federal depository insurance

D. GENERAL UNSECURED CLAIMS

(Includes balance of undersecured or limited priority claims together with all other claims proved and allowed or not covered by a priority category)

(1) Timely filed general unsecured claims and late claims where creditor had no notice or knowledge of the case to file in time but filed early enough to be able to participate.

(2) Other tardily filed general unsecured claims.

E. Claims for fines, penalties, forfeiture, or punitive damages, which are not compensation for actual pecuniary loss.

F. Interest on priority and general unsecured claims.

G. Any surplus remaining goes to the debtor.

———————————

*Most priority categories have limits. To the extent that a claim in the category exceeds the limit, the amount in excess of the limit is a general unsecured claim.

subject to setoff under §553. *Lien* is expansively defined in §101(37) to include all encumbrances, whether consensual or not. The requirement that the underlying claim be allowed reflects the principles introduced in Chapter 2 that a lien cannot exist in the abstract — it must secure a debt. Therefore, if the claim is disallowed, there is nothing to support the lien and the secured claim cannot exist. Section 506(d) reinforces this by voiding the lien on a disallowed claim. However (as stated in section 19.4), the lien is not voided if the claim was not allowed solely because it was not proved. A lienholder is entitled *not* to prove a claim against the estate, whereupon the lien survives as a charge against the property even though personal liability of the debtor is discharged. (*See* Example 1.)

b. Deficiency in Collateral Value: "Strip Down" and "Strip Off"

Section 506 states that a claim is secured to the extent of the collateral's value and is unsecured as to any deficiency. An undersecured debt is thus split into a secured and unsecured claim, thereby reflecting the reality (by now familiar) that security is necessarily limited by the value of the collateral. Under general principles of nonbankruptcy law, as long as the secured party does not foreclose on the security interest, any appreciation in the collateral's value will reduce or eliminate the deficiency, partially or fully restoring the secured portion of the debt. One of the questions that has long troubled courts is whether this general principle applies in bankruptcy. That is, if the debt is undersecured at the time of bankruptcy, it bifurcates into a secured debt, measured by the current value of the collateral and an unsecured debt for the deficiency. If the property is liquidated, the proceeds will be paid in partial satisfaction of the debt, fully paying the secured claim and leaving the deficiency as an unsecured claim in the estate. However, the property may not be liquidated. The trustee may abandon it as having no value to the estate, and the secured party may not move immediately to foreclose on it. (This may be simply because of a delay in foreclosure, or it could be that the secured party is willing to allow the debtor to keep it, subject to making payments on the secured debt.) If the value of the collateral rises after the value has been determined by the court, the question is whether that increase in value will restore the size of the secured debt, or will rather redound to the debtor's benefit. If the debtor is permitted to peg the amount of the secured claim at the value fixed by the bankruptcy court, the secured claim can never increase in size. As the deficiency is discharged in the bankruptcy, the secured party would never be able to obtain more than the court-determined value in the bankruptcy case. This is known as "lien stripping" or "strip down."

In *Dewsnup v. Timm*, 502 U.S. 410 (1992), the Ch. 7 debtor argued that §506(a) bifurcates an undersecured claim and therefore the deficiency cannot be classified as an "allowed secured claim." This means that it must be void under §506(d), which voids a lien "[t]o the extent that [it] secures a claim . . . that is not an allowed secured claim." The court rejected this argument and found that the language of §506(d) was only intended to cover situations in which the secured claim itself had been disallowed, not where the secured claim was allowed, but a deficiency remains that becomes an unsecured claim. In reaching its decision, the court was influenced by the fact that pre-Code law treated liens as passing through bankruptcy unaffected, and that if Congress had intended to change that result, it would have more clearly provided so. The effect of *Dewsnup* is that a Ch. 7 debtor cannot use §506(d) to reduce an undersecured claim to the present value of the collateral as judicially determined in the bankruptcy case. However, the court was concerned only with a consensual lien in a Ch. 7 case and did not indicate if the same rule would apply outside of Ch. 7 or to a nonconsensual lien. Subsequent lower court decisions have extended it to nonconsensual liens, but there remains some question over whether it would apply in a rehabilitation case. (We will see in Chapter 20 that in a Ch. 13 case, the U.S. Supreme Court has adopted an approach consistent with *Dewsnup* in relation to security interests in real property that is the debtor's principal residence. But that is based on the reading of a particular provision in Ch. 13.)

Since *Dewsnup*, a number of courts have grappled with its impact on secured claims that have completely lost all the value of their collateral. This occurs where there are two liens on property, and the value of the property is so low that it is sufficient to pay only the senior interest (in whole or in part) so that there is no value remaining to cover the junior interest. Debtors have argued that *Dewsnup* applies only to an undersecured lien, and that if a lien is totally unsecured on the debtor's bankruptcy the claim cannot be treated as secured at all and the lien must be void. (This is known as "strip off," as opposed to "strip down.") Courts have reacted differently to this argument. Some have agreed, but others, for example, *Ryan v. Homecomings Financial Network*, 253 F.3d 778 (4th Cir. 2001), have held that there is no principled distinction between this situation and that addressed by *Dewsnup*. Therefore, provided the lien is otherwise valid and unavoidable, the debtor should not be able to strip it off merely because the collateral does not have enough value to support it at the time of bankruptcy.

c. Interest, Costs, and Fees on Secured Claims

We have already encountered the principle that if the collateral is worth more than the debt, the surplus is applied to any junior claims to the property or, if there are none, belongs to the estate. This principle is subject to the oversecured claimant's right to interest and costs under §506(b) that was alluded to in section 19.5. Once the surplus is exhausted, the secured claim's right to interest, fees, and costs ends.

Under §506(b) a secured claimant is entitled to postpetition interest[2] on its claim to the extent of any surplus value in the collateral. Since *U.S. v. Ron Pair Enterprises*, 489 U.S. 235 (1989), it is clear that interest is not confined to consensual lienholders but is also available to oversecured nonconsensual liens. The rate of interest is the contract rate. In *In re Payless Cashways, Inc.*, 287 B.R. 482 (Bankr. W.D. Mo. 2002), the court noted that while §506(b) applies a reasonableness standard to costs and fees, it says nothing about reasonable interest. Therefore, the court should apply the contract rate, and as long as that rate is permissible under nonbankruptcy law, should not enquire into its reasonableness.

If the lien is consensual and the agreement so provides, the claimant can also recover reasonable costs and fees from the surplus. Unlike interest, these costs and fees are subject to a test of reasonableness and the court can reduce them if it considers them unreasonable, even if the contract authorizes them in the amount claimed. In *In re Welzel*, 275 F.3d 1308 (11th Cir. 2001), the court said that even if fees provided for in the contract are reduced as unreasonable, this does not mean that they are disallowed. The unreasonable portion of the costs and fees cannot be paid out of the surplus, but they can be proved in the estate as an unsecured claim.

d.   The Costs of Realizing or Preserving the Collateral

The trustee may need to take action to preserve or realize collateral. If so, §506(c) permits the reasonable and necessary costs and expenses of doing so to be recovered from the collateral to the extent of any benefit to the secured claimant. To be recoverable from the collateral, the expenses must be directly related to its preservation or disposition so that the secured claimant benefits by the protection or realization of its interest. (*See* Example 4.) If the expenditure benefits the claimant in part, a pro rata share of it is chargeable against the collateral. Expenses payable under §506(c) take precedence over the claimant's right to recover interest and costs and reduce any surplus that would otherwise be available for those charges.

Although the trustee is able to recover these costs from the secured party, the U.S. Supreme Court held in *Hartford Underwriters Ins. Co. v. Union Planters Bank*, 120 S.Ct. 1942 (2000), that §506(c), by its clear terms, is only available to the trustee. Therefore, if the trustee does not claim the expenses, the party who provided the services has no direct cause of action against the secured party for their recovery.

---

2. Although it does not expressly say so, §506(b) applies only to postpetition interest. Interest that had accrued prior to the petition is added to the claim. If the underlying contract or statute so provides, and if the collateral is valuable enough to accommodate it, the prepetition interest forms part of the secured debt.

e.   Valuation of the Collateral

The valuation of collateral is obviously crucial to the extent and treatment of a secured claim. Section 506(a) states the general principle that collateral must be valued in light of the purpose of the valuation and of the proposed use or disposition of the property. That is, the valuation must be fact-based and reasonable. Courts have struggled with the application of this general principle.

The valuation issue was addressed by the Supreme Court in *Associates Commercial Corp. v. Rash,* 117 S. Ct. 1879 (1997). The Ch. 13 debtor was a freight hauler. He owned a tractor-truck on which he owed about $41,000, secured by a security interest in the truck. The debtor proposed in his plan to keep the truck and to make payments to the secured creditor in the plan, equal to the present value of the secured claim. (This is what is required in Ch. 13, as explained in section 20.7.) Although the debtor would be keeping the truck, he argued that it should be valued on the basis of what the creditor would receive for it at a foreclosure sale, about $28,500. (On this valuation, the balance of the debt — the deficiency — would be treated as unsecured, and paid at the rate for unsecured claims). The creditor argued that the proper standard for valuation was the replacement value of the truck — what it would cost the debtor to buy it on the retail market. This value was equal to the outstanding debt, so that the claim would be fully secured. The Supreme Court favored the creditor's position. Because the debtor planned to keep and use the truck, and it was not intended that the truck would be sold in foreclosure, its replacement cost best reflected its value based on its proposed use and disposition.

Although the court spoke of replacement value, the opinion indicates that the court had in mind a fair market standard — what a willing buyer in the debtor's trade would pay a willing seller on the market for a truck of the age and condition of the truck in question. The court pointed out that the market that the debtor would use to buy the truck should be resolved as a factual question, and that the conventional market price may have to be adjusted by taking account of any augmentations of value added by the debtor, and deducting that portion of the market price that would be attributable to seller's costs that would not be incurred in fact because the debtor already owned the truck, and would not actually be buying it.

Rash was concerned with the valuation of collateral for the purposes of providing for a secured claim in a Ch. 13 case, so its scope outside that particular context has not been clear. Some courts have confined it narrowly and have held that replacement value is not always the proper standard under §506. For example, in *In re Henderson,* 235 B.R. 425 (Bankr. C.D. Ill. 1999), the court said that liquidation value is the more appropriate standard where the court is deciding on the redemption price under §722, because if the debtor did not redeem, the proposed disposition of the property would be the creditor's foreclosure. See also *In re Zell*, 284 B.R. 569 (Bankr. D. Md. 2002). The pending reform legislation would amend §506 to codify a replacement value standard based on *Rash* in both Ch. 7 and 13 cases.

§19.6.4   *Priority Claims*

While secured claims are satisfied by the collateral or its proceeds, all other claims are paid from the general fund of the estate. The Code recognizes 11 classes of priority unsecured claims which are payable, in descending order, before general unsecured claims are entitled to any share in the estate. The highest level of priority is occupied by claims of postpetition financiers who have been granted ultrapriority status by the court under §364(c)(1). (*See* section 17.3.2 and Example 5 of Chapter 17.) Next in line are deficiency claims granted superpriority status by §507(b) to compensate for failure of adequate protection. (*See* section 11.5.6, Example 3 of Chapter 11, and Example 5 of Chapter 17.) Although §507(b) claims are actually placed in the administrative expense category, they are treated as a separate, superior class within that category.

The remaining nine priority categories are listed in rank order in §507(a). Every subsection of §507(a) uses the word "allowed" to qualify the claims in each priority class. If a claim is disallowed, it does not participate in the estate as a priority claim or otherwise. Also, many of the priority categories have limits. To the extent that a claim exceeds the limit, it is a general unsecured claim. It is therefore possible for a single debt to be partly a priority claim and partly a general claim.

In examining the priority categories listed below, bear in mind that priorities reflect a legislative decision to give some claims special treatment at the expense of others. The motives for this preferential treatment vary. Some claims are given priority in the belief that it is needed to effect the aims of bankruptcy administration, and others are favored because Congress (with some help from lobbyists) concluded that the claimants deserve greater protection than other creditors. One cannot help feeling a sense of randomness in the selection of some priority categories and their place in the order of distribution.

It is also worth noting that the rules of discharge have an impact on the Code's priority scheme. As explained in Chapter 22, some debts are nondischargeable. If a nondischargeable debt is given priority, the debtor's postbankruptcy responsibility for the debt is reduced at the expense of creditors in junior classes. Conversely, a nondischargeable general unsecured claim (or junior priority claim) will have to be paid in full by the debtor after bankruptcy if priority claims (or senior priority claims) exhaust the fund of the estate.

1. Administrative Expenses (§507(a)(1))

Following superpriority claims, first priority is given to the expenses of administering the estate. The kinds of claims that are entitled to administrative priority are described in §503(b). The broadest group of expenses are the *actual and necessary costs of preserving the estate* referred to in §503(b)(1)(A). This encompasses all manner of expenditures deemed by the court to be reasonable in advancing the estate's interests, preserving or enhancing its assets, or furthering the debtor's efforts at rehabilitation. In addition to this general species of expense, §503(b) includes items such as trustee compensation, fees for professional services, and postpetition taxes due by the estate. Also, as mentioned in Chapters 17 and 18, postpetition credit and the performance under executory contracts are administrative expenses. The list in §503(b) is not definitive, and the court has the discretion to approve other expenses for inclusion in this category. (Administrative expense claims are illustrated in Examples 4 and 5(f).)

As administrative expenses are supposed to preserve the estate, it is not always clear how claims should be treated if they arise out of wrongful acts of the estate that ultimately diminish the estate. *Pennsylvania Dept. of Environmental Resources v. Tri-State Clinical Laboratories, Inc.*, 178 F.3d 685 (3rd Cir. 1999), provides a repulsive example. The Ch. 11 debtor in possession, a laboratory, improperly disposed of test tubes containing blood by putting them in a dumpster; when workers emptied the dumpster, they were splattered with the blood. The debtor was fined $30,000 for the violation. Shortly thereafter, the case was converted to Ch. 7 and the trustee challenged the state's assertion that the fine was an administrative expense. The court agreed with the trustee. It recognized that when an officer of the estate commits a tort in the course of the estate's business, this is not activity that preserves the estate. Nevertheless, because the injury occured as a result of the estate's business activity, principles of fairness require the injured party's damages to be given administrative expense priority. In the same way, if the claim was not a fine but the state's claim for reimbursement of cleanup costs incurred as a result of the pollution, this is correctly classified as an administrative expense. However, the court did not consider that the same considerations apply where a fine is involved. To treat this as an administrative expense would mean, in effect, that more junior creditors in the estate would be paying the penalty for the debtor's unlawful activity.

Unlike most other claims against the state, administrative expenses are incurred after the petition has been filed. The rationale for giving them top priority is that no one would be likely to render services or supplies to the estate without a reasonable assurance of being paid. Also, because bankruptcy administration is supposed to benefit creditors of the estate, it is regarded as appropriate that the expenses involved in the conduct of the estate's affairs come out of the fund before it is distributed to creditors. Of course, if the estate is so badly insolvent that there is only enough to pay administrative expenses, the benefit to unsecured creditors is cold comfort.

Because there is no internal hierarchy within each priority category, all administrative expenses (with the exception of §507(b) superpriority claims, of course) are of equal rank. If there is not enough money to pay all administrative expenses in full, they share pro rata. An exception to this rule is provided for where a case has been converted to Ch. 7. Section 726(b) splits administrative expenses into two categories and gives seniority to postconversion expenses. Most courts that have considered the question have held that when a case is converted to Ch.7, the priority given to the Ch. 7 administrative expenses by §726(b) takes precedence over all priority claims arising prior to the conversion, including superpriority claims under §§364(c)(1) and 507(b). In *In re Visionaire Corp.*, 290 B.R. 348 (Bankr. E.D. Mo. 2003), the court interpreted the language of §726(b) to be absolute in making the post-conversion expenses predominant, so that they were entitled to payment before the claim of a postpetition financer who had been given priority under §364(c)(1) in the Ch. 11 case. The court found that this interpretation strikes the correct balance between the need to protect postpetition lenders and the need to ensure that someone will be available to wind up the unsuccessful attempt at reorganization.

2.   Claims Allowed under §502(f) (§507(a)(2))

In an involuntary case, the debtor is entitled to continue operating its business or conducting its financial affairs in the period between the petition and the order for relief or appointment of a trustee. (*See* section 9.6.3.) Expenses incurred by the debtor in the ordinary course of business or financial affairs are allowed as a claim against the estate by §502(f). Section 503(b) expressly excludes these expenses from the first priority, but §507(a)(2) gives them second priority so they are paid immediately after administrative expenses. (*See* Example 5(c).)

3.   Unpaid Salary and Wages (§507(a)(3))

The third priority provides limited protection to claims of the debtor's employees for wages, salary, or commission (including vacation, severance, or sick-leave pay) that was unpaid at the time of bankruptcy. (*See* Examples 5(c) and 6.) The Bankruptcy Reform Act of 1994 added to this category individuals (or corporations with only one employee) who, while they are independent contractors and not technically employees, earn a large portion of their livelihood (75 percent or more of their income) from commissions paid to them by the debtor for the sale of goods or services.

The extent of third-priority claims is curtailed by both time period and amount. The modest dollar limit and relatively short temporal limit mean that the protection of priority will provide only a modicum of security to workers whose wages are unpaid at the time of bankruptcy. There is a $4,650 limit on each claim, and the remuneration must have been earned within 90 days of the petition or, if the debtor ceased business before that, within 90 days of the closing of the business. To the extent that the employee's claim exceeds these limits, it is a general unsecured claim. The monetary limit for this category was increased by the Bankruptcy Reform Act of 1994, which enacted §104. Under §104, the Judicial Conference of the United States adjusts dollar amounts in the Code every three years based on changes in the Consumer Price Index. The current adjustment was promulgated with effect from April 1, 2001. The figures will be adjusted again on April 1, 2004.

The third priority includes not only the employee's net earnings but also taxes due by the employee on those earnings which should be withheld from his or her pay. These third priority taxes due by the employee must be distinguished from employment taxes due by the debtor-employer and taxes that have already been withheld by the debtor-employer, both of which fall into the eighth priority category. The third priority covers only *prepetition* earnings: If the debtor's business is operated by the trustee after the petition, the salary of employees for that period is an administrative expense, entitled to first priority. (*See* Example 5(c).)

4. Contributions to Employee Benefit Plans (§507(a)(4))

The fourth priority must be taken in conjunction with the third, because amounts paid to employees for salary or wages under the third priority reduces the amount payable under the fourth. The fourth priority covers contributions to employee benefit plans, such as pensions, life insurance, or health insurance. Each plan's priority is limited to contributions relating to services rendered by covered employees in the 180 days before the earlier of the filing of the petition or the cessation of the debtor's business. The priority is also limited in amount. It cannot exceed $4,650 multiplied by the number of employees covered by the plan, less the aggregate amount paid to covered employees as salary or wages under the third priority. If there is more than one employee benefit plan, then the total payable to all plans under the fourth priority, together with amounts paid to covered employees under the third priority, cannot exceed the number of covered employees multiplied by $4,300. As noted above, this amount is administratively revised by the Judicial Conference of the United States every three years.

5.   Grain Farmers and Fishermen (§507(a)(5))

The fifth priority only applies to a debtor that operated a storage facility for grain or a storage or processing facility for fish. If the debtor became indebted to a grain farmer or fisherman in respect of grain or fish deposited with the debtor, the claimant is given a fifth priority for the claim, up to a maximum of $4,650. (Like the limits on the third and fourth priority categories, this amount is revised every three years. The $4,650 figure took effect on April 1, 2001.)

6.   Consumer Deposits (§507(a)(6))

An individual who deposited money with the debtor in connection with the purchase or lease of consumer goods or the purchase of consumer services, and did not receive the goods or services, is given a sixth priority claim for recovery of the deposit, up to an amount of $2,100 (as revised by the Judicial Conference under §104 with effect from April 1, 2001).

7.   Support, Maintenance, and Alimony (§507(a)(7))

The Bankruptcy Reform Act of 1994 enacted a set of provisions to protect dependents of the debtor by preventing the debtor from using bankruptcy to evade or delay obligations for support, maintenance, and alimony. We have already seen that such obligations are excluded from the stay (*see* section 10.4.2); if secured by a judicial lien, are not subject to lien avoidance (*see* section 13.5); and are not avoidable as preferences (*see* section 16.1.4). In addition, as discussed in section 22.5.4, they are not dischargeable. As part of this package of protections, the 1994 Act elevated these obligations to priority status, ranking them as a seventh priority, just before taxes.

To qualify for priority, the debt must satisfy the same requirements that are reflected in the other Code sections that accord special treatment to these obligations: The debt must be due to a spouse, former spouse, or child, arising out of a separation or property settlement agreement or an order of a court of record or a government agency; it must actually be for maintenance, support, or alimony, not simply a debt labeled as such, but actually arising from a property settlement or some other financial obligation; and it cannot be assigned, voluntarily or otherwise. No monetary limit has been placed on this priority category.

8.   Taxes (§507(a)(8))

The eighth priority covers a variety of taxes due to governmental units, defined in §101(27) to include federal, state, and local governments. Taxes that receive priority under §507(a)(8) are nondischargeable under §523(a) (1). In rehabilitation cases, these priority taxes must be paid in full under the plan unless the taxing authority agrees otherwise. In a Ch. 7 case, if the fund is inadequate to pay eighth priority taxes in full, the debtor remains liable after bankruptcy for any unpaid balance. When there are enough funds in the estate to pay claims up to and including the eighth priority, but not enough to pay general unsecured claims as well, the debtor benefits and general creditors are prejudiced by the eighth priority status of nondischargeable taxes. Payment of the taxes from the estate exhausts the fund that would otherwise have been distributed to the general creditors, while eliminating or reducing the debtor's undischargeable liability for the taxes. Under the right circumstances, therefore, the debtor's taxes are, in effect, paid by unsecured creditors. Although this may sound outrageous, bear in mind that federal and state governments have powerful collection rights under nonbankruptcy law too, and can usually trump unsecured creditors by perfecting a statutory lien on all the debtor's property.

A number of different taxes are included in the eighth priority. Many of them have priority only to the extent that they became due within a specified time before bankruptcy. Roughly speaking (and without examining the intricate qualifications of §507(a)(8), eighth priority is given to income taxes for three to four years prior to the petition; property taxes payable in the year before bankruptcy; "trust fund" taxes that the debtor withheld from its employees' salaries but failed to transmit to the taxing authority; employment taxes due by the debtor itself and payable by the debtor within approximately three years of bankruptcy (which differ from withholding taxes in that the debtor, rather than the employee, is liable for them); certain excise and customs duties; and compensatory penalties due on other eighth priority taxes. (Example 5(e) illustrates the tax priority.)

9.   Commitments to Maintain the Capital of an Insured Depository Institution (§507(a)(9))

The ninth priority was added to §507 in 1990 as part of a group of provisions enacted in response to the Savings and Loan crisis. It covers claims based on the debtor's commitment to the FDIC, RTC, and other governmental deposit insurers to maintain the capital of an insured depository institution.

§19.6.5   General Unsecured Claims and Lower Classes

As stated already, general unsecured claims share pro rata in any fund remaining after all priority claims have been paid. All unsecured claims that do not qualify for any priority fit into this category, as well as any deficiency due on undersecured claims and any amount over the limit on priority claims. (*See* Example 5.) Because most bankrupt estates are insolvent, general unsecured claims often receive only a partial distribution or are discharged with no payment at all. When the estate is solvent and general claims are paid in full, any remaining funds are distributed to the lowest priority claims listed in the table on page 409.

§19.7   Subordination under §510

Subordination is the demotion of a claim. In nonbankruptcy law, subordination may result from agreement or it may be imposed upon a claimant by a court of equity. Section 510 recognizes both these forms of subordination in bankruptcy.

§19.7.1   Consensual Subordination

A senior claimant may agree to subordinate its claim to induce another person to enter into a desirable transaction with the debtor. Say, for example, that a secured party has a security interest in the debtor's equipment. The debtor wishes to borrow money from another lender to upgrade the equipment, and the second lender will only advance the funds if it is given a first-priority security interest in the equipment to secure the loan. If the senior secured party believes that the equipment in its present state may not be worth enough to fully cover its loan, and that the renovations will enhance the equipment's value beyond the amount of the second secured loan, it may be willing to make an agreement with the second lender to subordinate its otherwise senior lien to that of the second lender. Section 510(a) recognizes such subordination agreements and makes them enforceable in bankruptcy to the extent that they are enforceable in nonbankruptcy law.

§19.7.2   Equitable Subordination

Courts of equity have the power to subordinate a claim where the equities so dictate. Section 510(c) authorizes the bankruptcy court to use principles of equitable subordination to reduce the rank of all or part of an allowed claim. If the subordinated claim is secured, the court may transfer the lien to the estate.

The most common basis for subordination is inequitable or dishonest conduct by the claimant that results in unfair advantage or prejudice to other creditors. Courts require both the elements of wrongful conduct and prejudice to be present. If a claim warrants subordination, it may be reduced slightly in rank or demoted to the lowest level in the order of distribution, depending on the nature and extent of the inequitable conduct. Subordination is meant to be an adjustment of rank to correct for the inequitable conduct, rather than a punishment, so the general rule is that the claim is subordinated only to the extent necessary to rectify the harm. For example, if a senior secured claimant made a misrepresentation to a junior lienholder, it may be appropriate merely to subordinate the senior secured claim to the junior and not to deprive it of secured status altogether. However, particularly unsavory behavior could justify a dramatic reduction in rank. For some illustrative cases, *see In re Fabricators, Inc.,* 926 F.2d 1458 (5th Cir. 1991); *In re Lemco Gypsum, Inc.,* 911 F.2d 1553 (11th Cir. 1990); *In re Giorgio,* 862 F.2d 933 (1st Cir. 1988).

A situation that looks like equitable subordination but is distinguishable occurs where the court recharacterizes a transaction as an investment, creating an ownership interest rather than a loan transaction. Where a person (commonly an existing shareholder in a debtor) provides funds to the debtor structured as a loan, but the true basis of the funding was an investment in the debtor, a court can use its equitable power to declare the transaction as creating equity, not debt. The significance of this is that the person who provided the funds is removed from the ranks of creditors and treated like an owner. This is more than merely a subordination. It does not just demote the claim in rank, but it reclassifies it so that it ceases to be a claim at all. The significance of the change is profound. As mentioned before, the owners of the debtor are at the very end of the line and do not share in the assets of the debtor unless all debts are first paid in full. The test used to decide whether to recharacterize a transaction as equity rather than debt involves the examination of the entire context of the transaction to ascertain the true nature of the funding and the intent of the parties at the time that it was provided. For an example of a case that conducts this analysis, see *In re Atlanticrancher, Inc.,* 279 B.R. 411 (Bankr. D. Mass. 2002).

The creditor's wrongful conduct is the clearest and most widely accepted basis for equitable subordination. However, some courts have exercised the discretion to subordinate a claim, even in the absence of wrongful conduct of the creditor, where they have found that the equities of the case demand it. This discretion to subordinate the claim of an innocent creditor, purely on the basis of general equitable considerations, has been called into doubt (or at least confined to the narrowest limits) by *U.S. v. Noland,* 517

U.S. 535 (1996). In that case, the IRS had proved a claim which included nonpecuniary tax penalties (that is, penalties imposed to punish the taxpayer for failure to pay the tax on time, rather than penalties in the form of interest to compensate the government for the late payment). The penalties were due by the estate on postpetition earnings, so they were entitled to first priority status as administrative expenses (as opposed to eighth priority status, accorded prepetition taxes). Although the IRS had not engaged in any inequitable conduct, the bankruptcy court found that the equities required its claim to be subordinated to those of general unsecured creditors, because it was unfair to pay penalties at the expense of general creditors who had claims based on actual value given to the debtor. The bankruptcy court's decision was affirmed by both the district court and the court of appeals, but the Supreme Court reversed.

The Court said that it need not decide if creditor misconduct must always be found as a basis for equitable subordination. However, it is not permissible for a court to simply subordinate a claim because it feels that the claim is less worthy of payment than claims in a lower class. Congress has set the priorities for payment, and it is not up to a court to use the equity powers recognized by §510(c) to reorder these priorities because it perceives the Code's ranking to be unfair.

EXAMPLES

1.   Abode in the Hand

Included in the Ch. 7 estate of Lester Pay is a house worth $100,000, subject to a mortgage held by Mori Bond Co. securing a debt of $120,000.

(a) Must Mori Bond Co. prove a claim in the estate to preserve its rights or to receive payment of its claim?

(b) Assume that the trustee abandoned the property as having no value or benefit to the estate. Because the property has been abandoned, Mori Bond may apply for relief from stay and foreclose on it immediately, or wait to foreclose after the case is closed. Lester commences proceedings to have the mortgage declared void under §506(d) to the extent that the debt exceeds the value of the collateral (i.e., by $20,000), and to peg the value of the secured claim at $100,000. Can Lester do this?

2.   High Claims and Mass Diseases

Cess Pools, Inc. manufactures pool chemicals. Some years ago it developed a revolutionary chemical that kept water clearer and brighter than any competing product. After the chemical had been marketed successfully for several years, it was discovered to be carcinogenic. Because it had been so popular, countless people had been exposed to it. Several hundred had already become ill, and an unknown number of people will probably develop cancer in the future as a result of contact with the chemical. In the face of this widespread tort liability, Cess Pools, Inc. has filed a Ch. 11 petition.

(a) Do the people with cancer have claims against the estate?

(b) May claims be proved in the estate by people who have been exposed to the chemical but do not have cancer? What is the impact of recognizing or refusing to recognize them as creditors of the estate?

3. Claiming over Spilt Muck

In the course of manufacturing the chemicals described in Example 2, Cess Pools, Inc. discharged hazardous substances into the ground. These discharges occurred prior to Cess Pools's bankruptcy and have since ceased because Cess Pools no longer makes the chemicals. Shortly before Cess Pools filed its Ch. 11 petition, the Environmental Protection Agency (EPA) identified the polluted land as requiring cleanup. Although the EPA could have ordered Cess Pools to clean up the waste, it exercised its statutory right to restore the site itself and to claim reimbursement from Cess Pools. No cleanup work had begun by the time of Cess Pools's bankruptcy, and the exact extent of the pollution and the cost of restoration are not yet known.

The EPA contends that its future claim for reimbursement following cleanup is not a dischargeable claim against Cess Pools's Ch. 11 estate, but will become a debt payable in full from the fresh-start assets of the reorganized debtor. It bases this contention on three arguments:

(a) Section 101(5) defines "claim" as "a right to payment." Cess Pools's liability under the Comprehensive Environmental Response, Compensation, and Liability Act (CERCLA) should be viewed as a statutory duty to restore the environment, rather than a monetary obligation. That is, it is in the nature of *an obligation to act* rather than *a right to payment.*

(b) Even if the EPA's rights against Cess Pools qualify as a right to payment, that right did not exist at the time of the petition, but will only arise following EPA's cleanup work. This should be treated as a postpetition claim against the reorganized debtor, not as a claim against the estate.

(c) If the court classifies Cess Pools's liability for the cleanup costs as a claim, thereby allowing it to be discharged in bankruptcy, it will undermine CERCLA's policy of placing the cost of rectifying pollution on the party responsible for causing it, rather than on the public.

Should the court accept any of these arguments and declare the cleanup costs to be a postpetition debt rather than a claim against the estate?

4. The Charge of the Light Brigade

Prior to its bankruptcy under Ch. 7, Withering Heights, Inc. owned and operated an office building. The property is subject to a mortgage securing a debt that exceeds the building's market value. The trustee continued to manage the building for a few months after the petition was filed, pending a determination of its value and a decision on what should be done with it. Eventually the building was abandoned to the mortgagee as having no value or benefit to the estate. During the period that the estate operated the building, the power company continued to supply electricity that was needed to keep the building habitable by tenants and to allow its electronic security system to function. The electricity bills for this period have not been paid. How should they be treated?

5. File and Rank

Trickle Downs, Inc. owned and managed an apartment complex. A group of its creditors petitioned to place it in Ch. 7 bankruptcy. A week after the petition, an interim trustee was appointed. The order for relief was granted a few weeks later. The trustee has sold the apartment complex as well as other estate property, and the estate will soon be distributed. The following are some of the claims that have been proved and allowed in the case:

(a) A first mortgage on the apartment complex, recorded ten years ago.

(b) A second mortgage on the complex, recorded five years ago.

(c) Salary due to the manager of the complex for the month prior to the petition and the month thereafter.

(d) The manager's claim for breach of contract, arising from the estate's termination of his employment contract which had two more years to run.

(e) Property taxes on the complex for the two years prior to the petition.

(f) An attorney's fee for services rendered to the trustee in connection with the sale of the complex.

(g) A claim by a landscaping service company for maintenance work done in the months before the petition and for charges for breach of contract arising out of the trustee's rejection of the contract for future services.

(h) Various claims by trade creditors who provided services and supplies to Trickle Downs in the months before bankruptcy.

Rank them.

EXPLANATIONS

1. **(a) Must Mori Bond prove a claim?**   A secured claim need not be proved to preserve the lien. Even though the debtor's personal obligation is dischargeable, the lien survives the bankruptcy provided that it is valid and not disallowed on grounds other than the lienholder's failure to prove a claim. However, Mori Bond is undersecured. If it wishes to receive a distribution on its deficiency (provided, of course, that nonbankruptcy law permits a mortgagee to claim a deficiency), it must prove a claim.

   (b) Is the mortgage void under §506(d) to the extent of the deficiency?   Lester's purpose is to peg the mortgage debt at the level of the current value of the property — that is, to have the court declare that the undischarged mortgage survives the bankruptcy only to the extent of $100,000, not to the full extent of the debt of $120,000. The advantage to Lester is that if the property appreciates before foreclosure so that it realizes more than $100,000, any surplus will belong to Lester and cannot be claimed by the mortgagee up to the amount of $120,000. Another advantage would be that if Lester was able to redeem the property, the redemption price would be $100,000 rather than $120,000, irrespective of any appreciation in the property. The tactic being tried by Lester is called *lien stripping*. As discussed in section 19.6.3, *Dewsnup v. Timm* precludes a Ch. 7 debtor from stripping down a consensual mortgage. Even though the reach of the case is uncertain beyond that, it clearly applies here, and the mortgage survives to the full extent of $120,000, even though Lester's personal liability is discharged.

2. **(a)** The people who are already stricken clearly have claims against the estate. These claims may still be unliquidated or disputed, but they qualify as claims under §101(5). During the course of the case, their claims will be resolved by litigation or negotiation. Under §502(c), the claims can be estimated if the normal process of resolution would cause undue delay in the administration of the case.

   (b) It is difficult to know how to deal with people who have been exposed to the chemical but are still healthy. They are potential claimants: The harmful act has been committed, but it has not yet caused physical injury. Some of these people will become ill, and others will not. They could be treated as contingent claimants, in that potential liability has been created, contingent upon the advent of illness. Alternatively, the approach could be taken that no tort has been committed and no liability exists unless and until an actual injury is manifested. This would mean that potential victims have no claim against the estate, but may later acquire a postbankruptcy claim against the debtor. State law is not uniform in the classification of such potential tort liability.

The choice between these two alternatives has significant consequences for claimants, the estate, and the debtor. If Cess Pools, Inc. has a good prospect of successful reorganization, potential victims may do better if their claims are treated as arising postpetition, because they can be asserted against the rehabilitated debtor when they arise, and need not be proved in the estate for fractional distribution. This classification creates serious trouble for Cess Pools, Inc., which cannot settle its liability in the bankruptcy case. If Cess Pools's prospects of survival following reorganization are not good, potential claimants are better served by having their claims treated as contingent. This allows them to prove claims in the estate so that they can share in the fund. (The same would be true if the debtor is to be liquidated: Because it will not survive the bankruptcy, the characterization of the incipient claims as contingent prepetition claims allows the potential victims to participate in the estate.) If the claims are treated as contingent, it may be difficult, if not impossible, to identify all potential claimants and to give them notice of the bankruptcy. When claims are made, they must be estimated by taking into account both the likely extent of injury and the probability of contracting the disease.

To deal with the problem of characterizing potential claims and to provide for the compensation of victims while permitting the rehabilitation of the debtor, the device of the trust fund has been used in some multivictim tort cases. A trust fund for tort victims is established under the plan. All tort claims, both existing and future, are channeled into the trust as they arise. The debtor is discharged from liability, and the court issues an injunction compelling all future claims to be made against the trust. Although the creation of a trust ameliorates some of the difficulties mentioned above, it does not solve a number of problems. One of the most serious concerns is that the size of the fund must be estimated, and there is a danger that it will prove inadequate to cover all claims that arise. Furthermore, it is not clear that future victims who have not proved claims in the fund should be bound by the discharge.

In the Bankruptcy Reform Act of 1994, Congress recognized the need to make some provision for the handling of mass tort claims in bankruptcy, and enacted §524(g). However, §524(g) falls short of providing any kind of detailed or comprehensive system for dealing with mass claims. It does nothing more than authorize the issuance of an injunction to supplement the discharge injunction in cases involving asbestos-related injury, in which a trust has been set up in the plan of reorganization. Because the section does not deal with other types of mass claims, and does not fully provide for the creation of a trust, it does not make it clear that the trust device can be generally used to deal with mass claims in bankruptcy. However, the section says nothing to preclude the use of this device either and could be read to recognize it implicitly. In its 1997 report, the National Bankruptcy Review Commission noted the inadequacy of current legislation and recommended that the Code be amended to include an express recognition of the power to deal with mass claims in bankruptcy, and to provide for a structure for dealing with them.

3. **(a)** The first argument cannot stand in light of *Ohio v. Kovacs,* 469 U.S. 274 (1985). Prior to the debtor's Ch. 7 bankruptcy, a state agency had obtained an order authorizing it to clean up the debtor's prepetition pollution and to recover the costs from the debtor's property. The Supreme Court held that the debtor's liability for the cleanup costs was a claim because it had been converted into an obligation to pay money. It said that the definition of claim in §101(5) was broad enough to include liability arising out of statute or court order, provided that this liability gave rise to a right to payment. Because the EPA has elected to pursue a right of reimbursement in lieu of an order compelling the debtor to restore past pollution, a monetary obligation has been created that qualifies as a claim. (This issue is discussed further in connection with the discharge in section 22.2.)

Therefore, on the facts of this example, because the EPA has elected to clean up the site itself, the classification of the obligation as a claim is clear. Conversely, where the relief sought by the government agency is unquestionably nothing more than an order to cease polluting (that is, to stop unlawful activity in the future), this is an injunction on prospective activity which cannot be translated into money. (The agency has no authority to elect to allow the pollution to continue and to claim compensation for it.) Therefore, the debtor's obligation to cease pollution is not a claim. Although an injunction prohibiting future pollution is the clearest case of a nonclaim, an order to clean up past pollution is also so classified where the agency is not empowered by legislation to perform the cleanup itself and claim reimbursement, but is permitted only to seek a cleanup order. Some state legislation is structured in this way. *See In re Industrial Salvage, Inc.* 196 B.R. 784 (Bankr. S.D. Ill. 1996). The fact that the estate would have to spend money to comply with the order does not in itself make the cleanup obligation into a claim.

A more difficult case is presented where the agency has the power to elect either to obtain a cleanup order or to perform the work itself and seek reimbursement. Some courts have held that even if the agency has not chosen to do the cleanup, the fact that it has the option of doing so makes the obligation into a claim. *See In re Torwico Electronics, Inc.,* 8 F.3d 146 (3d Cir. 1993). Therefore, in our example, even if the EPA had not yet decided to perform the cleanup, if it still had the option to do this, Cess Pools's liability could be treated as a claim.

(b) Although EPA's right to payment would only fall due if and when the cleanup costs are incurred, this does not necessarily mean that the claim arises (comes into existence) only when the costs are incurred. It is possible that liability on the claim arose earlier, contingent upon EPA performing the cleanup. That is, even if the claim would not yet be payable under nonbankruptcy law, it could be a contingent claim, which is included in the definition

427

of "claim" under §101(5), and must, therefore, be handled as a claim against the estate. (If the cleanup will not be performed for a period of time, and waiting for this contingency to be removed would unduly delay administration of the estate, the contingent claim can be estimated under §502(c).

Courts have had difficulty in deciding when a claim arises where the pollution occurred prepetition, but the cleanup and resulting monetary liability for reimbursement will only take place postpetition. This determination can be very significant, especially given the high cost of rectifying pollution. The dating of the claim can have a great impact on the estate and on the government's ability to recover from the polluter: If the claim arose when the pollution occurred, it would be an unsecured prepetition claim. However, if it arises only when the cleanup costs are incurred, it is a postpetition claim. If the cleanup takes place during the course of the administration of the estate, the claim would qualify as an administrative expense with first priority. If the cleanup occurs after the case has been closed, the claim could be seen as a postbankruptcy claim against the fresh start estate of the debtor. Obviously, the government would prefer to have its claim treated as arising after rather than before the petition if this means elevating it into a priority claim. Sometimes, where the rehabilitation is successful and the debtor is likely to have wealth in the future, it is better still for the claim to be treated as postbankruptcy.

The Code does not prescribe any specific test for deciding when a claim arises, and this must be decided with reference to nonbankruptcy law. The general rule under nonbankruptcy law is that a claim comes into existence as soon as the act giving rise to liability takes place. Some courts have held that as the release of the pollutant creates liability, the claim arose when the pollution occurred. Other courts, going to the opposite side of the spectrum, have held that the claim does not arise until the cost of cleaning the pollution is incurred. However, most courts feel that neither of these tests is satisfactory because neither adequately balances the fresh start policy of bankruptcy against the environmental policy of imposing cleanup liability on the polluter: To fix the claim at too early a date tends to favor the debtor's fresh start too heavily by making most liability for prepetition pollution into dischargeable general unsecured claims. Conversely, to fix the claim as arising only upon cleanup tends in some cases to permit the claim to be a charge against the fresh start estate and nondischargeable in the bankruptcy. To attempt a better policy balance, these courts have favored a more complex test under which the claim comes into existence at some point between these poles.

In *In re Chateaugay Corp.*, 944 F.2d 997 (2nd Cir. 1991), the court drew an analogy to contract law, because it felt that the EPA as regulator has a relationship with the debtor similar to that between parties to a contract. On this theory, the claim arises as soon as EPA became aware of the problem site and could reasonably have contemplated the need for cleanup. Later courts have built on and refined *Chateaugay*'s "reasonable contemplation" test by adding a requirement of fairness: The claim arose, not simply when the EPA had a general awareness that there was a pollution problem, but only when it became aware and could fairly have contemplated that the site would require remediation. *See In re National Gypsum Co.*, 139 B.R. 397 (N.D. Tex. 1992); *In re Texaco, Inc.*, 182 B.R. 937 (Bankr. S.D.N.Y. 1995); *Signature Combs, Inc. v. U.S.* 253 F. Supp. 2d. 1028 (W.D. Tenn 2003). The "fair contemplation" test has become the more widely accepted one.

Our facts are not full enough to enable us to decide at what point the EPA fairly contemplated that Cess Pools's site would require remediation, which shows that the "fair contemplation" standard is much more complex than a test based on an identifiable, discrete event. To answer the question, the court will have to conduct a factual inquiry into the history of EPA's relationship with the debtor and the site, including the extent of its investigation and the action taken over a period of time.

(c) This argument focuses on the policy issues raised in the answer to argument (b) and also revives the point made in Example 2 of Chapter 5 and in section 5.5: When bankruptcy policy pulls in a different direction from the policies served by another federal statute, the court must try to balance and reconcile the conflicting aims of the statutes as well as it can. Sometimes Congress gives clear guidance on which goal should predominate. If it has not, the court must do its best to ascertain the policy balance from the legal rules.

The inclusion of the cleanup obligation as a claim in the estate serves at least two bankruptcy goals. It permits the debtor a fresh start by discharging the claim, and it advances the aim of evenhanded treatment of creditors by according the environmental claim no higher status than any other claim of its class (provided, of course, that its classification either as a general unsecured claim or as an administrative expense is proper).

The dominant goal of CERCLA is to ensure that the person responsible for pollution, rather than the public treasury, pays for its remediation. Treating the cleanup responsibility as a postbankruptcy claim will usually best serve this goal unless the debtor has no assets and no likelihood of rehabilitation. Because Congress has not clearly articulated the balance in either statute, the judicial approaches that seek an intermediate point for dating the claim may most fairly strike the balance.

4. Provided that the trustee had court authority to operate the debtor's business under §721 for the purpose of orderly liquidation, the electricity charges qualify as an administrative expense under §§364(a), 503(b)(1), and 507(a)(1). However, the trustee may argue that the consumption of electricity was a reasonable, necessary expense for the preservation of the building that was incurred for the benefit of the mortgagee. As such, it is recoverable from the property under §506(c).

In *In re Delta Towers, Ltd.*, 924 F.2d 74 (5th Cir. 1991), the case on which this question is based, it was conceded that the expenses were necessary and reasonable, which is probably true in the present case as well. The focus was therefore on the issue of whether they were beneficial to the mortgagee. The court emphasized that the expenses must be primarily for the benefit of the secured claimant, and that the benefit must be quantifiable and direct — it is not enough that some tangential or speculative benefit is conferred. The court concluded that no such direct benefit was received by the mortgagee. Its interest extended only to the property itself, and was not enhanced or protected by the continued supply of utilities that were not needed to prevent deterioration of the property or to maintain its realizable value.

The question of benefit is a factual one, and it does not inevitably follow that the present case would be resolved the same way as *Delta Towers* was. The facts indicate that power was needed to operate a security system and to allow tenants to inhabit the building. It could be argued that the security system protected the building itself (rather than only the tenants), and that failure to provide the tenants with services would have resulted in lease cancellations that would have reduced the building's value. The facts would need to be examined more fully to decide if these arguments are tenable. If the electricity costs were partially beneficial to the mortgagee, they must be apportioned so that only those attributable to the preservation of the property are charged against it.

5. These claims should be ranked as follows.

(a-b) The first and second mortgages are secured claims that will both be paid in full out of the proceeds of the apartment complex — provided that the property realizes enough to cover them both. If the property's proceeds are sufficient to cover both mortgages, their relative priority is not practically significant because they are both paid in full. As there do not appear to be interests in the property junior to the mortgages, any surplus goes into the general fund of the estate for ultimate distribution to unsecured creditors. However, if the property is not valuable enough to pay both claims in full, they must be ranked. The order of priority between them is determined by nonbankruptcy law, which most likely follows the first-in-time rule based on the date of recording the mortgages. Therefore, for example, if the proceeds are sufficient to pay the first mortgage in full but only to satisfy the second in part, the deficiency due to the second mortgagee is an unsecured claim.

(c) The manager's salary for the month prior to the petition is a third priority claim under §507(a)(3), but only to the extent of $4,650. If the claim is larger than that, the excess is a general unsecured claim. The manager's salary for the month after the petition should be split into two. The salary for the week between the petition and the appointment of the trustee is a claim under §502(f). It seems to be an ordinary course expense incurred by the debtor in operating its business before the trustee's appointment in an involuntary case. As such, it is excluded from administrative expenses by §503(b) and is given second priority by §507(a)(2).

The claim for salary for the period following the trustee's appointment arises out of the trustee's short-term operation of the debtor's business in the course of liquidation. Provided that the court authorized this operation under §721, the claim results from the ordinary course of operating the debtor's business as permitted by §364(a), and it is a first priority administrative expense claim under §507(a)(1).

In summary, the salary debt due to the manager splits into three separate claims, having first, second and third priority. In addition, if the prepetition claim exceeds $4,650, the debt also produces a fourth claim that is a nonpriority general claim.

(d) The manager's damages claim for breach of contract arises out of the estate's rejection of the executory employment contract. As discussed in section 18.4, §365(g) treats the rejection as a prepetition breach and §502(g) provides for the damages claim to be handled as if it arose prepetition. Section 502(b)(7) disallows the claim for damages to the extent that it exceeds one year's compensation measured from the petition date or the date on which the employee's performance terminated. Therefore, not only is this claim a general unsecured claim, but it will also be reduced to the extent that it exceeds the limits imposed by §502(b)(7).

(e) Property taxes qualify for eighth priority under §507(a)(8)(B) provided that they were assessed before the petition and were last payable, without penalty, within a year of the petition. The tax claim represents two years' unpaid property taxes. Although the latest year probably satisfies the conditions for priority, the tax for the prior year only does so if the debtor could have paid it in the year before bankruptcy without being liable for a penalty. The state tax statute must be consulted to determine this. To the extent that the tax claim does not qualify for eighth priority, it is a general unsecured claim. (The exception to discharge in §523(a)(1) does not apply to the portion of the tax that does not qualify for priority status.)

(f) The attorney's fee relating to the sale of the complex is a cost of administering and liquidating the estate. It qualifies as an administrative expense under §503(b)(2), provided that the trustee's employment of the attorney is authorized under §327 and the fee is awarded by the court under §330. As an administrative expense, it is given first priority under §507(a)(1).

(g) The landscape company's claim for prepetition work fits into no priority category. It is a general unsecured claim. The same is true of the damages claim for breach arising out of the rejection of the executory contract which, like the manager's claim is deemed to be a general unsecured prepetition claim. Unlike the manager's claim, there is no limit imposed by §502 on the extent of damages claimable.

(h) The trade claims are all general unsecured claims.

In summary, the claims are ranked in the following order:

Secured Claims (to the extent of the proceeds of the collateral):
1. First mortgage
2. Second mortgage

Superpriority: None

Priority Claims:

First.	Manager's salary for period after trustee's appointment Attorney's fee
Second.	Manager's salary during gap between petition and trustee's appointment
Third.	Manager's prepetition salary, up to $4,650
Eighth.	Property taxes, to the extent that they qualify under §507(a)(8)(B)

General Unsecured Claims (all of equal rank):

Deficiency on mortgages, if any

Property taxes, to the extent not qualified for seventh priority

Manager's prepetition salary above $4,650

Manager's claim for breach of contract, subject to limit it §507(b)(7)

Landscape company's claims for prepetition work and for damages for breach of contract

Trade claims

20

The Chapter 13 Plan

§20.1 Introduction and Review

Rules and principles applicable in Ch. 13 cases have been discussed in each of the preceding chapters. The focus here is on the Ch. 13 proceedings and the plan. A comprehensive review of all the issues involved in a Ch. 13 case would take too long. However, a reminder of some of the central features of Ch. 13 is a useful starting point for the present discussion:[1]

(1) Unlike Ch. 7, in which the debtor's nonexempt assets are liquidated and the proceeds distributed to creditors, Ch. 13 is designed to enable the debtor to keep all or most of his or her property and to use part of future income over a period of years to pay creditors at least as much as — and ideally more than — they would have received from the liquidation of prepetition assets.

(2) It is a general policy of bankruptcy law to favor rehabilitation under Ch. 13 over liquidation under Ch. 7, on the theory that creditors are likely to do better in a Ch. 13 case. Whether or not this assumption is correct, it motivates many provisions of the Code that provide incentives to the debtor to choose Ch. 13 over Ch. 7. Until now, the Code has relied on these incentives to channel debtors into Ch. 13 voluntarily, but there has been a long-standing debate about their effectiveness. As noted in sections 8.5 and 9.7, pending reform legislation will, if passed, impose a means

---

1. The Appendix has a tabular comparison of the essential differences between Ch. 13 and other forms of bankruptcy.

test on debtors that will preclude Ch. 7 relief if they can afford to support a Ch. 13 plan.

(3) Eligibility for Ch. 13 relief is restricted. Only an individual with regular income, whose debts fall within the limitations of §109(e), can be a debtor under Ch. 13. (These limitations are discussed in section 8.4.2.) Ch. 13 debtors are commonly wage-earning consumers, but the debtor could derive income from other sources, including self-employment in business.

(4) A Ch. 13 case must be commenced voluntarily. Creditors have no right to petition for an involuntary Ch. 13 bankruptcy. Similarly, only the debtor may convert a case to Ch. 13. Under §1307, the debtor has the right to convert the Ch. 13 case to Ch. 7 or to have it dismissed. Creditors may convert a Ch. 13 case to Ch. 7 or have it dismissed for cause, which includes dilatory, abusive, or noncompliant behavior by the debtor. Section 1307 does not expressly include lack of good faith as a cause for dismissal, but courts have recognized that this is a basis for cause, as discussed in section 20.6.

(5) In a Ch. 13 case, the automatic stay is extended by §1301 to any individual who is codebtor or surety of the debtor on a consumer debt.

(6) Under §1306, the Ch. 13 estate consists not only of property covered by §541 but also of all such property, including postpetition earnings, acquired by the debtor between commencement of the case and its close. Postpetition property is included in the Ch. 13 estate because the debtor's performance under the plan is dependent on it. On confirmation of the plan, the property vests in the debtor, except as provided for in the plan. (This is explained further in section 20.2.)

(7) A trustee is appointed in all Ch. 13 cases. Districts with a large volume of Ch. 13 cases have a standing Ch. 13 trustee. The principal duty of the Ch. 13 trustee is the collection and disbursement of payments under the plan. In addition, under §1302, the trustee must account for property of the estate, investigate the debtor's affairs, examine and object to proofs of claim, help the debtor to formulate the plan, and participate in the confirmation and discharge hearings.

(8) Ch. 13 does not recognize the concept of a debtor in possession. However, if the debtor operated a business at the time of the petition, §1304 permits the debtor to continue to run the business after bankruptcy. The debtor retains control of the business under §1304 and performs the trustee's functions under §§363 and 364 with regard to the sale, use, and lease of estate property and postpetition credit. Other trustee's powers are exercised by the trustee who is required under §1302(c), read with §§1106(a)(3) and (4), to monitor the debtor's business activities until the close of the case.

(9) The exemptions available to an individual debtor are less directly applicable in Ch. 13 than they are in Ch. 7, because the general effect

of Ch. 13 is to enable the debtor to keep all property that is not designated for liquidation in the plan. However, exemptions are relevant in a Ch. 13 case, in that they are taken into account in deciding how much the debtor must pay under the plan to meet minimum requirements for confirmation. This is discussed in section 20.7.

(10) Finally, remember that all the provisions in Chs. 1, 3, and 5 apply in a Ch. 13 case unless specifically excluded.

§20.2   Outline of the Ch. 13 Proceedings

A Ch. 13 case begins much like the Ch. 7 case described in section 9.3, with a voluntary petition and supporting documents that are much the same, except for the plan.

Section 1321 requires the debtor to file a plan. Under Rule 3015(b), the plan must be filed with the petition or within 15 days thereafter unless the court extends the time. Only the debtor may file a plan. (Unlike Ch. 11, creditors have no right to file competing plans.) Section 1323 allows the debtor to modify the plan before confirmation without court approval. This enables the debtor to respond to any objections informally before the plan is submitted to the court for confirmation.

A trustee is appointed after the petition has been filed. There is no provision for the trustee's election at the meeting of creditors, as there is in a Ch. 7 case. Rule 2003(a) requires the meeting of creditors to be called within 20 to 50 days after the petition, and under Rule 3002 claims must be proved within 90 days of the meeting.

Unless the court orders otherwise, §1326(a)(1) requires the debtor to begin making payments within 30 days of filing the plan. Section 1302(b)(5) imposes the duty on the trustee to ensure that such payments are made. Under §1326(a)(2), until the plan is confirmed, the trustee retains the payments. Distribution begins as soon as practicable after confirmation of the plan. If the plan is not confirmed, payments are released to the debtor after the deduction of administrative costs.

Section 1324 deals with the confirmation hearing. Neither the Code nor the rules specify when the hearing must occur. It could take place soon after the meeting of creditors, or only after the bar date for proof of claims. Under Rule 2002(b), 25 days notice of the hearing must be given to parties in interest. Rule 3015(d) requires the notice to include a copy of the plan or a summary of it. Even if no one objects to the plan, the hearing must be held, and the court must scrutinize the plan to ensure that it complies with the statutory standards. (The term of art "after notice and a hearing" is not used in §1324, so the hearing is not dispensed with in the absence of objections.) If confirmation is refused, the debtor has the opportunity to correct objectionable elements in the plan by amendment. If the plan is not satisfactorily amended, a party in interest can apply under §1307 for dismissal of the case or its conversion to Ch. 7.

Upon confirmation of the plan, the trustee distributes the debtor's preconfirmation payments under §1326(a), and the debtor begins the course of payments required by the confirmed plan. If necessary, the court is able to issue a form of garnishment order under §1325(c), compelling the person from whom the debtor receives income to transmit the plan payments to the trustee. Section 1326 contemplates that the debtor makes payments to the trustee, who disburses them in accordance with the plan after deducting trustee's fees and other administrative expenses. However, in appropriate circumstances the court has the discretion to confirm a plan that provides for the debtor to make some payments directly to particular creditors. The debtor's default in the performance required under the plan is grounds for dismissal or conversion under §1307.

Section 1327(a) states the effect of confirmation: The plan binds the debtor and all creditors, whether or not their claims are provided for by the plan or whether they accepted or rejected it. Creditors do not vote on the Ch. 13 plan, as they do in a Ch. 11 case.[2] Their only opportunity to challenge the plan is by objection to confirmation on the grounds that the plan does not meet statutory standards. If a creditor fails to object or the objection is unsuccessful, the creditor is bound by the plan. Even if creditors do not like the plan, it is imposed on them (*crammed down*, in bankruptcy jargon), provided that it satisfies the prerequisites for confirmation.

Under §§1327(b) and (c), confirmation of the plan vests all property of the estate in the debtor, free and clear of any claim or interest in it, except as otherwise provided in the plan or the order of confirmation. Although the debtor's postpetition property continues to enter the estate under §§1306 and 541, all the estate property passes back to the debtor upon confirmation except for that property or income committed to performance of the plan. The estate therefore continues to exist as a legal entity, separate from the debtor, even though the bulk of its property vests in the debtor.

Unlike Ch. 11, in which confirmation of the plan discharges preconfirmation debts, the Ch. 13 confirmation does not operate as a discharge. Therefore, if the debtor defaults on the plan and the case is converted to Ch. 7 or dismissed, the balance of the claims against the debtor remain recoverable. The debtor is only discharged under §1328 after the plan has been consummated, unless cause exists for a premature discharge on grounds of hardship (discussed more fully in Chapter 22).

---

2. In a limited number of situations, a secured or priority creditor can accept a plan that gives it less than its statutory entitlement. This is not a general requirement for creditor assent, but applies only where the plan falls short of the minimum treatment prescribed for a secured or priority claim. *See* sections 20.7.1 and 20.7.2.

In appropriate circumstances, the plan may be revoked or modified after confirmation. Revocation may be ordered under §1330 after notice and a hearing if a party in interest applies for it within 180 days after the entry of the order of confirmation and shows that the confirmation was fraudulently procured. Modification may be applied for under §1329 by the debtor, the trustee, or an unsecured claimant, if the debtor's circumstances change after confirmation. This is discussed in section 20.10.

§20.3 Overview of the Plan and the Prerequisites for Confirmation

The plan is the debtor's proposal for the resolution of the Ch. 13 case. Its provisions are based on the information disclosed in the schedules filed in connection with the petition. Broadly speaking, the plan has three components: It states what income and assets will be used to fund the plan, it proposes the treatment to be given to claims, and it provides for various optional matters, such as the election on whether to assume or reject executory contracts. Sections 1322 and 1325 contain the crucial provisions on the contents of the plan and the standards for its confirmation. In summary, they are as follows:

(1) **Optional provisions under §1322(b).** Section 1332(b) lists optional provisions that may be included in the plan. It covers matters such as the classification of unsecured claims, the modification of claims, the cure of default, and other terms that may be useful to the debtor and appropriate in the case. The list in §1332(b) is not exclusive: §1332(b)(10) allows the debtor to include in the plan any provision that is not inconsistent with the Code.

(2) **Mandatory provisions under §1322(a).** Section 1332(a) states that the plan must comply with three rules. First, it must bind the debtor to pay future earnings to the trustee, in an amount sufficient to execute the plan. (*See* section 20.4.) Second, it must provide for the full payment of priority claims, unless the claimant agrees otherwise. (*See* section 20.7.2.) Third, if it classifies claims, it must treat claims in the same class equally. (*See* section 20.7.3.)

Because these requirements are mandatory, they must be satisfied and the court does not have the discretion to confirm a plan that does not comply with them. In *In re Escobedo*, 28 F.3d 34 (7th Cir. 1994), the court even allowed the trustee to object to a plan after it had been consummated because it had failed to provide for the full payment of priority claims. Even though no one objected at the time of confirmation, the court said that the plan could not validly omit the full payment of a priority claim without the agreement of the claimant.

(3) **Confirmation requirements under §1325(a).** Section 1325(a) requires the court to confirm a plan if it meets six criteria and if confirmation is

not precluded by §1325(b). On its face, §1325(a) gives the court no power to refuse confirmation if the requirements are satisfied. However, the court does have some discretion in determining whether or not the criteria have been met. Section 1325(a) is couched in affirmative terms; although it says that the court shall confirm a complying plan, it does not forbid the court from confirming a plan that falls short of full compliance. Notwithstanding, a court is not likely to confirm a plan that deviates from §1325(a) unless the parties whose rights are affected have acquiesced or the shortcoming in the plan is trivial and the spirit of the Code is not contravened by the noncompliance. (In *Escobedo*, the court distinguished the discretionary nature of the requirements in §1325 from the mandatory nature of those in §1322.) The debtor's failure to meet the standards of §1325(a) may be challenged through an objection to confirmation by a party in interest, or it could be raised by the court *sua sponte*, even in the absence of objection. Section 1325(a) is examined more carefully in the following sections. In summary, its six criteria are:

(a) The plan must comply with Ch. 13 and all other applicable provisions of the Code.

(b) All fees required to be paid before confirmation must have been paid.

(c) The plan must be proposed in good faith and not by any means forbidden by law. (*See* section 20.6.)

(d) The distribution to be paid to each unsecured claimant under the plan must be at least equal to what it would have received had the estate been liquidated under Ch. 7. Because the payments under the plan will be made over time, interest must be added to the amount distributed to each claimant so that the claimant receives the present value of its hypothetical Ch. 7 distribution. (*See* section 20.7.3.)

(e) Unless a secured claimant accepts different treatment, the plan must either provide for the collateral to be surrendered to the claimant, or it must preserve the claimant's lien and provide for full payment of the present value of the secured claim. Present value is determined by adding interest to the face amount of the claim. (*See* section 20.7.1.)

(f) The plan must be feasible. Based on the financial data furnished in the schedules, it must be apparent that the debtor will be able to make all payments under the plan and to comply with it. (*See* section 20.4.)

(4) Confirmation requirements under §1325(b).   Section 1325(b) contains a further requirement for confirmation that cannot be enforced by the court of its own accord but must be raised by objection by the trustee or an unsecured claimant. In the simplest terms, the trustee or an unsecured creditor who would receive less than full payment under the plan may object to the plan if the debtor has not committed to the plan all of his or her disposable income for a three-year period. (*See* section 20.7.3.)

§20.4 The Funding of the Plan and the Debtor's Obligation to Make Payments

As stated before, the Ch. 13 debtor usually seeks to keep the property that would otherwise have been liquidated under Ch. 7 and to substitute a series of payments to be distributed by the trustee to creditors. Although the premise of Ch. 13 is that the plan will be funded from the debtor's future income, it does not have to rely exclusively on that source. The debtor may liquidate some property to supplement the monies contributed from income, and is authorized to do so by §1322(b)(8). Also, §1325(a) permits the debtor to surrender property subject to a security interest, rather than retain the property and pay off the debt. Whatever the source of funding may be, the plan must specify it as well as set out the proposed periodic payments to be made by the debtor and the length of the payment period. Section 1322(a) requires the plan to provide for income to be submitted to the trustee sufficient to support the plan, §1302 obliges the trustee to ensure that payments are commenced, and §1326 regulates payments by the trustee.

Because the debtor's payments are the lifeblood of the plan, the court must be satisfied at the outset that the debtor can afford to make the payments. As stated in section 8.4.2, a debtor must have regular income to be eligible for Ch. 13 relief. A debtor with unpredictable or unstable income cannot be permitted to undertake Ch. 13 bankruptcy. This principle is also reflected in §1325(a)(6), which includes as one of the criteria for confirmation that the debtor appear to be able to make payments under the plan. Sections 109(e) and 1325(a)(b) impose a minimum standard of affordability on the debtor. At the other end of the scale, §1325(b) enables the trustee or an unsecured creditor to insist that the debtor commits all disposable income to the plan. This is discussed in section 20.7.3.

§20.5 The Length of the Plan

When it enacted Ch. 13 in 1978, Congress felt there should be a limit on the length of time that a debtor could be committed to payments under a Ch. 13 plan. Section §1322(d) absolutely forbids payments under a plan to extend beyond five years. Even within that five-year period, the court can only approve payments over more than three years if cause for the longer period is shown. (*See* Example 2.) This means that in the absence of a justification for a longer payment period, Ch. 13 plans last no more than three years. The wording of §1322(d) suggests that the time limit is reckoned from the first payment under the plan, which must be made 30 days after the petition. This issue is in some doubt, however, and there are courts that have measured it from the date of plan confirmation. As discussed in section 20.10, even if a plan is modified the statutory limit is still measured from the original date and not from the date of the modification.

No minimum period of payment is prescribed. However, a debtor who proposes to pay relatively small amounts over a short period will probably not satisfy the good faith and best interests tests described below. In addition, the disposable income test in §1325(b) gives creditors grounds to challenge a plan that does not commit all the debtor's disposable income for three years.

The pending bankruptcy reform legislation would, if passed, change §1322 to eliminate the need for court approval for a five-year plan where the debtor's income exceeds the median family income.

§20.6   Good Faith

Section 1325(a)(3) requires the plan to be proposed in good faith and not by any means forbidden by law. Good faith is a pervasive requirement in Ch. 13. Apart from being one of the prerequisites for plan confirmation, it is also a ground for dismissal or conversion under §1307. Section 1307(c) does not expressly mention lack of good faith in its non-definitive list of causes for conversion or dismissal, but courts have recognized it as encompassed within their general power to dismiss or convert for cause. See *In re Leavitt*, 171 F.3d 1219 (9th Cir. 1999); *In re Lancaster*, 280 B.R. 468 (Bankr. W.D. Mo. 2002). Courts use the same standards (discussed below) to measure good faith, whether they are dealing with a motion to dismiss or convert the case, or an objection to plan confirmation.

The above cases show the practical difference between using lack of good faith as grounds for dismissal or using it as the basis of refusing to confirm a plan. In *In re Leavitt*, the debtor had cheated his business partner and had filed successive bankruptcy petitions, including this one, to attempt to evade his liability to the partner. He had concealed assets and listed inflated expenses. The court dismissed the case with prejudice because the debtor had been motivated by bad faith in filing the case. This meant that the debtor was precluded from refiling under any Chapter for the purpose of obtaining a discharge. In *In re Lancaster* the debtor had behaved abominably prior to the case. Upon hearing that his estranged wife was seeing another man, he entered the other man's home, cut the brake line on his motorbike, and then rampaged through his home, smashing property. In the process, he broke plumbing, causing water to flood into the house, and also broke the gas line leading to the furnace, causing a gas leak that ultimately led to an explosion that destroyed the house. The owner of the house and his insurer sued the debtor for claims totaling about $200,000 and obtained judgments against him. He then filed a petition under Ch. 13. These two creditors moved for dismissal of the case on the ground that the debtor's primary purpose in filing under Ch. 13 was to discharge his debt for wilful and malicious injury that could not be discharged in Ch 7. (This is explained below and in Example 1). In the alternative, they objected to confirmation of the plan on grounds that the payments that he proposed under the plan were minimal — they amounted to about 3 percent of the claim — and he could afford to pay more. (This is also explained below and in Example 1.) The court found that there was no basis for dismissing the case because the debtor had the right to take advantage of the more generous discharge under Ch. 13 and he had not otherwise acted dishonestly in filing the petition. However, it refused to confirm the plan on the basis that he was trying to take advantage of the broader Ch. 13 discharge without making a sincere effort to pay more to creditors. As a result, the case was not terminated and the debtor had the opportunity to file an amended plan that proposed a more conscientious effort at payment.

The scope and meaning of good faith is not defined by the Code, but it has been developed judicially. The inquiry is directed at the debtor's state of mind in seeking Ch. 13 relief or in proposing the plan. The debtor's honesty is a factual issue to be decided under all the circumstances of the case. There is no definitive list of factors to be considered. However, the following are some of the areas that are often the subject of inquiry: The accuracy and honesty of the debtor's financial disclosures; the circumstances under which debts were incurred (*e.g.*, whether they arose from tortious or dishonest conduct); the debtor's prepetition dealings with creditors (*e.g.*, whether the debtor had used delaying tactics to avoid payment or had otherwise misled or deceived creditors); the debtor's dealings with property (*e.g.*, whether there had been avoidable preferences, fraudulent transfers, or attempts to conceal assets); the reason for the debtor's financial distress (*e.g.*, whether it was caused by unfortunate circumstances or by irresponsible or dishonest dealings); the advantages sought by the debtor in choosing relief under Ch. 13 instead of under Ch. 7 (*e.g.*, whether there is a substantial debt that is dischargeable under Ch. 13 but not under Ch. 7, as illustrated by Example 1); the debtor's financial history (including, for example, the frequency with which the debtor has sought bankruptcy relief in the past); the degree of effort undertaken by the debtor to pay claims and to give creditors fair treatment.

The last factor has given courts difficulty. There are objective criteria in §1325 for deciding whether the payment proposed for each class of claims is adequate. *See* section 20.7. The apparent intent of §1325 is that if these criteria are satisfied, the level of payment proposed by the debtor is legally sufficient. Therefore, the fact that the debtor could pay more, or that creditors receive little benefit beyond what they would have recovered from a Ch. 7 liquidation should not, of itself, be treated as bad faith. Although courts do tend to follow this reasoning and to separate the issues of good faith and sufficiency of payment, it is not always possible to draw a sharp line between them. The debtor's honesty is questionable when he or she receives a clear advantage under Ch. 13 without providing any more for creditors than they would have recovered under Ch. 7. Therefore, while courts do not generally find bad faith solely on the basis that the debtor can afford to pay more than the minimum required to satisfy the objective payment criteria, the sincerity of the debtor's effort to pay and to treat creditors fairly is one of the factors taken into account in determining whether good faith exists in the totality of the circumstances. *See, e.g., In re Doersam,* 849 F.2d 237 (6th Cir. 1988); *In re Smith,* 848 (F.2d 813 (7th Cir. 1988); *In re LeMaire,* 898 F.2d 1346 (8th Cir. 1990). *In re Keach,* 243 B.R. 851 (1st Cir. B.A.P. 2000); *In re Lancaster* (above). *See also* Example 1.

§20.7   The Classification of Claims and the Standards Applicable to Each Class

The plan deals with secured, priority, and general claims separately. In addition, §1322(b)(1) allows the debtor to divide unsecured claims into classes. The treatment of claims in each of the three principal classifications is subject to different rules.

§20.7.1   Secured Claims

The debtor has three alternatives for the treatment of secured claims in a Ch. 13 plan.[3] The first two do not require the creditor's acquiescence but can be crammed down provided that the plan meets the statutory requirements. The alternatives are:

(1) *Payment of the claim.* Under §1325(a)(5)(B), the plan may provide for the payment of the allowed amount of the secured claim,[4] valued as at the effective date of the plan. This is the present value of the claim, as explained before, calculated by adding interest to the claim's face value to compensate the holder for having to wait for its money instead of receiving it immediately in a Ch. 7 liquidation.

The face value of the claim is not always self-evident because, unless the collateral is found to be worth more than the amount of the debt, the secured claim is fixed at the value of the collateral. In such a case, the collateral must be valued to determine how much of the claim is to be treated as secured, and how much is to be

---

3. As a fourth alternative, the debtor can simply not provide for the claim in the plan, in which case it is not affected by the bankruptcy and survives the discharge.

4. The pending reform legislation would enhance the amount of payment required under §1325(a)(5)(B) by also requiring that periodic payments to the secured claimant are sufficient to assure adequate protection of the claim.

relegated to the unsecured category as a deficiency. The valuation of secured claims is discussed in section 19.6.3, in which the decision in *Associates Commercial Corp. v. Rash,* 117 S. Ct 1879 (1997) is explained. The court held that where the debtor proposes to keep and use the collateral in a Ch. 13 case, the proper measure of value is its replacement value (apparently equivalent to its fair value on the market in which the debtor would purchase it) rather than the value that it would realize at a foreclosure sale.

Although *Rash* settles the question that the rate of interest must be based on a market standard, courts since *Rash* have not agreed on the way in which to calculate the market rate. Some use a "cost of funds" approach that measures the interest rate in reference to what the lender would pay on the market to replace the funds tied up in the bankruptcy. Others prefer a "coerced loan" approach that is based on what the debtor would have to pay to get an equivalent loan on the commercial loan market under similar circumstances. Still others favor a "formula" approach that uses an objective interest rate (say the rate for treasury bonds) adjusted to take the creditor's risk into account. For some cases that discuss the merits and drawbacks of these different ways of determining the interest rate, see *In re Chiodo,* 261 B.R. 499 (Bankr. M.D. Fla. 2000); *In re Till,* 301 F.3d 583 (7th Cir. 2002); *In re Kidd,* 315 F.3d 671 (6th Cir. 2003).

If the plan provides for the payment of the secured claim, it must also preserve the holder's lien to secure payment. Therefore, although collateral vests in the debtor upon confirmation, it remains subject to the lien until the claim is paid in full. Except in the case of home mortgages, the payment schedule under the plan may be different from the original payment terms governing the secured debt. Also, the plan may provide for the cure of default and for the payment of long-term debt beyond the period of the plan. This is discussed in sections 20.8 and 20.9.

(2) *Surrender of the collateral.* Section 1325(a)(5)(C) permits the debtor to surrender the collateral to the holder of the claim, thereby disposing of the secured claim and freeing the debtor of the obligation to pay it under the plan. Of course, if the collateral is worth less than the debt, the deficiency is provable as an unsecured claim, provided that the creditor is entitled to claim the deficiency under nonbankruptcy law.

(3) *Consensual treatment.* Section 1325(a)(5)(A) allows the debtor to handle the secured claim in a manner different from that provided above if the holder of the claim accepts the plan. Acceptance is indicated most clearly by an affirmative act, but the claimant may be held to have accepted the plan if it fails to object.

§20.7.2   *Priority Claims*

Section 1322(a)(2) requires all priority claims to be paid in full by deferred cash payments unless the holder agrees to different treatment. Because priority claims must be paid in full, the order of priority in §507 is not as directly relevant in a Ch. 13 case as it is in Ch. 7. However, the ranking has some impact on the treatment of claims. If a class of priority claims would have received nothing had the case been filed under Ch. 7 (because the fund would have been exhausted by senior classes), the plan need provide only for full payment of the face amount of claims in that class. However, if the class would have been paid in full under Ch. 7, the best interests test described in section 20.7.3 requires that the class receives the present value of the Ch. 7 distribution, which includes interest on the face amount of the claims. If the priority class would have been treated somewhere between these extremes had the case been filed under Ch. 7 so that the claims would have received a pro rata payment, the amount paid under the plan must be the greater of the face value of the claims and the present value of the hypothetical pro rata Ch. 7 distribution. That is, if the Ch. 7 distribution plus interest is higher than the face value of the claim, this higher amount must be provided for in the plan to satisfy the best interests test.

§20.7.3   *Unsecured Claims*

The standards for confirmation relating to unsecured claims are prescribed by §§1325(a)(4) and (b). The former sets a minimum level of payment for unsecured claims and is known as the *best interests test* because its purpose is to ensure that the Ch. 13 plan serves the best interests of unsecured creditors by providing at least as much for them as they would have received in liquidation. Section 1325(b), added to the Code in 1984, requires the debtor to commit all disposable income for three years to payments under the plan. As mentioned before, this requirement only applies if invoked by the trustee or by an unsecured claimant whose claim is not to be paid in full under the plan.

a.   The Best Interests Test

Section 1325(a)(4) requires that the amount paid on each allowed unsecured claim have a value as of the effective date of the plan that is no lower than what would have been paid on the claim had the estate been liquidated under Ch. 7. To determine present value, a hypothetical Ch. 7 distribution must be calculated based on the value of estate property at the petition date, and to that amount a market interest rate for the period of payments under the plan must be added. The principle here is similar to that applicable to secured claims, in that interest must be added to compensate the claimant for payment over time. Note, however, that the formula for calculating present value differs between secured and unsecured claims. The present value of a secured claim is determined by adding interest to the allowed amount of the claim (*i.e.,* its face value); the present value of an unsecured claim is confined to the Ch. 7 distribution plus interest. This is because secured claims are paid in full out of the collateral in a Ch. 7 case, but unsecured claims receive only a partial distribution unless the estate is solvent.

If the Ch. 7 estate would have been so badly insolvent that general unsecured claims would have received no distribution, the best interests test provides no relief to them. As they would have received nothing under Ch. 7, a plan that provides for no distribution to general creditors satisfies the test. In such a case, a creditor cannot complain of inadequate payments unless there are grounds for invoking the disposable income test or the good faith standard.

b. The Disposable Income Test

If an objection is made by the trustee or by the holder of an allowed unsecured claim that is not to be paid in full under the plan, §1325(b)(1) forbids the court's approval of the plan unless the debtor has committed all his or her disposable income to the plan for the three years following the date on which the first payment is due. *Disposable income,* defined in §1325(b)(2), is income received by the debtor which is not reasonably necessary for the maintenance or support of the debtor or a dependent and, if the debtor is in business, for the necessary operation and preservation of the business.

By requiring the plan to apply all the debtor's "projected" disposable income over the three-year period, §1325(b)(1)(B) calls for a prediction of the debtor's future income over the life of the plan, and not simply the bare use of the debtor's earnings at the time of confirmation. However, because prediction is difficult, courts are not inclined to speculate on all the contingencies that might occur, and do not move much beyond the base of current income unless there is some indication that a specific anticipated event would alter income in a reasonably foreseeable way. Therefore, projected income is typically the debtor's current income, with some adjustment for reasonably expected and quantifiable future changes. As discussed in section 20.10, the plan can always be modified later if the projections of income turns out to be wrong.

The question of what constitutes "income" can also give rise to questions. "Income" is a wider term than "earnings," and it includes funds received by the debtor from various sources beyond wages. It could even include funds that would otherwise be exempt. In *In re Koch,* 109 F.3d 1285 (8th Cir. 1996), the court held that workers' compensation benefits paid to the debtor, although exempt under state law (and hence under §522, because the state had opted out of the federal exemptions), nevertheless, qualify as disposable income. The court reasoned that Ch. 13 had no language excluding exempt income from §1325(b)(1)(B), and the purpose of Ch. 13 was best served by requiring the debtor to apply it to the plan. The court observed that exemptions are intended to protect the debtor from penury and to bolster his fresh start, and if the debtor elects to obtain his fresh start by using Ch. 13 and making payments instead of sacrificing his otherwise executable assets, there is no unfairness in making him pay what he can afford.

As disposable income consists of that income not needed for the support of the debtor and his dependents and the payment of any of his business expenses, the court must also determine the debtor's reasonable living and work expenses. Like income, this is based on the debtor's current situation, with some adjustment for reasonably predictable changes over the plan period.

In deciding how much of the estimated income will be necessary for the debtor's reasonable needs, the court must examine the debtor's budget and decide what standard of living is appropriate for the debtor. Obviously, it is not justifiable for the debtor to live sumptuously while creditors are paid a fraction of their claims. On the other hand, while some sacrifice is to be expected, the debtor should not be reduced to desperate deprivation. (*See* Examples 1 and 2.)

The Religious Liberty and Charitable Contributions Protection Act was enacted by Congress in 1998 for the purpose of protecting the contributions made by the debtor to religious and charitable organizations. Its principal focus is on limiting the trustee's power to avoid such prepetition transfers as fraudulent transfers under §§544(b) and 548. (*See* sections 15.1.3 and 16.3). However, the 1998 amendments also added language to §707(b) on substantial abuse (*see* section 9.7) and to §1325(b)(2)(A) that ensure that religious or charitable contributions are taken into account in determining the debtor's reasonable expenditures. Section 1325(b)(2)(A) allows such contributions to be included as reasonable living expenses provided that they meet the requirements set out in §548 and the Internal Revenue Code, and they are made to a qualified religious or charitable organization as defined in those sections. They are capped at 15 percent of the debtor's gross income for the year in which they are made. The effect of this, of course, is to water down the disposable income test and to allow the debtor to continue to be charitable at the expense of unsecured creditors.

The language of §1325(b)(2)(A) gives the court little flexibility to decide if contributions under 15 percent of the debtor's annual gross income are reasonable. However, the good faith requirement of §1325(a)(3) is distinct from the disposable income test in §1325(b), and even if the contribution fits within the 15 percent cap, the court can still evaluate the debtor's good faith in claiming it as an expense. This is illustrated by *In re Cavanagh,* 250 B.R. 107 (9th Cir. B.A.P. 2000). The debtor originally filed a plan that made no provision for charitable or religious contributions.

He then amended his plan to show higher earnings offset by a tithe to be paid to his church, amounting to 7 percent of his gross income. He had not previously made church contributions. The trustee objected to the tithe. The court noted that §1325(b)(2)(A) deemed a contribution of under 15 percent to be a reasonably necessary expense so that the court could not enquire into whether the contribution was necessary. However, that did not mean that the court could not examine the debtor's motivation in making the contribution to determine if he was in good faith. Although the sudden decision to begin paying tithes was suspicious, the court deferred to the bankruptcy court's factual determination, based on its own extensive enquiries, that the debtor had undergone a genuine religious conversion after filing the petition.

c. The Classification of Unsecured Claims

Section 1322(b)(1) gives the debtor the discretion to place unsecured claims in separate classes. There are three guidelines that apply to claim classification: Claims in the same class must be treated alike (§1322(a)(3)), the plan must not discriminate unfairly against any class (§1322(b)(1)), and claims can only be classed together if they are substantially similar (§1322(b)(1) read with §1122).

Section 1322(b)(1) expresses only one justification for separate classification: If an individual is liable with the debtor on a consumer debt, that claim may be separated from other unsecured claims. The purpose of this provision is to allow the debtor to treat a consumer debt preferentially in order to eliminate or reduce the liability of a friend or relative who is codebtor or surety. The rationale behind the provision is that it prevents financial hardship to the codebtor and eliminates any pressure that the debtor would otherwise feel to pay the debt outside the plan, thereby endangering his or her rehabilitation.

The separate classification of guaranteed or joint consumer debts is presumptively fair discrimination (but the extent of the discrimination may be too excessive to be fair). However, when the debtor proposes to separate other types of claim into classes and to provide more favorable treatment to one or more of those classes, there must be good reason for the discrimination. The debtor's rationale for discriminatory treatment must be weighed against the general policy of evenhanded creditor treatment. Therefore, a court is likely to approve a claim classification only if it is necessary to the execution of the plan and the debtor's rehabilitation, it is proposed in good faith, and the degree of discrimination is no greater than it needs to be to achieve its purposes. For example, courts have not found discrimination to be fair where a debtor has classified a nondischargeable claim separately and provided for its full payment for the purpose of getting rid of the claim so that it would not have to be paid after the bankruptcy. By loading the full amount of the nondischargeable claim onto the plan, the debtor would devote a disproportionate amount of her disposable income toward the payment of the dischargeable claim, thereby reducing the fund that would otherwise be available to pay other creditors. See *In re Groves*, 39 F.3d 212 (8th Cir. 1994) (the debtor proposed to pay a nondischargeable student loan in full, while other unsecured creditors would receive only 40 percent of their claims); *In re Crawford*, 324 F.3d 539 (7th Cir. 2003) (the plan provided for almost full payment of a nondischargeable support debt, while other unsecured creditors got nothing); *In re Simmonds*, 288 B.R. 737 (Bankr. N.D. Tex. 2003) (the student loan would be paid in full, while other unsecured creditors were paid nothing.) For a further illustration, *see* Example 5. In addition, the best interests and disposable income tests require that even the class of claims that is treated least generously in the plan receives the level of payment required by §1325.

§20.8   The Modification of a Claimant's Rights and the Cure of Default

§20.8.1   *Introduction and General Note on Cure*

Section 1322(b)(2) allows the plan to modify the rights of all claimants except those whose claims are secured only by a security interest in real property used by the debtor as a principal residence. Section 1322(b)(3) allows the plan to provide for the cure or waiver of any default; this cure or waiver of default applies to all debts, including an otherwise nonmodifiable home mortgage.

The cure of default is a pervasive concept in §1322. It is permitted both by §1322(b)(3), which covers claims to be fully disposed of during the plan period, and by §1322(b)(5), which covers long-term debt to be paid off beyond the period of the plan. (Long-term debt is discussed in section 20.9.) This note states some general principles of cure, but the subject recurs in the remainder of this section and in section 20.9. As noted earlier, the cure of default is not regarded as a modification of the contract, so it applies, both under §1322(b)(3) and §1322(b)(5), to specially protected, nonmodifiable home mortgages. Although §1322(b)(3) provides in general terms for the cure of any default, its primary use is in connection with a secured debt in default. The debtor's motivation to propose the cure is her desire to retain property subject to a security interest. To do this, she is obliged, not only to pay the amounts due prospectively on the secured claim, but also to pay arrears or to remedy other breaches. That is, if the debtor has fallen into arrears in payments or has otherwise breached the contract, the right to cure enables her to reinstate the agreement by providing in the plan for payments or performance to remedy the breach. That is, of course, in addition to provisions in the plan (or in and beyond the plan for long-term debt) for the payment of future installments.

The amount payable to cure a default is stated in §1322(e) to be the amount determined in accordance with the agreement and applicable law. This provision was enacted in 1994 to make it clear (contrary to what the U.S. Supreme Court held in *Rake v. Wade*, 508 U.S. 464 (1993), that the secured claim is entitled to no more, as a cure, than the contract itself provides.

There is a difference of opinion among courts on whether §§1322(b)(3) and (5) apply only to prepetition defaults, or if they can also be used by a debtor who defaults during the course of the case by failing to perform the obligations assumed in the plan. If the cure right is available postpetition, a debtor who stumbles in making plan payments could then apply for a modification of the plan to include a cure of the default, thereby preventing dismissal or conversion to Ch. 7. *In re Mendoza*, 111 F.3d 1264 (5th Cir. 1997) is one of the cases that interpreted the cure provisions as applicable to postpetition default. The court noted that the general policy of §1322 is to encourage and facilitate the cure of default, and there is nothing in the language of the section that confines it to prepetition defaults. The court did recognize, however, that the debtor would be precluded from curing a postpetition default if the plan contained a "drop-dead" clause, which allows the creditor to foreclose in the event of default.

§20.8.2   The Modification and Cure of Claims Other Than Specially Protected Home Mortgages

The ability to modify rights enables the debtor to extend contractual installment periods that would otherwise have ended before the proposed period of the plan. This is most helpful when the debtor wishes to keep property subject to a security interest. Say, for example, that the debtor purchased a car on secured credit prior to bankruptcy, and the contractual payment period has two years to run. If the debtor proposes a three-year plan, §1322(b)(2) allows the payment period to be extended an extra year, thereby reducing the size of the monthly payments. In addition, if the debtor defaulted on the contract, §1322(b)(3) permits cure of the default so that the plan may provide for the payment of arrears as well as future installments. In effect, §§1322(b)(2) and (3) give the debtor the opportunity to redeem collateral by installments — something that cannot be done in a Ch. 7 case. The debtor's ability to modify a claimant's rights is limited by the confirmation criteria in §§1322 and 1325. So, for example, unless the claimant accepts the plan, the debtor cannot modify a security agreement by canceling the lien, substituting collateral, or giving the secured claimant less than it is entitled to receive under §1325(a)(5). If it passes, the pending bankruptcy reform legislation would restrict the debtor's right to modify a purchase money security interest in a motor vehicle acquired for personal use, if incurred within three years of bankruptcy, as well as other significant secured debts incurred within a year of bankruptcy.

§20.8.3   *The Special Treatment of Claims Secured Only by a Security Interest in Real Property That Is the Debtor's Principal Residence*

The bar on the modification of a security interest in the debtor's residence is intended to protect home mortgagees so that they will not be discouraged from providing home financing to individuals. Even though the debtor has some flexibility in restructuring other debts, the terms of the debtor's home mortgage must be complied with if the debtor wishes to keep the home. The plan cannot alter the payment schedule or otherwise propose to ease the debtor's commitments under the security agreement.

The prohibition on modification applies only to future payments. Default on the mortgage may be cured under §§1322(b)(3) and (c)(1) by providing in the plan for payment of the arrears by installments. Section 1322(c)(1), added by the Bankruptcy Reform Act of 1994, makes it clear that the cure provisions in §§1322(b)(3) and (5) are not affected by the antimodification rule in §1322(b)(2). The new subsection also specifies that the right to cure is not cut off by foreclosure until such time as the foreclosure sale has been completed. In states that recognize a statutory redemption period, courts have held that the right to cure extends even beyond the sale, until the end of the redemption period. (*See* Example 3.) The debtor has the right to cure defaults whether the mortgage is a short-term loan, payable within a period of the plan, or a long-term loan that may be dealt with under §1322(b)(5), as discussed in section 20.9.

The language used in §1322(b)(2) to exclude home mortgages from the debtor's modification power covers claims that are "secured only by a security interest in real property that is the debtor's principal residence." The word "only" means that if the mortgage covers other property in addition to the debtor's home (such as a second piece of real property, or personal property and appliances on the premises) or a multifamily dwelling, the antimodification rule does not apply. Similarly, it does not apply to a security interest in, say, a mobile home if state law does not classify it as real property,[5] nor to property that is not the debtor's principal residence (*e.g.*, a summer beach cottage).

Section 1322(c)(2), also added in 1994, creates another situation in which the antimodification rule is inapplicable. If the final payment under the mortgage falls due within the period of the plan (that is, the original

---

5. The pending bankruptcy reform legislation would include mobile homes and trailers as well as condominiums in the definition of "principal residence."

contractual due date for the final payment occurs within the plan period), the payment schedule can be amended by the plan so as to stretch out the mortgage payments over the entire length of the plan.

Section 1322(b)(2) expressly applies to secured claims. The antimodification rule is, therefore, clearly applicable when the home mortgage is fully secured (that is, the property is worth as much as or more than the debt). However, the section does not indicate what happens when the debt is only partially secured because the value of the home is worth less than the amount owing to the mortgagee. As a general rule, we have seen that when a claim is undersecured, §506(a) bifurcates it into a secured claim to the extent of the collateral's value, and an unsecured claim for the deficiency.

Prior to *Nobelman v. American Savings Bank,* 508 U.S. 324 (1993) it was unclear if the antimodification rule applied only to the secured debt, so that the unsecured debt could be stripped down, pegging the home mortgage at the value of the collateral as determined in bankruptcy. (The concept of lien stripping is explained in section 19.6.3). *Nobelman* made it clear that a debtor cannot strip down an undersecured mortgage on his principal residence. The court placed emphasis on the language of §1322(b)(2), which does not merely forbid modification of the claim secured by the mortgage, but prohibits the modification of the *rights* of the claimholder. The court acknowledged that a contrary reading of the section was possible on the plain grammar of §1322(b)(2) (to say nothing of the bifurcation principle in §506), but it considered that such a reading was not practicable because any stripping of or interference with the unsecured deficiency would inevitably be an interference with the holder's rights, and the section calls for the protection of those rights. (*See also* Example 6.)

Nobelman has the effect of extending the principle of *Dewsnup v. Tim,* 502 U.S. 410 (1992) to protected residential mortgages in Ch. 13. (*Dewsnup* was discussed in section 19.6.3. It held that a Ch. 7 debtor cannot use §506(d) to strip down an undersecured lien on real property by pegging it at the judicially determined valuation of the property at the time of bankruptcy. Recall, however, that *Dewsnup* was expressly confined to Ch. 7 cases, and *Nobelman* is limited to protected home mortgages in Ch. 13. In the case of other secured claims, the Supreme Court has not forbidden lien stripping, and many lower courts have held it to be permissible.)

An issue similar to that which has vexed courts under *Dewsnup* has arisen under §1322(b)(2) and *Nobleman.* The Supreme Court has dealt with the strip down of a partially secured mortgage, but not with the strip off of a fully unsecured second mortgage—that is, one that would be paid nothing in bankruptcy because, at the time of bankruptcy, the property is not worth enough to cover any portion of the junior lien. (Again, *see* section 19.6.3.) Courts dealing with this issue under §1322(b)(2) have been similarly divided. Some have held that *Nobleman* was premised on the creditor having at least some existing interest in the property at the time of bankruptcy, so if there is no value in the property to support the mortgage, it cannot qualify as a secured claim and is entitled to no protection under §1322(b)(2). See, for example, *In re Hoskins*, 262 B.R. 693 (Bankr. E.D. Mich. 2001); *In re Zimmer*, 313 F.3d 1220 (9th Cir. 2002); *In re German*, 258 B.R. 468 (Bankr. N.D. Okla. 2001). (*German* made the policy observation that junior mortgages—in the form of home equity loans—are often not in fact used to acquire or add value to a home, but for consumer purchases, so the policy of protecting home financiers is not necessarily furthered by giving junior mortgages the protection accorded by §1322(b)(2).) Other courts have taken the view that the crux of *Nobleman* is the protection of the "rights" of the claimholder, and as long as the mortgage is valid, those rights exist, even if they have no present economic worth. See for example, *In re Bauler*, 215 B.R. 628 (Bankr. D.N. Mex. 1997); *In re Lewandowski*, 219 B.R. 99 (Bankr. W.D. Pa. 1998).

§20.9   Long-Term Debt

While §1322(b)(2) enables the plan to extend payments on short-term debt, §1322(b)(5) allows the debtor to take advantage of a contract payment period that is longer than the period of the plan. Section 1322(b)(5) applies to all debts, including those secured by a home mortgage. The example of the car purchase, used in section 20.8.2, can be modified to explain this provision's operation: Say that the contractual payment period for the car has not two, but four years to run, and the debtor proposes a three-year plan. Section 1322(b)(5) allows the debtor to adhere to the contractual payment schedule, rather than accelerating it to bring it within the term of the plan. The debtor maintains regular installment payments while the plan is pending (these may be paid through the trustee or directly to the claimant) and continues to make contract payments after the conclusion of the plan until the debt is satisfied. Because payments on the claim will extend beyond the period of the plan, §1328(a)(1) excludes the debt from the Ch. 13 discharge. (For a further illustration of the use of §1322(b)(5), *see* Example 3.)

If the debtor had defaulted on the debt, §1322(b)(5) requires cure of the default within a reasonable time. Therefore, in addition to paying the regular installments as they become due, the debtor must provide in the plan for payments to be made on the arrears. The question of what time is reasonable for affecting the cure depends upon the circumstances of the case. The debtor is not necessarily entitled to spread the cure payments over the whole length of the plan.

§20.10   Modification of a Confirmed Plan

As mentioned in section 20.2, before confirmation, §1323 permits the debtor to modify the plan easily, and without court approval. Modification after confirmation is a more onerous process, which does require an application to court. Section 1329 provides for the modification of a confirmed plan, at any time before completion of payments, on request of the debtor, the trustee or the holder of an unsecured claim. Under §1329(a), the modification may either increase or reduce payments to a particular class, alter the time period for such payments, or change the amount of the distribution to a creditor to take account of payments outside of the plan. For the modification to be approved, §1329(c) states that the plan as modified must satisfy the same standards and requirements under §§1322 and 1325 as govern the original confirmation of a plan (such as the full payment of priority claims, the good faith and feasibility standards, and "best interests" test — as discussed in sections 20.3 through 20.7). Upon approval of the modification, the modified plan substitutes for and supercedes the original. Under §1329(c), even if a plan is extended by modification, it cannot exceed the permissible length measured from the date of the first payment under the original plan. That is, the modification cannot increase the payment period beyond the maximum prescribed by §1322(d) of three years (or, for cause, up to five years) from the time of the first payment made in the case.

Prior to 1984 only the debtor could apply for modification of the plan, but the ability to ask for modifications was extended to the trustee and creditors by the 1984 amendments to the Code. The odd thing about the amendment is that it was passed in conjunction with the disposable income test, yet §1329(b) subjects the modification to all the standards applicable to the original confirmation in §§1322(a) and (b) and 1325(a), but does not mention the disposable income test in §1325(b). The omission was probably an oversight because the intent was to allow the trustee and creditors to apply for modification where the debtor's income increased.

A debtor's request for modification is typically aimed at reducing or extending obligations assumed under the original plan — the debtor has found that the original commitment was too onerous, or circumstances have changed making it so, and she seeks to reduce her payments or to increase the length of the payment period to make the amount of periodic payments more manageable. (Of course, this can be done only to the extent that the plan, as modified, still satisfies the confirmation and length requirements of §§1322 and 1325.) Beyond adjusting the length or amount of payments, the debtor's ability to make substantive modification to the plan is limited. For example, in *In re Nolan*, 232 F.3d 528 (6th Cir. 2000), the debtor had retained a car subject to a security interest and had provided in the plan for the full payment of the secured claim in an amount of $8,200. After plan confirmation, the debtor decided that she wanted to get rid of the car and buy a better one. The debtor proposed to amend the plan to surrender the car to the secured party at its present value of $4,000, and to reclassify the deficiency on the secured claim as an unsecured claim. The court refused the modification. It held that once the claim had been classified as secured and fixed in amount, it could not be modified merely because the collateral had become less valuable and the debtor no longer wanted to keep it.

Debtors' requests to reduce the burden of the plan constitute the majority of modification applications, but applications by trustees and creditors to modify by increasing or accelerating payments, based on an improvement in the debtor's financial situation, have become common. Some courts have declined to modify a plan to allow for increased payments if the increase in the debtor's income was foreseeable and should have been taken into account at the time of plan confirmation. Modification under such circumstances would offend the principle of res judicata. These courts require there to have been a substantial and unanticipated change in the debtor's circumstances since confirmation. Some courts have applied a less rigorous test, requiring at least some change in circumstances to justify modification. Other courts have held that res judicata is not applicable and there should be no threshold test for a plan modification. For a selection of cases that discuss this issue, *see In re Brown,* 219 B.R. 191 (6th Cir. B.A.P. 1998); *In re Witkowski,* 16 F.3d 739 (7th Cir. 1994); *In re Thomas,* 291, B.R. 189 (Bankr. M.D. Ala. 2003); *Barbosa v. Soloman,* 235 F.3d 31 (1st Cir. 2000). A creditor's request for modification is illustrated in Example 2.

§20.11 Postscript on the Ch. 12 Plan

Sections 1221 through 1227 are almost identical to §§1321 through 1327. In fact, most of the Ch. 12 provisions are exact replicas of the corresponding Ch. 13 sections discussed in this chapter. For most purposes, therefore, the rules and principles discussed in this chapter are helpful to an understanding of the Ch. 12 plan.

EXAMPLES

1. Foul Faith and Credit

Fido Semper applied to the bank for a loan. Fido was heavily in debt, and he knew that the bank would not lend him money if it was aware of the full extent of his obligations. He therefore deliberately omitted several debts from the financial statement submitted as part of his loan application. The bank reasonably relied on the information in the application and granted the loan. Fido never repaid the loan, and the bank sued him and obtained judgment.

A short time afterwards, Fido filed a Ch. 13 petition. His plan proposes payment to the trustee of 25 percent of his monthly income over 30 months. It is clear that Fido cannot afford to pay more than 25 percent of his earnings to the trustee because he needs the balance for reasonable living expenses. The plan will pay general creditors, including the bank, five percent of their claims.

If Fido's estate had been liquidated under Ch. 7, the proceeds would not have been enough to pay any dividend to general unsecured creditors. However, the bank's claim would not have been discharged in the Ch. 7 case, because it was induced by a fraudulent financial statement on which the bank reasonably relied (§523(a)(2)(B)). Under §1328, many of the exceptions to discharge in §523, including this one, are made inapplicable to Ch. 13. Therefore, Fido will be able to discharge this debt upon completion of the distribution provided for in the plan. (*See* Chapter 22 for further details.)

What grounds does the bank have for objecting to Fido's plan?

2. For Whom Belle Toils

Belle Lated filed a Ch. 13 petition two years ago. At the time, she was employed as a sales representative and earned $50,000 per annum in salary and commission. She proposed a three-year plan under which general unsecured creditors would receive payment of 20 percent of their claims. The plan met the standards of §§1322 and 1325 and was confirmed.

One of Belle's creditors has now discovered that Belle was recently promoted to sales manager, and that her annual earnings have increased to $100,000. The creditor has applied for modification of the plan under §1329, asking for the size of the payments to be doubled and for the payment period to be extended by two years. Belle opposes the modification. She argues that the extra income is a reward for her hard work, and that a modification would be unfair because the original plan met all the standards of the Code. She also points out that if modification is allowed under these circumstances, debtors would have no incentive to better themselves because any increase in income simply enlarges the commitment under the preexisting plan. Belle has also submitted a budget which shows that her expenses have increased commensurate with her income because her managerial position necessitates housing of executive quality, membership in an exclusive golf club, and fine accoutrements. In fact, Belle's budget shows that her disposable income is no higher than it was when the plan was originally confirmed.

Should the court approve the modification?

3. House-Keeping

Bill Overdew owned a home subject to a mortgage. He defaulted on his monthly mortgage payments, and the mortgagee accelerated the debt, initiated foreclosure proceedings, and eventually obtained a judgment of foreclosure. The mortgage would have had 20 more years to run had it not been accelerated. The house is worth considerably more than the balance of the debt.

Shortly after the judgment, and before a foreclosure sale took place, Bill filed a Ch. 13 petition. In his plan, he proposes to pay the arrears owing on the mortgage over a few months. (Assume that the period of the proposed cure is reasonable.) He will also pay the current installments on the mortgage as required in the mortgage note. These payments will extend beyond the period of the plan, for the remaining term of the mortgage.

Is this provision in the plan acceptable?

4. Maximum Relief

Sal Vage borrowed money secured by a mortgage on a piece of land. Sal defaulted on the loan, and the mortgagee began suit to foreclose on the collateral. While the foreclosure proceedings were pending, Sal filed a Ch. 7 petition. His personal liability on the loan was ultimately discharged in the Ch. 7 case, but the mortgage on the property was not affected by the discharge. (*See* section 19.4.) After the close of the Ch. 7 case, the mortgagee resumed its foreclosure action. However, before the foreclosure sale could be held, Sal filed a Ch. 13 petition. In his Ch. 13 plan, Sal proposes to retain the property and to pay off the mortgage claim in installments. Is this permissible?

5. Class Struggle

Katie Gorize, a debtor under Ch. 13, has proposed a plan under which she will commit her disposable income for three years to the payment of claims. The lowest class of unsecured claims will receive a total distribution of ten percent of the value of their claims. These claims would have received no payment in a Ch. 7 liquidation. Although the plan seems to be acceptable in other respects, objections have been made to the following three claims. Are they objectionable?

(a) Three years ago, Katie bought a car on credit, and gave the seller a security interest to secure the debt. The term of the loan is five years, so it has two years to run. The car is worth less than the balance of the debt. Katie proposes to keep the car. The plan provides for the seller's retention of its lien, and for payment of the full balance owing on the car over the three years of the plan.

(b) Katie failed to pay the property taxes due on her house for the tax year ending prior to her petition. The taxes had been assessed, and they should have been paid a few months before the petition to avoid penalties. The state did not file a lien, so the claim is unsecured. Katie has classified it with other unsecured claims, and will pay ten percent of it over the three years of the plan.

(c) A short time before Katie's bankruptcy, a friend loaned her some money to help her cope with her financial difficulties. Katie is grateful to the friend, and feels bad about not having repaid the loan. She has therefore classified the friend's claim separately and proposes to pay 100 percent of it over the three years of the plan.

6. Strip Tease

(a) Prior to Leanne Stripper's bankruptcy, Junior Loan Co. lent her $25,000, secured by a second mortgage on her home. At the time of the transaction, the home, Leanne's principal residence, was subject to a first mortgage in favor of Senior Security Co. Leanne has now filed a petition under Ch. 13. The balance due to Senior under the first mortgage is $180,000, and the balance of the debt due to Junior is $20,000. The value of the home has been reliably appraised at $160,000. In her plan, Leanne proposes to treat Senior's first mortgage as a secured claim to the extent of $160,000, and an unsecured claim to the extent of the deficiency of $20,000. The proposed plan treats Junior's claim in its entirety as a general unsecured claim. The plan provides for a 10 percent distribution on general unsecured claims. Does either Senior Security Co. or Junior Loan Co. have grounds to object to the plan?

(b) Would your answer change if, at the time of the transactions, Leanne was using the home as her principal residence, but by the time of the petition, she had moved out of the house to live elsewhere, and was renting it to a tenant?

EXPLANATIONS

1. On the facts, there are three possible grounds on which the bank could object to confirmation of the plan:

(a) **Good faith.** Good faith is a factual matter to be decided under all the circumstances of the case. It is not per se bad faith for a debtor to choose Ch. 13 because of its more generous discharge. This remains true even if the debt to be discharged was incurred dishonestly. Fido is, after all, merely taking advantage of an opportunity given to him by the Code. However, as the court remarked in *In re Caldwell*, 895 F.2d 1123 (6th Cir. 1990), where a Ch. 13 plan proposes to pay only a small portion of a debt that would be nondischargeable in Ch. 7, the plan must be given particular scrutiny to decide whether it conforms to the good faith standard. See also *In re Francis* 273 B.R. 87 (6th Cir. B.A.P. 2002).

In evaluating the totality of the circumstances to decide if the plan is dishonest or abusive, the court takes into account factors such as those listed in section 20.6. Among the relevant considerations are the following facts: Fido obtained the loan through a misrepresentation; the transaction occurred a short time before bankruptcy; the filing followed soon after the judgment; Fido would not have been released from the debt under Ch. 7. If the debt to the bank constitutes a substantial portion of Fido's total indebtedness, that would bolster the suspicion that Fido chose Ch. 13 for the primary purpose of escaping it. The sufficiency of Fido's proposed payments is also a factor to be included in the totality of the circumstances. However, because the best interests and disposable income tests provide objective standards for determining the adequacy of payment, this factor should not be emphasized too heavily in the good faith test.

In re Norwood, 178 B.R. 683 (Bankr. E.D. Pa. 1995) illustrates the application of the "totality of the circumstances" approach where a debtor seeks to discharge a debt in Ch. 13 that would be nondischargeable under Ch. 7. The Ch. 13 debtor had sexually assaulted another man, and the victim of the assault obtained a judgment against him. Shortly after the judgment, the debtor filed a petition under Ch. 13 and proposed a plan that would have paid secured and priority claims in full, but would make no payment to the assault victim, who was by far his largest creditor. (The tort claim represented 76 percent of his indebtedness.) Because the claim arose out of a willful and malicious injury, it would have been excluded from a Ch. 7 discharge under §523(a)(6), but that section is not applicable in a Ch. 13 case. Taking into account the totality of the circumstances, the court found that the Ch. 13 filing was an attempt to manipulate the Code to obtain an unfair advantage, and the plan was not proposed in good faith and should not be confirmed. The court was most strongly influenced by the fact that the tort debt was the predominant claim against the estate; it derived from the debtor's deliberately wrongful conduct; it would not have been dischargeable in Ch. 7, and the debtor proposed no effort to make any payment of it under the plan. (The debtor claimed that he could not afford any payment to unsecured claims, but the court was unconvinced about this.) There were also indications that, at the time of the tort suit, the debtor had already determined to discharge the full debt under Ch. 13. He did not bother to defend the tort suit, assuming that he was "judgment proof" and would simply evade |responsibility by filing a Ch. 13 petition. (See also *In re Lancaster*, 280 B.R. 468 (Bankr. W.D. Mo. 2002), discussed in section 20.6.)

In summary, if, on the totality of the circumstances, the court concludes that the sole purpose of the Ch. 13 filing was to discharge the debt, with no advantage to creditors and no sincere effort to pay as fully as possible, the court should not confirm the plan. *See also In re Schaitz*, 913 F.2d 452 (7th Cir. 1990).

(b) The best interests test. Because general unsecured creditors would receive nothing in a Ch. 7 liquidation, the best interests test provides no minimum payment for them, so the five-percent distribution exceeds the standard prescribed by §1325(a)(4). The bank may argue that because its claim is nondischargeable in Ch. 7, it would have had the potential of full payment if Fido had filed under Ch. 7. However, §1325(a)(4) speaks clearly of giving creditors no less than they would be paid on their claims in a Ch. 7 liquidation. The portion of the nondischargeable debt that survived the bankruptcy would not have been paid on the claim, but would have been claimable from the debtor's postbankruptcy estate. It must therefore not be taken into account in applying the best interests test. *See In re Rimgale*, 669 F.2d 426 (7th Cir. 1982).

(c) **The disposable income test.** The facts indicate that Fido had submitted a reasonable budget for his living expenses and has committed the remainder of his monthly income to the plan. He apparently satisfies the disposable income test with regard to the amount to be submitted to the trustee each month. However, he has proposed a 30-month plan, and §1325(b)(1) requires disposable income to be committed for three years. Unless Fido extends the plan by six months, it cannot be confirmed if the bank objects under §1325(b).

2. (a) **The increase in the size of payments.** Section 1329(a)(1) allows an unsecured creditor to apply for modification of a plan to increase the amount of installments. Section 1329(b) subjects the modification to all the standards that apply to the original confirmation under §§1322(a) and (b) and 1325(a), but it makes no reference to §1325(b) (the disposable income test). However, as noted in section 20.10, the omission of §1325(b) is likely an oversight and courts do apply the disposable income test to modifications.

In the case on which this Example is based (*In re Arnold*, 869 F.2d 240 (4th Cir. 1989)), the court expressed no qualms about using the disposable income test to justify modifying the debtor's plan by doubling the required payments when the debtor's annual earnings as a sales representative had increased from $80,000 to $200,000. The court was unimpressed by the debtor's arguments that an increase in plan payments thwarted his fresh start, were unfair, and would be a disincentive to hard work. It pointed out that the debtor's fresh start is supposed to begin after the bankruptcy case and that it is appropriate for creditors to benefit from any substantial increase in the debtor's income before the case is closed. This prospect, it observed, should not be a disincentive to a responsible debtor, who should be willing to work hard to pay off as much of his debt as possible.

Arnold suggested that not every increase in the debtor's income would justify a modification, and that the doctrine of res judicata would preclude modifications based on changes in income that were reasonably foreseeable and should have been taken into account when the plan was confirmed. As noted in section 20.10, some courts have agreed with this, but others have not required a substantial and significant change in the debtor's circumstances.

The debtor in *Arnold* also produced a budget reflecting higher living expenses which consumed the increase in income. The court saw through that ploy quite easily; the expenses were unreasonably high and could be reduced so that some of the debtor's new wealth could be applied to the payment of creditors. The debtor's budget must reflect a reasonable standard of living. Belle is neither expected to live in poverty nor should she live luxuriously at the expense of creditors.

(b) The increase in the payment period. In addition to requesting an increase in the size of payments, the creditor has asked that the plan be extended to five years. Section 1329(a)(2) permits such a modification, subject to the standards for plan confirmation. Section §1322(d) allows the court, for cause, to approve a plan for a period up to five years. Under §1329(c), the statutory time limit is measured from the date of the original plan, not from the time of modification. The extension from three to five years is within the limits of §§1322(d) and 1329(c). However, cause must be shown for the court to approve a period of more than five years. Congress did not intend courts to rubber-stamp plans over three years long. The mere fact that five years of payments gives more to creditors and can be afforded by the debtor is not enough to constitute cause. If this was all that was needed, cause would be present in most cases. Some further special circumstances must be shown to justify extending the plan beyond three years. For example, a debtor may need to pay over five years to reduce the monthly installments, and yet still meet the best interests test.

In the *Arnold* case, the creditor sought to modify the length of the plan period as well as the size of the payments. The bankruptcy court extended the plan to five years. Because the debtor did not object to this, the Court of Appeals declined to consider whether there had been an abuse of discretion. It did say, however, that cause may have been present because the debtor's income had increased steadily over the two and a half years since confirmation, so the debtor had had excess disposable income for some time. The creditor had only discovered this near the end of the plan period. To confine the increased payments to the few months remaining on the existing plan would not give creditors what they deserved.

3. Bill proposes to deal with the mortgage under §1322(b)(5) by curing the default within a reasonable time and making payments during and beyond the plan period for the remaining term of the contract. The debt would be excluded from the discharge by §1328(a)(1). Had the mortgage not been accelerated and foreclosed prior to bankruptcy, this arrangement would be unobjectionable because the cure is reasonable and Bill would not be attempting to modify the mortgage in violation of §1322(b)(2). However, the mortgage can only be paid beyond the plan period under §1322(b)(5) if the final payment is due after the last payment under the plan. The acceleration of the mortgage terminates the debtor's right to pay over the next 20 years and makes full payment due immediately.

Prior to 1994, courts developed a wide range of views on whether §1322(b)(5) could be used by a debtor to reverse a prepetition acceleration and foreclosure. The Bankruptcy Reform Act of 1994 settled the question by adding §1322(c)(1), which adopts the position most favorable to cure, allowing it to take place at any time up to the completion of the foreclosure sale.[6] State law need no longer be consulted to decide at which stage of the foreclosure process the debtor's interest in the property is extinguished. Whatever state law may provide, once the debtor files a Ch. 13 petition, the cure may be affected at any time up to the conclusion of the sale. However, there is one situation in which state law still seems relevant. Section 1322(c)(1) does not itself extend the debtor's right to cure beyond the sale, but some courts have held that if state law provides for a statutory post-sale redemption period, the right to cure in bankruptcy will go beyond the sale, and will not terminate until the end of the redemption period. The reasoning behind this approach is illustrated by *In re Sims,* 185 B.R. 853 (Bankr. N.D. Ala. 1995), in which the court permitted cure up to the end of the statutory redemption period allowed by state law. The court felt that the recognition of this extension of the cure right, even beyond the stage articulated in §1322(c)(1), best serves the clear aim of §1322, which seeks to provide the debtor with every opportunity to cure. In addition, it is consistent with §541(a) (the provision making state law determinative of what property rights enter the estate), because where a state allows redemption after the sale, the debtor's rights in the property are not completely divested until the redemption period ends.

4. The tactic employed by Sal has come to be known as "Chapter 20." Sal has contrived to first discharge his personal liability on the debt in the Ch. 7 case, and then to use Ch. 13 to prevent foreclosure on the surviving lien so that he can keep the property and force the lienholder to accept payment of the secured claim under the plan. In this way, he is able, in effect, to force the secured claimant into accepting a redemption by installments through Ch.13, while at the same time keeping his payments under the Ch. 13 plan to a minimum by shedding his dischargeable debt in the prior Ch. 7 case.

As unsavory as this practice may be, the Supreme Court decided in *Johnson v. Home State Bank,* 501 U.S. 78 (1991), that it is permissible. First, it resolved the question of whether a mortgage could qualify as a claim where the debtor's personal liability had been discharged. It held that the mortgage still met the definition of "claim" in §101(5) in that, even in the absence of any recourse against the debtor, a mortgage remains a right to payment or to an equitable remedy. Second, it found that although the Code precludes

---

6. Section 1322(c)(2) is not directly applicable here because it deals with the stretching-out of payment on a short term home mortgage, whose contractual due date falls before the end of the plan period. That is, covers extension of a short-term debt to correspond to the longer plan length, rather than payment of a long-term debt beyond the plan. However, this subsection does reinforce the principle of §1322(c)(1) by focusing on the contractual due date of the debt, notwithstanding any acceleration.

serial Ch. 7 discharges under §727, there is no equivalent restriction on filing for a Ch. 13 discharge immediately after obtaining a Ch. 7 discharge. The court did recognize, however, that the good faith standard in §1325(a)(3) can be used by a court to refuse confirmation of a Ch. 13 plan that has an abusive or dishonest motive. One consideration that might be taken into account in the good faith analysis is that the debtor had entered Ch. 13 as part of a scheme to undermine the policies and purposes of the Code.

Since *Johnson*, several courts have applied the good faith standard to "Chapter 20" serial filings. Although the serial filings are surely abusive, lower courts cannot simply find the serial filings to be per se bad faith in light of *Johnson*, so they have used the well-established "totality of the circumstances" approach to decide if there is something beyond the mere use of the successive Ch. 7 and 13 filings that shows a dishonest or improperly manipulative motive. Two cases illustrate the relativity of trying to apply a "totality of the circumstances" approach to action that is in itself a manipulation of the Code. In *In re Cushman*, 217 B.R. 470 (Bankr. E.D. Va. 1998), the court said that "Chapter 20" filings must be carefully scrutinized. The debtor had discharged all his debt without any payment under Ch. 7, including the deficiency on his car loan. He then filed Ch. 13 for the purpose of paying off the stripped down secured portion of the loan. The court found that the debtor had acted in bad faith in the totality of the circumstances: The serial filings were planned before the Ch. 7 case was filed; no payment was made to unsecured creditors in the Ch. 7 case; although the debtor could have afforded to pay the claim secured by the car more quickly, he proposed to take four years to pay it; although he could not have stripped the lien in Ch.7 in light of *Dewsnup*, and he could not have redeemed by instalments, he had used Ch. 13 to force the creditor into accepting payments over time.

By contrast, in *In re Keach*, 243 B.R. 851 (1st Cir. B.A.P. 2000), the court did allow the debtor to get away with a "Chapter 20." The case shows the use of this process for a different purpose than that in Sal's case and *Cushman*. The debtor first used Ch. 7 to discharge all debts that were dischargeable under Ch. 7. Then, after getting the discharge, but even before the Ch. 7 case was closed, he filed a Ch. 13 case to deal with a fraud debt that was excepted from the Ch. 7 discharge, but was dischargeable under Ch. 13. In his plan, he proposed to pay 5 only percent of that debt. The court found that even though the debtor may have acted unfairly and immorally, he was not guilty of bad faith as that concept should be applied under the Code.

5. **(a)** **The claim secured by the car.** Katie proposes to pay this claim under §1325(a)(5)(B) after modifying the payment period under §1322(b)(2). If the claim was fully secured, this treatment would be unobjectionable, provided that the full payment amount is adjusted to present value. The problem with the proposal is that the car is worth less than the debt, so part of the claim is unsecured. Katie has in fact classified the seller's secured and unsecured claims together and is proposing full payment of both. This could be challenged under §1322(b)(1) by another creditor or the trustee, or disapproved by the court of its own accord. The secured and unsecured claims are not substantially similar as required by §1122, and the discrimination is unfair because there is no appropriate justification for treating this unsecured claim differently from others.

(b) The property taxes. The property tax meets the qualifications for priority under §507(a)(8)(B): It was assessed before the petition and was last payable without penalty within a year before the petition. Section 1322(a)(2) requires full payment of priority claims unless the holder agrees to a different treatment. This claim has been misclassified, and the proposed payment is inadequate.

(c) The friend's loan. The friend's claim is a general unsecured claim which Katie has placed in a separate class. She is entitled to do this by §1322(b)(1), as long as the discrimination is not unfair. Other creditors, who are being paid only a tenth of their claims, are likely to object to the favored treatment of Katie's friend, given that the additional payment to her will reduce the disposable income available to pay their claims.

For discrimination to be fair, there must be a reasonable basis for the separate classification, and the discrimination should serve some legitimate purpose in the debtor's attempt at rehabilitation. The desire to favor a friend is not adequate justification for paying him more at the expense of other creditors. Katie may argue that her proposed treatment of a friend who came to her aid is analogous to the one form of discrimination that is expressly sanctioned by §1322(b)(1): The separate classification of a consumer debt on which another individual is liable as codebtor or surety. It could be said that, even though the Code does not address this situation expressly, the policy of preventing financial hardship to a friend and avoiding pressure on the debtor to pay the balance of the debt outside the plan is just as applicable here as it is for sureties and codebtors.

6. (a) Leanne's proposal to bifurcate Senior's mortgage and to treat the deficiency as an unsecured claim, payable at the rate of 10 percent is a clear contravention of *Nobelman v. American Savings Bank*, 508 U.S. 324 (1993). The mortgage is a claim secured only by a security interest in real property that is the debtor's principal residence, and §1322(b)(2) forbids any modification of the rights of the holder. *Nobelman* held that the section's use of the word "rights" extends the protection beyond the portion of the debt that qualifies as a secured claim, and includes any deficiency that would otherwise qualify as an unsecured claim. Leanne's attempt to strip Senior's lien to correspond to the present appraised value of the property is not allowed, and Senior has grounds to object.

Junior's position is less clear because the senior lien covers the entire value of the property, leaving nothing over for Junior. Its mortgage is therefore not merely undersecured, but completely unsecured. As noted in section 20.8.3, courts differ on whether a completely unsecured mortgage is protected from "strip off" by §1322(b)(2).

(b) Section 1322(b)(2) gives no indication of the point in time at which the use of the property must be determined. This issue had to be resolved in *In re Smart,* 214 B.R. 63 (Bankr. D. Conn. 1997), in which the court held that the time of the original transaction, not the time of the petition, was the proper point for determining the property's use. The court reasoned that the purpose of §1322(b)(2) was to encourage lenders to make home loans, and this incentive would be undermined if they could not rely on the state of affairs that existed at the time of the loan. It imports a risk, inconsistent with the goals of the section, to deprive a lender of the protection from modification if, after the transaction, the debtor converts the use of the property from that of principal residence. On this reasoning, the answer to question (a) would not change merely because Leanne was no longer using the home as her principal residence at the time of her bankruptcy.

21

The Chapter 11 Plan

§21.1 Introduction to Ch. 11 and Its Debtors

§21.1.1 General Introduction

Many aspects of Ch. 11 bankruptcy have been covered in previous chapters. The focus here is on the Ch. 11 process and the creation, confirmation, and execution of the plan. This is an intricate and complex topic; all that is attempted here is a broad overview of the central issues relating to the Ch. 11 process and the plan. Because so much basic explanation is needed on this topic, this chapter is purely textual and does not have Examples and Explanations.

Although there are many significant differences between Chs. 11 and 13, they have close conceptual and structural affinities. The differences between them are necessitated by their intended scope of application: While Ch. 13 is designed to fit the needs of an individual — typically a consumer — with relatively small debt, Ch. 11 accommodates debtors with more complex affairs, such as individuals whose debts exceed the Ch. 13 limitations or large commercial enterprises with armies of creditors, employees, and shareholders.

§21.1.2 Eligibility for Ch. 11 and Distinctions between Ch. 11 Debtors

Section §109(d) makes Ch. 11 relief available to most debtors who qualify for Ch. 7. (*See* section 8.4.2.) Although Ch. 11 is generally associated with corporate debtors or other commercial entities such as partnerships or associations, it may be used by individuals as well. Any doubt that may have existed on this point has been put to rest by the Supreme Court in *Toibb v. Radloff*, 111 S. Ct. 2197 (1991). Ch. 13 is generally more appropriate for an individual than Ch. 11 unless the debts exceed the Ch. 13 limitations or the debtor owns a business and has affairs that are complex enough to require the flexibility of Ch. 11.

An ongoing issue in Ch. 11 is the need for and appropriate extent of different treatment for large and small businesses. The old Bankruptcy Act provided separate chapters for large public corporations (Ch. X) and smaller businesses (Ch. XI). When the Code was enacted in 1978, this distinction was eliminated in favor of the unitary treatment of the current Ch. 11. However, this did not put the issue to rest. There continues to be criticism of the unnecessary complexity of Ch. 11 in the reorganization of small businesses, and discussion of the desirability of providing a simpler, more expeditious procedure for them. Congress took up this issue when it debated the Bankruptcy Reform Act of 1994. Original proposals called for extensive changes, which would have made Ch. 11 applicable only to large corporate bankruptcies and would have created a new Ch. 10, with streamlined procedures and different substantive rules and standards for small businesses. However, the proposal was too controversial and it was abandoned in favor of more modest and limited changes, which were not formed into a separate Chapter, but were incorporated into Ch. 11. These changes are purely procedural, designed to speed up cases involving small businesses, and do not alter the substantive standards to be satisfied for the confirmation and performance of the plan.

A "small business" is defined in §101(51C), not on the basis of the actual size of its operations, assets, or volume of business, but on the extent of its liabilities existing at the time of filing: It is a person engaged in commercial or business activities, having aggregate noncontingent, liquidated, secured and unsecured debts, as of the date of the petition, that do not exceed $2 million. A debtor whose primary activity is owning and operating real property (that is, a single-asset real estate operation) is expressly excluded from the definition, and cannot be treated as a small business.[1] If a debtor qualifies as a small business, three changes in procedure come into effect. However, only one of them takes effect merely by virtue of the debtor falling within the definition. For the other two to apply, the debtor must both satisfy the definition and elect to be treated as a small business. These special procedures for small businesses are discussed in the appropriate places below, but it may be helpful to identify them here as well:

---

1. Single asset real estate cases are those in which the debtor's primary business is operating a single piece of investment property, and substantially all of the debtor's income is generated by that property. (*See* §101(52B).) Cases of this kind were discussed in section 11.4.3 and Example 4 of Chapter 11, where it was noted that the Bankruptcy Reform Act of 1994 established special grounds for relief from stay in such cases to prevent debtors from abusing the bankruptcy system by filing a Ch. 11 petition to stay foreclosure on the real estate where there is little prospect of rehabilitation.

(1) A means is provided for creditors to avoid the appointment of a creditors' committee if this would be unnecessary and cumbersome. (This does not require the debtor to elect to be treated as a small business.)

(2) If the debtor elects to be treated as a small business, the period for plan formulation is reduced.

(3) If the debtor elects to be treated as a small business, the procedures for approving the disclosure statement and the solicitation of acceptances or rejections is simplified.

The 1994 amendments may not be the end of the process of reforming Ch. 11 for the purpose of creating different rules for small businesses. In its 1997 report, the National Bankruptcy Review Commission found that small business bankruptcies, which constitute the bulk of Ch. 11 filings, have a poor rate of success and require a tighter, more controlled process to expedite cases that are likely to be successful and to more speedily get rid of those in which the debtor has little prospect for rehabilitation. It endorsed the move to create more efficient procedures for small businesses, and recommended further steps in this direction. For example, it recommended that the debt ceiling for inclusion in this category be substantially increased and that all the special rules apply universally to qualifying debtors, and none are made applicable only at the debtor's election; it recommended that procedures be added for closer supervision of and reporting by the debtor in possession; it also recommended that the periods for plan filing and confirmation be shortened; and the grounds for dismissal or conversion be expanded. The pending bankruptcy reform legislation has adopted many of these recommendations.

§21.2   The Purpose of a Ch. 11 Case

It has been reiterated throughout this book that the goal of a Ch. 11 case is the rehabilitation of the debtor. The rehabilitative function of Ch. 11 is particularly important to corporate debtors, which cannot survive liquidation bankruptcy. By filing a Ch. 11 petition, the debtor is able to continue the operation of its business under the shelter of the automatic stay. It is thereby able to preserve its profitable activities and assets while it negotiates with creditors and attempts to develop a strategy for the satisfaction of debts and the revitalization of its failing enterprise. If the negotiations are fruitful, the debtor formulates a plan, which is the blueprint for its rehabilitation. The plan contains proposals for the treatment of debt and sets out the course to be taken by the debtor in seeking financial recovery.

If the plan satisfies the requirements of the Code, it is confirmed by the court. The debtor then tries to implement the plan. A successful consummation depends on the accuracy of the business judgments underlying the plan, the competence of the debtor's management, and the prevailing economic conditions. If all these factors are favorable, the terms of the plan will be performed, the Ch. 11 case will eventually be closed, and the debtor will emerge from bankruptcy freed of its prepetition debts and in fiscal health. From the perspective of creditors, a successful reorganization holds the promise of a greater recovery on their claims. For the owners of the debtor, rehabilitation offers a chance of preserving some or all of an investment that would have been lost in liquidation. Society as a whole is benefited by the preservation of the profitable elements of the enterprise with its jobs and products. Of course, not all Ch. 11 cases achieve this cheerful result. Many Ch. 11 debtors cannot be rehabilitated and end up in liquidation. (Liquidation may take place following conversion to Ch. 7 or, where there has not been substantial consummation of the plan, by modifying the plan to provide for the debtor's liquidation.)

Apart from liquidation following an unsuccessful attempt at reorganization, a debtor can choose from the outset to liquidate under Ch. 11. Section 1123(a)(5)(D) expressly permits liquidating plans. Although the end result of liquidation under Ch. 11 is legally the same as liquidation under Ch. 7, a Ch. 11 liquidation can provide practical advantages to the debtor and creditors. For example, the debtor can usually retain greater control of the liquidation process, take more time to wind up its affairs, and enhance the ultimate liquidation value of its estate.

§21.3   The Importance of Negotiation and Business Judgment in a Ch. 11 Case

Ch. 11 is much more intricate than Ch. 13 because the affairs of a Ch. 11 debtor can be very complex and require greater flexibility and more extensive participation by parties in interest. Two aspects of a Ch. 11 case stand out and distinguish it dramatically from the other forms of bankruptcy. The first is the great leeway given to the debtor and other parties in interest to negotiate during the case for the purpose of reaching agreement on the terms of the plan. Provision is made for representative committees, for the communication of information, and for voting. Ideally, a Ch. 11 plan should be a consensual document, although Ch. 11 does have some mechanisms for overriding opposition to it and imposing its terms on unwilling parties. The role played by Code provisions in encouraging negotiation or providing bargaining leverage to one or another party is a constant theme in any discussion of Ch. 11.

The second distinguishing feature of Ch. 11 is the extent to which it interacts with difficult issues of corporate and business law and business strategy. Particularly in corporate reorganizations, the Code provisions, complex as they may be, are mere skeletal structures. They are augmented by nonbankruptcy laws such as those governing corporations, labor relations, commercial law, securities, and taxation. Of course, nonbankruptcy law and economic considerations are relevant in all forms of bankruptcy, as has often been pointed out before. However, the scope and scale of the application of nonbankruptcy business law and business judgment is typically much greater in a complex Ch. 11 case.

§21.4   Outline of the Ch. 11 Case

The progress of the Ch. 11 case is set out in this section, which provides a broad description of essential features in an approximate chronological sequence. (Many of the issues mentioned have been dealt with previously and are included for the purpose of review.) In sections 21.6 and 21.7 the contents of the plan and the requirements for confirmation are explained more fully. The diagram on page 470 charts the Ch. 11 process.

§21.4.1   Commencement of the Case

A Ch. 11 case may be commenced either voluntarily or involuntarily. Under Rule 1007, the debtor must file a schedule of assets and liabilities, a statement of financial affairs, and a statement of executory contracts, as described in section 9.3. In addition, a corporate debtor must file a list of equity security holders, and all Ch. 11 debtors must file a list of the 20 largest unsecured creditors, so that the U.S. Trustee can appoint a creditors' committee.

A case can be converted involuntarily to Ch. 11 only from Ch. 7, and it can be dismissed or converted to Ch. 7 by a party other than the debtor for cause. Section 1112 gives the debtor broader rights of conversion to and from Ch. 11.

The automatic stay goes into effect on commencement of the case, and prepetition property enters the estate as in a Ch. 7 case. Unlike Chs. 12 and 13, postpetition property does not automatically become property of the estate.

§21.4.2   The Roles of the Debtor in Possession, Creditors, and Interest Holders

As mentioned before, the debtor in possession normally exercises the trustee's functions in a Ch. 11 case and operates the debtor's business under §1108.

However, a trustee may be appointed if the court so orders under §1104. The order for appointment of a trustee must be based on an application by the U.S. Trustee or a party in interest who must show cause (usually in the form of dishonesty or mismanagement by the debtor in possession) or that the appointment serves the interests of creditors and equity security

The Progress of a Ch. 11 Case

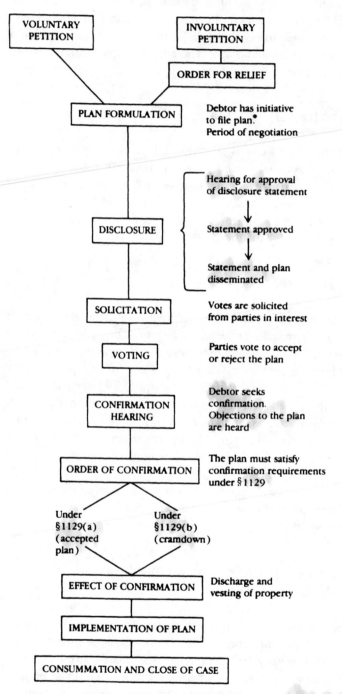

Some of the other activity during this period:
· Relief from stay litigation
· Applications for the appointment of trustee or examiner, if appropriate
· Continued operation of business
· Creditors meeting
· Appointment of committees

*If the debtor is unable to develop an accepted plan within the period of exclusivity, other parties in interest may file plans. This diagram does not reflect the possibility of competing plans.

holders. After the court orders the appointment of a trustee, the U.S. Trustee makes the appointment unless, within 30 days of the order, a party in interest requests under §1104(b) that the trustee be elected. If an election is requested, the U.S. Trustee must call a meeting of creditors and the election follows the procedures set out for the election of a Ch. 7 trustee. In cases where the maladministration is not dire enough to justify the appointment of a trustee to take over the administration of the estate, but there are questions of competence or honesty to be investigated, the court may, on the application of a creditor or the U.S. Trustee, and for cause, order the appointment of an examiner to conduct the appropriate investigation.

The creditors' committee plays a significant role in many Ch. 11 cases, particularly when the case is large enough to warrant the attention and interest of an influential group of creditors. However, in smaller cases, especially where creditors do not have large debts at stake, or have little optimism about getting substantial payment, it can be difficult to establish and maintain an active committee. Section 1102 requires the U.S. Trustee to appoint at least one committee of unsecured creditors as soon as practicable after the order for relief. If appropriate, the U.S. Trustee may appoint additional committees of creditors and equity security holders. However, when the debtor qualifies as a small business (*see* Section 21.1.2), the U.S. Trustee's duty to appoint a committee is qualified by §1102(a)(3), which allows the court to dispense with the appointment of a committee on request of a party in interest and for cause.

Where a committee is appointed, its purpose is to represent the creditors' interests and to keep an eye on the debtor's conduct of estate affairs. Section 1103 sets out the committee's powers. Among other things, it may hire attorneys and accountants, investigate the conduct of the business, participate in the plan formulation, raise and be heard on any issue in the case, and otherwise participate in the case to protect the interests of its constituency.

Many Ch. 11 debtors are corporations, and shareholders in the debtor have an obvious stake in the reorganization. Because their shares constitute an ownership interest in the debtor, they would be the last to receive any distribution in a liquidation. However, if the debtor is successfully reorganized, they may salvage all or part of their investment. Shareholders fall within the definition of equity security holders in §§101(16) and (17), and they are included as parties in interest in a Ch. 11 case. Ch. 11 constantly refers not merely to *claims* but to *claims and interests,* signifying that shareholders are entitled to be full participants in the case. They may be represented by an equity security holders' committee, which is appointed by the U.S. Trustee, and their interests are dealt with in the plan.

Creditors and equity security holders are divided into different classes in the plan, as explained in section 21.6.2. Bear in mind that a class of claims or interests is treated as a unit for many purposes in a Ch. 11 case. This is particularly significant in the context of voting when the time comes for the approval or disapproval of a proposed plan.

In a Ch. 11 case, a creditor does not need to prove a claim unless its claim is omitted from the debtor's schedule or is listed as disputed, contingent, or unliquidated (§1111(a) and Rule 3003). If the claim is so listed, or is not scheduled at all, the creditor must file a proof to vote and participate in the distribution. Section 1111(a) also refers to a proof of interest, which reflects the rights of equity security holders. Under Rule 3003, equity security holders do not have to file proofs of interest. Their participation and voting in the case is based on the official records of ownership in the debtor.

§21.4.3   *The Formulation of the Plan by the Debtor or Other Parties in Interest*

Section 1121(a) says that the debtor may file a plan with the petition or at any time thereafter. It is possible that the debtor may have formulated a plan before the petition has been filed.[2] However, because the plan is often developed by negotiation and consultation, serious work on the plan often begins only after the petition. In fact, many debtors need the protection of bankruptcy filing to stay collection activity while the plan is being worked out.

As stated in section 20.2, in a Ch. 13 case the debtor is the only person who may file a plan, and it must be done within a prescribed period after the petition. The approach in Ch. 11 is very different. It has no absolute time limit for the filing of the plan. Section 1121 gives the debtor the exclusive right to propose a plan in the 120 days after the order for relief. If a trustee is appointed in the case, this period is cut short and ends upon the trustee's appointment. If the debtor does not file a plan in the exclusivity period, any party in interest may file a plan. If the debtor filed a plan in the 120-day period, and it was accepted during that period by each impaired class (*see* section 21.6.2), no one else may file a plan: The debtor's plan is the only one available for confirmation. If the plan was filed but not accepted by the end of the 120-day period, the debtor has a further 60 days to try to get the plan (or an amended version of it) accepted. If the debtor fails, any party in interest may propose a plan. The court is able to reduce or increase the exclusivity period after notice and a hearing, provided that a party in interest applies before the expiry of the period and shows cause.

Where the debtor qualifies as a small business and elects to be treated as such, §1121(e) provides shorter time periods for proposing the plan. As explained in section 21.1.2, this provision was added in 1994 for the purpose of expediting bankruptcies involving business debtors with relatively small liabilities. Because the truncated time periods apply only if the debtor so chooses, §1121(e) is only brought into effect where the debtor perceives this

---

2. In fact, it is possible that the debtor may have negotiated a plan before the petition has been filed, so that it has a "prepackaged" plan in hand at the time of the petition. This is discussed in section 21.5.

to be in its interests. It is therefore only of limited value to creditors, who cannot take the initiative to use it to put pressure on the debtor to move more quickly in proposing a plan and getting it accepted. Section 1121(e) reduces the debtor's exclusivity period to 100 days, and the period for filing all proposed plans to 160 days. The court has the discretion, upon request by a party in interest before the expiry of the period in question, to reduce either period for cause. The court may increase the 100-day exclusivity period if the debtor shows that the need for the increase was caused by circumstances for which it was not responsible.

Although single asset real estate debtors are excluded from the definition of "small business" (as explained in section 21.1.2) and cannot elect the shorter periods, there is a less direct but possibly more effective mechanism for expediting plan formulation in such cases. As discussed in section 11.4.3, if a debtor falls within the definition of a single asset real estate operation (§101(51B)), a creditor holding a claim secured by the real property is entitled to relief from stay under §362(d)(3), unless the debtor has filed a feasible plan or has commenced to make interest payments to all mortgage holders within 90 days of the order for relief.

The possibility for competing plans gives creditors negotiating power and puts pressure on the debtor to devise an acceptable and feasible plan as quickly as possible. The debtor knows that if it does not produce a plan that satisfies creditors, alternative plans may be put forward that are less advantageous. They may provide for the sale of desirable assets, the elimination of ownership interests, or even the debtor's liquidation. When the plans are voted on, dissatisfied creditors may favor a plan that the debtor does not want. Therefore, even if no competing plan emerges, the threat of alternative plans has an impact on the debtor's thinking as it deals with creditors in the negotiating process.

If competing plans are proposed, each must comply with the disclosure requirements and confirmation standards discussed below. If, in the end, there are two or more plans that satisfy the requirements for confirmation, §1129(c) requires the court to consider the preferences of creditors and equity security holders in deciding which to confirm. Only one plan can be confirmed. (Although the possibility is raised here that a plan may be proposed by someone other than the debtor, the remainder of this chapter operates on the assumption, for the sake of simplicity, that no competing plan has been proposed.)

§21.4.4 Disclosure

In a Ch. 11 case, creditors and equity security holders vote to accept or reject the plan, as described in section 21.4.5. To ensure that these parties are given sufficient information on the plan and the debtor's affairs before they vote,

§1125 requires the proponent of the plan to draft a disclosure statement containing *adequate information*. The statement must be approved by the court after notice and a hearing, and it must then be transmitted to all creditors and equity security holders, together with a copy of the plan or a summary of it. Section 1125 prohibits the postpetition[3] solicitation of acceptances or rejections of a plan prior to the dissemination of the plan and the court-approved disclosure statement.

Section 1125(a)(1) defines adequate information very loosely to give the court discretion in evaluating a disclosure statement in light of the complexity of the debtor's affairs and the circumstances of the case: Enough information must be given, as far as reasonably practicable in light of the debtor's nature and history and the state of its records, to enable a hypothetical reasonable investor with attributes of the members of the class in question to make an informed judgment about the plan. Typically, a disclosure statement provides a history of the debtor and a description of its business operations. It explains the plan (which has been formulated by this time) and alerts parties to any options available under the plan. It describes the proposed course of consummation of the plan and provides financial information so that the debtor's prospects of rehabilitation can be evaluated and its liquidation value assessed.

The disclosure statement is analogous to the prospectus published by a corporation in connection with the issuance of stock. If the Ch. 11 case involves a corporation and the plan is complex, the disclosure statement could be as lengthy and intricate as a prospectus. If the debtor is an individual or a smaller business, the statement is likely to be considerably shorter and simpler.

If the debtor qualifies as a small business (*see* section 21.2.1) and elects to be treated as such, §1125(f) provides for a less stringent process for approval of the disclosure statement. The statement can be conditionally approved by the court, and the debtor can immediately begin to solicit acceptances and rejections based on the conditionally approved disclosure, as long as the debtor provides adequate information to those holders of claims and interests who are solicited. Final approval of the statement may be combined with the confirmation hearing.

Outside of bankruptcy, the disclosure required by a corporate prospectus is subject to securities regulation. Section 1125(d) allows regulatory agencies such as the SEC to address the court on the adequacy of disclosure, but makes it clear that the standards of bankruptcy law ultimately determine the extent of disclosure required. A statement that does not fully satisfy nonbankruptcy standards could be adequate for Ch. 11 purposes.

Section 1125(c) allows different statements to be approved for different classes, but all members of a particular class must receive the same statement.

---

3. Section 1125 applies only to postpetition solicitation of votes. Sometimes the debtor may negotiate a plan with creditors before filing the petition. This is discussed in section 21.5.

Variations in the statement sent to different classes may be appropriate based on the nature of the claims or interests in that class and the depth of information that they require to exercise informed judgment.

Section 1125(e) contains what is called a *safe harbor* provision, which protects persons who violate nonbankruptcy regulations in the solicitation of votes or the issuance of securities under the plan, provided that they act in good faith and in accordance with the Code. The effect of this provision is to protect parties, such as creditors' committees, attorneys, or creditors, who solicit votes on the plan by using the court-approved disclosure statement. The protection only applies if the party acts in good faith, without knowledge of some defect or omission in the statement, and in compliance with the solicitation requirements of the Code.

§21.4.5 *Voting on the Plan*

When the court approves the disclosure statement, it fixes the period for voting on the plan. Holders of claims or interests who are eligible to vote on the plan receive ballots with the disclosure statement and must return them within the prescribed time, indicating acceptance or rejection of the plan. (Rules 3017, 3017.1, and 3018.) Acceptance of the plan is not based on a simple majority of all the votes. Instead, all claims and interests are divided into classes as explained in section 21.6.2. Each class forms a voting block. If the requisite majority of members of that class votes in favor of the plan, the class as a whole accepts it, even though some of its members may have voted to reject the plan. It is the vote of the class that is significant for confirmation purposes, and the o utvoted dissenters are bound by the majority. However, when the class has accepted the plan, the minority who favored rejection is given some protection by provisions that set minimum standards for the treatment of their claims and interests. (This is discussed in section 21.7.2.)

The voting majority for acceptance by a class of claims is slightly different from that for a class of interests. Under §1126(c), a class of claims accepts the plan if at least two-thirds in amount and more than half in number of the voting creditors with allowed claims in that class have accepted the plan. Under §1126(d), a class of interests accepts the plan if at least two-thirds in amount of the voting holders of allowed interests in that class have accepted the plan. Section 1126(e) allows the court, on request of a party in interest and after notice and a hearing, to exclude from the vote any entity whose acceptance or rejection was not in good faith or was not solicited or procured in good faith or in accordance with the provisions of the Code.

In two situations, the vote of a class is presumed as a matter of law, so no actual voting takes place. First, a class that is unimpaired does not vote on the plan, but is conclusively deemed by §1126(f) to have accepted the plan. (As explained in section 21.6.2, a class is impaired unless the rights of its members are left unaltered by the plan, except for the cure of default.) Second, a class of claims or interests that will receive or retain no property under the plan is deemed under §1126(g) to have rejected the plan and is not required to vote.

§21.4.6   Confirmation

After the period for voting has closed and notice of hearing has been given, §1128 requires a confirmation hearing to be held. Parties in interest may object to confirmation. An *objection* to confirmation differs from a vote to *reject* the plan: Rejection is motivated by the preference of the holder, and its perception of its best interests; objection must be based on the legal ground that the plan fails to meet the requirements for confirmation prescribed by §1129. (*See* section 21.7.) If the plan satisfies those requirements, the objection fails and the court issues an order of confirmation under Rule 3020.

§21.4.7   Modification of the Plan

Section 1127 permits the proponent of a plan to modify it before or after confirmation. Any modification must comply with the requirements applicable to the original plan under §§1122 and 1123 and a disclosure statement must be approved by the court and disseminated for the modified plan in accordance with §1125. A holder of a claim or interest who accepted or rejected the original plan is deemed to have voted the same way on the modified plan unless the holder changes its vote.

Prior to confirmation, §1127(a) allows the proponent to modify the plan simply by filing a modified plan with the court. This gives the proponent some flexibility to make changes in the plan to overcome opposition and achieve a higher degree of acceptance. Modification after confirmation is more disruptive, so §1127(b) imposes restrictions on postconfirmation modification. The plan may only be modified with court approval following notice and a hearing and upon a showing that circumstances warrant modification. In addition, the modification must be made before *substantial consummation* of the plan. This is defined in §1101(2) to mean the transfer of all or substantially all of the property proposed to be transferred by the plan, assumption by the debtor or its successor of the business or of the management of all or substantially all of the property dealt with by the plan, and commencement of distribution under the plan.

§21.4.8   The Effect of Confirmation

The effect of confirmation is stated by §1141. In general, §1141(a) makes the provisions of the confirmed plan binding on all parties in interest — including the debtor, creditors, and shareholders — whether or not their claims were impaired and whether or not they accepted the plan. This general rule is subject to the exceptions to discharge mentioned below. Under §§1141(b) and (c), confirmation also vests all the estate's property in the debtor, free and clear of all claims and interests except to the extent that the plan provides otherwise. (The plan may provide otherwise for the purpose of preserving liens pending payment of secured claims or because some property is to be transferred or liquidated to settle claims.)

Section 1141(d) discharges the debtor upon confirmation of the plan, so that the debtor's original obligations fall away and are replaced by the obligations assumed under the plan. In this respect, Ch. 11 differs from Ch. 13, in which discharge only occurs after consummation of the plan. The discharge relates to all prepetition debts as well as postpetition debts allowed under §§502(g), (h), and (i), whether or not a proof of claim was filed, the claim was allowed, or the plan was accepted by the holder. The discharge is subject to the provisions of the plan and the confirmation order, which may curtail its scope and exclude otherwise dischargeable debts. Quite apart from the provisions of the plan, §§1141(d)(2) and (3) contain exceptions to discharge: §1141(d)(2) excepts from the discharge of an individual debtor any debts that are nondischargeable under §523. Section 1141(d)(3) denies a discharge to debtor, whether it is an individual or a corporation, if the plan liquidates all or substantially all of its property, the debtor does not engage in business after consummation of the plan, and it would not have been entitled to a discharge if the case had been filed under Ch. 7. (This is explained further in section 22.6.)

Section 1141(d)(1)(B) deals with the effect of confirmation on ownership interests in the debtor: Except as otherwise provided in the plan or the confirmation order, confirmation terminates the rights and interests of equity security holders and general partners provided for by the plan. In other words, §1141(d)(1)(B) sets out a general rule that ownership interests in the debtor cannot survive Ch. 11 bankruptcy unless the debtor is able to have a plan confirmed that preserves them in whole or in part. To achieve confirmation of a plan with such provisions, the debtor must provide sufficient payment to gain acceptance of the plan by creditors, or to meet the stringent *cramdown* standards explained in section 21.7.3.

§21.4.9   *Consummation of the Plan*

Unlike Ch. 13, Ch. 11 prescribes no time limit for performance of the obligations under the plan. The payment periods and the timetable for implementation of the plan are stipulated by the plan itself. These periods are settled in the preconfirmation negotiation process and are based on the business realities of the debtor's situation. Section 1142 requires the debtor to proceed with implementation of the plan upon confirmation. If the plan is successfully consummated, the case is closed. Otherwise, the debtor's failure to perform are grounds for dismissal or conversion to a Ch. 7 under §1112.

§21.5   Prepackaged Plans

The above outline presupposes that the plan is developed and votes are solicited after the petition has been filed. This is the conventional approach, but the debtor may be able to work out a plan with creditors before filing the petition. The Code recognizes this possibility and accommodates it in §§1121(a) and 1126(b). The former section allows the debtor to file a plan with the petition, and the latter treats prepetition acceptances and rejections as valid, provided that proper disclosure was made under nonbankruptcy disclosure regulations or, if none exist, under the *adequate information* standard of §1125(a).

A plan that is wholly or substantially settled prior to the petition is called a *prepackaged plan*. It is essentially an out-of-court settlement between the debtor and creditors (or at least the most important creditors), followed by a Ch. 11 filing so that the Code can be used to effectuate the settlement, to deal with dissenters, and to obtain the court's imprimatur. If a prepackaged plan can be formulated, the reorganization usually proceeds much more quickly, which reduces the risk, delay, and uncertainty of the postpetition process.

Of course, a prepackaged plan is not a possibility for every debtor. The prospect of settling the reorganization before filing is only open to those debtors who are in a position to approach creditors without the protection of the bankruptcy stay. In addition, the feasibility of prepetition resolution of the plan is affected by factors such as the scope and complexity of what is to be achieved in the reorganization and the range of claims and interests to be accommodated.

§21.6   The Content of the Plan

§21.6.1   Overview

As stated before, Ch. 11 favors consensual plans formulated by negotiation. Section 1123 therefore gives the debtor considerable flexibility to develop a plan that best meets its needs while accommodating the legitimate demands of creditors and other parties in interest. Section 1123(a) contains six mandatory provisions for the plan, and §1123(b) sets out a range of permissive provisions that may be included in it. The content of the plan is also affected by §1129, which prescribes the standards that it must meet for confirmation. While some of the mandatory provisions and standards are absolute, others may be varied by consent so that they give bargaining power to a party whose consent is sought.

Ch. 11 plans vary greatly. Some are quite short and simple, while others are lengthy and complex. Obviously, this depends on the size of the debtor and the scale of its operations. Notwithstanding, the plan is likely to follow a typical pattern: It begins with an introductory section that defines terms and provides background material. It may provide some historical data to explain the debtor's situation, and it may offer a synopsis of the plan provisions and a justification for the decisions that have been made. It then classifies claims and interests into classes, states which classes are impaired, and specifies the treatment to be given to each class. This, a crucial part of the plan, is one of the mandatory components. The plan then sets out the means for implementation and the terms, time periods, and undertakings regarding performance. This is another vital component. Finally, the plan contains a variety of optional provisions, governing such matters as the treatment of executory contracts, the sale or liquidation of assets, any amendments to the debtor's charter, the employment of professionals, the retention of jurisdiction by the bankruptcy court to resolve certain postconfirmation matters, and so on.

§21.6.2   The Mandatory Provisions under §1123(a)

Section 1123(a) requires the plan to deal with the following matters:

(1) Designation of classes of claims and interests (§1123(a)(1)). The basic principles of claim classification were addressed in section 19.6, which described the tripartite classification into secured, priority, and general claims, and in section 20.7, which discussed the classification of unsecured claims in a Ch. 13 plan. The classification of claims and interests assumes a particularly important role in the Ch. 11 case because it not only affects the distribution to be received, but also the voting power of the creditor or interest holder. Section 1123(a)(1) merely requires the designation of classes. The principles governing classification are set out in §1122 and in caselaw. Because classification has an impact on the substantive and voting rights of parties, the debtor's discretion in establishing classes is controlled to prevent unfair discrimination and manipulation of voting power. The following principles apply:

(a)   Section 1122 requires claims and interests in a class to be substantially similar. The Code does not say what constitutes substantial similarity, but this is generally taken to mean that the claims must be of the same priority and quality. Therefore, for example, a debtor cannot place in the same class a secured and an unsecured claim, or claims having different priorities. Although unsecured claims of equal rank are often placed in the same class, each secured claim is usually given a class of its own because secured claims are not substantially similar to each other — they are either secured by different collateral or have a different priority in the same collateral.

One group of dissimilar claims may be combined in a single class under §1122(b). Unsecured claims of relatively low value may be classed together for convenience, so that they can be dealt with in the same way. This classification requires court approval, which is granted only if the ceiling amount is reasonable and the classification is necessary for administrative convenience.

(b) Although §1122 prevents the inclusion of dissimilar claims in a class, it does not forbid the debtor from placing similar claims in different classes. However, the debtor's ability to classify similar claims separately is subject to the requirement that the classification has a reasonable basis. This is intended to prevent manipulations of the classification process for the purpose of diluting the votes of unsympathetic creditors or providing preferential treatment for favored creditors.

(c) Three types of priority claims are not subject to classification in the plan. Administrative expenses with first priority under §507(a)(1) and operating expenses incurred by the debtor in the gap period in an involuntary case, having second priority under §507(a)(2), are not classified. This is because §1129(a)(9)(A) requires all these claims to be fully paid in cash on the effective date of the plan. Because they are settled before the plan goes into effect, no purpose is served by classifying them. The rights of the holders of such claims cannot be impaired without their consent, and they do not vote on the plan. Tax claims that fall into the eighth priority under §507(a)(8) are not classified either. Section 1129(a)(9)(C) requires that they be paid in full over a period of not more than six years from assessment. As with administrative expenses, the debtor has no discretion to impair these claims without the consent of the holder, so classification serves no purpose.

(d) Like claims, interests may also be divided into classes. For example, a corporate debtor may have issued preferred stock that has priority over common stock. The same rules apply to prevent the placing of dissimilar interests in the same class or dividing up similar interests into arbitrary or manipulative classifications.

(2) Specification of unimpaired classes of claims and interests (§1123(a)(2)). *Impairment* is a central concept in Ch. 11. It has already been referred to in connection with voting, and its significance in the confirmation of the plan is discussed in section 21.7. Section 1123(a)(2) requires the plan to specify any class of claims or interests that is not impaired under the plan. It follows that it will also be apparent from the plan which classes are impaired.

The meaning of impairment is set out in §1124, which states that a class of claims or interests is impaired unless each claim or interest in the class is treated in one of the two ways specified in the section. (Notice that although it is the *class* that is impaired, the test for nonimpairment is applied to *each claim or interest* in the class.) In short, for a claim or interest to be unimpaired, the rights of the holder must be unaltered, or they must be unaltered except for cure of a default and deacceleration of the debt, with full compensation for any damages incurred in reasonable reliance on the default or acceleration clause. More specifically, the meaning of these requirements is:

(a) *No alteration of rights (§1124(1)).* A claim or interest is not impaired under the plan if the legal, equitable, and contractual rights of the holder are left unaltered. In other words, the plan proposes to give the holder exactly what it is entitled to receive under the terms of its contract or applicable nonbankruptcy law. Any change in those rights (apart from those described in the next paragraph) is an impairment.

(b) *No alteration of rights except for the cure of a default and deacceleration with compensation for loss (§1124(2)).* If the debtor defaulted on an obligation prior to bankruptcy, §1124(2) allows it to provide in the plan for cure of the default and reversal of the acceleration. If the holder of the claim or interest is compensated for any damages resulting from reasonable reliance on the term of the contract or on nonbankruptcy law that permitted acceleration, and if all other rights of the holder of the claim or interest are left intact, the provision for cure and reinstatement of the original maturity date does not constitute an impairment.

(3) Specification of the treatment of impaired classes of claims or interests (§1123(a)(3)). The preceding explanation of impairment shows that, as a general matter, almost every deviation from the nonbankruptcy rights of a claimant or interest-holder results in impairment of the claim or interest. Because impaired parties will not receive exactly what they had the right to expect under nonbankruptcy law, the plan must set out precisely how they are to be treated: what value they will receive, if any, and when and in what form they will receive it. A plan that fails to do this cannot be coherent or competent.

Section 1123(a)(3) merely requires the plan to specify the treatment of the impaired classes. Section 1129 sets out some minimum standards for that treatment, which are discussed in section 21.7. Subject to those standards, the debtor, as proponent of the plan, decides how impaired claims are to be provided for. Of course, to secure confirmation of the plan, the debtor needs to consult and negotiate with impaired parties in devising provisions that are practicable, affordable, and acceptable.

There are many different ways in which impaired claims could be treated. The following examples illustrate what the plan may provide: It may undertake full or partial payment over an extended time or in a lump sum; it may propose that a class of claims be paid pro rata out of a particular fund or the proceeds of specified property; it may propose to issue stock or to transfer property to creditors in satisfaction of their claims; it may even provide for no distribution at all to a particular class or classes.

(4) Equal treatment of claims or interests in a class (§1123(a)(4)). The principle of equal treatment of members of a class was introduced in the Ch. 13 context in section 20.7.3. Once claims or interests have been classified together, they must be treated the same unless the holder of a particular claim or interest agrees to a less favorable treatment.

(5) Adequate means for the plan's implementation (§1123(a)(5)). A plan is meaningless unless it has provisions for its implementation. Section 1123(a)(5) requires the plan to set out the manner in which the plan will be funded and the course that will be followed to bring the reorganization to a successful conclusion. Section 1123(a)(5) has a nonexclusive list of some of the implementation provisions that may be included in the plan. Creation of the means of implementation is one of the important areas of flexibility in Ch. 11. It gives a wide range of options to the debtor for devising a reorganization scheme that best satisfies claims, while allowing the debtor to take advantage of resources available for the salvation of its business. The plan's implementation provisions can range from a simple funding scheme derived from future income and the liquidation of unwanted assets to a much more complex arrangement involving such strategies as the issuance of new stock, the creation of new investment or credit, or merger with another entity.

(6) Voting powers for corporate debtors (§1123(a)(6)). If the debtor is a corporation, the plan must provide for matters of voting power in the charter of the debtor and of any corporations with which it proposes to become associated. The charter of the reorganized debtor must forbid the issuance of nonvoting securities. If there are different classes of security, the voting power among them must be appropriately distributed.

(7) The selection of officers (§1123(a)(7)). The provisions in the plan concerning the selection of any officer, director or trustee must be consistent with public policy and the interests of creditors and equity security holders.

§21.6.3   Permissive Provisions under §1123(b)

Section 1123(b) is similar in tone to §1322(b) in that it provides a broadly drafted list of provisions that can be included in the plan if the proponent so desires. The decision on which classes of claims to impair or leave unimpaired is one example. Other matters that may be provided for include the assumption or rejection of executory contracts or the sale of property.

Section 1123(b)(5) duplicates in a Ch. 11 case the modification-of-rights provision of §1322(b)(5). Section 1123(b)(5) was added by the Bankruptcy Reform Act of 1994 to incorporate into the Ch. 11 case of an individual the same rule as applies in Ch. 13: The debtor can modify the rights of holders of unsecured claims and secured claims, except for the rights of the holder of a claim secured only by a security interest in real property that is the debtor's principal residence. The addition of §1123(b)(5) overrules case law that held that the protection from strip-down, available to home mortgagees under Ch. 13, was not available in a Ch. 11 case. An individual debtor may therefore no longer use Ch. 11 to get around the prohibition on modification discussed in section 20.8.3.

In short, the plan may deal with any appropriate matters that are not inconsistent with the Code. As mentioned before, the range and detail of these optional provisions can be far-reaching in the reorganization of a large debtor.

§21.7   Confirmation Requirements

§21.7.1   Overview

Section 1129 imposes the standards and requirements for plan confirmation. It provides for two alternative means of confirmation: §1129(a), which sets out the prerequisites for confirmation when the plan has been accepted by all impaired classes, and §1129(b), which governs confirmation in the absence of universal acceptance by all impaired classes, known as *cramdown*. Cramdown confirmation under §1129(b) is subject to all the requirements of §1129(a), except for §1129(a)(8), which specifies acceptance by all classes. In addition, the further requirements of §1129(b) must be satisfied. The diagram on page 458 shows these alternative means of confirmation.

§21.7.2   Confirmation under §1129(a)

There are 13 requirements for confirmation in §1129(a). (Section 1129(d) has a further requirement which is not discussed here.) Some of the requirements are quite technical, and are omitted from this overview. Coverage is

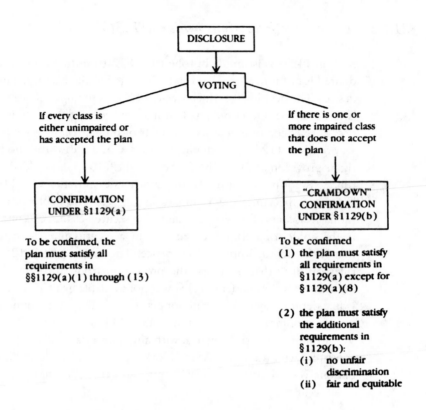

confined to those that are necessary to an understanding of confirmation under §1129(a).

(1) Lawfulness and good faith (§§1129(a)(1), (2) and (3)).   Both the plan itself and the proponent's conduct in proposing it must comply with the Code. In addition, the standard of good faith that was discussed in connection with the Ch. 13 plan applies to a Ch. 11 plan as well. The court has the power to refuse confirmation of a plan that is abusive, manipulative or counter to the spirit and purpose of Ch. 11.

(2) The treatment of impaired claims and interests (§1129(a)(7)). Unimpaired classes are deemed to have accepted the plan, so their consent is presumed as a matter of course. Impaired classes vote on the plan. Those members of the class that vote for acceptance are also treated as having consented to the plan. Even though an impaired class may have accepted the plan by the requisite majority, some class members may have voted against the plan. Section 1129(a)(7)(A) protects these dissenters by imposing a best interests test for their claims and interests that is similar to the test discussed in section 20.7 in connection with §1325(a): If a class is impaired, each member of that class who did not vote to accept the plan must receive a distribution under the plan at least equal to the present value, on the effective date of the plan, of what would have been received had the debtor been liquidated under Ch. 7.

Section 1129(a)(7)(B) prescribes the minimum distribution to be provided for undersecured claims who have made the election under §1111(b). *See* section 21.7.4.

(3) Acceptance by classes of claims and interests (§1129(a)(8)). Section 1129(a)(8) sets out the acceptance requirements that must be satisfied for a plan to be confirmed under the consensual standards of §1129(a): Each class of claims or interests must either be unimpaired or must have accepted the plan. Remember that an unimpaired class does not vote because its acceptance is presumed, and a class who receives no value under the plan is deemed to have rejected it. If even one impaired class does not accept the plan §1129(a)(8) is not satisfied, and confirmation can only be achieved by complying with the additional requirements for cramdown confirmation under §1129(b).

(4) The required treatment for priority claims (§1129(a)(9)). Except to the extent that the holder of a particular claim has agreed to a different treatment, §1129(a)(9) requires priority claims to be provided for as follows:

(a) Administrative expenses and claims arising out of the conduct of the debtor's business during the gap period in an involuntary case (*i.e.,* claims under §§507(a)(1) and (2)) must be paid in cash, to the extent of the allowed amount of the claim, on the effective date of the plan.

(b) Priority tax claims under §507(a)(8) must be paid in full in installments over a period of not more than six years from the date of assessment of the tax. The deferred payments must equal the present value, as of the plan's effective date, of the allowed amount of the claim.

(c) All other priority claims from the third to the seventh priority categories (the ninth is not mentioned) must be paid in full. If a class of priority claims has accepted the plan, the claims in that class may be paid in installments. The amount paid must equal the present value of the allowed claim as at the effective date of the plan. If a class has not accepted the plan, claims in that class must be paid in cash on the effective date of the plan.

(5) Acceptance by at least one impaired class (§1129(a)(10)). If any class of claims is impaired under the plan, §1129(a)(10) requires that at least one impaired class of claims has accepted the plan. In counting votes for this purpose, the affirmative votes of any insiders in that class are disregarded.

This provision is of limited effect in a confirmation under §1129(a), because §1129(a)(8) requires acceptance by all impaired classes. In most cases, compliance with §1129(a)(10) follows as a matter of course from satisfaction of the requirements of §1129(a)(8), but this is not always so. Section 1129(a)(10) excludes the acceptance votes of any insiders in the class. Therefore, if the acceptances of impaired classes was achieved only by the affirmative vote of insiders in those classes, the plan cannot be confirmed.

In cramdown under §1129(b), §1129(a)(10) serves as a control by ensuring that there is some modicum of creditor support for the plan. Although dissenting classes may exist, at least the majority of noninsider creditors in one impaired class has voted in favor of the plan.

(6) The plan must have a reasonable prospect of success (§1129(a)(11)). Section 1129(a)(11) requires, as a condition of confirmation, that the plan not be likely to be followed by liquidation or further financial reorganization, except as provided for by the plan. (The caveat makes it clear that this standard does not prevent a liquidating plan when that is the resolution contemplated by the plan.) This requirement, the *feasibility standard*, places the burden on the proponent to satisfy the court that the plan has a reasonable prospect of achieving its goals and allows the court to refuse confirmation if the plan is impracticable or over-optimistic.

§21.7.3   Confirmation under §1129(b)

The purpose of §1129(b) is to give the debtor a means of confirmation even though some classes of creditors or interest holders have refused to accept the plan. Essentially, §1129(b) prescribes a minimum level of treatment for claims and interests that was considered by Congress to be fair enough to justify imposition of the plan on unwilling classes.

In short, the plan will be confirmed by the cramdown method under §1129(b) if the following requirements are met:

(1) All the standards of confirmation in §1129(a) are satisfied, except for §1129(a)(8) which requires acceptance by all impaired classes.
(2) The plan does not discriminate unfairly against any impaired class that has not accepted the plan.
(3) The plan is fair and equitable with respect to each impaired class that has not accepted the plan.

The latter two additional standards for cramdown require explanation.

a. Unfair Discrimination (§1129(b)(1))

The question of whether a dissenting class has been unfairly discriminated against is largely a factual one that involves some degree of discretionary evaluation by the court. In general terms, the class that has rejected the plan must receive treatment under the plan consistent with that being given to other classes who have comparable legal rights. Thus, the treatment given to the dissenting classes must be compared with that of others with claims or interests of similar rank. If the dissenting class is not treated as well, this is discrimination. However, *discrimination is permissible if it is not unfair.* The question of fairness has to be resolved by evaluating the need and motive for the discrimination. If it is justifiable — it has some reasonable basis, it is not motivated by bad faith, and it is necessary to the success of the reorganization — it will likely not be unfair.

b. Fair and Equitable (§§1129(b)(1) and (2))

The requirement that impaired classes must be treated fairly and equitably covers an even broader range of considerations than the unfair discrimination standard. However, some specific content is given to the meaning of "fair and equitable" by §1129(b)(2), which prescribes the minimum level of treatment to be given to secured claims, unsecured claims, and interests for the plan to qualify as fair and equitable. Note that these are minimum standards: If they are not satisfied, the plan is not fair and equitable. However, even if they are met, this does not dispose of the issue. Other factors may lead to the conclusion that the plan is still not fair and equitable to an impaired class that has not accepted the plan.

i. Secured Claims

To be fair and equitable to an impaired class of secured claims,[4] the plan must at a minimum contain provisions that satisfy one of three alternative tests:

(1) **Retention of the lien and deferred payments (§1129(b)(2)(A)(i)).** To satisfy the first alternative test, the liens of the claimants in the class must be preserved to the full allowed amount of their secured claims. In addition,

---

4. As mentioned in section 21.6.2, it is usual for the plan to place each secured claim in its own separate class. Therefore, although §1129(b)(2) applies to a class of secured claims and refers to claims in the plural, there is often only one claim in each class.

each claimant in the class must receive deferred cash payments totalling at least the allowed amount of its secured claim having a value, as at the effective date of the plan, at least equal to the value of the holder's interest in the property. (As explained in section 20.7.3 in connection with Ch. 13, present value is the face value plus interest to compensate for the delay in payment.)

In other words, the first alternative test requires that claimants in the class retain their liens and also receive payment that cannot be less than the allowed amount of the claim, adjusted upwards to compensate for deferred payment. When the claimant is fully secured, these two tests mean that it must receive deferred payments equal to the present value of its fully secured claim. If the claimant is undersecured, matters become a little more complicated because of an election provided for under §1111(b). That is dealt with in section 21.7.4.

(2) Sale free and clear of liens, and a lien on the proceeds (§1129(b)(2)(A)(ii)).   The second alternative test applies if the debtor wishes to sell the property free and clear of liens, so that the lien cannot be preserved as required by §1129(b)(2)(A)(i). The debtor is permitted to sell the property free and clear of the lien under §363(K), which allows the claimant to bid at the sale; the lien attaches to the proceeds of the sale. The claimant is given the same rights to preservation of the lien in the proceeds and to payment, as are provided in §§1129(b)(2)(A)(i) and (iii).

(3) Indubitable equivalent (§1129(b)(2)(A)(iii)).   The third alternative is a broad provision that gives the court discretion to approve some other treatment of the secured claim that assures the claimant of receiving the *indubitable equivalent* of the claim. This term is also used in §361(3). *See* section 11.5.4. As in that context, the question to be decided is whether some alternative treatment proposed in the plan will result in the holders of claims receiving value that is unquestionably equal to their claims. For example, a proposal to surrender the collateral may satisfy this test.

ii.   Unsecured Claims

For the plan to be fair and equitable to a dissenting class of unsecured claims, it must satisfy one of two alternative requirements:

(1) Payment of the allowed amount of the claim (§1129(b)(2)(B)(i)). The plan must provide that each holder of a claim in the class receives property of a value, as of the effective date of the plan, equal to the allowed amount of the claim. This is the present value test again: If deferred payments are to be made, the amount of the distribution must equal the full face amount of the claim plus interest.

(2) No junior claim or interest receives or retains any property on account of its claim or interest (§1129(b)(2)(B)(ii)). As an alternative to full payment of the claims in the class, the plan can satisfy the fair-and-equitable standard by providing for no distribution or retention of property by anyone whose claim or interest is junior to the dissenting impaired class. This alternative is known as the *absolute priority* rule, because it is similar to a rule under the Bankruptcy Act that required senior classes to be fully paid before junior classes received anything. The effect of the rule is that if the senior nonaccepting class is not paid in full, the plan can only be crammed down if the debtor is willing to deprive all junior classes of all value.

Shareholders and other holders of ownership interests in the debtor are junior to creditors. Under the absolute priority rule, holders of equity in the debtor cannot remain owners unless general unsecured creditors are paid in full — they are "wiped out." Because cramdown results in the sacrifice of ownership equity, the debtor usually has a strong incentive to avoid this course, and to try to negotiate acceptance of the plan. However, if the debtor is willing to pay this price, or if no other alternative is feasible, the absolute priority rule allows cramdown of a plan that pays the dissenting class little or nothing on its claims.

This is qualified by the *best interests test* of §1129(a)(7), which applies to dissenting unsecured claimants even in a cramdown. They must receive at least the present value of what they would have received in a Ch. 7 liquidation.

There is one situation in which some courts have allowed equity holders to retain their interests even though a senior nonaccepting class has not received full payment: If the equity holders contribute new capital to the debtor, that is equal to or greater than the value of their interests, they can retain stock in the debtor in exchange for this new value. This is known as the *new value exception.* (Some commentators argue that it is not an exception at all, but a corollary to the rule, implicit in the wording of §1129(b).) The new contribution must be in money or money's worth; it cannot take the form of a promise of managerial services or other intangible benefits. The effect of the exception is that equity holders can buy out their equity by making a contribution of capital reasonably equivalent to the value of their interests in the debtor.

The new value exception was recognized under the Bankruptcy Act, but it is not expressly adopted in the Code. Courts disagree on whether the exception continues to exist under the Code. Several courts of appeal have considered the new value exception. Some have found that it still exists, and others have held that it does not. Even among courts that recognize the exception, there is a difference of opinion on its nature and extent. The Supreme Court has had opportunities to resolve this conflict, but it has not done so. In the most recent case in which the question was presented, *In re*

203 La Salle Street Partnership, 523 U.S. 1106 (1999), the court skirted the question of finally deciding if the new value exception exists under the Code by holding that even if it did exist, the equity holders had not given new value under circumstances that satisfied the language of §1129(b). In its 1997 report, the National Bankruptcy Review Commission recommended an amendment to the Code expressly recognizing the exception and setting forth specific standards to be met for its application.

iii.   Interests

The fair-and-equitable standard applicable to classes of interests that have not accepted the plan is similar to that relating to unsecured claims. If the class does not receive the present value of its interest, no junior interest may receive or retain any property under the plan. The present value of the interest must be based on the greater of the fixed liquidation preference or the fixed redemption price to which the holder is entitled, or the value of the interest. §§1129(b)(2)(C)(i) and (ii).

§21.7.4   Undersecured Creditors and §1111(b)

Ch. 11 has a protective device for undersecured creditors that is not available under any other chapter of the Code. It is provided for in §1111(b). On reading that section, one's first reaction is to wonder whether it was sneaked into the Code by visiting extraterrestrials. Although an exploration of all the ramifications of §1111(b) is beyond the scope of this overview of Ch. 11, the following explanation tries to give a sense of its purpose and effect.

Section 1111(b) has two essential components. First, it enhances the legal rights of nonrecourse undersecured creditors. Second, it provides some protection to all undersecured creditors by making it more difficult for the debtor to buy out their interests at depressed value. Each of these elements are discussed below. To understand them, bear in mind (as explained in section 19.6) that an undersecured claim is treated in bankruptcy as two claims: It is a secured claim to the extent of the value of the collateral and an unsecured claim for the deficiency. It therefore falls into two classes in the Ch. 11 plan, and these two classes are likely to be treated quite differently.

a.   Nonrecourse Undersecured Claims

A nonrecourse secured debt is one in which the holder of the security interest is confined to the collateral for satisfaction of the claim. The debtor has no personal liability on the claim, and if the collateral is worth less than the debt, the undersecured party cannot claim the deficiency from the debtor. The undersecured party may lack recourse either because the contract so provides, or because nonbankruptcy law forbids suit for any deficiency. (For example, in some states a mortgagee is held to an election of remedies on foreclosure, and is barred from claiming a deficiency if the price received at the foreclosure sale is not enough to fully satisfy the debt.)

In a Ch. 11 case, §1111(b) disregards nonrecourse provisions in contracts and under nonbankruptcy law. Even though the undersecured party could not have sued for the deficiency outside of bankruptcy, it is given an unsecured claim for the deficiency against the Ch. 11 estate. The undersecured party's rights are enhanced in this way to ameliorate the loss of an advantage that would usually be available under nonbankruptcy law: The secured party can normally bid at the foreclosure sale and has the chance of buying the property at a low price and later reselling it, thereby recouping the deficiency. This opportunity of acquiring the collateral at foreclosure is not available in a Ch. 11 case if the debtor proposes to keep the property rather than sell it. Furthermore, the amount to be paid out under the plan to the undersecured claimant could in fact be less than the actual value of the collateral, because the amount of the secured claim is determined by appraisal. By recognizing an unsecured claim for the deficiency, the Code provides some compensation to the undersecured creditor for having to abide by an appraisal of the collateral rather than seeking to offset its loss at a foreclosure sale. The unsecured claim for the deficiency is protected by all the usual rules governing unsecured claims, so that if the creditor does not accept the plan, the best interests test applies, and in a cramdown, the claim is subject to the unfair discrimination standard and the fair-and-equitable standard.

Because the recognition of the deficiency is compensation for the undersecured party's loss of opportunity to bid for the property, it is inapplicable when the property is sold by the estate and the holder of the undersecured nonrecourse claim is entitled to bid at the sale under §363. It is also inapplicable if the election under §1111(b)(2) is made, as explained below.

b. The Undersecured Creditor's Election under §1111(b)(2)

This election is available to all undersecured creditors, whether their claims are with or without recourse under nonbankruptcy law. The election must be made by the class as a whole by a vote of at least two-thirds in amount and more than half in number of the allowed claims in the class.[5] Section

---

5. As noted before, if the claim is placed in a class of its own, the voting majority is irrelevant.

1111(b)(1)(B) does not permit the election to be made if the members' interest in property is of inconsequential value or if a member of the class has recourse against the debtor on account of the claim and the property is sold under §363 or in the plan.

If the class of undersecured creditors makes the election under §1111(b)(2), the unsecured deficiency claim of each member of the class is eliminated and the full amount of the debt — both the secured and the unsecured portions — is placed in the secured category. As a result, the full allowed claim is treated as secured and exceeds the value of the collateral. This is, of course, an exception to the usual rule that the value of the collateral is the upper limit of the secured claim. However, the departure from general principle is not as drastic as it may seem. The election does not result in treatment of the entire claim as secured for all purposes; it is largely a tactical device that is not necessarily advantageous to creditors in the class and that, in some circumstances, would in fact be prejudicial. It is therefore not made as a matter of course, but only where the circumstances call for it. The effect of the election, listed below, suggests some of the considerations that must be taken into account by a class of undersecured creditors in deciding whether or not to make the election:

(1) By making the election, the class enlarges its secured claims, thereby preventing the debtor from leaving the claims unimpaired by paying only the present value of the collateral. To avoid impairing the claims and to keep them from being entitled to vote, the debtor has to pay the debts in full under either §1124(1) or §1124(3).

(2) Under the right circumstances, the election makes it more expensive for the debtor to cram down the plan. Under §1129(b)(2)(A), to be fair and equitable to secured creditors the plan must provide that they retain their liens on their full allowed claims and that they receive cash payments equal at least to the full face value of the claims, having a present value equal at least to the collateral's value. Thus, the level of payment must satisfy two standards: It must equal the present value of the collateral (that is, appraised value plus interest) as well as the face value of the claim. By adding the deficiency to the secured claim, its face value is increased. If the deficiency is large enough, it can inflate the face value of the claim beyond the present value of the collateral and the plan can only meet the fair and equitable standard if the debtor provides for full payment of this higher amount. (Of course, if the deficiency is not large enough to increase the face value of the claim beyond the present value of the collateral, the election has no effect on the payment level required under the plan.)

(3) Because the creditors' liens extend to the full allowed amount of their claims under §1129(b)(2), the election may be useful to the

class of undersecured creditors when the collateral is temporarily depressed in value or undervalued and there is a prospect that the reorganization may fail. If the plan is not consummated and the property is later liquidated, the full debt will have been preserved by the election so that it extends to the appreciated value of the collateral, rather than being confined to the collateral's value on the effective date of the plan.

(4)   The negative effect of the election, from the creditors' standpoint, is that the unsecured claims are lost. If the plan would have provided for a distribution to claims in that class, the loss of that distribution has to be weighed against any advantage achieved by the election. In addition, having lost their unsecured claims, the creditors also lose their right to vote in that unsecured class. Depending on the facts, that vote may have been useful because it could have given the creditors the power to create a dissenting class, thereby forcing the debtor into a cramdown.

The following hypothetical attempts to illustrate how the §1111(b)(2) election works: Suppose there is a mortgage on the debtor's property that secures a debt of $100,000. Because of a slump in property values, the collateral is appraised at only $80,000. (The collateral will probably appreciate in the future, when the real estate market improves.) The deficiency of $20,000 is allowed as an unsecured claim under §1111(b)(1), whether or not the mortgagee had recourse under nonbankruptcy law. The plan places the secured claim of $80,000 and the unsecured claim of $20,000 in two separate classes. Assume that each of these claims is placed in a class of its own.

If the mortgagee does not make the §1111(b)(2) election, its two claims remain separate. If the debtor proposes to keep the property, the plan needs only to provide for full payment of the secured claim of $80,000. This leaves the secured claim unimpaired, so that the secured claimant is conclusively deemed to have accepted the plan and has no right to vote to reject it. However, the unsecured claim for the deficiency of $20,000 gives the mortgagee voting rights in its unsecured class, and also entitles it to a distribution payable to claims of that rank. As the mortgagee is the only creditor in this class, the mortgagee has substantial influence in the confirmation process because it could vote to reject the plan, thereby forcing the debtor into a cramdown.

If the election is made under §1111(b)(2), the mortgagee loses the $20,000 deficiency claim, along with its voting rights and its share of the distribution for that class. In exchange, the mortgagee's secured claim increases from $80,000 to $100,000. The debtor can no longer pay only the present value of the collateral if it wishes to leave the claim unimpaired, but must pay the greater of the present value of the collateral or the face amount of the debt. If the debtor does not do this, the claim is impaired, the mortgagee becomes entitled to vote, and the debtor is forced to satisfy the cramdown standards for the secured claim. This means that the debtor must comply with one of the three alternative standards set out in §1129(b)(2). In addition, even if the debtor succeeds in having the plan confirmed, either by paying enough to prevent impairment or under the cramdown standards, the election gives the mortgage an advantage if the plan is not consummated and the debtor is subsequently liquidated: The mortgagee's lien against the property will be $100,000, not $80,000, and any appreciation in the collateral's value will go to the mortgagee, up to the full amount of the allowed secured claim (*i.e.*, the full debt).

A comparison of the alternatives available to the undersecured creditor shows that the election may or may not be advantageous. The gain in the secured claim comes at the cost of the unsecured claim. To decide on the election, claimants in the class have to decide whether it is worth sacrificing the vote and distribution in the unsecured class to gain leverage and possible financial advantage in the secured class. Also, as is true with so much of Ch. 11, the debtor's awareness that undersecured creditors are thinking about the election may influence its approach and make it more amenable to negotiation.

22

The Debtor's Discharge

§22.1   Introduction

The debtor's discharge has been referred to frequently in prior chapters. The discharge is the statutory forgiveness of the balance of debts that are not paid in full in the bankruptcy case. The debtor's right to receive a discharge as a matter of law, even in the absence of creditor assent, is one of the features that distinguishes bankruptcy from insolvency proceedings under state law. For many debtors, it is the principal incentive for seeking bankruptcy relief. The discharge is one of the most important manifestations of bankruptcy's fresh start policy. However, as was observed in the general discussion of bankruptcy policy in Chapter 5, the goal of providing a fresh start to the debtor must be balanced against other public policies served by the Code. To give due deference to these policies, limits and qualifications are imposed on the debtor's right to a discharge. Before covering the detailed rules of the discharge, it is useful to identify some of the broad themes that arise from the Code's attempt to balance the debtor's right to a fresh start against other bankruptcy goals.

Bankruptcy's fresh start is meant to help the honest debtor and not to provide a means for the unscrupulous evasion of debt. For this reason, there are provisions in the Code that deny or limit the discharge where the debtor has dealt dishonestly with creditors or has tried to abuse the spirit and purpose of the Code. However, these penalties are not comprehensive. They cover only specified conduct in particular situations. They also do not apply equally in all forms of bankruptcy; for example, many rules applicable in Ch. 7 do not apply in Ch. 13. Therefore, although one can state as a general proposition that undeserving conduct may affect the debtor's discharge, one has to examine the Code provisions carefully to determine whether particular behavior has an impact on the discharge.

As an alternative to denying or restricting the discharge to penalize bad faith conduct, the court has the power, upon cause being shown by a party in interest, to dismiss the bankruptcy case. (*See* section 9.7.) Dismissal denies all bankruptcy relief to the debtor, including the discharge, and is therefore another means of preventing abuse of bankruptcy's discharge privilege. Of course, grounds for dismissal must be present, and not all forms of unworthy conduct constitute a basis for dismissal.

Wrongful conduct is not the only basis for denying or limiting the discharge. Some debts are excluded from the discharge because Congress has decided that the claims in question should not be forgiven. This is exemplified by the nondischargeability of certain taxes, support obligations, and student loans. These limits on dischargeability are very specific and only apply to debts that meet the statutory qualifications.

The extent and scope of the discharge varies between the different Chapters of the Code. Each chapter has its own discharge provisions, namely §§727, 1141, 1228, and 1328. In addition, §§523, 524, and 525 apply to all chapters except to the extent that they are excluded by the specific provisions of a particular chapter. These variations in the discharge result in part from the policy favoring rehabilitation over liquidation. (This is most strikingly apparent in the comparison between discharge under Chs. 7 and 13.) However, divergence in the discharge provisions also reflects the particular structure of each chapter and the premises on which it is based.

Distinctions are also made in the Code between the availability of the discharge to individuals and to corporate entities. Unless there are grounds for denial of or exclusions from the discharge, an individual may obtain a discharge irrespective of which form of bankruptcy relief has been chosen. However, a corporation can only receive a discharge if it undergoes rehabilitation under Chs. 11 or 12. If it is liquidated under Ch. 7 or under Ch. 11, it becomes a mere shell. Bankruptcy does not actually terminate its existence (this is left to nonbankruptcy law), but if the corporation is not deregistered under nonbankruptcy law, the Code provides a strong disincentive to the revitalization of the corporate shell: Its undischarged prepetition debts remain in existence and are claimable from its new assets. (For an example of a case in which a successor to a defunct corporation was held liable for its prepetition debt, *see In re Goodman*, 873 F.2d 598 (2d Cir. 1989).)

§22.2   The Scope of the Discharge

The discharge applies only to debts that fall within the bankruptcy case. As a general rule, this covers only prepetition debts that were or could have been proved in the estate. Most postpetition debts incurred by the debtor are obligations of the fresh start estate and are not affected by the discharge. There are exceptions to this rule. In an involuntary Ch. 7 case, §727(b) includes in the discharge all debts incurred in the gap period between the petition and the adjudication of bankruptcy; in a Ch. 11 case, §1141(d)(1) includes in the discharge all debts that arose before the order of confirmation; and in cases under Chs. 12 and 13, the discharge covers all claims provided for in the plan (§§1228 and 1328).

Only *debts* are discharged: §§727, 1141, 1228, and 1328 all specifically refer to this term in providing for the discharge. "Debt" is defined in §101(12) to mean liability on a claim, which is in turn defined, in very broad terms, in §101(5). (*See* section 19.2.) Although most obligations are encompassed by this broad definition, some prepetition obligations of the debtors do not qualify as claims. If they are not claims, they are not covered by the discharge. The Supreme Court dealt with this issue in *Ohio v. Kovacs,* 469 U.S. 274 (1985). (*See* Example 3 of Chapter 19). In *Kovacs* the court held that a prepetition court order directing the debtor to clean up hazardous waste was a claim because the state agency had the alternative, under the state environmental statute, to conduct the cleanup itself and to seek reimbursement from the debtor. The court indicated that if there had been no alternative of a monetary remedy, the order compelling the debtor to clean up the site would not have been a claim. In *Pennsylvania Department of Public Welfare v. Davenport,* 495 U.S. 552 (1990), the Supreme Court held that the debtor's obligation to make restitution as a condition of probation in a criminal case is a right to payment and hence a debt. (Congress responded to *Davenport* by making the debt nondischargeable in a Ch. 13 case, as discussed in Example 2.) Since *Kovacs* and *Davenport,* lower courts have followed this distinction in a variety of different cases. For example, in *Kennedy v. Medicap Pharmacies, Inc.* 267 F.3d 493 (6th Cir. 2001), the court held that an injunction to enforce a covenant not to compete did not constitute a claim under *Kovacs* because the plaintiff had no alternative right to payment. The equitable relief of an injunction was premised on the absence of an adequate legal remedy for damages.

§22.3 The Effect of the Discharge

As explained in sections 19.4 and 19.6.3, the discharge affects only the debtor's personal liability on the debts and does not terminate any lien on the debtor's property which remains collectable from the collateral to the extent of its value. The discharge of debts eliminates all the debtor's personal liability. Section 524(a) enjoins all further proceedings and activity to collect or recover the debt. The injunction created by the discharge succeeds the automatic stay that had been in effect during the case and turns the temporary bar of the stay into a permanent prohibition on collection activity in respect of a discharged debt.

The enforcement of the injunction is by means of the court's civil contempt power under §105. In *Walls v. Wells Fargo Bank, N.A.*, 276 F.3d 502 (9th Cir. 2002), the court held that a civil contempt order is the only remedy available to the debtor, who is granted no independent private right of action under §524. However, the court pointed out that no remedy beyond a contempt order is needed because the court can make a compensatory contempt order to reimburse the debtor for any loss suffered as a result of the violation. The awesome power of the contempt remedy is illustrated by *In re Vivian*, 150 B.R. 832 (Bankr. S.D. Fla. 1992). Although the creditor knew of and tried to obey the discharge, it apparently could not get its computer to stop sending monthly dunning letters to the debtor. The court found the creditor's computer to be in contempt and fined it 50 megabytes of hard drive memory and 10 megabytes of R.A.M. Section 524(e) makes it clear that the discharge of the debtor does not operate as a discharge in favor of any other person who is liable on the debt.

Sections 525(a) and (b) prohibit discrimination against the debtor by governmental units or by a private employer solely on the ground of the debtor's bankruptcy, insolvency, or nonpayment of a discharged debt. The word "solely" allows a governmental unit or employer to justify adverse treatment by showing that it was based on grounds other than the debtor's bankruptcy or the nonpayment of a discharged debt. Courts have disagreed on the meaning and effect of "solely." Some have given it an interpretation favoring the debtor, and find discrimination if the bankruptcy played a significant role in the decision to refuse government services or to dismiss an employee. Others have adopted a plain-meaning approach and require only that the government or employer show that the action was motivated by legitimate reasons other than the debtor's bankruptcy. For a discussion of these two approaches, see *Laracuente v. Chase Manhattan Bank*, 891 F.2d 17 (1st Cir. 1989), in which the court adopted the latter interpretation of §525. There is some difference of opinion about whether §525 extends to discrimination against a debtor who intends to file bankruptcy. In *In re Majewski*, 310 F.3d 653 (9th Cir. 2002), the court held that §525 does not preclude an employer from dismissing an employee who revealed that he was in financial difficulty and planned to file a petition.

Subsection (c) to §525 (added in 1994) makes it clear that a debtor, ex-debtor, or person associated with a debtor who seeks a student loan or loan guarantee is included in the protection from discrimination under §525. Section 525(c) merely clarifies that applications for student loans are included in the protection against discrimination, and does not confer any higher level of protection on them. Therefore, although the debtor cannot be discriminated against solely because of the bankruptcy or discharge, the loan or guarantee can still be denied for other, legitimate, reasons. That is, the debtor's eligibility for the loan or guarantee must be evaluated as if the bankruptcy or discharge never existed.

§22.4 Wavier of the Discharge and Reaffirmation of the Debt

Section 524(a)(2) states that the injunctive force of the discharge and the release of the debtor from liability is not affected by any waiver of the discharge. This provision generally invalidates waivers, but it is qualified by §§727(a) (10), 1228(a), and 1328(a), which give effect to a waiver executed by the debtor in writing after the order for relief and approved by the court. Although Ch. 11 does not have a provision with the same wording, §1141(d) has the same effect, in that it permits the debtor to waive a discharge in the plan. The discharge can also be waived by a reaffirmation agreement, discussed in section 13.7. Reaffirmation is subject to controls even more stringent than waiver. Although wavier or reaffirmation is unenforceable unless the prescribed requirements are satisfied, §524(f) allows the debtor to repay a debt voluntarily. (Of course, if the creditor puts undue pressure on the debtor to pay, this would violate the injunction.)

§22.5 The Ch. 7 Discharge

§22.5.1 Procedure and Scope

As stated before, the Ch. 7 discharge is available only to an individual debtor. Unlike other chapters of the Code, Ch. 7 does not specify the point in the proceedings at which the discharge occurs. Rule 4004 requires objections to the discharge to be filed within 60 days of the creditors' meeting. If an objection is filed, or the U.S. Trustee has moved to dismiss the case for substantial abuse, the discharge is granted only after the court hears the matter and determines the debtor's right to a discharge. In the absence of such challenges, the discharge is granted as soon as possible after the expiry of that period. Within 30 days of the order granting or denying the discharge, the court may hold a discharge and reaffirmation hearing under Rule 4008 and §524(d), at which the court deals with any reaffirmation agreement that the debtor has made.

Under §727(b), the discharge covers all prepetition debts as well as postpetition claims treated as prepetition debts by §502. (This includes, for example, claims arising out of the rejection of an executory contract or the avoidance of a transfer, as explained in section 19.2.) These debts and claims are discharged whether or not they were proved or allowed. The debtor's right to a discharge is qualified by §§727 and 523. It is important to distinguish the effects of these two sections: §727 deprives the debtor of the discharge completely, while §523 excludes certain debts from it.

§22.5.2   *Denial of the Discharge under §727*

The denial of a discharge deprives the debtor of one of the most important (for some debtors, the most important) benefits of bankruptcy — forgiveness of the unpaid balance of debts provable against the estate. The grounds for denial of a discharge are set out in §727(a). If any one of them is applicable, the trustee, a creditor, or the U.S. Trustee may object to the grant of the discharge. Under Rule 4004, the objection is tried by the court as an adversary proceeding. Rule 4005 places the burden of proving the objection on the objecting party. Most of the grounds for denial are intended to penalize wrongful conduct or to prevent abuse of the fresh start policy. However, two of them, mentioned already, are not based on fault: §727(a)(1) precludes the discharge of a debtor that is not an individual, and §727(a)(10) allows the court to approve a written waiver of discharge, executed by the debtor after the order for relief. The grounds for denial based on fault or abuse can be placed into three broad categories.

(1)   The debtor is denied a discharge as punishment for certain kinds of dishonest, unlawful, or uncooperative conduct in anticipation of or in connection with the case. These grounds are set out in §§727(a)(2) through (6), and include:

    (a)   fraudulent transfer, concealment, or damage to property
    (b)   unjustified failure to keep records or the falsification or destruction of records
    (c)   inability to explain a loss or deficiency in assets
    (d)   obstructive behavior, such as the refusal to obey court orders, answer questions, or testify without justification based on the privilege against self-incrimination.

See Examples 1 and 3.

(2)   In some cases, the debtor's bankruptcy is linked to the bankruptcy of another individual or corporation whose financial affairs are related to those of the debtor. For example, the failure of a corporation could result in the personal bankruptcy of its owner as well. Where this has occurred, a debtor who has behaved dishonestly or obstructively in connection with the other bankruptcy may be denied a discharge in his or her own case. Section 727(a)(7) provides for this by authorizing the court to deny a discharge to a debtor who has committed any act specified in §§727(a)(2) through (6) in connection with the bankruptcy of an insider, either while the debtor's own case is pending, or within a year before the debtor's petition.

(3) To prevent a debtor from obtaining immediate successive Ch. 7 discharges, §727(a)(8) precludes the debtor from obtaining another Ch. 7 discharge until at least six years have elapsed since the filing of an earlier case under either Ch. 7 or Ch. 11 in which the debtor received a discharge. (The pending bankruptcy reform legsislation proposes to increase this period for Ch. 7 cases and to establish a similar rule on successive Ch. 13 petitions.) If the prior discharge was obtained under Chs. 12 or 13, the same rule applies unless the plan paid unsecured claims in full or paid at least 70 percent of such claims, and the plan was proposed in good faith and was the debtor's best effort. The six-year rule applies only where the later case has been filed under Ch. 7. With the exception of liquidation plans under Ch. 11 (discussed below), it does not apply where the debtor's subsequent case has been filed under another chapter of the Code. (See Example 4 of Chapter 20.)

§22.5.3   Revocation of the Discharge

Section 727(d) allows a creditor, the trustee, or the U.S. Trustee to apply for revocation of the debtor's discharge on one of three grounds: The debtor obtained the discharge through fraud that was not discovered by the appli-cant until after the discharge was granted; the debtor deliberately withheld or concealed property that would have been property of the estate; or the debtor disobeyed a court order or refused to testify or respond to a material question without justification based on the privilege against self-incrimina-tion. Section 727(e) requires an application for revocation under the first ground to be made within a year after the grant of the discharge, and an application on either of the other two grounds to be made within the later of one year after the grant of the discharge or the close of the case.

§22.5.4   Exclusions from the Ch. 7 Discharge by §523

Even when the debtor is entitled to a discharge under §727, the discharge may not include all the debts that are provable against the estate. Section 523 excludes several types of debt from the discharge. As noted in section 22.1, the reasons for these exclusions differ. Some of them are primarily aimed at penalizing wrongful conduct by the debtor, while others are more concerned with the protection of debts which Congress felt should not be reduced or eliminated in bankruptcy. There are 19 categories of nondischargeable debts listed in §523(a). The most generally applicable exclusions are summarized below, and some of them are illustrated by Examples 2, 3, 4, and 5.

All the exclusions in §523 are applicable in a Ch. 7 case. (Their applica-bility under other chapters is discussed below.) Most of the exclusions do not have to be adjudicated during the bankruptcy case and simply take effect if the debt meets the criteria for exclusion, but §523(c)(1) requires creditors whose debts qualify for exclusion under §§523(a)(2), (4), and (6) (generally speaking, these are grounds relating to fraud or intentional wrongs) and (15) (relating to nondischargeable marital property settlements) to apply to the court on notice for a determination of dischargeability. Rule 4007 governs this application, which must normally be filed within 60 days of the creditors' meeting unless the court grants an extension of the time. When a determination of nondischargeability is required, the creditor loses the right to exclude the debt from the discharge if the matter is not brought before the court for determination in time. The creditor's responsibility to make timely application for a dischargeability determination presupposes that the creditor knew or should have known of the bankruptcy. If the debt was not scheduled or listed and the creditor did not otherwise obtain knowledge of the bankruptcy in time to apply for the determination, §523(a)(3) excludes the debt from the discharge despite the lack of a court determination.

Some of the 19 categories of exclusion are quite narrow and specialized. The following are those that are most likely to arise:

(1) **Priority taxes (§523(a)(1)).**   Taxes that are entitled to priority under §507(a) (*see* section 19.6.4) are not discharged. In addition, taxes are excluded from the discharge if a required return was not filed, if it was filed late within two years before bankruptcy, or if the debtor filed a fraudulent return or tried to evade the tax. Under §523(a)(14), if the debtor borrows money to pay a nondischargeability tax, the loan itself becomes nondischargeable.

(2) **Obligations incurred fraudulently (§523(a)(2)).**   Section 523(a)(2) must surely be the most extensively invoked exception to discharge. It has slightly different rules for two distinct types of fraudulent misrepresentation made by the debtor to induce the debt. The first, dealt with in subsection (A), is the more general ground of fraud covering debts induced by the debtor's false representations, whether made orally or in writing. In cases involving last-minute consumer spending sprees, subsection (A) is augmented by a presumption set out in subsection (C). The second, dealt with in subsection (B), is a more specific basis for nondischargeability when the debt was induced by a materially false written financial statement. (Further discussion of nondischargability for fraud can be found in Examples 2 and 5.)

(a) *Nondischargeability for actual fraud under §523(a)(2)(A).*   Section 523(a)(2)(A) excludes from the discharge a debt for money, property, services or new or renewed credit to the extent that it was obtained by false pretenses, a false representation, or actual fraud. This covers all types of oral or written fraudulent misrepresentations by the debtor except for one, which is explicitly excluded: A statement representing the debtor's or an insider's financial condition. This form of representation in writing is dealt with separately in §523(a)(2)(B). (An oral statement of this kind is not covered in either subsection and is therefore not a basis for exclusion from the discharge under §523(a)(2).)

The type of conduct, that will make a debt nondischargeable under subsection (2)(A), is equivalent to common law fraud. Although the elements to be satisfied are not expressly stated in the subsection, they are well established under common law:

(1) The debtor must have made a *false representation*. There is some question about whether the representation must be *material*. Some courts articulate the materiality requirement, and others do not. In most cases, this is not really an issue, because it is hard for a creditor to prove the element of justifiable inducement when the misrepresentation relates to a trivial fact.

(2) At the time of making the misrepresentation, the debtor must have had knowledge of its falsity and intent to deceive. (This knowledge and deliberate purpose of deceit are known as *scienter*).

(3) The creditor must have justifiably relied on the false representation in entering into the transaction — it must have been induced by the misrepresentation to give the debtor the money, property, services, or credit. In *Field v. Mans,* 516 U.S. 59 (1995), the Supreme Court held that as §523(a)(2)(A) does not prescribe a test for reliance, the common law standard of justifiable reliance applies. This standard is distinguished from a stricter test of reasonable reliance, which is more objective and does not take into account the debtor's attributes and circumstances.

(4) The misrepresentation must have resulted in some injury. (Where the debtor has not repaid the debt, and seeks to discharge it in bankruptcy, the issue of injury is clear-cut.)

If a debt is excluded from the discharge under §523(a)(2)(A), the exclusion covers both the original debt and any award of punitive damages made by a court to penalize the debtor for the fraudulent conduct. This was not clear until settled by the Supreme Court in *Cohen v. De La Cruz,* 523 U.S. 213 (1998). The court determined that, on a grammatical reading of §523(a)(2), the section included not only the initial fraudulently incurred debt, but the full liability adjudged due, including any punitive damages, that is traceable to the fraud.

In *Archer v. Warner,* 123 S.Ct. 1462 (2003), the Supreme Court held that where a fraudulently incurred debt is later included in a settlement agreement and released in exchange for a promise to pay under the settlement, it retains its fraudulent character for the purposes of nondischargeability under §523(a)(2). The Court rejected the reasoning of the court of appeals that the settlement agreement constituted a novation of the debt that extinguished the fraud claim and replaced it with an ordinary contract claim.

Section 523(a)(2) excludes the debt from the discharge if it is for money, property, services, or credit "obtained by false pretenses . . . or actual fraud." Therefore, on a literal reading, the exclusion does not actually say that the debtor must have himself been guilty of the fraud. It could apply even where the debt was induced by the fraud of a third party. Although this situation is not likely to arise very often, it can happen, as illustrated by *In re M.M. Winkler & Associates*, 239 F.3d 746 (5th Cir. 2001). The debtor's partner in an accountancy firm had defrauded clients. Although the debtor was not involved in the fraud, he was liable to the clients by virtue of a partner's joint and several liability for partnership debts. The court held that the language of §523(a)(2) focuses on the character of the debt, not necessarily on the conduct of the debtor. Therefore, the fraud claim was nondischargeable in the debtor's bankruptcy, and even though he was not himself guilty of fraud, liability was imputed to him by virtue of the partnership relationship and the debtor received no benefit from the fraudulent transaction.

(b) The presumption of fraud in last-minute consumer spending sprees under §523(a)(2)(C). As discussed below, the creditor normally bears the burden of proving fraud. However, §523(a)(2)(C) makes one exception to this by creating a presumption of fraud for the purposes of §523(a)(2)(A) when, shortly before filing the petition, the debtor went on a consumer spending splurge. The presumption only applies to consumer debt incurred by an individual. It takes effect in one of two alternative circumstances.

First, the presumption applies if, within 60 days before the order for relief, the debtor incurred consumer debts for luxury goods or services (defined in the subsection as those not reasonably acquired for the support or maintenance of the debtor or her dependent), aggregating more than $1,150, owed to a single creditor. There can be an interpretational issue about what constitute luxuries, and one debtor's luxury may be another's necessity. For example, in *In re Hall*, 228 B.R. 483 (Bankr. M.D. Ga. 1998), the court held that while credit given to a debtor by a casino is a luxury when the gambling is recreational, it does not so qualify when the debtor is a longtime, high-stakes gambler trying to save his business by making a big win.

Second, fraud is presumed if within 60 days before the order for relief, the debtor obtained cash advances aggregating more than $1,150 and constituting an extension of consumer credit under an open-end credit plan. (This is a plan under which the debtor is given a line of credit and repeated transactions are contemplated.) This provision is worded so as not to include the requirements that the advances be used to buy luxury goods or services, or that they all be obtained from the same creditor.

The amount of the debt stated in the subsection — $1,150 — is one of those monetary amounts subject to periodic administrative adjustment under §104(b) by the Judicial Conference of the United States. The figure was established with effect from April 1, 2001 and will be adjusted again with effect from April 1, 2004. The pending bankruptcy reform legislation would extend the reachback period and change the dollar amounts.

It is worth stressing that §523(a)(2)(C) does not make debts incurred under the stated circumstances automatically nondischargeable, but merely establishes a presumption that a debt so incurred is fraudulent. This places the burden on the debtor to prove that the elements of fraud are not satisfied despite the suspicious circumstances.

(c) Nondischargeability for materially false financial statements under §523(a)(2)(B). Section 523(a)(2)(B) applies only to situations in which money, property, services, or new or renewed credit is obtained by a false written financial statement concerning the debtor or an insider. Unlike subsection (a)(2)(A), this subsection does set out the required elements: The statement must be written; it must be materially false; the debtor must have published it or caused it to be published with intent to deceive; and the creditor must have reasonably relied on it. As you can see, the elements are quite similar to those for common law fraud, with two differences: Only written statements are covered, and the test for reliance is the more stringently objective reasonableness standard. As mentioned above, a false oral financial statement is not a ground for nondischargeability at all, because it is not covered by either subsection.

The legislative history of §523(a)(2)(B) and *Field v. Mans* explain why this subsection articulates the elements of a false financial statement and imposes the stricter reasonable reliance standard: Congress did not want a creditor to claim nondischargeability on the basis of some unimportant misstatement or inaccuracy in a credit application or financial statement.

Cohen was concerned with a case involving §523(a)(2)(A), but its interpretation involved the language common to both subsections, so its conclusion about punitive damages is equally applicable to §523(a)(2)(B).

(d) The dischargeability hearing and the burden of proof. Section 523(a)(2) is one of the subsections listed in §523(c)(1), so the debt is not automatically excluded from the discharge, and the creditor must seek a determination of dischargeability from the court following notice and a hearing.

At the hearing, the creditor has the burden of proving that the debt qualifies for exclusion from the discharge. This includes proving the element of deliberate fraud, unless, of course, the case is one in which the presumption of §523(a)(2)(C) applies. In *Grogan v. Garner,* 498 U.S. 279 (1991), the Supreme Court made it clear that fraud must be proved on the normal preponderance-of-the-evidence standard, and need not be established on the more rigorous clear-and-convincing standard.

(e) Sanctions for an unsuccessful application for nondischargeability. To discourage creditors from making vexatious or groundless applications for the nondischargeability of consumer debts on grounds of fraud, §523(d) gives the court the discretion to award costs and attorneys fees for the proceedings to the debtor if the creditor's application for nondischargeability was not substantially justified and there are no special circumstances that would make the award unjust.

(3) Unlisted or unscheduled debts (§523(a)(3)). Although the discharge normally extends even to those debts for which no proof of claim was filed, §523(a)(3) protects creditors who did not know of the bankruptcy in time to file a claim. If the debtor did not timely list or schedule the debt, so that the creditor did not receive notice of the bankruptcy and did not otherwise find out about it in time to file a proof of claim, the debt is excluded from the discharge.

As mentioned earlier, §523(a)(3) also precludes discharge of a debt covered by §523(a)(2), (4), or (6) where the creditor's failure to make timely application for a nondischargeability determination resulted from lack of knowledge of the bankruptcy because the debtor failed to list or schedule the debt. When §523(a)(15) was added in 1994, reference to it was included in §523(c) as one of the debts that was not automatically excluded from the discharge, but required a dischargeability hearing. However, apparently as a result of an oversight, it was omitted from §523(a)(3).

(4) Debts arising out of the debtor's dishonesty as a fiduciary, or from embezzlement or larceny (§523(a)(4)). If, while acting in a fiduciary capacity, the debtor committed fraud or defalcation or if, acting in any capacity, the debtor embezzled money or committed larceny, the liability arising from that wrongful act is excluded from the discharge. This is one of the exclusions for which a determination of dischargeability must be requested. Note that the requirement that the debtor was acting in a fiduciary capacity qualifies only fraud and defalcation. The exclusion applies to debts arising from embezzlement or larceny even when the debtor was not a fiduciary. (*See* Example 2.)

Courts disagree on the scope of that portion of §523(a)(4) that applies to fraud or defalcation committed in a fiduciary capacity. Some restrict it to trusts in the formal sense — that is, express or technical trusts (*see*, for example, *In re Burress*, 245 B.R. 871 (Bankr. D. Colo. 2000) — while others interpret "fiduciary capacity" more broadly to include any relationship in which the debtor stands in a position of trust and confidence towards the creditor which demands a duty of loyalty and care (*see*, for example, *In re McDade*,

282 B.R. 650 (Bankr. N.D. Ill. 2002)). An attorney-client relationship is an example, and some courts have been willing to apply §523(a)(4) when the debt arose as a result of the attorney's faithless conduct, even if the wrong did not involve the misappropriation of trust funds. However, even among courts that adopt the broader approach, there seems to be general agreement that there must at least be some kind of genuine trust relationship between the parties, so it is not appropriate to apply §523(a)(4) when the debtor is deemed by equity or statute to be a constructive trustee purely for the sake of affording a remedy to the victim of the fraud or defalcation. For example, in *In re Marchiando,* 13 F.3d 1111 (7th Cir. 1994) the debtor, who owned a convenience store, failed to remit to the state the proceeds of lottery tickets that she had sold. The state statute provided that the proceeds of ticket sales would constitute a trust fund until paid to the state. The state sought to have the debt for the unpaid proceeds excluded from the debtor's discharge under §523(a)(4), but the court found the section inapplicable. Although the court agreed with a wider definition of fiduciary capacity, the debtor here was merely a ticket agent without any special power, expertise, or duty of loyalty. The statutory device of deeming the funds to be in trust was really nothing more than the creation of a constructive trust for remedial purpose — a collection device.

Because §523(a)(4) covers fraud and defalcation, it may be possible, on some facts, to exclude the debt from the discharge under §523(a)(2) without having to prove fiduciary capacity. However, that subsection is not helpful unless money, property, services, or credit was obtained by the fraud, and this link between the fraud and the giving of value may not be present, or may be difficult to establish.

(5) Debts for alimony, maintenance, or support (§523(a)(5)). Debts to a spouse, former spouse, or child of the debtor for alimony, maintenance, or support are excluded from the discharge. The debt must have arisen from a divorce decree or other court or governmental order or from a separation or property settlement agreement. The substance of the obligation governs, rather than its form, so a creditor spouse cannot protect a property settlement or commercial debt by labeling it a support payment in the divorce agreement. A support obligation cannot be excluded from the discharge to the extent that it has been voluntarily or involuntarily assigned to someone other than the state or federal government.

This provision ties in with other sections protecting claims for support, alimony, and maintenance in bankruptcy, such as those excluding them from the stay, granting them priority status, and precluding their avoidance. (While these other provisions were enacted as a package by the Bankruptcy Reform Act of 1994, §523(a)(5) has been part of the Code ever since its enactment in 1978). Section 523(a)(18) also excepts from the discharge a support debt owed to a state or municipality.

(6) Debts for willful and malicious injury (§523(a)(6)).   A debt resulting from the debtor's willful and malicious injury to another entity or the property of another entity is excluded from the discharge. This is one of the exclusions for which a determination of dischargeability must be requested.

Although the precise scope of the term "willful and malicious" is subject to doubt, it is clear that this exclusion applies to liability for deliberate wrongful conduct. It is concerned with intentional rather than negligent behavior. Any doubt on this issue was settled by the Supreme Court in *Kawaauhau v. Geiger*, 523 U.S. 57 (1998). The debtor had been sued for medical malpractice. It was apparent that his conduct had been reckless, rather than merely negligent, and the question was whether the exclusion from discharge covered recklessness. The court said that it did not. The use of the words "willful and malicious" make it clear that §523(a)(6) is confined to intentional injuries: the actor must not only intend the act, but also its consequences. To read the subsection as covering reckless conduct, or even intentional conduct that is not accompanied by the intent to do the harm, violates the plain meaning of its language, and renders superfluous other subsections that cover reckless injury, namely §523(a)(9) (debts for injury caused by driving while intoxicated) and §523(a)(12) (malicious or reckless failure to fulfill commitments due to a federal depository institution regulatory agency). (*See* Examples 3 and 4.)

(7) Governmental fines, penalties, and forfeitures (§523(a)(7)).
Debts due to the government for fines, penalties, or forfeitures that are not compensation for actual pecuniary loss, are excluded from the discharge. (*See* Example 2.) This category includes penalties on taxes that are nondischargeable under §523(a)(7), but does not include penalties on dischargeable taxes or on a transaction that occurred more than three years before the petition.

It can be a difficult factual question to decide whether a debt due to the government qualifies for one of the categories excluded from discharge under §523(a)(7). For example, *In re Taggart*, 249 F.3d 987 (9th Cir. 2001), concerned the question of whether a penalty was compensation for actual pecuniary loss. A state statute allowed the state bar to collect the costs and fees of disciplinary proceedings from an attorney who was disciplined. The court held that on an interpretation of the statute in question, the recovery of the costs and fees were compensation for pecuniary loss—a simple fee-shifting provision—and not a punishment. The court distinguished cases that interpreted statutes from other states, in which the payment of costs had a punitive purpose. The issue in *In re Nam*, 273 F.3d 281 (3rd Cir. 2001) was the meaning of the word "forfeiture" in §523(a)(7). The father of an accused murderer had posted bail of $1 million for his son. The son jumped bail and fled the country. In the father's subsequent Ch. 7 case, the city (as beneficiary of the bond) argued that the bail bond was excluded from the discharge and the court agreed. It was not necessary that the debt arise from punishment because the plain language of the subsection included forfeitures as well as punishments. There was also no question that the bail bond was not compensation for pecuniary loss. The court bolstered its finding by the policy observation that it would defeat the purpose of bail to allow a friend or relative to escape liability by filing bankruptcy because the accused criminal would have little incentive not to flee if he knew that the bond could be discharged in bankruptcy. (The court confined its decision to bonds given by family members, recognizing that different considerations may apply to a professional bail bondsman.)

(8) **Educational loans and benefits (§523(a)(8)).** Section 523(a)(8) excludes from the discharge educational loans and other repayable educational benefits, if they were made, insured, or guaranteed by the government, or were made under a program wholly or partially funded by the government or a nonprofit institution. The obvious intent of this provision is to protect governmental and institutional student loan programs by preventing graduates from using bankruptcy to discharge liability for loans. Section 523(a)(8) used to be confined to loans whose first payment date occurred within seven years of bankruptcy. This was eliminated by an a amendment in 1998, which bars the discharge of student loans, no matter how old they may be, in all cases commenced after the effective date of the amendment.

Even if the debt is nondischargeable under §523(a)(8), the section gives the court the discretion to discharge the debt if exclusion from the discharge would cause undue hardship to the debtor or dependents. The Code does not indicate what constitutes undue hardship. In deciding whether it exists, courts examine not only the debtor's financial resources and expenses, but also efforts made to repay the loan, to obtain suitable employment and to control expenses, and, in general, the debtor's good faith in seeking bankruptcy relief. Where hardship may not be enough to discharge the entire debt, the court may discharge part of the debt to the extent necessary to relieve the hardship. See *In re Saxman*, 325 F.3d 1168 (9th Cir. 2003).

(9) **Liability for driving under the influence of drugs or alcohol (§523(a)(9)).** If the debtor incurred liability for death or personal injury, caused by the unlawful operation of a vehicle while under the influence of drugs, alcohol, or another substance, such liability is nondischargeable. This subsection formerly applied only to judgments and consent decrees relating to such liability, but it was amended in 1990 to make it clear that the liability is nondischargeable even if no judgment had been obtained by the time of the petition.

(10) **Debts from a prior case in which a discharge was waived or denied (§523(a)(10)).** Section 523(a)(10) deals with the situation of a debtor who has been bankrupt before and waived the discharge in the prior

case or was denied it under any of the grounds in §§727(a)(2) through (7). Such a waiver or denial makes all debts in that case permanently nondischargeable. Therefore, if the debtor subsequently seeks bankruptcy relief again, the discharge in the later case does not cover any balance still owing on undischarged debts from the earlier case. Note that §523(a)(1) does not prevent the discharge in a current bankruptcy of debts that survived an earlier case because a discharge was denied under the six-year rule of §§727(a)(8) or (9). Therefore, in the debtor's third or later bankruptcy, debts from the preceding bankruptcy may be discharged if a discharge had been denied in that case solely on the grounds of the six-year rule. These surviving debts are treated differently because the denial of the earlier discharge was based on an objective time period, rather than on the debtor's dishonest or obstructive behavior, or on the debtor's consensual waiver of the right to discharge.

Section 523(a)(10) only applies where the earlier discharge was denied in its entirety under §727. It is not applicable to debts that survived an earlier discharge under §523. The treatment of such debts is discussed in section 22.5.5.

(11) Payments under an order of restitution in federal cases (§523(a)(13)). As discussed in Section 22.7, the Supreme Court held in *Pennsylvania Department of Public Welfare v. Davenport*, 495 U.S. 552 (1990) that liability under a restitution order is a claim, and was therefore dischargeable under Ch. 13. In response to that decision, Congress added §1328(a)(3) to exclude from the Ch. 13 discharge any debt for restitution included in a sentence on the debtor's conviction of a crime. It was assumed that it was not necessary to include a similar provision in §523, because such a debt would be covered by the exclusion of debts for willful and malicious injury under §523(a)(6), or of penalties, fines, and forfeitures payable to and for the benefit of the government in §523(a)(7). (As explained in Section 22.7, these exclusions are not applicable in a Ch. 13 case.) However, following some decisions that found those sections inapplicable to a criminal restitution order, the Bankruptcy Reform Act of 1994 sought to close the gap by adding §523(a)(13). However, it does not fill the gap entirely because it only covers restitution orders in federal cases. A debt arising from a restitution order under state law will therefore be dischargeable outside of Ch. 13 unless it can be made to fit within §§523(a)(6) or (7).

(12) Matrimonial debts that do not qualify as alimony, maintenance, or support (§523(a)(15)). The Bankruptcy Reform Act of 1994 added this section to give some protection to matrimonial or support debts that do not qualify for exclusion from the discharge under §523(a)(5) because they are not for alimony, maintenance, or support. These non-support debts are not unqualifiedly excluded from the discharge, but are subject to a balancing test that requires the court to take into account the debtor's ability to pay them and the relative needs of the debtor and creditor spouse.

Because the court must evaluate these questions, a dischargeability hearing is required under §523(c). Section 523(a)(15) applies to debts incurred in the course of a divorce or separation, or under a separation agreement, divorce decree, or other order of a court or government agency. To decide whether or not they should be excluded from the discharge, the court must make two determinations. First, it must decide if the debtor can afford to pay the debt from his postpetition income without undue hardship. The test to be used is based on the disposable income test of §1325(b): Will the debtor have enough left over to make payments to the ex-spouse, after paying for the reasonable support of himself and his dependents, and for any necessary business expenses? Second, the court must balance the benefit to the debtor of discharging the debt against the harm that the discharge would cause to the creditor spouse.

§22.5.5   *The Discharge of Nondischargeable Debts in a Subsequent Case*

As discussed above, if the debtor was denied a discharge entirely under §§727(a)(2) through (7) in a prior bankruptcy, or waived the discharge, the surviving debts are excluded from the discharge in the later bankruptcy by §523(a)(10). Surviving debts that were excluded from a prior discharge under §523 are not covered by §523(a)(10), but are dealt with in §523(b). Provided that the grounds for exclusion no longer apply, §523(b) allows the discharge in a later bankruptcy of three types of debt that were excluded from the discharge in an earlier case: nondischargeable tax debts under §523(a)(1), unscheduled debts under §523(a)(3), and education loans under §528(a)(8).[1] Because these are the only debts included in §523(b), all other debts that were not discharged in the prior case are excluded from the discharge in the later case as well. The basis for the exclusion from the subsequent discharge is that the exclusion in the prior case is res judicata. Once the debt is held nondischargeable, it is always nondischargeable. *In re Paine* 283 B.R. 33 (9th Cir. B.A.P. 2002).

§22.6   The Ch. 11 Discharge

Unlike Ch. 7, Ch. 11 grants a discharge to both individuals and corporate entities. Under §1141(d), the discharge takes effect upon confirmation of the

---

1. As noted in section 22.5.4, one of the grounds for avoiding nondischargeability of a student loan — the age of the debt — is no longer available in cases commenced after the effective date of the 1998 amendment to the section. Therefore, in such cases, the only basis for changing the grounds of nondischargeability will be hardship that arose since the prior bankruptcy.

plan. It covers all debts that arose before the date of confirmation, including debts deemed under §§502(g), (h), and (i) to have arisen prepetition. The discharge of a debt is not dependent on the proof or allowance of the claim or on the holder's acceptance of the plan. The plan itself may contain provisions that expand or reduce the extent of the discharge.

Ch. 11 does not have an equivalent of §727. However, §727 applies in a Ch. 11 case where the debtor is being liquidated under the plan. Section 1141(d)(3) states that confirmation of the plan does not discharge the debtor if the plan provides for the liquidation of all or substantially all of the debtor's estate, the debtor does not engage in business after consummation of the plan, and the debtor would have been denied a discharge under §727(a) if the case had been filed under Ch. 7. The simple point of this provision is that if the debtor is to be liquidated under Ch. 11 and will not remain in business, there is no reason to treat the Ch. 11 discharge differently from that under Ch. 7. Therefore, if the debtor is a corporation, the discharge is precluded by §727(a)(1). If the debtor is an individual, any grounds for the denial of a discharge under any other provision of §727 apply in the Ch. 11 case.

If the debtor is an individual, §1141(d)(2) excludes from the discharge all debts that are nondischargeable under §523, so that the exceptions to the individual debtor's discharge are the same in Chs. 7 and 11 — with one qualification: Under §1141(d) the plan may provide for the discharge of a debt that would otherwise be excluded from the discharge under §523. Of course, a provision of this kind is only feasible where the debtor has enough negotiating leverage to include it in the confirmed plan and the plan satisfies the confirmation standards discussed in Chapter 21. When the Ch. 11 debtor is not an individual, the exclusions from discharge in §523 are not applicable.

Section 1144 permits the court to revoke an order of confirmation, including the grant of the discharge, if the confirmation order was obtained by fraud. Revocation must be requested by a party in interest within 180 days from the entry of the order and can be granted only after notice and a hearing.

§22.7   The Ch. 13 Discharge

Unlike Ch. 11, the Ch. 13 discharge does not take effect on confirmation of the plan. Section 1328(a) requires the court to grant the discharge only after the debtor has completed payments under the plan. (However, an earlier discharge can be granted on the grounds of hardship, as discussed below.) The Ch. 13 discharge includes all debts provided for by the plan or disallowed under §502. "Provided for" means not that payment must be provided for in the plan, but merely that the debt is dealt with, even if no payment will be made.

As one of the incentives for selecting debt adjustment over liquidation, Congress has provided for a more liberal discharge in Ch. 13 by limiting the applicability of §523(a) in a Ch. 13 case. As noted several times before, the rationale for encouraging debtors to choose Ch. 13 is that creditors are expected to receive a higher level of payment in a Ch. 13 case than they would have received in a liquidation. When the creditor body as a whole does in fact benefit by a larger Ch. 13 distribution, the policy of granting a broader discharge can be justified on the argument that the rights of creditors with otherwise nondischargeable debts are curtailed for the common good. However, the rationale for a broader Ch. 13 discharge is unconvincing when a debtor uses Ch. 13 for the primary purpose of discharging a substantial debt that is otherwise nondischargeable and the plan provides a level of payment to creditors that just satisfies the minimum standard required by law.

To police against this kind of abuse, courts apply the good faith requirement of §1325(a)(3). Although it is not per se bad faith for a debtor to choose Ch. 13 to take advantage of its broader discharge, the plan may fail the good faith test if the dominant purpose of the Ch. 13 filing was to discharge an otherwise nondischargeable debt, the plan provides no substantial advantage to creditors, and there is an absence of sincere effort to pay to the best of the debtor's ability. (*See* section 20.6 and Example 1 of Chapter 20.) Congress has also given some attention to this problem. The addition of the disposable income test to §1325 by the 1984 amendments to the Code (*see* section 20.7.3) partially responds to the concern about minimal payment. More directly, §1328 was itself amended in 1990 to make more of §523 applicable in Ch. 13 cases. (If the pending bankruptcy reform legislation passes, it will continue this trend by adding debts incurred by fraud and embezzlement to the list of debts not dischargeable in Ch. 13.) Notwithstanding, the Ch. 13 discharge remains much more generous than that granted under Ch. 7, and it includes debts incurred dishonestly and most debts arising out of deliberate injury. There are in fact only six categories of nondischargeable debts in a Ch. 13 case. Five of them are excluded from the discharge under §1328(a) and the sixth is excluded by §1328(d). They are:

(1) Debts provided for in §1322(b)(5) that are to be paid beyond the payment period of the plan (*see* section 20.9). These debts necessarily remain enforceable after the discharge, because the plan contemplates that they will continue to be paid off after bankruptcy.

(2) Debts excluded from the discharge by §523(a)(5) for familial support, maintenance, and alimony.

(3) Debts excluded from the discharge by §523(a)(8) for student loans.

(4) Debts excluded from the discharge by §523(a)(9) for death or personal injury caused by the debtor while driving under the influence of drugs or alcohol.

(5) Debts for restitution, or a criminal fine imposed on the debtor as part of a criminal sentence. As originally added in 1990, this provision covered only debts for restitution under a criminal sentence. It was a response to *Pennsylvania Department of Public Welfare v. Davenport,* 495 U.S. 552 (1990), in which the Supreme Court held that a criminal restitution obligation satisfied the definition of "claim" and, since it was not excluded from the Ch. 13 discharge, it was dischargeable. (*See* Example 2.) Because a criminal fine is different from a sentence requiring restitution, the section was amended by the Bankruptcy Reform Act of 1994 to make it clear that criminal fines are nondischargeable in Ch. 13 as well. (They are nondischargeable in other Chapters by virtue of §523(a)(7). The exclusion in §523(a)(7) is broader than under §1328 because it covers all fines and penalties, not only those included in a criminal sentence.)

(6) Debts based on a claim for consumer necessities, allowed under §1305(a)(2), for which prior trustee approval was practicable but not obtained. As explained in section 19.2.3, §1305(a)(2) allows a creditor to prove a claim for a postpetition consumer debt incurred by the debtor for household or personal necessities, so that the debt can be handled in the estate. If the debtor obtained the prior approval of the trustee, or such approval was not practicable, any balance of the debt unpaid by the Ch. 13 distribution is discharged. However, if the debtor failed to obtain the trustee's approval when practicable, the debt is excluded from the discharge under §1328(d). (If the creditor knew that trustee approval was practicable but not obtained, the claim will be disallowed under §1305(c), so its dischargeability would not be in issue.)

The above list does not cover priority tax claims which are nondischargeable under §523(a)(1). However, because such tax claims must be paid in full under the plan unless the holder agrees to a different treatment, the discharge of any unpaid balance of the claim either does not arise at all, or else relates only to present value enhancement of the claim. (*See* sections 19.6.1 and 20.7.2.)

The grounds for denial of discharge in §727 are not applicable in a Ch. 13 case. Any dishonest, manipulative, or uncooperative conduct by the debtor must be dealt with under the good faith standard for confirmation, or as grounds for conversion or dismissal. Because §727 does not govern a Ch. 13 case, §727(a)(8) and (9) do not apply to bar the grant of a Ch. 13 discharge within six years of a previous case. Therefore, unless the successive filings are abusive or constitute bad faith, the debtor can obtain full Ch. 13 relief, even if a recent prior discharge was granted in a case under Ch. 13 or any other chapter.[2] Section 1328(a) recognizes a written waiver of discharge, executed by the debtor after the order for relief and approved by the court.

Section 1328(e) permits the court to revoke the discharge on grounds of the debtor's fraud if the applicant for revocation did not know of the fraud until after the discharge was granted. The application for revocation must be made within a year of the discharge and can only be granted after notice and a hearing.

As stated earlier, the debtor must normally complete payments under the plan to receive the discharge. However, §1328(b) gives the court the discretion, after notice and a hearing, to grant a *hardship discharge* to a debtor who has not been able to complete payments under the plan. A hardship discharge may only be granted to the debtor if three conditions are satisfied: The failure to complete payments must result from factors beyond the debtor's control; the distribution actually made to unsecured claims must satisfy the best interests test (*i.e.,* the payments actually made to unsecured creditors under the plan up to the time of discharge must be at least equal to the present value of what unsecured creditors would have received in a Ch. 7 liquidation); and modification of the plan must be impracticable. Because the hardship discharge is given to a debtor who has not consummated the plan, it is not as generous as the normal Ch. 13 discharge and is fully subject to the exclusions in §523(a). In sum, under §§1328(c) and (d), the hardship discharge does not extend to secured debts, debts excluded from the plan under §1322(b)(5), postpetition debts for consumer necessities incurred without trustee approval, and all debts excluded from the discharge by §523(a).

§22.8 The Ch. 12 Discharge

The Ch. 12 discharge provisions are modeled on those in Ch. 13, with some variations. Like Ch. 13, the Ch. 12 discharge is normally granted only upon consummation of the plan (§1228(a)). The Ch. 12 discharge is not as generous as that under Ch. 13, and the exclusions from the discharge in §523(a) apply fully in a Ch. 12 case. In addition, the Ch. 12 discharge does not

---

2. The issue of a Ch. 13 filing within six years of a prior Ch. 7 case was raised in *Johnson v. Home State Bank*, 501 U.S. 78 (1991). The central issue in the case was whether the debtor could deal with a mortgage in a Ch. 13 plan where personal liability on the debt had been discharged in a prior Ch. 7 case. (*See* Example 4 of Chapter 20.) One of the ancillary arguments made in the case was that serial filings under Chs. 7 and 13 violated the limits Congress intended for the bankruptcy remedy. The Court disagreed, pointing out that where Congress intended to prevent serial filings, it has done so (*e.g.,* in §727(a)(8)). In the absence of such a bar in Ch. 13, a recent prior discharge under Ch. 7 does not preclude full Ch. 13 relief unless the serial filings offend the requirement of good faith.

extend to long-term debts paid outside the plan under §1222(b)(5) (a provision almost identical to §1322(b)(5)) or to debts to be settled by the transfer of property after the plan period under §1222(b)(10). Section 1228(a) allows the debtor to waive the discharge in writing after the order for relief, subject to court approval.

As in Ch. 13, the grounds for denial of discharge in §727 are not applicable in a Ch. 12 case, and policing of debtor conduct must take place under the good faith test for plan confirmation in §1225 or the grounds for dismissal or conversion in §1208. Similarly, there is no bar to a discharge in Ch. 12 within a six-year period from the commencement of a prior case in which a discharge was obtained, so unless consecutive filings are abusive, the debtor can obtain a Ch. 12 discharge at any time after a discharge in a prior bankruptcy.

As in Ch. 13, the Ch. 12 discharge can be revoked on grounds of fraud under §1228(d) within a year of discharge. Section 1228(b) provides for a hardship discharge very similar to that in Ch. 13. The grounds for granting the hardship discharge are the same as in Ch. 13, and the discharge is also less generous than normal. Because nondischargeable debts under §523 are excluded from the Ch. 12 discharge in any event, this is not a point of difference in the hardship discharge. However, the hardship discharge does not cover administrative expenses that would otherwise be discharged, and it does not cover secured debts.

EXAMPLES

1. Physician, Shield Thyself

Hippocrates Oaf is a successful physician whose hobby was real estate speculation. He embarked upon a large suburban development project, using all his savings as well as borrowed funds. The venture failed, rendering Dr. Oaf insolvent and forcing him into default on his loan. Dr. Oaf plans to seek Ch. 7 relief. Dr. Oaf's state of domicile has enacted legislation under §522(b), making nonbankruptcy exemptions applicable in bankruptcy cases. Under the state's exemption law most exemptions are subject to low dollar limits. However, two classes of exempt property — the debtor's homestead and musical instruments — have no value limitations at all.

Dr. Oaf owns a home worth $500,000, subject to a mortgage of $300,000. He is tone deaf, and has no musical instruments. In the few weeks before the filing of his Ch. 7 petition, Dr. Oaf sold a number of valuable nonexempt assets, realizing proceeds of $450,000. (This is the fair market value of the assets sold.) He used $300,000 of this fund to pay off the mortgage on his house, and bought an antique pipe organ with the balance. When this process was complete, he filed his Ch. 7 petition. A debtor can effectively convert nonexempt assets into exempt assets prior to bankruptcy provided that this is not a violation of good faith. (See Example 5 of Chapter 13.) Would or should Dr. Oaf's prepetition conduct have any impact on his discharge?

2. Crime Does Not Pay Less

While employed as a personnel manager, Penny Tentiary padded the company's payroll by adding fictitious names to it. When checks were issued to these nonexistent employees, Penny cashed them and kept the money. She did this for a few months, until her employer discovered her subterfuge, dismissed her, and filed criminal charges. Penny was convicted and was sentenced to a term of imprisonment, suspended on condition that she pay back the stolen funds by specified monthly installments over three years. Under the state's probation statute, Penny was required to make payments to the probation department, which would transmit the funds to the victim of the crime.

Penny paid the installments for about six months, and then filed a petition under Ch. 7. She listed the restitution obligation as an unsecured debt. Neither the employer nor the state proved a claim against her estate. She ultimately received a discharge.

    (a)   Has the restitution obligation been discharged?

    (b)   Would the answer be different if Penny had filed under Ch. 13?

3. Necessity Is the Mother of Inventory

Will Fully owned and operated a retail store as a sole proprietor. He recently filed a Ch. 7 petition. In the months prior to his bankruptcy, Will fell behind in payments due to his suppliers and could no longer buy inventory on credit. To raise cash to buy new inventory, Will sold all his office equipment and furnishings. This property was subject to a valid and perfected security interest in favor of a bank that had financed its purchase. Will realized that the sale was a violation of an express term of the security agreement.

Will sold the new inventory in the course of business and used its proceeds to pay expenses. This enable him to operate for a while longer, but his business eventually failed and he filed his Ch. 7 petition. It was only after the filing that the bank discovered that its collateral had been sold and its proceeds dissipated, leaving the bank with an unsecured claim against the estate. (The buyer of the collateral cannot be found, so the bank cannot recover it from him.)

The bank has applied for a determination of nondischargeability under §523(c).

    (a)   Should the debt be excluded from Will's discharge?

    (b)   Would the answer be different if Will had filed under Ch. 13?

4. With Malice toward None

Comic Kazi has a wonderful sense of humor. He is employed by an auto parts and tire store. One day, as a prank, he threw a lighted firecracker into the store's basement for the purpose of scaring a fellow employee. Because there were gas fumes in the basement, the firecracker set off an explosion that injured the coworker. The coworker sued Comic for damages and obtained a judgment for actual damages of $1,000,000 and punitives of $500,000.

Comic filed a petition under Ch. 7. Is the tort judgment dischargeable?

5. Mail-a-fide

On opening his mail one day, Falsus N. Omnibus found a letter and glossy brochure from Reliance Bank, inviting him to apply for a credit card. The letter assured Falsus that he had already been approved for a $2,000 line of credit. Falsus was pleasantly surprised. He was so heavily in debt and had such a poor payment record that no one who obtained a credit report would give him any credit at all. Reliance had not checked his credit. Its offer was part of a large promotion mailed to names on a mailing list that the bank had purchased.

Falsus immediately completed and returned the application form. It was a short and simple document that asked for no information about the applicant's financial affairs. The new card arrived in the mail a few weeks later. To celebrate, Falsus hastened to his local shopping mall, where he made purchases to the full credit limit on the card. He never made any payments to Reliance. About a month later, Falsus, feeling the pressure of all his unpaid debts, filed a Ch. 7 petition.

Reliance filed an application for a nondischargeability determination on the grounds that Falsus had made a false representation under §523(a)(2)(A). Reliance conceded that Falsus had made no express misrepresentations, but argued that his application and subsequent use of the card constituted an implied representation that he was financially responsible and would pay for purchases charged to the account. Should the debt be excluded from the discharge?

EXPLANATIONS

1. "Prepetition planning," as Dr. Oaf's efforts may euphemistically be called, becomes fraudulent if the debtor engaged in dishonest conduct to achieve it. If fraud is present, it could result in denial of the exemption or denial of the discharge under §727(a)(2) on the basis that Dr. Oaf transferred property within a year of the petition with intent to hinder, delay, or defraud a creditor. (This is not a case for exclusion of a debt from the discharge under §523(a)(2) because there is nothing to suggest fraud in the procuring of credit.)

Dr. Oaf's sale of nonexempt assets clearly was a transfer of property within a year of the petition. The issue is whether the disposition had those additional elements of dishonesty that make it fraudulent. This *extrinsic fraud,* as it is sometimes called, can take many forms. For example, the debtor may have used new credit to acquire the exempt property, or may have taken steps to conceal the conversion from creditors, or may have sold nonexempt property at sacrifice prices to get rid of it quickly and complete the conversion before creditors can find out about it. *See e.g., In re Reed,* 700 F.2d 986 (5th Cir. 1983); *In re Smiley,* 864 F.2d 562 (7th Cir. 1989); *In re Bowyer,* 916 F.2d 1056 (5th Cir. 1990); *In re Armstrong,* 931 F.2d 1233 (8th Cir. 1991).

There is no indication of such extrinsic fraud in the present case. Dr. Oaf appears simply to have taken advantage of the unlimited exemptions that the legislature has seen fit to provide. However, there is some authority that if the conversion is on a great enough scale, the court will be less concerned with finding evidence of extrinsic fraud. In *Norwest Bank Nebraska v. Tveten,* 848 F.2d 871 (8th Cir. 1988), the court denied a discharge to the debtor, a physician, who converted $700,000 worth of nonexempt property into fully exempt insurance and annuity policies. Although there was no evidence of extrinsic fraud, the court considered that the excessive size of the conversion so perverted the Code's fresh start policy that it could not be tolerated. In a subsequent case, *In re Johnson,* 880 F.2d 78 (8th Cir. 1989), the court qualified its approach in *Tveten* to some extent. In that case the debtor (also a doctor) converted nonexempt property into a fully exempt homestead, musical instruments and annuities. The court said that its decision in *Tveten* did not apply to the large-scale investment in the homestead because the legislature clearly intended to confer a homestead exemption without a monetary limit. However, it reaffirmed its position that with regard to the other exemptions, the size of the conversion is relevant to the issue of fraud. These cases indicate that a debtor like Dr. Oaf walks a fine line in conducting extensive "prepetition planning." Even in the absence of accompanying dishonest behavior, the circumstances and scale of the conversion could result in a finding of fraud under §727(a)(2). Advising a prospective debtor on this kind of prepetition activity requires careful judgment by the debtor's attorney, who must inform the client of his legal rights so that he can make legitimate planning choices, but must not participate in or encourage fraudulent manipulations.

2. (a) The Ch. 7 case.   In *Kelley v. Robinson,* 479 U.S. 36 (1986), the Court dealt with issues similar to those presented by these facts. The debtor had been convicted of welfare fraud and had been given a suspended prison sentence. As a condition of her probation, she was required to make restitution payments over a period of years. The state did not prove a claim against the estate, and took the position that the restitution obligation was excluded from the discharge. The court found that the obligation was a noncompensatory penalty, excluded from the discharge by §523(a)(7). The court so characterized it because a criminal restitution obligation goes beyond mere compensation of the victim and serves the state's broader goal of punishing and rehabilitating offenders and enforcing its criminal law.[3]

In Penny's case, the restitution obligation arises from the embezzlement of funds, so it could also be excluded under §§523(a)(2) or (4). The same was true of the welfare fraud in *Kelley*. The Court observed, however, that those grounds are less desirable from the state's point of view, because they require a timely determination of dischargeability under §523(c). (In addition, these grounds do not apply to all restitution obligations. For example, restitution for negligent homicide could be excluded only under §523(a)(7).)

In summary, although the restitution obligation is a debt, it is excluded from the Ch. 7 discharge by §523(a)(7), even if the state did not seek a determination of dischargeability under §523(c).

(b) If the case were under Ch. 13. Section 523(a)(7) does not apply in a Ch. 13 case, as it is not one of the grounds of nondischargeability preserved by §1328(a). Similarly, the alternatives of §§523(a)(2) and (4) are inapplicable in a Ch. 13 case. In *Pennsylvania Department of Public Welfare v. Davenport*, 495 U.S. 552 (1990), the Court held that a restitution obligation arising out of welfare fraud was dischargeable under Ch. 13. As a result of *Davenport*, Congress amended §1328 in 1990 to include §1328(a)(3), which expressly excluded criminal restitution obligations from the Ch. 13 discharge. Note that the restitution obligation must be part of the sentence on the debtor's conviction of a crime. If Penny had agreed to repay the money to avoid prosecution, the debt would not be covered by §1328(a)(3).

In short, the answer to the question would not change if Penny had filed under Ch. 13, but the result is reached by direct application of §1328(a)(3) rather than through §523(a).

3. (a) Exclusion from the Ch. 7 discharge. Courts have recognized that the debtor's disposal of collateral in breach of a security agreement constitutes an injury to the property of the secured creditor. If the injury was inflicted willfully and maliciously, the debt is nondischargeable under §523(a)(6). (Although willful and malicious injury is normally associated with tortious conduct, it could arise in a breach of contract too, if that breach is malicious in its motive or itself constitutes a tort such as conversion or intentional interference with contract rights.) For example, in *In re Jercich*, 238 F.3d 1202 (9th Cir. 2001), the court noted that a mere breach of

---

3. In a dictum, the court expressed doubt that a restitution obligation is a debt at all under §101(12). If it does not qualify as a debt, it cannot be discharged, even if none of the exclusions in §523 apply. However, in *Pennsylvania Department of Public Welfare v. Davenport*, 495 U.S. 552 (1990), the court reversed itself on its dictum in *Kelley* and held that a restitution obligation is a debt and is therefore dischargeable unless one of the grounds for nondischargeability in §523 applies.

contract, even if deliberate, does not preclude discharge of the debt under §523(a)(6). However, if the breach is not just deliberate, but made with intent to injure the other party, the breach could rise to the level of a deliberate tort for purposes of §523(a)(6).

An injury is willful if it is deliberate and intentional, rather than negligent or accidental. It is malicious if the debtor acted with intent to harm or realized that harm would be caused. In short, *willfulness* describes the debtor's volition in causing the injury, while *malice* focuses on his motivation or state of mind. Liability for the injury is excluded from the discharge under §523(a)(6) only if both these elements are present. Often, malice can be easily inferred from the fact that the injury was willfully inflicted, but this is not necessarily always so. Therefore, the existence of malice must be treated as a distinct requirement; one should not simply assume that it automatically follows willfulness in all cases. This was clearly enunciated by the Supreme Court in *Kawaauhau v. Geiger*, 523 U.S. 57 (1998), which stresses the importance of the element of intent to injure. *Kawaauhau* has been applied in many cases in the conversion context where the debtor realized that he was violating the lienholders rights, but without the deliberate intent to harm. See, for example, *In re Thiara*, 258 B.R. 420 (9th Cir. B.A.P. 2002); *In re Longley*, 235 B.R. 651 (10th Cir. B.A.P. 1999). The facts of *Longley* are instructive: The debtor had reneged on a drug deal. The dealer threatened to do physical harm to him unless he gave the dealer his car in compensation. The debtor knew that the car was subject to a security interest, but gave it to the dealer notwithstanding. The court said that the creditor had not proved malice because the debtor's motive was not to harm the creditor, but to avoid physical harm.

Will's sale of the collateral was a deliberate act. There has clearly been a willful injury to the property interest of the bank. The circumstances strongly indicate that malice was present as well. Will knew that the sale was a breach of the security agreement, and he intended to spend the proceeds, rather than to remit them to the bank. Given his financial circumstances, he must have realized, as a person with some business experience, that he was depriving the bank of its protection against nonpayment at a time when default was a definite possibility. Therefore, even though the bank has lost its security, it may obtain some consolation by having its unsecured debt excepted from the discharge.

This question has concentrated on excluding the debt from the discharge under §523. Remember, however, that some forms of dishonest prepetition conduct could disqualify the debtor from a discharge in its entirety under §727. On the facts of this case, §727(a)(2) is worth considering, in that Will transferred property within a year of bankruptcy with apparent intent to hinder, delay or defraud a creditor. In addition, the fact that the buyer of the collateral cannot be found may suggest that Will's recordkeeping was deficient. This could cause him problems under §727(a)(3).

(b) What if Will had filed under Ch. 13? Section 523(a)(6) is not one of the exclusions incorporated into Ch. 13 by §1328(a). Will's debt is therefore dischargeable in Ch. 13 even though he was guilty of willful and malicious injury to the bank's property interest.

4. In Example 3 nondischargeability based on willful and malicious injury was illustrated by a deliberate sale of collateral. The intentional tort is perhaps a more obvious example of this ground for exclusion from the discharge. Often, the tort involves a deliberate and malicious physical injury to person or property, but the claim can arise from other torts too. For example, in *In re Peck*, 295 B.R. 353 (9th Cir. B.A.P. 2003), the court excluded from the discharge a claim arising from the debtor's slander of the plaintiff. The plaintiff, the debtor's former landlord, had evicted her for failure to pay rent. In revenge, the debtor falsely accused the plaintiff of having sexually molested her daughter.

Both willfulness and malice must be proved. Comic's act was clearly willful — it was deliberate and intentional. Malice is more difficult to decide. Comic did not desire or intend to injure his coworker. His behavior was idiotic rather than malicious. In *In re Hartley*, 869 F.2d 394 (8th Cir. 1989), a case with similar facts, the court found that malice had not been established and the debt was therefore dischargeable. This accords with *Kawaauhau* (cited in Example 3), in which the court held that recklessness is not enough to satisfy the requirement of malice. Nevertheless, the case is not clear cut. An intentional reckless act is close to the borderline and proof of malice could be inferred from deliberate conduct that will likely cause injury, performed with callous indifference to the consequences.

In this case, the coworker's claim has already been adjudicated in state court. The facts do not say if the state court made a specific finding to willfulness and malice. If it did (which seems likely, because it awarded punitive damages) the bankruptcy court may accept that finding without requiring the creditor to prove those elements again in the nondischargeability hearing. For example, in *In re Braen*, 900 F.2d 621 (3d Cir. 1990), damages for malicious prosecution were held nondischargeable without further evidence because the necessary elements had already been proved in the tort case.

If the injury is found to have been inflicted willfully and maliciously, does the exclusion from discharge apply to punitive damages as well? In *Cohen v. De La Cruz*, 523 U.S. 213 (1998), the court found that the language of §523(a)(2) covered punitive damages as well as the original debt. Although the court did not address whether the same result would be called for by §523(a)(6), its reasoning, based on a grammatical interpretation of §523(a)(2), would be equally applicable to §523(a)(6) because the structure of the language is the same. In fact, if anything, the language of §523(a)(6) even more strongly leads to the conclusion that punitive damages are covered, because it simply excludes from the discharge "any debt . . . for willful and malicious injury."

5. This question is inspired by the constant stream of cases in which a debtor has incurred debt on a credit card at a time that his financial circumstances indicate that he has little prospect of paying the debt, or where the debtor has "loaded up" the card with charges or cash advances that are clearly beyond his ability to pay. When the debtor eventually files bankruptcy and seeks to discharge the debt, the credit card issuer moves to exclude the debt from the discharge on the grounds that use of the card under the debtor's financial circumstances was fraud. To have the debt declared nondischargeable under §523(a)(2)(A), the creditor must prove the common law elements of fraud. (Since *Grogan v. Garner*, 498 U.S. 279 (1991), it is clear that the standard of proof is the preponderance of the evidence.) The elements are: a false representation (possibly, the creditor must also show that the misrepresentation related to a material fact); knowledge of its falsity and intent to deceive (scienter); justifiable reliance by the creditor in entering the transaction; and injury.

Where the debtor simply used the credit card, without making any express representations about his intent or ability to pay, three questions are most commonly in issue.

(a) Can a representation be implied merely from the use of the credit card? Most courts are willing to recognize that the mere use of a credit card is enough to constitute an implied representation that the debtor will pay the debt, even if not on due date, at least at some time in the future.

(b) If the implied representation is false, was the representation made with fraudulent intent? Fraud does not follow inevitably from the determination that the debtor realized his poor financial circumstances when making the implied representation. Courts generally employ a "totality of the circumstances" test to decide fraudulent intent: Based on all the facts of the case, can it be concluded that the debtor used the card with the present intention of not paying the debt. The test is subjective because the honest or dishonest state of the debtor's mind is the issue. The question is what the debtor actually intended, not what she reasonably should have realized or believed. In *In re Mercer*, 246 F.3d 391 (5th Cir. 2001), the court stressed that the use of the card is a representation of intent to repay, not ability to repay. Some of the factors taken into account are: the length of time between the charges and the petition; whether there were any indications that the debtor had been contemplating bankruptcy at the time of the charges; the debtor's financial condition, employment status, and future prospects at that time; whether the charges were for luxuries or necessities; whether the spending pattern of the charges was unusual or frenetic; and the degree of the debtor's financial sophistication.

For example, the courts found intent not to pay the debt at the time of incurring the charges in the following cases: *In re Ward*, 857 F.2d. 1082 (6th Cir. 1988), (on similar facts, the court found that the debtor had used the opportunity of receiving the card to go on a buying spree, intending it to be at the creditor's expense.); *In re Burge*, 198 B.R. 773 (B.A.P. 9th Cir. 1996), (a few weeks before filing her petition, the debtor made 47 purchases of luxury goods on her credit card totaling about $8,600, at a time when she was not earning enough to cover her monthly living expenses.); *In re Hashemi,* 104 F.3d 1122 (9th Cir. 1996) (the debtor spent more than $60,000 on a six-week European vacation at a time when he already owed $300,000 on other credit cards.)

By contrast, there are other situations in which courts have found that the creditor had failed to prove intent not to pay because the circumstances suggested that when the debtor incurred the charges, he hoped and expected to pay the debt at some time. For example, in *In re Shartz,* 221 B.R. 397 (B.A.P. 6th Cir. 1998), after losing her job, the debtor manipulated several credit cards to pay her living expenses and mortgage, thereby managing to keep going for about a year and accumulating a total credit card debt of $67,000. The court found that the debtor was not responsible for her financial crisis — she was laid off; she diligently looked for a new job and expected to find one, but it took longer than she expected and the situation got out of control; the charges and cash advances were not for luxuries, but just to tide herself over during a difficult time. A similar approach was taken in *In re Kountry Korner Store,* 221 B.R. 265 (Bankr. N.D. Okla. 1998), in which the debtor incurred about $3,800 in credit card charges in the three weeks before her bankruptcy in an effort to keep her struggling business in operation, in the unrealistic hope that she would eventually repay her debt.

Sometimes a court may give too much credence to the debtor's undue optimism: In *In re Rembert,* 141 F.3d 277 (6th Cir. 1998), the debtor used his credit card to obtain a cash advance so that he could gamble. The court found that dishonest intent was not established because the debtor hoped that he would win, and planned to use some of the proceeds to repay the debt. A similar argument did not work in *In re Herrig,* 217 B.R. 891 (Bankr. N.D. Okla. 1998), in which the court found fraudulent intent on the totality of the circumstances where the gambling debtor used the card to its limit in a short time without any ability to repay the debt, and no regard for whether he could do so.

(c) Justifiable reliance. Under *Field v. Mans,* 516 U.S. 59 (1995), the creditor does not have to prove reliance on the strictly objective test of reasonableness, but rather on the less stringent test of justifiable reliance, which takes into account the attributes of the creditor — its own knowledge, experience, and circumstances.

Even when a creditor is able to establish that the debtor incurred the debt without intent to repay it, the creditor will still not obtain an order of nondischargeability unless it can also show that it justifiably relied on the misrepresentation. Some courts have very little sympathy for the credit card industry with its good profits and easy credit policies. If the issuer made little or no inquiry, it assumed the risk of default, and if it did check the debtor's credit reports, it relied on them, rather than on any misrepresentation made by the debtor. Other courts take a more balanced approach, weighing the debtor's dishonesty against the creditor's justifiable confidence that the card would not be abused. That is, provided that some investigation is made, the creditor is entitled to assume, in the absence of suspicious indications to the contrary, that the debtor is honest and will use the card in good faith.

In *In re Mercer*, 246 F.3d 391 (5th Cir. 2001), the court said that the creditor's justisfiable reliance should be measured at the time that the debtor uses the card because the use of the card is the debtor's representation of intent to repay. Therefore, provided that there was some preapproval credit-worthiness screening with no red flags arising from the debtor's credit history or his prior misuse of the card, the creditor is justified in relying on the debtor's implied representation that by using the card, he intends to pay the debt. See also *Herrig* (where the creditor conducted a preapproval screening that revealed no problems, and was held justified in relying on the debtor's implied representation, made by use of the card, that he intended to repay it); *Burge* (unless suspicious circumstances are apparent, a creditor is justified in relying on a debtor's credit record, and has no duty of further inquiry); *In re Samani,* 192 B.R. 877 (Bankr. S.D. Tex. 1996) (the creditor's continued extension of credit was justified by the debtor's past payment record on the card, even though it was sporadic.)

Reliance Bank does not appear to qualify under the justifiable reliance standard articulated by these cases. It does not seem to have made any investigation of creditworthiness and is likely to fail the test of justifiable reliance.

Appendix
Summary of the Significant Differences between Chs. 7, 11, 12, and 13

Warning:

This table is intended as a broad guide to the significant differences between the chapters. It is a summary and simplification, and should be treated as such.

Issue	Ch. 7	Ch. 11	Ch. 12	Ch. 13
1. Is an involuntary petition for relief competent?	Yes	Yes	No	No
2. Does the filing of a petition bring the automatic stay into effect under §362?	Yes	Yes	Yes	Yes
3. Will the automatic stay protect certain codebtors of the debtor?	No	No	Yes (§1201)	Yes (§1301)

Issue	Ch. 7	Ch. 11	Ch. 12	Ch. 13
4. What assets become property of the estate?	Debtor's property at commencement, with a few exceptions. Postpetition property is generally excluded (§541).	Same as in Ch. 7.	Prepetition property as in Ch. 7, as well as postpetition property (§§541 and 1207).	Same as in Ch. 12 (§§541 and 1306).
5. What is the disposition of estate property?	Liquidation and distribution of proceeds to creditors (possibility of redemption under §722 or the retention of encumbered property by reaffirmation under §524).	Revested in debtor on confirmation of the plan (§1141).	Revested in debtor on confirmation of the plan (§1227).	Revested in debtor on confirmation of the plan (§1327).
6. What impact will bankruptcy have on the debtor's postpetition income?	Unaffected. The debtor keeps this income.	No set rule. It depends on the terms of the plan.	The debtor's disposable income must be applied to payments under the plan (§§1225(b), 1222(a)).	Same as in Ch. 12 (§§1322(a), 1325(b)).
7. Who will administer the estate and operate any business of the debtor?	Trustee administers the estate and conducts short-term business operations. Business is liquidated as soon as possible (§§701-703, 721).	"Debtor in possession" retains control of estate and operates business. A trustee or examiner can be appointed if necessary (§§1104, 1108).	Debtor continues to operate farm as "debtor in possession" under the supervision of a trustee (§§1202-1203).	Trustee performs investigative and supervisory function and distributes payments under plan. Debtor continues to operate any business under trustee's supervision (§§1302, 1304).
8. May the case be converted to a case under another chapter? If so, who may apply to court for conversion?	Debtor has a broad right of conversion (§707). Creditors can convert to Ch. 11 for cause (§706).	Debtor has the right to convert with some limitations (§1112). Creditors can convert to Ch. 7 for cause (§1112).	Debtor has a broad right of conversion (§1208). Creditors have very limited grounds to convert to Ch. 7 (§1208).	Debtor has a broad right of conversion (§1307). Creditors can convert to Ch. 7 for cause (§1307).

Issue	Ch. 7	Ch. 11	Ch. 12	Ch. 13
9. May the case be dismissed voluntarily or involuntarily?	May be dismissed by debtor or other party in interest only for cause, or by U.S. trustee or court.	May be dismissed by debtor, other party in interest, or U.S. trustee, only for cause (§1112).	Debtor has broad right to dismiss. Other parties in interest can dismiss for cause (§1208).	Debtor has broad right to dismiss. Other parties in interest can dismiss for cause (§1307).
10. What is the likely source of funding for payment of creditors' claims?	The proceeds of nonexempt property of the estate (§§704, 726).	Debtor is given flexibility in devising sources for funding the payments or making property distributions under the plan (*i.e.,* the sale of assets, future income or loans). Corporate debtor may offer securities to creditors (§1123).	Generally, future income, but property of the estate may be sold for the purpose of generating funds (§1222).	Same as in Ch. 12 (§1322).
11. What is the time period for payment?	Liquidation and distribution as expeditiously as possible (§704).	No statutory limit. Period of payments set by plan.	Payments must be made over a period of not more than 3 years or, with court approval, 5 years (§1222).	Same as in Ch. 12 (§1332).
12. What are the standards fixing the minimum level of payment to creditors?	Creditors cannot get more than the total proceeds realized from estate property. *Secured claims* are satisfied from proceeds of collateral. *Priority claims* are paid in order of rank, followed by general unsecured claims. Members of each class share pro rata. Once the fund is exhausted, junior classes are excluded (§§506-507, 726).	The standards for minimum payment in Ch. 11 are too complex to be summarized here. They are governed by §1129 and summarized in Chapter 21.	Plan must give *secured creditors* the present value of the secured claim, and preserve their liens. *Priority claims* must be paid in full. Payments to *unsecured creditors* must meet "best-interests" and "disposablein-income" tests. Creditors can consent to lesser payments (§§1222, 1225).	Same as in Ch. 12 (§§1322, 1325).

Issue	Ch. 7	Ch. 11	Ch. 12	Ch. 13
13. To what extent may the debtor discriminate in favor of a preferred creditor or class of creditors in the bankruptcy distribution?	No discrimination is allowed. Creditors in each category (secured, priority and unsecured) must be treated on the same basis as other creditors in that category.	The plan may designate classes of creditor and discriminate - between them. Creditors in the same class must be treated equally unless they agree otherwise. The debtor may not "discriminate unfairly" against an "impaired" class (§§1122, 1123, 1129).	The plan may designate classes of unsecured creditor and may discriminate between them. However, it cannot discriminate unfairly against any class and cannot discriminate between creditors in a class (§1222).	Same as in Ch. 12 (§1322).
14. Does the debtor have the power to cure prior default on or to restructure payments on or to modify secured obligations?	No, unless the secured creditor agrees to the modification in a reaffirmation agreement under §524.	Cure, restructuring and modification in the plan are generally possible with the exception of modification of home mortgages (§1123).	Same as in Ch. 11, but without the bar on home mortgage modification (§1222).	Same as in Ch. 11 (§1322).
15. Do creditors have any power to participate in the formulation of the plan, or to propose their own plan?	Not applicable. No plan is filed.	Creditor comittees participate in plan formulation and under some circumstances, creditors may file their own plan (§§1103, 1121).	Only the debtor may propose a plan (§1221).	Same as in Ch. 12 (§1321).
16. To what extent is creditor consent necessary to validate the proposed bankruptcy distribution?	Creditor consent does not feature in the Ch. 7 distribution, which is fixed by the Code (§726).	Creditors vote on the plan. Voting takes place within each class, and class vote is determined by a majority. A plan can be imposed on a dissenting class ("cramdown") provided that certain conditions are satisfied (§1129).	Creditors have no vote on the debtor's plan, but are confined to objecting if it fails to meet confirmation standards. Creditors can consent to treatment less favorable then that to which they are entitled under the Code (§§1225, 1227).	Same as in Ch. 12 (§§1325, 1327).

Summary of Differences between Chs. 7, 11, 12, and 13

Issue	Ch. 7	Ch. 11	Ch. 12	Ch. 13
17. May a corporation receive a discharge?	No, only an individual (§727).	Yes (§1141).	Yes, if the corporation is eligible for Ch. 12 relief as a family farmer (§1228).	Corporations are not eligible for Ch. 13 relief.
18. What is the breadth of discharge?	All prepetition debts are discharged except for those listed in §523. A debtor may be denied a discharge on the grounds set out in §727.	All debts arising prior to plan confirmation are discharged. The exceptions to discharge in §523 apply to individuals, and the grounds for denial of discharge in §727 apply in liquidating plans (§1141).	All debts provided for in the plan, or disallowed against the estate are discharged. The exceptions in §523 apply, but not the grounds for denial of discharge in §727. A hardship discharge is permitted under certain circumstances where the plan is not fully consummated (§1228).	All debts provided for in the plan or disallowed as claims against the estate are discharged. Most of the exceptions to discharge in §523 are excluded in a Ch. 13 case. §727 is inapplicable. A hardship discharge is permitted under certain circumstances where the plan is not fully consummated (§1328).
19. When is the discharge granted?	During the course of the case, after expiry of the period for filing objections to discharge (Rule 4004).	At the time of confirmation of the plan (§1141).	After completion of payments under the plan, unless a hardship discharge is granted (§1228).	Same as in Ch. 12 (§1328).

Glossary

Abandonment. 1. The trustee's relinquishment of estate property that is burdensome to the estate or of inconsequential value or benefit to the estate. (§554)

   2. With reference to the debtor's homestead: The debtor's permanent termination of residence in the property, so that it no longer qualifies for the exemption.

Absolute priority rule. In a Ch. 11 case, the principle that no junior class of claims or interests may receive anything of value from the estate unless a more senior nonaccepting class of unsecured claims or interests is paid in full. (§§1129(b)(2)(B) and (C))

Abstention. The court's dismissal of suspension of a bankruptcy case, or its refusal to entertain related proceedings, on grounds of fairness or in deference to another court. (§305; 28 U.S.C. §1334(c))

Acceleration. The termination of the debtor's right to pay a debt in installments or at a future maturity date, so that the debt becomes immediately payable.

Acceleration clause. A contractual provision entitling the creditor to accelerate payment under the contract upon the happening of a specified event, usually the debtor's default.

Acceptance (of a Ch. 11 plan). The determination, by a majority vote of the members of a class of claims or interests, to acquiesce in a proposed Ch. 11 plan. (§1126)

Account. A right to payment for goods sold or services rendered. (Also called a "receivable" or "account receivable.")

Account receivable. *See* Account.

Adequate protection. If the estate retains property in which a person other than the debtor has an interest, that interest is entitled to adequate protection. That is, the value of the interest must be maintained during the period of retention, so that when the interest is ultimately realized, the holder will receive no less than would have been received had the property been surrendered or liquidated immediately. (§§361, 1205)

Administrative expenses. Expenses incurred by the trustee or debtor in possession in the conduct of the estate's affairs or the preservation of its property. If allowed under §503, these expenses are paid as a first priority under §507.

Adversary proceedings. Litigation in the bankruptcy case that is required by Rule 7001 to take the form of a civil suit, initiated by complaint; a full civil lawsuit within the bankruptcy case. *See* Contested matter.

After-acquired collateral. Property acquired by the debtor that, by contract or operation of law, automatically becomes subject to a lien created in advance of the debtor's acquisition of the property.

After notice and a hearing. *See* Notice and a hearing.

Alias writ. A second writ of execution, issued after the first writ failed to generate sufficient proceeds to satisfy the judgment.

Allowed claim. A claim that is accepted as owing by the estate under §502 either because it is not objected to or because the court has upheld it following a hearing on the objection.

Antecedent debt. A debt due by the debtor that arose before the debtor made a transfer to the creditor in respect of the debt.

Antiassignment provision. A provision in a contract or in law that prohibits the transfer of rights or the delegation of duties by the original holder of those rights and duties. *See* Assignment.

Artisan's lien. A common law lien (now codified in many states) that may be asserted in personal property by a person who has repaired or improved it. The lien secures the agreed or reasonable cost of the work performed. At common law, it must be perfected by possession, but a statutory alternative of perfection by filing may be available.

Assignment (of contract). Strictly speaking, assignment is the transfer of rights under a contract. The transfer of contractual duties is called "delegation." However, "assignment" is often used to mean the transfer of both rights and duties by one of the parties to a contract. It is used in this sense in §365, which empowers the trustee to assume (*i.e.,* take transfer of) an executory contract of the debtor and then to realize its value by assigning (*i.e.,* selling) the debtor's package of rights and obligations to a third party.

Assignment for the benefit of creditors. An insolvency procedure under state law under which the debtor makes a voluntary transfer of property in trust to another person (the assignee), with instructions to liquidate the property and to distribute its proceeds to creditors who have elected to participate.

Assumption (of contract). The estate's adoption of an executory contract entered into by the debtor prior to bankruptcy, so that the estate is substituted for the debtor as party to the contract. (§365)

Attachment. 1. A prejudgment remedy under which property of the defendant is seized by the sheriff and held in legal custody pending final resolution of the case, so that it can be sold in execution if the plaintiff succeeds in obtaining judgment.

   2. The creation of a lien, valid and enforceable as between the lienholder and the debtor. (For most liens, the further step of perfection is required to make the lien effective against any third parties who acquire rights in the property.)

Attachment lien. A judicial lien obtained by the creditor on property levied upon under a writ of attachment. The lien secures the plaintiff's claim while the case is pending, and the property is executed upon to satisfy the claim if the plaintiff ultimately obtains judgment.

Automatic perfection. The perfection of a lien immediately upon its attachment, without the need for any further action by the lienholder.

Automatic stay. The injunction that arises by operation of law, without the need for a court order, immediately upon the filing of a bankruptcy petition. The stay bars creditors from initiating or continuing with efforts to collect or enforce secured or unsecured debts, or to enforce claims against estate property. (§362)

Avoid. To annul; to make void or cancel.

Avoidance power. 1. The trustee's power under §§544 to 553 to overturn certain dispositions or obligations improperly made or incurred by the debtor prior to bankruptcy, as well as certain unauthorized postpetition dispositions of estate property.

   2. The debtor's right under §522(f) to set aside specified interests to the extent that they impair qualified exemptions in property.

Backdating. Upon timely completion of the prescribed act of perfection, some liens are given retrospective effect so that their priority will date from some specified earlier time.

Badge of fraud. Suspicious circumstances leading to the inference that a transfer made by the debtor was motivated by the actual intent to defraud creditors.

BAFJA. The Bankruptcy Amendments and Federal Judgeship Act of 1984, which made several significant amendments to the Code.

Balance sheet test. *See* Insolvency.

Bankruptcy Act. The predecessor to the present Code, which was enacted in 1898 and repealed in 1978.

Bankruptcy Reform Act. The 1978 statute which, with amendments, forms the present Code. (The same name was given to the act that amended the Code in 1994.)

Bankruptcy test. *See* Insolvency.

BAP (Bankruptcy Appellate Panel). A court, consisting of three bankruptcy judges, established in some circuits to hear appeals from bankruptcy courts.

Best interests test. One of the standards for plan confirmation, which requires that the total amount to be paid on a claim under the plan has a present value at least equal to what the claimant would have received had the estate been liquidated under Ch. 7. The requirement of present value is intended to compensate the claimant for having to await distribution over time instead of receiving immediate payment upon liquidation of the estate. The present value of the distribution is determined by adding interest at the market rate to the face value of the hypothetical Ch. 7 payment. (§1129(a)(7), 1125(a)(4) and 1325(a)(4))

Bifurcation of claim. *See* bifurcation.

Bona fide purchaser. (Latin: "good faith.") A person who, in a consensual transaction, acquires rights in property in good faith (*i.e.*, with subjective honesty) for value and without actual or constructive notice that the purchase violates rights in the property held by a person other than the transferor. *See* Good faith purchaser.

Business judgment rule. A standard for court approval of the trustee's decision to assume or reject an executory contract, under which the court declines to interfere with the trustee's decision if it was made in good faith and was a reasonable business judgment.

Cash collateral. Cash or cash equivalent that is subject to an interest (such as a security interest) held by a person other than the estate. (§363(a))

Chapter 20. An unofficial name for the debtor's tactic of filing sequentially under Chs. 7 and 13 for the purpose of discharging personal liability on a secured claim in the Ch. 7 case, and thereafter preventing foreclosure of the undischarged lien by providing for payment of it by installments in the Ch. 13 plan.

Claim. Any secured or unsecured right to payment arising in law or equity. (§101(5))

Claim and delivery. *See* Replevin.

Claim bifurcation. The splitting of an undersecured debt into a secured claim to the extent of the collateral's value and an unsecured claim for the deficiency. This division is required by §506.

Class (of claims or interests). Claims or interests that have been placed in the same category for treatment in bankruptcy, either because they fall within one of the statutory priority classifications or because the debtor has properly grouped them together in a plan under Ch. 11, 12, or 13.

Codebtors. Persons who are both liable on the same debt. (Also called "joint debtors," not to be confused with debtors in joint cases.)

Cognovit note. (Latin: "acknowledgment") *See* Confession to judgment.

Collateral. The property subject to a lien or security interest.

Collective proceedings. General name for proceedings such as assignments for the benefit of creditors, compositions, and bankruptcy, under which the claims of creditors are dealt with collectively to avoid the disruption and inequality of individual creditor action.

Common law lien. A lien arising by operation of common law, not dependent on agreement, statute, or judicial process. Common law liens are typically intended to provide security for the agreed or reasonable charges owing to a person who has repaired, improved, or preserved personal property or provided personal services at the owner's request. They must usually be perfected by possession.

Composition. A contract between a debtor and creditors, under which partial payment is promised and accepted in full settlement of claims.

Confession to judgment. The debtor's waiver of the right to contest a collection suit, authorizing the creditor to obtain judgment by consent. A confession during the course of litigation (also called a "stipulation") is enforceable if freely made. However, a confession made before default, particularly one contained in the instrument of debt itself (called a "cognovit note" or "warrant of attorney") is subject to particular scrutiny and is usually unenforceable in a consumer transaction.

Confirmation. 1. With reference to a plan under Chs. 11, 12, or 13: The court's determination that the plan meets the requirements of the Code, and that it will form the basis for the treatment of claims, disposition of estate property, and conduct of the estate's affairs.

2. With reference to a sale in execution: The court's approval of an execution sale of real property.

Consensual lien. A lien granted in a contract between the lienholder and the debtor, such as a mortgage or a UCC Article 9 security interest.

Consolidation of cases. 1. *Procedural consolidation:* The consolidation of two separate petitions filed in relation to the same debtor.

2. *Substantive consolidation:* The combination of the estates of two closely related debtors, so that assets are pooled and creditors of each become creditors of the combined estate.

Construction lien. *See* Mechanic's lien.

Constructive fraud. Fraud established not by proof of actual dishonest intent but by facts that are, as a matter of legal policy, treated as giving rise to an irrebuttable presumption of fraud.

Constructive notice. *See* Notice.

Constructive trust. An equitable remedy under which a person who has acquired property by a wrongful act is deemed to hold the property in trust for the victim of the wrong.

Consumer debt. A debt incurred by an individual primarily for personal, family, or household purposes. (§101(8))

Contested matter. A proceeding within the bankruptcy case, initiated by motion or objection rather than by the filing of a complaint. *See* Adversary proceedings.

Contingent claim. A claim in which the debtor's potential liability has been created by contract or wrongful act, but actual liability will only arise upon the happening of a future event that may not occur.

Conversion. 1. A chance in the Code chapter governing the case, altering the form of bankruptcy relief sought. For example, a case originally filed under Ch. 13 may be converted into a liquidation under Ch. 7 if the debtor's attempt at debt adjustment fails.

2. The realization of nonexempt property and the use of the proceeds to acquire exempt property. *See* Prepetition planning.

3. The tort of unauthorized use or taking of another's property.

Core proceeding. A proceeding in a bankruptcy case that involves the adjudication of rights created by the Code, or concerns issues that, by their nature, could only arise in a bankruptcy case. Because core proceedings involve substantive rights granted under the Code, they may be finally determined by the bankruptcy court itself. A nondefinitive list of core proceedings is set out in 28 U.S.C. §157(2). *See* Related proceedings.

Cramdown. The confirmation of a plan despite opposition from some creditors, where the plan satisfies the Code's prerequisites for nonconsensual confirmation. (§§1129(b), 1225, and 1325)

Creditor's bill. An equitable suit available to a creditor for the purpose of locating and recovering executable property that has been concealed or wrongfully transferred by the debtor or for reaching assets that otherwise cannot be executed upon using procedures at law.

Creditor's committee. A committee of creditors appointed by the U.S. Trustee in Ch. 11 cases, and sometimes in Ch. 7 cases, to represent the interests of the creditor body as a whole or, if more than one committee is appropriate, a class of creditors.

Creditors' meeting. The statutory meeting of creditors required in all bankruptcy cases by §341. The meeting must be convened by the U.S. Trustee within a prescribed time following the order for relief. Its primary business is the examination of the debtor.

Cross-collateralization. A term in a contract for the provision of postpetition credit to the estate, under which collateral furnished by the estate to secure the new credit also covers an unsecured or undersecured prepetition claim of the lender.

Cure of default. The payment of arrears or the rectification of any other breach of contractual obligations, so that the party's performance is brought into compliance with the terms of the contract.

Custodian. Any person appointed to take charge of the debtor's property under nonbankruptcy law, such as a receiver or an assignee for the benefit of creditors. (§101(11))

Debt. An obligation to pay money. In §101(12) "debt" is defined as liability on a "claim," which is defined in §101(5) as a right to payment.

Debt adjustment. A case under Ch. 12 or 13.

Debtor. A person liable on a debt. In bankruptcy, the debtor is the person concerning whom a bankruptcy case has been commenced. (§101(13))

Debtor in possession. 1. The new legal personality acquired by the debtor in a Ch. 11 case, under which the debtor administers the estate and fulfills the role of trustee for most purposes. (§§1101(1) and 1107)
   2. In a Ch. 12 case, the debtor is also called a "debtor in possession," but does not exercise the functions of the trustee beyond the conduct of business operations.

Debtor's equity. The debtor's unencumbered ownership interest in property.

Default. The debtor's material breach of contract, such as the failure to pay a debt on the due date. Some contracts provide that the insolvency or bankruptcy of the debtor constitutes *ipso facto* default. Such a provision is not enforceable in bankruptcy.

Default judgment. A judgment granted on application of the plaintiff when the defendant has failed to file an answer or other required pleading.

Deficiency. The shortfall that results when a debt is undersecured, that is, when the collateral securing the debt is worth less than the amount owing, so that realization of the collateral does not fully satisfy the debt. *See* Equity cushion; Surplus.

Delegation. *See* Assignment.

Delivery (of writ). The transmission of a writ to the sheriff with instructions to execute it.

Delivery bond. *See* Redelivery bond.

Discharge. The debtor's release from liability for the unpaid balance of all debts that are provable in bankruptcy and that are not excluded from discharge under the Code.

Discharging/Dissolution bond. A bond posted by the debtor for the purpose of releasing property from attachment. The bond is an undertaking by the debtor, supported by a surety, to pay any judgment ultimately obtained by the creditor. Its effect is to terminate the attachment and restore the property to the debtor. *See* Redelivery bond.

Disclosure statement. The statement required by §1123 to be disseminated by the proponent of a Ch. 11 plan, providing sufficient information on the plan to enable the holders of claims and interests to make an informed judgment on it.

Dismissal. The court's termination of the bankruptcy case upon voluntary withdrawal by the petitioner or on the motion of a party in interest.

Disposable income test. A test for confirmation of a Ch. 12 or 13 plan that requires the debtor to commit all his or her disposable income to payments under the plan for a period of three years. "Disposable income" is that portion of the debtor's income not reasonably necessary for the maintenance and support of the debtor or a dependent and not necessary for the operation and preservation of any business in which the debtor is engaged. The test is only applied upon objection to confirmation by a competent party.

Distraint/Distress. The seizure of property to secure or satisfy a debt. For example, a landlord's right to seize a tenant's goods on the leased premises to satisfy a claim for unpaid arrear rent.

Distress sale. A forced sale, such as an execution or foreclosure sale. Because of the circumstances of the sale, the price obtained for the property is usually depressed.

Docket. A record of proceedings in court or the act of making an entry in such record.

Dormant (judgment). A judgment that has become unenforceable because it has not been executed upon within the prescribed time. It can be revived by application. (*Dormancy* must be distinguished from *expiry* of a judgment: When a judgment reaches the end of its statutory lifespan, it becomes ineffective and cannot be revived.)

"Drop-dead" clause. A provision in a contract or rehabilitation plan that requires exact compliance with the debtor's obligations and gives the creditor an immediate right of action (for example, to accelerate the debt or to foreclose) in the event of default.

Elegit. An early common law writ, available as an alternative to fieri facias, that enabled a judgment creditor to obtain personal property of the debtor or to receive revenues from portion of the debtor's lands. *See* Fieri facias.

Enabling loan. Purchase money security interest.

Encumbrance. A right to or interest in property, such as a lien, which diminishes the extent of the owner's title.

Entity. A general term used in the Code to encompass a wide variety of legal persons, including individuals, corporations, and governmental units. (§101(15))

Equitable lien. A lien recognized under principles of equity in the absence of legal lien rights, in order to do justice between the parties and to provide effective relief to an otherwise unsecured creditor.

Equitable subordination. *See* Subordination.

Equity. 1. In addition to its general meaning of fairness or justice, "equity" denotes the body or rules and principles developed by Courts of Chancery (and now applied by courts of combined legal and equitable jurisdiction) to afford relief where remedies at law are inadequate.

2. An owner's unencumbered interest in property. *See* Debtor's equity.

Equity cushion. The amount of surplus realizable equity held by the debtor in collateral beyond the amount of the secured debt plus any senior claims. This excess value in the collateral is called an "equity cushion" because it provides a margin of safety for the lienholder to cover any adverse change in the collateral-debt ratio caused by future depreciation of the property or the accumulation of interest or costs.

Equity of redemption. The mortgagor's right to save property from foreclosure by paying the mortgage debt before the foreclosure sale. The equity of redemption arises from principles of equity and applies only in the presale period. It must be distinguished from statutory redemption, which extends beyond the sale date and may be exercised against the purchaser of the property. *See also* Redemption.

Equity receivership. *See* Receiver.

Equity security. A share in a corporation or a limited partner's interest in a partnership. (§101(16))

Equity test. *See* Insolvency.

Estate. 1. The total property held by a person.
2. In bankruptcy, the legal entity created by the filing of the petition, which succeeds to the debtor's property rights under §541.

Examiner. A person appointed by the court under §1104(b) to investigate the management or conduct of the debtor in a Ch. 11 case.

Exception to discharge. A debt that is excluded from the debtor's discharge on one of the grounds enumerated in §523.

Exclusivity period. The period following the filing of a Ch. 11 petition, during which the debtor has the exclusive right to file a plan. (§1121)

Executable property. Property of the debtor that is not exempt or otherwise immune from execution, so that it can be subjected to the claims of creditors.

Execution. The enforcement of a judgment by the seizure and sale of nonexempt property of the debtor.

Execution lien. A judicial lien created in property of the debtor levied upon under a writ of execution.

Executory contract. A contractual relationship in which the obligations of both parties are so far unperformed that the failure of either to complete performance would be a material breach. Upon the bankruptcy of one of the parties to such a contract, his or her trustee must elect to reject or assume the contract under §365.

Exemption (Exempt property). A right granted by statute to an individual debtor to hold specified property free from the claims of creditors. (§522)

Extension. A contract between a debtor and a creditor or creditors, under which the debtor is allowed an extension of time in which to pay debts.

Fair and equitable standard. A Ch. 11 plan can only be confirmed by the cramdown method if classes of claims and interests are treated in a fair and equitable manner. This requires not only fair treatment in the usual sense, but also that the specific requirements of §1129(b) (such as the absolute priority rule) are satisfied.

Family farmer. A debtor (including an individual, spouses, or a family-held corporation or partnership) that is engaged in farming operations and meets the other eligibility requirements for Ch. 12 relief. (§§101(18) to (21))

Feasibility standard. The requirement for plan confirmation that the debtor has demonstrated a reasonable prospect of being able to make the payments and meet the rehabilitative goals set out in the plan.

Fieri facias. Originally, a common law writ commanding the sheriff to seize chattels of the debtor to satisfy a judgment. The term is still used in some jurisdictions as the name for the writ of execution. (Abbreviated as "fi fa.") *See* Elegit.

Financing statement. The document filed in public records to perfect a security interest under UCC Article 9.

First-in-time rule. The general rule of priority under which an earlier perfected lien or interest in property takes precedence over a later one.

Floating lien. A security interest that extends to collateral of a specified type acquired by the debtor, to advances made to the debtor after the execution of the security agreement, or to both. *See* After-acquired collateral; Future advance.

Foreclosure. The process whereby a lienholder enforces the lien following the debtor's default and subjects the collateral to satisfaction of the debt. Following seizure, the collateral is normally sold and its proceeds applied to payment of the debt. However, strict foreclosure (forfeiture of the property to the lienholder in full satisfaction of the debt) is permitted as an alternative in the case of some liens.

Foreign judgment. As used in the Uniform Enforcement of Foreign Judgments Act, "foreign" means judgments of the courts of other states and federal courts, not judgments of the courts of foreign nations.

Fraudulent transfer/conveyance. A disposition of property by a debtor with the actual or constructive intent to defraud creditors or to delay or hinder their collection efforts.

Fresh start. The rehabilitation of a debtor through the process of bank-ruptcy, achieved by the resolution and discharge of prepetition debt.

Future advance. A loan or credit advanced to the debtor after a security inter-est has been created, and secured by such preexisting security interest.

Gap creditor. A person who extends credit or financing to the debtor during the period between two legally significant events, such as between the attachment and perfection of a security interest or between the filing of an involuntary petition and the order for relief.

Garnishment. A creditor's (garnishor's) levy on property of the debtor in the possession of a third party (garnishee), or on a debt or obligation due by the garnishee to the debtor.

Garnishment lien. A judicial lien that arises in property upon which gar-nishment has been levied.

Going concern value. The value of a business based on its sale as a continu-ing operation, rather than on the proceeds that would be realized upon the liquidation of its assets.

Good faith. Subjective honesty and (in the bankruptcy context) compliance with the spirit of the Code.

Good faith purchaser. This term is sometimes used synonymously with bona fide purchaser. However, it is also sometimes used to denote a pur-chaser who acts honestly, but does not satisfy all of the other elements necessary to qualify as a bona fide purchaser. *See* Bona fide purchaser.

Holder of a claim. A creditor of the debtor whose claim is provable in the estate.

Homestead exemption. A exemption granted under state law or §522(d)(1) in an individual debtor's interest in property in which the debtor or a dependent resides.

Hypothetical status of trustee. The legal fictions created by §544, permit-ting the trustee to exercise avoidance rights that would have been available to a bona fide purchaser of real property, a lien creditor, and an execution creditor, had such persons existed on the date that the bankruptcy petition was filed.

Illiquid. Inability to convert assets into cash. *See* Insolvency.

Impaired (Class of claims or interests). In a Ch. 11 case, a class is impaired unless the rights of each member are unaltered except for the cure of any default and deacceleration of the debt. (§1124)

Improvement in position test. One of the requirements for the avoidance of a transfer under §547 is that the transfer enabled the creditor to improve on the position that it would have occupied without the transfer. Improvement in position occurs where the transfer has enabled the creditor to receive more on its claim than it would have been paid in a hypothetical Ch. 7 distribution in the absence of the transfer.

In custodia legis. (Latin: "In the custody of the law.") The retention of property for safekeeping by the sheriff, a receiver, or some other person with legal authority.

Individual. A natural person, as distinct from a corporate entity.

Indubitable equivalent. A broad standard for measuring adequate protection under §361(3). The court must be satisfied that a proposed method of protecting an interest in property will undoubtedly provide the claimant with value equal to the value of the interest. Indubitable equivalence is also used as a standard for determining whether a secured claim has been treated fairly and equitably in a cramdown confirmation. (§1129(b)(2)(A)(iii))

Insider (of the debtor). A person who has such a close relationship with the debtor that he or she has special access to information and opportunities for favorable treatment. Defined by §101(31) to include relatives of an individual debtor and persons in control of a corporate debtor.

Insolvency. Inability to pay debts, determined by one of two tests: inability to pay debts as they fall due (called the "equity test") or an excess of liabilities over assets (called the "bankruptcy" or "balance sheet" test). (§101(32))

Interim trustee. A trustee appointed under §701 following the order for relief in a Ch. 7 case, to serve until a permanent trustee is appointed or elected at the meeting of creditors.

Involuntary case. A case under Ch. 7 or 11 initiated against the debtor by a creditor or creditors who qualify to seek bankruptcy relief. (§303)

Ipso facto clause/provision. (Latin: "By the fact itself.") A provision in a contract or in nonbankruptcy law under which the insolvency or bankruptcy of the debtor is treated as a default.

Joint administration. The administration of the estates of closely related debtors for the purpose of convenience and the reduction of administrative costs. *See* Consolidation of cases.

Joint case. A bankruptcy case in which a single voluntary petition is filed by both spouses, placing both their estates in bankruptcy. Although the estates are administered jointly, their assets and liabilities are not consolidated unless appropriate. (§302)

Joint debtors. *See* Codebtors.

Judgment lien. A judicial lien arising on all the real property owned by the debtor in the county in which the judgment is docketed or recorded. In some states, a judgment recorded in UCC filing records creates a judgment lien on the debtor's personal property.

Judicial lien. Any lien arising out of court proceedings. (§101(36))

Knowledge. *See* Notice.

Leverage. 1. In negotiations, bargaining power or the ability to exert pressure on the other party to obtain a desired resolution.

2. In financing, making an investment consisting largely of borrowed funds.

Leveraged buyout. The purchase of stock in a corporation with borrowed funds, financed by the corporation itself or secured by its assets.

Levy. The sheriff's seizure or taking control of property pursuant to a writ.

Lien. Used broadly, any charge against or interest in property to secure a creditor's right to payment, so that if the debt is not paid, the creditor may have recourse to the property to satisfy the debt. (*See* §101(32).) "Lien" is sometimes used more narrowly to denote only such interests that arise by operation of law or court order, as distinct from interests created by contract, called "security interests."

Lienholder/Lienor. The holder of a lien. (Note: The person who grants the lien is simply called a debtor; there is no such thing as a "lienee," except in Australia.)

Lien stripping. A strategy whereby the debtor attempts to peg an undersecured debt or a debt that has become unsecured at the value of the collateral as determined by the bankruptcy court, so that if the collateral appreciates after the bankruptcy case, the lien (which survives the bankruptcy) cannot extend to the increase in equity but is frozen at the bankruptcy valuation. Where the lien is undersecured, the fixing of the amount of the lien at the current value of the collateral is called "strip down." If the lien has become fully unsecured (because it is a junior lien and the senior lien has taken up the full value of the collateral) the fixing of the lien value at zero is called "strip off."

Liquidated claim. *See* Unliquidated claim.

Liquidating plan. A Ch. 11 plan that provides for the liquidation of the debtor, rather than its rehabilitation.

Liquidation. The realization of the debtor's executable assets for the purpose of generating proceeds to be applied to the payment of debts.

Lis pendens. (Latin: "Pending suit.") The doctrine, deriving from common law, that a person who acquires an interest in realty while litigation is pending concerning title, possession, or other rights to it, is bound by the court's ultimate resolution of the controversy. A party wishing to be protected by the doctrine must file a notice of pendency in the real estate records to give constructive notice of the litigation to any potential transferee.

"Loading up." Excessive spending or borrowing on a credit card or other line of credit, with the effect of increasing the debt just before filing a bankruptcy petition.

Marshalling of assets. An equitable doctrine that applies when two creditors are competing for satisfaction of their claims from the same fund and one of them has another fund available for application to its debt. Marshalling requires that creditor resort to the other fund before having recourse to the shared fund.

Materialman's lien. *See* Mechanic's lien.

Mature claim. *See* Unmatured claim.

Mechanic's lien. A statutory lien on real property available to a person who, at the request of the owner or the owner's agent, has furnished services or labor on credit in connection with the improvement of the property. The supplier of materials used in the construction may assert a similar statutory lien called a "materialman's lien." These traditional names for the liens have been abandoned in some states in favor of the more modern "construction lien."

Meeting of creditors. *See* Creditors' meeting.

Net result rule. An exception to the avoidance of transfers under §547(c)(4), which validates an otherwise avoidable transfer to the extent that the creditor-transferee gave new unsecured value to the debtor after receiving the transfer.

New value exception. An exception (or corollary) to the absolute priority rule that enables equity holders to retain their interests in the debtor, even though a senior non-accepting class has not been paid in full, if the equity holders contribute new capital to the debtor equal to or greater than the value of their interests.

No-Asset case. A liquidation case in which there are insufficient assets to allow for a distribution.

Nonbankruptcy law. The term used in the Code to describe the entire body of law prevailing in the jurisdiction, both state and federal, apart from bankruptcy law.

"Non-core proceedings." *See* Related proceedings.

Nondischargeable debt. A debt that is excluded from the discharge under §523.

Nonrecourse secured debt. A secured debt for which the debtor has no liability beyond the value of the collateral, so that the debtor cannot be held responsible for any deficiency following foreclosure.

Notice. Information concerning a fact, whether deriving from actual knowledge or imputed as a legal consequence of proper recording or other publicity. Imputed knowledge is called "constructive notice."

Notice and a hearing. When a Code provision states that particular action can only be taken after notice and a hearing, this means that appropriate notice must be given, but a hearing is only required if a party in interest requests it. (§102(2))

Nulla bona return. (Latin: "No goods.") The report returned by the sheriff following an attempt at levy in which no executable property could be found.

Objection. A written response required by the Bankruptcy Rules to challenge certain actions or assertions by another party, such as a claim, a claim of exemption, a proposed plan, or the discharge of a debt.

Order for relief. In an involuntary case, the court's grant of the petition for bankruptcy relief. In a voluntary case, no actual adjudication of bankruptcy is required. The filing of the petition itself constitutes the order for relief.

Perfection. The process of making a lien effective against persons other than the debtor, who may subsequently acquire rights in the collateral. Perfection is normally accomplished by an act of publicity such as recording the lien or taking possession of the collateral.

Petition. The pleading filed to initiate a bankruptcy case.

Plenary jurisdiction. Full jurisdiction over the subject matter of the case and the parties, as distinguished from the more limited "summary" jurisdiction of the bankruptcy court. These terms were used in connection with bankruptcy jurisdiction prior to 1978, but have become outmoded under the Code and the current jurisdictional provisions of Title 28.

Pluries writ. A writ of execution issued after the second ("alias") writ. *See* Alias writ.

Preference. An avoidable advantage given by the debtor to a creditor through payment or some other transfer that results in the creditor receiving greater satisfaction on its claim than that to which it is entitled under bankruptcy law.

Prejudgment remedy or process. Provisional and ancillary relief available to the plaintiff during the pendency of a civil case to prevent loss or harm before the case is finally resolved. Most prejudgment remedies aim at the preservation of property that is claimed in the suit or may ultimately be sold in execution to satisfy the judgment.

Prepackaged plan. A Ch. 11 plan that is wholly or substantially settled by the debtor and creditors before the Ch. 11 petition is filed.

Prepetition planning. The debtor's reordering of his or her affairs prior to filing a bankruptcy petition by realizing nonexempt property and using the proceeds to acquire exempt property.

Present value. *See* Best interests test.

Priority. The ranking of liens and other interests in the same property.

Priority claim. An unsecured claim (or that portion of it) that qualifies for inclusion in one of the categories entitled to precedence in payment under §507.

Proceedings in aid of execution. *See* Supplementary proceedings.

Proceeds. Any property or money received in exchange for an asset.

Proof of claim. A creditor's formal submission of a claim against the estate under §501.

Provisional remedy or process. *See* Prejudgment remedy or process.

Purchase. The acquisition of rights in property by voluntary act. "Purchase" is not simply a synonym for "buy," but includes also the consensual acquisition of other rights, such as a security interest. (§§101(43) and 101(54))

Purchase money security interest (PMSI). A security interest in property, to the extent that it secures a loan or credit given to the debtor for the express purpose of acquiring the property and actually used by the debtor for that purpose.

Reach-back period. The period immediately before the filing of a bankruptcy petition within which transfers are vulnerable to avoidance.

Reaffirmation. The debtor's contractual undertaking, executed in compliance with prescribed procedures during the period between the petition and the discharge, to pay an otherwise dischargeable debt.

Receivable. *See* Account.

Receivership. A proceeding, originating in equity, under which a person (receiver) is appointed to take control of property and to preserve and administer it as the court directs.

Reclamation. A seller's limited right to reclaim goods when the buyer was insolvent upon receipt of the goods and the seller was unaware of the insolvency. Reclamation is governed by UCC §2.702 and is given qualified recognition in bankruptcy by §546(c).

Redelivery bond. A bond posted by the debtor for the purpose of regaining possession of attached property pending final determination of the suit. In the bond, the debtor undertakes to redeliver the property or its value if the creditor ultimately obtains judgment. Unlike a discharging bond, a redelivery bond does not release the attachment lien.

Redemption. The debtor's right to buy back property that has been foreclosed upon or otherwise subjected to realization for the satisfaction of debt. Redemption is available only where recognized by principles of equity or by statute (*e.g.*, execution statutes or §722). In some cases creditors junior to the foreclosing party are also given redemption rights. *See* Equity of redemption.

Referee. The original name for a bankruptcy judge under the Bankruptcy Act of 1898.

Rehabilitation. In a general sense, resolution of the debtor's financial difficulties through bankruptcy, so that the debtor's fiscal viability is restored. More specifically, bankruptcy relief by means of a plan under Ch. 11, 12, or 13 as distinct from liquidation.

Rejection (of a contract). The estate's repudiation of a prepetition executory contract of the debtor, so that the estate acquires no performance rights and obligations under the contract and the other party has a general unsecured claim for damages.

Related proceedings. Litigation concerning a matter of nonbankruptcy law, the outcome of which affects the rights, liabilities, or administration of the estate. Because the controversy has an impact on the estate, it falls within the nonexclusive jurisdiction of the district court. In the absence of consent by the parties, related proceedings cannot be finally determined by the bankruptcy court, but must be returned to the district court for final judgment. *See* Core proceedings.

Relation-back. *See* Backdating.

Reorganization. The rehabilitation of a debtor under Ch. 11. Sometimes this word is used in a more general sense to mean rehabilitation under Ch. 11, 12, or 13.

Remand. The bankruptcy court's return of a matter to the court from which it was removed.

Removal. The transfer of related proceedings from another court to the bankruptcy court.

Replevin. A possessory action for the recovery of specific tangible personal property that has been wrongfully taken or retained. As a prejudgment remedy, replevin enables a plaintiff to obtain provisional seizure and possession of property which is the subject matter of the underlying suit. (Replevin is called "claim and delivery" in some states.)

Return. The report submitted by the sheriff that states the action taken on a writ or other process.

Revival (of judgment). The renewal of a judgment that has become dormant because it has not been executed upon during its period of enforceability.

"Ride-through." An arrangement between the debtor and a secured claimant under which the debtor is permitted to retain the collateral in return for a commitment to maintain payments on the debt as originally contracted. The "ride-through" is an alternative in Ch. 7 cases to the more formal reaffirmation.

Safe harbor. A provision in a statute that shields a person from liability for breach of a statutory duty, on condition that the person meets minimum standards of good faith compliance. (*E.g.*, under §1125, a person who solicits acceptance or rejection of a plan in compliance with the Code is protected from liability for any violation of securities laws.)

Secured debt/claim. A debt is secured to the extent that the debtor's personal obligation to pay is reinforced by a lien on property of the debtor, so that if the debtor defaults, the secured creditor may have recourse to the property to satisfy the debt. In bankruptcy, provided that the secured debt is allowed as a claim, it is treated as secured to the extent of the value of the collateral. (§506)

Security agreement. A contract under which a security interest is created. (§§101(50) and (51))

Security interest. Although this term is sometimes used to denote a lien of any kind, it is usually confined to mean a consensual lien. (§101(51))

Self-help. The pursuit of a remedy without court proceedings, such as a lienholder's seizure of collateral upon default without court authority. Self-help seizure and foreclosure are permitted only in connection with certain liens and are subject to restrictions even when allowed.

Sequestration. An equitable remedy, similar to attachment, under which the plaintiff may remove property from the defendant's control pending the final resolution of a case. Sequestration is usually available only when the defendant's property interest is equitable in nature and cannot be reached by attachment.

Setoff. When two persons are mutually indebted, the two debts may be treated as canceling each other out so that neither need be paid. If one of the debts is smaller than the other, setoff operates to the extent of the smaller debt.

Spendthrift trust. A trust with restrictions on alienation designed to protect the fund from dissipation by the beneficiary or seizure by the beneficiary's creditors.

Standing trustee. A person appointed by the U.S. Trustee to serve as trustee for all Ch. 12 and 13 cases filed in a region. (More than one standing trustee may be appointed if the volume of cases is large.)

Statutory lien. A lien arising by virtue of a statutory provision that confers lien rights on otherwise unsecured creditors in particular types of transactions, under specified circumstances. Statutory liens owe their existence to the rights conferred by statute and are not created by contract or judicial process. (§101(53))

Stay. *See* Automatic stay.

Straight bankruptcy. Liquidation under Ch. 7.

Strict foreclosure. A method of foreclosure under which the lienholder acquires ownership of the collateral in full satisfaction of the debt and is not required to conduct a foreclosure sale. The lienholder is therefore not accountable to the debtor for any value in the collateral in excess of the debt and may not claim any deficiency from the debtor if the collateral is worth less than the debt. Strict foreclosure is available only in connection with some liens, and is subject to restrictions, even where permitted.

Strip down and strip off. See Lien stripping.

Strong-arm clause. The traditional name given to the trustee's avoidance powers under §544(a) and its predecessor in the Bankruptcy Act.

Subordination. The demotion of a claim, either by consent of the claimant (consensual subordination) or under principles of equity (equitable subordination). Equitable subordination is appropriate where fairness so requires, typically when the claimant has behaved in a dishonest or inequitable manner to the prejudice of a more junior party or of creditors in general. (§510)

Substantial abuse. An abuse of the spirit and purpose of Ch. 7 by a consumer debtor that provides grounds for dismissal of the case under §707(b).

Summary jurisdiction. *See* Plenary jurisdiction.

Superpriority. Special priority classifications given to two types of claim: (1) Priority at the top of the administrative expense category, granted by §507(b) to a claimant where adequate protection was attempted but proved to be insufficient to fully protect its interest; (2) An even more elevated priority position, senior to all administrative expenses (including superpriority claims under §507(b)), granted to a postpetition financer under §364(c) as consideration for the extension of credit to the estate.

Supplementary proceedings. Statutory proceedings in aid of execution, under which a judgment creditor may seek discovery of executable assets or take other steps to subject the debtor's executable property to the satisfaction of the judgment.

Surplus. The amount in excess of the debt after collateral or property seized in execution has been realized. *See* Deficiency; Equity cushion.

Title 11. The Bankruptcy Code. (11 U.S.C. §§101-1330)

Transfer. Any disposition of property or an interest in property. In the Code, "transfer" is usually used to describe the debtor's transmission of property rights to some other person, resulting in impoverishment of the estate. (§101(54))

Trustee. A private person appointed by the U.S. Trustee (or elected in some Ch. 7 cases) who represents, administers, and distributes the bankruptcy estate. (§§321, 322, and 323)

Turnover. The surrender of estate property to the trustee by any person in possession of it. (§§542 and 543)

UCC. The Uniform Commercial Code. A uniform code, adopted in all states except Louisiana, covering sales, negotiable instruments, security interests in personal property, and other commercial transactions.

UFCA/UFTA. The Uniform Fraudulent Conveyance Act of 1918 and its successor, the Uniform Fraudulent Transfer Act of 1984. Uniform Acts, adopted in one version or the other in most states, providing for the avoidance of fraudulent dispositions by a debtor.

Undersecured debt. *See* Deficiency.

Unfair discrimination. Unjustified differentiation in a plan between claims of comparable rank that should be treated equally.

Unimpaired (class of claims or interests). *See* Impaired (class of claims or interests).

Unliquidated claim. A claim on which the debtor's liability has arisen, but the amount of which is uncertain and cannot be calculated arithmetically from known data.

Unmatured claim. A claim for a debt that has come into existence but whose date of payment has not yet fallen due.

U.S. Trustee. A federal official, appointed under 28 U.S.C. §581, who is responsible for the appointment and supervision of bankruptcy trustees and for the general oversight of bankruptcy cases.

Venue. The appropriate federal district for the conduct of the bankruptcy case or related proceedings.

Voluntary case. A bankruptcy case initiated by the debtor.

Wage earner plan. The name for the plan under the predecessor of Ch. 13 in the Bankruptcy Act. The term is obsolete but is still sometimes used to describe a Ch. 13 plan.

Warrant of attorney. A provision in a contract or instrument of debt, appointing the creditor to act as the debtor's agent in confessing to judgment if the debtor should default. *See* Confession to judgment.

Wildcard provision. A nickname for §522(d)(5) (or an equivalent provision in a state statute) under which the debtor may apply a general exemption to any property selected, up to a prescribed value.

Workout. A negotiated settlement under which the debtor and creditors resolve the debtor's financial difficulties by agreeing to terms of payment. A workout may occur outside of bankruptcy, resulting in a composition and extension, or it may take place in the process of formulating a plan in a bankruptcy case.

Writ. A written order issued pursuant to court authority, requiring the sheriff or some other official to perform an act, such as the levy of execution.

Index

[*References are to sections. This index does not include references to the Examples and Explanations.*]

557